Memory for
Everyday and Emotional Events

Memory for Everyday and Emotional Events

Edited by

Nancy L. Stein
University of Chicago

Peter A. Ornstein
University of North Carolina at Chapel Hill

Barbara Tversky
Stanford University

Charles Brainerd
University of Arizona

 LAWRENCE ERLBAUM ASSOCIATES, PUBLISHERS
1997   Mahwah, New Jersey

Lawrence Erlbaum Associates, Inc., Publishers
10 Industrial Avenue
Mahwah, New Jersey 07430

Cover design by Semadar Megged

Library of Congress Cataloging-in-Publication Data

Memory for everyday and emotional events / edited by Nancy L. Stein . . . [et al.].
    p.   cm.
    Papers presented at a conference, University of Chicago, May 1993.
    Includes bibliographical references and indexes.
    ISBN 0-8058-1443-4 (cloth : alk. paper). — ISBN 0-8058-2609-2 (pbk : alk. paper).
    1. Memory—Congresses. 2. Recollection (Psychology)—Congresses. I. Stein, Nancy L.
    BF371.M4486   1996
    153.1'2—dc20   96-35580
                                        CIP

Printed in the United States of America
10 9 8 7 6 5 4 3 2 1

We dedicate this volume to Irving Harris. It was through his generosity that this conference came about. He has supported the Center for Developmental Studies and the Developmental Program in Psychology at the University of Chicago for the last 10 years. Not only does he provide financial support, but his intellectual support and integrity have been unwavering. He is astute about important new research findings, is always focused on what would make a better life for children and people in general, and has definitive ideas when considering just how it is that we should create a better place to live. For these things, we give a special thanks to Irving Harris.

CONTENTS

Participants at the Conference on Everyday and Emotional Memory

Larry Barsalou
Department of Psychology
University of Chicago
5848 S. University Avenue
Chicago, IL 60637

Charles Brainerd
Department of Educational
  Psychology
University of Arizona
6060 Calle Ojos Verdes
Tucson, AZ 85721

William Brewer
Department of Psychology
University of Illinois, Urbana–Champaign
605 E. Daniel Street
Champaign, IL 61820

Stephen Ceci
Department of Human Development
  and Family Studies
Cornell University
Maithran Renselear Hall
Ithaca, NY 14853

Paul Ekman
Department of Psychiatry
UCSF
401 Parnassus Avenue
San Francisco, CA 94143

Robyn Fivush
Department of Psychology
Emory University
Atlanta, GA 30322

Susan Folkman
UCSF
74 New Montgomery Street
Suite 600
San Francisco, CA 94105

Gerd Gigerenzer
Department of Psychology
University of Chicago
5848 S. University Avenue
Chicago, IL 60637

Gail Goodman
Department of Psychology
University of California, Davis
Davis, CA 95616

Janellen Huttenlocher
Department of Psychology
University of Chicago
5848 S. University Avenue
Chicago, IL 60637

Marcia Johnson
Department of Psychology
Princeton University
Princeton, NJ 08544-1010

Jean Mandler
Department of Psychology
University of California, San Diego
La Jolla, CA 92093

Mary Ann Mason
School of Social Welfare
University of California, Berkeley
120 Haviland Hall
Berkeley, CA 94720

Peter Ornstein
Department of Psychology
University of North Carolina
CB# 3270, Davie Hall
Chapel Hill, NC 27599-3270

Douglas Peters
Department of Psychology
University of North Dakota
Grand Forks, ND 58202

Michael Ross
Department of Psychology
University of Waterloo
Waterloo, Ontario N2L 1C3
Canada

Peter Salovey
Department of Psychology
Yale University
P.O. Box 11A Yale Station
New Haven, CT 06520-7447

Nancy L. Stein
Department of Psychology
University of Chicago
5848 S. University Avenue
Chicago, IL 60637

Tom Trabasso
Department of Psychology
University of Chicago
5848 S. University Avenue
Chicago, IL 60637

Barbara Tversky
Department of Psychology
Stanford University
Jordan Hall, Bldg. 420
Stanford, CA 94305-2130

Maria Zaragoza
Department of Psychology
Kent State University
Kent, OH 44242

1

AN AGENDA FOR RESEARCH IN EVERYDAY AND EMOTIONAL MEMORY

Nancy L. Stein
University of Chicago

Peter A. Ornstein
University of North Carolina at Chapel Hill

This book is the outgrowth of a conference on the nature of everyday memory held at the University of Chicago during May 1993. The editors of this volume worked to bring together a diverse set of people to discuss issues and implications for the study of everyday and emotional memory. We wanted to include researchers who, under ordinary circumstances, would not come into contact with one another but whose work was closely related. Thus, investigators from cognitive, developmental, social, decision-making, legal, and health psychology were invited to participate in an ongoing interchange (and often debate) that spanned 4 days.

The conference topics were wide ranging, but revolved primarily around five major issues: (a) the role of knowledge and appraisal processes in determining everyday memory; (b) the contributions of both nonverbal and verbal processes during encoding and retrieval of memory; (c) the role of trauma, emotion, and pain in determining memory; (d) constraints inherent in the legal and social systems that facilitate or diminish the probability of measuring and assessing everyday memory; and (e) issues related to the validity and accuracy of eyewitness testimony.

PART I: KNOWLEDGE- AND APPRAISAL-BASED MODELS OF EVERYDAY AND EMOTIONAL MEMORIES

In the first part of this volume, four teams of researchers focus on the processes and mechanisms that underlie the construction of everyday and emotional memories. Although memory for everyday events results from a constructive process that involves interpretation and inference, the four contributions in this section show that memory is both accurate and inaccurate, depending on the conditions under which information is encoded and retrieved. The thrust of each chapter is to describe the conditions that lead to accuracy versus inaccuracy and distortion. The contributions of Stein, Wade, and Liwag and of Ornstein, Shapiro, Clubb, Follmer, and Baker-Ward focus on the types and organizations of the events in question, the amount of prior knowledge children and adults have already acquired about the to-be-remembered event, and the circumstances under which people are asked to remember.

The conclusions of both sets of investigators are that young children are quite accurate in remembering many different types of events that occur in everyday interaction, from the routine to the very emotional; that many of the errors made in remembering occur during encoding rather than at retrieval; that the errors during encoding often occur because of a lack of accurate knowledge and inappropriate inferences made about the event in question; and that the causal structure and organization of an event is one of the most critical dimensions that predicts whether an event will be remembered accurately or not.

Folkman and Stein make a further contribution to the study of everyday memory by describing the content and organization of everyday memory in reports of emotionally stressful events. These investigators take an unusual stance in examining memories for everyday events. Rather than choosing to focus on the inaccuracies or suggestibility of memories for emotional and stressful events, such as in the eyewitness testimony literature, Folkman and Stein focus on the contents of everyday memories to describe the appraisals and coping strategies people carry out to maintain states of psychological well-being. They examine memories of men who are caregivers and partners to men who have AIDS.

By analyzing caregiver narratives about stressful and emotional events, Folkman and Stein are able to predict which men will be able to retain positive states of well-being, despite the fact that they will experience or have experienced the loss of their partner. They focus on the positive or negative beliefs caregivers hold; their emotions, goals, successes, and failures that were remembered during ongoing stressful events; and the ways in which caregivers revise or restructure goals in response to success or failure. According to Folkman and Stein, critical dimensions that characterize caregivers who are able to maintain a positive view of their world, despite ongoing loss, are the ability to revise deeply held beliefs in the face of changing circumstances, the ability to generate new goals that give meaning to current existence, and the ability to replace goals that are no longer tenable.

Ross also focuses on the nature and organization of everyday memory, but he does so from a different perspective. Although he clearly indicates that memories can be both accurate and inaccurate, and he provides examples of the ways in which memories become faulty, he focuses on different measures of accurate memory and asks whether any one measure can be used to guarantee the accuracy and veridicality of a specific memory. Ross shows by many examples, some quite humorous, that the criteria researchers use to establish accurate memory are relative and approximate. Even though researchers score memories for their accuracy, scoring procedures involve approximations of the original stimulus, not verbatim accuracy. Investigators often do not have access to the original event under consideration and are relegated to guessing about the nature of the input by using different types of memory measures.

Ross provides an excellent example of not having access to what subjects experienced and encoded by using examples from the Challenger disaster. Because the tapes of the Challenger disaster received such wide television and newspaper distribution, it was assumed that most people would have a solid command of the detailed nature of the tragedy. As a result, no attempt was made to question or verify the nature of information subjects encoded about the disaster. Ross points out that the veridicality of the memories for the disaster may well reflect what parts of the Challenger event subjects actually saw and encoded correctly. He then focuses on three criteria to determine memory accuracy: the source and quality of the memory, such as its cohesiveness; the uniqueness and nature of the event; and the consistency of memory in the light of other memories that have been reported.

PART II: PERCEPTUAL AND VERBAL PROCESSES IN EVERYDAY MEMORY

All too often researchers forget that much of everyday memory is not verbal. Incoming information from participating in social interaction and from observing the unfolding of everyday events is encoded in visual, auditory, tactile, gustatory, and motoric representations, as well as strictly "verbal" linguistic representations. Both children and adults use all sensory capacities to encode and recollect what has happened to them. They often have access to only visual or auditory representation during the initial phases of encoding. At opportune times, however, even children can verbally recall a past event that was originally encoded only in a nonverbal representation. Mandler and McDonough elegantly describe instances such as these, and they also describe the different types of methodologies and results that support the notion that very young children encode and use sophisticated information about remembering temporal sequences of events that underlie everyday memory.

Huttenlocher and Prohaska elaborate on the ability of people to remember one part of a temporal sequence: the time-specific day on which an event occurred. These investigators report a definite bias in the dating of daily events. People tend to cluster dates around the endpoints of the week rather than in the middle. Huttenlocher and Prohaska focus on the conditions that lead to memory errors and accuracies. If multiple events have occurred and if the events are similar to one another, the probability of making a dating error increases. Each incoming event is stored in relation to similar events that preceded it. Information about a previous event may be merged with incoming information, making it difficult to distinguish between the two events. If integration across event representations occurs, retrieving the representation of a unique event often becomes difficult.

Tversky then describes the types of errors and biases that exist in spatial representations of the environment. In several different studies of memory for spatial locations of objects, Tversky showed that people have a bias in terms of the axis they remember the best, with the vertical being remembered better than the horizontal. One reason for the bias is that people use their bodies as referents to encode the locations of objects. The vertical asymmetry of the body make this axis more distinguishable than the horizontal axis. Tversky shows the implications of using the body as a referent by having people lie down when they attempt to remember the spatial location of objects. The bias then operates in favor of the horizontal because of the change in body position.

Brainerd examines basic research on age differences in the forgetting of verbal material and discusses the implication of his results for eyewitness testimony. He argues that verbal list memory parallels memory for everyday events and that suggestibility of memory in both situations increases as the original memory fades. Brainerd demonstrates that in some situations forgetting is routinely shown to decrease with age, and that children as well as adults benefit significantly from the effects of repeated testing on subsequent remembering. In regard to the effects of repetition on memory, the implications Brainerd draws for eyewitness testimony are quite different from those of researchers who conclude that, generally, repetition results in the transformation of a specific memory.

Brainerd also addresses the nature of memory representations by distinguishing between verbatim or gistlike memory. As a verbatim memory representation fades, memory becomes more gistlike and more prone to additions and transformations, unless the input is structured in such a way as to resist fading. An interesting implication of Brainerd's work is the determination of which memories resist fading and which are prone to transformation.

PART III: STUDIES OF EMOTIONAL
AND PAINFUL MEMORIES

These chapters address the importance of the situation and input from other people in determining what gets remembered and what gets recalled. Fivush and Kuebli illustrate how mothers, in the process of talking to their children, frame and elaborate situations in terms of their emotional content. These investigators show that mothers talk to their daughters differently than they talk to their sons. The mother–daughter conversations are more detailed in terms of discussions about past feelings and appraisals of situations. Fivush and Kuebli contend that mothers influence not only the encoding of the immediate situation, but they also influence how children will encode future situations.

Goodman and Quas also show that maternal input at the time of encoding is critical in predicting memory for an emotional event in a medical setting. These researchers present data they collected as they observed children undergo a medical procedure, called a voiding cystourethrogram fluoroscopy (VCUG), that was fairly invasive but was also critical to children's physical well-being. The procedure enables urologists to use fluoroscopic filming to determine whether anatomical abnormalities are present in the bladder or urethra. The procedure involves urinary catheterization, filling, and then voiding of the bladder.

Goodman and Quas conclude that the ways in which mothers interact with their children directly influence the children's memory representation of the entire event. When mothers and children show a secure attachment, children are more likely to retain a detailed representation of the medical procedure as opposed to children who are insecurely attached to their mothers. The description of mother–child relationships is critical because parents serve as children's primary teachers, especially during the pre-school years. The nature and type of parent–child interaction becomes the focus, just as it does in formal instructional settings. The quality and structure of parental input is critical to accurate encoding. Many studies on narrative memory, both with young children and adults, have shown that structuring input in such a way as to ensure detailed unambiguous representations of an event is critical to both immediate and long-term memory.

Mothers who had secure relationships with their children may have been able to ease the fears of their children before the children underwent the VCUG experience. These mothers may also have a tendency to explain future events to their children so that their children are not anxiety ridden and know what to expect. If this is the case, the types of information that mothers give to their children, in addition to the emotional sustenance that is derived from the interaction, becomes important. Future studies will need to describe the more detailed nature of parent–child interaction to determine the specific dimensions that account for better memory. It is clear from both the Fivush and Kuebli chapter and the Goodman and Quas chapter, that the nature of parental input is a fundamental issue in learning about and remembering everyday events.

Salovey and Smith explore the closely linked domains of pain perception and memory for pain in adults, assessing both by the use of questionnaires. Based on a comparison of immediate and delayed ratings of a painful experience, they demonstrate that adults quite accurately recall painful experience, especially the intensity of the painful event. They show, however, that the intensity of perceived pain during a prior event is influenced by the intensity of pain that a subject is experiencing during the delayed test of memory. These data are critical in supporting the contention that past memories are always influenced, to some extent, by the current feeling states and attitudes of participants.

PARTS IV AND V: THE NATURE AND ACCURACY OF EYEWITNESS TESTIMONY

The contributors in Parts IV and V focus on ways in which findings from their research could be applied to the area of eyewitness testimony. Mason's contribution focuses on the adults' perceptions of children's memories of sexual abuse, and the implications these perceptions have on clinical and legal practices. Mason's work is the most directly related to the real exploration of eyewitness testimony. She shows the difficulties of accepting children's testimony in courts of law when they serve as witnesses to or victims of sexual abuse. At the heart of Mason's chapter is an effort to discern whether or not judges actually use children's testimony as valid evidence to incriminate an accused abuser.

The difficulties begin with the criteria that are used to determine whether or not children have suffered from sexual abuse. Most experts who testify, Mason reports, are clinicians who base their conclusions on lists of abuse characteristics they have compiled from previously treated children, not on any independent research that they or other expert witnesses are conducting. Mason shows that the criteria for identifying sexually abused children are quite contradictory. Some experts assert that testimony of these children is often inconsistent, delayed, and prone to recanting. Other experts testify that abused children are quite truthful and very consistent in their reporting. Further, some experts contend that children know quite a bit about abuse, and others contend that abused children are naive and ignorant.

Judges will consider and accept expert testimony but mostly when this testimony is used as a rebuttal to testimony given by a child. More than anything else, Mason underscores the need to acquire more accurate information about the uses and abuses of testimony, especially in terms of what judges and lawyers really do and whether or not these practices correspond to the findings in ongoing research about children's memory for abuse.

Ekman focuses on those dimensions of testimony and nonverbal behavior that can be used to catch a liar. He first points out that different definitions of deception exist and that we need to be sensitive to the conscious aspects of reporting information that we know is not correct. He then discusses the various behaviors that can be used to detect deception or lying. Although verbal inconsistencies can be used as evidence of lying, as in the work lawyers do, Ekman uses a broader array of behaviors, including the prosody (melody) of speech and facial and body patterns expressed during an interview and interaction. He shows that the identification of lying is not always associated with the level of expertise a person has acquired about deception or testimony. The results from some of his studies show that untrained adolescent women are sometimes better judges of who is lying and who is not. The fact that multiple criteria must be used to detect lying is similar in nature to the claim made by Ross about criteria for assessing the veridicality of a memory. Multiple criteria need to be used.

The section on the development of children's testimony focuses primarily on issues surrounding children's capability of remembering events accurately and the conditions that lead to the suggestibility of memory. Peters is most concerned with the nature of traumatic experience and the role that psychological arousal plays in determining memory accuracy. He shows quite nicely that traumatic experience often involves a high level of physiological arousal and that this type of response often precludes the encoding of accurate memory for an ongoing situation. He also suggests that the linkage between the level of physiological responsiveness and memory is an area that is very much in need of more exploration, especially in relationship to the conclusions that we reach about the role of emotion in the retention of accurate memories.

Bruck and Ceci focus primarily on the phenomenon of suggestibility and the ways in which questioning procedures during legal interviews make children vulnerable to suggestible influence. These investigators adopt a broad definition of suggestibility and show the extent to which a variety of factors, internal and external to the child, can affect all aspects of testimony reporting. Bruck and Ceci then present the results from some of their current studies that are modeled on specific aspects of the forensic context. Their studies focus on efforts to induce certain elements of stereotype induction, repeated bouts of suggestible and leading questions, and the presence of interviewers who have strong hypotheses about the facts surrounding a particular event.

Under these conditions, Bruck and Ceci show the relative ease of getting children to incorporate inaccurate information into their testimony. Some children are more prone than others to inaccurate accounting, and much remains to be learned about factors that would ensure a more accurate report of events, especially in legal situations. The disastrous effects that interviewers and the interview can have on the accounting of events, however, is clearly a factor that increases the probability of error.

Zaragoza, Lane, Ackil, and Chambers then present the results from studies where children of varying ages have been asked to recall accurately event information that occurs in different modalities (e.g., visual and verbal). They show that children often make source errors and confuse modalities. Their data also show that younger children are more prone than older children to these errors, and younger children also evidence more suggestibility in their recall than do older children.

PART VI: CRITICAL COMMENTARIES
ABOUT A THEORY OF EVERYDAY
AND EMOTIONAL MEMORY

Trabasso, Gigerenzer, and Brewer then discuss issues that are critical to the advancement of a theory of emotional and everyday memory. All three researchers advocate the need for future studies to be more theoretically bound and explanatory in nature. Trabasso emphasizes the need to study the social context in which these everyday memories occur and to focus on the nature of the input and the process of understanding, especially in terms of the collaboration of thinking and understanding that occurs during the unfolding of an event. He also emphasizes that very few studies have access to the original event or to the ways in which the understander encoded the original event. His list of recommendations for future research focuses on the necessity of getting both videotapes and audiotapes of the interviews in regard to legal testimony. Trabasso also recommends systematic analysis of verbal and visual protocols produced during these interviews. At the present time, interview data are analyzed in an unsystematic way, and the results support the initial biases of an investigator only because the data have not been analyzed in a more complete fashion.

Gigerenzer focuses on several issues surrounding the development of a theory of everyday memory, especially the necessity to document and explore the situated contextual basis of memory. He contends that if everyday memory is really dependent on what we know about an event, then the measurement of memory must always reflect this knowledge to some extent. Gigerenzer also discusses the effects of repetition on the belief that an event did or did not occur, showing that in some instances, repetition increases the probability that a person will say that an event has occurred. On the other hand, the willingness to say that an event occurred is determined by how the event was understood initially in relation to other events that occurred. Gigerenzer again emphasizes the necessity to explore and describe in a more theoretical and explanatory fashion the role that prior knowledge and specific information play in regulating a memory representation.

Brewer concludes the volume by focusing on implications that all of the presentations have for theories of autobiographical and schematic memory. He asserts at different points throughout his chapter that the ways in which testimony researchers have studied the veridicality issue do not necessarily result in any advances in our understanding of how children remember events and what they are capable of understanding. Although Brewer professes admiration for many of the advances that have occurred in current eyewitness testimony studies, he maintains that current studies still lack important variables that are necessary to understand the nature of memory processes. In particular, Brewer asserts that visual memories are as critical to accurate recall as are the verbal memory of a sequence of events. His claim is similar in nature to those of Stein et al., Ross, Mandler and McDonough, Tversky, and Ekman. We need to broaden the types of memory representations that are encoded during an event not only to increase the accuracy of reporting an event, but also to come to a better understanding of how memory processes operate. Although people may not be able to recount an event accurately in one modality, they may be able to access a more detailed representation in another modality.

The second issue that Brewer raises focuses on distinguishing between the use of a generic memory representation to recall a specific event versus the use of information to encode a representation that is specific only to the event being recalled. Brewer points out that encoding of any event relies on prior knowledge that is often organized in schematic form, having been integrated across a number of situations. When people attempt to remember events, they are able to remember the event because the information in the current event corresponds to information in the knowledge scheme that is guiding their interpretation of the event. People use prior knowledge schemes by activating and pulling out critical information in that scheme to help them interpret incoming information. As a result, incoming information from a current event is often merged with information from prior events. Many times, people are not able to isolate and distinguish information learned during one time period from that learned during another time period.

Advancement of a Theory of Memory for Everyday and Emotional Events

Although Brewer's concern about the generic quality of memory is quite valid, especially in reference to how most researchers have chosen to study memory, the uniqueness of many emotional and traumatic events must be considered as well as the conscious efforts people often take to ensure that their memories for everyday events are accurate. Most laboratory studies of memory for everyday events, despite efforts to consider the ecological validity of the specific events being studied, are a far cry from the types and sequences of events that lead up to the major cases tried in our legal system. Furthermore, many examples of children's inability to testify accurately and in detail in court settings ignore those situations and cases where children were extremely accurate in their testimony and where adult testimony corroborated the recall of children.

An advancement in this area would be one that recognized the multiplicity of conditions and circumstances in cases involving child as well as adult witnesses. One reason that expert witnesses contradict each other in describing the behavioral characteristics of abused children is that more than one prototype exists. In many cases, children have extremely accurate and detailed memories of their abuse because of the conditions under which it occurred. They were at attention when the events unfolded, they understood that the perpetrator intended to harm them, and they understood the nature of the actions. We should not forget that many children become habituated to violence before 3 years of age not only from adults but also from sibling interaction. Understanding that someone else does not like you and fully intends to harm you is one of the first things children understand about other people, including members of their own families. The degree of liking among two people, including young children, is communicated not only verbally, but by facial expression (disgust, contempt), failure to attend to or engage in interaction in a meaningful fashion, changing the topic of conversation, physical distancing of another person, and other verbal and nonverbal characteristics. Further, children are often given clear warning that abuse will follow by the name calling that precedes abuse, verbal threats that are later enacted, and being told how much their attackers enjoy watching children suffer.

At the same time, there are many instances of abuse that are ambiguous, that are not clearly encoded by children, and therefore are not readily understood in terms of the intent to harm or abuse. Many situations of abuse occur when children least expect the abuse, when it is not clear exactly what the abuser is doing, and when children have become partial partners to the abuse. To distinguish among the different types of situations will require more careful description of the actual unfolding of abuse sequences, and an increased effort to describe the many types of abuses that occur, similar to the way in which Mason collected her data to describe adults' perceptions of children's testimony in the courtroom. By necessity, our studies will need to become more anthropological—more broadly conceived to include children from different types of ethnic groups and different socioeconomic levels.

The consequences of not arriving at a more accurate description of the different conditions under which testimony is both accurate and inaccurate are many. By believing that children cannot provide accurate testimony regarding people who have harmed them and who could harm them in the future, we are readily exposing these children to another event that could be life threatening. At the same time, we must consider the fact that some children are very influenced by social pressure of the testimony situation and by their likes and dislikes of a person who stands accused of abuse. Thus, it is quite easy for children to report incorrect and inaccurate information, not necessarily because they are suggestible, but because their incorrect testimony serves goals other than relating the truth of a situation. Children and adults who are strongly predisposed toward either guilt or innocence of a person are quite capable of confabulating their reports and transforming their account of an original event.

Many of these accounts are quite coherent and invulnerable to the detection of falsification. In these cases, not being able to detect deception results in the conviction of innocent people being found guilty and being relegated to suffering for an act they did not commit. Similarly, efforts to ensure the verdict of innocence can allow a guilty person to be freed to commit another crime, often a more harmful one. Thus, understanding and being able to operate with the complexities of testimony situations will require research that integrates methodologies used across different disciplines.

Most important will be efforts to collect data before or during a situation that results in abuse. To date, most studies on children's testimony focus on children's memories for medical procedures, memories for events that were carried out in children's classrooms, or retrospective memories for trauma (see Trabasso's discussion). Ironically, few investigators have observed children in family situations where a high rate of abuse occurs. Investigators need to become sensitive to the fact that some ethnic communities are more prone to abuse and violence than other communities. Thus, examining preschool children's understanding of abuse and violence in cases in which the children's parents or brothers have been killed in a gang war is quite different from getting a report of abuse from a child who has been through a routine medical procedure.

In situations in which repetitive violence occurs, we need to remind ourselves that generic memory structures may be used to interpret ongoing events because the generic memory representation contains a strict causal sequence in terms of the roles that individuals play and the actions that are undertaken in every violent or abusive encounter. Recalling an individual event in a generic fashion may allow a person to ensure that the memory representation is accurate. Thus, in determining whether memory is accurate for harmful and abusive events, the type of memory storage (e.g., generic vs. situated) may not be the issue.

A missing component from our conference concerned the ways in which young children and adults used nonverbal memories to enhance or constrain their representations of an emotional event. Mandler and McDonough showed how powerful nonverbal representations could be in toddlers' ability to retain accurate information from sequences of events. Ekman, Brewer, and Trabasso underscored the need to be able to elicit and describe these types of representations. To our knowledge, however, few testimony researchers look at enactment recall along with verbal and recognitory recall of a situation, especially in young children.

Finally, as many conference participants noted during their conversations with one another, more emphasis needs to be put on two dimensions: individual differences in skill in accurately recalling an event and the stabilities that exist in memory representations as well as the changes that occur to these representations. Bruck and Ceci as well as Goodman reported that large individual differences occurred in children's skill in accurately recalling the unfolding of an event. These findings suggest that children come to the situation with differing amounts of knowledge and exposure to the events in question. To the extent that children have prior knowledge of an event, and understand and interpret the event in the correct frame of reference, their recall will be accurate (e.g., see Stein et al. and Ornstein et al.). Thus, a critical advance in our understanding of how individual differences operate during everyday memory situations would focus on gaining access to the prior knowledge and thinking of children before they enter a situation.

Similarly, many situations exist in which children's memory is quite resistant to change, even when a restructuring and change in the memory representation would be beneficial to their understanding of a situation. The conditions that result in stability of memory are just as important as those that lead to restructuring of memory. The study of stability and change must proceed together because most memory representations evidence both of these dimensions. What remains stable and accurate has received less attention than the changes or transformation in memory. Understanding why some memories are accurate can only improve our understanding of the inaccuracies and changes that occur in memory representations.

KNOWLEDGE-BASED AND APPRAISAL MODELS OF EVERYDAY AND EMOTIONAL MEMORY

2

A THEORETICAL APPROACH TO UNDERSTANDING AND REMEMBERING EMOTIONAL EVENTS

Nancy L. Stein
Elizabeth Wade
Maria D. Liwag
University of Chicago

The goal of this chapter is to present theory and data that describe how children and adults understand, evaluate, and subsequently remember real-life events that result in emotional reactions. Events result in emotion when they are perceived to affect the status of physical or psychological well-being. Understanding how people recall and report emotional events is important because such events are often the primary focus of legal and psychothera-peutic testimony (Brewin, Andrews, & Gotlib, in press; Goodman & Bottoms, 1993; Lindsay & Read, in press).

In this chapter, we lay out an explanatory framework that describes the understanding of everyday emotional events. It is during understanding that events take on meaning, significance, and emotional valence, all of which shape subsequent recall. Thus, in order to predict the content and organi-zation of event memory, we focus on the role of understanding and emo-tional reactions. To this end, we highlight the importance of prior knowledge and beliefs brought to a situation, we illustrate how these beliefs and knowl-edge systems affect the goals, plans, and actions carried out in emotion-elic-iting situations, and we demonstrate how specific meaning attributed to an event affects its importance, its subsequent memory representation, the probability that a person will lie about the event, and future states of psychological well-being. In essence, we are advancing a theory of intelli-gent, motivated remembering that is driven by a person's goals and desires as well as by dynamic working knowledge about external reality and the ways in which this reality constrains or facilitates goal achievement.

Because our theory is both knowledge- and emotion-based, we assume that the organization and content of event memory is always influenced by the nature of the specific event under consideration (for support for this assumption, see Anderson & Pitchert, 1978; Barsalou, 1992; Chi & Ceci, 1987; Schank, 1982; Schank & Abelson, 1977; Stein & Glenn, 1979; Stein & Trabasso, 1982a, 1982b; Stein, Trabasso, & Liwag, 1992, 1994). Therefore, we do not make predictions about the quality and organization of event memory unless the specific parameters of a given situation can be described in detail. The topic, the functional significance of the event, and its organization affect the focus of attention during encoding, the knowledge brought to bear, the understanding process, and subsequent decision making and action. In turn, appraisal and understanding processes regulate the content and accuracy of memory. Thus, memory is inherently constructive in nature (i.e., memory is always a result of the interpretative process as described in Stein & Glenn, 1979; Stein & Trabasso, 1982a, 1982b, 1985; Stein et al., 1992, 1994; Trabasso & Stein, 1994) and rarely corresponds directly to the content and organization of incoming information.

The indirect correspondence between incoming information and memory, however, is not in itself conclusive evidence that memory is inherently or universally poor, prone to error, fuzzy, or highly suggestible. Rather, it suggests that there will be conditions under which memory is likely to be highly accurate and stable as well as others in which it will be inaccurate or suggestible, and that these conditions can be described by the match or mismatch between construction processes and the nature of the to-be-remembered event. For this reason, we argue that it is vital to characterize both the constructive processes of memory and the nature of the event in question. Without such characterization, we cannot make general conclusions about memory accuracy or stability. We cannot categorically conclude that children are more suggestible than adults (see Pezdek, in press), that they lack strategic abilities to lie or deceive (see Chandler, Fritz, & Hala, 1989; Ekman, 1989, for supporting evidence on children's ability to deceive and understand deception), or that they are unreliable as witnesses in legal testimony situations (see Goodman & Bottoms, 1993, for supporting evidence about children's abilities to give testimony in different situations).

The nature of the event, what is known about it, the way incoming information is interpreted, and the perceived function of testimony influence understanding and accuracy of recall. We argue that memory can be clear, unambiguous, and accurate in certain types of situations. Moreover, certain memories are extremely accurate, robust, and not sensitive to updating, even when updating serves a powerful function (see Chinn & Brewer, 1993; Johnson & Siefert, in press; Stein, Bernas, Calicchia, & Wright, 1996; Stein & Miller, 1993a, 1993b).

At the same time, we contend that people do make errors during event understanding and that these errors directly affect memory. Some errors can be predicted by analyzing the structure and content of the input in conjunction with an analysis of the prior knowledge and inference process activated during encoding (Stein, 1979, 1988; Stein & Glenn, 1979; Stein & Nezworski, 1978; Stein & Trabasso, 1982a, 1982b; Suh & Trabasso, 1993; Trabasso, Secco, & van den Broek, 1984; Trabasso, Stein, Rodkin, Munger, & Baughn, 1992).

In this chapter, we describe some of the mental structures and operations that guide thinking and knowledge activation during understanding. We show that inferences made during understanding often become part of the memory representation itself. To the extent that these inferences accurately reflect the content and structure of the input, memory will be veridical (Stein & Glenn, 1979; Stein & Nezworski, 1978; Stein & Trabasso, 1982a, 1982b; Suh & Trabasso, 1993). To the extent that the inferences are ancillary or irrelevant, memory will not correspond to an ideal (Suh & Trabasso, 1993). Therefore, the encoding of the original event is critical to our formulation of memory, for it is during the online encoding process that we can examine the content and quality of understanding.

To determine the validity of our hypotheses, we review a body of research on memory for both narratives and everyday events, and we discuss the results of our own studies within this context. We conclude that a serious obstacle to determining whether everyday memory is accurate has been the lack of a conceptual methodology for identifying the content and structure of the prior knowledge and inferences activated during event understanding. We contend that this lack has made it difficult to meaningfully characterize the content and structure of the resulting memory representation.

With this concern in mind, we lay out a framework of event understanding that enables us to describe the content and structure of the knowledge base, the inference processes, and the resulting memory representation. We pose questions about the accuracy of memory within this framework, and we propose future studies to examine accuracy in a systematic way that takes advantage of such research on knowledge structure.

ACCURACY OF EVERYDAY MEMORY

Several current reviews of the literature on event memory (Brewin et al., in press; Ceci & Bruck, 1993; Goodman & Bottoms, 1993; Goodman, Hirschman, Hepps, & Rudy, 1991; Goodman, Quas, Belterman-Fauce, Riddlesberger, & Kuhn, in press; Loftus, 1993; Ornstein, Larus, & Clubb, 1991) have found mixed patterns of memory accuracy across subjects and situations. On the one hand, investigators have concluded that, in certain situations, children and adults are quite accurate in recalling real-life events, especially those that are relevant to their physical and psychological well-being (Ceci & Bruck, 1993). A number of researchers, notably Goodman (Goodman et al., 1991; Goodman et al., in press), Bower (1992), Reisberg and Heuer (1992), and Brewin et al. (in press) have argued that when the to-be-remembered event is personally meaningful, memory is quite accurate because of its emotional and stressful nature.

On the other hand, researchers have also concluded that children and adults often do not report an event accurately (Ceci & Bruck, 1993; Loftus, 1992, 1993; Peters, 1991; Ross, 1989; Ross & Buehler, in press). Errors in memory are observed in the same types of stressful or emotional situations where high rates of accuracy have been reported. In many cases, errors are found as the result of suggestions or leading questions asked by an interrogator. However, in a number of cases, poor memory has been reported even when suggestive questioning is not administered (Ceci & Bruck, 1993).

Broadly speaking, the events that have been studied in eyewitness testimony research can be characterized as more or less important to the physical and psychological well-being of the person involved. Reporting memory of these events normally involves assigning blame to a person who is responsible for wrongdoing and giving testimony or a justification in support of or against the perpetrator's innocence or guilt (Doris, 1991; Goodman & Bottoms, 1993; Mason, chapter 13, this volume; Stein, in press; Stein & Miller, 1993a, 1993b).

The events that researchers have characterized as relevant to eyewitness testimony are quite varied. Some events bear a closer resemblance than others to the situations that are the actual problems of legal and psychiatric testimony (such as child abuse, incest, or quality of parenting in divorce proceedings) or those that are theoretically defined as a stressful event (see Folkman & Stein, chapter 5, this volume). In one group of studies, investigators have examined memory for routine, emergency, or diagnostic medical procedures (Goodman et al., 1991; Ornstein, Shapiro, Clubb, Follmer, & Baker-Ward, chapter 4, this volume), visits to a dentist (Peters, 1991), naturally occurring tragedies (Bohannon & Symons, 1992; Boyce et al., 1991), emergencies such as fire alarms (Peters, 1987, 1991; Pillemer, 1992a), and staged "harmful" actions directed at inanimate objects (Clarke-Stewart, Thompson, & Lepore, 1989). Another group of investigators has focused on children's and adults' self-generated reports of emotional and traumatic events (Fergusson, 1993; Fivush, 1993; Folkman & Stein, chapter 5, this volume; Liwag & Stein, 1995; Stein & Liwag, 1994; Stein, Trabasso, & Liwag, 1992, 1994; Wade & Stein, 1994) or self-generated reports of conflictual interaction (Ross & Holmberg, 1990; Stein et al., 1994; Stein et al., 1996).

In this section, we describe several findings from research on comprehension, emotion, and perspective taking that may prove useful to disentangling some of the complexities of this eyewitness testimony research. We begin by describing some conditions that lead to memory accuracy and inaccuracy.

Memory errors can be divided into three general categories (Stein, 1979, in press; Stein & Glenn, 1979): the addition of information not included in the original event, the deletion of information included in the original event, and the reorganization of the original sequence of events. In legal testimony (Mason, chapter 13, this volume) and in studies of memory for social and personal events (Stein & Trabasso, 1982a), all three types of errors co-occur in a single report, along with an accurate report of the remainder of the event information. Additions of new information rarely occur without deletions or reorganization of other event information.

Findings from studies of memory for narrative or actual events have found a number of conditions that predict the accuracy of recall. We focus here on the following: (a) the ability to infer explicit causal relations that link events, (b) prior knowledge about the event or similar events, (c) the potential for multiple interpretations of the meaning of the event, and (d) the presence of an emotional reaction to the event. In addition, we discuss the effect of the purpose of reporting memory, and how motivations may affect a report's accuracy.

The Ability to Infer Causal Relations

At the moment, the relationship between memory accuracy and understanding causal relations has not been examined in the framework of current eyewitness testimony research. However, this relationship has been considered in a number of studies on narrative comprehension. In such studies, errors in comprehension (and subsequently memory) can almost always be induced if incoming information is manipulated in such a way as to prevent or inhibit inferences about causal connections between events. Two sets of studies best illustrate the importance of causal inferences during comprehension. The first set of studies (Stein, 1979; Stein & Glenn, 1979; Stein & Nezworski, 1978; Trabasso, Stein, & Johnson, 1981) focused on two types of manipulations: varying the temporal sequence in which events occur and deleting information that is critical to maintaining a causally relevant representation of an episode.

By creating flashbacks, flashforwards, and randomly organized sequences, Stein and her colleagues (Stein & Glenn, 1982; Stein & Nezworski, 1978) investigated how the causal and temporal organization of an event affects subsequent memory. They found that both children and adults could remember 80–90% of canonically presented stories (e.g., stories with all of the functionally and causally relevant information made explicit). This high level of accuracy was found even for 4- and 5-year-old children (Stein, Day, Shirrey, & Trabasso, 1979). If the narrative contained any disruption of the causal sequence, however, comprehension was significantly worse. In the following example from Stein and Nezworski (1978), for instance, the narrative was reordered such that the end outcome of a series of events was presented out of the canonical temporal order (line numbers indicate order in the canonical version):

1. Once there was a big gray fish named Albert
2. who lived in a big icy pond near the edge of a forest.
11. Albert felt sad
12. and wished he had been more careful.
3. One day, Albert was swimming around the pond
4. when he spotted a big juicy worm on the top of the water.
5. Albert knew how delicious worms tasted
6. and wanted to eat that one for his dinner.
7. So he swam very close to the worm
8. and bit into him.
9. Suddenly, Albert was pulled through the water into a boat.
10. He had been caught by a fisherman.

When children and adults were asked to recall an inverted sequence containing this sort of flashforward, a number of them recalled the outcome twice, once in the beginning, where the outcome actually occurred and once at the end, where it belonged in a causal or psychological sense. Thus, the primary error in these flashforwards was one of addition: that of reporting that the outcome occurred twice.

Subjects who recalled the outcome twice often generated an additional scenario around the first occurrence. Rather than leaving this outcome to stand alone, they felt compelled to construct an explanation for why such an event would occur more than once in an episode. In the process of devising an explanation, however, they could not focus as clearly on the remainder of the incoming information, and their comprehension was poorer than that of subjects who heard or saw a canonically constructed episode. Therefore, there were two sources of error: the perceived need to explain apparent anomaly, and the resulting shift in attention away from subsequent incoming information.

In another series of studies, Stein (1979) and Nezworski, Stein, and Trabasso (1982) manipulated the causal sequence of narratives so that critical information was either deleted from the narrative sequence or put in different positions such that an explanation for action would come before or after the action was carried out. Stein (1979) found that when either the event that motivated action or the outcome of action was deleted from a narrative, recall of the narrative sequence was impaired. The remainder of the narrative did not make much sense without these two types of information, and subjects spent their time trying to figure out just what sorts of events and outcomes could have occurred, given the character's actions. In addition, the effort of attempting to figure out what could fill in the gap interfered with comprehension for the remainder of the sequence. When incoming information is not immediately sensible, attention is focused on the retrieval of knowledge that would aid in constructing a meaningful representation or explanation for such an event. In the process, the demands of explaining an event often force attention to shift away from the remainder of the incoming information. Thus, there is a trade-off between trying to explain puzzling events and being able to keep attention focused on new incoming information. Subjects cannot do both well.

Other parts of the event sequence, such as the goals and actions of a person, can sometimes be deleted from a narrative sequence without causing a loss of understanding for the remainder of the events. In these instances, however, subjects make another type of memory error: that of addition. Stein (1979) showed that when goal or action information was deleted from a goal-directed episode, subjects could easily infer the correct goal or action. However, they included these inferences in their recall, as if the inferred goals and actions had actually been presented in the narrative.

When subjects are exposed to information that they do not understand or information that they find difficult, they often remember that the information was difficult for them. Even young children will volunteer the fact that they have been given a sequence of events that does not make sense. What they often attempt to do is to put the events back into an order that makes correct causal sense (Stein & Glenn, 1982; Stein & Nezworski, 1978), knowing full well that they did not see such a sequence. Subjects will often report, accurately, just where their understanding broke down and what proved difficult for them to encode. Thus, in these difficult-to-understand situations, subjects still attempt to attribute meaning to the incoming information, even if the meaning is a tag signifying that the information is not understood. Therefore, if a sequence of events violated the expected causal order, subjects will put it into an order that conforms to their logical expectations, but they will remember that they transformed it because it didn't make sense.

Just as the absence of an explicit goal-directed causal sequence decreases comprehension, the presence of an explicit causal sequence increases comprehension and subsequently memory. The importance of causal relationships has been noted by almost every researcher studying narrative or script comprehension since the late 1970s (Bauer, 1992; Bauer & Mandler, 1992; Beck, McKeown, Sinatra, & Loxerman, 1991; Fivush, 1993; Mandler, 1984; Nelson, 1991; Rumelhart, 1975; Schank & Abelson, 1977; Stein, 1979; Stein & Glenn, 1979; Stein & Policastro, 1984; Trabasso et al., 1984; Trabasso & Sperry, 1985).

Although this research has not directly addressed suggestibility; that is, the stability of memory in the face of contradiction, it has found that spontaneous memory errors are systematically related to the explanation strategies and knowledge activated during the encoding process. The quality and detail of a representation formed at encoding predict the quality of representation generated both immediately and over the long term (see Bransford, 1979; Mandler, 1984; Stein & Glenn, 1979; Stein & Trabasso, 1982a, 1982b; Trabasso et al., 1984). We would argue that the same factors that cause spontaneous errors should also lead to increased suggestibility. If a person has had difficulty understanding some event or portion of an event sequence, then he or she should also be more open to suggestions about what really happened.

Although the analysis of causal relationships has yet to be applied to the study of eyewitness testimony, from our examination of several of these studies, it is clear that the causal organization, content, and clarity of situations and events presented to children has varied widely. We have argued here that the extent to which a situation is understandable and causally coherent predicts the amount of new information incorporated into a memory representation. The contradictory findings about developmental differences in suggestibility may be due to the fact that some researchers use events that are familiar to young children, so that the children can form a causally cohesive representation of the event, whereas other researchers use events that are not easily organized or represented in a causal fashion. In order to compare results across studies, it is necessary to analyze understandability of each variation in stimulus materials. To this point, cross-study comparisons have consisted of rough counts of how many studies show that children are suggestible and how many do not. Unfortunately, many studies have not measured the understandability of their stimulus materials, nor do some even report what the children actually witnessed. What is needed is a more robust and systematic analysis of the specific types of events used in each study, a description of the actual sequence and organization of each stimulus event, and a measure of the resulting comprehension.

Prior Knowledge

Although children have been shown to be suggestible and prone to error when recalling physical pain, harm, or abuse (see Ceci & Bruck, 1993, for a review of these studies; Clarke-Stewart et al., 1989), we do not know how children have understood these events at the time of encoding and whether they experienced difficulties in constructing an accurate representation of the event. Moreover, we do not know what or how much knowledge children have acquired about different real life scenarios prior to their participation in these studies.

Contradictory results from studies on children's memory for physical touch might be explained by children's knowledge and expectations about the specific situation under consideration, and whether touching violated social and moral principles of interaction. Some studies of children's memories for physical touch involve visits to a doctor, where children undergo an elaborate painful medical procedure to aid in the diagnosis of a serious or chronic disease (Goodman et al., in press; Ornstein et al., chapter 4, this volume); some involve visits to the dentist (Peters, 1991); some involve genital touching during routine doctor visits (Goodman et al., 1991), others involve instructions not to allow an adult to touch children while in the act of bathing (Peters, 1991), whereas still others involve observing whether or not an adult touched a doll improperly (Clarke-Stewart et al., 1989).

The difficulty of arriving at any consistent set of conclusions from these studies is that, without further specification of children's prior knowledge of each situation, we cannot know how the children interpreted each situation. The function and consequences of touching are quite different across these situations. In some situations, the physical well-being of the child is at stake if a technical procedure involving touch is *not* carried out; in other situations, the physical or psychological well-being of the child is at stake if touching is carried out; and, in a third type of situation, the physical well-being of the child is neither enhanced nor worsened as a function of touching. However, it is unclear how much the children involved understood about these functions and consequences.

Our hypothesis is that differing degrees of accuracy regarding the act and sequence of touching will result, depending on children's prior knowledge about the function of touching, their knowledge about the procedures being carried out during the touching episode, their expectations and experience regarding pain that occurs as part of a medical examination or social interactive situation, their knowledge of the consequences that will result if the touching is or is not carried out, their conceptions of what constitutes a moral or social violation, and their motives for engaging in the touching episode in the first place.

A similar hypothesis should hold for situations that result in harm but do not entail physical abuse or physical pain. It will be necessary to extend the study of everyday memory to a broader range of situations that include but are not limited to those resulting in physical pain and abuse. Although memory for physical and sexual abuse clearly needs more detailed study and support, many other types of wrongdoing and harm get carried out on a daily basis, in the context of the family, school, and the workplace. These harms are more psychologically based but are just as significant as the harm resulting from physical or sexual abuse (Stein & Liwag, 1994; Stein et al., 1994).

Although some investigators acknowledge the importance of prior knowledge and the nature of the specific situation in predicting memory for an everyday event (see Goodman et al., in press; Loftus, 1993; Pillemer, 1992b), these two factors remain to be considered in a theoretical fashion across a wide range of studies. None of the current reviews of eyewitness testimony has characterized the thematic nature of the specific situations encountered. However, we know from research on narrative, social, and scientific understanding that a specific description of the to-be-remembered situation is necessary for determining the accuracy of a memory representation. Previous research has found a number of situation-based factors that contribute to either accuracy or inaccuracy of event memory (Beck et al., 1991; McNamara, Kintsch, Songer, & Kintsch, 1993; Mandler, 1984; Simon, 1990; Stein, 1979; Trabasso & Stein, in press).

Potential for Multiple Interpretations

Studies of memory for both text and real events have provided evidence that a person's perspective influences his or her memory for an event. Because events are complex, they may be understood in different ways; for example, events may be interpreted differently based on expectations, outcomes may be given different meanings depending on what the observer desires, and different details may be seen as more or less important by different people.

Understanding and memory for an event relies on an interpretation of what actions or words mean in context. Event sequences may be difficult to remember if an understander has no clear referent at the time the information is being presented. Bransford (1979) gave the clearest example of the need for reference using a passage describing how to do laundry. Unless the reader knows that the actions describe washing clothes, however (e.g., "The procedure is actually quite simple. First you arrange the items in different groups. Of course one pile may be sufficient depending on how much there is to do," etc.), it is very difficult to remember the passage because the actions make no sense. Most of the reader's time is spent trying to figure out just what the passage is about. Even with some effort at rehearsal, much of the passage is not retained. If the reader is told in advance that the passage is about washing clothes, however, comprehension and memory improve dramatically.

This source of errors is not confined to information presented as text. Memory errors for the actions of other people may often be due to ambiguity in the way those actions can be interpreted. We take as an example the results from a study by Clarke-Stewart and her colleagues (Clarke-Stewart et al., 1989). These researchers tested children's memory for the actions of "Chester the Molester," an adult whose behavior could be interpreted in different ways. Of particular interest to Clarke-Stewart et al. was the issue of whether children would defend or denounce Chester after they had observed him carrying out actions toward a doll in one of two different contexts. Chester—actually a research assistant posing as a janitor—picked up the doll, sprayed it in the face with water, looked under its clothes, straightened its arms and legs, and bit a loose thread off its clothing. As he carried out these actions, he explained to the child that he was either cleaning the doll or playing with it. Afterward, the child was questioned either nonsuggestively (using open-ended questions like "What did Chester do?"), in an incriminating manner (using language that became increasingly accusatory, ranging from suggesting that Chester sometimes played with the toys instead of cleaning them to "Chester was playing, right?"), or in an exculpating manner (using suggestions that Chester was really only cleaning). Clarke-Stewart et al. found that, although the children's memories were fairly good after nonsuggestive questioning, the reports of children who received either kind of suggestive questioning strongly reflected the interviewer's position, regardless of what they had seen Chester do.

Although Clarke-Stewart et al. concluded that children were indeed suggestible, there is an alternative explanation. Children may have different concepts of what is defined as a harmful action. If children initially believed that the actions of Chester were not harmful, they would not believe that Chester violated any moral or social code. Therefore, his reasons for his actions—whether he was playing or cleaning—may not have seemed important to the children, and what is more, the children may not have understood them very well. If the children did not see the act as harmful, they would be less likely to pay attention to it, think about it afterwards, or believe they should denounce it. Because they did not attach importance to the event, they would be less likely to insist that their version was right, and more likely to give in to suggestive questioning.

In order to determine whether differences in understanding were responsible for children's decisions, their appraisals of the situation must be evaluated before or during the presentation of scenario information. Had children been told about the types of actions that are deemed harmful, and had they agreed that these actions were indeed harmful, our prediction is that their memories for Chester's actions would have been less suggestible, even under leading questioning.

Research on children's understanding of moral events has provided evidence that children may have different concepts of what is wrong or harmful. In a study of 5-, 8-, and 13-year-old children, Stein and Trabasso (1982a) found that all three groups of children had little difficulty remembering the details of different moral dilemmas, in which a person had to decide on an action to take when any action would result in negative consequences. The dilemmas were similar to those used by Kohlberg (1969) to study moral decision making.

Stein and Trabasso (1982a) used dilemmas that were simple and clear enough that all of the children had little difficulty understanding, evaluating, or remembering the basic facts. The developmental differences that emerged were in the course of action children chose to resolve the dilemma, the consequences they inferred, given that one course of action versus another would be chosen, and the reasons they gave for valuing one course of action over another. The oldest children consistently chose a course of action where a protagonist should make a medicine to save her husband's life, even if making the medicine entailed stealing a tiger's whiskers. The younger children chose to allow the husband to die because they could not sanction harming the tiger in order to make the medicine.

On detailed probing of the younger children, it was clear that they understood that the husband would die if he did not get medicine. However, some of these children did not believe that a medicine made from the whiskers of a tiger was going to help in the healing process. They felt that the husband would die anyway, despite the efforts that would be made to save his life. Other children believed that the medicine would indeed help the husband, but they felt that the wife could get another husband once this one died.

Although these explanations are somewhat fanciful, they do represent the different bases on which children and adults make decisions in moral and conflictual contexts. Often, it is not the memory for a situation that differs among children and adults but rather its interpretation. Asking children if a person performed a "good" or "bad" act must occur in the context of knowing beforehand what children conceive to be "bad" or "good." When children testify in abuse cases, they may go along with what their parents think is bad or good because they understand the social consequences of contradicting their parents. They are also made to feel heroic if they can give a coherent account of the "bad things" an accused person has done. In reality, however, it is often unclear that the child believes that the accused has done anything immoral or unethical. Therefore, a more systematic basis for examining children's understanding of harmful situations will involve making a priori assessments of what each child believes to be harmful, and then relating subsequent memory to these beliefs.

Apparent "errors" in memory can also result from the fact that two comprehenders have different goals during an interaction, and thus report different details from the event. Although reviews of eyewitness testimony studies give the impression that only one correct interpretation of an event sequence is possible, multiple interpretations can often be constructed, each focusing on different information in the event. The difference in memory due to perspective has been labeled the *Rashomon phenomenon* (see Stein et al., 1994), and is a frequent characteristic of eyewitness testimony proceedings.

In situations where there are two different perspectives, memories for the event sequence overlap on critical points, but also differ significantly. The effect of perspective has been illustrated nicely in a study by Anderson and Pitchert (1978). Subjects read a passage describing the contents of a house under instructions to take the perspective of either a home buyer or a burglar. When taking a burglar's perspective, subjects remembered more items that were valuable and portable, like a color television set. When taking the perspective of a home buyer, subjects remembered more items that affected the value of the house, like a leak in the roof. Therefore, the goal of the participant at the time of the event is critical to determining just what is remembered. However, as this study illustrates, the different accounts are not necessarily inaccurate. The major error in these situations is generally one of deletion; thus two accounts may appear to conflict, but may actually each tell accurate (but incomplete) parts of the story.

Conflicting perspectives often arise in emotional events, especially in events that involve anger. In a study of memories for episodes involving anger, Baumeister, Stillwell, and Wotman (1990) found that the roles of perpetrator and victim in the conflict were associated with different subjective interpretations and memories of the interpersonal conflict. Perpetrator narratives often rendered the events as isolated incidents with no lasting implications, whereas victim narratives contained a lingering sense of loss and harm for the aggrieved party.

Our analysis of parent and child memories for the same events (Stein et al., 1994) also indicates that parents and children provide discordant reports because they have different goals and different knowledge bases even in the same situation. When asked to recall an event when their child had expressed anger, many parents reported conflicts between themselves and their children where a parent's prohibitions, denials, or punitive behaviors caused the child's anger. In such situations, the parent and child often have mutually opposing goals. Each one understands the situation according to personal goals operating at the time. Therefore, even though parents and children are participating in a common situation, they may encode the event quite differently, each focusing attention on a different part of the event or creating a different interpretation of the situation.

The current assumption in testimony research is that only one accurate representation of an event exists. Our data, however, strongly suggest that it is possible to have two different but accurate representations of the same situation. What happens when parents and children are in conflict with each other is that they each take in and encode a partial reality. The information that is included in each account of the event could be veridical. However, each may fail to recall critical information that the other reports, either because the focus of attention was different during the encoding of the event, or because some information was never available to one participant. That is, only the experiencer of the emotion has direct access to mental events, such as feelings and plans, that take place during emotional episodes, and only the experiencer may understand how these internal states are linked to his or her subsequent actions. Such internal states become privileged information for the experiencer and are not included by the person who observed only the focal event. Therefore, future research can be more be sensitive to the possibilities of multiple but equally valid interpretations of harmful or emotion-provoking events, and the significant role that goals play in the participants' understanding of these situations.

Emotional Reactions

Emotionally laden events have been hypothesized to be either more memorable or less memorable than emotionally neutral events. Some researchers have suggested that the effect depends on the intensity of the emotion, such that moderately intense emotional reactions improve memory, but extremely intense emotional reactions impair memory (e.g., Deffenbacher, 1983; Eysenck, 1982; Loftus & Doyle, 1987; Mandler, 1975). In a review of relevant literature, however, Christianson (1992) did not find unequivocal support for this hypothesis.

Several investigators (Bower, 1992; Goodman et al., 1991; Reisberg & Heuer, 1992) have argued that emotional events are remembered accurately because of their personal relevance to the subject. Although these researchers generally have not measured the intensity of emotion, in practice they have tended to study moderate levels. From our theoretical perspective, personal relevance is defined by the stakes a person has in the to-be-remembered event (see also Lazarus & Folkman, 1984). To have a stake in an event, a person must believe that ongoing events will have direct consequences for the attainment or maintenance of goals that lead to states of physical and psychological well-being. Such emotionally laden events are memorable for a number of reasons.

Because these events have personal consequences, they draw notice, require ongoing attention, and often provoke subsequent rumination (Nolen-Hoeksema, 1991). We have argued (Stein & Levine, 1990; Stein et al., 1992, 1994) that the experience of emotion almost always activates a causal inference process, the outcome of which becomes part of the representation of the emotional event. Emotions cannot be experienced without some appraisal and meaning analysis of the precipitating event. Therefore, asking people to recall an emotional experience almost always results in a report that is at least partially coherent, even in 3- to 4-year-old children (Liwag & Stein, under review).

When arousal is at the midlevel, a person can activate causal inference processes that focus on the goals that have been blocked or threatened, who or what caused the blockage or threat, what can be done about the success or failure of goals, and the consequences of carrying out action in the service of a goal.

The degree to which a person can remain focused on the appraisal of incoming information, depends, in large part, on whether there is a need either for action or for internal regulation of physiological processes. In situations that cause intense fear or startle reactions, the physiological response may saturate the system to the point where it shuts down in order to reduce the physiological damage of the stimulation. Although people can endure stressful situations for some length of time, the intensity of such situations is known to be a critical component in determining the amount of damage caused by a stressor (Rachman, 1978). A racing heart, an intense adrenaline reaction, and profuse sweating all require physiological equilibration in order for the organism to continue to function properly. Therefore, one strategy people use in highly emotional situations is to focus on internal equilibration. Rather than continue to focus on the external incoming information, they turn their attention inward in order to control their physiological responses.

When attention is shifted inward, people can no longer attend to incoming information in a meaningful fashion. The self-regulatory processes in which they are engaged require too much effort and attention. A shift to an internal self-regulatory focus can be seen most clearly in response to intense pain. Individuals in severe pain may attempt to control the perceived level of pain by attending to specific aspects of the situation that lessen the pain or by attempting to deflect the perception of pain to other elements of the situation. These strategies, however, require attention to internal regulatory processes and enormous amounts of cognitive effort.

Rachman (1978) argued that this shift in attention involves a narrowing phenomenon because people in intense states of fear almost always lock their attention on certain components of the situation and fail to process other components. We argue instead that attention indeed becomes focused on one or two elements of an ongoing situation, but not because of a narrowing of attention. Rather, additional attention must be focused on the planning and action processes that the situation requires. Sometimes, the situation requires the development of a strategy to control internal processes. Other times, the situation demands that attention be focused on plans of action to escape or to resolve the situation. Therefore, the "narrowing" of attention may not change processing capacity. Rather, the focus of attention shifts inward to the construction of plans, either to regulate and equilibrate internal processes or to develop plans for future action.

The intensity of an emotional response may also influence subsequent processing of the event in memory. People who experience intensely emotional or highly stressful events often continue to ruminate and reflect about these events for quite a while after the event occurs (Nolen-Hoeksema, 1991). Children, for instance, actively seek out other people who will listen and talk to them about these events (Gottman & Parker, 1986). Confidants include but are not limited to parents; close friends and trustworthy siblings are just as likely to hear about a child's emotional experiences. Through such conversations as well as through private rumination, children continue to think about an event until some type of resolution is reached.

We would argue that ruminations and active thinking about a stressful event should be studied in a more systematic manner. At the moment, many researchers believe that ruminations transform the nature of the memory representation of an emotional event into a less accurate account of the situation. However, the claim that the accuracy of the memory representation is affected by the integration of additional information will have to be explored more analytically. An initial analysis of parent–child emotion memories (Stein et al., 1994) suggests that parents often provide their children with information that enables the children to construct a more accurate representation of an emotion-provoking event. For instance, parents may challenge their children and ask them to provide evidence that they had indeed experienced harm. When they are asked to provide factual evidence to support their perceptions and beliefs (e.g., that a monster is under the bed; that their cousins really hate them, etc.) children may engage in a more systematic analysis of past events or in a consideration of possible inaccuracies in their understanding of the situation. Therefore, it is possible to speculate that everyday types of postevent suggestion could actually increase the accuracy of an event representation.

In addition, in highly emotional situations, new information may be incorporated only if it is consistent with the preexisting interpretation of the event. Reminding oneself about traumatic events is often an opportunity to review painful facts in the drive toward future-oriented problem solving. Abramson, Alloy, and Metalsky (1990) found that people who tend toward depression or who are actively depressed report negative events more accurately than people who have higher positive morale scores and lower depression scores. One of the therapeutic strategies often used with these depressed people is that of deflecting attention from true information that would lead to a negative mood state. Although these deflection attempts do not actively encourage transformations of the original memory, the use of such techniques often results in altered memories of the original situation. There are times, however, when therapists and researchers fail in their attempts to deflect attention from these painful events, simply because the event is too well encoded in memory and too coherently organized. In fact, recent studies on providing causally coherent explanations for unexpected harmful events illustrate how difficult it is to change the representation of an event once a coherent organization of that event has formed.

The Function or Purpose of Testifying

When people report what they remember, they always have some purpose for doing so, and this purpose or function of testimony may well affect the accuracy of their report. In situations as varied as giving legal testimony, participating in psychological experiments, and tattling to one's mother, the consequences of reporting can be considerable. Will the testimony be used as evidence against the person who recounts a scenario? (See Mason, chapter 13, this volume, for the legal ramifications of reporting certain details in court cases.) Will negative or harmful consequences follow if information is either included in or deleted from the report? What will happen to the reporter if he or she gives an accurate rendition of the episode? Will any gains accrue from generating an inaccurate report? The purpose of the testimony must be considered in all studies (Pillemer, 1992b; Ross & Buehler, in press), even in those carried out on very young children. Several current studies (denBak & Ross, 1993; Chandler et al., 1989; Dunn, 1993; Ekman, 1989; Miller, 1991; Wimmer, 1992) have illustrated that young children are capable of deception in interaction with their peers and adults, especially when a child wants something and cannot get it except by lying. Children will tattle on their siblings if they deem it appropriate, and they will also lie about the details of their own actions in attempts to win arguments and avoid punishment.

The conditions that promote lying are often associated with the goals of self-protection and self-enhancement. Many individuals will not hesitate to lie if lying will result in attaining important personal or social goals. Despite the social, moral, legal, and religious prohibitions against deception, lying occurs routinely, even in the most unsuspecting "moral" circumstances. Bok (1978, 1984) and Ekman (1989, 1992) have both carried out systematic analyses of the situations that promote lying and deception. In addition, recent studies of conflict interaction provide evidence that siblings intentionally lie about each other to get revenge (denBak & Ross, 1993); that peers, especially two girls or two women intent on forming a coalition (Goodwin, 1995; Shuman, 1986), actively engage in collaborations to create a false account of a situation that will harm another woman and that teenagers will lie about their positions just to end an argument session (Stein et al., 1996).

Asking children to recount their experiences of emotional events may also give them the "right" to engage in pretense and fantasy narration. Because emotion episodes often involve goals and plans that are not carried out, we use a questioning procedure that examines thoughts and actions as separate components of memories for emotional experiences. In our studies (Liwag & Stein, 1995; Stein & Levine, 1989; Stein & Liwag, 1994; Stein & Trabasso, 1989; Wade & Stein, 1994), children are always asked three different questions: what they wanted to do when a particular emotional event occurred, what they planned to do, and what they really did. Desiring, planning, and acting are distinctly different parts of a goal-directed action episode. The results from our studies confirm that children often make clear distinctions between plans and actions (Stein & Levine, 1989; Stein & Trabasso, 1989; Wade & Stein, 1994), and they can report both of these components of a goal-directed episode.

One child's report of memory for an anger episode will serve to demonstrate these distinctions. Michael, aged 3 years, 10 months, distinguished clearly between desired plans of actions and the actions he really carried out. He was asked how he felt when, on a trip to Canada with his mother, a little girl that he was visiting broke his new toy gun. Michael responded with the following narrative:

Goal
I don't like broken guns; I like fixed guns.

Initiating Event
She was jumping on her knees.
She was this big *(child shows experimenter how big the girl was).*
And she jumped and then *(makes noise)*—
It broke.

Emotional Response
I was medium mad
when she broke it.

Initial Actions
I told my momma, boy!
She get in trouble,
and I told her momma.

Plans of Action (Fantasy Actions)
Then, I was about to call the police.
I beat her
I did a backward flip
I knocked her right out of—right off my bed.
She fell on the concrete and busted her lip.

Actions That Got Carried Out
I went away
I never talk to her before
I never ever showed her things that I be doing
I never do anything with her.

When probed with three questions that distinguish among desires, plans, and actions, it was evident that Michael knew he had not beaten up the little girl, that he had not done a backward flip, that he had not knocked the little girl off of his bed, and that she did not get a busted lip. He was able to fully acknowledge this. In reality, what did happen was that Michael went to his mother to complain, and that after complaining and tattling on the little girl, he never spoke to her or played with her again.

The accuracy of Michael's report and his ability to distinguish between fantasy and reality was confirmed in two ways. First, his mother agreed that the little girl was responsible for breaking his gun. The mother also reported the same sequence of actions that led up to and followed the breaking of the gun. Both reported that Michael came to the mother and told her what happened. In addition, the mother reported that Michael wanted her to spank the little girl. The mother told him she couldn't do it because the little girl wasn't hers to spank.

That Michael made a clear distinction between his desired plans and the actions he carried out was evident when he told us what he had really done. During the recounting of his real actions, Michael's emotional expression changed from anger to one of marked sadness, as captured in both video and audio recording. The shift in his emotional state signaled an awareness that his plan for revenge on the little girl could not be achieved. Instead, he had to focus on the loss of his gun. He could not get his mother to replace the gun, and this upset him. He told us that he liked fixed guns, not broken ones. He had just gotten the gun as a present right before his trip to Canada, and along with the gun, he got several targets and ducks for shooting practice. Ruminating about all of the negative outcomes he had to consider caused him to volunteer that he wasn't able to act toward the little girl the way he had wanted. However, he did carry out a series of punitive acts toward the little girl. He first tattled on her, and then refused to interact with her anymore.

That very young children sometimes distinguish between fantasy and reality is important for several reasons (see also Garvey, 1992; Haith, 1994; Harris & Kavanaugh, 1993, for extended discussions of children's understanding of pretense). First, in our data (Stein & Levine, 1989; Stein & Miller, 1993a, 1993b; Stein & Trabasso, 1989; Wade & Stein, 1994), children frequently include fantasies in their emotion narratives. However, so do adults. Given appropriate instructions for recounting emotional experience (Stein & Levine, 1989; Stein & Trabasso, 1989; Wade & Stein, 1994), subjects demonstrate that they are aware of the difference between reality and wishful thinking. They often produce different answers to questions about what they wished they could do and questions about actual actions. In recounting angry, fearful, and sad experiences, children and adults almost always have plans of actions that remain unfulfilled, because in these episodes, an important goal has generally failed. If children are not probed correctly or if questioning procedures do not allow for the elicitation of these "fantasy" plans, judgments about the ability to produce accurate representations of an emotional event may be erroneous. That is, children may know exactly what is true and what is not true, but the pragmatic constraints under which they narrate may predispose them to include events that did not occur.

In a recent study on negotiation, we found that adolescents often engage in this type of "erroneous" reporting when they verbally capitulate to or compromise with an opponent in an argument (Stein et al., 1996). When asked to talk about whether they had really supported their opponent as they had asserted during negotiation, arguers often confessed that they had intentionally deceived their opponent, and reverted back to denying the validity of their opponent's argument. That is, many arguers did not believe in or support the position they took during negotiation. In the context of the negotiation, they chose to lie or exaggerate compliance in order to bring the session to a close.

Despite the fact that both children and adults are sometimes motivated to produce erroneous reports, we would argue that they rarely confuse their plans with the actions they carry out, especially in situations that involve conflict (Stein et al., 1996). Such confusion is unlikely because the consequences of alternative plans are usually quite different from the consequences of the actions that actually occurred. The outcomes and emotions that would be experienced in the two cases do not overlap. For example, the consequences of really busting a girl's lip are incompatible with the consequences of not busting her lip. If Michael were successful, he would probably experience happiness because he succeeded in retaliation. He might also experience additional consequences, such as punishment, and the emotions that go along with them, such as pain or anger. If he did not successfully carry through the plan (as was the case), the memories would be ones of frustration and sadness at the inability to retaliate.

The absence of confusions in emotionally laden situations, however, does not mean that people are always able to maintain this distinction. In a study of reality monitoring, Johnson and Foley (1984; Foley & Johnson, 1985) have found that people sometimes confuse what they did with what they merely thought about doing. For example, subjects sometimes recalled actually tracing letters or wrapping a package when they had previously only imagined doing so. In this experiment, however, there were no important differences between the consequences of carrying out the action or merely imagining doing so. In both cases, the subjects simply left the laboratory and returned later to provide recall; thus they did not have an important memory cue like that which enabled Michael to differentiate between his fantasy of revenge and the reality of frustration.

We are arguing, then, that in emotional events, people often have multiple cues to distinguish actual events from those only imagined. Whether they will be motivated to report this difference, however, is another concern. We propose that the utmost care should be taken to examine the social and personal payoffs of telling the truth within the context of both experimental and real-life remembering. Furthermore, questioning techniques should be used to probe for both real events and internal states, especially when the subjects are young children.

A KNOWLEDGE-BASED THEORY OF MEMORY
FOR EMOTIONAL EVENTS

One reason that a knowledge-based theory of everyday memory has not received active consideration in the eyewitness testimony literature is that researchers have believed that the complexities of describing the knowledge used to understand emotional situations are overwhelming. Although a diversity of knowledge is used to understand emotional events, there are important constraints on the knowledge, thinking, and reasoning used in these situations. The results from studies on narrative (Stein & Trabasso, 1982a, 1982b, 1992) and argument understanding (Hart & Honoré, 1956; Morris, 1956; Stein & Miller, 1993a, 1993b) indicate that the process of event understanding is structured by a framework of causal inference in the context of social knowledge. Many researchers (D'Andrade & Strauss, 1992; Hammond, 1989; Mandler & Johnson, 1977; McLaughlin, Cody, & Read, 1992; Ross, 1989; Searle, 1983; Schank, 1982; Schank & Abelson, 1977; Stein & Glenn, 1979; Stein & Levine, 1990; Stein & Trabasso, 1982b; Suchman, 1987; Suh & Trabasso, 1993; Trabasso et al., 1984; Trabasso & Stein, in press) have noted this consistent structure, and have attributed it to the cross-situational importance of personal beliefs, goals, emotions, plans, actions, and their outcomes.

The Content and Organization of Goal-Structured Knowledge

We have labeled the knowledge that involves goals, actions, and outcomes of actions as *goal-structured knowledge* (Stein & Levine, 1990; Stein & Trabasso, 1992; Stein et al., 1993; Stein, Trabasso, et al., in press; Trabasso & Stein, in press). This knowledge is similar to that described by Heider (1958) and Searle (1983) in their writings on human intentionality, Suchman (1987) in her description of everyday planning knowledge, and Schank (1982) in his description of social and personal knowledge used during remembering.

The content and organization of goal-structured knowledge is constrained by the functions of human social interaction and by built-in processing constraints of the nervous system (Mandler, 1984; Mandler & Johnson, 1977; Schank & Abelson, 1977; Stein & Glenn, 1979; Stein & Trabasso, 1982a; Trabasso et al., 1984). Goal-structured knowledge is activated in any situation which involves a change in the status of goals that are relevant to psychological and physiological well-being, and it is intimately related to the experience of emotion (Lazarus, 1991; Mandler, 1984; Oatley & Johnson-Laird, 1987; Roseman, 1991; Stein et al., 1993). Therefore, goal-based knowledge is accessed and updated during many daily interactions. The content and organization of this knowledge can be described in terms of appraisals that are made during an ongoing event. Here we outline these appraisals using as an example a situation that provoked an intense emotional reaction in a young child.

In one of our recent studies (Liwag & Stein, 1995; Stein et al., 1994), a 4½-year-old boy, Robert, was asked to recall a recent incident that took place when his parents invited a guest over for Friday-night dinner. According to his mother, Friday-night dinners are especially meaningful to Robert. Dinner guests normally focus much of their attention on him, making him an active part of the dinner conversation. In this incident, a new guest was invited, but the consequences for Robert were unexpected and unpleasant. During the course of the evening, Robert initiated a conversation with the new guest by relating some of his recent activities. The male guest, however, did not think it was appropriate for Robert to talk so much. According to Robert's mother, the guest wanted the floor, and when Robert kept talking, he told Robert that, "When you are little, you can't talk, and . . . only when you grow up and become an adult, then you get to talk."

We ask how this event was understood from Robert's perspective. How did he go about appraising the guest's behavior toward him? What was his emotional reaction to the guest's reprimand? What exactly did Robert do? Table 2.1 contains a series of questions that represent the types of appraisals that are carried out when an event evokes an emotional response in an individual. The three major classes of appraisals are:

1. "What happened?"
2. "What can I do about it?"
3. "What did I do and what are the results of my actions?"

These three categories of appraisals are both temporally and causally constrained by one another. Thinking about possible plans of action cannot occur until some appraisal has been carried out about the significance of the emotion precipitating event. Evaluating the consequences of action cannot occur until plans have been generated and actions have been carried out.

The first category of appraisals, "What happened?" focuses on identifying the event that affected the status of desired goals and assessing its impact. The questions included in this category refer to appraisals made about whether desired goals have been blocked or facilitated, who or what caused the change in status of important goals, what the consequences of the status change are or will be, and what beliefs have been violated and updated as a result of the precipitating event. Robert appraised what happened like this: He concluded that the guest interfered with his ability to get attention, maintain the floor in a dinner conversation, and feel an important part of a social transaction. The consequences of the dinner guest lecturing Robert were that none of Robert's goals were realized.

TABLE 2.1
The Content of Appraisals Made During the
Experience of an Emotional Event

What happened?

---

1. What type of event occurred?
2. Have my goals been affected?
3. Which goals have changed in status?
4. How have the goals changed (have they failed or succeeded)?
5. Who or what caused the change in the status of the goal?
6. What are the consequences of the change in the goal's status?
7. What beliefs have been violated and updated due to the change?

What can I do about it?

---

1. What do I want to do about it?
2. Do I think the goal can (should) be reinstated?
3. Is an action plan available that would reinstate or modify the desired goal?
4. How do I feel about it?
5. What are the reasons for my emotional reactions?

What did I do and what were the results of my actions?

---

1. Did I carry out actions in the service of attaining or maintaining the goal?
2. What were the actions?
3. What were the outcomes?
4. Did any unintended outcomes result from goal achievement or failure?
5. Did the unintended outcomes cause a reappraisal or reevaluation of the goals at stake?
6. How will the immediate outcomes affect other desired goals?

The appraisal "What can I do about it?" involves assessing the feasibility of new goals. The person focuses on setting a new goal when a valued goal has failed. In Robert's case, he wanted to reinstate his original goals; he wanted to recapture the focus of attention, and he wanted the guest to consider him a valuable conversation partner. According to both Robert and his mother, however, Robert failed to attain these goals. The guest insisted that young children should not participate in adult conversation. Therefore, Robert's answer to the question "Can my goal be reinstated?" was no. When he found that he could not reinstate his initial goals, Robert had a number of options, including telling the guest that he was wrong to say that young children should not contribute to dinnertime conversation.

The appraisal "What did I do and what were the results of my actions?" involves assessing the outcome of actions taken in the service of new goals. According to his mother, Robert first defended children's rights by telling the guest that his comments were unfair and that children did not have to wait until they were grown up to enter into dinner conversation. However, the man's lecture also made Robert cry, and he needed a lot of holding from his parents. According to Robert, he felt very sad because he had to wait a long time to talk. However, he also reported, "I thought about why don't I stick my tongue out at him. And I went into the kitchen and stuck my tongue out . . . on him." So Robert was not able to attain his initial goals of participating in the dinner time conversation, but he did defend himself by telling the guest that he disagreed with him, and he did seek revenge, but behind the scenes. Therefore, the consequences of having some of his goals blocked were the formation of substitute goals of telling the guest that he disagreed with him and seeking revenge surreptitiously.

The full transcript of Robert's and his mother's reports is provided in Table 2.2. The answer to almost every question that appears in Table 2.1 was given either by Robert or by his mother, who observed Robert's emotional reactions and behavior. The question remains, however, whether these appraisal processes are carried out in all emotional situations. In order to answer this question, we asked preschool children and their parents to recall real-life emotion episodes (Liwag & Stein, 1995; Stein & Liwag, 1994; Wade & Stein, 1994). We then used a goal-based approach that incorporated the basic components of these three appraisal categories to examine the content and structure of the emotion narratives generated by the children.

Memory for Emotional Events

In our studies on memory for emotional events, we elicited children's narrations using two different methods. In the first (Wade & Stein, 1994), 85 children were asked to nominate and then narrate about events that caused happiness, anger, sadness, and fear. In the second (Liwag & Stein, 1995; Stein & Liwag, 1994), the same children were asked to recall and narrate about incidents where their parents had observed the children express happiness, anger, sadness, and fear. In both studies, children were first asked to recall as much as they could about the event. Then they were asked a series of probe questions, including: "What did you think about?" "What did you do?" "Why did (the event) make you feel (emotion)?" "What did you wish you could do?" and "What did you actually do?" Children in the second experiment were also asked to remember how they felt.

Our data indicate that children were quite capable of narrating about emotion episodes. In the first study, the children were able to nominate emotion-eliciting events 80% of the time. In the second study, children recognized 87% of the events nominated by their parents, and were able to narrate about the event for 90% of those events that they recognized. In 90% of these narratives, the children reported having felt an emotion.

In both situations, children organized their narrative recall around the three categories of appraisals outlined in Table 2.1. The majority of narra-

TABLE 2.2
Mother–Child Report of an "Anger" Episode: "The Dinner Guest"

Time Line for Mother's Narrative	Time Line for Son's Narrative
Events and states prior to focal episode	
Setting: "Recently, we had guests for a meal. This happened two weeks ago. They were people actually that we didn't know that well."	*Setting:* "There were two guests over, then th- they were talking"
Child's expectations: "Robert, when we have guests, he's used to getting a lot of attention, and he's very excited, and he sort of expects that um, they'll want to talk to him"	*Child's belief:* *Child has a belief that guests shouldn't say words that aren't nice.* "It wasn't nice words to say to someone"
Goals	
"Robert was vying for attention, he wanted attention very much, and he was hoping for it and expecting it ..."	*Child wanted to join in the adults' conversation. He wanted to talk.*
Focal Episode	
Precipitating event	
"He (guest) said something to Robert to the effect of '... When you're little ... you can't talk ... and sort of only when you grow up and become an adult, then you get to talk.' "	"And then, um, he (guest) said, 'When, when when I was little, I was quiet and I let the parents talk. The older you grow up, the more you can talk.' "
Change in status of goal	
Goal failure: Aversive state: "From Robert's perspective, the man was interrupting him, because each of them was trying to get, you know, different attention." "He was excited about whatever it was he had wanted to tell people, he was mad at the lack of attention he was getting ..."	*Goal failure: Aversive state:* *He wasn't able to participate in the conversation* "And I had to wait a long time (to talk)"
Emotional reaction	
"He was very angry, um, and upset" "And he sulked a bit" "He was very confused ... he was baffled by it."	"Sad"
Reasons for emotional reaction	
"Robert immediately sensed it (comment) as quite cruel and discriminating" "When he got it, in his own sense, what he said, was really how it struck him that's not fair."	"Because it wasn't nice words to say to someone"

(Continued)

TABLE 2.2
(Continued)

Time Line for Mother's Narrative	*Time Line for Son's Narrative*
Reasons for emotional reaction (cont.)	
"He was angry because, all his expectations were shot down. He was excited about whatever it was he had wanted to tell people, he was mad at the lack of attention he was getting and he was mad at this man for so clearly telling him, 'You don't matter. I matter!'"	
New goals	
Revenge (?): "Maybe part of him wanted to, to tell the man off. "On the other hand, he was baffled by it. I'm not sure he knew what he wanted to do."	*Goal reinstatement:* "I wish he would let me talk."
Possible plan of action	
	"I thinked about ... why don't I stick out my tongue at him." *This plan corresponds to a desire for revenge.*
Actions	
"But he said something like, 'That isn't fair.' Um, and he came back with it. He said, 'That's not fair. Children can talk too. That isn't fair that you have to wait til you're grown up.'" "He, he started to cry, Oh, he cried. He cried and he sulked a bit, and he needed a lot of holding from us" "That's why the tears came, in part. because it was also confusing to him."	"I went into the kitchen." "And I stuck my tongue out on him, at him." *Note that the plan was enacted, although he didn't explicitly state the goal.*
Consequences	
Goal success: Attainment: "I thought he did a good job defending children's rights." *In mother's view, Robert was successful in "telling the man off." Note that we don't know what effect this had on the guest who made the comment.*	*Not stated:* *We don't know how sticking out his tongue or going into the kitchen affected the goal of wanting to be allowed to talk, or the inferred goal of revenge.*

tives contained the basic elements of a goal-directed appraisal of "What happened." Across the two studies, children mentioned or clearly implied goals in 85% of their narratives, goal success or failure in 87%, and agency in 60%. Children also provided information on subsequent wishes and plans ("What can I do about it?") in 63% of narratives. They described subsequent actions ("What did I do?") in 70%.

Recall of emotion episodes mirrors the prototypic pattern found in studies that examine recall of more complex goal-directed narratives (Mandler & Johnson, 1977; Stein & Glenn, 1979; Stein & Trabasso, 1982b; Trabasso & Sperry, 1985; Trabasso et al., 1984). The emotion-eliciting event, its consequences to the protagonist's goals, the emotional reaction to the change in a goal's status, the setting of a new goal, and actions carried out in the service of the new goal are almost always recalled.

Our data from children's emotion narratives thus support the hypothesis that children structure their memories of emotional events around goals, outcomes, and actions. Although the focus and purpose of these studies did not involve assessing accuracy, we propose that this method of analyzing the content and structure of narratives should prove useful in assessing event memory. Many current studies of eyewitness testimony assess memory for isolated facts or details, without reference to how those details relate to the observer's goals or to events that affect those goals. We propose using questioning techniques to elicit information about goal relevance and coding schemes to take goal-structured knowledge into account.

CONCLUSIONS

What implications, then, do studies of understanding emotional events have for further studies of everyday memory, especially those related to testimony issues, public policy regarding children's eyewitness abilities, and the legal community? First, we have found in almost every study we have carried out or reviewed, that by the age of 3, children understand and can talk about their emotional experiences in terms of causes and consequences. Their accounts include appraisals that describe the event, its meaning, its consequences, their emotional response, the goal set in reaction to the event, the actions carried out in the service of the goal, and the consequences of such actions. We have also found that children have highly accurate memories for events when these events are understandable and presented in a coherent fashion (Nezworski et al., 1982; Stein & Levine, 1989; Stein & Trabasso, 1982a, 1982b). We propose that these two lines of research be combined; that is, we need to study the veridicality of memory for real-life emotional events within the framework of goal-structured knowledge. Are some elements of a goal-based narrative more likely to be veridical than others? Which elements are critical to overall accuracy? For example, when children verbally distinguish between real actions and mere wishes, do they accurately differentiate between things that did and did not actually occur?

We have argued throughout this chapter that the online understanding of emotional events needs more systematic and creative study. To understand the veridical nature of memories for these kinds of events, more complete descriptions of the originally encoded situation are necessary. These descriptions should take into account the causal coherence of the event, the ease or difficulty with which each of the events was understood, and the prior knowledge that individuals bring to the situation. In addition, because most emotional, stressful, and harmful experiences take place in a social context, memories of these events must be considered in light of the participants' differing goals and motivations, which often lead to conflicting interpretations as well as lying and deception.

Finally, we propose that future research on memory for emotional events may profit from the use of a goal-based knowledge approach that specifies the online inferences and appraisals made during emotional experience. Knowledge of personal and social desires, changes in the ability to attain these desires, the conditions under which these desires can and cannot be achieved, plans of action, and actions in the service of goal attainment are the necessary components of understanding emotional events. To the extent that we can document how event understanding takes place, we can examine the nature of memory representations and predict the content and accuracy of event memories.

ACKNOWLEDGMENTS

This research was funded in part by grants from the Smart Foundation on Early Learning, the National Institute of Child Health and Human Development (Grant No. HD 25742), and the Spencer Foundation. Maria D. Liwag was supported by an Irving B. Harris Fellowship from the Harris Center for Developmental Studies and the Harris Foundation. Our thanks are due to Susan Folkman, Peter Ornstein, Mike Ross, Tom Trabasso, and Barbara Tversky for their comments on an earlier version of this chapter. We wish to thank all of the preschools, parents, and children in Hyde Park who have so generously given their time, memories, and support throughout our projects on everyday memory for emotional and harmful events.

REFERENCES

Abramson, L. Y., Alloy, L. B., & Metalsky, G. I. (1990). The hopeless theory of depression. In N. L. Stein, B. Leventhal, & T. Trabasso (Eds.), *Psychological and biological approaches to emotion* (pp. 333–358). Hillsdale, NJ: Lawrence Erlbaum Associates.

Anderson, R. C., & Pitchert, J. W. (1978). Recall of previously unrecalled information following a shift in perspective. *Journal of Verbal Learning and Verbal Behavior, 17,* 1–12.

Barsalou, L. (1992). Frames, concepts, and conceptual fields. In A. Lehrer & E. F. Kittay (Eds.), *Frames, fields, and contrasts* (pp. 21–74). Hillsdale, NJ: Lawrence Erlbaum Associates.

Bauer, P. J. (1992). Holding it all together: How enabling relations facilitate young children's event recall. *Cognitive Development, 7,* 1–28.

Bauer, P. J., & Mandler, J. M. (1992). Putting the cart before the horse: The use of temporal order in recall of events by one-year-old children. *Developmental Psychology, 28,* 441–452.

Baumeister, R. F., Stillwell, S., & Wotman, S. R. (1990). Victim and perpetrator accounts of interpersonal conflict: Autobiographical narratives about anger. *Journal of Personality and Social Psychology, 59*(5), 994–1005.

Beck, I. L., McKeown, M. G., Sinatra, G. M., & Loxerman, J. A. (1991). Revising social studies text from a text-processing perspective: Evidence of improved comprehensibility. *Reading Research Quarterly, 27,* 251–276.

Bohannon, J. N., & Symons, V. L. (1992). Flashbulb memories: Confidence, consistency, and quantity. In E. Winograd & U. Neisser (Eds.), *Affect and accuracy in recall: Studies of "flashbulb" memories* (pp. 65–94). Cambridge, England: Cambridge University Press.

Bok, C. (1978). *Lying: Moral choice in public and private life.* New York: Pergamon.

Bok, C. (1984). *Secrets: On the ethics of concealment and revelation.* New York: Pergamon.

Bower, G. (1992). Emotion and memory. In S. A. Christianson (Ed.), *Handbook of emotion and memory* (pp. 3–31). Hillsdale, NJ: Lawrence Erlbaum Associates.

Boyce, W. T., Chesterman, E. A., Martin, N., Folkman, S., Cohen, F., & Wara, D. (1991, April). *Immunological changes occurring at kindergarten entry predict respiratory illness following Loma Prieta Earthquake.* Paper presented at the 1991 Meeting of the Society for Pediatric Research, New Orleans, LA.

Bransford, J. D. (1979). *Human cognition: Learning, understanding, and remembering.* Belmont, CA: Wadsworth.

Brewin, C. R., Andrews, B., & Gotlib, I. H. (in press). Psychopathology and early experience: A reappraisal of retrospective reports. *Psychological Bulletin.*

Ceci, S. J., & Bruck, M. (1993). The suggestibility of the child witness: An historical review. *Psychological Bulletin, 113,* 403–439.

Chandler, M., Fritz, A. S., & Hala, S. (1989). Small scale deceit: Deception as a marker of 2-, 3-, and 4-year olds' early theories of mind. *Child Development, 60*(6), 1263–1277.

Chi, M. T. H., & Ceci, S. J. (1987). Content knowledge: Its role, representation, and restructuring in memory development. In *Advances in child development and behavior* (Vol. 20, pp. 91–142). New York: Academic Press.

Chinn, C., & Brewer, W. F. (1993). The role of anomalous data in knowledge acquisition: A theoretical framework and implications for science instruction. *Review of Educational Research, 68*(1), 1–49.

Christianson, S. A. (1992). Emotional stress and eyewitness memory: A critical review. *Psychological Bulletin, 112*(2), 284–309.

Clarke-Stewart, A., Thompson, W., & Lepore, S. (1989, March). *Manipulating children's interpretations through interrogation.* Paper presented at the Biennial meeting of the Society for Research in Child Development, Kansas City, MO.

D'Andrade, R., & Strauss, C. (1992). *Human motives and cultural models.* New York: Cambridge University Press.

Deffenbacher, K. A. (1983). The influence of arousal on reliability of testimony. In S. M. A. Lloyd-Bostock & B. R. Clifford (Eds.), *Evaluating witness evidence* (pp. 235–251). New York: Wiley.

denBak, I., & Ross, H. (1993, March). *Truths, lies, and justice: Tattling in the family context.* Paper presented at the Biennial meeting of the Society for Research in Child Development, New Orleans, LA.

Doris, J. (1991). *The suggestibility of children's recollections.* Washington, DC: American Psychological Association.

Dunn, J. (1993). *Young children's close relationships: Beyond attachment.* Newbury Park, CA: Sage.

Ekman, P. (1992). *Telling lies.* New York: Norton.

Ekman, P. (1989). *Why kids lie.* New York: Penguin.

Eysenck, M. W. (1982). *Attention and arousal: Cognition and performance.* Berlin: Springer.

Fergusson, P. (1993). *Writing about traumatic events using the third person pronoun: Psychological and health effects.* Unpublished doctoral dissertation, University of Waterloo, Ontario, Canada.

Fivush, R. (1993). Developmental perspectives on autobiographical recall. In G. Goodman & B. Bottoms (Eds.), *Child victims, child witnesses* (pp. 1–24). New York: Guilford.

Foley, M. A., & Johnson, M. K. (1985). Confusions between memories for performed and imagined actions: A developmental comparison. *Child Development, 54,* 1145–1155.

Goodman, G., Hirshman, J., Hepps, D., & Rudy, L. (1991). Children's memory for stressful events. *Merrill–Palmer Quarterly, 37*(1), 109–158.

Goodman, G., & Bottoms, B. (1993). *Child victims, child witnesses.* New York: Guilford.

Goodman, G., Quas, J., Balterman-Faunce, J. M., Riddlesberger, M., & Kuhn, G. (in press). Predictors of accurate and inaccurate memories of stressful event. In K. Pezdek & W. P. Banks (Eds.), *The recovered memory/false memory debate.* San Diego, CA: Academic Press.

Goodwin, H. H. (1995). *Games of stance. Conflict and footing in hopscotch.* Paper presented at Linguistic Institute Conversational Symposium, University of New Mexico, Albuquerque.

Gottman, J. M., & Parker, J. G. (1986). *Conversations of friends: Speculations on affective development.* Cambridge, England: Cambridge University Press.

Haith, M. (1994). Visual expectations as the first step toward the development of future oriented processes. In M. Haith, J. B. Benson, R. J. Roberts, & B. I. Pennington (Eds.), *The development of future oriented processes.* Chicago: University of Chicago Press.

Hammond, K. J. (1989). *Case-based planning.* San Diego, CA: Academic Press.

Harris, P. L., & Kavanaugh, R. D. (1993). Young children's understanding of pretense. *Monographs of the Society for Research in Child Development, 58*(1), 1–91.

Hart, H. L. A., & Honoré, A. M. (1956). Causation and the law. *Law Quarterly Review* LXXII, Pt. I, 58–90. Reprinted in H. Morris (Ed.), *Freedom and responsibility: Readings in philosophy and law* (pp. 325–342). Stanford, CA: Stanford University Press.

Heider, F. (1958). *The psychology of interpersonal relations.* New York: Wiley.

Johnson, H. M., & Siefert, C. M. (in press). Sources of the continued influence effect. When misinformation in memory affects later inferences. *Journal of Experimental Psychology: Learning, Memory, & Cognition.*

Johnson, M. K., & Foley, M. A. (1984). Differentiating fact from fantasy: The reliability of children's memory. *Journal of Social Issues, 40,* 33–50.

Kohlberg, L. (1969). Stage and sequence: The cognitive developmental approach to socialization. In D. Goslin (Ed.), *Handbook of socialization theory and research* (pp. 347–480). Chicago: Rand McNally.

Lazarus, R. S. (1991). Cognition and motivation in emotion. *American Psychologist, 46*(4), 352–67.

Lazarus, R. S., & Folkman, S. (1984). *Stress, appraisal, and coping.* New York: Springer-Verlag.

Lindsay, D. S., & Read, J. D. (in press). Psychotherapy and memories of childhood sexual abuse: A cognitive perspective. *Journal of Clinical and Consulting Psychology.*

Liwag, M. D., & Stein, N. L. (1995). Children's memory for emotional events: The importance of emotion enactment cues. *Journal of Experimental Child Psychology, 60,* 2–31.

Loftus, E. F. (1992). When a lie becomes memory's truth: Memory distortion after exposure to misinformation. *Current Directions in Psychological Science, 1*(4), 121–123.

Loftus, E. F. (1993). Desperately seeking memories of the first few years of childhood: The reality of early memories. *Journal of Experimental Psychology, General, 122*(2), 274–277.

Loftus, E. F., & Doyle, J. M. (1987). *Eye-witness testimony. Civil and criminal.* New York: Kluwer.

Mandler, G. (1975). *Mind and emotion.* New York: Wiley.

Mandler, G. (1984). *Mind and body: Psychology of emotion and stress.* New York: Norton.

Mandler, J. M., & Johnson, N. S. (1977). Remembrance of things parsed. *Cognitive Psychology, 9,* 111–151.

McLaughlin, M. L., Cody, M. J., & Read, S. J. (1992). *Explaining one's self to others: Reason-giving in a social context.* Hillsdale, NJ: Lawrence Erlbaum Associates.

McNamara, D. S., Kintsch, E., Songer, N. B., & Kintsch, W. (1993). *Text coherence, background knowledge, and levels of understanding in learning from text* (Tech. Rep. No. 93–04). Boulder: The University of Colorado.

Miller, C. A. (1991). *Learning to disagree: Argumentative reasoning skill in development.* Unpublished doctoral dissertation, University of Chicago.

Morris, H. (1961). *Freedom and responsibility.* Stanford, CA: Stanford University Press.

Nelson, K. (1991). Remembering and telling: A developmental story. *Journal of Narrative and Life History, 1*(2–3), 109–128.

Nezworski, T., Stein, N. L., & Trabasso, T. (1982). Story structure versus content in children's recall. *Journal of Verbal Learning and Verbal Behavior, 21,* 196–206.

Nolen-Hoeksema, S. (1991). Responses to depression and their effects on the duration of depressive episodes. *Journal of Abnormal Psychology, 100*(4), 569–582.

Oatley, K., & Johnson-Laird, P. N. (1987). Towards a cognitive theory of emotion. *Cognition and Emotion, 1*(1), 29–50.

Ornstein, P. A., Larus, D., & Clubb, P. A. (1991). Understanding children's testimony: Implications of research on the development of memory. In R. Vasta (Ed.), *Annals of child development* (Vol. 8, pp. 145–176). London: Jessica Kingsley.

Pezdek, K. (in press). Children's eyewitness memory: How suggestible is it? *Consciousness and Cognition.*

Peters, D. (1987). The impact of naturally occurring stress on children's memory for events. In S. Ceci, M. Toglia, & D. Ross (Eds.), *Children's eyewitness memory* (pp. 122–141). New York: Springer-Verlag.

Peters, D. (1991). The influence of stress and arousal on the child witness. In J. Doris (Ed.), *Suggestibility of children's recollections* (pp. 60–76). Washington, DC: American Psychological Association.

Pillemer, D. B. (1992a). Preschool children's memories of personal circumstances: The fire alarm study. In E. Winograd & U. Neisser (Eds.), *Affect and accuracy in recall: Studies of "flashbulb" memories* (pp. 121–140). Cambridge, England: Cambridge University Press.

Pillemer, D. B. (1992b). Remembering personal circumstances: A functional analysis. In E. Winograd & U. Neisser (Eds.), *Affect and accuracy in recall: Studies of "flashbulb" memories* (pp. 236–273). Cambridge, England: Cambridge University Press.

Rachman, S. J. (1978). *Fear and courage.* San Francisco: Freeman.

Reisberg, D., & Heuer, F. (1992). Remembering the details of emotional events. In E. Winograd & U. Neisser (Eds.), *Affect and accuracy in recall: Studies of flashbulb memories* (pp. 162–190). New York: Cambridge University Press.

Roseman, I. J. (1991). Appraisal determinants of discrete emotions. *Cognition and Emotion, 5*(3), 161–200.

Ross, H. S., & Conant, C. L. (1992). The social structure of early conflict. Interaction, relationships, and alliances. In C. U. Shantz & W. W. Hartup (Eds.), *Conflict in child and adolescent development.* New York: Cambridge University Press.

Ross, M. (1989). Relation of implicit theories to the construction of personal histories. *Psychological Review, 96,* 341–357.

Ross, M., & Buehler, R. (in press). Creative remembering. In U. Neisser & R. Fivush (Eds.), *The remembering self.* New York: Cambridge University Press.

Ross, M., & Holmberg, D. (1990). Recounting the past: Gender differences in the recall of events in the history of a close relationship. In J. M. Olson & M. P. Zanna (Eds.), *Self-inference processes: The Ontario Symposium* (Vol. 6, pp. 135–152). Hillsdale, NJ: Lawrence Erlbaum Associates.

Rumelhart, D. E. (1975). Notes on a schema for stories. In D. G. Bobrow & A. Collins (Eds.), *Representation and understanding* (pp. 211–236). New York: Academic Press.

Searle, J. R. (1983). *Intentionality*. New York: Cambridge University Press.

Schank, R. (1982). *Dynamic memory*. New York: Cambridge University Press.

Schank, R., & Abelson, R. (1977). *Scripts, plans, goals, and understanding*. Hillsdale, NJ: Lawrence Erlbaum Associates.

Shuman, A. (1986). *Storytelling rights*. New York: Cambridge University Press.

Stein, N. L. (1979). How children understand stories: A developmental analysis. In L. Katz (Ed.), *Current topics in early childhood education* (Vol. 2, pp. 261–290). Norwood, NJ: Ablex.

Stein, N. L. (1988). The development of storytelling skill. In M. Franklin & S. Barten (Eds.), *Child language: A reader* (pp. 282–297). New York: Oxford University Press.

Stein, N. L. (in press). Children's memory for emotional events. Implications for testimony. In K. Pezdek & W. P. Banks (Eds.), *The recovered memory/false memory debate*. San Diego, CA: Academic Press.

Stein, N. L., Bernas, R., Calicchia, D., & Wright, A. (1996). Understanding and resolving arguments: The dynamics of negotiation. In B. Britton & A. G. Graesser (Eds.), *Models of understanding* (pp. 257–287). Mahwah, NJ: Lawrence Erlbaum Associates.

Stein, N. L., Day, J., Shirrey, L., & Trabasso, T. (1979, March). *A study of inferential comprehension: The use of a story schema to remember picture sequences*. Paper presented at the Biennial meeting of the Society for Research in Child Development, San Francisco, CA.

Stein, N. L., & Glenn, C. G. (1979). An analysis of story comprehension in elementary school children. In R. O. Freedle (Ed.), *New directions in discourse processing* (Vol. 2, pp. 53–119). Norwood, NJ: Ablex.

Stein, N. L., & Glenn, C. G. (1982). Children's concept of time: The development of a story schema. In W. J. Friedman (Ed.), *The developmental psychology of time* (pp. 255–282). New York: Academic Press.

Stein, N. L., & Levine, L. (1989). The causal organization of emotion knowledge: A developmental study. *Cognition and Emotion, 3*(4), 343–378.

Stein, N. L., & Levine, L. (1990). Making sense out of emotional experience: The representation and use of goal-directed knowledge. In N. L. Stein, B. Leventhal, & T. Trabasso (Eds.), *Psychological and biological approaches to emotion* (pp. 45–73). Hillsdale, NJ: Lawrence Erlbaum Associates.

Stein, N. L., & Liwag, M. D. (1994). *Parents' and children's memory for real-life emotional events*. Unpublished manuscript, University of Chicago.

Stein, N. L., & Miller, C. A. (1993a). The development of memory and reasoning skill in argumentative contexts: Evaluating, explaining, and generating evidence. In R. Glaser (Ed.), *Advances in instructional psychology* (Vol. 4, pp. 285–335). Hillsdale, NJ: Lawrence Erlbaum Associates.

Stein, N. L., & Miller, C. A. (1993b). A theory of argumentative understanding: Relationships among position preference, judgments of goodness, memory, and reasoning. *Argumentation, 7,* 183–204.

Stein, N. L., & Nezworski, M. T. (1978). The effect of organization and instructional set on story memory. *Discourse Processes, 1,* 177–193.

Stein, N. L., & Policastro, M. (1984). The concept of a story: A comparison between children's and teachers' viewpoints. In H. Mandl, N. L. Stein, & T. Trabasso (Eds.), *Learning and comprehension of text* (pp. 113–155). Hillsdale, NJ: Lawrence Erlbaum Associates.

Stein, N. L., & Trabasso, T. (1982a). Children's understanding of stories: A basis for moral judgment and resolution. In C. J. Brainerd & M. Pressley (Eds.), *Verbal processes in children* (pp. 161–188). New York: Springer-Verlag.

Stein, N. L., & Trabasso, T. (1982b). What's in a story: An approach to comprehension and instruction. In R. Glaser (Ed.), *Advances in instructional psychology* (Vol. 2, pp. 213–267). Hillsdale, NJ: Lawrence Erlbaum Associates.

Stein, N. L., & Trabasso, T. (1985). The search after meaning: Comprehension and comprehension monitoring. In F. Morrison, C. Lord, & D. Keating (Eds.), *Advances in applied developmental psychology* (Vol. 2, pp. 33–57). New York: Academic Press.

Stein, N. L., & Trabasso, T. (1989). Children's understanding of changing emotion states. In C. Saarni & P. L. Harris (Eds.), *Children's understanding of emotion* (pp. 50–77). New York: Cambridge University Press.

Stein, N. L., & Trabasso, T. (1992). The organization of emotional experience: Creating links among emotion, thinking, language, and intentional action. *Cognition and Emotion, 6*(3–4), 225–244.

Stein, N. L., Trabasso, T., & Liwag, M. D. (1992). The representation and organization of emotional experience. Unfolding the emotional episode. In M. Lewis & J. Haviland (Eds.), *Handbook of emotion* (pp. 279–300). New York: Guilford.

Stein, N. L., Trabasso, T., & Liwag, M. D. (1994). The Rashomon phenomenon: Personal frames and future-oriented appraisals in memory for emotional events. In M. Haith (Ed.), *Future-oriented processes*. Chicago: University of Chicago Press.

Suchman, L. A. (1987). *Plans and situated actions*. New York: Cambridge University Press.

Suh, S., & Trabasso, T. (1993). Inferences during online processing: Converging evidence from discourse analysis, talk-aloud protocols, and recognition priming. *Journal of Memory and Language, 32*, 279–301.

Trabasso, T., Secco, T., & van den Broek, P. (1984). Causal cohesion and story coherence. In H. Mandl, N. L. Stein, & T. Trabasso (Eds.), *Learning and comprehension of text* (pp. 83–111). Hillsdale, NJ: Lawrence Erlbaum Associates.

Trabasso, T., & Sperry, L. (1985). Causal relatedness and importance of story events. *Journal of Memory and Language, 24*, 595–611.

Trabasso, T., & Stein, N. L. (1994). Using goal-plan knowledge to merge the past with the present and the future in narrating online events. In M. Haith (Ed.), *Future-oriented processes*. Chicago: University of Chicago Press.

Trabasso, T., Stein, N. L., & Johnson, N. (1981). Children's knowledge of events: A causal analysis of story structure. *The Psychology of Learning and Motivation, 15*, 237–282.

Trabasso, T., Stein, N. L., Rodkin, P. C., Munger, G. P., & Baughn, C. (1992). Knowledge of goals and plans in the online narration of events. *Cognitive Development, 7*, 133–170.

Wade, E., & Stein, N. L. (1994, July). *Children's understanding of real and hypothetical emotional events*. Paper presented at the annual meeting of the Society for Text and Discourse, Washington, DC.

Wimmer, H., & Perner, J. (1983). Beliefs about beliefs. Representation and constraining functions of wrong beliefs in young children's understanding of deception. *Cognition, 13*, 103–128.

3

VALIDATING MEMORIES

Michael Ross
University of Waterloo

Bartlett is perhaps the most influential advocate of the constructivist approach to memory. In his book on remembering, Bartlett (1932) noted that "the description of memories as 'fixed and lifeless' is merely an unpleasant fiction" (p. 311). In the first sentence of the preface of that very same book, Bartlett recalled that the Laboratory of Experimental Psychology at Cambridge was formally opened on "a brilliant afternoon in May 1913." Although Bartlett did not describe the basis of this personal memory, he offered no indication that he felt a need to check the records of the national weather service or consult with others who had been present. Instead, this noted constructivist apparently accepted the accuracy of his own recall. Interestingly, another person who was at the opening of the Laboratory, Sir Godfrey Thompson, subsequently remembered that it poured rain (Zangwill, 1972).

A much anticipated ballet, *Le Sacre du Printemps* (Rites of Spring), opened in Paris that same spring of 1913. Various people provided firsthand accounts of the event (Eksteins, 1989) and their descriptions differ on significant details. Some reported that spectators either booed or applauded loudly, completely drowning out Stravinsky's music. Others described the audience as relatively quiet. Some remembered fights; others did not. Some recalled that protesters were ousted from the performance; others did not remember expulsions. Jean Cocteau published an account of an event that followed the performance: Along with Stravinsky, Najinsky, and Diaghilev, Cocteau drove to the Bois de Boulogne and Diaghilev, tears streaming down his face, recited Pushkin. Stravinsky subsequently denied that this episode

occurred. Finally, there are even disputes about who attended the performance. The vanguard of the Parisian cultural community would not want to
miss such an epic event. This may help explain why some people who
apparently were not there wrote detailed personal descriptions of opening
night, which, in turn, could help explain some of the discrepancies in the
stories.

Conflicting accounts of the past are not limited to events that occurred
in 1913. Announcements of Nobel Prizes are sometimes accompanied by
disputes among scientists concerning the origins of their ideas and the
nature of their respective contributions (Ross, 1981; Sutton, 1984). Politicians
who write memoirs are praised for honesty by some former associates and
accused of distorting history by others. Divorcing spouses often offer discrepant accounts of events in their marriage. In recent years, increasing
numbers of adults report recovering at middle age previously "lost" memories of being sexually abused when they were children. In many cases, the
alleged perpetrators maintain their innocence, reacting to the accusations
of abuse with apparent surprise and outrage.

Psychologists have long recognized that (other) people's memories are
fallible. At the beginning of this century, Stern asked individuals to describe
pictures they had seen. He summarized his findings as follows: "Perfectly
correct remembrance is not the rule but the exception" (cited in Undeutsch,
1988, p. 102). Stern (1910) noted that his findings called into question the
accuracy of eyewitness testimony in legal contexts.

More recently, Brown and Kulik (1977) appeared to provide evidence that
contradicted Stern's claims about the unreliability of memory. Many people
reported vivid recollections of the circumstances in which they learned
about unexpected, consequential events (e.g., the death of President John
F. Kennedy). Assigning the label *flashbulb memories* to such remembrances,
Brown and Kulik suggested that people's memory for the context in which
they hear about momentous events "is very like a photograph that indis-
criminately preserves the scene" (p. 74).

Brown and Kulik did not assess the validity of people's recall; subsequent
research has discredited the photographic analogy. Flashbulb memories are
not pristine. Over time, people sometimes alter their accounts of the circumstances in which they learned about important events (Brewer, 1992;
McCloskey, Wible, & Cohen, 1988; Neisser & Harsch, 1992).

Memory researchers often assess the accuracy of recollections. Outside
of the psychological laboratory, people make similar evaluations during
their everyday lives. Sometimes it is crucially important that individuals get
the assessment right—as, for example, when they serve as jurors. How do
people distinguish truth from falsity within and outside of the psychology
experiment? In this chapter, I discuss factors that influence individuals'
evaluations of memories, as well as the efficacy of their verification proce-

dures. I examine whether the verification process provides definitive tests of the validity of everyday memories. I begin by analyzing the recollection process with the goal of developing definitions of accurate recall.

THE RECOLLECTION PROCESS

My analysis of recall falls within the general framework of constructivist approaches to memory as developed by Bartlett (1932), Mead (1929/1964) and many others. Consider a simplified scheme of the recollection process that includes four main components: an external event, an internal representation of that event in long-term memory, a current recollective experience of the event, and a verbal description of that experience. How are these components related to each other? Although the internal representation normally resembles the external event, it is often not a precise copy for at least three reasons: (a) A perceiver is unlikely to notice or pay attention to all the particulars of a situation. In most everyday contexts, there is simply too much going on for a perceiver to take it all in. Also, what perceivers detect depends, in part, on the circumstances of observation (e.g., lighting, vantage point, distance, and so forth) and their emotional and physical states (Stein, Trabasso, & Liwag, in press). (b) Perceivers do not transfer everything that they observe from short-term to longer term memory. (c) People use their existing knowledge to observe, understand, and interpret episodes. They integrate incoming information into a coherent schema and add material from their general knowledge to eliminate contradictions or inconsistencies (Bransford & Franks, 1971; Bruner & Goodman, 1947; Mead, 1929/1964; Spiro, 1977).

Just as internal representations are not normally exact copies of external events, recollective experiences are not necessarily precise reproductions of the initial, internal representations in long-term memory. Both encoding and retrieval processes contribute to differences between recollections and initial representations. People's original encodings of events vary in strength and quality (depending, for example, on the importance and distinctiveness of the event), with the result that individuals forget some episodes more rapidly than others (Brewer, 1988, 1992; Johnson, Hashtroudi, & Lindsay, 1993; Moscovitch & Craik, 1976; Spiro, 1977). Repeated experiences of similar events may become confused with each other and combined into a generic memory that Neisser (1981) labeled *repisodic*. The details of particular events are difficult to extract from these generic memories (Brewer, 1988; Linton, 1982).

During retrieval, people's current knowledge and beliefs influence their recollective experiences. Memories consistent with people's present knowledge are often more accessible than memories containing contradictory information; also, people tend to interpret ambiguous memories as congruent with their current knowledge (Anderson & Pichert, 1978; Bartlett, 1932;

Cantor & Mischel, 1977; Hastie, 1981; Markus, 1977; Mischel, Ebbeson, & Zeiss, 1976; Ross, 1989; Schank & Abelson, 1977; Snyder & Uranowitz, 1978; Taylor & Crocker, 1981). When individuals are unable to recall relevant information, they may guess at the past, using their present knowledge as a guide for inferring what must have ocurred (Bellezza & Bower, 1981).

Finally, people's motivation for engaging in recall affects their retrieval and reporting of memories (Kunda, 1990; Ross & Buehler, 1994). Similar to present knowledge, people's goals and motives can influence the recollective experience by altering what individuals remember and how they interpret that information. For example, Santioso, Kunda, and Fong (1990) induced individuals to believe that extroversion is superior to introversion, or vice versa; later, those individuals who favored extroversion more readily recalled engaging in extroverted behaviors than did those who preferred introversion. People's goals and motives also affect how they choose to describe their recollective experience to others. Rememberers alter their reports of their memories in response to attributes of their listeners such as status, age, interests, knowledge, and attitudes (Brown & Levinson, 1978; Cansler & Stiles, 1981; DePaulo & Coleman, 1986; Higgins & Rholes, 1978; Schlenker & Weigold, 1992; Turnbull, 1992).

Memories and verbal reports may differ for an additional reason. Individuals may be unable to translate their private experiences into words. What is the relation between a recollection and its verbal expression? In his novel *The Genius and the Goddess*, Huxley (1955) observed: "What a gulf between *im*pression and *ex*pression! That's our ironic fate—to have Shakespearean feelings and (unless by some billion-to-one chance we happen to *be* Shakespeare) to talk about them like automobile salesmen or teenagers or college professors" (p. 47). Although Huxley may be overstating his case, it seems likely that people often fail to duplicate in words their feelings and emotions. I am not aware of research that directly addresses whether people believe that they are able to convey their impressions adequately.

Finally, let us subtract a couple of elements from the scheme of the recollection process. Suppose that there was no external event, and hence no internal representation of that event in long-term memory. Imagine, however, that people think about an event and discuss it with others. They may subsequently mistake the source of their recollection, believing that the thoughts stem from an external event that occurred to them (Johnson et al., 1993; Johnson & Raye, 1981). Researchers have also shown that leading questions and misleading information can produce such false memories (Ceci & Bruck, 1993; Loftus, 1993; Ofshe, 1992; Stern, 1910). Piaget's (1962) memory of an attempted kidnapping provides an example of the impact of misleading information:

> One of my first memories would date, if it were true, from my second year. I can still see, most clearly, the following scene, in which I believed until I was

about fifteen. I was sitting in my pram ... when a man tried to kidnap me. I was held in by the strap fastened round me while my nurse bravely tried to stand between me and the thief. She received various scratches, and I can still see vaguely those on her face. Then a crowd gathered, a policeman with a short cloak and a white baton came up, and the man took to his heels. I can still see the whole scene and even place it near the tube station. When I was about fifteen, my parents received a letter from my former nurse saying that she had been converted to the Salvation Army. She wanted to confess her past faults, and in particular to return the watch she had been given as a reward on this occasion. She had made up the whole story, faking the scratches. I therefore must have heard, as a child, the account of the story, which my parents believed, and projected it into the past in the form of a visual memory, which was a memory of a memory, but false. (p. 188)

Piaget noted an important implication of his anecdote: Accurate memories can reflect the same process as his false memories. Even a remembrance that is demonstrably valid may be a memory of a memory, rather than a recollection of an actual episode that the rememberer witnessed. This issue bedevils psychological studies of early recollections (e.g., Howes, Siegal, & Brown, 1993; Usher & Neisser, 1993). Researchers cannot be certain whether individuals recall their own experiences or whether they inadvertently include information that other people have provided about an event.

DEFINING AND ASSESSING ACCURACY

Correspondence of Recall to External Reality

A constructivist analysis of memory implies that people who attempt to recall the past accurately may inadvertently misremember events. How do individuals assess whether or not an episode is misremembered? Common sense suggests that a recollection is correct if it corresponds to an external, target event. In laboratory studies of memory, researchers typically operationalize accuracy in this way. Psychologists could debate the meaning of *corresponds* ad nauseam, but researchers usually manage to convince themselves and others that people's memories do or do not conform to the target stimulus. Bartlett's (1932) strategy was to juxtapose the initial passage or picture that he presented to research participants and examples of their subsequent reproductions. The differences between the original stimulus and the recollections were often quite striking.

It is not clear whether Bartlett reported representative examples of subjects' memories. Furthermore, he disdained any attempt to quantify his findings. Therefore, readers have no means of assessing the amount of accuracy exhibited by his respondents. Many other researchers have attempted to measure degree of accuracy. For instance, some researchers present subjects with lists of words and assess the number of items that participants can later reproduce. Even if participants remember all the words, however, their recollections are not necessarily exact copies of the stimulus: They may be unable to report the order in which the words were presented, their spelling, whether the words were written in capital or small letters, and so forth.

Usually psychologists settle for a form of bounded accuracy that is limited to specific aspects of the stimulus. One sensible approach is to condition the definition of accuracy on the task demands presented to research participants at the time of encoding. If the participants' goal is to remember a list of words, then their accuracy is typically determined by their recall of the words. Individuals who expected to be tested on words would probably think it quite unsporting to be asked questions about the pictures on the wall of the experimental room. Note, however, that recall of features of a stimulus or event that seem inconsequential at the time of encoding is an important aspect of some eyewitness testimony.

A focus on people's goals also enabled psychologists to develop a definition of accuracy for recall of texts. In real life, individuals rarely have to remember the exact words in a passage. Recently, I read a list of rules that govern visitors' behavior in a nature reserve. To conform to these rules, I do not need to remember the precise words, merely their meaning. Accordingly, psychologists studying recall of texts normally associate accurate recall with memory for gist. Rememberers are correct if they reproduce the essence of a passage.

In the context of psychological research, then, sensible people can produce reasonable operationalizations of accuracy. To declare a recollection accurate, psychologists typically do not insist that it be an exact copy of an external stimulus. In addition, rememberers are more or less accurate: Accuracy is not an all or nothing thing. Finally, there is no critical test of validity; rather, psychologists have developed norms that define accuracy in bounded terms and allow researchers to continue with their work. The operationalization and quantification of accuracy are greatly simplified by the fact that researchers generally possess the original stimulus that rememberers strive to recall.

Correspondence of Recall to an Initial Representation

Next, consider a second definition of accuracy: A recollection is accurate if it corresponds to people's original reality, by which I mean their initial representation of an event in long-term memory. We cannot ask more out of memory than that recollections reflect the person's original reality; otherwise, we may confound errors in memory with errors in perception. Suppose a person remembers that the word "sex" appeared in a list of words that contained the term "sect," not "sex." If the experimenter presented the list verbally, then one might be tempted to classify the individual's error as a mistake in hearing rather than remembering (and provide a Freudian interpretation of his or her error).

It is difficult for investigators to measure accuracy by the degree of correspondence between the initial representation and a recollection. Researchers do not have direct access to an individual's initial representation of an episode. On the other hand, researchers are sometimes unable to observe the target episode, but able to obtain an approximation of a rememberer's original reality by assessing his or her recall shortly after the event occurred.

A recent set of flashbulb memory studies concerned the explosion of the U.S. space shuttle Challenger (e.g., Neisser & Harsch, 1992; McCloskey et al., 1988). Researchers were unable to observe the circumstances in which people learned about the explosion. Instead, researchers assessed participants' recollections of where and how they heard about the blast shortly after the event (usually within days) and then much later, as long as several years later.

In these studies, researchers compared very long-term recall to an approximation of the rememberers' original reality. A reading of the articles suggests, however, that researchers presumed that they were doing more than this. They appear to assume that people's early recollections mirror external reality. Therefore, later recollections that paralleled the earlier memories also depicted external reality. This reasoning is plausible, but concordance demonstrates reliability, not validity. While composing their initial reports, subjects may engage in interpretation and inference; they may also adapt their reports to suit their audience.[1]

The evaluation of the validity of later memories will depend, in part, on an assessor's definition of accuracy. A thought experiment illustrates the importance of the definition. Loftus (1993) showed that leading questions incorporating false information foster inaccurate memories. Suppose that she revised the paradigm of her studies. Imagine that the experimenter's leading questions included accurate information that research participants failed to perceive on their own, details that were not part of participants' original reality. In comparison to controls, participants who received leading questions might then exhibit more accurate or less accurate recall, depending on the definition of accuracy. Participants receiving leading questions would demonstrate enhanced accuracy, as assessed by the correspondence between a recollection and an external stimulus. Individuals exposed to

---

[1]Note that these researchers were primarily concerned with assessing whether delayed and more immediate recall were alike. A lack of concordance between these two reports is evidence against the flashbulb hypothesis.

leading questions would demonstrate reduced accuracy, as evaluated by the correspondence between recollections and participants' original representations.

The second definition of accuracy suggests an alternative approach to the study of memory. Instead of asking rememberers to recall an external reality, ask them to recollect their original reality. In the studies of the shuttle explosion, for example, experimenters could have prompted individuals to recall their initial experimental reports, rather than the event itself. The advantage of this approach for flashbulb memory studies is that it induces participants to recollect the very same material that researchers use to evaluate the accuracy of recall. Individuals' responses might differ depending on whether researchers ask them to remember what they reported earlier versus what "really happened."[2] A discrepancy may be particularly likely if individuals recognize that they received later information that led them to alter their accounts.

I provide an anecdote that reinforces the point that the nature of the question matters. For the first 54 years of her life, my mother believed that she was born on January 24th. At the age of 55, she required a birth certificate to register for her pension. When she received the certificate, she was startled to discover that her date of birth was February 10th. She asked her mother, my grandmother, about the discrepancy. My grandmother asserted that her husband must have been befuddled when he registered the birth; my mother was the fourth child in the family and her father must have confused the birth dates of his children. January 24th, the day my mother had always celebrated, was indeed her birthday. Now dead, my grandfather was unable to defend himself.

My mother decided to correct the error; a January birthday would allow her to start her pension a month earlier than a February birthday. She telephoned the hospital at which she was born to obtain a record of her birth. According to this record, she was not born February 10th, as reported on the birth certificate, but she was also not born January 24th, as her mother claimed. Instead, she was born February 12th. Accepting the hospital records as valid, my mother has not forgiven either of her parents for their errors, although 20 years have now passed since she discovered the apparent mistakes.

If psychologists had asked my mother to report her date of birth 60 years ago, she would have responded January 24th. If they asked now she would answer February 12th. But if they asked her to recall how she had responded 60 years ago, she would surely answer January 24th. Different questions sometimes produce different answers.

---

[2]It is actually more complicated than this. What they said earlier may not be precisely what they remembered earlier.

VALIDATING EVERYDAY MEMORIES

The difficulties of validating memories are compounded when one leaves the psychology laboratory. In everyday life, individuals generally want to know whether a recollection accurately depicts an external event. Unfortunately, people typically are unable to evaluate personal memories by comparing the recollections to the original event. They do not have the initial text or word list that is available to the memory researcher. As the anecdote involving my mother illustrates, people can sometimes compare dates and other details of recollections to documentation compiled at or near the time of the target event. Even this documentation can err: Should my mother believe the birth certificate or the hospital record? She apparently chose to accept the evidence that was closest in time to the target event, but anyone who has worked in hospitals will concede that their records are fallible. Moreover, documentation of this sort is lacking for most episodes in everyday life.

Observers' dependence on verbal reports of recollections further complicates the validation of everyday memories. Other people can only know what rememberers say they recall, not what they actually recollect. Consequently, observers may evaluate memories for evidence of either deception or misremembering. Deception involves the intentional verbal misrepresentation of remembered events (Ekman, 1985). In contrast, misremembering is inadvertent: People believe their own inaccurate recollections. Conceptually, deception and misremembering are independent processes. I can mislead people about what I remember, regardless of whether my memories are valid or invalid. I can accurately report what I remember, although what I remember might be wrong. There can be a fine line, however, between deception and reporting an episode selectively or tailoring an account for an audience.

Participants in psychological studies of memory typically have no reason to deceive researchers about their recollections. Often, researchers can access the remembered event, so lying would be futile. Furthermore, there is no apparent motivation to lie in most memory research. On the other hand, in everyday life people may often be tempted to falsify their reports of their memories for personal and social reasons. My major purpose in this chapter is to examine how rememberers and their audiences attempt to differentiate misremembering from accurate remembering. Nonetheless, research on deception is relevant to some parts of my analysis because observers are not always able to know whether a memory might be an inadvertent or intentional misrepresentation.

Proxies for External Reality: Truth Criteria

People often devise proxies for external reality when evaluating the accuracy of everyday memories. Sometimes memory researchers also have to settle for an alternative to the original circumstance—this was the case in studies of flashbulb memories of the shuttle explosion, for example. Nonetheless, these researchers had a decided advantage over the average person—they possessed people's written accounts of the event shortly after its occurrence. Rememberers and their audiences typically have no similar document. How do people judge whether remembrances mirror external reality in the absence of external reality?

One answer to this question is that people typically do not subject memories to extensive evaluation. Individuals may accept many of their recollections uncritically. There is research evidence that in some contexts, at least, people are too confident of the accuracy of their memories (e.g., Neisser & Harsch, 1992; Trope, 1978). In our culture, individuals may also generally assume the truthfulness of other people's recollections. Grice (1975) suggested that in everyday conversation listeners typically presume that others tell the truth. Studies of deception provide evidence of people's credulity. Observers detect deception at only slightly better than chance levels, and their errors are systematic; observers tend to believe liars (DePaulo, Stone, & Lassiter, 1985; Ekman & O'Sullivan, 1991; Fleming, Darley, Hilton, & Kojetin, 1990; Krauss, 1981). The propensity to trust communicators is one of the most consistent findings in the deception literature (DePaulo et al., 1985).

Sometimes people do not accept memories as true. Factors both external and intrinsic to the memory may induce people to seek verification. If people's memories conflict, then the rememberers and their audiences may be prompted to evaluate the accuracy of each recollection. People's tendency to seek verification also varies with the importance of accurate recall; for example, individuals may be more inclined to document memories in legal than in social contexts. In addition, people may try to verify recollections that seem vague, incomplete, or unusual.

In the absence of external reality, rememberers and their audiences invoke a variety of truth criteria to assess the validity of recollections. These standards may be psychological or epistemological in nature. Next, I describe some major criteria and examine their efficacy.

Psychological Criteria

To evaluate a memory, people can examine attributes of the remember (source characteristics). Individuals judge some rememberers to be more credible than others. They can also consider the context in which the memory occurred. Assessors can determine whether the situation might induce misremembering or deception. Finally, people can study the quality and nature of the memory itself for clues regarding its accuracy.

Source Characteristics. A number of traits are related to perceptions of credibility, including the remember's expertise, gender, age, personality, and character (Johnson et al., 1993; Ross, Karr, & Buehler, 1992; Undeutsch,

1988). Do such source characteristics provide convincing evidence of the veracity of memories? Some attributes are diagnostic. Expertise is related to memory accuracy. For example, observers should prefer a master chess player's memory of the alignment of pieces on a chess board to the recollections of weaker players. The effects of expertise are limited, however. The memory advantage of master chess players disappears when the pieces are placed randomly on the board (Chase & Simon, 1973).

A connection has also been espoused between gender and age on the one hand, and credibility on the other. Stern, the originator of experimental research on eyewitness testimony, commented on the credibility of female and adolescent witnesses in actual child sexual abuse cases. In the absence of experimental data, Stern accepted the cultural beliefs of his day. He deemed women to be untrustworthy witnesses in sex cases and adolescents often to be incapable of distinguishing between sexual fantasy and reality due to the influence of hormonal changes (Undeutsch, 1988). Cultural stereotypes have changed and people would presumably be likely to reject Stern's claims today.

Nonetheless, gender and age continue to influence credibility assessments. Ross and Holmberg (1990) asked husbands and wives to evaluate the accuracy of each other's memories for various events in their relationship (e.g., their first date together). Both spouses rated the females' memories as superior. Because Ross and Holmberg were unable to assess the accuracy of the couples' memories, it is unclear whether spouses' assessments reflected their experiences, sexual stereotypes, or both. As for age, there is a stereotype in our culture that older people evidence a decrease in memory ability (e.g., Rothbaum, 1983). This stereotype seems to be partly true. The findings from research on memory and aging are complex: Age-related decline does occur, but only under some conditions and on some tests of memory (Craik & Simon, 1980; Craik & Trehub, 1982; Ferguson, Hashtroudi, & Johnson, 1992; Hashtroudi, Johnson, & Chrosniak, 1989).

Like older people, young children are also commonly assumed to exhibit memory deficiencies (Bottoms, 1993; Ceci & Bruck, 1993; Goodman, Bottoms, Herscovici, & Shaver, 1989; Whipple, 1911). A recent article by Howes et al. (1993) on the accuracy of early memories illustrates how psychologists' acceptance of this belief may affect their assessments of the validity of memories. These researchers asked university students to record their earliest recollections and then contact other people present at the time of the original event, soliciting their recall of the episodes. When an adult witness remembered the event differently than the subject, Howes et al. judged the subject's recall to be distorted. In contrast, if a child witness (e.g., a sibling) recalled the episode differently, then Howes et al. simply coded the recollections as different.

Howes et al. (1993) implicitly assumed that adults' memories of events that occur during their adult lives are more valid than their memories from childhood, even when the recall interval is identical. This assumption has not received close scrutiny from researchers. If I consider only events that *can* be remembered from childhood, not episodes shrouded by childhood amnesia, I am unaware of investigations that permit a definitive evaluation of the validity of the two sets of memories. Most researchers compare children's memories to adults' memories (Ceci & Bruck, 1993). Young children's memories are sometimes, but not always, inferior. Moreover, differences in the memory abilities of chidren of the same age appear to exceed differences in memory across ages (Wells, Turtle, & Luus, 1989). In summarizing research on eyewitness testimony, Dunning (1989) concluded that relative to older children, younger children (under the age of 9) "provide less complete and accurate testimony, although the deficit is small and depends on the questions confronted" (p. 231). Compared to older children and adults, younger children do appear to be more susceptible to leading questions and misleading information (e.g., Ceci, Ross, & Toglia, 1987; Raskin & Yuille, 1989; Wells et al., 1989).

People may use their assessments of a rememberer's personality or character as indicators of credibility (Undeutsch, 1988). From an actuarial perspective, this strategy probably does make good sense, if the assessments of character are valid and the trait is associated with the accuracy of people's recollections. The potential problem with the strategy is that behavior is often inconsistent across contexts. Everyone inadvertently misremembers some episodes and deliberately lies about others; everyone also reports events accurately. Thus, Undeutsch argued against using character as a basis for judging the credibility of adult witnesses in child abuse cases. Typically honest people may lie when the truth is especially damaging to them and they anticipate that their falsehoods will be believed.

Besides considering rememberers' traits, audiences can scrutinize rememberers' behaviors for clues concerning the accuracy of their recollections. Rememberers' apparent confidence in their memories may be a particularly important cue for observers. Wells, Lindsay, and Fergusson (1979) had subjects observe the questioning of an eyewitness to a theft. Subjects then judged whether the witness correctly identified the thief from a set of pictures and estimated the witness's confidence in his or her memory. The correlation between subjects' attributions of confidence to the witnesses and their belief in the accuracy of the the witnesses' decisions was high, r = .71. Other researchers have obtained similar results (e.g., Goodman et al., 1989; Lieppe, Manion, & Romanczyk, 1993; Wells et al., 1989).

Whether a rememberer's confidence is a valid cue will depend on whether observers can successfully estimate a rememberer's confidence as well as whether a rememberer's confidence predicts the accuracy of his or her recall. In the eyewitness study conducted by Wells and his associates (Wells et al., 1979), observers assessed the eyewitnesses' confidence in their memories fairly well ($r = .55$), but eyewitnesses' confidence failed to predict the accuracy of their recall ($r = .01$). Not surprisingly, then, observers showed little ability to differentiate accurate from inaccurate witnesses. In a study involving child witnesses, Goodman et al. (1989) found that mock jurors' impressions of the children's confidence in their testimony predicted the jurors' assessment of the accuracy of that testimony; there was no relation, however, between jurors' estimates of the children's confidence and the actual accuracy of the testimony.

More generally, research on the relation between rememberers' confidence and the accuracy of their recall has produced mixed results: Some researchers find a relationship (e.g., Brewer, 1988) and others fail to do so (e.g., Neisser & Harsch, 1992; for reviews see Bothwell, Deffenbacher, & Brigham, 1987, as well as Loftus, 1979). Consequently, observers' estimates of confidence are unlikely to provide foolproof measures of the validity of memories.

Obviously, confidence is not the only possible behavioral cue. Research on deception indicates that observers view hesitations, speech disfluencies, elevated voice pitch, and gaze aversion as reasons for doubting a speaker's honesty (DePaulo et al., 1985; Ekman, 1985). The first three behavioral cues are valid indicators of deception (eye gaze is not), and presumably reflect the anxiety many people experience while deliberately telling lies (DePaulo et al., 1985). In deception studies, observers have difficulty identifying liars from nonliars (DePaulo et al., 1985; Ekman & O'Sullivan, 1991). Presumably, observers would experience even greater difficulty detecting unintended fabrications. In assessing everyday recall, observers may confront individuals who believe what they are saying and yet are wrong. The anxiety-based behavioral cues associated with lying may often not be helpful in differentiating people who believe their false memories from people who believe their true memories.

Although I have discussed source characteristics from the perspective of an audience, many of the same factors are likely to influence rememberers' judgments of their own memories. Therefore, rememberers may be more persuaded that their recall is accurate in domains in which they are expert. Also, young children may have greater faith in their parents' memories than in their own recollections.

Context. People use context as a basis for evaluating memories. For example, employers may suppose that job applicants are inclined to exaggerate their past accomplishments. Accordingly, some potential employers require candidates to provide references that verify their recollections. I concentrate here on a contextual factor that has received considerable research attention from psychologists: the effect of questions on recall.

As the extensive literature on self-fulfilling prophesies indicates, individuals often seem to underestimate the impact of their own behavior on other people's behavior. Of particular relevance to my present concerns, interrogators and therapists sometimes appear to underestimate the influence of their own questions and investigative techniques on people's reports of their recollections (Loftus, 1993; Ofshe, 1992). Questioners tend to believe that they facilitate the recall of true memories, but they may inadvertently lead people to fabricate their pasts. Consequently, some psychologists suggest that spontaneous recall may often be more valid than recall that occurs in response to extensive probing (e.g., Ceci & Bruck, 1993; Loftus, 1993).

Research on leading questions provides some support for this claim (Loftus, 1993). It is not evident, however, that questions, leading or otherwise, necessarily yield inaccurate information. Stern (1910) speculated that leading questions are most apt to produce falsification when individuals feel compelled to respond to queries about events that they remember only vaguely, if at all. Consistent with this reasoning, psychologists who experimentally evoke false memories typically ask subjects leading questions about episodes that either never happened or that occurred in the context of complex, fast-moving events; presumably, subjects' memories for these episodes are impoverished.

Furthermore, open-ended recall is not necessarily more valid than recall prompted by questioning. Younger children tend to need questions and cues to provide detailed accounts of past events, even relatively recent episodes (Fivush, 1993). Moreover, contrary to the usual concern with leading questions, some authorities advocate their use in special circumstances. MacFarlane (1985) argued that leading questions help investigators to gather accurate information from child witnesses in sexual abuse cases. Leading questions may encourage accurate reporting if witnesses remember an event well, but are reluctant to disclose it because of embarrassment, fear, or other reasons.

Memory Qualities. People can evaluate the accuracy of memories by examining the qualities of the memory itself. Johnson and her colleagues found that actual memories contain more perceptual and contextual details, more information about subjective emotional states, and less information about cognitive operations than fantasized events. Individuals use these properties in their attempts to distinguish reality from fantasy in their own and other people's accounts (Johnson, 1988; Johnson, Foley, Suengas, & Raye, 1988; Johnson et al., 1993; Johnson & Raye, 1981; Steller, 1988; Undeutsch, 1988). Memory qualities may have especially profound implications for people's assessments of their own recollections. What can individuals believe about their pasts if they cannot assume the accuracy of remembrances that contain abundant perceptual and context information? If forced to doubt such recollections, people may feel that they are losing their sanity.

The use of memory qualities to validate recollections has an intriguing implication that to my knowledge has not yet received research attention.

Suppose that a woman recalls an argument with her spouse in vivid detail. Also imagine that her husband is unable to recall the event and denies its occurrence. Such denials are necessarily devoid of detail; the man cannot provide sensory and context information for an episode that he does not remember. Consequently, both rememberers and audiences may judge positive instances of remembering to be more credible than claims that an event did not occur.

Despite their usefulness, memory qualities do not appear to provide a definitive basis for evaluating memories. According to Johnson et al. (1993), people judge the source of a memory (e.g., fantasy versus genuine experience), in part, by using heuristics such as "if the amount of perceptual detail exceeds X, the event was probably perceived" (p. 5). Johnson and her colleagues did not specify the level of "X." Indeed, they noted that its value can change. For instance, people might expect memories of a recent event to contain more perceptual detail than recollections of an earlier event.

Nature of Recalled Event. Individuals can examine the nature of the recalled event to assess the accuracy of a memory. Individuals possess theories about how memorable or forgettable events are, as the following quote from a fifth-grade yearbook illustrates: "We all had a great time at the zoo and we probably will all remember this time forever." People are likely to accept the validity of a recollection if it seems to encapsulate an unforgettable event (Ross et al., 1992).

How valid are individuals' assessments of whether they are likely to remember particular episodes? The evidence that people are sometimes overconfident about the accuracy of their recollections (e.g., Neisser & Harsch, 1992; Trope, 1978) suggests that people's intuitions about memory are fallible. Moreover, it is not always easy to specify which events will be retained. Some episodes are memorable because they occur at a particular time or in a context that gives them special meaning. The same event may be memorable for some people and forgettable for others. For example, the following experience will be familiar to many professors: A student expects a professor to remember a previous conversation in the same vivid detail as he or she apparently does; unfortunately, the professor can hardly remember the student's name, let alone the conversation. For the professor, the conversation constituted one of many discussions with different students; for the student, a conversation with a professor is a relatively rare event. Also, the topic of discussion (e.g., grades) may be more personally important to the student than to the professor. For these and other reasons, the student is likely to possess a more detailed memory of the conversation. Therefore, whether events are memorable or not may depend in part on the nature of the episodes, and in part on the relation between individuals and events.

In sum, rememberers and their audiences use a variety of psychological criteria to evaluate recollections. Some of these criteria relate to the memory itself, and others to the source of the recollection or the context in which it occurs. There is no evidence, however, that any of these standards provides a decisive assessment of the accuracy of a memory.

Epistemological Criteria

Individuals may use epistemological standards to evaluate the accuracy of memories. The most important criteria include internal consistency, reliability, congruence with other knowledge, and consensus. A number of theorists have proposed that people use some or all these standards for distinguishing reality from fantasy and deliberate fabrication (e.g., Johnson et al., 1993; Johnson & Raye, 1981; Pennington & Hastie, 1986; Ross et al., 1992; Steller, 1988; Undeutsch, 1988). I evaluate each standard in turn.

Internal Consistency. It is often supposed that actual memories are likely to be internally consistent (e.g., Johnson et al., 1993; Ross et al., 1992). Incoherence and internal contradiction, the stuff of dreams and delirium, seem good reasons to deny the reality of recollections. Ross et al. asked rememberers and their audiences to assess the accuracy of memories and explain their judgments. About 90% of rememberers and 50% of their audiences invoked an internal consistency criterion as one justification for their validity judgments.

Not all social observers agree, however, that internal consistency is a hallmark of valid memories. Well-told stories are coherent, but real life may not be: "Reality never makes sense. . . . Fiction has unity, fiction has style. Facts possess neither. In the raw, existence is always one damn thing after another" (Huxley, 1955, p. 9). Along these same lines, Steller (1988) suggested that false testimonies tend to be more coherent that than true testimonies. Mead (1929/1964) agreed that life is disorderly, but argued that people normally impose organization while recollecting the past.

In sum, the internal consistency criterion may have contradictory implications. On the one hand, incoherence and internal contradiction seem to provide a basis for rejecting the reality of recollections. On the other hand, high coherence may also render memories suspect. I do not see any way to establish a priori where the cut-off points are: When is a memory sufficiently (in)coherent to be a believable depiction of an episode in a person's life?

Reliability. Assessors can consider whether a memory remains consistent over time, judging reliable memories to be more valid than recollections that shift. Reliability does not guarantee validity, however. I could describe an event incorrectly the first time and then continue to report it in the same erroneous manner on subsequent occasions. Indeed, there is research evidence that errors in memory tend to persist (Neisser & Harsch, 1992; Schooler, Foster, & Loftus, 1988). It may seem, though, that low reliability is strong evidence of a lack of validity. However, what does low reliability invalidate? The first report? Later reports? All reports? Baddeley and Wilson (1986) interpreted a lack of reliability as evidence that their brain-injured patients confabulated their initial reports (and perhaps their subsequent descriptions) of an episode. In contrast, Neisser and Harsch did not question the first report of a flashbulb memory when a second report contradicted it. Instead, they used the recall interval as a basis for assuming the validity of the first recall, and the falsity of the second. Finally, Fivush (1993) reported data on preschool children that directly address the reliability–accuracy issue. She asked the children to recount the same episodes over a series of interviews. She found that they were markedly inconsistent in what they recalled at each interview: For example, only 10% of the information that children recalled about an event on the second interview overlapped with what they recalled about that same episode on the first interview. Inconsistency did not signal inaccuracy, however. About 90% of what the children recalled was accurate as determined by their parents.[3]

I suggest, therefore, that high reliability does not guarantee validity and that low reliability does not necessarily discredit any particular recollection. Nonetheless, low reliability should inspire doubt and lead individuals to attempt to verify the memories in other ways.

Congruence With Other Knowledge and Experiences. People may examine a memory to determine if the facts agree with their previous experiences, as well as with their knowledge of the world and people. People frequently invoke the congruence criterion to evaluate the accuracy of their own and other people's memories (Johnson et al., 1993; Ross et al., 1992; Steller, 1988; Undeutsch, 1988). The usefulness of this criterion will depend primarily on the accuracy of the assessor's knowledge. Freud may have repudiated seduction theory, in part, because he believed that his patients recalled more sexual abuse than they could possibly have experienced during their childhood. Recent surveys provide more accurate information on the frequency of sexual and physical abuse of children. These findings have led some psychologists to argue that abuse is important in the etiology of mental illness (Bliss, 1988; Masson, 1984).

At times, people might be quite justified in rejecting a recollection that contradicts their everyday knowledge. For example, I doubt the validity of an article in the *National Inquirer* in which an Oklahoma farmer reports being

---

[3]In the spirit of the current argument, I would, of course, not necessarily assume the accuracy of parental memories.

carted off in an alien spaceship. At best, however, the usefulness of testing a memory against everyday knowledge is one-sided. People may be able to reject some reports as false (although they could be mistaken if their knowledge base is fallacious), but they cannot know with certainty that a report is true simply because it is consistent with their everyday knowledge. Moreover, most memories are not as outrageous as my Oklahoma example; some degree of inconsistency between memories and everyday knowledge may be common. It is unclear how much inconsistency assessors should or will tolerate before they reject a memory (Johnson et al., 1993).

Consensus. The final and perhaps most convincing epistemological standard is consensus: Do other people remember the episode in the same way that the rememberer does? For audiences, the most important test of consensus may be the degree to which the rememberer's recollection corresponds to their own memory of the same event. In the face of conflicting memories, people tend to view their own memories as valid (Ross et al., 1992). The consensus criterion is often applied in legal settings to evaluate the accounts of various witnesses. In simulated trials, mock jurors take corroborated testimony more seriously than noncorroborated testimony (Duggan et al., 1989).

As evidence of the special status of consensus, consider again the Howes et al. (1993) study of early memories. Recall that these researchers accorded greater weight to lack of corroboration by an adult witness than to lack of corroboration by a child witness. Howes et al. changed the rules governing their coding when the witness corroborated, rather than contradicted, the subject's remembrance. If either a child or adult witness recalled the episode similarly to the subject, then Howes et al. judged the memory to be verified and presumably accurate. The rule shift suggests that agreement, whatever its source, offers strong evidence of validity.

Agreement is no guarantee of accuracy, however. Consensus provides convincing evidence only if the observations are independent. In everyday life, observations are often not independent. Fifty million Frenchmen can be wrong because they may share an erroneous perspective on their environment. Similarly, Platt (1980) observed that consensus among family members about events in their lives is no guarantee of validity. Family members may hold norms and values that differ from those evidenced by their neighbors or members of other socioeconomic classes.

If consensus does not affirm accuracy, can we at least state that disagreement indicates that some people's memories are false or distorted? I think not. Conflicting accounts may both be "true" in the sense that each captures some aspect of external reality, as well as the person's original or current understanding of events. For example, because of differing vantage points or expectations, observers may perceive different events and faithfully remember what they saw. Some of the discrepancies in people's accounts of the opening night of *Le Sacre du Printemps* might reflect differential observation. Platt (1980) made a parallel point in his analysis of the validity of interviews: Low agreement between informants' reports does not necessarily imply that a measure has poor validity.

In recent years, reliance on the consensus criterion contributed to therapists' apparent misinterpretation of the recollections of patients with multiple personality disorder, or MPD (Ganaway, 1989). Many MPD patients report memories of childhood ritual abuse: They provide detailed recollections of cannibalistic revels, and adolescent experiences such as being forced by satanic cults to provide untraceable infants for ritual sacrifices. These memories contain considerable context and perceptual information; moreover, different patients describe nearly identical tales to their therapists. Believing these stories, numerous therapists supposed that satanic abuse is a major cause of MPD. Ganaway observed, however, that the detail and consensus may result from patients' exposure to books and TV programs on satanic cults, as well as discussions among patients and among therapists (during seminars, workshops, and group therapy sessions) who share information and cross-validate each other's histories. There has been virtually no physical evidence to corroborate any of the stories of satanic abuse.

Summary. Epistemological truth criteria seem to offer no guarantee of success. Even if people apply these standards systematically and impartially, the criteria fail to provide a definitive basis for accepting or rejecting a memory. Moreover, as I observe next, individuals do not tend to use these or other truth standards systematically.

CREATIVE APPLICATIONS OF THE TRUTH CRITERIA

People seem to be creatively inconsistent in the application of truth standards: They will sometimes use evidence that typically would support the validity of a memory as evidence against it. For example, although people may normally reject memories that contradict their everyday experiences, they occasionally appear to accept memories for the very same reason. A 26-year-old New Jersey woman was imprisoned for 5 years due to "the most absurd testimony ever credited in an American courtroom" (Rabinowitz, 1993, p. D3). A preschool worker, Ms. Michaels was charged with repeatedly raping 4- and 5-year-old children with various instruments including knives, Lego blocks, and wooden cooking spoons. She was also charged with making these children drink her urine and eat her feces, and with smearing the children's genital areas with peanut butter and then licking it off. She allegedly committed these crimes during regular school hours in a busy church. A jury found Ms. Michaels guilty even though none of her coworkers saw or heard any of these episodes, there was no physical evidence that the children had been abused, and none of the children complained about Michaels' behavior before the investigation.

From my description of the case, it is probably difficult to understand how a jury could convict her. Why would people believe such outlandish accusations in the absence of external corroboration? Now put yourself in the place of the jurors. They heard child after child testify that the abuse occurred. The children's testimony thus satisfies the consensus criterion. In addition, jurors heard the horrible details of sexual abuse from the mouths of babes. The stories are so bizarre, so beyond the ken of most 4- and 5-year-old children, that it may be hard to believe that the children concocted them (everyday knowledge criterion). In psychological research, mock jurors sometimes judge younger witnesses' testimony about sexual assault to be more credible and trustworthy than the testimony of older witnesses (thereby reversing people's usual tendency to question the memories of very young children); the jurors assume that young children have neither the motivation nor knowledge to fabricate stories of sexual assault (Bottoms, 1993; Goodman et al., 1989; Raskin & Yuille, 1989).

Although perceptual and contextual details in a memory usually provide support for its validity (Johnson et al., 1993), Karr (1990) found that people will occasionally argue that a memory is too detailed to be credible. In this instance, people's intuitions about memory (no one could remember that much detail so long after the event) clash with their tendency to view detail favorably. Similarly, whereas people typically use reliability to support the validity of a memory, they are capable of arguing the opposite. Eileen Franklin reported to the police that she had recovered a repressed memory in which her father murdered her friend 20 years earlier. Her recollection of the murder changed somewhat with repeated telling (Loftus, 1993; MacLean, 1993). Lenore Terr, a well-known psychiatrist, testified at the father's trial that such alterations would be expected as repression gradually lifts. According to Terr, unreliability provided evidence that Franklin was recovering memories of actual experiences. I also suspect that a jury may interpret such changes as evidence of Franklin's good intentions. They might assume that she could have produced a consistent story if she simply wanted to convict her father. Inconsistency, like lack of detail, can sometimes be a virtue.

People are no doubt correct if they suppose that the meaning of the truth criteria varies across contexts. Perhaps, then, people's creative use of the criteria should be recognized as evidence of cognitive flexibility and good judgment. Although I am sympathetic with this argument, I am troubled by the lack of a theory that allows us to specify, a priori, how context alters the meaning of the truth standards. Also there is reason to suppose that people's interpretations were false in some of the examples that I provided. In the preschool sexual abuse case, the children were apparently pressured into telling the stories by investigators. A New Jersey appellate court reversed Ms. Michaels' conviction.

THE INFLUENCE OF RECEIVER CHARACTERISTICS

I have discussed criteria that individuals can explicitly use to evaluate the accuracy of a memory. In addition, attributes of the evaluators, themselves, bias their assessments. Sometimes evaluators recognize the impact of these attributes; more often, perhaps, assessors are unaware of their influence.

Evaluators' relation to and attitudes toward rememberers are likely to affect their judgments of credibility. People may be more inclined to give the benefit of doubt to their friends than to their enemies. When appraisals are public, assessors may also be influenced by social factors. Consider, for example, the judgments of a group of American senators. In the fall of 1991, Professor Anita Hill confronted Judge Clarence Thomas, a nominee for the Supreme Court, before the Senate Judiciary Committee. A professor of law at the University of Oklahoma, Hill accused Thomas of sexually harassing her when she worked for him 10 years earlier in the Department of Education. Hill described, in detail, incriminating conversations with Thomas, who forcefully denied making the statements that Hill ascribed to him. After listening to hours of testimony the senators solemnly weighed the evidence—and voted primarily along party lines.

I presume that some senators acted on their private convictions, whereas others voted contrary to their beliefs, conforming to political pressures. In either case, individuals may not ignore the truth criteria, but rather use them judiciously. Such selectivity may provide a basis for people's private beliefs, or be a ploy to justify decisions and gain the support of others. Some of the senators who defended Thomas observed that he worked with many women, but that no one other than Hill claimed that he sexually harassed them (consensus criterion). They also noted that Hill continued to work for Thomas after the alleged harassment; she even followed him to a new job. These actions violated the senators' professed belief (knowledge criterion) that a person who is sexually harassed will attempt to avoid the perpetrator. In contrast, some of the senators who supported Hill emphasized her detailed and vivid descriptions of the harassment (memory qualities), as well as her glowing reputation and lack of ulterior motive to harm Thomas (source characteristics).

The impact of the assessor's relation to the rememberer is perhaps most apparent when the assessor and rememberer are the same person. Suppose that a rememberer's recollections diverge from those of someone else. Rememberers may, then, use their subjective experience as a basis for evaluating the conflicting memories (Ross et al., 1992). In reconstructing a conversation, a woman may "hear" her spouse asking her to close the windows. His claim that he instructed her to open the windows cannot eliminate her sensory experience. Moreover, the wife lacks direct access to the vivid, perceptual information that her spouse possibly derives from his own recall of the conversation. As this example suggests, people may infer that their own memories contain more sensory detail than does another person's recall of the same event. Rememberers may, then, judge their own recollections to be more accurate on the basis of presumed differences in memory quality. Ross et al. obtained preliminary support for this hypothesis: Rememberers judged their own accounts to be more vivid and accurate than another person's conflicting memory of the same event.

The tendency to use the truth criteria selectively is not limited to people's judgments of their own memories or to biased assessors. Generally, people do not have the time, resources, or motivation to cycle through the entire list. Instead, individuals may dwell on criteria that are readily determined and seem especially relevant to the case at hand.

RIPOSTE

I have proposed that recollections are imperfect copies of events, copies that may differ from both the episodes themselves and from people's original representations of the episodes. I have also described criteria that individuals can invoke to evaluate the validity of memories when the remembered event is unavailable for scrutiny. I suggested, though, that the usefulness of these standards is limited. There is no definitive test of the validity of people's recollections. I now consider arguments that I am too pessimistic.

Memories Are Typically More Accurate Than I Imply

In my simplified scheme of the memory process, I noted that internal representations can differ from external events, and recollections from internal representations. By positing these differences, I may seem to assert that individuals are totally out of touch with external reality. Most people likely find it hard to believe that their recollections are completely or largely inaccurate, and indeed I do not make that claim. The degree of accuracy depends on the magnitude and importance of the discrepancies among the components of the recollection process. Memories need not be precise copies to represent events sufficiently well for people's everyday purposes. The constructivist argument is that individuals often store the gist of events rather than the precise details. In addition, rememberers act on the stored material, retrieving and interpreting information selectively according to their current knowledge, goals, emotional states, and so forth. None of this necessarily implies that individuals lose total contact with previous realities.

Is there evidence that people inadvertently engage in extensive confabulation when recollecting the past? Psychologists sometimes present Piaget's kidnapping anecdote as an illustration that individuals can construct and accept as real a detailed memory of an important life event that never occurred (e.g., see previous discussion; also, Loftus, 1993). The literatures on hypnosis, guided imagery, and leading and coercive questioning provide additional instances of demonstrably false memories (e.g., Ceci & Bruck, 1993; Loftus, 1993; Ofshe, 1992). The memories of satanic abuse reported by MPD patients also seem doubtful (Ganaway, 1989).

The significance of such fabrications for everyday remembering is unclear. Perhaps psychologists' continued reliance on Piaget's striking anecdote illustrates the rarity of such constructions. The effects of hypnosis, leading questions, and so forth may indicate, in part, that rememberers say what they suppose an interrogator wants to hear, instead of what they truly remember. Also, some people may report, and certain circumstances may produce, false memories; however, that does not mean that erroneous conceptions permeate the everyday recall of the average person. I may remember my childhood quite accurately even though MPD patients do not.

There are several diary studies that suggest that people's autobiographical memories may be quite accurate (e.g., Larsen, 1992; Linton, 1982; Wagenaar, 1986). In each of these studies, the researcher recorded the most salient or important events that happened to him or her each day for extended periods of time (6 years, in Linton's case). The researchers then tested their memory for the date or content of these events at various retention intervals. They found that although the amount of detail that they recalled diminished somewhat over time, the information they did recall was generally correct. In another well-known case history, Neisser (1981) examined the validity of John Dean's testimony during the Watergate hearings. Although his testimony was self-aggrandizing and rife with bias and error, Dean accurately reported some of the major themes of his conversations with President Nixon. Paraphrasing Dean's own claims about his memory, Neisser concluded that Dean's testimony "was fairly close to the mark: His mind was not a tape recorder, but it certainly received the message that was being given" (p. 21).

These are significant and interesting studies, but it is difficult to draw general inferences about the accuracy of everyday memories from case histories. Moreover, the diarists targeted events that they deemed special in some way. Brewer (1988) found much more rapid forgetting of randomly sampled autobiographical events. The diarists also recorded the episodes—

the attention that the researchers accorded to these events may have rendered them more memorable. More importantly, perhaps, the diarists based their remembrances on accurate records. For example, Litton read her initial description of an episode before trying to date it; Wagenaar cued himself with one or more details from his diary such as the time or location of an event to determine how much he could recall about it. John Dean also had access to external records: He reported that he triggered his memories by going through newspaper clippings of Watergate related events (Neisser, 1981). In everyday life, people would usually not have records such as diaries or newspaper reports that they could use to cue their autobiographical memories.

Additional research suggests that people should not be too sanguine about the validity of their memories. In his study of randomly sampled autobiographical events, Brewer (1988) found that about 50% of subjects' recollections were erroneous. Here I briefly describe two other types of evidence, source misattributions, and errors in the scholarly literature. As Piaget (1962) recognized, people may commonly mistake the source of their memories. Johnson and her colleagues have described the bases of people's source attributions for everyday memories (Johnson et al., 1988; Johnson et al., 1993; Johnson & Raye, 1981). The inference processes that people use to deduce the origins of their memories often produce correct attributions; occasionally, however, the same processes lead people astray. How significant are source misattributions? I am not totally out of touch with reality if I remember that I said "X" when I only thought it, or if I suppose that you said said "Y" when your friend said it. One can imagine situations, however, in which such misattributions have grave consequences for the people involved. Johnson and her colleagues argued that mistakes in source monitoring contribute to delusions, errors in eyewitness testimony, inadvertent plagiarism, and other memory inaccuracies. Vicente and Brewer (1993) recently demonstrated source confusion in the psychological literature: Researchers and textbook writers sometimes attribute findings to the wrong investigators.

Detailed examination of the scientific literature reveals other types of errors. These include erroneous stories about the origins of major discoveries, as well as inaccurate reporting of the methodological details and findings of research in books and journal articles (Harris, 1979; Mahony, 1986; Ross & Buehler, 1994; Vicente & Brewer, 1993). Many of these inaccuracies are not trivial. They potentially affect people's understanding of past work and their plans for their own research.

To my knowledge, no one has computed the frequency of such errors in scientific writing. Surely textbook authors get the source right most of the time and writers of journal articles are usually accurate in their referencing and descriptions of past research. Nonetheless, the presence of these errors is surprising and troubling for several reasons. First, accuracy is highly valued in science. The primary criteria for good scientific writing are accuracy and clarity; humor, style, and creative writing are subsidiary virtues. Second, scholars submit their work to experts for review. Presumably, many errors are discovered and eliminated before publication. In addition, scholars communicate their published work to knowledgeable and critical audiences. I assume that scholars want and strive to get the details right, in part, because their errors are likely to be detected and harm their reputations. Finally, scholars can often access the original material rather than simply rely on their recall. Textbook writers could read De Groot's (1965) own description of his chess studies before writing about them and Freud could read his process notes before recording his case histories; however, serious misreporting occurred in both instances. In describing De Groot's research, textbook writers sometimes incorporate a control group that De Groot omitted but that subsequent investigators included (Vicente & Brewer, 1993); Freud's published case histories exaggerate the effectiveness and orderliness of his therapy sessions (Mahony, 1986).

Contrast everyday remembering to scholarly reporting. Unlike scholars, rememberers typically cannot compare their memories to original, written reports. Also, the demands for accuracy are generally not as strong in everyday life. Consequently, rememberers may not work as hard as scholars at encoding events precisely, retrieving episodes correctly, and verifying their memories. Rememberers may also be less motivated to report their memories accurately. People's everyday recollections serve social functions. Their audiences may well prefer amusing embellishments to accurate but boring tales (Ross & Holmberg, 1990). Moreover, social audiences are usually accepting; rememberers do not face the prospect of passing their life stories through the hands of anonymous, carping reviewers and authoritative editors (although I have occasionally proposed that wives serve a similar kind of surveillance function concerning the truthfulness of their husbands' tall tales). There is ample reason to suppose, then, that errors should be much more common in everyday remembering than in scientific reporting.

People Can Be Trained to Use the Truth Criteria Effectively

I have argued that people use the truth standards selectively. That is a problem with individuals, not the criteria. Would people's performance improve if they were trained to use the criteria appropriately? Researchers have identified qualitative differences between people's reports of accurate memories and inaccurate memories, with accurate recall including more sensory detail and contextual information (Johnson et al., 1993; Schooler,

Clark, & Loftus, 1987; Schooler, Gerhard, & Loftus, 1986). The distinctions are subtle, however, and observers' ability to discriminate between the two kinds of descriptions is typically only slightly better than chance. Telling observers which cues to attend to improves their accuracy somewhat, but their overall classification performance remains unimpressive (Schooler et al., 1986). Training in the detection of deliberate lies has also yielded modest results, at best (Ekman & O'Sullivan, 1991). More research is needed but the available evidence provides little grounds for optimism: Instruction in the use of truth criteria seems to yield minimal improvement in the detection of misremembering or deception.

Who Needs an Acid Test?

At the beginning of this chapter I observed that even memory researchers who can access the remembered event itself lack an acid test of validity. Rather, they conform to norms that define accuracy in bounded terms. If I can settle for this kind of looseness from researchers, why do I seek definitive standards for evaluating everyday memories?

Memory researchers achieve a degree of precision by offering an operational definition of accuracy and using it to quantify the level of accuracy exhibited by rememberers. In everyday remembering, the original episode is usually unavailable for comparison; therefore, it is difficult to specify the amount of error. Theoretically, it should be feasible to assess the *probability* that everyday memories are true or false, given that they satisfy a certain number or combination of truth criteria. However, psychologists have not proposed rules that formally connect the various truth criteria to estimates of accuracy. In the absence of explicit statements of probability, I believe that it is important to emphasize that no single criterion is definitive.

Individual Criteria Versus Combinations

Perhaps I have revealed flaws in the individual criteria, but the standards may be quite effective in combination. Conceivably, the criteria possess compensating strengths and thus complement each other. This intriguing possibility remains to be demonstrated empirically. Currently, I do not know which combinations of criteria might be especially effective, or how to weight the various standards.

I Am Looking in the Wrong Place

I based the list of truth criteria on the standards people commonly use (or propose using) in both psychological research and everyday life to distinguish accurate recall from misremembering. Memory researchers have discovered a number of other factors that may be positively associated with accurate recall of an event, including its uniqueness, how much emotion the event originally aroused, its importance to the individual, the individual's ability to understand the event, his or her tendency to rehearse the event in memory, and so forth (Bower, 1992; Brewer, 1988, 1992; Johnson et al., 1993; Stein, Wade, & Liwag, chapter 2, this volume). On the basis of such results, an additional list of truth criteria could be developed that would conceivably enable both rememberers and observers to distinguish accurate recall from misremembering. I suspect, however, that this new list would not fare any better than the standards that I have discussed. For example, the relation between emotion and memory is complex: Emotional events are not necessarily better remembered than neutral episodes (Christianson, 1992). Also, in everyday life most episodes are not totally incomprehensible or unique. How intelligible or rare does an event have to be before it will be remembered accurately?

DISTINGUISHING FACT FROM FICTION

One reason that it is so difficult to derive definitive standards is that truth and fiction are fuzzy categories; many autobiographical memories are both true and false (as Neisser, 1981, neatly documented in his analysis of John Dean's memory). Perhaps, then, we should abandon the search for measures of objective truth. If perception and memory are constructions influenced by a variety of transient subjective and contextual factors, then why not agree that everything is in the mind of the beholder? Along these lines, Edwards and Potter (1992) argued that original events can never be established objectively and thus cannot be used to verify memories. Instead, individuals strive to develop a mutually acceptable story of what happened during everyday conversational remembering. For Edwards and Potter, memories are the only reality.

This extreme constructivist approach to the study of memory has met with a barrage of criticism (e.g., Baddeley, 1992; Neisser, 1992). The critics emphasize that what really happened matters because it often serves to constrain people's memories (they do not remember just anything) and it has significant implications for the present and future. Consider where an extreme constructivist view takes us. Suppose that a woman recovers a childhood memory of being sexually abused by her father. From the standpoint of both society and the individuals involved, it matters whether the abuse occurred. If guilty, the father should be dealt with by the legal system and prevented from harming others. If innocent, the father may be needlessly subjected to a horrendous ordeal.

There is one intriguing instance in which biological and cognitive processes seem to spare people the need to distinguish fact from fiction. Many authors have theorized about the functions of dreams. In addition, many have speculated about the mechanisms that cause people to forget the vast majority of their dreams. I do not know why people dream, but I am fairly confident that I know why humans evolved with a facility for forgetting their dreams. Imagine how life would be if we retained all of our dreams and faced the daily task of differentiating them from reality. Poets seem to enjoy fantasizing about such a circumstance (as the following excerpt reveals), but I believe that for most people it would be a nightmare:

> Once upon a time, I, Chuang Tsu, dreamed I was a butterfly flying happily here and there, enjoying life without knowing who I was. Suddenly I woke up and I was indeed Chuang Tsu. Did Chuang Tsu dream he was a butterfly, or did the butterfly dream he was Chuang Tsu? (Chuang Tsu, 4th century B.C.)

For society to function effectively, people need be able to differentiate truth from fantasy and falsehood. If the distinction proves difficult or contentious, the public sometimes turns to psychologists for help. When society or the legal system calls on psychologists, it is often in the hope of obtaining an unequivocal assessment of the validity of a specific memory (e.g., MacLean, 1993; Undeutsch, 1988). In my view, we should be very clear that no such test exists. Psychologists cannot state with scientific authority that a particular memory is true or false. With further research, we may achieve a more modest goal, however. We may be able to link people's standing on various truth criteria to probability estimates of the accuracy of their memories. Given the importance of assessing validity, I believe that this objective is worth pursuing.

ACKNOWLEDGMENTS

I thank Hildy Ross, Barbara Tversky, and Elizabeth Wade for their comments on an earlier draft of this chapter. My research is supported by the Social Sciences and Humanities Research Council of Canada.

REFERENCES

Anderson, R. C., & Pichert, J. W. (1978). Recall of previously unrecallable information following a shift in perspective. *Journal of Verbal Learning and Verbal Behavior, 17*, 1–12.

Baddeley, A. (1992). Is memory all talk? *The Psychologist, 5*, 447–448.

Baddeley, A., & Wilson, B. (1986). Amnesia, autobiographical memory, and confabulation. In D. C. Rubin (Ed.), *Autobiographical memory* (pp. 225–252). New York: Cambridge University Press.

Bartlett, F. C. (1932). *Remembering: A study in experimental and social psychology*. Cambridge, England: Cambridge University Press.

Bellezza, F. S., & Bower, G. H. (1981). Person stereotypes and memory for people. *Journal of Personality and Social Psychology, 41,* 856–865.

Bliss, E. L. (1988). A reexamination of Freud's basic concepts from studies of multiple personality disorder. *Dissociation, 1,* 36–40.

Bothwell, R., Deffenbacher, K., & Brigham, J. (1987). Correlation of eyewitness accuracy and confidence: Optimality hypothesis revised. *Journal of Applied Psychology, 72,* 691–695.

Bottoms, B. L. (1993). Individual differences in perceptions of child sexual assault victims. In G. S. Goodman & B. L. Bottoms (Eds.), *Child victims, child witnesses* (pp. 229–261). New York: Guilford.

Bower, G. H. (1992). How might emotions affect learning? In S. Christianson (Ed.), *The handbook of emotion and memory* (pp. 3–31). Hillsdale, NJ: Lawrence Erlbaum Associates.

Bransford, J. D., & Franks, J. J. (1971). The abstraction of linguistic ideas. *Cognitive Psychology, 2,* 331–350.

Brewer, W. F. (1988). Memory for randomly sampled autobiographical events. In U. Neisser & E. Winograd (Eds.), *Remembering reconsidered: Ecological and traditional approaches to the study of memory* (pp. 21–90). New York: Cambridge University Press.

Brewer, W. F. (1992). The theoretical and empirical status of the flashbulb memory hypothesis. In E. Winograd & U. Neisser (Eds.), *Affect and accuracy in recall: Studies of "flashbulb" memories* (pp. 274–305). New York: Cambridge University Press.

Brown, P., & Levinson, S. (1978). Universals in language use: Politeness phenomena. In E. Goody (Ed.), *Question and politeness* (pp. 56–310). Cambridge, England: Cambridge University Press.

Brown, R., & Kulik, J. (1977). Flashbulb memories. *Cognition, 5,* 73–99.

Bruner, J. S., & Goodman, C. C. (1947). Value and need as organizing factors in perception. *Journal of Abnormal and Social Psychology, 42,* 33–44.

Cansler, D., & Stiles, W. (1981). Relative status and interpersonal presumptuousness. *Journal of Experimental Social Psychology, 17,* 459–471.

Cantor, N., & Mischel, W. (1977). Traits as prototypes: Effects on recognition memory. *Journal of Personality and Social Psychology, 35,* 38–48.

Ceci, S. J., & Bruck, M. (1993). Suggestibility of the child witness: A historical review and synthesis. *Psychological Bulletin, 11,* 403–439.

Ceci, S. J., Ross, D. F., & Toglia, M. P. (1987). Suggestibility of children's memory: Psycholegal implications. *Journal of Experimental Psychology: General, 116,* 38–49.

Christianson, S. (1992). *The handbook of emotion and memory: Research and theory.* Hillsdale, NJ: Lawrence Erlbaum Associates.

Chuang Tsu (1974). *Inner chapters* (G. Feng & J. English, Trans.). London: Wildwood House. (Original chapters written circa 4th Century B.C.)

Chase, W. G., & Simon, H. A. (1973). Perception in chess. *Cognitive Psychology, 4,* 55–81.

Craik, F. I. M., & Simon, E. (1980). Age differences in memory: The roles of attention and depth of processing. In L. W. Poon, J. L. Fozard, L. S. Cermak, D. Arenberg, & L. W. Thompson (Eds.), *New directions in memory and aging: Proceedings of the George A. Talland Memorial Conference* (pp. 95–112). Hillsdale, NJ: Lawrence Erlbaum Associates.

Craik, F. I. M., & Trehub, S. E. (1982). *Aging and cognitive processes.* New York: Plenum.

De Groot, A. D. (1965). *Thought and choice in chess.* The Hague, The Netherlands: Mouton.

DePaulo, B., & Coleman, L. (1986). Talking to children, foreigners, and retarded adults. *Journal of Personality and Social Psychology, 51,* 945–959.

DePaulo, B. M., Stone, J. I., & Lassiter, G. D. (1985). Deceiving and detecting deceit. In B. R. Schlenker (Ed.), *The self and social life* (pp. 323–370). New York: McGraw-Hill.

Duggan, L. M., III, Aubrey, M., Doherty, E., Isquith, P., Levine, M., & Scheiner, J. (1989). The credibility of children as witnesses in a simulated child sexual abuse trial. In S. J. Ceci, D. F. Ross, & M. P. Toglia (Eds.), *Perspectives on children's testimony* (pp. 71–99). New York: Springer-Verlag.

Dunning, D. (1989). Research on children's eyewitness testimony: Perspectives on its past and future. In S. J. Ceci, D. F. Ross, & M. P. Toglia (Eds.), *Perspectives on children's testimony* (pp. 230–247). New York: Springer-Verlag.

Edwards, D., & Potter, J. (1992). The chancellor's memory: Rhetoric and truth in discursive remembering. *Applied Cognitive Psychology, 6,* 187–215.

Ekman, P. (1985). *Telling lies. Clues to deception in the marketplace, marriage, and politics.* New York: Norton.

Ekman, P., & O'Sullivan, M. (1991). Who can catch a liar? *American Psychologist, 46,* 913–920.

Eksteins, M. (1989). Rites of Spring: *The great war and the birth of the modern age.* Boston: Houghton Mifflin.

Ferguson, S. A., Hashtroudi, S., & Johnson, M. K. (1992). Age differences in using source-relevant cues. *Psychology and Aging, 7,* 443–452.

Fivush, R. (1993). Developmental perspectives on autobiographical recall. In G. S. Goodman & B. L. Bottoms (Eds.), *Child victims, child witnesses* (pp. 1–24). New York: Guilford.

Fleming, J. H., Darley, J. M., Hilton, J. L., & Kojetin, B. A. (1990). Multiple audience problem: A strategic communication perspective on social perception. *Journal of Personality and Social Psychology, 58,* 593–609.

Ganaway, G. K. (1989). Historical versus narrative truth: Clarifying the role of exogenous trauma in the etiology of MPD and its variants. *Dissociation, 2,* 205–220.

Goodman, G. S., Bottoms, B. L., Herscovici, B. B., & Shaver, P. (1989). Determinants of the child victim's perceived credibility. In S. J. Ceci, D. F. Ross, & M. P. Toglia (Eds.), *Perspectives on children's testimony* (pp. 1–22). New York: Springer-Verlag.

Grice, H. P. (1975). Logic and conversation. In P. Cole & J. Morgan (Eds.), *Syntax and semantics: Vol. 3. Speech acts* (pp. 41–58). New York: Academic Press.

Harris, B. (1979). Whatever happened to Little Albert? *American Psychologist, 34,* 151–160.

Hashtroudi, S., Johnson, M. K., & Chrosniak, L. D. (1989). Aging and source monitoring. *Psychology and Aging, 4,* 106–112.

Hastie, R. (1981). Schematic principles in human memory. In E. T. Higgins, C. P. Herman, & M. P. Zanna (Eds.), *Social cognition: The Ontario Symposium* (Vol. 1, pp. 39–88). Hillsdale, NJ: Lawrence Erlbaum Associates.

Higgins, E. T., & Rholes, W. S. (1978). Saying is believing: Effects of message modification on memory and liking for the person described. *Journal of Experimental Social Psychology, 14,* 363–378.

Howes, M., Siegel, M., & Brown, F. (1993). Early childhood memories: Accuracy and affect. *Cognition, 47,* 95–119.

Huxley, A. (1955). *The genius and the goddess.* New York: Harper.

Johnson, M. K. (1988). Reality monitoring: An experimental phenomenological approach. *Journal of Experimental Psychology: General, 117*(4), 390–394.

Johnson, M. K., Foley, M. A., Suengas, A. G., & Raye, C. L. (1988). Phenomenal characteristics of memories for perceived and imagined autobiographical events. *Journal of Experimental Psychology: General, 117*(4), 371–376.

Johnson, M. K., Hashtroudi, S., & Lindsay, D. S. (1993). Source monitoring. *Psychological Bulletin, 114,* 3–28.

Johnson. M. K., & Raye, C. L. (1981). Reality monitoring. *Psychological Review, 88,* 67–85.

Karr, J. W. (1990). *Assessing the accuracy of conflicting memories for the same event.* Unpublished masters thesis, University of Waterloo, Ontario, Canada.

Krauss, R. M. (1981). Impression formation, impression management, and nonverbal behaviors. In E. T. Higgins, C. P. Herman, & M. P. Zanna (Eds.), *Social cognition: The Ontario Symposium* (Vol. 1, pp. 323–341). Hillsdale, NJ: Lawrence Erlbaum Associates.

Kunda, Z. (1990). The case for motivated reasoning. *Psychological Bulletin, 108,* 480–498.

Larsen, S. F. (1992). Potential flashbulbs: Memories of ordinary news as the baseline. In E. Winograd & U. Neisser (Eds.), *Affect and accuracy in recall: Studies of "flashbulb" memories* (pp. 32–64). New York: Cambridge University Press.

Lieppe, M. R., Manion, A. P., & Romanczyk, A. (1993). Discernibility or discrimination?: Understanding jurors' reactions to accurate and inaccurate child and adult eyewitnesses. In G. S. Goodman & B. L. Bottoms (Eds.), *Child victims, child witnesses* (pp. 169–202). New York: Guilford.

Linton, M. (1982). Transformations of memory in everyday life. In U. Neisser (Ed.), *Memory observed* (pp. 77–91). San Francisco: Freeman.

Loftus, E. F. (1979). *Eyewitness testimony*. Cambridge, MA: Harvard University Press.

Loftus, E. F. (1993). The reality of repressed memories. *American Psychologist, 48*, 518–537.

MacFarlane, K. (1985). Diagnostic evaluations and the use of videotapes in child sexual abuse cases. *Miami Law Review, 40*, 135–155.

MacLean, H. N. (1993). *Once upon a time*. New York: HarperCollins.

McCloskey, M., Wible, C., & Cohen, N. J. (1988). Is there a special flashbulb-memory mechanism? *Journal of Experimental Psychology: General, 117*, 171–181.

Mahony, P. J. (1986). *Freud and the rat man*. New Haven, CT: Yale University Press.

Markus, H. (1977). Self-schemata and processing information about the self. *Journal of Personality and Social Psychology, 35*, 63–78.

Masson, J. M. (1984). *The assault on truth: Freud's suppression of the seduction theory*. New York: Farrar, Straus & Giroux.

Mead, G. H. (1964). The nature of the past. In A. J. Reck (Ed.), *Selective writings: George Herbert Mead* (pp. 345–354). Chicago: University of Chicago Press. (Original work published 1929)

Mischel, W., Ebbesen, E. B., & Zeiss, A. M. (1976). Determinants of selective memory about the self. *Journal of Consulting and Clincial Psychology, 1*, 92–103.

Moscovitch, M., & Craik, F. I. M. (1976). Depth of processing, retrieval cues, and uniqueness of encoding as factors in recall. *Journal of Verbal Learning and Verbal Behavior, 15*, 447–468.

Neisser, U. (1981). John Dean's memory: A case study. *Cognition, 9*, 1–22.

Neisser, U. (1992). The psychology of memory and the sociolinguistics of remembering. *The Psychologist, 5*, 451–452.

Neisser, U. (1994). Self narratives: True and false. In U. Neisser & R. Fivush (Eds.), *The remembering self* (pp. 1–18). New York: Cambridge University Press.

Neisser, U., & Harsch, N. (1992). Phantom flashbulbs: False recollections of hearing the news about Challenger. In E. Winograd & U. Neisser (Eds.), *Affect and accuracy in recall: Studies of "flashbulb" memories* (pp. 9–31). New York: Cambridge University Press.

Ofshe, R. J. (1992). Inadvertent hypnosis during interrogation: False confession due to dissociative state; misidentified multiple personality, and the satanic cult hypothesis. *International Journal of Clinical and Experimental Hypnosis, 40*, 125–156.

Pennington, N., & Hastie, R. (1986). Evidence evaluation in complex decision making. *Journal of Personality and Social Psychology, 51*, 247–258.

Piaget, J. (1962). *Plays, dreams and imitation in childhood*. New York: Norton.

Platt, S. (1980). On establishing the validity of "objective" data: Can we rely on cross-interview agreement? *Psychological Medicine, 10*, 573–581.

Rabinowitz, D. (1993, May 1). A sex case built on air. *The Globe and Mail*, p. D3.

Raskin, D. C., & Yuille, J. C. (1989). Problems in evaluating interviews of children in sexual abuse cases. In S. J. Ceci, D. F. Ross, & M. P. Toglia (Eds.), *Perspectives on children's testimony* (pp. 184–207). New York: Springer-Verlag.

Ross, M. (1981). Egocentric biases in attributions of responsibility: Antecedents and consequences. In E. T. Higgins, C. P. Herman, & M. P. Zanna (Eds.), *Social cognition: The Ontario Symposium* (Vol. 1, pp. 305–322). Hillsdale, NJ: Lawrence Erlbaum Associates.

Ross, M. (1989). The relation of implicit theories to the construction of personal histories. *Psychological Review, 96*, 341–357.

Ross M., & Buehler, R. (1994). Creative remembering. In U. Neisser & R. Fivush (Eds.), *The remembering self* (pp. 205–235). New York: Cambridge University Press.

Ross, M., & Holmberg, D. (1990). Recounting the past: Gender differences in the recall of events in the history of a close relationship. In J. M. Olson & M. P. Zanna (Eds.), *Self-inference processes: The Ontario Symposium* (Vol. 6, pp. 135–152). Hillsdale, NJ: Lawrence Erlbaum Associates.

Ross, M., Karr. J. W., & Buehler, R. (1992). *Assessing the accuracy of conflicting autobiographical memories.* Unpublished manuscript, University of Waterloo, Ontario, Canada.

Rothbaum, F. (1983). Aging and age stereotypes. *Social Cognition, 2,* 171–184.

Santioso, R., Kunda, Z., & Fong, G. T. (1990). Motivated recruitment of autobiographical memories. *Journal of Personality and Social Psychology, 59,* 229–241.

Schank, R. C., & Abelson, R. P. (1977). *Scripts, plans, goals and understanding.* Hillsdale, NJ: Lawrence Erlbaum Associates.

Schlenker, B. R., & Weigold, M. F. (1992). Interpersonal processes involving impression regulation and management. *Annual Review of Psychology, 43,* 133–168.

Schooler, J. W., Clark, C. A., & Loftus, E. F. (1987). Knowing when memory is real. In M. M. Gruneberg, P. E. Morris, & R. N. Sykes (Eds.), *Practical aspects of memory: Current research and issues* (Vol. 1, pp. 83–88). New York: Wiley.

Schooler, J. W., Foster, A. F., & Loftus, E. F. (1988). Some deleterious consequences of the act of recollection. *Memory & Cognition, 16,* 243–251.

Schooler, J. W., Gerhard, D., & Loftus, E. F. (1986). Qualities of the unreal. *Journal of Personality and Social Psychology, 12,* 171–181.

Snyder, M., & Uranowitz, S. M. (1978). Reconstructing the past: Some cognitive consequences of person perception. *Journal of Personality and Social Psychology, 36,* 941–950.

Spiro, R. J. (1977). Remembering information from text: Theoretical and empirical issues concerning the "state of schema" reconstruction hypothesis. In R. C. Anderson, R. J. Spiro, & W. E. Montague (Eds.), *Schooling and the acquisition of knowledge* (pp. 137–165). Hillsdale, NJ: Lawrence Erlbaum Associates.

Stein, N. L., Trabasso, T., & Liwag, M. (in press). The Rashomon phenomenon: Personal frames and future-oriented appraisals in memory for emotional events. In M. Haith (Ed.), *Future-oriented processes.*

Steller, M. (1988). Recent developments in statement analysis. In J. C. Yuille (Ed.), *Credibility assessment* (pp. 135–154). Dordrecht, The Netherlands: Kluwer.

Stern, W. (1910). Abstracts of lectures on the psychology of testimony and on the study of individuality. *American Journal of Psychology, 21,* 270–282.

Sutton, C. (1984). A breakdown in symmetry. *New Scientist, 26,* 34–35.

Taylor, S. E., & Crocker, J. (1981). Schematic bases of information processing. In E. T. Higgins, C. P. Herman, & M. P. Zanna (Eds.), *Social cognition: The Ontario Symposium* (Vol. 1, pp. 89–134). Hillsdale, NJ: Lawrence Erlbaum Associates.

Trope, Y. (1978). Inferences of personal characteristics on the basis of information retrieved from one's memory. *Journal of Personality and Social Psychology, 36,* 93–106.

Turnbull, W. (1992). A conversation approach to explanation, with emphasis on politeness and accounting. In M. L. McLaughlin, M. J. Cody, & S. J. Read (Eds.), *Explaining one's self to others: Reason giving in a social context* (pp. 105–129). Hillsdale, NJ: Lawrence Erlbaum Associates.

Undeutsch, U. (1988). The development of statement reality analysis. In J. C. Yuille (Ed.), *Credibility assessment* (pp. 101–120). Dordrecht, The Netherlands: Kluwer.

Usher, J. A., & Neisser, U. (1993). Childhood amnesia and the beginnings of memory for four early life events. *Journal of Experimental Psychology: General, 122,* 155–165.

Vicente, K. J., & Brewer, W. F. (1993). Reconstructive remembering of the scientific literature. *Cognition, 46,* 101–128.

Wagenaar, W. A. (1986). My memory: A study of autobiographical memory over six years. *Cognitive Psychology, 18,* 225–252.

Wells, G. L., Lindsay, R. C., & Fergusson, T. J. (1979). Accuracy, confidence, and juror perceptions in eyewitness identification. *Journal of Applied Psychology, 64*, 440–448.

Wells, G. L., Turtle, J. W., & Luus, C. A. E. (1989). The perceived credibility of child eyewitnesses: What happens when they use their own words? In S. J. Ceci, D. F. Ross, & M. P. Toglia (Eds.), *Perspectives on children's testimony* (pp. 23–36). New York: Springer-Verlag.

Whipple, G. M. (1911). The psychology of testimony. *Psychological Bulletin, 8*, 307–309.

Zangwill, O. L. (1972). Remembering revisited. *Quarterly Journal of Experimental Psychology, 24*, 123–138.

4

THE INFLUENCE OF PRIOR KNOWLEDGE ON CHILDREN'S MEMORY FOR SALIENT MEDICAL EXPERIENCES

Peter A. Ornstein
Lauren R. Shapiro
Patricia A. Clubb
Andrea Follmer
University of North Carolina at Chapel Hill

Lynne Baker-Ward
North Carolina State University

Recent studies of young children's long-term retention have examined age differences in the recall of salient, personally experienced events. For example, children have been asked to remember positive events such as family vacations (Hamond & Fivush, 1991) and school outings (Fivush, Hudson, & Nelson, 1984; Hudson & Fivush, 1991), more neutral events such as well-child visits to the doctor (Baker-Ward, Gordon, Ornstein, Larus, & Clubb, 1993), and decidedly negative experiences, including medical procedures involving inoculations and venipuncture (e.g., Goodman, Hirschman, Hepps, & Rudy, 1991; Peters, 1987) and urinary catheterization (Merritt, Ornstein, & Spicker, 1994). These studies, and others in the emerging developmental literature on long-term retention (see Howe, Brainerd, & Reyna, 1992), provide important demonstrations of young children's abilities to remember the details of personal experiences over extended periods of time. In general, memory performance can be quite good, at least under optimal conditions of interviewing, although age differences in both initial recall and degree of forgetting are observed.

In this chapter, we explore one aspect of young children's long-term retention, that of the linkage between their memory performance and prior knowledge of the events being reported (see Ornstein, Larus, & Clubb, 1991). A considerable amount of evidence indicates that what an individual knows can have a serious impact on the processing and retention of information (e.g., Bartlett, 1932; Binet & Henri, 1894; Bjorklund, 1985; Chi, 1978; Chi & Ceci, 1987; Nelson & Gruendel, 1981; Ornstein & Naus, 1985). Indeed, there is substantial agreement that prior knowledge can influence how one monitors the world, codes material for storage, and subsequently retrieves information from memory (Brainerd & Ornstein, 1991; Brewer & Nakamura, 1984; Ornstein et al., 1991). We explore these knowledge-driven processes in the present chapter by focusing on our efforts to understand the abilities of children between 3 and 7 years of age to remember their experiences with various medical procedures (see Ornstein, Gordon, Baker-Ward, & Merritt, in press).

The research presented here is thus embedded in two partially overlapping literatures, one concerned with the development of long-term retention and forgetting and the other dealing with the operation of the "knowledge base" in permanent memory. From our perspective, however, the insights available from both literatures are quite limited. For example, several serious problems arise in considering the available corpus of research on long-term retention. At the most basic level, there is an absence of systematic data concerning what children of different ages are able to remember about various types of events at various points in time. Moreover, in order to understand these retention functions (and in fact to adequately score recall performance), it is essential to have detailed information concerning the events that were experienced, information that is unfortunately lacking in most studies of children's long-term memory for salient experiences. It is equally important to have some indication of the subjects' interpretation and encoding of the events that were experienced; direct indices of encoding are obviously difficult to obtain, but a proxy measure can often be derived from an assessment of immediate memory performance.

Specification of those aspects of an event that are encoded and stored is clearly relevant to understanding subsequent memory reports. In fact, there is suggestive evidence from the comprehension literature that the initial representation of an event determines to a considerable extent the course of later remembering and forgetting (e.g., Mandler, 1983, 1984; Stein & Trabasso, 1982). In order to come to grips with the initial encoding and representation, however, it is necessary to consider children's prior knowledge of the events that are being experienced, which returns us to the knowledge-base literature. Unfortunately, it can be argued that the field has not progressed much beyond demonstrations of the influence of extant knowledge and that a great deal remains to be learned about the mechanisms by which knowledge affects memory (see Brewer & Nakamura, 1984; Ornstein, 1991; Ornstein & Naus, 1985). Hence, there is a critical need for a precise delineation of both the course of retention and of the role played by prior knowledge in the understanding, encoding, transformation, and retrieval of information over long intervals of time.

With these caveats concerning the limitations of the current literatures, we outline here some of our initial efforts to examine the impact of underlying knowledge on children's memory for specific medical experiences. In the course of our investigations of 3- to 7-year-olds' memory for the details of routine physical examinations, we became interested in the role played by knowledge in the generation of children's accounts of their experiences. Our main concern was to ascertain whether prior knowledge of office-visit routines fosters the general reconstruction of the event or serves as a guide for retrieving specific memories. If children's reports are based primarily on reconstruction, then we would expect that recall would be susceptible to script-based errors. That is, as memory fades, activities that are congruent with mental scripts for doctor visits would tend to be included in children's accounts of a specific episode, even though they had not occurred (see Ross, 1989; Stein & Trabasso, 1982). Alternatively, mental scripts may help children to recall particular visits to the doctor by serving as frameworks for maintaining experiences as organized wholes, leading to consistent reports across interviews (Fivush & Slackman, 1986).

This initial concern led us to additional questions about the mechanisms by which prior knowledge might influence children's memory for the details of specific medical experiences. For example, how does children's understanding of office visits and medical procedures affect encoding and the construction of a coherent representation of a specific experience? A considerable body of evidence suggests that initial expectations about events, generated in part by mental scripts, can affect perception and interpretation and consequently influence what gets into memory (see Hudson & Nelson, 1984; Nelson, 1986). A second issue concerns the influence of preexisting knowledge on the recall of novel events. For example, are children able to use their mental scripts for routine physical examinations as a basis for understanding and remembering an unusual medical procedure heretofore not experienced?

In order to explore this set of issues concerning the role of knowledge in children's long-term retention, we contrast memory for two different medical experiences, one quite familiar and the other very novel. Specifically, in this chapter we discuss the abilities of 3- to 7-year-olds to remember the details of a routine physical examination and a radiological procedure involving urinary catheterization. Our presentation is organized around three sets of data: (a) children's recall of a specific visit to the doctor for a regularly scheduled pediatric checkup (Baker-Ward et al., 1993); (b) children's knowledge of the details of what usually happens during such a physical examination (Clubb, Nida, Merritt, & Ornstein, 1993); and (c) children's recall of an invasive radiological procedure, a voiding cystourethrogram (VCUG; Merritt et al., 1994). Because we know more about children's memory for visits to the doctor than we do about their recall of the VCUG at this point, the bulk of the chapter is devoted to a treatment of the role of knowledge factors in remembering the medical checkup.

To illustrate children's memory for pediatric checkups, we first present the data gathered by Baker-Ward et al. (1993) in what we refer to here as the Doctor Visit Study. A major section of the chapter is then dedicated to a consideration of how information about children's knowledge of physical examinations can help us account for the recall performance of the children in the Doctor Visit Study. We explore these issues by presenting normative data on children's understanding of pediatric checkups that were recently reported by Clubb et al. (1993) in a project that we call the Knowledge Study. Our discussion of the linkage between knowledge and remembering revolves around three separate analyses that relate the data obtained in the Doctor Visit and Knowledge Studies. One of these analyses (the Feature Analysis) was included in Clubb et al.'s (1993) write-up of the Knowledge Study, whereas two others (the Script and the Profile Analyses) represent follow-up efforts by Shapiro, Clubb, and Ornstein (1994) and Clubb and Ornstein (1992), respectively. We then turn to a discussion of Bender, Wallsten, and Ornstein's (1996) efforts to characterize the performance of the Doctor Visit subjects in terms of a multinomial model that examines encoding and retrieval processes. Of particular interest for the present discussion is the linkage between the normative knowledge data and the encoding and retrieval parameters derived from the model. Finally, we present Merritt et al.'s (1994) exploration of children's memory for the VCUG.

Because the work outlined here reflects the sustained activities of a core group of collaborators, the first-person plural is often used in our accounts of studies, even though not all of the present authors were involved in all reports and analyses. When necessary, moreover, we differentiate between an interpretation that was presented in a published article (e.g., that of Baker-Ward et al., 1993) and that which we are developing here.

THE DOCTOR VISIT STUDY

In the Doctor Visit Study, we explored the abilities of 3-, 5-, and 7-year-old children to remember the details of a routine, regularly scheduled pediatric examination. Because we were able to obtain checklists from the parents and the medical personnel, the details of the children's individual examinations could be specified, and the accuracy of the children's memory reports could be verified. The overall design of this experiment is illustrated in Fig. 4.1 in which it can be seen that four groups of subjects were established at each age level. Children in three of these conditions were interviewed immediately after their physical examinations and then at a delay of either 1, 3, or 6 weeks. The fourth group of children, in a partial effort to control for

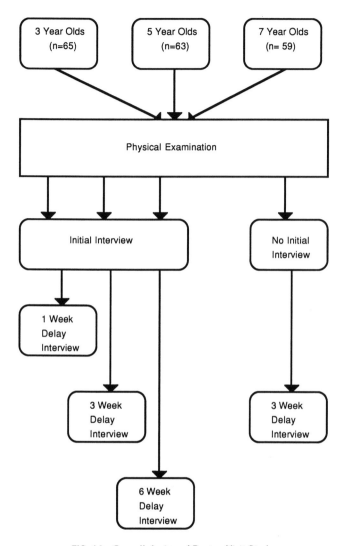

FIG. 4.1. Overall design of Doctor Visit Study.

the effects of the initial memory assessment, was interviewed only once, at a delay interval of 3 weeks. These interviews were designed to probe for the children's memory of the component features of the physical examination that are illustrated in Table 4.1. The mode of questioning followed a general-to-specific pattern, beginning with open-ended probes (e.g., "Tell me what happened during your checkup."), continuing with more specific questions (e.g., "Did the doctor check any parts of your face?"), and concluding with yes/no questions about aspects of the checkup not already reported

TABLE 4.1
Standard Features of the Physical Examinations

Visit With Nurse	Visit With Doctor
Measure height	Check eyes
Measure weight	Check ears
Administer vision test	Check mouth
Administer hearing test	Check knees
Obtain urine sample	Check elbows
Obtain blood sample	Check wrists
Measure blood pressure	Check heels
Administer TB tine test	Check bottoms of feet
Administer inoculation (shot)	Listen to chest (heart)
Give out prize	Listen to back (lungs)
	Check stomach
	Check private parts
	Ask child to walk forwards
	Ask child to walk backwards
	Ask child to walk on tiptoes
	Ask child to walk on heels
	Ask child to touch nose

(e.g., "Did she [he] check your eyes?"). Although individual checkups varied somewhat as a function of the particular child's age and medical history, the typical examination included approximately 75% of the 27 procedures presented in Table 4.1.

The basic recall findings are illustrated in Fig. 4.2. Memory performance is indicated in terms of the percentage of the component features of each child's checkup that were remembered in response to both open-ended and more specific questions, as a function of the delay interval. As can be seen, the overall performance of the children is quite good, although there are clear age differences in both immediate and delayed recall. Moreover, as would be expected (Dent & Stephenson, 1979; Ornstein, Gordon, & Larus, 1992), the younger children provide less information than the older subjects in response to open-ended questions, which suggests that they rely more on the specific probes to search their memory. Further, inspection of Fig. 4.2 indicates that retention over time varies directly with age, such that little forgetting is observed among 7-year-olds and a considerable amount of forgetting is seen among the 3-year-olds. Finally, the performance of the control subjects indicates that the high levels of recall observed at the delayed interviews cannot be attributed to the potentially facilitative effects of multiple interviews.

A series of potentially misleading questions about actions not part of the children's examinations was also included in the Doctor Visit Study. Because the checkups differed across children, the use of a standard interview protocol resulted in each child being asked some questions about aspects of a

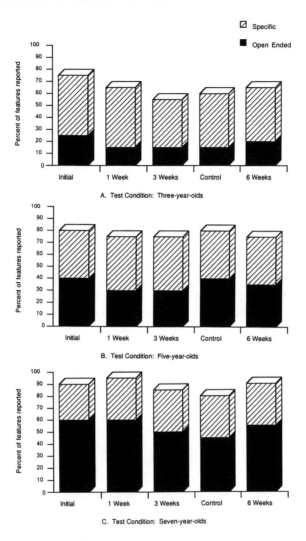

FIG. 4.2.   Percentage of features correctly reported in response to open-ended and specific probes by test condition at ages 3 (Panel A), 5 (Panel B), and 7 (Panel C) in the Doctor Visit Study. From Baker-Ward et al. (1993). © 1993 by Society for Research in Child Development. Adapted with permission.

physical examination that he or she had not experienced. These "absent-feature" questions clearly varied from child to child. For example, a query about an inoculation would be considered to be an absent-feature question for children who had not been inoculated in their checkups. In addition, all children were asked "extra-event" questions about eight actions that were never included in any physical examination.

In general, we found that the children in the Doctor Visit Study responded appropriately to the absent-feature and extra-event questions. As can be seen in Table 4.2, performance almost always exceeded the .50 rate of correct denials that would be expected on the basis of chance alone. There were, however, clear developmental differences, with the 3-year-olds making more errors than the older children with both types of questions. Moreover, a comparison of responses to the two types of questions indicates that all subjects responded more appropriately to the extra-event questions than to the absent-feature questions. Finally, as is also indicated in Table 4.2, the children's rates of correct denials to these misleading questions are relatively stable over the 6-week delay interval.

The findings of the Doctor Visit Study indicate that young children's reports of personally experienced events can be both extensive and accurate. Even the 3-year-olds were able to encode the bulk of the component features of the physical examination, as seen in their initial recall of the event, and performance increased with age such that the 7-year-olds remembered approximately 90% of the features at each assessment. These impressive levels of performance, however, raise a fundamental question about the validity of the data: Do the children's reports reflect their memory for

TABLE 4.2
Mean Proportion of Correct Responses (Denials) to Absent-Feature and
Extra-Event Questions by Age and Delay (Standard Deviations in Parentheses)

	Question Type			
Age (Years)	Absent-Feature		Extra-Event	
3				
Initial	.72	(.30)	.87	(.19)
1 Week	.80	(.28)	.90	(.13)
3 Weeks	.62	(.39)	.74	(.31)
Control	.67	(.31)	.75	(.28)
6 Weeks	.71	(.26)	.87	(.26)
5				
Initial	.93	(.14)	.96	(.07)
1 Week	.89	(.16)	.98	(.05)
3 Weeks	.84	(.19)	.96	(.07)
Control	.68	(.29)	.95	(.08)
6 Weeks	.80	(.32)	.91	(.13)
7				
Initial	.88	(.18)	.99	(.06)
1 Week	.85	(.23)	.95	(.11)
3 Weeks	.90	(.13)	.97	(.07)
Control	.82	(.14)	.94	(.10)
6 Weeks	.76	(.29)	.98	(.04)

Note. Data from Baker-Ward et al. (1993). © 1993 by the Society for Research in Child Development. Adapted with permission.

the particular checkup experienced in the context of this study or their more generalized knowledge of medical examinations?

To address this issue, Baker-Ward et al. (1993) presented several lines of evidence in support of the claim that the children were not just reporting their mental scripts for visits to the doctor, but rather were remembering a specific checkup. As discussed earlier, the children's correct denials to the absent-feature questions exceeded chance expectancy and did not change systematically over time. If the children were generating responses primarily on the basis of their prior knowledge about visits to the doctor, performance with these misleading questions would have been less impressive and most likely would have deteriorated somewhat over time. In addition, the children made essentially no intrusions in response to the initial open-ended questions. If they were relying primarily on their mental scripts, they should have reported acts that were absent from their physical examinations but typically are part of the experience. Further support that the data are indicative of a specific experience was provided by children's recall of having their pictures taken by the nursing staff, a novel, unexpected feature that was added to the standard medical examination. In general, recall for this particular feature was comparable to that of the standard features of the checkup.

THE KNOWLEDGE STUDY

The arguments presented earlier suggest that the children who participated in the Doctor Visit Study were able to remember the details of a specific visit to the doctor for a routine checkup. From this perspective, therefore, it seems unlikely that the children's memory performance was driven by reconstructive processes at retrieval. Of course, the claim that recall was not based primarily on their office-visit mental scripts does not imply that prior knowledge of medical routines did not affect the children's memory performance. Indeed, as Ornstein et al. (1991) indicated, it seems very likely that prior knowledge of medical procedures can affect memory performance in at least three additional ways. Specifically, prior knowledge can influence: (a) the encoding and storage of information about the checkup; (b) the strength and organization of the memory trace of the checkup; and (c) constructive changes over time in the nature of the underlying memory representation.

Teasing apart these alternative contributions of knowledge to remembering requires an examination of the nature and strength of the linkage between knowledge of visits to the doctor and recall of a specific checkup. Clubb et al.'s (1993) Knowledge Study was designed to do this by gathering basic normative data about what 5-year-olds know about routine visits to the pediatrician. Rather than identifying children who could be classified dichotomously in terms of their expertise (cf. Chi, 1978; Schneider, Korkel, & Weinert, 1989), Clubb et al. (1993) reasoned that children, "experts" and "novices" alike, would most likely have different degrees of knowledge concerning the various activities that comprise routine pediatric checkups. As such, the Knowledge Study was designed to focus on differences in what children understand about the component features of the physical examination.

We recruited a sample of 5-year-olds who had not recently been seen by their pediatricians and asked them to provide information about what generally happens when they go to the doctor. Paralleling the interview structure of the Doctor Visit Study, the questions followed a general-to-specific format. In the report (Clubb et al., 1993), however, we focused on the features of routine checkups that the children nominated in response to open-ended questions that could elicit multiple responses, such as, "What does the doctor (nurse) do to check you?" The fundamental unit of analysis in the Knowledge Study was that of the individual feature of the physical examination. After the protocols of each child were coded, the data were pooled across subjects, so as to determine the degree to which the sample as a whole provided information about each component of the checkup. We then constructed composite "knowledge scores" for the features by calculating the proportion of the children who nominated each action in response to the open-ended questions. In this manner, the different components were rank ordered in terms of the frequency with which they were mentioned by the sample.

The knowledge scores for the various features are displayed in the first column of Table 4.3. As shown in Table 4.3, the knowledge scores indicated that the features of the physical examination varied considerably in terms of how salient they were to the children, perhaps reflecting the degree to which these components had been experienced previously. Some components of the pediatric visit were reported spontaneously by large segments of the sample, whereas others were barely mentioned by any subjects. For example, receiving a prize (.77), getting a shot (.64), and checking the heart (.64) and the mouth (.55) were the features most often nominated by the sample. On the other hand, walking forward (.00) and checking the wrist (.05) were rarely mentioned in response to the open-ended questions. In addition to the features defined by the physicians, the children frequently nominated four other components of the doctor visit: laying down (.27), undressing (.27), getting a Band-Aid (.46), and experiencing discomfort (.59).

How does this characterization of the children's differential understanding of the various features of the physical examination relate to the immediate and delayed recall of specific checkups? To explore this issue, we now turn to three analyses of the knowledge–memory linkage.

TABLE 4.3
Knowledge Scores and 5-Year-Olds' Memory Scores by Delay Interval

| Feature | Knowledge | Memory | | | |
		Initial	1 Week	3 Weeks	6 Weeks
Back	.18	.31	.18	.38	.25
Blood pressure	.09	.16	.06	.13	.13
Blood test	.27	.93	.75	.60	.67
Ears	.55	.63	.47	.25	.56
Elbows	.18	.23	.08	.20	.13
Eyes	.27	.51	.29	.44	.56
Feet	.32	.10	.15	.13	.13
Hearing	.14	.43	.24	.19	.19
Heart	.64	.47	.35	.25	.38
Heels	.05	.14	.19	.15	.07
Height	.50	.67	.53	.56	.44
Knees	.41	.57	.56	.47	.60
Mouth	.55	.55	.24	.25	.44
Private parts	.09	.29	.35	.19	.13
Prize	.77	.73	.63	.64	.73
Shot	.64	.76	.71	.62	.56
Stomach	.41	.45	.47	.25	.31
TB tine	.14	.59	.33	.33	.14
Touch nose	.00	—	—	—	—
Urinalysis	.05	.07	.00	.17	.21
Vision	.18	.51	.35	.40	.47
Walk backwards	.09	.50	.50	.17	.33
Walk forwards	.00	.04	.00	.00	.14
Walk on heels	.00	—	—	—	—
Walk on toes	.00	—	—	—	—
Weight	.50	.67	.35	.44	.44
Wrist	.05	.00	.07	.09	.00

Note. Data from Clubb et al. (1993). © 1993 by Ablex Publishing Corporation. Adapted with permission.

Feature Analysis

In order to relate the obtained knowledge scores to children's actual memory of the details of the pediatric checkup, Clubb et al. (1993) reanalyzed the recall protocols obtained in the Doctor Visit study. Therefore, even though Baker-Ward et al. (1993) had not reported the memory data at the level of the individual feature, it was possible to rescore the protocols to determine the proportion of children who recalled each component of the checkup in response to open-ended questions. In this manner, "memory scores" were constructed for each of the features of the physical examination. These scores are conceptually parallel to the knowledge scores discussed previously.

With comparable knowledge and memory scores for the individual features of the physical examination, it is possible to determine the extent to which the recall of one sample can be predicted by the normative knowledge data generated by a different sample. In a sense, this approach to the knowledge–memory relation is similar to that utilized by researchers in verbal memory and learning who have obtained normative data about varying characteristics of stimulus items (e.g., associative frequency, emotionality, meaningfulness, imagery) and related these stimulus dimensions to recall performance (see, e.g., Friendly, Franklin, Hoffman, & Rubin, 1982; Rubin & Friendly, 1986). To illustrate this perspective, the memory scores of the subsample of 5-year-olds who participated in the Memory Study are presented in Table 4.3, in conjunction with the knowledge scores of the children who participated in the Knowledge Study. These memory scores are displayed in the second, third, fourth, and fifth columns of Table 4.3 for the initial, 1-, 3-, and 6-week memory assessments, respectively.

Inspection of the recall data indicates that the components of the physical examination varied considerably in their memorability. Thus, for example, the blood test was remembered by almost all of the 5-year-olds initially (.93), perhaps because it involved an uncomfortable finger prick, and was still recalled by a majority of the children (.67) after 6 weeks, even though substantial forgetting took place over time. In contrast, the pediatrician's check of the wrist was not remembered well at any time. It should be noted that memory scores were not calculated for a number of features because they occurred infrequently in the children's physical examinations.

The data presented in Table 4.3 also indicate considerable similarity in the patterns of variability among the knowledge and memory scores. To examine the knowledge–recall association more directly, the knowledge scores were correlated with the memory scores at each delay interval. The resulting correlation coefficients were .68, .63, .64, and .74 ($ps < .01$) for the initial, 1-, 3-, and 6-week interviews, respectively. A pictorial representation of the linear relations that were obtained at each delay interval is presented in Fig. 4.3, which illustrates a scatter plot of the knowledge scores and the memory scores obtained from the interview 6 weeks after the physical examination. This interview was selected for analysis because recall following an extended delay would most likely be more sensitive to any involvement of mental scripts than would reports obtained at earlier assessment periods.

How shall these correlations between knowledge and remembering be interpreted? As indicated earlier, Baker-Ward et al. (1993) argued that their subjects' effective recall did not stem primarily from reconstructive activities based on the activation of children's mental scripts for visits to the doctor. To explore further this claim, Clubb et al. (1993) examined the language used by the children in the Knowledge and Doctor Visit studies. These analyses

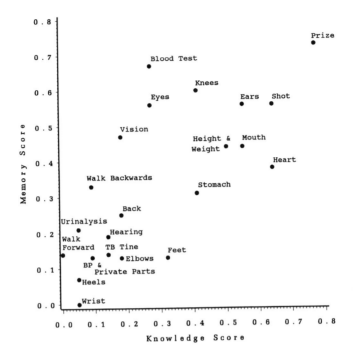

FIG. 4.3. Scatter plot of knowledge and memory scores at 6 weeks for 5-year-olds in the feature analysis of the Knowledge Study. From Clubb et al. (1993). © 1993 by Ablex Publishing Corporation. Adapted with permission.

were based on the suggestions of Fivush (1984), Nelson (1986), and their colleagues that specific forms of verb usage may be diagnostic of the reliance on mental scripts. If the protocols obtained in the Knowledge Study reflected the operation of the children's scripts for doctor visits, but the recall protocols were based on their recollections of specific checkups, then it would be expected that they would be characterized by quite different language. For example, script reports typically are made in the present tense, whereas memory reports are related in the past tense (see Hudson & Shapiro, 1991).

Our analysis focused on those segments of the 5-year-olds' protocols in which information was provided about features nominated spontaneously in the Knowledge Study or recalled at the open-ended level after a delay of 6 weeks in the Doctor Visit Study. Indeed, the data of Myles-Worsley, Cromer, and Dodd (1986) suggest that as memory for the details of a particular event (a day at preschool) fades, young children's reports may come to be based on their scripted knowledge. Consistent with the expectations of script theory (e.g., Nelson, 1986), we found that the children's discussions of what generally happens when they visit the doctor seemed to reflect the operation of their underlying scripts: The 5-year-olds in the Knowledge Study used the present and/or future tense to discuss 68% of the features of the checkup. This finding contrasts with both the recall protocols and the expectations of the Myles-Worsley et al. (1986) study because the language used to describe a specific office visit 6 weeks earlier did not seem to be script-driven: The 5-year-olds in the Doctor Visit Study only used the present and/or future tense when they talked about 10% of the features that were recalled at the open-ended level.

Script Analysis

Clubb et al. (1993) demonstrated a strong relation between children's knowledge and recall of the features of a routine physical examination using a methodology in which the item, as opposed to the subject, was the unit of analysis. Converging evidence for their conclusions was obtained in a recent reanalysis of both the knowledge and recall data carried out by Shapiro et al. (1994) that focused on the subject as the unit of analysis rather than the feature. Our approach was to identify a "master" script for the visit to the doctor that would reflect a mental representation that was shared, to some extent, by the 5-year-olds who generated the knowledge protocols for the Knowledge Study. More specifically, the master script was comprised of those components of the checkup that were nominated spontaneously by at least 25% of the children in the knowledge sample, thereby portraying the more salient event features. We found that 12 of the 24 standard items of the physical examination included in the Knowledge Study met the master script criterion; these features were labeled *scripted*, whereas those not nominated at the 25% level were called *nonscripted*. Three of the 27 standard features assessed in the Memory Study were eliminated because they were infrequently administered. As can be seen in the first column of Table 4.3, some of the scripted features included receiving an inoculation (.64) and having a blood test (.27), whereas being asked to walk backwards (.09) and being asked for a urine specimen (.05) were examples of nonscripted procedures.

Having identified the scripted and nonscripted components of the physical examination, Shapiro et al. (1994) recoded the Doctor Visit memory protocols to calculate the 5-year-olds' recall of these features. For each child, the proportion of scripted items remembered was defined as the number of master script features recalled in response to open-ended questions divided by the total number of scripted features actually included in his or her checkup. The proportion of nonscripted features recalled was calculated in a similar fashion, with the denominator being the number of nonscripted features represented in the actual physical examination. Using these subject-based measures, we observed that the children recalled more scripted than nonscripted features of the checkup at each of the four memory assessments. Indeed, the 5-year-olds in the Doctor Visit Study remembered .58, .43, .41, and .49 of the scripted items at the initial, 1-, 3-, and 6-week interviews, respectively; comparable values for the recall of nonscripted items were .27, .19, .23, and .18. Further, comparison of retention of the scripted and nonscripted items over time indicated that the scripted items were recalled more consistently than the nonscripted items.

Profile Analysis

Although the analyses presented thus far provide converging evidence for the linkage between knowledge about the component features of the physical examination and recall at each of the four assessment points, they do not focus directly on the form of the retention function over the course of the 6-week delay interval. To what extent do individual features of the checkup exhibit similar or contrasting profiles of retention over this interval? Moreover, is it possible to identify groups of features that exhibit similar retention profiles over time? And if so, can these profiles be related to the children's underlying knowledge of the component features?

To explore these questions, Clubb and Ornstein (1992) used hierarchical cluster analysis procedures (see Aldenderfer & Blashfield, 1984) in an effort to identify groups of features with similar profiles of retention over the course of 6 weeks. Beginning with the recall data presented in Table 4.3 (four memory scores for each of 24 features of the physical examination), we calculated the Euclidean distance between all possible pairs of features. To do so, the recall associated with each feature of the physical examination was characterized as a vector composed of four memory scores, one for each of the immediate, 1-, 3-, and 6-week assessments. Generalizing the classic formula for the distance between two points, for each pair of examination features the distance that was computed was a function of the differences in recall at the immediate assessments (imm) and the interviews at 1 (1), 3 (3), and 6 (6) weeks. As an example, consider the first two features in Table 4.4, *back* (b) and *blood pressure* (bp). The "distance" (D) between the two recall profiles would be defined as follows:

$$D_{(b,bp)} = [(b_{imm} - bp_{imm})^2 + (b_1 - bp_1)^2 + (b_3 - bp_3)^2 + (b_6 - bp_6)^2]^{1/2}$$

Because the resulting distance scores have no upper bounds, these measures were transformed into proximity scores that ranged between 0 and 1, such that larger values represented greater degrees of similarity among pairs of profiles. The similarity between any two profiles (e.g., *back* and *blood pressure*) was defined as:

$$S_{(b,bp)} = 1 - [D_{(b,bp)} - D_{(min)}] / [D_{(max)} - D_{(min)}]$$

The resulting similarity scores were entered into a proximity matrix, and a hierarchical cluster analysis was conducted using an average linkage solution (Legendre & Legendre, 1983). This solution was employed because it represents a compromise between liberal and conservative clustering algorithms that result in the establishment of few (inclusive) groupings and many (exclusive) groupings.

The results of this clustering analysis are seen in the tree structure diagram indicated in Fig. 4.4, with the nodes in the dendogram corresponding to points at which various features of the physical examination can be viewed as joining together in clusters. For example, checks of *heels* and *feet* have a proximity value of 1.0, indicating that their recall profiles over the 6-week delay period are identical. Inspection of Fig. 4.4 suggests the existence of four basic groups of examination features that share contrasting profiles of recall over time. For convenience, these groups are labeled 1, 2, 3, and 4 and are identified in the figure.

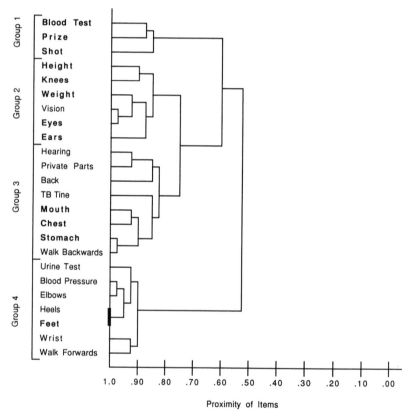

FIG. 4.4. Dendrogram of memory score data in the Profile Analysis of the Knowledge Study.

Average memory scores at each delay interval were then computed for the examination features in each of the four groups, and the composite recall profiles are illustrated in Fig. 4.5. As can be seen, although similar patterns of high initial recall were observed for the features of the physical examination that comprise Groups 1 and 2, the two retention functions differed substantially over the 6-week delay interval. Despite some loss over this period of time, recall of the features in Group 1 at all four interviews was clearly superior to immediate recall of the other groups. In contrast, retention of the features in Group 2 was characterized by a pattern of some loss at 1 and 3 weeks, followed by recovery at 6 weeks. Moreover, initial recall of the items in Group 3 was at a lower level, and performance declined

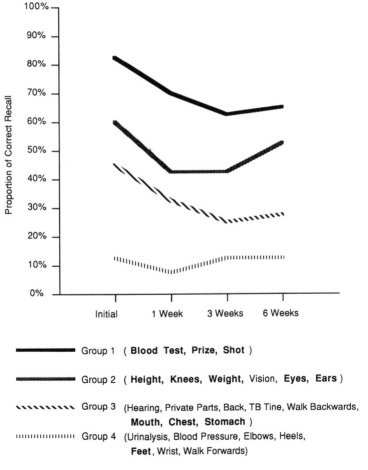

FIG. 4.5.   Mean proportion of correct recall at each delay interval in the Profile Analysis of the Knowledge Study.

substantially over time. Finally, the features of Group 4 were not well remembered at any assessment interval.

These findings indicate that various component features are recalled at different levels during the initial and delay intervals. To understand how children's knowledge about visits to the doctor might be related to these contrasting retention functions, composite knowledge scores for these four groups of examination features were calculated. As expected, the average knowledge scores associated with Groups 1 ($M = .56$) and 2 ($M = .40$) were higher than those for Groups 3 ($M = .28$) and 4 ($M = .11$). Therefore, high knowledge features were associated with good long-term retention, whereas low knowledge items were less memorable over time. In a similar fashion, the four groups of features of the physical examination may also be characterized in terms of Shapiro et al.'s (1994) distinction between scripted and nonscripted features of the checkup. In fact, inspection of Figs. 4.4 and 4.5, in which scripted features are indicated in boldface type and nonscripted features are shown in plain print, reveals that Groups 1 through 4 differ substantially in terms of the representation of these two types of items, with more scripted items being found in Groups 1 and 2 than Groups 3 and 4.

Why were some features of the event recalled better than others? Clearly, the features in Group 1 typically involved emotional reactions, both positive (e.g., *prize*) and negative (e.g., *shot*), which may have served to enhance recall. Prior knowledge, however, also affects recall, as evidenced by the association of high knowledge in Groups 1 and 2 with good recall across time. In contrast, less familiar features are associated with low recall, as shown by Groups 3 and 4. These features may be less salient to the child for a variety of reasons; for example, components of the checkup may not involve instruments (e.g., *check tummy*), are less invasive (e.g., *check wrist*), are performed in subtle ways (e.g., *walk forwards*), or are simply not well understood (e.g., *check back, urinalysis*). Reporting bias due to social norms may also affect which features children include in their memory interviews (see Saywitz, Goodman, Nicholas, & Moan, 1991). Finally, emotionality, prior knowledge, salience, and social inhibition may also interact in various ways to affect initial and delayed recall.

LINKING KNOWLEDGE TO ENCODING
AND RETRIEVAL OPERATIONS

Additional insights concerning the role of knowledge in children's memory for visits to the doctor come from a consideration of the implications of a simple multinomial model (Riefer & Batchelder, 1988) developed in collaboration with Wallsten and Bender to characterize the findings of the Doctor Visit Study. This model (Bender et al., 1996) involves the translation of our empirical data into statements about factors that separately influence the probability that a component feature of a medical procedure is encoded and, given that it is encoded, that it is also retrieved at different points in time. Bender et al.'s major interest was in the extent to which the encoding and retrieval parameter values of the model vary across both age levels and specific components of the pediatric checkup. We can also ask how the parameter values for individual components of the checkup relate to children's knowledge of those features.

In the initial application of the model to the routine physical examination (Bender et al., 1996), equations were written to relate probabilities of hypothetical encoding and retrieval operations involving individual features to the relative frequencies of four experimental outcomes: the recall of a given feature immediately after the checkup and at a delay (YY); the recall of the feature immediately, but not after a delay (YN); the failure to remember the feature initially, combined with successful recall after a delay (NY); and recall failure at both tests (NN). For example, if for a given age group and component feature (e.g., *obtaining a urine specimen*), q is the probability that the feature is encoded, r_1 the probability that it is recalled immediately and r_2 the probability that it is recalled after a delay, then the probability that it is recalled both times is qr_1r_2, the probability that it is recalled the first time, but not the second is $qr_1(1 - r_2)$, and so on. By setting these expressions equal to the observed relative frequencies, we could solve for estimates of the encoding and retrieval parameters.

Our approach to the Doctor Visit data was to test a hierarchy of alternative forms of the basic model by imposing increasingly restrictive constraints on the parameter space corresponding to the major hypotheses of interest. Thus, beginning with the full model, which included nine parameters (one encoding and two retrieval parameters for each age group) and was essentially a rewriting of the data, we explored alternative models to test hypotheses about age and delay effects in encoding and retrieval. These processes were carried out separately for the 15 features of the physical examination for which each of the four outcomes (YY, YN, NY, NN) occurred with nonzero frequencies for the 3-, 5-, and 7-year-olds in the Doctor Visit Study. The form of the model that seemed most consistent with the data was one in which encoding was age-invariant but retrieval varied developmentally and as a function of time (i.e., immediate vs. delayed recall). This outcome, however, should not be taken to suggest that the encoding parameter was constant across the components of the physical examination, because as can be seen in Table 4.4, some features were clearly encoded more readily than others. Nonetheless, for any given component of the checkup, the major age differences that we obtained were in terms of retrieval. Indeed, inspection of Table 4.4 indicates that age-related increases were observed for the majority of the 15 features.

Given the successful fit of the model, what can be said about the relations between children's knowledge of the features of the doctor visit and the parameter values indicated in Table 4.4? To examine this issue, we correlated

TABLE 4.4
Encoding and Retrieval Parameters by Age

| | | Retrieval | | | | | |
| | | Age 3 | | Age 5 | | Age 7 | |
Feature	Encoding	Time 1	Time 2	Time 1	Time 2	Time 1	Time 2
Blood pressure	.83	.11	.09	.20	.13	.58	.28
Ears	.93	.35	.16	.47	.69	.89	.81
Hearing	.86	.25	.25	.50	.24	.85	.74
Heart	.87	.31	.22	.54	.38	.77	.72
Knees	.76	.66	.43	.85	.82	.89	.83
Mouth	.88	.32	.12	.64	.36	.84	.74
Picture	.50	.37	.25	.30	.11	.38	.38
Private parts	.49	.55	.50	.65	.51	.49	.62
Prize	.94	.77	.53	.76	.69	.73	.70
TB tine	.90	.75	.43	.69	.29	.87	.58
Stomach	.79	.33	.22	.56	.44	.63	.66
Urinalysis	.41	.15	.22	.18	.30	.74	.62
Vision	.84	.14	.14	.62	.49	.87	.81
Weight	.98	.13	.15	.68	.43	.89	.80
Walk on toes	.69	.29	.29	.80	.54	.76	.87

Note. Data from Bender et al. (1996). © by the Psychonomic Society. Adapted with permission.

the knowledge scores obtained in the Knowledge Study with the encoding and retrieval parameters obtained for specific examination features. These analyses revealed a significant correlation between the knowledge scores and the encoding parameters, $r = .65$, $p < .01$. In addition, of the six correlations carried out between the knowledge scores and retrieval parameters, only one was significant, that for the delayed recall of the 5-year-olds, $r = .52$, $p < .05$. Because the knowledge scores were derived from 5-year-olds, knowledge–retrieval linkages might be more likely with children of this age than with the 3- and 7-year-olds. Nonetheless, within the context of this model, knowledge clearly influences encoding and has a lesser impact on retrieval.

CHILDREN'S MEMORY FOR AN AVERSIVE AND NOVEL EXPERIENCE

To supplement our explorations of children's memory for routine physical examinations, we have begun to explore recall for medical experiences that are both more novel and aversive than the pediatric checkup. In one of these studies, Merritt et al. (1994) examined young children's memory for the details of a VCUG, a radiological procedure involving urinary catheterization. Administered when a child's symptoms (e.g., frequent urinary tract infections) suggest the need for fluoroscopic examination of the urinary system, the VCUG is not only a less familiar event, but also more stressful than the routine physical examination. The most notable features of the procedure include cleansing the genital area, inserting a catheter into the urethra, filling the bladder with contrast fluid, fluoroscopic filming, and voiding the fluid (i.e., urinating) on the examination table.

Merritt et al.'s (1994) sample included 24 children, ranging in age from 3 to 7 years, who were referred by their physicians to a radiology clinic for the VCUG. Each child was interviewed about his or her VCUG experience immediately following the examination and again after a 6-week delay. The questioning followed the same type of hierarchical interview sequence that we have employed in our series of doctor-visit studies, with increasingly more specific probes being employed when information was not elicited by open-ended questions. In addition to assessing the children's recall perform- ance, efforts were made to obtain behavioral and physiological measures of children's stress and to examine the linkage between stress and remem- bering. In particular, children's behavioral reactions during the VCUG were coded according to the Observational Scale of Behavioral Distress (OSBD; Elliott, Jay, & Woody, 1987), and their fearfulness and cooperation were rated on Likert scales by the radiology technologists. Moreover, physiologi- cal correlates of distress were obtained by means of salivary cortisol assays. Finally, to examine the link between individual differences in temperament and children's recall, parents completed the Temperament Assessment Bat- tery for Children (TABC; Martin, 1988).

The children's overall recall was very impressive. These 3- to 7-year-olds reported 88% of the components of the VCUG immediately after the proce- dure, a level of performance that was comparable to that of the 5-year-olds in the Doctor Visit Study. Most interestingly, the children in the VCUG study evidenced higher levels of recall in response to open-ended questions ($M = 65\%$) than the 5-year-olds in the Doctor Visit Study ($M = 42\%$), indicating that they were able to retrieve most of the features of this invasive procedure with minimal prompting. The delayed recall performance of the children was also excellent. Indeed, as measured by both overall ($M = 86\%$) and open-ended ($M = 60\%$) recall, the children demonstrated little forgetting over a period of 6 weeks. In addition, the children's responses to questions about activities that were not part of the VCUG procedure indicated little suggesti- bility; indeed, they correctly denied 95% of the misleading questions that were posed in the initial interview and 93% of the questions presented during the delayed assessment.

The children who took part in the VCUG study exhibited levels of stress considerably higher than those observed in our studies of memory for the details of the physical examination. Indeed, both salivary cortisol assays and behavioral measures (i.e., the behavioral coding of the videotapes of the procedure and the technologists' ratings) indicated that the VCUG subjects were very distressed by the procedure. Moreover, negative associations were observed between the behavioral measures of stress and recall, especially remembering at 6 weeks. Thus, for example, partial correlations (holding age constant) between delayed recall and the behavioral coding of the videotapes and the technologists' judgments of the children's fear were $-.56$ and $-.58$ ($ps < .01$), respectively. Interestingly, there was no association between the salivary cortisol measure and recall performance.

We also found that both immediate and delayed open-ended recall was positively correlated with Adaptability ($rs = .62$ and $.69$, $ps < .001$) and Approach–Withdrawal ($rs = .72$ and $.81$, $ps < .001$), as assessed by the TABC. Not surprisingly, children with low scores on Adaptability were rated by the radiology technologists as exhibiting high levels of fear during the VCUG ($r = -.67$, $p < .001$). Although these correlations are impressive, it must be noted that little is known about the ways in which temperament may influence recall performance. Nonetheless, it is interesting to speculate about the possible impact of temperament on both the encoding and retrieval of information. Indeed, it seems likely that temperament can influence the extent to which children are attending actively to the events during the VCUG, seeking additional information about the procedure, and so forth, as well as their reactions while being interviewed.

Thus, encoding might be enhanced for those children who adapt well to new situations and reduced for those who are less able to adapt. For example, a child who shuts his or her eyes as a means of coping with an unbearable situation is obviously not likely to encode many aspects of the event. Moreover, temperament may affect the adjustment of the child to the interview context which, in turn, influences the amount of retrieval and/or reporting. For instance, slow-to-warm-up children, in comparison with outgoing children, may engage in only a modicum of discussion during the interview, thereby providing less information about the event than others who are more at ease with the situation.

DISCUSSION

The evidence presented here indicates clear linkages between children's knowledge and memory. By focusing on the individual features of the physical examination, the complementary analyses of the Knowledge Study provide convincing evidence for relations between knowledge of the checkup and several aspects of recall performance. Thus, differences in children's understanding of specific components of the pediatric examination are associated with corresponding variation in children's memory of those features. Indeed, recall performance increases directly with gains in underlying knowledge. Moreover, not only are our measures of knowledge predictive of immediate and delayed recall, they are also associated with corresponding differences in retention profiles over time.

Were the Children "Confabulating"?

Given these connections between knowledge and recall, can we be sure that the children were actually remembering the details of specific visits to the doctor and not providing reports that are based primarily on their generic knowledge of office visits? Converging evidence from several types of analyses leads us to have confidence in the view that the children were reporting the details of specific visits to the doctor and that their accounts did not reflect script-based constructions. Nonetheless, we readily admit that such knowledge-driven generation of probable features would quite likely be observed if the delay intervals were extended considerably, especially if the children had other intervening medical experiences.

How Does Knowledge "Work"?

If the children's reports discussed here do not reflect script-generated constructive processes, how does knowledge influence performance? Application of Bender et al.'s (1996) model suggests that knowledge of physical examinations impacts both encoding and retrieval processes. Even though knowledge exerted a stronger influence on encoding than retrieval, this general conclusion is consistent with our earlier analysis (Ornstein et al., 1991) of the possible impact of knowledge on the flow of information within the memory system. Indeed, we feel it likely that prior knowledge affects the children's encoding and retrieval, as well as the status of information in memory during the interval between memory storage and recovery. Unfortunately, however, relatively little direct evidence is available to provide a credible account of the mechanisms underlying these presumed influences of knowledge on remembering.

Consider, for example, the role played by knowledge in encoding. Consistent with the comprehension literature (e.g., Stein & Trabasso, 1982), we are comfortable with the position that knowledge has a direct influence on children's understanding of an event that is being experienced and hence on the construction of an underlying representation. We recognize, of course, that we have no direct evidence of encoding per se, but rather must rely on immediate recall to provide a proxy measure of encoding. The use of "talk-aloud" procedures or other "online" measurements may help us gain leverage on this problem by generating information about encoding that is more-or-less independent of recall.

On initial inspection, the absence of age-related changes in the encoding parameter in Bender et al.'s (1996) model may seem inconsistent with the argument that knowledge affects encoding. Because older children are almost certain to possess more knowledge about familiar life experiences than younger ones, age-related changes in encoding might be expected if encoding is to some degree driven by knowledge (see Farrar & Goodman, 1990, for a similar argument). Several characteristics of the study, however, are relevant in evaluating the absence of age-related changes in this particular model. Note that the knowledge "norms" were developed on the basis of the reports of only one age group, and hence may not accurately represent the information available to other age groups. In addition, because the event was so familiar, even the youngest children may have possessed a sufficient amount of prior information to enable encoding at the global feature level. If so, age-related differences in this parameter may be present when more detailed information is requested in recall, or when the event is less familiar to the children.

Let us now consider the question of retrieval. If script-driven construction as a mechanism is rejected in interpreting our findings, just how does prior knowledge influence the retrieval process? Our working hypothesis is that doctor-visit scripts may be used as retrieval guides, with children retrieving highly probable activities and then self-testing for information concerning the presence of those activities in the target physical examination. This account could be viewed as a variant of generate-recognition models of recall, although we have no real data concerning how children (or adults for that matter) carry out the implied generic versus episodic memory discrimination. Finally, we must admit that with the doctor visit as a "stimulus event" being remembered over the course of 6 to 12 weeks, we have no evidence of the impact of knowledge on changing the underlying memory trace during the delay interval, although classic constructive accounts of memory (e.g., Bartlett, 1932) provide ample evidence for the phenomenon.

Problems in Measuring Knowledge

Although the findings presented here provide clear support for a linkage between knowledge and remembering, several limitations in our assessment procedures may have resulted in an underestimation of the impact of knowledge on event memory. Our measurement of knowledge was confined to children's verbal responses to general questions about physical examinations. For a number of reasons, this technique may have led to a quite conservative account of what children actually know about doctor visits. Because young children routinely require specific probes to provide elaborate accounts of their experiences (Baker-Ward et al., 1993; Dent & Stephenson, 1979), a more complete description of their knowledge might result from more detailed questioning. It is also possible that children's understanding of events would be reflected more accurately by behavioral enactment procedures rather than verbal assessments (e.g., Ratner, Bukowski, & Foley, 1992). Another limitation of our assessment was that our measure focused solely on the individual features of the physical examination and did not incorporate elaborative detail or information regarding the structure of knowledge in memory. Further, the present data on knowledge and memory were generated by separate samples of children that may have received somewhat different routine pediatric care. It is quite likely that a within-subjects assessment would enable a more accurate charting of the degree of correspondence between knowledge and memory.

Memory in the Absence of Extensive Knowledge

Thus far, our discussion has revolved around positive associations between knowledge and memory. Within the context of the physical examination, recall of individual features clearly improves directly as a function of children's knowledge of those components, even with our imperfect measure of knowledge. Given this account, how can we understand the excellent recall of the children in the VCUG sample? These children were required to undergo a novel medical procedure that was both aversive and stressful. The complete unfamiliarity of the VCUG would most likely have eliminated any possibility of the children's reports being constructed on the basis of their prior knowledge. If this were the case, however, how was the event understood and encoded so that it could later be effectively retrieved?

Although follow-up studies are necessary to interpret the performance of the VCUG subjects, we can identify three factors that could have contributed to their elevated levels of recall. First, it seems possible that the children were able to interpret the VCUG procedure on the basis of some general representation of their previous experiences with physicians and medical personnel, ranging from those associated with routine checkups to those involving treatments for illnesses and accidents. From this perspective, the children could have viewed the VCUG as an event that was somewhat discrepant from an underlying composite script for medical experiences (see Graesser, Gordon, & Sawyer, 1979; Graesser, Woll, Kowalski, & Smith, 1980). Second, the arousal associated with the intensively personal nature of the VCUG might have led to heightened attention and encoding of individual features (e.g., the insertion of the catheter) of the radiological procedure. Therefore, even though the children could not have completely understood the VCUG procedure, at least from an adult perspective, individual features may have received extended processing that could facilitate subsequent recall.

A third possibility is that the underlying structure of the VCUG was supportive of enhanced recall. Although the VCUG is composed of unfamiliar components, the central features are linked together by a set of temporally invariant causal enablements; thus, for example, the bladder cannot be filled with contrast fluid before the catheter is inserted, and the contrast fluid cannot be voided until the bladder is filled. In contrast, even though the physical examination is composed of features that are more familiar to the children, their interrelations can be temporally variable and to some extent arbitrary. Recent demonstrations (e.g., Bauer, 1992; Bauer & Mandler, 1989) that even infants are able to remember causally constrained events more readily than arbitrarily structured experiences suggest that the superior performance of the VCUG subjects may stem, at least in part, from the nature of the event itself.

Putting It All Together

These observations about the contrasting nature of the physical examination and the VCUG procedure suggest that accounts of children's memory for salient experiences require that we consider both (a) the knowledge that children bring to those experiences and (b) the basic structural properties of the events that are to be remembered. In addition, the findings of the VCUG study, as well as other work conducted in our laboratory (e.g., Gordon et al., 1993), indicate that we cannot understand children's memory for these types of events without considering the impact of a range of individual difference variables. For example, the strong correlations between remembering and the Adaptability and Approach–Withdrawal dimensions of temperament suggest that personality characteristics likely influence the deployment of attention and the subsequent encoding and storage of information. Moreover, the negative correlations between behavioral measures of stress and recall, in combination with the absence of such a linkage between salivary cortisol levels and remembering, suggest that the degree of distress experienced is driven to some extent by the children's personal interpretation of the events that they experience.

How can these different observations be brought together? It seems clear that we need to work toward the development of formal models of children's encoding, storage, and retrieval of the details of salient personal experiences. The themes discussed here underscore the fact that many characteristics of the individual and the situation contribute to the construction of a stable representation in memory. Models of memory thus need to articulate a type of conversion process whereby an "objective" stimulus event (e.g., the VCUG) is transformed into something that may be quite unique from the perspective of the individual. These models must also specify the conditions under which established representations are likely to be stable over time, as opposed to being susceptible to interference and modification. Finally, it is essential that we work toward the construction of models of children's memory that are developmental in their orientation, thus focusing on age-related changes in the critical encoding and retrieval processes.

ACKNOWLEDGMENTS

The research discussed in this chapter was supported in part by grant MH 49304 from the United States Public Health Service. During the preparation of this chapter, Lauren Shapiro was supported by a postdoctoral fellowship from the Carolina Consortium on Human Development. Thanks are due Charles J. Brainerd for his helpful comments on an earlier draft of the manuscript.

REFERENCES

Aldenderfer, M. S., & Blashfield, R. K. (1984). *Cluster analysis*. Beverly Hills, CA: Sage.

Baker-Ward, L., Gordon, B. N., Ornstein, P. A., Larus, D. M., & Clubb, P. A. (1993). Young children's long-term retention of a pediatric examination. *Child Development, 64*, 1519–1533.

Bartlett, F. C. (1932). *Remembering: A study in experimental and social psychology*. New York: Cambridge University Press.

Bauer, P. (1992). Holding it all together: How enabling relations facilitate young children's event recall. *Cognitive Development, 7*, 1–28.

Bauer, P., & Mandler, J. (1989). One thing follows another: Effects of temporal structure on 1–2-year-olds' recall of events. *Developmental Psychology, 25*, 197–206.

Bender, R. H., Wallsten, T. S., & Ornstein, P. A. (1996). Age differences in encoding and retrieving details of a pediatric examination. *Psychonomic Bulletin and Review, 3*, 188–198.

Binet, A., & Henri, V. (1894). La mémoire des phrases (mémoire des idées). [Memory for prose]. *L'Année Psychologique, 1*, 24–59.

Bjorklund, D. F. (1985). The role of conceptual knowledge in the development of organization in children's memory. In C. J. Brainerd & M. Pressley (Eds.), *Basic processes in memory development* (pp. 103–142). New York: Springer-Verlag.

Brainerd, C., & Ornstein, P. A. (1991). Children's memory for witnessed events: The developmental backdrop. In D. J. Doris (Ed.), *The suggestibility of children's recollections* (pp. 10–20). Washington, DC: American Psychological Association.

Brewer, W. F., & Nakamura, G. V. (1984). The nature and functions of schema. In R. S. Wyer, Jr., & T. K. Srull (Eds.), *Handbook of social cognition* (Vol. 1, pp. 119–160). Hillsdale, NJ: Lawrence Erlbaum Associates.

Chi, M. T. H. (1978). Knowledge structures and memory development. In R. S. Siegler (Ed.), *Children's thinking: What develops?* (pp. 73–96). Hillsdale, NJ: Lawrence Erlbaum Associates.

Chi, M. T. H., & Ceci, S. J. (1987). Content knowledge: Its role, representation, and restructuring in memory development. In H. W. Reese (Ed.), *Advances in child development and behavior* (Vol. 20, pp. 91–142). Orlando, FL: Academic Press.

Clubb, P. A., Nida, R., Merritt, K., & Ornstein, P. A. (1993). Visiting the doctor: Children's knowledge and memory. *Cognitive Development, 8*, 361–372.

Clubb, P. A., & Ornstein, P. A. (1992, April). Visiting the doctor: Children's differential retention of individual components of the physical examination. In D. F. Bjorklund & P. A. Ornstein (Chairs), *Children's memory for real-world events: Implications for testimony*. Paper presented at the meeting of the Conference on Human Development, Atlanta, GA.

Dent, H. R., & Stephenson, G. M. (1979). An experimental study of the effectiveness of different techniques of questioning child witnesses. *British Journal of Social and Clinical Psychology*, *18*, 41–51.

Elliott, C. H., Jay, S. M., & Woody, P. (1987). An observation scale for measuring children's distress during medical procedures. *Journal of Pediatric Psychology*, *12*, 543–551.

Farrar, M. J., & Goodman, G. S. (1990). Developmental differences in the relation between scripts and episodic memory: Do they exist? In J. Hudson & R. Fivush (Eds.), *Knowing and remembering in young children* (pp. 30–64). New York: Cambridge University Press.

Fivush, R. (1984). Learning about school: The development of kindergartners' school scripts. *Child Development*, *55*, 1697–1709.

Fivush, R., Hudson, J. A., & Nelson, K. (1984). Children's long-term memory for a novel event: An exploratory study. *Merrill–Palmer Quarterly*, *30*, 303–316.

Fivush, R., & Slackman, E. A. (1986). The acquisition and development of scripts. In K. Nelson (Ed.), *Event knowledge: Structure and function in development* (pp. 71–96). Hillsdale, NJ: Lawrence Erlbaum Associates.

Friendly, M., Franklin, P. E., Hoffman, D., & Rubin, D. C. (1982). The Toronto Word Pool: Norms for imagery, concreteness, orthographic variables, and grammatical usage for 1,080 words. *Behavior Research Methods and Instrumentation*, *14*, 375–399.

Goodman, G. S., Hirschman, J. E., Hepps, D., & Rudy, R. (1991). Children's memory for stressful events. *Merrill–Palmer Quarterly*, *37*, 109–158.

Gordon, B. N., Ornstein, P. A., Nida, R. E., Follmer, A., Crenshaw, M. C., & Albert, G. (1993). Does the use of dolls facilitate children's memory of visits to the doctor? *Applied Cognitive Psychology*, *7*, 459–474.

Graesser, A. C., Gordon, S. E., & Sawyer, J. D. (1979). Recognition memory for typical and atypical actions in scripted activities: Tests of a script + pointer tag hypothesis. *Journal of Verbal Learning and Verbal Behavior*, *18*, 319–332.

Graesser, A. C., Woll, S. B., Kowalski, D. J., & Smith, D. A. (1980). Memory for typical and atypical actions in scripted activities. *Journal of Experimental Psychology: Human Learning and Memory*, *6*, 503–515.

Hamond, N. R., & Fivush, R. (1991). Memories of Mickey Mouse: Young children recount their trip to Disneyworld. *Cognitive Development*, *6*, 433–448.

Howe, M. L., Brainerd, C. J., & Reyna, V. F. (Eds.). (1992). *Development of long-term retention*. New York: Springer-Verlag.

Hudson, J. A. (1986). Memories are made of this: General event knowledge and the development of autobiographical memory. In K. Nelson (Ed.), *Event knowledge: Structure and function in development* (pp. 97–118). Hillsdale, NJ: Lawrence Erlbaum Associates.

Hudson, J. A., & Fivush, R. (1991). As time goes by: Sixth graders remember a kindergarten experience. *Applied Cognitive Psychology*, *5*, 347–360.

Hudson, J. A., & Nelson, K. (1984). Differentiation and development in children's event narratives. *Papers and Reports on Child Developmental Research*, *23*, 50–57.

Hudson, J. A., & Shapiro, L. R. (1991). Children's scripts, stories, and personal narratives. In A. McCabe & C. Peterson (Eds.), *New directions in developing narrative structure* (pp. 89–136). Hillsdale, NJ: Lawrence Erlbaum Associates.

Legendre, L., & Legendre, P. (1983). *Numerical ecology*. New York: Elsevier.

Mandler, J. M. (1983). Representation. In J. H. Flavell & E. M. Markman (Eds.), *Handbook of child psychology: Vol. 3. Cognitive development* (pp. 420–494). New York: Wiley.

Mandler, J. M. (1984). *Stories, scripts, and scenes*. Hillsdale, NJ: Lawrence Erlbaum Associates.

Martin, R. P. (1988). *Temperament assessment battery for children*. Brandon, VT: Clinical Psychology Publishing Company.

Merritt, K. A., Ornstein, P. A., & Spicker, B. (1994). Children's memory for a salient medical procedure: Implications for testimony. *Pediatrics*, *94*, 17–23.

Myles-Worsley, M., Cromer, C., & Dodd, D. (1986). Children's preschool script reconstruction: Reliance on general knowledge as memory fades. *Developmental Psychology, 22,* 22–30.

Nelson, K. A. (1986). *Event knowledge: Structure and function in development.* Hillsdale, NJ: Lawrence Erlbaum Associates.

Nelson, K. A., & Gruendel, J. (1981). Generalized event representations: Basic building blocks of cognitive development. In M. E. Lamb & A. L. Brown (Eds.), *Advances in developmental psychology* (Vol. 1, pp. 131–158). Hillsdale, NJ: Lawrence Erlbaum Associates.

Ornstein, P. A. (1991). Commentary: Putting interviewing in context. In D. J. Doris (Ed.), *The suggestibility of children's recollections* (pp. 147–152). Washington, DC: American Psychological Association.

Ornstein, P. A., Gordon, B. N., & Larus, D. H. (1992). Children's memory for a personally experienced event: Implications for testimony. *Applied Cognitive Psychology, 6,* 49–60.

Ornstein, P. A., Larus, D. M., & Clubb, P. A. (1991). Understanding children's testimony: Implications of research on the development of memory. In R. Vasta (Ed.), *Annals of child development* (Vol. 8, pp. 145–176). London: Jessica Kingsley.

Ornstein, P. A., Gordon, B. N., Baker-Ward, L. E., & Merritt, K. A. (in press). Children's memory for medical experiences: Implications for testimony. In D. Peters (Ed.), *The child witness in context: Cognitive, social, and legal perspectives.* Dordrecht, The Netherlands: Kluwer.

Ornstein, P. A., & Naus, M. J. (1985). Effects of the knowledge base on children's memory strategies. In H. W. Reese (Ed.), *Advances in child development and behavior* (Vol. 19, pp. 113–148). Orlando, FL: Academic Press.

Peters, D. P. (1987). The impact of naturally occuring stress on children's memory. In S. J. Ceci, M. P. Toglia, & D. P. Ross (Eds.), *Children's eyewitness memory* (pp. 122–141). New York: Springer-Verlag.

Ratner, H. H., Bukowski, P., & Foley, M. A. (1992, April). *Now you see it, now you don't: The role of action and outcome in event memory.* Paper presented at the Conference on Human Development, Atlanta, GA.

Riefer, D. M., & Batchelder, W. H. (1988). Multinomial modeling and the measurement of cognitive processes. *Psychological Review, 98,* 318–337.

Ross, M. (1989). Relation of implicit theories to the construction of personal histories. *Psychological Review, 96,* 341–357.

Rubin, D. C., & Friendly, M. (1986). Predicting which words get recalled: Measures of free recall, availability, goodness, emotionality, and pronunciability for 925 nouns. *Memory & Cognition, 141,* 79–94.

Saywitz, K. J., Goodman, G. S., Nicholas, E., & Moan, S. (1991). Children's memories of physical examinations involving genital touch: Implications for reports of child sexual abuse. *Journal of Consulting and Clinical Psychology, 59,* 682–691.

Schneider, W., Korkel, J., & Weinert, F. E. (1989). Domain-specific knowledge and memory performance: A comparison of high- and low-aptitude children. *Journal of Educational Psychology, 81,* 306–312.

Shapiro, L. R., Clubb, P. A., & Ornstein, P. A. (1994, April). *The effect of knowledge on children's memory reports for their five-year-old checkups.* Poster presented at the meeting of the Conference on Human Development, Pittsburgh, PA.

Stein, N. L., & Trabasso, T. (1982). What's in a story: An approach to comprehension and instruction. In R. Glaser (Ed.), *Advances in instructional psychology* (Vol. 2, pp. 213–267). Hillsdale, NJ: Lawrence Erlbaum Associates.

5

A GOAL-PROCESS APPROACH TO ANALYZING NARRATIVE MEMORIES FOR AIDS-RELATED STRESSFUL EVENTS

Susan Folkman
University of California, San Francisco

Nancy L. Stein
University of Chicago

> *It is a life and death matter to hang on to your beliefs, but it can also be a life and death matter to know when it's time to say "They aren't working any more, and they must be revised."*
> —Tony Kushner, from his play *Angels in America*.

Since ancient times people have attempted to understand how it is that some individuals seem to be able to surmount difficult circumstances, while others succumb, both psychologically and physically. In recent years, understanding individual differences in response to the demands of difficult circumstances has been advanced with the help of theoretical models that explore the appraisal of meaning, emotion responses, and coping under conditions of loss, threat, and challenge. In this chapter we draw on two of these models, Lazarus and Folkman's (1984) cognitive theory of stress and coping and Stein and Trabasso's (1992; Stein, Trabasso, & Liwag, 1992, 1994) theory of emotional understanding.

Our goal is to use these models to demonstrate how individual differences in the appraisal of stressful events lead to different outcomes with respect to psychological well-being. In this chapter, we focus specifically on a sample of male caregivers who are caring for partners with AIDS. These men were asked to recall, at regular 2-month intervals, a stressful event within the past week that they had experienced in the process of providing care for their partner. As such, our corpus of remembered events exemplifies personally significant happenings that are largely uncontrollable and signal continuously deteriorating conditions, for both the caregivers and their partners.

Using memories of stressful events to predict psychological well-being is not a new enterprise, in and of itself. As Kihlstrom (in press-b) demonstrated, Freud had most of his ingenious insights into psychological well-being while studying the past memories of his patients. Freud believed that the ways in which people structured their memories would directly predict current and future states of psychological lucidity and mental health. Indeed, many current investigations of mental health (Beck, 1988; Gottman, 1994; Meichenbaum, 1994; Traue & Pennebaker, 1993) use narrative interviews or written reports of conversations between partners (Ross & Holmberg, 1990) to predict the success of a relationship or personal states of psychological well-being

Lazarus and Folkman (1984) used a cognitive theory of stress and coping to understand how people manage the vicissitudes of ordinary daily life. One of the major tenets of this theory is that *coping processes* link the ways in which stressful events are appraised and adaptational outcomes. These outcomes include psychological well-being, social functioning, and physical health. The study of coping based on the Lazarus–Folkman model thus focuses on specific thoughts and behaviors that people use to manage the demands of particular stressful situations.

Folkman and Lazarus (1980, 1985, 1988b) developed a self-report measure of 67 coping thoughts and behaviors called the "Ways of Coping" to assess these coping processes. Studies using this measure have shown that: (a) coping is multidimensional in that it involves a variety of emotion-regulating and problem-solving functions; (b) people use strategies to regulate both their emotional responses and problem-solving skill in virtually every type of stressful encounter; (c) the specific coping strategies used are influenced by the demands of specific situations; and (d) coping is dynamic in that strategies change within a stressful episode as the episode unfolds (Folkman, 1992; Folkman & Lazarus, 1980, 1985; Lazarus & Folkman, 1987; Tennen & Herzberger, 1985).

Stein and Trabasso (1992) and their colleagues (Stein & Jewett, 1986; Stein & Levine, 1987, 1989, 1990; Stein et al., 1992; Trabasso, Stein, Rodkin, Munger, & Baughn, 1992; Trabasso & van den Broek, 1985) developed a theoretical model that describes how people represent and understand events that lead to emotional reactions and subsequent action after an emotion is experienced. The model has been used to demonstrate how people remember both real-life and hypothetical emotion episodes in social and personal situations.

The heart of the model embodies a description of the ways in which people use information to evaluate the status of events, actions, and goals that are judged to be personally meaningful. Stein and Trabasso (Stein et al., 1992) illustrated the ways in which people make appraisals and experience emotional reactions while carrying out plans of action in the service of maintaining their goals. Their model describes the temporal unfolding and causal sequence of the specific cognitive appraisals that are made in an attempt to preserve personally meaningful goals that lead to states of well-being (Stein & Levine, 1989; Stein et al., 1992, 1994). As a result of their studies, Stein and Trabasso's research with children and adults has increased understanding of the causal relationships among beliefs, the status of valued goals, and individual emotional and behavioral responses to changes in the status of valued beliefs and goals in stressful situations.

We use a combination of these two theories to describe how psychological well-being can be assessed better in stressful situations. Despite the progress that has been made in understanding coping processes in the context of stressful situations, we still lack precise knowledge of whether and how people maintain their psychological well-being under highly stressful circumstances. In this chapter we propose cognitive and affective processes through which individuals appraise and cope with what is happening to them. These processes describe how individuals understand and impute meaning to their circumstances in terms of their valued goals, and how this meaning changes as stressful circumstances unfold. Our goal is to describe with precision a set of cognitive mechanisms through which individuals adapt to highly stressful circumstances, especially circumstances that are personally significant, largely uncontrollable, and continuously deteriorating. Our model will allow researchers to investigate more systematically the mechanisms for maintaining psychological well-being in difficult circumstances, and to evaluate the adaptive significance of these mechanisms relative to other coping mechanisms, such as the effective use of social support.

GOAL PROCESSES

We posit that the maintenance of psychological well-being under circumstances that are personally significant, largely uncontrollable, and continuously deteriorating is directly related to the ways in which appraisals of events and actions are made in relationship to current beliefs and goals of individuals. These appraisals sometimes change current beliefs and goals, and they are critical in regulating emotional reactions and subsequent coping processes. The critical aspects of these appraisals hinge on the individual's ability to (a) recognize when previously held beliefs and goals are no longer tenable; (b) revise untenable beliefs that lead to unattainable goals; and (c) generate new goals that are meaningful and attainable. *Beliefs* refer to individuals' understanding of how things are and their expectations about how things will be (Lazarus & Folkman, 1984; Stein & Levine, 1990; Stein et al., 1992, 1994). *Goals* refer to any valued object, activity, or state that the individual desires (Stein et al., 1992).

We refer to the general sequence of appraisal and reappraisal of events and actions as *goal processes*. Although people continually appraise different events and actions in everyday stressful situations, for the most part they do so for the purpose of maintaining valued goals. We provide an example of the appraisal of a stressful event to illustrate the centrality of goals in this process.

Normally, the appraisal process is initiated by an event that violates an individual's belief or expectation about what should have happened or what will happen in the current context. The violation occurs because the prior knowledge that individuals have acquired about a particular event, with respect to being able to maintain (or attain) personally significant goals, runs counter to that which has been experienced. The violation is appraised as a harm, loss, threat, or challenge to a valued goal (or goals) and almost always involves emotional responses. In the case of appraising an event as resulting in harm/loss, for example, anger or sadness ensue; in the case of threat, worry or fear ensue; and in the case of challenge, excitement or eagerness ensue (Folkman & Lazarus, 1985, 1988a; Lazarus, 1991; Stein & Jewett, 1986; Stein & Levine, 1987, 1989, 1990).

The individual's appraisal of the precipitating event, and the fact that its occurrence violated a set of prior beliefs, may lead him or her to decide that, notwithstanding this event, the prior beliefs are still realistic or, alternatively, that the beliefs need to be revised regarding how things are now and how they are expected to be. Emotions signal that the status of a valued goal has changed, and they also signal the degree and magnitude of the harm/loss or threat. Appraisals of harm and loss, for example, can generate anger, sadness, or guilt, depending on specific appraisals made about the causes of the event and the reinstatability of a goal. Appraisals of threat can generate fear and anxiety, depending on appraisals made about the prevention of goal failure and the consequences of coping with possible failure (Lazarus, 1991; Lazarus & Smith, 1988; Scherer, 1984; Stein & Jewett, 1986; Stein et al., 1992).

Depending on the type of appraisal made about the viability of maintaining a blocked goal, an individual will attempt to reinstate the previous goal or attempt to generate a new goal that may serve as a substitution for the failed goal. During this phase of appraisal and decision making, individuals often experience negative emotions such as sadness, because setting a new goal involves letting go of another valued goal that is no longer tenable (Carver & Scheier, 1990; Folkman & Lazarus, 1985; Stein & Levine, 1989, 1990). At the same time, setting a new goal can help mobilize different individual resources and create positive emotions (Carver & Scheier, 1990). For example, in the case of a caregiver, the recognition that the partner's health is deteriorating can generate sadness and fear, but the decision to make a very special meal for him or to create special occasions can generate eagerness. The caregiver will then construct a plan and initiate action in service of the new goal.

As we noted earlier, a goal refers to any valued object, activity, or state that an individual desires (Stein et al., 1992). Goals, therefore, can include not only wanting something other than what one already has, but also wanting things to remain as they are. The plans that derive from goals can range from clearly thought through, purposeful, and deliberate behavior, to decisions to do nothing, which to the observer may appear to represent the absence of a plan. The setting of realistic goals can lead both to the feeling of being challenged in a positive manner and to the feeling of being threatened, to the extent that a possibility of goal failure exists (Folkman & Lazarus, 1985; Stein & Jewett, 1986).

The appraisal of an event, especially in the case of goal failure, forces a reconsideration of current beliefs (whether they should be revised or not revised), the appropriateness of the current goal, and options for responding to goal failure (whether the goal should be reinstated, revised, or abandoned). These appraisals lead to subsequent positive or negative emotions, or a combination thereof, depending on the content of the specific belief challenged and the types of alternative responses considered.

The processes and sequence of appraisals we have described are summarized in Fig. 5.1. It should be noted that goal processes are inherently dynamic, and appraisals may shift rapidly depending on the current operating conditions. Beliefs and goals that are realistic one week may not be realistic the next. A person with AIDS, for example, may believe realistically that he is able to maintain his weight by eating well during a period of relative health. Once chronic diarrhea sets in, signaling the beginning of uncontrollable wasting, however, it may no longer be realistic for the individual to believe he can control his weight by eating well. His previous beliefs and goals no longer fit the circumstances and need to be revised.

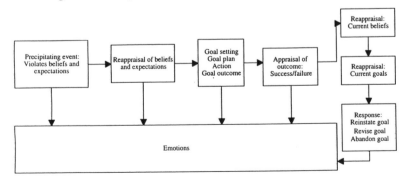

FIG. 5.1. The processes and sequence of event appraisals.

ADAPTIVE AND MALADAPTIVE GOAL PROCESSES

One of the goals of any theory of coping is to specify conditions under which processes lead to adaptive and maladaptive outcomes. Our theoretical expectations regarding adaptive and maladaptive goal processes rest on three assumptions:

1. Individuals act in a goal-directed and purposeful fashion, continuously appraising and attempting to maintain valued goals and positive states of well-being (Beach, 1985; Emmons, 1992, in press; Emmons & King, 1988; Heckhausen & Kuhl, 1985; Klinger, 1975, 1977, 1987; Lazarus, 1991; Lazarus & Folkman, 1984; Martin & Tesser, 1989; Pervin, 1989; Semmer & Frese, 1985; Stadler & Wehner, 1985; Stein & Jewett, 1986; Stein & Levine, 1987, 1990; Stein & Trabasso, 1992). Even in situations that are ostensibly uncontrollable, as in the case of a chronic or terminal illness, individuals attempt to identify meaningful and attainable goals. A chronically ill person, for example, can decide to maintain a healthy diet and get enough rest (Taylor, Helgeson, Reed, & Skokan, 1991), or a terminally ill person can decide to mend relationships, turn attention towards helping others, or set things in motion to carry out a final wish. At the final stages of a disease process, an individual may decide that his or her goal is to die quickly and to seek immediate relief.

2. To maintain psychological well-being in changing circumstances, especially in deteriorating circumstances, the individual must first recognize and understand that the state of the world is different from the way it was expected to be and the way the person wants it to be (Stein et al., 1992). We call this process of recognition and understanding *belief revision*. When belief revision occurs, an individual has been able to reevaluate whether personally important goals can still be attained in the current set of changed circumstances (Stein & Levine, 1990; Stein et al., 1992).

3. To maintain psychological well-being in circumstances that are deteriorating, the individual must relinquish untenable goals and substitute new or revised goals that are personally meaningful and realistic in the context of the changing circumstances. The importance of adjusting beliefs and goals in relationship to changing events and noncontrollable outcomes is well established in clinical practice and 12-step programs, and it is implicit in theories of stress (Breznitz, 1983; Janis & Mann, 1977).

4. Specific types of goal processes (i.e., belief and goal revision) are important because they increase the probability of goal success, and goal success leads to positive states of emotion and psychological well-being (Brunstein, 1993; Emmons, in press; Stein & Jewett, 1986; Stein & Levine, 1987, 1990).

Maladaptive goal processes occur when individuals fully understand that they are blocked from pursuing a valued goal, but at the same time, refuse to give up their investment in this goal or are blocked from generating new goals that would lead to more positive outcomes. If these situations occur, a person is likely to become frustrated, angry, discouraged, and ultimately hopeless. Eventually, the individual is likely to resort to reminiscing about the past or fantasizing that the past is still present (Frese & Sabini, 1985; Martin & Tesser, 1989). Although most everyone engages in these types of thought processes at one time or another, continual rumination about lost goals and failure to impute value to other goals leads to deepened states of depression (Beck, 1988; Horowitz, 1991; Nolen-Hoeksema, Girgus, & Seligman, 1992).

Adaptive goal processes occur when people understand that they are blocked from pursuing a valued goal, revise their beliefs and expectations accordingly, and substitute new goals that eventually take on the same or greater value as goals that were blocked from attainment. Even when the probability of achieving a new goal is uncertain, the process of trying to attain it can lead to new knowledge, skill, or opportunity. People can choose a new goal that is similar to their blocked goal to help maintain an important superordinate goal. For example, a caregiver may no longer be able to enjoy emotional closeness through sexual intimacy with his partner, but he may enjoy emotional closeness when massaging his partner to help ease his partner's discomfort.

In this chapter we describe the method we have developed for analyzing goal processes in narratives produced by the caregiving partners of men with AIDS. We describe the study of caregiving partners, provide definitions of 11 theoretically relevant facets of goal processes, illustrate our analytic approach with the narratives from one caregiver, and summarize data across five caregivers to illustrate the quantification of scores from the narrative analysis.

UCSF COPING PROJECT

The UCSF Coping Project is a longitudinal study of HIV-positive and HIV-negative caregiving partners of men with AIDS. Advanced HIV disease, or AIDS, is essentially uncontrollable, relentlessly progressive, and culminates in death. The nature of this disease makes caregiving extremely demanding psychologically, emotionally, and physically. One of the caregivers in our project wrote a letter that provides a summary of the disease course in his partner over a 2-year period of time. The following is an excerpt from that letter:

> As AIDS progresses it takes over your life, both for the person with AIDS and for his caregiver. I suspect it must be like being an amputee: you don't consciously think about your missing limb every minute of the day, but the fact is always somewhere in mind. It is your reality. It is your life. In less than 2

years, my lover has had lymphoma and three rounds of chemo, a brain infection that has partially paralyzed one hand and caused multiple Grand Mal seizures, pneumonia six times, disseminated TB which damaged his liver and heart, an infection of the eyes that left him partially blinded and continues to threaten his sight, and a gastrointestinal problem of undetermined origin which makes it impossible for him to eat. . . . At the least, one result is the feeling that you can't escape this thing. You get through one crisis and, BAM, you're hit with another. (Folkman, Chesney, & Christopher-Richards, 1994, p. 38)

The major purpose of the UCSF Coping Project is to identify processes that contribute to maintenance, the decline of physical and psychological well-being, or both throughout caregiving and subsequent bereavement process. Data collection began in April 1990 and will continue through September 1997.

To be included in the study, men had to identify themselves as gay or bisexual, be in a committed relationship and share living quarters with their partner, be willing to be tested for HIV antibodies, have no more than two symptoms of HIV disease, and not be an intravenous drug user. The men's partners had to have a diagnosis of AIDS, need assistance with at least two instrumental tasks of daily living, and be living at home.

Participants were recruited between April 1990 and June 1992 from the San Francisco Bay area using advertisements in the gay press, public service announcements on radio and television, referrals from clinics and gay organizations, and annual mailings to residents of selected San Francisco zip codes.

The initial sample included 86 HIV-positive caregivers and 167 HIV-negative caregivers. The sample is 90% White, 3% African American, 4% Hispanic, and 3% other. This distribution is representative of the San Francisco gay community. The average age of the participants is 36.6 years, and most earn between $20,000 and $29,000 a year. The average length of the relationship between study participants and their partners is 6.2 years.

Each participant is followed bimonthly for 2 years and semiannually for 3 follow-up years. Semiannual clinical assessments are made of physical health, neuropsyhological performance, and major depressive disorders; during the first 2 years, bimonthly psychosocial interviews assess positive and negative states and stress, coping, and social support. These interviews are conducted semiannually for the 3 follow-up years.

The analysis of goal processs focuses on the regulation and maintenance of psychological well-being in the midst of highly stressful circumstances. We assess psychological well-being with two measures: the Bradburn Positive Morale Scale (Bradburn, 1969), which is an assessment of positive mood states, and Positive States of Mind (Horowitz, Adler, & Kegeles, 1988), which is an assessment of the individual's success in achieving desired mental states. Negative mood is measured with the Centers for Epidemiological Studies–Depression measure (Radloff, 1977), the Spielberger State Anxiety

Inventory (Spielberger, Gorsuch, & Lushene, 1970), and the Spielberger Anger Inventory (Spielberger, 1988).

As part of the psychosocial interview, each participant is asked to describe the most stressful event that occurred during the previous week related to caregiving. The interview was guided by questions designed to generate details about the context of the stressful situation. Interviewers asked: "What happened?", "When did it happen?", "Who was involved?", "What made it stressful?" and "What emotions did you feel?" For each emotion that was reported, the caregiver was asked, "What made you feel [emotion name]?" Answers to the questions concerning what made the event stressful and what made the caregiver feel each emotion he reported tended to contain critical information regarding beliefs and goals.[1]

This chapter is confined to narrative data from five men that were collected in bimonthly interviews during the period of caregiving prior to their partner's death. The interviews were conducted at our project offices or the participant's home. On average, each caregiver narrated eight stressful events.

Table 5.1 contains the definitions of functional categories that we used to code the narrative data. These categories were derived from a theory of emotional understanding (Stein & Levine, 1987; Stein et al., 1992) and refer to the causal sequence of goal process that are carried out during a stressful encounter (e.g., the precipitating stressful event, the belief that was violated, goals, plans, goal outcomes, and goal responses). The functional categories also capture caregivers' thoughts about stressful events. Therefore, we have access to specific content of beliefs, goals, and their revisions as an event unfolds. The answer to a particular question, the presence of a specific linguistic marker, or a statement's relationship to another statement is used to classify each clause in a narrative into a given functional category.

We present three narratives from one caregiver, whom we refer to as Caregiver 1, to provide an example of a caregiver's experience during the 8 months leading to his partner's death. The caregiver's narratives were generated in response to the questions we described earlier, beginning with a request to describe a stressful event related to caregiving that occurred during the previous week. In Session 5, approximately 8 months prior to the partner's death, Caregiver 1 said:

> The story has to do with Todd getting the right side of his body sort of locked up, getting shooting pains from his shoulder down his right arm and into his hand; and his neck was very stiff which created headaches. He was in so much pain he couldn't move.
>
> And so he was taking pain pills but they weren't working. And I kept wanting him to call the doctor. I guess for me that situation is that whenever anyone's

---

[1]In this sense, the caregiver interview about a recent stressful event was similar to the interviews that Stein and Trabasso (Stein et al., 1994) have carried out on young children's and their parents' memory of emotional events.

in pain I feel I've got to do something about it. I was feeling helpless around the situation because I didn't feel it was my place to call the doctor.

So he finally called the doctor on Thursday. And I had gone to work. And he called me and said: "Well, the doctor said I should come there right away."

So I picked him up and dropped him off at the hospital, at Ward 86 [AIDS ward]. And I just dropped him off. Usually I go up—I've been going up with him lately.

And I guess that was most stressful about this situation was that I was extremely busy, getting ready for an extremely busy weekend, and this happened. Plus I was having problems at work, and this was one more thing I had to field, plus all the planning and organizational things I had to do at work. And I also had to be at this volunteer thing that I had to be at that afternoon.

So Todd was at the hospital and I hadn't heard and I hadn't heard. And finally he called at about 1:34. We were just starting to have lunch at work. I needed to pick him up and be somewhere at 2. So I gobble my food down, I pick him up, I get home—I get him home, and then I get to the office at 2.

I guess what I was upset about was that I was sort of angry at his—at him being sick, interfering with—just adding one other thing to my life. . . . And overall what's really been very upsetting about him getting sick—I'm starting to worry that maybe this is the beginning of the end. But what I was *really* pissed off about was, you know, he may not be around anymore. And *that's* what I was really angry about; not that I had to take him to the doctor and pick him up.

TABLE 5.1
Functional Categories Used to Code Narrative

Functional Category	Definition
Precipitating stressful event	An event that is unexpected in some fashion and that challenges current beliefs about the world. Precipitating events can be physical events, human actions, or the activation of a memory of an event. In all cases, the precipitating event leads to the appraisal of current states of well-being and to an evaluation of the status of current goals. The identification of the precipitating event is determined by the participant's answer to the question, "What event was stressful for you this week?" Additional probes that ask, "What about the occurrence was stressful?" help clarify exactly what caused the precipitating event to violate expectations.
Violation of beliefs	Relevant beliefs that have been challenged or violated by the precipitating stressful event. Violation of belief is scored using the linguistic criteria of violation of normality: "It wasn't supposed to happen"; "I couldn't believe what was happening"; "I hadn't expected him to get sick this fast"; "I really had to change my thinking about the situation"; "My way wasn't going to work"; "I had the wrong approach, and I changed it." A violation of belief is almost always explicitly stated in the narrative of the stressful event because it defines what is meant by a stressful event. Explicit mention of the violation consists of two parts: mention of the change that has occurred ("He got sick really fast") and mention of the fact that this change violated what was expected ("I didn't expect him to get sick so fast").

(Continued)

TABLE 5.1
(Continued)

Functional Category	Definition
Belief revision	Response to the violation of belief. Does the participant reinstate his beliefs about how things were before they were challenged by the stressful event, or does he revise them? Belief revision is scored by examining the semantic content and relational significance of adjacent clauses, such as, "His CD4 cells took a dive. I guess he's really getting sick," which represents a belief update in the form of a revision. "His CD4 cells took a dive, but he'll bounce back. He'll be okay" represents a reinstatement of a belief prior to the event. In this latter case, a prior belief is challenged but not revised.
Emotional reactions	Emotions experienced during the event. Emotions are identified using an emotion word taxonomy (Stein & Carstensen, 1993) that incorporates current analyses and standardized norms (Johnson-Laird & Oatley, 1989) used to specify different emotion labels. The taxonomy includes slang expressions, e.g., "pissed off" and "bummed out," the emotional meanings of which are inferred from the context. Ten categories capture different degrees and types of affective expressions: happiness; other positive emotions (e.g., proud, excited), neutral (e.g., indifferent, okay), general distress (e.g., bothered, unhappy, upset); sadness; anger; fear/anxiety; disgust; other negative emotions (e.g., embarrassed, guilty); and surprise. Emotions are distinguished from positive dispositional states (kind, receptive, smart, capable), neutral dispositional states (normal, average), and negative dispositional states (stern, picky).
Reasons for emotions	Participants generate explanations of emotions in terms of the goals, beliefs, and outcomes that are necessary conditions for experiencing a particular emotion. Reasons are frequently marked linguistically by causal conjunctions such as: "I was really terrified BECAUSE I knew that this was the beginning of the end." The clause after the marker normally serves as the reason for the unmarked beginning clause. Reasons for emotions include acknowledgment of beliefs or standards that have been violated, goals that have failed or succeeded, acknowledgment of the person or event that caused the change in the status of a goal, and future implications of losing or gaining something that is desired.
	Information in a narrative that does not carry an explicit causal marker can serve as a reason by using two criteria: answers to "why" questions and counterfactual reasons for questions. If a narrative clause can be inserted as an answer to a "Why" question such as, "Why did he get angry (or any other emotion)?", the clause usually serves as a reason for an emotion. If a clause is necessary for an emotion, counterfactual reasoning criteria of the form: If not A, then not B, can be applied. For example, if the partner's CD4 count had not dropped suddenly, then the caregiver would not have been frightened. Note that this is similar to answering the question "Why was the caregiver frightened?" with "His partner's CD4 count dropped suddenly." If a clause satisfies the counterfactual criterion or serves as an answer to a why question, it is scored as a reason for the emotion.

(Continued)

TABLE 5.1
(Continued)

Functional Category	Definition
Goals	Goals are statements about a caregiver's desires or those of his partner. A goal is defined as a desire to go from one state to another or a desire to maintain a current state. Goals refer to any valued object, activity, or state that the participant or partner with AIDS wants to attain. Goals may occur in conjunction with statements of preferences. The language of preference almost always includes some reference to liking, loving, missing, hating, avoiding, or disliking: "I really like it when we can just spend some quiet time, without any more painful things occurring"; "I really hate the way the doctors talk to you about these visits." Goals can also be identified by auxiliaries such as: wish, want, decide, going to do, try to do, must do: "I really wish he weren't in so much pain and suffering"; "I wish I could transform him back to his old self"; "I really don't want him to go through all of this suffering"; "I wish he would have a more positive attitude so he could beat this thing." Finally, goals can be identified from stated reasons or purposes for actions that were taken. Goals or purposes motivate action and are often connected to them by prepositions such as "to," "for," or "in order to" in clauses. For example, "I read some of his favorite short stories to him in order to relax him and distract him from the recent bad news."

Goals do not exist in isolation. They are related to the events that activate them and to other goals. Goal relationships are hierarchical: some goals are formulated in order to achieve other goals. The hierarchical order can be determined by asking "Why" questions on actions or goals. Consider the following example. In a stressful event where a partner with AIDS refused to take a workshop, the caregiver made the following statements: 1) "So I tried *to get him to take a workshop*." 2) "It teaches you *to increase the quality of your life*." 3) "I guess this is the bottom line. It is hard *to motivate him to continue to live*." The goals in each sentence are italicized.

To determine the hierarchical organization of goals, we ask "Why did the caregiver want his partner to take the workshop?" Answer: So that he could increase the quality of his life. Then we ask "Why does the caregiver want his partner to increase the quality of his life?" Answer: He wants to motivate him to live. In this example, the caregiver's highest order goal is to motivate the partner to continue to live. His first subordinate goal is to improve the quality of the partner's life. His second subordinate goal is to get the partner to take the workshop.

The goal that is highest in a hierarchy can be considered the most important. Evidence of its importance comes from the number of goals subordinate to it and the number of times that events affect it. For example, one caregiver might report five contextual goals related to the higher order goal of motivating a partner to live, while another caregiver might report only one such contextual goal. Information about the importance of goals can be obtained either within or across narratives. For this particular caregiver, seven of his nine narratives were organized around the superordinate goal of motivating his partner to live. This goal was repeatedly frustrated by the partner's apathy. In this instance, what might seem to have been a minor event—to get the partner to take a workshop—takes on major significance because it is related to a central goal of motivating the partner to live.

(Continued)

TABLE 5.1
(Continued)

Functional Category	Definition
Plans of action	The types of plans the caregiver considered before attempting to deal with the problem created by the precipitating event. Plans are identified by the use of verbs that are either conditional or future oriented and refer to desires: "Here's what I'd really like to do"; "Here's what I thought about doing"; "Here's how I planned to handle the disaster." Plans are normally expressed as subordinate goals to a higher order goal mentioned previously in the narrative. They usually contain goals that can be directly enacted to achieve a superordinate goal.
Actions	Actions are identified in terms of verbs of movement. Actions may be identified using Hopper and Thompson's (1984) transitivity criteria, where certain types of changes in the state of the actor or the object of action occur. Therefore, actions are identified by movement from one state to another, and their identification depends on the verb used in each sentence: "I took him to the hospital"; "I changed the sheets three times that night"; "I tried to make him as comfortable as possible." Most actions are voluntary and are intended to achieve a particular goal.
Consequences or goal outcomes	The outcomes that result from the actions taken with respect to the attainment or maintenance of goals. Was there goal success, failure, success and failure, partial success, or partial failure? Success and failure are identified in terms of the language of outcomes: "I did it"; "I got it"; "I really accomplished a lot" or "I really blew it"; "It just didn't happen." Outcomes generally include reference to the result of an action or to the ending of an action. "I gave him a massage *and he felt better*" or "Although I gave him the medicine, *he got worse.*"
Assessment of the stressful experience	The caregiver makes an explicit appraisal of the experience as positive, negative, mixed, or none. Assessment is scored by using linguistic criteria that include positive and negative reference to valuable experiences: "I learned a lot of valuable things about myself even though it was hard to take care of him"; "I couldn't really succeed no matter what I did"; "It was a real turnoff."
Reinstatement, revision, or abandonment of goals	Reinstatements or changes in goals and plans that were made as a result of goal success or failure. Did the participant abandon, revise, or reinstate the successful or failed goal? Reinstatement is identified by examining the content of the goal statement: "I'll try to do it again," "I didn't give up on it," or by repeated actions that are in the service of a goal. Revision is scored by identifying language that signals replacement: "I tried something else," "I tried a new strategy," or by actions that clearly serve a goal different from the one that failed. Goal revision, reinstatement, or abandonment may also be signaled by clauses that contain an original goal that is modified or altered, by a restatement of the same goal, or by the substitution of a new goal that replaces the original goal.

In Session 6, approximately 6 months prior to the partner's death:

Actually, it [stressful event] was a few days ago. Todd had just talked to the doctor. The last time he had been to see the doctor he had asked to have his T-cell count, so that was what the doctor called about on Thursday.

It was three. His T-cell count was three. And I was thinking: Mine is 1140. Now I'm gonna relate some other things that were going on and how it all ties together, why it was so stressful. Todd's weight has come down 20 pounds. He's 140 now. He goes through three T-shirts a night while in bed. He's just dripping wet. What it is on a very deep level, is that this is just a constant stressor. His weight loss, his inability to get around like he used to is just a stressor. It's there constantly.

So the thing is, when he told me, my grieving process started to come up and I was shocked. I looked at him. Maybe "shocked" is too strong a word. Stunned, or whatever.

So I looked into his face and I could see that his own fear was up. So I had to put my own feelings on hold so I could be where he was at. So I had to tell him that those were the facts but the truth was that he was still healthy to some degree, that he could still get around. I was trying to look for the positive.

And I guess what I was trying to do was convince myself, as well as him, that just because his T-cell count is three, that doesn't mean his life is over, that the grave is imminent. That there are things to be joyous about still.

Now I want to end the story is that as I'm telling the story and I'm pausing as Sam [the interviewer] writes, that I'm sitting here with my emotions and I'm really aware of how frightening the prospect of death can be. And I ask is my belief system going to support me through this next phase—the next phase of this process or experience?

There's only one other thing I wanna say and that's that I feel I'm not really being honest with Todd because I don't share this with him, because I put it aside to be with him when he's going through his emotional upheaval.

In Session 8, approximately 2 months prior to the partner's death:

Todd's decided to go home to his family because according to him it's getting very close to the end. And he's doing that because he feels he's being a burden to me.

The thing is he got some boxes and he was starting to pack the other day and I was really resistant to it. We both wear the same size clothes, and we've even bought clothes together. And there's this shirt. It cost $300. And I got very angry about the shirt because, I thought, this is supposed to be my shirt, he's supposed to leave it to me. And I couldn't believe how angry I got about the shirt and about the packing. And I thought, is this what the relationship has come down to—a fight about the belongings, the goods?

And I guess what I'm feeling about this situation is that he's packing and leaving and I feel gypped.

Not only the caregiving, but the relationship. I feel that I've put in all this time and something is being taken away from me, the final stage of the relationship, the dying. The ending. It's not just the shirt—and believe me, it's gorgeous.

I feel I need an ending to this story, too. I don't know what it is, except to tell him what's going on."

(Interviewer: I'd like to know what about all this was especially stressful for you.)

Well, I guess the conflict that created the stress was, on the one hand—this has to do with a belief—if I'm such a good person, why am I being possessive about a shirt? So the stressor was, those feelings aren't valid, I shouldn't have them. I only have to think about Todd—I shouldn't think about myself. And the other stressor is that he's going to be leaving. Whether he goes home to Ohio, or stays here, he's going to die.

(A postscript to this interview: Todd returned to Ohio, and Todd's family called his partner to come be with Todd before he died. Todd has since died.)

Analysis of the Narrative

Table 5.2 contains an analysis of Caregiver 1's fifth session to illustrate the beliefs that were violated by the stressful event, the goals and plans that were stated by the caregiver, the outcomes of the goals and plans (success, failure, or some of both), and the caregiver's response to outcomes (reinstatement, abandonment or revision of goal).

Summary of One Caregiver's Narratives

Table 5.3 summarizes the coding of goals for eight narratives that were generated by Caregiver 1 prior to his partner's death. The columns list the initiating stressful event, the goal plan, the goal outcome, and the goal response. A similar table can be created to describe challenged or violated beliefs and belief revisions. Note the extent to which Caregiver 1 is able to generate attainable goals during the time when his partner's death is approaching.

Summary of Five Caregivers' Narratives

Table 5.4 depicts the results from analyses of the narratives generated by five caregivers. For each individual, the table lists the total number of events, goals, goal outcomes (successes and failures), and goal responses (abandonments, goal revisions, and goal reinstatements) under conditions of goal success and goal failure. Although other variables may be related to psychological well-being (see Stein, Folkman, Trabasso, & Christopher-Richards, 1995), we chose the number of successful or failed goals and responses to the goal outcomes to illustrate the relationship between appraisal processes and psychological well-being. From these data, a score can be calculated for each subject regarding the proportion of successes given successes and

TABLE 5.2
Single Narrative From Caregiver 1: Analysis of Beliefs and Goals

Underlying Belief That Is Violated	Belief Update	Goal Plans	Goal Outcome	Goal Response
"Whenever anyone's in pain, I feel I've got to do something about it."	"I was feeling helpless around the situation because I didn't feel it was my place to call the doctor."	To have Todd call a doctor. "And I kept wanting him to call the doctor."	Success: "So he finally called the doctor on Thursday."	Goal abandoned Note: Goal was abandoned because closure was achieved.
[Inferred]: The end stages of AIDS have not yet begun.	"And overall what's really been very upsetting about him getting sick—I'm starting to worry that maybe this is the beginning of the end."	To get back to work by 2:00. "I needed to pick him up and be somewhere by 2."	Success: "So I gobble my food down, I pick him up, I get home—I get him home, and then I get to the office at 2."	Goal abandoned Note: Goal was abandoned because closure was achieved.

TABLE 5.3
Summary of Goal Analysis Across Event Narratives of Caregiver 1

Event	Goal Plan	Goal Outcome	Response
#1: PWA[a] exhibiting violent psychotic behavior in reaction to psychotropic drugs or dementia	1. To protect PWA (Persuade him not to leave the house)	1. Success	1. Reinstatement
	2. To calm him down	2. Success	2. Reinstatement
	3. To get PWA hospitalized	3. Success	3. Abandonment
#2: Appearance of unexpected illness creates conflict between caregiving and job	1. To assess how ill the PWA is	No information	—
	2. To provide care if it is needed	No information	—
#3: PWA wanted caregiver to cancel a doctor's appointment for him and caregiver didn't want to do it	1. To get PWA to phone doctor	1. Success	1. Abandonment
#4: PWA wouldn't meditate with caregiver	1. To get PWA to meditate (good for his health and the relationship)	1. Failure	1. Reinstatement
#5: Anticipating PWA's death Conflict between caregiving and work roles	1. Wants PWA to call his doctor	1. Success	1. Abandonment
	2. Pick up PWA at hospital and return to work on time	2. Success	2. Abandonment
#6: Anticipatory grief Disease progression	1. To put feeling on hold	1. Success	1. Reinstatement
	2. To provide hope to self and partner	2. Success	2. Reinstatement
#7: Caregiver suppresses emotions because of PWA's dementia	1. To stop his anger and rage	1. Success	1. Revision (find another way to deal with it)
#8: PWA is leaving caregiver to go to his family to die	1. To have the final stage of the relationship	1. Failure	1. Reinstatement
	2. To think about his partner and not just himself	2. Success	
	3. To be there at the end	3. Not known at time of interview, but ultimately successful	

[a]PWA = Partner with AIDS.

TABLE 5.4
Goal Outcome Frequencies Across Five Caregivers' Narratives

	Caregiver Number				
Functional Category	1	2	3	4	5
Total narratives	11.0	13.0	8	12	9.0
Total goals	22.0	25.0	15	25	24.0
Total failures	15.5	7.0	2	2	12.5
Total successes	7.5	8.0	11	14	7.5
Given failure: Total abandonments	1.0	1.0	0	0	5.0
Total reinstatements	13.0	5.5	2	0	5.0
Total revisions	0.5	0.0	0	2	1.5

failures, or the proportion of goal reinstatements given goal failures. These scores, in turn, can also be related to psychological well-being.

Goal Success, Depressive Mood, and Positive Morale

A major goal of the UCSF Coping Project is to increase understanding of how people maintain psychological well-being in very difficult circumstances. We expected that the participants in this study would have high levels of depressive mood because of the circumstances of caregiving for a partner with AIDS. Our expectations were confirmed: At the initial assessment of all study participants, the mean CES–D score was 19.18 ($SD = 10.89$) for the HIV-positive caregivers and 17.30 ($SD = 9.40$) for the HIV-negative caregivers. These scores are more than a standard deviation higher than community norms (Folkman, Chesney, Cooke, Boccellari, & Collette, 1994). The difference between the HIV-positive caregivers and the HIV-negative caregivers was not significant.

Although we expected caregivers to be depressed, we did not know how they would score on tests of positive morale. The norms for the Bradburn Positive Morale are reported for each of four items as proportions of individuals who report that they never felt that way, sometimes felt that way, or always felt that way during the previous week (McDowell & Praught, 1982). The four items are rated on a 4-point Likert scale (not at all, once, several times, often) following the prompt: "How often last week did you feel . . . ?" The items include "on top of the world," "particularly excited or interested in something," "pleased about having accomplished something," and "proud because someone complimented you on something you had done."

A comparison of the responses of individuals in our sample and community norms for males in the 25–54-year range indicated that 21% of caregivers and 9% of the community sample reported never feeling any of the four positive states, 65% of caregivers and 62% of the community sample reported feeling the four positive states an average of several times, and 12% of caregiver and 29% of the community sample reported feeling the four positive states often. Therefore, the samples are largely comparable in that a large majority of both reported feeling positive states some of the time. In short, although the great majority of caregivers reported high levels of depressive mood, they also reported feeling positive at least some of the time. Feeling bad does not preclude also feeling good.

The key question suggested by these findings is: What contributes to positive morale when people are simultaneously feeling depressed? Our formulation of adaptive goal processes would suggest that achieving goals, even goals that are transitory and trivial to the casual observer, should contribute to positive well-being, even in situations that are deteriorating and essentially uncontrollable.

We explored the answer to this question in a very tentative way with five subjects for whom we had scored goal successes and goal failures. A score describing the proportion of goal successes to total goal successes and goal failures was calculated for each of the five participants and related to measures of depression and positive morale. The goal success scores ranged from .32 to .87. The correlation between the goal success score and depressive mood was $-.28$, and the correlation between the goal success score and positive morale was .44.

Although these observations are preliminary, they illustrate that having successes while in the midst of deteriorating conditions contribute to positive morale, even when the individual is feeling depressed about everything else that is going on. In future analyses of recent stressful events, we will explore again the relationship between goal success or failure and states of psychological well-being. In our recent analysis of the bereavement narratives of these caregivers (Stein et al., 1995), where each caregiver recounted many different events that occurred at the time of the PWA's death, the proportion of successful and failed goals has been shown to be significantly related to indices of both positive and negative mood. Therefore, the perception of being able to succeed at some level of goal attainment is quite important, especially in situations where traumatic events have already occurred and caregivers are attempting to distill the meaning of these events.

CONCLUSION

We have described a theoretical framework for examining individuals' cognitive, emotional, and behavioral responses to stressful events. In the present study, the stressful events we examined were generated by caregiving partners of men with AIDS. The events usually involved losses ranging from relatively minor ones, such as having a carefully prepared meal rejected, to losses associated with a partner's deteriorating health and, ultimately, the loss of the partner's life. Our theoretical framework focuses on describing the meaning of these losses in terms of the specific beliefs and goals that are challenged in the context of a stressful encounter. We argue that the maintenance of psychological well-being in deteriorating circumstances involves being able to revise one's beliefs about how things are and how they will be, being able to relinquish goals that are no longer tenable, and being able to substitute new, meaningful goals that provide opportunities for success. In effect, suffering loss requires that individuals devalue the importance of a blocked goal, generate a new goal that can be linked to a current goal that is still operative, and increase the value of the new goal to equal or surpass the value of the failed goal.

One of the ways these processes can be measured is by examining the ways in which individuals talk about their current goal successes and failures. Using a small sample of data, we showed that the proportion of successful goals that caregivers mentioned significantly predicted the strength of concurrent states of psychological well-being. We (Stein et al., 1995) have been able to replicate this finding in an analysis of the bereavement reports that caregivers provide at the death of their partners. The relative proportion of positive to negative emotional states expressed also predict both current and long-term states of psychological well-being.

The ability to focus on the positive implications of personal goals, even while in the midst of experiencing tremendous trauma, appears to be a significant indicator of psychological well-being, especially when positive states of mind are considered. It is not that these successful caregivers fail to express their deep grief and commitment to a relationship; it is that the nature of the relationship and the meaning of the relationship enables some caregivers to consider the positive outcomes in the face of and in relationship to disaster or trauma. In our future studies, we planned to explore the longitudinal nature of these complex assessments of coping strategies. If we are able to better describe the nature of positive coping strategies in the face of disastrous outcomes, we may be able to develop better intervention techniques that can be applied when coping strategies are not psychologically productive.

Our approach requires individuals to consider a specific situation when reporting their thoughts, feelings, and behavior. Many appraisal approaches focus on the nature of general beliefs about the self and the world that are less situated (e.g., Catlin & Epstein, 1992; Collins, Taylor, & Skokan, 1990; Janoff-Bulman, 1989; Taylor & Brown, 1988). The extent to which general beliefs predict and are related to specific situational beliefs about how things are, how they are expected to be, and what can be done about them, has only begun to be explored. To date, only modest relationships have been reported. For example, Taylor and her colleagues (Taylor et al., 1992) found a modest relationship ($r = .18$) between dispositional and specific event-based optimistic expectations in a cohort of gay men, and other studies have found modest relationships between generalized and situated-based expectancies for control (Folkman, 1984).

The lack of a powerful relationship between situated and general appraisals suggest one of two possible explanations. The first concerns the specific situations considered when paper and pencil measures are used to report general appraisals about the self. Individuals may focus only on one or two highly memorable events to assess their beliefs about the self and the world. The situations that people experience and relate in the process of reporting stressful events, such as those that caregivers report about caregiving, however, may be quite different and atypical of those used to assess the general self-concept. Therefore, different situations may be considered when assessing dispositional versus situation-specific self-concepts.

The second possibility is that individuals do have more complex assessments of their sense of a general self, but current paper and pencil measures do not permit or do not capture this more complex sense of self. Given that we have demonstrated significant correlations between appraisals of situationally based behavior and psychological well-being, we need to determine whether a general appraisal of self involves these situations. In this way, we will be able to describe what a general self-assessment measure involves, compared to a situated self-assessment measure. The technique of using situated judgments to assess general conceptual beliefs may be necessary to improve measurements of current and long-range psychological well-being.

Our focus on goal-related processes is also different from other researchers who have focused on the importance of goals (Martin & Tesser, 1989; Nolen-Hoeksema et al., 1992). We are concerned with the maintenance of positive morale over time under deteriorating conditions (see also Wortman & Silver, 1987) as well as with the precipitation of depressive and ruminative processes. The mechanisms that lead to positive psychological well-being may be different from the mechanisms that lead to depression and rumination. Moreover, the nature of depression, in terms of the length of the normal recovery process, needs a more elaborated description. Although Nolen-Hoeksema et al. showed clearly that focusing on specific aspects of a depressive situation can be more debilitating than helpful, we (Stein, Ross, Wright, & Wiens, 1995) have shown that talking about a traumatic occurrence in specifically constrained ways improves depressive mood. Therefore, not all talk and attention to depression is harmful or causes further depression. The outcomes depend on the initial level of depression, the type of trauma considered, and the nature of the talk about the trauma.

The fact that we are able to describe and assess the dynamic aspects of thinking, feeling, planning, and acting also distinguishes our approach from other researchers who focus on the nature and importance of situation based appraisals. Little's (1983) concept of *personal projects*, Emmons' (1992; Emmons & King, 1988) *personal strivings*, Brandstadter and Renner's (1990) *personal preferences*, and Smith and Lazarus' (1990, 1993; Smith, Haynes, Lazarus, & Pope, 1993) *goal congruence* all consider situationally based appraisal processes. Most of these analyses, however, tend to be static. They do not explore the process of goal setting and goal revision, nor do they describe the temporal and causal nature of the planning process. Most importantly, the learning and change processes that occur as a function of coping are not addressed.

Finally, our approach differs from traditional qualitative approaches in which investigators typically describe the spectrum of different responses, identify patterns, and from those patterns suggest hypotheses. In contrast, we are guided by a theoretical framework, which shapes the definition and operationalization of coding categories. Our approach is designed to test hypotheses rather than generate them and to explore the nature of the connections between feeling, thinking, and acting (Stein & Trabasso, 1992).

Although our theory is still in a formative stage, we hope to develop our framework with sufficient precision so that other researchers can use their own narrative data to test and extend our model. Our theory is neutral with respect to the importance of specific contexts and, therefore, should be applicable to a wide range of circumstances. Because we initially tested our theory on a sample of caregivers who are gay, in committed relationships, and living with partners with AIDS, our hypotheses and findings about the maintenance of psychological well-being in difficult circumstances need to be examined in other contexts to determine their generalizability.

ACKNOWLEDGMENTS

This research was supported by grants MH44045 and MH52517 from the National Institute of Mental Health, a grant from the Smart Foundation Center on Early Learning, and grant HD25742 from the National Institute of Child Health and Human Development. We would like to thank Liz Albro, Anne Christopher-Richards, and Lynae Darbes for their assistance in the analysis of the narratives.

REFERENCES

Beach, L. R. (1985). Action: Decision implementation strategies and tactics. In M. Frese & J. Sabini (Eds.), *The concept of action in psychology* (pp. 123–133). Hillsdale, NJ: Lawrence Erlbaum Associates.
Beck, A. T. (1988). *Love is never enough.* New York: Harper & Row.
Bradburn, N. M. (1969). *The structure of psychological well-being.* Chicago: Aldine.
Brandstadter, J., & Renner, G. (1990). Tenacious goal pursuit and flexible goal adjustment. *Psychology and Aging, 5,* 58–67.

Breznitz, S. (1983). *The denial of stress*. New York: International Universities Press.

Brunstein, J. C. (1993). Personal goals and subjective well-being: A longitudinal study. *Journal of Personality and Social Psychology, 65*, 1061–1070.

Carver, C. S., & Scheier, M. F. (1990). Origins and functions of positive and negative affect: A control-process view. *Psychological Review, 97*, 19–35.

Catlin, G., & Epstein, S. (1992). Unforgettable experiences: The relation of life events to basic belief about self and world. *Social Cognition, 10*, 189–209.

Collins, R. L., Taylor, S. E., & Skokan, L. A. (1990). A better world or a shattered vision? Changes in life perspectives following victimization. *Social Cognition, 8*, 263–285.

Emmons, R. A. (1992). Abstract versus concrete goals: Personal striving level, physical illness, and psychological well-being. *Journal of Personality and Social Psychology, 62*, 292–300.

Emmons, R. A. (in press). Striving and feeling: Personal goals and subjective well-being. In J. Bargh & P. Gollwitzer (Eds.), *Motivation and action*. New York: Guilford.

Emmons, R. A., & King, L. A. (1988). Conflict among personal strivings: Immediate and long-term implications for psychological and physical well-being. *Journal of Personality and Social Psychology, 54*, 1040–1048.

Folkman, S. (1984). Personal control and stress and coping processes: A theoretical analysis. *Journal of Personality and Social Psychology, 46*, 839–852.

Folkman, S. (1992). Making the case for coping. In B. Carpenter (Ed.), *Personal coping: Theory, research, and application* (pp. 31–46). New York: Praeger.

Folkman, S., Chesney, M. A., & Christopher-Richards, A. (1994). Stress and coping in partners of men with AIDS. *Psychiatric Clinics of North America, 17*, 35–54.

Folkman, S., Chesney, M. A., Cooke, M., Boccellari, A., & Collette, L. (1994). Caregiver burden in HIV+ and HIV− partners of men with AIDS. *Journal of Consulting and Clinical Psychology, 62*, 746–756.

Folkman, S., & Lazarus, R. S. (1980). An analysis of coping in a middle-aged community sample. *Journal of Health and Social Behavior, 21*, 219–239.

Folkman, S., & Lazarus, R. S. (1985). If it changes it must be a process: Study of emotion and coping during three stages of a college examination. *Journal of Personality and Social Psychology, 48*, 150–170.

Folkman, S., & Lazarus, R. S. (1988b). *Ways of Coping Questionnaire*. Palo Alto, CA: Consulting Psychologists Press.

Frese, M., & Sabini, J. (1985). *The concept of action in psychology*. Hillsdale, NJ: Lawrence Erlbaum Associates.

Gottman, J. (1994). *Why marriages succeed or fail*. New York: Simon & Schuster.

Heckhausen, H., & Kuhl, J. (1985). From wishes to action. The dead ends and short cuts on the long way to action. In M. Frese & J. Sabini (Eds.), *The concept of action in psychology* (pp. 136–160). Hillsdale, NJ: Lawrence Erlbaum Associates.

Hopper, P. J., & Thompson, S. A. (1984). The discourse basis for lexical categories in universal grammar. *Language, 60*, 703–752.

Horowitz, M., Adler, N., & Kegeles, S. (1988). A scale for measuring the occurrence of positive states of mind: A preliminary report. *Psychosomatic Medicine, 50*, 477–483.

Horowitz, M. J. (1991). *Person schemas and maladaptive patterns*. Chicago: University of Chicago Press.

Janis, I., & Mann, L. (1977). *Decision making*. New York: The Free Press.

Janoff-Bulman, R. (1989). Assumptive worlds and the stress of traumatic events: Applications of the schema construct. *Social Cognition, 7*, 113–136.

Johnson-Laird, P. N., & Oatley, K. (1989). The language of emotions: An analysis of a semantic field. *Cognition and Emotion, 3*, 81–123.

Kihlstrom, J. (in press-a). Exhumed memory. In S. J. Lynn & N. P. Spanos (Eds.), *Truth in memory*. New York: Guilford.

Kihlstrom, J. (in press-b). Trauma and memory. *Consciousness and Cognition* [Special issue on the recovery of lost childhood memories for traumatic events].

Klinger, E. (1975). Consequence of commitment to and disengagement from incentives. *Psychological Review, 82*, 1–25.

Klinger, E. (1977). *Meaning and void: Inner experience and the incentives in people's lives*. Minneapolis: University of Minnesota Press.

Klinger, E. (1987). Current concerns and disengagement from incentives. In F. Halisch & J. Kuhl (Eds.), *Motivation, intention, and volition* (pp. 337–347). Berlin: Springer.

Lazarus, R. S. (1991). *Emotion and adaptation*. New York: Oxford University Press.

Lazarus, R. S., & Folkman, S. (1984). *Stress, appraisal, and coping*. New York: Springer.

Lazarus, R. S., & Folkman, S. (1987). Transactional theory and research on emotion and coping. In L. Laux & G. Vossel (Eds.), *Personality in biographical stress and coping research* (pp. 141–169). Berne: Verlag & Huber.

Lazarus, R. S., & Smith, C. A. (1988). Knowledge and appraisal in the cognition–emotion relationship. *Cognition and Emotion, 2*, 281–300.

Little, B. R. (1983). Personal projects: A rationale and methods for investigation. *Environmental Behavior, 15*, 273–309.

Martin, L. L., & Tesser, A. (1989). Toward a motivational and structural theory of ruminative thought. In J. S. Uleman & J. A. Bargh (Eds.), *Unintended thought* (pp. 306–326). New York: Guilford.

McDowell, I., & Praught, E. (1982). On the measurement of happiness: An examination of the Bradburn Scale in the Canada Health Survey. *American Journal of Epidemiology, 116*, 949–958.

Meichenbaum, D. (1994). *A clinical handbook/practical therapist manual for assessing and treating adults with posttraumatic stress disorder*. Waterloo, Ontario, Canada: Institute Press.

Nolen-Hoeksema, S., Girgus, J. S., & Seligman, M. E. P. (1992). Predictors and consequences of depressive symptoms in children: A 5-year longitudinal study. *Journal of Abnormal Psychology, 101*, 405–422.

Pervin, L. A. (1989). Goal concepts in personality and social psychology: A historical perspective. In L. A. Pervin (Ed.), *Goal concepts in personality and social psychology*. Hillsdale, NJ: Lawrence Erlbaum Associates.

Radloff, L. S. (1977). The CES-D Scale: A self-report depression scale for research in the general population. *Applied Psychological Measurement, 1*, 385–401.

Ross, M., & Holmberg, D. (1990). Recounting the past: Gender differences in the recall of events in the history of a close relationship. In M. Olson & M. P. Zanna (Eds.), *Self-inference processes: The Ontario symposium* (Vol. 6, pp. 135–152). Hillsdale, NJ: Lawrence Erlbaum Associates.

Scherer, K. R. (1984). On the nature and function of emotion: A component process approach. In K. R. Scherer & P. Ekman (Eds.), *Approaches to emotion* (pp. 293–317). Hillsdale, NJ: Lawrence Erlbaum Associates.

Semmer, N., & Frese, M. (1985). Action theory in clinical psychology. In M. Frese & J. Sabini (Eds.), *The concept of action in psychology* (pp. 296–310). Hillsdale, NJ: Lawrence Erlbaum Associates.

Smith, C. A., Haynes, K. N., Lazarus, R. S., & Pope, L. K. (1993). In search of the "Hot" cognitions: Attributions, appraisals, and their relation to emotion. *Journal of Personality and Social Psychology, 65*, 916–929.

Smith, C. A., & Lazarus, R. A. (1990). Emotion and adaptation. In L. A. Pervin (Ed.), *Handbook of personality: Theory and research* (pp. 609–637). New York: Guilford.

Smith, C. A., & Lazarus, R. A. (1993). Appraisal components, core relational themes, and the emotions. *Cognition & Emotion, 7*, 233–269.

Spielberger, C. D. (1988). *State–Trait Anger Expression Inventory*. Lutz, FL: Psychological Assessment Resources, Inc.

Spielberger, C. D., Gorsuch, R. L., & Lushene, R. E. (1970). *STAI Manual for the State–Trait Anxiety Inventory*. Palo Alto, CA: Consulting Psychologists Press.

Stadler, M., & Wehner, T. (1985). Anticipation as a basic principle in goal-directed action. In M. Frese & J. Sabini (Eds.), *The concept of action in psychology* (pp. 67–79). Hillsdale, NJ: Lawrence Erlbaum Associates.

Stein, N. L., & Carstensen, L. (1993). *Natural language descriptions of the face: A working internal state and event taxonomy*. Unpublished manuscript.

Stein, N. L., Folkman, S., Trabasso, T., & Christopher-Richards, A. (1995, January). *The role of goal appraisal processes in predicting psychological well-being*. Paper presented at the Rashomon Conference, Center for the Study of AIDS Prevention, University of California, San Francisco.

Stein, N. L., & Jewett, J. (1986). A conceptual analysis of the meaning of negative emotions: Implications for a theory of development. In C. Izard & P. Read (Eds.), *Measuring emotions in infants and children* (pp. 238–267). Cambridge, England: Cambridge University Press.

Stein, N. L., & Levine, L. (1987). Thinking about feelings: The development and organization of emotional knowledge. In R. Snow & M. Farr (Eds.), *Aptitude, learning and instruction* (pp. 165–197). Hillsdale, NJ: Lawrence Erlbaum Associates.

Stein, N. L., & Levine, L. (1989). The causal organization of emotion knowledge: A developmental study. *Cognition and Emotion, 3*(4), 343–378.

Stein, N. L., & Levine, L. (1990). Making sense out of emotion: The representation and use of goal-structured knowledge. In N. L. Stein, B. Leventhal, & T. Trabasso (Eds.), *Psychological and biological approaches to emotion* (pp. 45–73). Hillsdale, NJ: Lawrence Erlbaum Associates.

Stein, N. L., Ross, M., Wright, S., & Wiens, B. (1995). *Adolescents talking about trauma: Its relationship to states of psychological well-being*. Unpublished manuscript, University of Chicago.

Stein, N. L., & Trabasso, T. (1992). The organization of emotional experience: Creating links among emotion, thinking, language and intentional action. *Cognition and Emotion*, 225–244.

Stein, N. L., Trabasso, T., & Liwag, M. (1992). The representation and organization of emotional experience. Unfolding the emotional episode. In M. Lewis & J. Haviland (Eds.), *Handbook of emotion* (pp. 279–299). New York: Guilford.

Stein, N. L., Trabasso, T., & Liwag, M. (1994). The Rashomon phenomenon: Personal frames and future-oriented appraisals in memory for emotional events. In M. Haith (Ed.), *Future-oriented processes*. Chicago: University of Chicago Press.

Taylor, S. E., & Brown, J. D. (1988). Illusion and well-being: A social psychological perspective on mental health. *Psychological Bulletin, 103*, 193–210.

Taylor, S. E., Helgeson, V. S., Reed, G. M., & Skokan, L. A. (1991). Self-generated feeling of control and adjustment to physical illness. *Journal of Social Issues, 47*, 91–109.

Taylor, S. E., Kemeny, M. E., Aspinwall, L. G., Schneider, S. G., Rodriguez, R., & Herbert, M. (1992). Optimism, coping, psychological distress, and high-risk sexual behavior among men at risk for Acquired Immunodeficiency Syndrome (AIDS). *Journal of Personality and Social Psychology, 63*, 460–473.

Tennen, H., & Herzberger, S. (1985). Ways of coping scale. In D. J. Keyser & R. C. Sweetland (Eds.), *Test critiques* (pp. 686–697). Kansas City, MO: Test Corporation of America.

Trabasso, T., Stein, N. L., Rodkin, P. C., Munger, G. P., & Baughn, C. (1992). Knowledge of goals and plans in the on-line narration of events. *Cognitive Development, 7*, 133–170.

Trabasso, T., & van den Broek, P. (1985). Causal thinking and the representation of narrative events. *Journal of Memory and Language, 24*, 612–630.

Traue, H. C., & Pennebaker, J. W. (1993). *Emotion, inhibition, and health*. Göttingen, Germany: Hogrefe & Huber.

Wortman, C., & Silver, R. (1987). Coping with irrevocable loss. In G. R. VandenBos & B. K. Bryant (Eds.), *Cataclysms, crises, and catastrophes: Psychology in action* (pp. 189–235). Washington, DC: American Psychological Association.

Perceptual and Verbal Processes in Everyday Memory

6

NONVERBAL RECALL

Jean M. Mandler
University of California, San Diego
University College London

Laraine McDonough
University of California, San Diego

When the term *recall* is used, most people think of a verbal recollection of a past event, probably because when they share a memory with others they typically do so by means of a verbal account. Psychologists have concentrated their efforts on the study of these accounts, typically treating them as synonymous with recall itself. However, verbal protocols are constructions; they are only very partial descriptions of what has been perceived and is now being remembered. Recall of events also consists of images of what has happened that may not appear in the verbal account at all. Indeed, these imaginal components are often used to construct the verbal account. Therefore, a verbal account provides evidence that recall has taken place, but is not necessarily all that has come to mind.

Many memories are entirely nonverbal—for infants all are so. It is thus surprising how little information is available about nonverbal recall. Indeed, there is not even a generally accepted definition that covers the verbal and nonverbal cases equally well. Many psychologists manage without a definition of recall at all, although if pressed they may espouse the commonsense definition of bringing something to mind. Others would reject even this definition. To bring something to mind means bringing it to consciousness, and some psychologists refuse to use this term on the (rather outdated) grounds that it is not scientifically respectable. The problem with this approach is that it leaves the term recall undefined. However, everyone uses the term without, apparently, feeling uneasy about its lack of formal definition.

We see no choice but to define recall for what it is: bringing information that is not perceptually present to conscious awareness. Interestingly, this definition also constitutes one of the main senses of the Piagetian term *representation*: re-presenting something to oneself that is not perceptually present. This association between recall and representation is not accidental. One cannot bring to mind a past event without having represented it, in the sense of having conceived of it in some way; one cannot recall an uninterpreted event. The essence of conscious recollection is an interpretation of the past. Unless it is conceptualized, an event will not be stored in such a way as to make the information retrievable at a later time. Another way to state this criterion is to say that recall requires that information be encoded into the declarative (explicit) knowledge system. This is why amnesia, which involves the inability to recall, is considered to be a disorder of the declarative memory system (Squire, 1987).

That recall requires the declarative knowledge system is not particularly controversial when dealing with verbally expressed memories. When people describe a past event the verbalization itself makes it clear that the knowledge is explicit; they have conceptualized the event and are *declaring* or telling us about that conceptualization. How, then, can infants tell us whether they have recalled the past when they have no language to express what they have experienced? Following observations of Piaget (1951) and also work by Meltzoff (1988a, 1988b), we have been using deferred imitation as a nonverbal measure of recall. This work depends on the assumption that to *reenact* an event after it happened requires the same type of conceptualization of the event and the same kind of retrieval as to *retell* what happened. Enactment will not produce exactly the same information as verbalization, because it will *show* what happened rather than *tell* what happened, but we claim that the overall recall requirement is equivalent.

We had never heard any objections to Piaget's use of deferred imitation as a type of recall, and so we were somewhat surprised to find that our claim is considered controversial by some of our colleagues. It has been suggested to us that perhaps the ability to enact an event does not require the same kind of higher cognitive functions as verbal recall. Perhaps enactment can be done in some automatic way without bringing the absent information to awareness. One of our colleagues suggested that unless we could show that amnesic adults could not do deferred imitation, we could not begin to contemplate calling it recall without providing verbal evidence as well (see discussion section of J. Mandler, 1990).

The requirement that recall be verbal is obviously too restrictive, but what should we use in its place when we want to study preverbal children or other nontalking creatures? What should we use as evidence that recall has taken place? How can we be sure that we are studying recall and not some simpler kind of retention? That is the force of the just cited remark:

Without verbal evidence we might really only be observing the operation of a previously learned sensorimotor procedure, or perhaps a form of repetition priming of the kind that remains intact in amnesia.

One goal of the present chapter, therefore, is to distinguish between procedural, implicit memory in infancy that does not make use of the higher order recall function, and declarative, explicit memory that involves bringing conceptual information to mind. As Piaget's work makes clear, if we are to understand early development we must know how and when conceptual functioning begins in infancy; recall is one piece of evidence for that development. Obviously, if recall begins before the onset of language, then we must have a nonverbal method of measuring it. Therefore, a second goal of the chapter is to elucidate deferred imitation as such a method, and to show that reenacting events does involve explicit memory; that is, it requires the ability to bring information about the past to conscious awareness. Along the way, we reiterate the point that the same kinds of retrieval and constructive processes take place in deferred imitation as in verbal recall. We also want to note that we do not discuss the spatiotemporal dating of recall. We have no evidence that when infants reproduce an event by acting it out that they remember when or where it happened. Although as adults we tend to think of our recall memories as being spatiotemporally dated, they often are not. It is quite possible to recall an event in considerable detail and not be able to remember when or where it took place.

PROCEDURAL VERSUS DECLARATIVE MEMORY IN INFANCY

Some form of memory is operative at least from birth, because learning itself requires memory. Many of the kinds of information that are stored during learning, however, cannot be brought to mind; they are not explicit. Prominent among these are the perceptual and motor skills called *sensorimotor schemas*. Simple motor skills such as crawling or walking, and more complex skills such as typing or driving a car, have long been used as classic examples of *procedural knowledge*, which is displayed without awareness of how the actions are performed and thus without the ability to describe them. The same is true for *perceptual recognition*; people know that someone looks familiar but do not know the information they are using to make this judgment and cannot describe (or draw) how the face looks. This lack of awareness does not mean, of course, that people learned to walk or talk or play the piano in an unconscious state. However, most of the information acquired during the learning of perceptual–motor schemas is not accessible, regardless of what was being thought about at the time. For those of us who as youngsters were forced to learn the piano, a little reflection on what we thought about when endlessly practicing scales dramatizes this point. The repetitive practice had the desired refining and unitizing effect in spite of our conceptual inattention. The absence of conscious reflection is most obvious for the sensorimotor procedures of infancy, because these are presumably even less dependent on conscious conceptualizations for their refinement into smoothly functioning and efficient procedures than more advanced skills such as learning to play the piano.

Sensorimotor procedures are the sole kind of representation that Piaget (1952) ascribed to infants. He duly noted that infants learn to handle objects and to treat them as familiar. What was missing, according to his theory, was conceptual representation, or what today would more typically be called *declarative* or *explicit knowledge*. During the sensorimotor period the baby was said not yet to have concepts, and therefore to be incapable of recalling the past, imagining the future, or doing mental problem solving. These mental activities require a declarative knowledge base of concepts from which information can be accessed to consciousness. Until such a base is built up, conscious thought, recollection, and planning for the future is simply not possible.

It may be noted that there is rough but not perfect synonymy among the sets of terms that are used to divide knowledge into two types. Piaget's distinction was between sensorimotor and conceptual knowledge. In current research this distinction is more apt to be called the difference between *inaccessible* and *accessible knowledge*, or *procedural* and *declarative knowledge* (e.g., Squire, 1987), or *implicit* and *explicit knowledge* (e.g., Schacter, 1987). There are some minor differences in the definition of these terms (e.g., sensorimotor knowledge is only a subset of procedural knowledge because it does not include mental procedures such as retrieval), but for all of them the defining characteristic is whether information can be brought to conscious awareness or not. The plethora of terminology for what is basically the same distinction seems to be due to the reluctance to talk about consciousness. However, it should be understood that in this chapter recall is defined in terms of accessibility to consciousness, which means that it requires conceptual, declarative, or explicit knowledge.

It is not our intention to debate the status of procedural and declarative knowledge. It is widely agreed that there is something different between factual knowledge, whether that be remembering events of the past or knowledge of history more widely conceived, and perceptual and motor skills. It is still a matter of debate how much these differences are due to different storage systems, including different formats for the two types of knowledge, or how much they are due to different kinds of processing within a single storage system. Rather, our intention is to discuss the onset of one particular kind of knowledge (or the onset of one particular kind of processing) that involves explicit (conscious) memory; namely, recall of the past.

Recall has traditionally been classed as one of the higher cognitive functions just because it requires a re-presentation, or conceptualization, of the world. As discussed earlier, when someone verbally summarizes a recent experience, it is obvious that they have a conceptualization of what has happened. It may be less obvious that nonverbal recall also requires conceptualization. In the nonverbal case, recall requires the partial reproduction of an experience through imagery. However, people do not create images from uninterpreted perceptual records, but from perceptual information that has been interpreted or construed (Intons-Peterson & Roskos-Ewoldsen, 1989; Intraub & Richardson, 1989; Kosslyn, 1980). Therefore, images do not consist of the re-creation of raw perceptual data, but rather are composed of conceptually interpreted scenes. In this sense they are just as conceptual as a verbal construal of a scene.

One of the simplest demonstrations of the conceptual nature of imagery was shown many years ago by Carmichael, Hogan, and Walters (1932). These investigators showed people nonsense line drawings that were given different labels. For example, a figure consisting of two small circles connected by a horizontal line was labeled either as eyeglasses or a dumbbell. When the subjects were later asked to draw the forms from memory, it became obvious that the labels had influenced the nature of the image that was recalled. The figures subjects drew were recognizably more like eyeglasses or dumbbells depending on the label that had originally accompanied them. This example involves verbalization, of course, but the principle is the same for nonverbal processing. How we conceptualize a figure at the time of encoding is what is potentially accessible at a later time. If we have conceptualized two circles connected by a line as eyeglasses, then something that looks like eyeglasses is what we will recall.

Piaget (1952; Piaget & Inhelder, 1971) realized the significance for early development of the fact that images are conceptually interpreted and that we do not recall raw perceptual data. Because in his theory infants have only sensorimotor knowledge during the first year of life and have not yet achieved conceptual representations of the world, this meant they cannot form images (and therefore cannot recall). He understood that to form an image of an object is a type of conceptual functioning, and this was exactly the sort of representation that he claimed is absent during the first year of life. If infants could form images, by definition that would mean that they were conceptualizing what they saw, and therefore they would not be confined to an exclusively sensorimotor form of representation.

Piaget (1951) used recall (which he variously called *evocative memory* or the *symbolic evocation of absent realities*) as one of the hallmarks of the achievement of the conceptual (declarative) system. He called the earliest form of evocative memory that he observed *deferred imitation*, and he used it as one of the signs that a representational, conceptual capacity had evolved. When children can reproduce a novel event that is no longer perceptually present, they must be able to re-present it to themselves. For example, at 16 months his daughter Jacqueline watched with fascination a visiting child throw a temper tantrum when he could not get out of his play pen, an event that was new and wondrous to her. The next day, being put in her own play pen apparently reminded her of the event because she reproduced the actions the boy had carried out. In addition, when she saw him again 2 weeks later, she repeated some of the gestures he had used. These were some of the observations Piaget took as an indication that the transition out of the sensorimotor period had taken place.

DEFERRED IMITATION
AS A LABORATORY TECHNIQUE

In the experimental version of deferred imitation one models some event for infants, typically using two or three objects as props. After a delay of a day or week or so, one then brings the infants back into the situation, presents the props that were used, and encourages the infants to reproduce what they had previously observed. A wide range of events has been studied using this technique. For example, Bauer and Mandler (1989) used three kinds of event sequences, each three actions in length. There were novel causal sequences that the children would not have seen before (such as making a frog jump by putting a small board on a wedge to make a teeter-totter, putting a toy frog on one end, and hitting the other end of the board). If this result is to occur, the sequence must be performed in the modeled order. There were also novel arbitrary sequences that could be done in any order (such as making a picture by putting a sticker on a chalkboard, leaning the board against an easel, and scribbling on the board). And there were familiar sequences representing common home routines that are mixtures of causally and conventionally connected actions (such as cleaning the table by spraying it with a spray bottle, wiping it with a paper towel, and throwing the towel away into a basket).

Until recently, deferred imitation was used as a laboratory technique primarily with children over a year of age, and therefore near the end of what would be considered the sensorimotor period. For example, in the Bauer and Mandler (1989) study, 16- to 20-month-olds were able to reproduce the causal and familiar sequences after delays of 2 weeks, and Bauer and Shore (1987) found that children this age could reproduce similar sequences after delays up to 6 weeks. Meltzoff (1988a) worked with slightly younger children (14-month-olds) and modeled several novel actions (such as lighting a panel on a box by touching it with the forehead). He found that they could reproduce these actions after a week's delay. These results are experimental replications of the kind of observations that Piaget described, using subjects of roughly the same age as his own children. However, Meltzoff (1988b) also replicated the phenomenon in 9-month-olds, using a 24-hour delay. He modeled several single-action events using novel objects, such as depressing a recessed button on a box and clapping together a hinged block of wood. The infants were not allowed to perform the actions themselves, but only observed the experimenter carry them out. Nevertheless, the next day, when given the novel objects, they were more likely than various control groups to carry out the actions they had observed the day before. These results surprised many people because according to Piagetian theory infants this young should not be able to recall events.

Meltzoff's data with children under a year involved only single actions and delays of 24 hours. In our laboratory we have expanded on his findings with young infants in two ways. We have shown that 11-month-olds can imitate event *sequences* (not just single actions) and can do so after delays considerably longer than 24 hours. In a recent study, we showed that 11-month-olds can reproduce two-action sequences after a delay of 3 months (Mandler & McDonough, 1995). We used both causally organized and arbitrarily organized events. An example of a causal event was making a rattle by putting a button through a slit in a box and shaking it. An example of an arbitrary sequence was putting a hat on a bunny and then feeding it a carrot.[1]

In the first experiment, before modeling each sequence the infants were given the props to play with as a baseline condition. This condition was used to measure the rate at which infants spontaneously produce the actions that were to be modeled. After the baseline period, four sequences were modeled. Following the modeling, the infants were given the props for each sequence either after a 20-second delay or after a 24-hour delay and the actions that they performed with them were recorded. The infants reproduced almost half of the actions that were modeled from both the causal and arbitrary events after the 20-second delay, and at this short delay did about equally well on the two types of events. However, differences began to appear when the delay was increased to 24 hours. The infants recalled the causal events just as well after 24 hours as after 20 seconds, but began to forget the arbitrary events over this period of time.

Because some of the infants reproduced only one of the two actions in a sequence, there were fewer whole sequences produced than individual actions. Nevertheless, 42% of the causal events were reproduced in their

---

[1]It may be noted that because of the motor incompetence of infants under a year of age we use actions that are simpler than those used with older children. Nevertheless, there are a wide variety of actions that even very young children perform on objects during baseline exploration. For example, in addition to the commonly occurring banging or manual examination, they sometimes hug the bunny or try to pull the foliage off the top of the carrot.

entirety (compared to 11% during baseline); all but one of these were reproduced in the correct order. Few arbitrary sequences were performed in their
entirety, and when they were the order in which the actions were carried
out appeared to be random.

In the second experiment (Mandler & McDonough, 1995) the infants were
brought back 3 months later (when they were 14 months old) and were
again given the props for the same sequences without modeling the actions.
Their performance was contrasted with that of a control group of 14-month-
olds who had not seen the events before. The performance of the control
group provided a base rate for spontaneous production of the relevant
actions by 14-month-olds. The returning subjects performed twice as many
actions from the causal events as the control group, providing clear evidence of retention of this kind of sequence. Not surprisingly, given the
relatively poor performance of the experimental subjects on the arbitrary
events after a 24-hour delay, there was no indication of memory for this kind
of sequence. Performance on the arbitrary sequences was no higher for the
returning subjects than their initial baseline performance at 11 months and
also was no higher than the baseline of the 14-month-old control subjects.

It is of interest that the difference between recall of causal and arbitrary
events should appear so early in development. Indeed, pilot work in our lab
suggests that the difference may have begun by 9 months of age; we have
had some success in getting 9-month-olds to reproduce two-action causal
events after 24 hours, but have had great difficulty in getting them to
reproduce two-action arbitrary events even for immediate imitation. This
difficulty reinforces the claim that deferred imitation requires conceptual
representation of what has been observed and that nonverbal recall is
subject to the same factors that influence verbal recall from its earliest
stages. Young infants have trouble understanding arbitrary event sequences
as meaningful wholes at the time of encoding and therefore cannot reproduce them from memory. These differences between causally organized and
arbitrarily organized events or between meaningful and nonmeaningful
events remain throughout development, from deferred imitation in 1- to
2-year-olds (Bauer, 1992; Bauer & Mandler, 1989), to early verbal comprehension and recall (Slackman, Hudson, & Fivush, 1986), to older children
(e.g., J. Mandler, 1978; Stein & Nezworski, 1978; Trabasso, Secco, & Van den
Broek, 1984), and continuing into adulthood (J. Mandler, 1986a, 1986b).

Of course, conceptual representation is important not only for recall of
the order in which events occur, but also for recall of the individual components themselves. McDonough (1992) found that when 11-month-olds observe a meaningless, albeit easy to perform, action on an object, they have
great difficulty recalling it after a 24-hour delay. Just as in adult studies of
verbal recall, meaningful items are easier to recall than nonsense syllables.
Other data from our lab show that 11-month-olds can recall single-action

events 1 year afterward if they are meaningful (McDonough & Mandler, 1994). In this case, we found that infants shown a novel version of a familiar event (feeding a toy bear with an object that looked a little bit like a bottle) were able to reproduce it after 24 hours and again at 23 months. Few 23-month-old control subjects performed such an action spontaneously when presented with the bottle-like object. In contrast, even more novel (although still meaningful) events, such as pushing on the nipple-like projection of the object to extrude a hidden toy, were also recalled after 24 hours, but were not reproduced a year later at rates higher than those of control subjects.

In conjunction with the work of Meltzoff (1988b), these experiments show that infants as young as 9 months can encode novel events from a brief period of observational learning and at least by 11 months can recall well-organized events after very long delays. We concluded from this work that recall begins relatively early in infancy, recallable memories are potentially long lasting from the start, and the earliest recall memories are influenced by the same kind of organizational factors that influence verbal recall in older children and adults.

WHAT DOES DEFERRED IMITATION MEASURE?

We did not consider the conclusion that infants can engage in long-term recall to be controversial, in part because so far as we knew Piaget's discussion of deferred imitation as a measure of recall was widely accepted, and in part because there already existed in the literature one piece of evidence for *verbal* long-term recall from the same period. Myers, Clifton, and Clarkson (1987) brought back to their laboratory five 33-month-old children who had participated in an extensive experiment between the ages of 6 weeks and 9 months. One of these children was able to recall verbally a picture of a whale used in the procedure that he had last experienced at 9 months, in spite of the fact that he did not know the word "whale" at that age. If long-term verbal recall is shown for experiences occurring at around 9 months, then one should not be unduly surprised by a demonstration of long-term nonverbal recall at the same age. Nevertheless, verbal recall in the infancy period is a rare event, and if recall memory during the preverbal period is to be thoroughly explored, an agreed on nonverbal measure is needed. We have been using a set of criteria that was derived in part from the conditions used in adult verbal recall experiments (J. Mandler, 1990). In each case the criteria are meant to differentiate a nonverbal reenactment task from other memory tasks that might be carried out on an implicit basis.

The first criterion is to eliminate an explanation of successful performance in terms of a conditioned response or a learned stimulus–response association. As mentioned earlier, some form of memory is required for any kind of learning in organisms. One of the simplest kinds of learning is operant conditioning. Lowly invertebrates such as the sea slug (Aplysia) and the flatworm (Planaria) show this kind of conditioning (Fantino & Logan, 1979) and so it cannot require declarative, explicit memory; in general, conditioning is not considered to be one of the higher cognitive functions. Operant conditioning can be demonstrated in young infants as well. Two-month-old infants can learn an operantly conditioned foot-kicking response and retain it over relatively long periods of time (e.g., Rovee-Collier, 1990). Nevertheless, when kicking occurs to the trained stimulus after a delay (or generalizes to a similar stimulus), one would not want to say that the infant has *recalled* earlier kicking episodes, because conditioned responding can occur in the absence of declarative, explicit memory.

One of the ways to avoid a conditioning interpretation of deferred imitation is to use novel events the infants have never seen before and to use actions they have only observed but not carried out themselves. The reason for these restrictions is to eliminate the conditions required for conditioning to take place. Operant conditioning requires multiple trials for an association between the stimulus and response to build up, especially in the case of multistep event sequences. It also requires that the organism make a response, not merely observe a single instance of an environmental contingency.

In the case of deferred imitation, one can interpret novelty more or less strictly. It does not seem necessary that the event be entirely novel, however that might be defined. The objective is not to mystify the baby but to avoid events that may have been seen at home often enough to automatically arouse a sequence of responses to an object cue. In the study of verbal recall, lists of words are often used; the words themselves are familiar, only their combination on the list is unpredictable. The same thing can be said of events; in a new event the individual actions or props may have been seen before but their combination is unpredictable. Similarly, one can contrast recall of words with recall of nonsense material; recall is obviously better for words. Again, however, even nonsense syllables are not totally novel because they follow the rules of English phonology; they are only relatively novel compared to familiar words. One needs to be able to make similar comparisons when studying recall of nonverbal material.

The same kind of argument applies to amount of practice. If the event is a multistep sequence and long delays are used, it does not seem unreasonable to allow the infant to enact the event once. This procedure ensures that the sequence was encoded. This procedure is comparable to letting an adult subject read a list of words out loud before testing for its recall on the following day.

The point of the first criterion is to ensure that performance requires explicit processing and cannot be accounted for by implicit processes such as conditioning, sensorimotor habits or any other kind of automated routine. In the verbal realm, experimenters studying recall of paired-associate lists avoid familiar associates, such as bread and butter. To respond with "butter" to the stimulus "bread" is an example of learning in which the items have become unitized. After many repetitions the first term automatically activates the second; no retrieval is required (Mandler, Rabinowitz, & Simon, 1981). Such well-known verbal associates are preserved in amnesia, and therefore can be produced in the absence of explicit memory (Shimamura & Squire, 1984), whereas new material cannot.

The second criterion for a nonverbal recall task is to eliminate recognition as an explanation of successful performance. This criterion is designed not to eliminate automatized sensorimotor responding but to require that a representation of something not perceptually present be activated. Both finding a hidden object and reproducing an event by deferred imitation fit this criterion, because in neither case is the relevant information there to be recognized. There are cues in both cases (the occluder in the object-hiding case, and the props used to reproduce the actions in the imitation case) but the issue is not cued recall versus noncued recall. Indeed, in one sense all recall must be cued by something; one is either reminded by something or is specifically asked to recall, in which case one is given relevant contextual information about the target. For example, a prosecutor asks, "Did you actually see the accused fire the gun or did you only hear it?" or an experimenter says, "Now I want you to recall the first of the two lists of words I gave you." The crucial points here are that the to-be-recalled information is not perceptually present, and that retrieval is required.

Third, there should be a delay between the event and its reproduction that exceeds the perceptual span so that one cannot read off the information from primary memory. This is another way of saying that a retrieval search has to take place.

These criteria were designed to eliminate a sensorimotor account of deferred imitation because, as Piaget (1951, 1952) documented, learning a sensorimotor schema is a protracted process and such a system is unable to represent objects or events when they are no longer present. Sensorimotor schemas only allow (a) primitive recognition[2] of familiar objects or events, (b) gradual learning of actions on objects and sequences of such actions, and (c) anticipatory expectations about the sequence in which already learned events take place. Another way of expressing these restrictions is to say that sensorimotor learning and primitive recognition involve

---

[2]*Primitive recognition* (J. Mandler, 1984), sometimes called perceptual enhancement (Jaccoby, 1983), is a form of priming. It refers to the fact that prior exposures to a stimulus have effects on behavior, but it does not imply awareness of familiarity. It is the kind of recognition that is involved in infant tests using habituation–dishabituation; these tests do not involve any measure of awareness of familiarity (e.g., saying "Old") such as used in adult tests of recognition.

the implicit, procedural knowledge system and do not require an explicit, declarative knowledge system (J. Mandler, 1988). It is the latter system that is engaged in recall.

We have heard two objections to this analysis of deferred imitation as a recall task. The first one is that it is unnecessary to distinguish between recall and other kinds of memory, that recall *is* the same form of retention found in conditioning. For example, it has been claimed that the 2-month-olds in Rovee-Collier's (1989, 1990) conditioning experiments are recalling the past. Rovee-Collier herself has indicated that her experiments are a form of cued recall (J. Mandler, 1990). As just discussed, in her work infants are trained to make a foot-kicking response. After a period of weeks this conditioned response appears to be forgotten. However, if given a brief reexposure to the learning context, the conditioned response is "reinstated." Apparently it is the reinstatement phenomenon, originally studied by Campbell (1984) in rats, that Rovee-Collier called *cued recall*. Cued recall is recall, however, and although conditioning involves the retention of information, it does not provide positive evidence for recall. Conditioned learning (and retention) is one of the most basic behavioral characteristics of organisms, and because it occurs in organisms as simple as insects, it cannot *require* higher order thought processes. On the contrary, it is a classic example of procedural learning. Of course, babies are not simple organisms and they *might* recall foot kicking in the presence of the reinstatement cue, but it is not necessary for them to do so in order for the conditioned response to occur. Therefore, it is not parsimonious to assume that they do.

The second objection we have heard to our analysis of deferred imitation is that the very essence of sensorimotor learning is that an object or an event is understood in terms of the possible actions that can be performed on it, and so recall is not required (see discussion section of J. Mandler, 1990). According to this argument, reproducing an event can be directly "triggered" by some cue in the situation, rather than requiring a mental representation of the event. The suggestion is that there is no difference between a perceived object and the action to be performed on it, even if it is an action the infant has not done before. If we understand this formulation correctly, it states that observational learning of a series of actions on an object is a kind of procedural learning that can take place in a single trial (because in many of our deferred imitation tasks, only a single trial is given) and does not require bringing absent information to mind. It only requires the repetition of the context in which the observational learning originally took place and the actions will automatically ensue.

This argument is more difficult to answer because it is not known exactly how observational learning takes place. We assume that observational learning takes place by attentive (conscious) analysis of whatever one is trying to learn (i.e., involves declarative knowledge), and requires recall when one tries to reproduce what has been analyzed at a later date. This is the situation involved in trying to learn the steps in a new office routine, or trying to remember a recipe produced by a chef on TV when one did not write the sequence down. At least in our experience, recall is required in order to reproduce such sequences. Unfortunately for our cooking, they do not seem to be automatically triggered.

An experiment by Murachver, Fivush, and Mandler (described in J. Mandler, 1986a) provides some relevant data. In this experiment adults were given novel sequences, such as making a ring or building a cement patio. Each sequence consisted of 15 simple statements, each of which described one action taken in the course of carrying out the event. These were presented in correct order to form a coherent story. After studying a given sequence, the subjects were given the statements in random order and asked to reproduce the correct sequence. Even though the statements were there in front of them as cues, subjects took an average of 2 minutes to reproduce each sequence and also made some ordering mistakes. The length of time taken to order the statements as well as the errors indicate that far from being able to reproduce the sequences in any automatic way, the subjects could not even recall the ordering with ease, although with effort they usually could figure out how the sequences should be put together.

It is less obvious that recall is involved in the kind of observational learning which occurs in mutual imitation. We have in mind the repetitive imitating games in which parents engage with children, such as peek-a-boo, vocal imitation, and so forth. In these situations the imitation is virtually simultaneous with the modeling; that is, the stimulus being reproduced is present, not absent, so that re-presentation may not be required. Notice that having the stimulus present is not the same as the procedure that Bauer and we have sometimes used to study immediate imitation (e.g., Bauer & Mandler, 1992; McDonough, 1992). Although we call our procedure immediate imitation, there is a delay of at least 10 to 15 seconds (and often somewhat longer) before the baby begins to reproduce what has been modeled. Typically, we have used "immediate" imitation to assess short-term recall, and contrasted it with deferred imitation to assess long-term recall.

Imitation after a delay of just a few seconds actually poses some interesting questions. It is usually assumed that recall is required to reproduce new material at any time after the immediate present or the span of consciousness. This was the reason for our third criterion, to insure that there is a delay between presentation and reproduction. However, there may be important differences between immediate and delayed recall having to do with the span of short-term memory. There appears to be a particular kind of memory for the current context in which one is situated that includes the surrounding objects. The surround seems to remain activated as long as the context remains in force, and therefore immediately available without having to engage in a retrieval search (G. Mandler, 1985). This kind of contextual memory has been relatively little studied, so it is not known for how long or how thoroughly objects remain activated. For example, a person may close her eyes and remember where the furniture is in a room, even if she has not been there before, as long as she stays within the room. On the other hand, we have all had the frustrating experience of putting a book down in a room and then not being able to locate it even a few minutes later.

We have some preliminary developmental data relevant to this issue. We have found that 7-month-old babies are able to remember where in the laboratory an attractive object is hidden for approximately 90 seconds. We provide two alternative locations, make sure the baby has encoded both of them, hide the object in one while the baby is watching, and then make sure the baby looks at the incorrect location and sees that it is empty. Then we play with the baby for the delay period to be sure its attention is distracted from the correct location. Under these circumstances, most babies will reach toward the correct location after the delay. (They are too young to retrieve the object from its hiding place, but their reaching tells us they remember where it is.) If instead of just distracting the baby's attention from the hiding place, we take the baby outside the room for the 90-second delay period, performance is somewhat worse but still above chance.

This finding needs to be systematically explored, but it suggests that there may be a relatively primitive ability to keep track of where the objects around one are located in the current situation even when they are hidden from view. This ability may reflect a state of activation of contextual information that does not require a retrieval process just because it is already active. If so, this kind of short-term object-hiding test may tap a different set of processes than the usual recall test. This issue is worthy of investigation because it affects the interpretation of some of the recent work on object permanence, such as Baillargeon's finding that 8-month-old infants can remember for a short period of time where an object in the current situation is hidden (e.g., Baillargeon, DeVos, & Graber, 1989). In the past, we have tentatively interpreted this kind of finding in terms of short-term recall (e.g., J. Mandler, 1988), but it may represent a more primitive kind of processing.

However one is to interpret the ability to find hidden objects after a few seconds delay, there does not appear to be any reason to think that events taking place within a given context remain active in the same way as the location of the objects surrounding one. If that is the case, then the tests of immediate imitation we have used (e.g., Bauer & Mandler, 1992) to assess recall seem reasonable. Nevertheless, the role played by the current context is a theoretical issue that needs work. One reason why we have so little information about the conditions of and limitations on recall of the current spatial surround may be because so much of the research on recall has used verbal material.

DEFERRED IMITATION TESTED WITH AMNESICS

We have claimed that adults cannot automatically reproduce a sequence of actions after a single exposure; they need to bring it to conscious awareness. Although we presented a certain amount of evidence in the Murachver, Fivush, and Mandler experiment that such recall is required to reproduce an observed sequence of actions, the evidence was somewhat indirect. It is also possible that some of the difficulty the subjects experienced in that experiment may have been due to the much greater length of the sequences they studied compared to the short sequences we have used with infants. Therefore, to settle the issue of whether or not it is possible to imitate without recall the kind of event sequences we use in our infant experiments, we decided to follow the suggestion mentioned at the beginning of this chapter and replicate the infant work as closely as possible with amnesic patients.

The rationale behind testing amnesics is the following: We claim that a person can do deferred imitation of novel events if and only if they can recall what they have seen. Amnesics cannot recall. Therefore, they should not be able to do deferred imitation. On the other hand, if event sequences can be learned through observation and activated by means of priming, it might be possible for amnesics to accomplish deferred imitation. It is possible that imitating a simple event sequence is similar to a stem-completion task, in which adults are asked to complete three-letter stems of words. Amnesics cannot do this task if they are asked to use words they have just studied, because they cannot recall them (Graf, Squire, & Mandler, 1984). However, when no explicit instructions to use the just studied words are given and subjects are simply asked to report the first words that come to mind, amnesics nevertheless tend to use the studied words (Warrington & Weiskrantz, 1974). The words on the list have been activated (primed) sufficiently for the patients to produce them over the various other possibilities. If amnesic patients could imitate events in the same way, our argument that deferred imitation requires recall would be considerably weakened.

In conjunction with Squire and McKee we have carried out such a test (McDonough, Mandler, McKee, & Squire, 1995). We devised eight three-action event sequences that mimic our baby tests but that are appropriate for adults; four of these sequences were causally ordered and four were arbitrarily ordered. An example of a causal sequence was demonstrating the Bernoulli effect by turning on a hair dryer, placing an inflated balloon in the air stream, and rotating the dryer to the side. An example of an arbitrary task was making a design by folding a piece of paper in half, cutting the corners off the paper, and drawing a star on it.

We followed as closely as possible the procedure we use with infants. The main difference was the use of verbal instructions. However, to make the imitation tasks roughly similar to the uninstructed conditions used with infants, we presented the tasks to the adults in the guise of distractor tasks. We gave amnesics and control subjects a list of words to remember, followed by the props for each event. The subjects were told that to distract them from the words they had heard they should do whatever they liked with the props. This condition provided a baseline measure of any tendency to do the sequences spontaneously. Then subjects were asked to recall as many of the words as they could. Next we told the subjects that they would be asked to repeat the words later, and we then modeled the sequences for them, explaining that this was another distractor task. They were then asked to recall the words again. Following recall we read the list once more, telling the subjects that recall would be tested again on the following day. On the next day, after a recall test for the words the subjects were handed the props to do with what they wished, again under the guise of being a distractor task. This condition served as an instructionless memory condition such as that used with infants, and such as has been found to be effective in priming tasks with amnesics. If deferred imitation tasks are analogous to priming tasks, there should be relatively little difference between the amnesics and the controls in this condition. Immediately afterwards, we asked the subjects explicitly to reproduce the event sequences we had shown them the day before. This was an instructed recall condition. If amnesics are only using priming processes in imitation tasks, they should do especially poorly in this condition in comparison to the normal controls. If they do equally poorly in both instructed and uninstructed conditions it indicates that priming plays little role in deferred imitation and that recall is required.

The results did not support a priming explanation. Overall, the control subjects reproduced 75% of the actions that had been modeled for them the day before; they produced only slightly more actions in the instructed than in the uninstructed condition. In contrast, the amnesic patients could not reproduce the action sequences in either the uninstructed or instructed memory conditions. There was a marginal increase in the number of actions they performed during deferred imitation in comparison to their baseline performance; this increase may have occurred because of having a second opportunity to produce a relevant action.[3] The comparison in performance between the two groups is shown in Fig. 6.1. Similarly, although little correct sequencing occurred in the baseline period, the control subjects significantly increased the amount of correct sequencing after the events had been modeled. In contrast, there was no improvement in sequencing by the amnesic subjects. This comparison between the two groups is shown in Fig. 6.2; the measure is pairs of actions performed in the correct order.

---

[3]The actions that were performed by the amnesics during the memory conditions were almost entirely those also performed correctly by control subjects during the baseline condition; that is, these were the actions most likely to be spontaneously discovered when given enough time to interact with the objects.

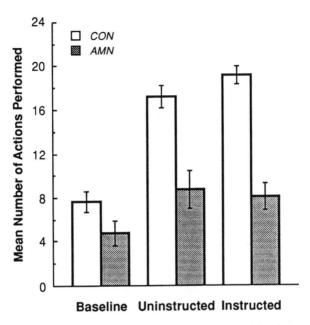

FIG. 6.1. Mean number of actions (max = 24) performed by the control subjects (CON) and amnesic patients (AMN).

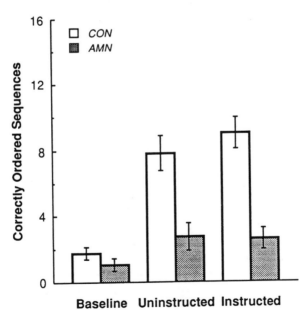

FIG. 6.2. Mean number of correctly ordered pairs of actions (max = 16) performed by the control subjects (CON) and the amnesic patients (AMN).

It is also of interest that just as with deferred imitation of events by babies, control subjects remembered causal events better than arbitrary ones. It is also worth noting that the only difference between uninstructed and instructed memory conditions was that sequencing of arbitrary events was somewhat better in the instructed condition. This finding suggests that part of the difference in sequencing causal versus arbitrary events that we have found in babies (Bauer & Mandler, 1989; Mandler & McDonough, 1995) may be due to the fact that deferred imitation by preverbal infants is essentially uninstructed performance. If there is no conceptual reason for an event to be ordered in a particular way, then unless explicit instructions are given to do so, adults and infants alike tend not to adhere to the presented order in their recall. This is another piece of evidence that neither children nor adults are merely repeating uninterpreted sequences but are recalling the gist of what they have understood.

As can be seen from Figs. 6.1 and 6.2, amnesics did not show better performance in the uninstructed memory condition. In priming tests, amnesics show better performance in uninstructed conditions (Graf et al., 1984), but in the deferred imitation test this was not the case. In sum, amnesic subjects cannot perform the deferred imitation of event sequences that babies can, thus offering further evidence that to imitate a previously seen series of actions, even simple ones such as the three-action sequences used in this experiment, requires recall processing and cannot be managed through repetition priming alone.

WHAT MEDIATES PREVERBAL RECALL?

To conclude, we want to say a few words about the representational system used to mediate the nonverbal recall that is shown by deferred imitation. Although there is not space to discuss this issue in detail, it is too important to omit entirely. We cannot stop with the demonstration of preverbal recall or even rest content with exploring its parameters; we need to understand the mechanisms by which it happens. We have provided evidence that recall requires the operation of the declarative knowledge system, but what is the form in which the knowledge being brought to mind is represented? We direct this question primarily to our preverbal subjects, because adult subjects, amnesic or not, may rely heavily on verbal representations even in situations in which no language is overtly used.

Introspection tells us that recall of past events is frequently in the form of imagery. Indeed, the only two ways we know of for information to be brought to mind is in the form of imagery or words (or other symbols such as numbers). Because babies do not have the use of words, one must assume that all of their conscious recollection takes place in images. That does not mean, however, that their underlying knowledge system is imaginal in the same sense. If there is one thing we have learned about conscious phenomena such as recall it is that they are constructed and do not directly reflect underlying processing (e.g., G. Mandler, 1985). There is no royal introspective road to the representational format of the declarative knowledge system. Even if the declarative knowledge system is not itself imaginal, however, it would make sense if the imagery that appears in conscious remembering were mediated by meanings (i.e., declarative representation) that were formed out of and were related to perceptual information (Kosslyn, 1980). Such meanings could be represented in analog form. There does not appear to be a compelling reason to assume that the declarative knowledge system assumes a propositional form of representation in nonverbal organisms. Indeed, psychologists' propensity to insist on propositional representational systems may arise because we humans are such language-saturated organisms that it is difficult for us to deal with other possible forms.

The series on how to build a baby (J. Mandler, 1988, 1992) attempted to specify what the format of the declarative knowledge system might look like in infants who are able to conceptualize and recall before they can talk. It was suggested there that the initial format for the declarative knowledge system is that of image-schemas. Image-schemas are abstract spatial schemas that are derived from the attentive analysis of perceptual displays. However, in spite of being derived from perceptual data (and having the word "image" in their name), they are not part of the perceptual system. Instead, image-schemas are abstract spatial representations that we hypothesize constitute the first meanings in the declarative knowledge system.

The usual functioning of the perceptual system is automatic and implicit; perceptual information is accrued and stored without effort or attention from the perceiver. From introspection, however, we know that it is possible to direct attention to what is being perceived and to analyze it. The proposal is that this kind of perceptual analysis creates the first meanings, and that before language begins these meanings consist of spatial summaries of what is being analyzed. We illustrate this process here by showing how a small set of meanings can form an initial concept of *animal*. The relevant meanings can be derived from analysis of the paths that objects take when they are in motion.

Consider a baby in the first month or so of life, a creature who shows a pronounced tendency to intently watch moving objects. If, as we assume, these intent periods of observation involve analysis of the paths that the objects take, the following sources of information are available, even when acuity is still relatively poor. First, the infant can see that some object is moving on a path across the visual field, even if there is not time (or acuity) to analyze details of the object's shape. Second, the infant can see whether or not the object starts its path by itself or is contacted (or pushed) by another object. Third, the infant receives enough perceptual information to categorize the path as "biological" as opposed to mechanical (see Bertenthal, 1993). Fourth, interactions of this object with other objects from a distance (as in linked paths or back and forth interaction) are also available to be observed. Each of these aspects of the scene can be abstracted to form a meaning: moving on a path, beginning-of-path, "biological" path, and linked paths. These meanings can be combined to form a primitive concept of animal as a thing that starts up on its own, moves in a distinctive kind of way, and interacts with other objects from a distance.

Each of these meanings is represented by a simple spatial schema. Combining two or more of them forms a concept, in the sense that the combination of the individual meanings tells the baby what kind of thing a given object is. For example, to the extent that young babies who are learning to perceptually categorize various kinds of animals such as dogs and cats (Quinn, Eimas, & Rosenkrantz, 1993) have any concept of what kind of things these categories are, it is these image-schemas that provide it. When these analyses have been carried out, the infant can think about these patterns as being "animal-like" things; that is, as things that move by themselves, and so on. Indeed, in our work there is clear evidence that by 7 to 9 months of age babies have attained a beginning concept of animal that they distinguish as conceptually different from vehicles (Mandler & McDonough, 1993) and from plants (work in progress). This concept is global in nature and lacks detail; for example, it makes few if any distinctions between one kind of animal and another. We assume it is this global concept that is evoked when some event involving an animal is recalled. How is it then that infants are able to reproduce a particular event with any accuracy? If the infant is using such highly general concepts as animal (rather than dog or cat), should recall not be inexact? Although we have not yet studied this problem specifically, we do have some data suggesting that early recall may indeed be global in nature or, at the least, inexact.

The data were collected in order to study induction in preverbal children (Mandler & McDonough, in press). Specifically, we were interested in how 1-year-old infants generalize what they observe about animals and vehicles to other members of the same class. For example, if a 1-year-old observes people eating and perhaps the family dog eating, will the infant generalize eating as a property applicable to all animals? The experiments we have conducted to investigate this issue have used the deferred imitation technique. In the experiment most relevant to the present chapter, we modeled for 14-month-olds feeding a dog from a cup, putting a dog in a bed, using a key on a car, and having a car give a person a ride. Later we gave the props back to the infants and encouraged them to imitate what they had seen. However, we did not give them back the original props, but instead gave them a different animal as well as a distractor object for each task. Therefore, if feeding a dog was to be imitated, we gave the infant the cup, a bird, and an airplane. Under these circumstances, the infants chose the conceptually correct object (the bird) 66% of the time, and only 12% of the time did they choose the inappropriate objects (the airplane). This preponderance of correct choice was the same whether the object provided was similar to the original object (substituting a cat for a dog) or dissimilar to the original (substituting a bird for a dog). This success rate compares favorably with our usual experiments in which the actual object used in the modeling is provided for the imitation test. In short, infants appear to be just as willing to carry out their imitation using a different exemplar as they are to use the particular exemplar they have seen.

Of course, to do a thorough assessment of the generality of the representation mediating the recall; that is, to determine if their recall was truly gist-like or whether the infants were merely recognizing that in a pinch one can substitute a dog for a bird, one would have to provide both the original object and its substitute and see how often the infant chose the original. Nevertheless, this example illustrates that deferred imitation is a conceptual task: In no sense are infants merely reproducing an uninterpreted display. Just as Piaget (1951) found that his children did not imitate actions of any degree of complexity until they had already analyzed them, we find that infants reproduce the overall meaning of what they have seen, and are not engaging in a mindless repetition of uninterpreted detail.

This example of inductive generalization illustrates how preverbal children can engage in conceptual thought. Such thought requires a preverbal representational system. The system we have described is similar to that suggested by Barsalou (1993). His concerns are primarily with the adult cognitive system, but we have come to similar conclusions on the basis of developmental data. As developmental psychologists interested in infancy, we find an image-schema system potentially able to account both for the conceptual successes and failures of preverbal infants. Infant conceptions of animate objects seem to be highly general and missing the many specific details that adults use to make fine differentiations among animals. Therefore, even though infants can see the difference between horses and zebras (Quinn & Eimas, 1992), they have little conceptual notion of the differences among them. Similarly, they seem quite happy to substitute a bird for a dog in a memory task about animals.

Huge changes in conceptual sophistication take place with development. However, we have no reason to think that the preverbal conceptual system and the meanings from which it is constructed die away or get replaced once language is learned. In fact, a plausible case has been made that the linguistic system itself is structured in terms of image-schemas (Johnson, 1987; Lakoff, 1987; Langacker, 1987; Talmy, 1983). In addition to image-schemas forming the meaning basis of language, we also assume that people continue to use underlying image-schematic meanings for purposes of analogical thought and problem solving and for creating new nonlinguistic ideas throughout life. These meanings come to consciousness in the form of real images but it seems plausible that the images themselves are constructed out of underlying image-schematic meanings. To the extent that the meanings in a scene are represented by schematic paths and other spatial relations, some of the work needed to reconstruct the visualized scene has already been accomplished. In this view, image-schemas play a double role in mediating recall. They provide a scaffolding for the construction of the concrete images that are brought to mind. At the same time, they provide the meaning of the scenes thus remembered.

In this way, the foundations of an accessible declarative knowledge system can begin early in the preverbal period. It is not yet known when in human development long-term recall first becomes possible, although it has been speculated to be about 8 to 9 months (Schacter & Moscovitch, 1984). Recall requires not only a storage system formatted in such a way that conscious access is possible, but also consolidation of the stored information and the development of retrieval mechanisms that do the accessing. At present, in line with Schacter and Moscovitch's speculation, there is no hard evidence that all of this system is in place before 9 months, but there is ample evidence for long-lasting nonverbal recall after that time.

ACKNOWLEDGMENTS

Preparation of this chapter was supported in part by NSF Research Grants BNS89–19035 and SBR92–21867.

REFERENCES

Baillargeon, R., DeVos, J., & Graber, M. (1989). Location memory in 8-month-old infants in a non-search AB task: Further evidence. *Cognitive Development, 4,* 345–367.

Barsalou, L. W. (1993). Flexibility, structure, and linguistic vagary in concepts: Manifestations of a compositional system of perceptual symbols. In A. C. Collins, S. E. Gathercole, M. A. Conway, & P. E. M. Morris (Eds.), *Theories of memories* (pp. 29–101). Hillsdale, NJ: Lawrence Erlbaum Associates.

Bauer, P. J. (1992). Holding it all together: How enabling relations facilitate young children's event recall. *Cognitive Development, 7,* 1–28.

Bauer, P. J., & Mandler, J. M. (1989). One thing follows another: Effects of temporal structure on 1- to 2-year-olds' recall of events. *Developmental Psychology, 25,* 197–206.

Bauer, P. J., & Mandler, J. M. (1992). Putting the horse before the cart: The use of temporal order in recall of events by one-year-old children. *Developmental Psychology, 28,* 441–452.

Bauer, P. J., & Shore, C. M. (1987). Making a memorable event: Effects of familiarity and organization on young children's recall of action sequences. *Cognitive Development, 2,* 327–338.

Bertenthal, B. I. (1993). Infants' perception of biomechanical motions: Intrinsic image and knowledge-based constraints. In C. E. Granrud (Ed.), *Visual perception and cognition in infancy* (pp. 175–214). Hillsdale, NJ: Lawrence Erlbaum Associates.

Campbell, B. A. (1984). Reflections on the ontogeny of learning and memory. In R. Kail & N. E. Spear (Eds.), *Comparative perspectives on the development of memory* (pp. 25–35). Hillsdale, NJ: Lawrence Erlbaum Associates.

Carmichael, L., Hogan, H. P., & Walters, A. A. (1932). An experimental study of the effect of language on the reproduction of visually perceived form. *Journal of Experimental Psychology, 15,* 73–86.

Fantino, E. J., & Logan, C. A. (1979). *The experimental analysis of behavior: A biological perspective.* San Francisco: Freeman.

Graf, P., Squire, L. R., & Mandler, G. (1984). The information that amnesic patients do not forget. *Journal of Experimental Psychology: Learning, Memory, and Cognition, 10,* 164–178.

Intons-Peterson, M. J., & Roskos-Ewoldsen, B. B. (1989). Sensory-perceptual qualities of images. *Journal of Experimental Psychology: Learning, Memory, and Cognition, 15,* 188–199.

Intraub, H., & Richardson, M. (1989). Wide-angle memories of close-up scenes. *Journal of Experimental Psychology: Learning, Memory, and Cognition, 15,* 179–187.

Jaccoby, L. L. (1983). Perceptual enhancement: Persistent effects of an experience. *Journal of Experimental Psychology: Learning, Memory, and Cognition, 9,* 21–38.

Johnson, M. (1987). *The body in the mind: The bodily basis of meaning, imagination, and reason.* Chicago: University of Chicago Press.

Kosslyn, S. M. (1980). *Image and mind.* Cambridge, MA: Harvard University Press.

Lakoff, G. (1987). *Women, fire, and dangerous things.* Chicago: University of Chicago Press.

Langacker, R. (1987). *Foundations of cognitive Grammar* (Vol. 1). Stanford, CA: Stanford University Press.

Mandler, G. (1985). *Cognitive psychology.* Hillsdale, NJ: Lawrence Erlbaum Associates.

Mandler, G., Rabinowitz, J. C., & Simon, R. A. (1981). Coordinate organization: The holistic representation of word pairs. *American Journal of Psychology, 94,* 209–222.

Mandler, J. M. (1978). A code in the node: The use of a story schema in retrieval. *Discourse Processes, 1,* 14–35.

Mandler, J. M. (1984). Representation and recall in infancy. In M. Moscovitch (Ed.), *Infant memory* (pp. 420–494). New York: Plenum.

Mandler, J. M. (1986a). The development of event memory. In K. Klix & H. Hagendorf (Eds.), *Human memory and cognitive capabilities* (pp. 459–467). Amsterdam: Elsevier.

Mandler, J. M. (1986b). On the comprehension of temporal order. *Language and Cognitive Processes, 1,* 309–320.

Mandler, J. M. (1988). How to build a baby: On the development of an accessible representational system. *Cognitive Development, 3,* 113–136.

Mandler, J. M. (1990). Recall of events by preverbal children. In A. Diamond (Ed.), *The development and neural bases of higher cognitive functions* (pp. 485–516). New York: New York Academy of Sciences.

Mandler, J. M. (1992). How to build a baby: II. Conceptual primitives. *Psychological Review, 99,* 587–604.

Mandler, J. M., & McDonough, L. (1993). Concept formation in infancy. *Cognitive Development, 8,* 291–318.

Mandler, J. M., & McDonough, L. (1995). Long-term recall in infancy. *Journal of Experimental Child Psychology, 59,* 457–474.

Mandler, J. M., & McDonough, L. (in press). Drinking and driving don't mix: Inductive generalization. *Cognition.*

McDonough, L. (1992, June). *Infant imitation and recall of familiar and novel actions.* Poster presented at the meetings of the American Psychological Society, San Diego, CA.

McDonough, L., & Mandler, J. M. (1994). Very long-term recall in infants: Infantile amnesia reconsidered. *Memory, 2*, 339–352.

McDonough, L., Mandler, J. M., McKee, R., & Squire, L. R. (1995). The deferred imitation task as a nonverbal measure of declarative memory. *Proceedings of the National Academy of Sciences, USA, 92*, 7580–7584.

Meltzoff, A. N. (1988a). Infant imitation after a 1-week delay: Long-term memory for novel acts and multiple stimuli. *Developmental Psychology, 24*, 470–486.

Meltzoff, A. N. (1988b). Infant imitation and memory: Nine-month-olds in immediate and deferred tests. *Child Development, 59*, 217–225.

Myers, N. A., Clifton, R. K., & Clarkson, M. G. (1987). When they were very young: Almost-threes remember two years ago. *Infant Behavior and Development, 10*, 123–132.

Piaget, J. (1951). *Play, dreams and imitation in childhood.* New York: Norton.

Piaget, J. (1952). *The origins of intelligence in children.* New York: International Universities Press.

Piaget, J., & Inhelder, B. (1971). *Mental imagery in the child.* New York: Basic Books.

Quinn, P. C., & Eimas, P. D. (1992, May). *Basic-level category development during the first half year of life.* Paper presented at the biennial meeting of the International Society for Infant Studies, Miami, FL.

Quinn, P. C., Eimas, P. D., & Rosenkrantz, S. L. (1993). Evidence for representation of perceptually similar natural categories by 3-month-old and 4-month-old infants. *Perception, 22*, 463–475.

Rovee-Collier, C. (1989). The joy of kicking: Memories, motives, and mobiles. In P. R. Solomon, G. R. Goethals, C. M. Kelley, & B. R. Stephens (Eds.), *Memory: Interdisciplinary approaches* (pp. 151–180). New York: Springer-Verlag.

Rovee-Collier, C. (1990). The "memory system" of prelinguistic infants. In A. Diamond (Ed.), *The development and neural bases of higher cognitive functions* (pp. 517–542). New York: New York Academy of Sciences.

Schacter, D. L. (1987). Implicit memory: History and current status. *Journal of Experimental Psychology: Learning, Memory, and Cognition, 13*, 501–518.

Schacter, D. L., & Moscovitch, M. (1984). Infants, amnesics, and dissociable memory systems. In M. Moscovitch (Ed.), *Infant memory* (pp. 173–216). New York: Plenum.

Shimamura, A. P., & Squire, L. R. (1984). Long-term memory in amnesia: Cued recall, recognition memory, and confidence ratings. *Journal of Experimental Psychology: Learning, Memory, and Cognition, 14*, 763–770.

Slackman, E., Hudson, J., & Fivush, R. (1986). Actions, actors, links, and goals: The structure of children's event representations. In K. Nelson (Ed.), *Event knowledge: Structure and function in development* (pp. 47–70). Hillsdale, NJ: Lawrence Erlbaum Associates.

Squire, L. R. (1987). *Memory and brain.* New York: Oxford University Press.

Stein, N. L., & Nezworski, T. (1978). The effects of organization and instructional set on story memory. *Discourse Processes, 1*, 177–194.

Talmy, L. (1983). How language structures space. In H. L. Pick, Jr. & L. P. Acredolo (Eds.), *Spatial orientation: Theory, research, and application* (pp. –). New York: Plenum.

Trabasso, T., Secco, T., & Van den Broek, P. (1984). Causal cohesion and story coherence. In H. Mandl, N. L. Stein, & T. Trabasso (Eds.), *Learning and comprehension of text* (pp. 83–111). Hillsdale, NJ: Lawrence Erlbaum Associates.

Warrington, E. K., & Weiskrantz, L. (1974). The effect of prior learning on subsequent retention in amnesic patients. *Neuropsychologia, 12*, 419–428.

7

RECONSTRUCTING THE TIMES OF PAST EVENTS

Janellen Huttenlocher
University of Chicago

Vincent Prohaska
Lehman College of the City University of New York

People remember, more or less well, many aspects of nonemotional, mundane events: objects and persons involved, actions that occurred, settings (time and place), and so on. However, in response to specific questions, people may try to recover more exact information than they actually can retrieve.

It is well known that when people are unsure about the details of an event, their reconstructions may be influenced by categorical or schematic information (e.g., Bartlett, 1932; Brewer & Nakamura, 1984). For example, a person who spent the summer in Sweden and saw a car accident in early September may report the car as being shaped similar to a recent Saab and the date as more central to the summer than actually was the case. This tendency toward the typical in reporting can be described as a bias, but we suggest it is better viewed as an adjustment process or statistical correction.

We discuss a model developed by Huttenlocher and Hedges that explores processes involved in reconstructing past experience from inexact memories. The model has been used to examine people's estimates of the times of occurrence (Huttenlocher, Hedges, & Bradburn, 1990; Huttenlocher, Hedges, & Prohaska, 1988, 1992) and the spatial locations (Huttenlocher, Hedges, & Duncan, 1991) of events, and of the properties of objects, such as their sizes and colors (Huttenlocher, Hedges, Engebretson, & Vevea, 1995).

The present chapter focuses on memory for the time when events occurred. The Huttenlocher and Hedges model was first evaluated in the temporal domain for several reasons. One reason was that temporal coding is clearly both multilevel (i.e., an event occurs on a certain day in a certain

season or year) and schematic (i.e., temporal units have unique characteristics—Sunday as a day of rest, September as the opening of school, noon
as lunchtime, etc.). Another reason was that, although temporal coding at
the time an event occurs is likely to be quite exact, research indicated that
temporal memory becomes increasingly inexact over time (e.g., Baddeley,
Lewis, & Nimmo-Smith, 1978; Burt, 1992; Thompson, 1982; Thompson, Skowronski, & Lee, 1988). Finally, there was some tentative evidence in the
literature of bias in temporal reports; namely, a specific bias called *forward
telescoping* (Loftus & Marburger, 1983; Neter & Waksberg, 1964; Thompson
et al., 1988). Forward telescoping consists of a tendency to report events as
more recent than they really were. One of the first tests of the model was
to explain forward telescoping; specifically, how inexact but unbiased memory might give rise to biased reports. We begin our discussion with some
general issues concerning the representation of time.

THE REPRESENTATION OF TIME

Consider the representation of time in written records and verbal communication. After all, these conventional forms may provide clues about mental
representation. People use a variety of temporal schemes based on calendars and clocks. First, there are noncyclic schemes that keep track of time
over unbounded periods, notably the calendar year (e.g., 1815, 1921). In
addition, there are cyclic schemes of varying scope. These include hour of
the day, day of the week, and month of the year. Information about the time
of occurrence of an event in different temporal schemes is independent.
Therefore, to specify the day of the week of an event indicates nothing about
the time of day, month, or year. When temporal schemes are used in combination, they can uniquely specify the particular time of an event to any
level of detail (e.g., the conference took place on January 5, 1989; she arrived
at 3 p.m. on the third Wednesday of February).

Another way of specifying the times of events, without necessary re-
course to calendars and clocks, is to embed events within temporally organized narratives. That is, events can be linked to one another within a
narrative that forms a structure or frame in which any target event can be
located. Frames for noncyclic schemes consist of either public historic
narratives or private autobiographical narratives. For example, in historic
documents a target event may be described as occurring after a particular
earthquake, before a particular famine, or during the reign of a particular
king. In autobiographical documents, a target event may be described as
occurring before a marriage, after the birth of a child, while living in a
particular city, or while holding a particular job. Virginia Woolf said that
different epochs in her life were defined by the different houses she inhab-

ited. Notice that major events of known date might exist within a narrative (e.g., a king's coronation, a wedding) that can be used to link the narrative to clocks and calendars.

Frames for cyclic schemes consist of a different sort of narrative; namely, one involving recurring patterns of human activity. Such patterns can be conceptualized as scripts or schemata. These are terms that have typically been used to describe recurring types of activities (e.g., the much cited "restaurant script"), but they also can be applied to the temporal patterning of activities. For example, the week is an historically pervasive temporal unit that, as many authors have noted (Colson, 1926; Lauer, 1981; Zerubavel, 1985), forms a structure or frame in which certain events have fixed positions. Across a host of cultures, the week includes a day of rest, or Sabbath, each seventh day.

For many people, whole sets of activities have regular temporal positions in a weekly pattern. For example, a salesperson may meet with his boss on Wednesdays, summarize his sales on Fridays, do his food shopping on Saturdays, and go to church on Sundays. Such a cyclic narrative may locate events that can occur on any day (such as running into an old friend on the street before talking to the boss). Other cyclic schemes also form narratives, such as time of day (e.g., getting up in the morning, eating lunch at noon, going to bed in the evening, etc.). An event can also be located within such a frame (e.g., getting an important call just after breakfast). Narratives for time of day, day of the week, and for historical time may be independent of one another, just as clock and calendar schemes are. Therefore, the fact that an event occurred just after breakfast is independent of whether it occurred on a shopping day or in the year of Kennedy's inauguration.

THE MENTAL REPRESENTATION OF TIME

The temporal narratives discussed earlier also may be important in the mental representation of the time of occurrence of an event, both within noncyclic and cyclic schemes. Within narratives, certain "landmark" events may have fixed positions that are associated with dates, such as birthdays, holidays, and so on. By relating a target event to a landmark event in such a scheme, the event's time of occurrence within the scheme can be specified. Loftus and Marburger (1983) showed people's use of landmark events such as the eruption of Mount St. Helens and New Year's Day in placing target events (crime victimizations) within specified temporal periods. Baddeley et al. (1978) found that associating a visit to the lab (their target event) to a personal event lead to more accurate date estimates. Brown, Shevell, and Rips (1986) found that representing the historic time of a public target event (e.g., signing of a treaty, death of a famous person) may involve placing the event in relation to framing events of known dates, such as presidential terms. Friedman and Wilkins (1985) and Friedman (1987) found that people reported using personal events to date public and autobiographical events. However, data collected by Friedman and Wilkins and Friedman demonstrate that different landmarks or framing events were used to reconstruct reports for different temporal schemes. The reliability of framing events may vary for different temporal schemes and, on occasion, may even provide misleading cues. Friedman and Wilkins noted that a number of British pilot subjects reported Kennedy's assassination (which occurred in November) as occurring during a summer month, because they remembered he was wearing a short-sleeved shirt and riding in an open car when shot.

Events in memory may be represented via a *time line*, a single continuing narrative or an endless appointment book with conventional clock and calendar markings. Temporal information at different levels is coordinated, and, at retrieval, a person recovers a single composite temporal entry for an event. A person who can enter the time line at a particular point, perhaps the day of the week of an event, would also know the month and year on which it occurred. In such a representation, the time of an event would simply be recovered, not reconstructed, at the time of retrieval. Baddeley et al. (1978) found that people indicated using day of the week as a cue to retrieve other temporal information. However, use of this cue was rare. Thompson, Skowronski, and Betz (1993) also found that people used day of the week as a cue to retrieve dates when asked to mark the date of an event on a blank calendar page. However, because a calendar necessarily forces coordination of levels these data also do not necessarily reflect the representation of time in memory.

Shanon (1979) found that people were faster to report what day of the week "tomorrow" will be when the question was asked in the evening than in the morning. People also were faster to report what day "yesterday" was when the question was asked in the morning than in the evening. These data suggest a time line representation for time of the day and day of the week at the time of encoding an event in memory. However, these data may reflect the use of cues present at during questioning rather than the representation of time in memory.

The fact that there are a variety of temporal schemes suggests that the mental representation of temporal information for an event may involve multiple entries rather than a time line. Each entry would specify time within a particular scheme. For a multiple-entry representation, the retention or loss of information in one scheme would not have implication for retention or loss in other schemes. At retrieval, the time of an event is reconstructed from a number of retrieved entries.

There is evidence supporting separate, multiple-entry representations. Friedman and Wilkins (1985) found that reports of the year, month, day of the month, day of the week, and hour of the day of public events were independent of one another. Friedman (1987) replicated these results using an autobiographical event—an earthquake that people had experienced. Huttenlocher et al. (1990) found that people asked to date a home interview did not spontaneously use the date, but instead reported the number of days that had elapsed since the interview. Indeed, many of their subjects could not even be persuaded to guess the date.

HIERARCHICAL ORGANIZATION OF MULTILEVEL REPRESENTATIONS

Before we began our research program, note that there was no convincing evidence that time is hierarchically organized in memory although there were data suggesting that it might be. Existing studies focused on the academic year; in particular, on whether semesters form temporal units in memory. It was found that students' reports of school-related events pile up at the beginnings and ends of semesters (Pillemer, Rhinehart, & White, 1986; Robinson, 1986). This finding could reflect a bias involving semesters as temporal categories. A limitation of these studies is that the actual dates of events were not available; hence, there are several possible explanations of the pile up of reports. Not all of these explanations have to do with temporal memory or hierarchical organization. First, more memorable events may actually occur at the beginnings and ends of semesters. Second, the beginnings and ends of the semesters may be good retrieval cues, so events at these times may be more easily recovered, even if the number of events in memory were equal over the school year.

Finally, a pile up of reports at boundaries could involve temporal memory, but not hierarchical organization. Temporal coding might be most accurate near semester boundaries, because these are landmarks. In space, locating objects is more accurate near landmarks (e.g., Kosslyn, Pick, & Fariello, 1974; Nelson & Chaiklin, 1980; Newcombe & Liben, 1982; Thorndyke, 1981). If temporal coding is more accurate at the beginnings and ends of semesters, reports would include both events that actually occurred then, plus other events misplaced there because of greater coding inaccuracy at other times. Use of landmarks at retrieval to improve dating accuracy was found by several investigators (e.g., Baddeley et al., 1978; Brown et al., 1986; Friedman & Wilkins, 1985; Loftus & Marburger, 1983; Thompson, 1982).

For the week, there is evidence that the boundaries separating the weekday and weekend periods play a role in people's awareness of the current day of the week. Koriat and Fischhoff (1974) found that Israeli subjects were more rapid in reporting the current day of the week on the days bounding the Sabbath. Shanon (1979) found that Americans were more rapid in accessing information about the current day of the week on the days bounding the weekend (Monday or Friday). Of course, speed of accessing the current day may reflect the salience of the day's activities and need not reflect memory organization.

A MODEL OF REPORTING FROM HIERARCHICALLY ORGANIZED MEMORY

Our model concerns the combination of specific and categorical information to reconstruct a report from hierarchically organized memory. The general claims of the model are not novel. The first is that information about a particular event in memory is multilevel, including both categorical and particular or "individuating" information (e.g., Barsalou, 1988; Neisser, 1988). The second is that, at retrieval, people recover fragments of information from memory and reconstruct an overall account of an event (e.g., Brown, 1991; Brown et al., 1986; Wagenaar, 1986). That is, different aspects of an event are represented separately, and when retrieved, are added together to form an overall reconstruction of the event.

The novelty in the model is the claim that even different levels of information about a single aspect of an event may be represented separately. For example, reconstructing when an event occurred might include retrieving information that it occurred in a freezing rain (similar to rain that occurs in March and April) and also retrieving that the event occurred in the spring academic quarter (that began on April 1). Information at different levels is mutually constraining; therefore, contrary to unrelated pieces of information, it cannot simply be added together in reconstructing an event. The weight given to the particular memory versus the category will depend on the uncertainty of the particular memory.

The model concerns the way mutually constraining information is combined in estimation. It shows how this process may lead to bias toward the typical in reconstructing events, even when memory for those events is not itself biased. In particular, when memory is multilevel and inexact, bias arises from blending mutually constraining information at different levels. Consider a person pouring milk from a Wedgewood pitcher that was grayish in color rather than the usual blue. Later the person tries to recall the color of the pitcher. Given an inexact memory for the particular Wedgewood pitcher and categorical information about the usual color of such pitchers, the report is likely to be intermediate (grayish-blue) between the two (cf. Belli, 1988; Loftus, 1977).

The model refers to the most detailed level of information in memory as a *fine-grain value*. Fine-grain values may be inexact relative to the information a person is seeking to recover. An inexact fine-grain memory can be conceptualized as a distribution of values centered at the true stimulus value; for example, the actual shade of green of an object, or the actual date of an event. At retrieval, a person samples a value from this distribution. A sense of the uncertainty of a memory can be obtained by sampling a few values.

A category covers a range of fine-grain values; a range of particular shades are greens, a range of particular dates are in a month. In reconstructing a report, a recollected fine-grain value (e.g., a remembered date) is combined with category information (e.g., that an event occurred in the fall quarter). We have proposed two processes—truncation and prototypes—by which category information may be combined with a fine-grain value. We have found that truncation due to category boundaries is the critical adjustment process for temporal categories.

To understand truncation, consider a student attempting to remember a stimulus; specifically, the date of an event. Memory for this fine-grain value is inexact. The true value (actual date) will be at the center of a distribution of fine-grain values (e.g., the actual date is December 3; the distribution might extend from October 1 to February 1). Suppose the student also remembers the category in which the stimulus falls (e.g., the fall academic quarter, which extends from October 1 to December 15). Note that the distribution of fine-grain values (October 1 to February 1) extends past the category boundary (December 15). If a stimulus has been coded as in the category, its value must fall inside the category boundary. This leads to truncation of the distribution by the boundary. Truncation can be considered a process in which a person draws a value from an underlying unbiased distribution, and, if it falls outside the boundary, discards it and draws another (e.g., the student will discard any dates after December 15). The overall effect of truncation is to move the mean of people's reports inward from the true stimulus value toward the center of the category. The process leads to bias, but decreases variance. Bias arises because the retrieved value and the retrieved category must be consistent with each other. In the previous example, the boundaries of the quarter constrain the range of possible dates. Bias is greatest for stimulus values very near the boundaries, because a sizable portion of the distribution lies outside the boundary. In addition, the more inexact a remembered value, the greater the bias. This is because when the distribution at any particular location is wider, more of it falls outside the boundary.

Truncation effects due to hierarchical organization explain the phenomenon of forward telescoping. Because memory for the fine-grain values becomes less exact over time, the forward bias at the beginning of any category should be greater than the backward bias at the end of the category. Overall, then, there should be forward telescoping of reports.

HIERARCHICAL ORGANIZATION OF THE
ACADEMIC YEAR REVEALED BY THE MODEL

Our first study, Huttenlocher et al. (1988), continued the tradition of examining the hierarchical organization of the academic year. In late May, the end of the academic year at the University of Chicago, we telephoned students and asked them to report the dates of movies they had seen at the University over the year. We knew the true dates of these movies and thus compared people's reports of the dates of events to the actual dates.

Our data are presented in Fig. 7.1. Along the horizontal axis are actual dates. Along the vertical axis is bias, the difference between actual dates and mean reported dates. If the mean of people's reports on a particular actual date lies at that date, bias is zero. Means above zero indicate forward bias. Means below zero indicate backward bias. The bias in Fig. 7.1 consists of misplacement away from the boundaries of the quarters, indicating that dates were organized into academic quarters. In addition, as predicted, a net forward telescoping was evident—forward misplacement was greater than backward misplacement—reflecting greater uncertainty in memory for events further in the past. Finally, there was striking evidence for our model. The observed bias could be explained by positing that people combined inexact but unbiased information about the date with information about the quarter. Subsequently, other investigators also have found that truncation

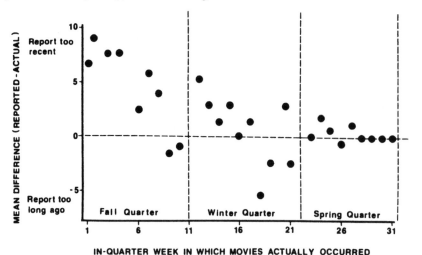

FIG. 7.1. Plot of the mean differences (reported in-quarter weeks minus actual in-quarter weeks) by in-quarter week in which the movies actually occurred, for the 8-month group. From Huttenlocher, J., Hedges, L. V., and Prohaska, V. (1988). Hierarchical organization in ordered domains: Estimating the dates of events. *Psychological Review, 95*(4), 471–484. Copyright American Psychological Association, 1988. Reprinted with permission.

by boundaries can account for observed bias (e.g., Burt, 1992; Rubin & Baddeley, 1989).

TIME LINE VERSUS MULTIPLE ENTRY REPRESENTATIONS

Huttenlocher et al. (1992) directly examined whether temporal schemes— specifically, time of day, day of the week, and day of the month—are independent of one another in memory. In addition, we evaluated whether the week itself might be hierarchically organized into weekday and weekend periods—whether people code an event on a particular day and as in the weekday or weekend period. Organization of a single cyclic scheme may well be hierarchical; if an event took place at work, it was during the weekday period, but not on any particular day. If the week is hierarchically organized, there would be constraints across levels, so our model of bias should apply. The critical assumptions of the model are the same as in Huttenlocher et al. (1988)—that fine-grain memory is inexact, consisting of a distribution centered at the actual value, and that time is represented at two levels of detail. For an actual day near a boundary (i.e., Monday or Friday), the distribution of uncertainty may extend into the weekend. However, if the event is categorized as being in the weekday period, then a weekend day will not be reported. Therefore, the distribution of uncertainty will be truncated, and the mean of reports will be moved from the actual value toward the center of the category. In the original form of the model, the uncertainty of a fine-grain memory depended only on the elapsed time since the event. For day of the week, certainty may vary with day because of the distinctiveness and salience of the scripts for different days (e.g., Sunday with church, sports events, etc.).

Huttenlocher et al. (1992) focused on reports of a relatively unique target event, an interview in people's homes that lasted approximately 2 hours. This home interview was part of a survey carried out each year by the National Opinion Research Center (NORC), a survey organization associated with the University of Chicago. The people interviewed included a cross section of the U.S. population. Interviews occurred on arbitrary days over a period of months, on all days of the week, and at various hours of the day. The day of the week, the date, and the starting time of the interview were known. In large surveys, it is common to make a follow-up telephone call (a "validation call") to a percentage of people interviewed to verify the data collected during the interview. We inserted three temporal questions into the validation call; the first two questions concerned the day of week and time of day of the home interview. The third question concerned unbounded time. Validation calls were made to 814 people and were made 7 to 75 days after the home interviews. The people called represented a broad range of social classes, areas of the country, age groups, and so on.

The percentage correct of day of the week reports ranged from slightly under 60% correct after 1 week to about 40% correct after 10 weeks. Even after 10 weeks, this percentage was well above the 14% expected by chance. Percentage correct also was significantly above the 34% that would be expected by chance if subjects divided the week into two categories, week-end and weekday periods, retained only these categories, and guessed within category. Thompson et al. (1993) also found that day of the week was well retained up to 10 weeks. However, Friedman and Wilkins (1985) and Prohaska and Fellner (1993) found that day of the week for public events was not well retained over intervals longer than 10 weeks.

To test whether memory for when the interview occurred involved a time-line or multiple entry representation, we examined two relations. First, we examined the relation between reports of day of the week and reports of elapsed time. A particular number of elapsed days specifies a particular day of the week. For example, a subject whose validation call was on a Tuesday and who reported that the interview took place 12 days ago is placing the interview on a Sunday. In a time line representation, these retrieved values are coordinated, so there should be matches between reported day of the week and the day of the week calculated from a subject's report of elapsed days. In contrast, a multiple entry representation predicts independence of different schemes. Therefore, matches between reported day of the week and the day of the week calculated from a subject's report of elapsed days should be at chance, except when subjects independently know both pieces of information, in which case they would necessarily match.

Our data allowed us to compare calculated day of the week to the subject's report of day of the week to determine whether they matched. A nonsignificant χ^2 is evidence of independence (i.e., a nonsignificant number of matches). Displayed in Table 7.1 is the χ^2 for each actual elapsed week. Data were combined for the first 2 and last 2 weeks in order to have enough cases for a χ^2 analysis. Results showed that reported day of the week and reported elapsed time were independent after 2 weeks.

However, our analysis of the first 2 weeks may overestimate matches, because at such a short delay people may independently remember both the elapsed time since the event and the day of the week. To reexamine data from the first 2 weeks, we recomputed the χ^2 statistic including only the 96 cases in which either reported elapsed time or reported day of the week or both were incorrect. In this reanalysis, the χ^2 statistic for the first 2 weeks was nonsignificant, $\chi^2 = 9.15$, $df = 6$, n.s., suggesting that reports were independent even with only a 2-week delay.

The second relation we examined was the relation between memory for day of the week and time of the day. Shanon (1979) found that time of day

TABLE 7.1
Chi-Square Statistics for Reported Day
and Day Calculated From Elapsed Time

Actual Elapsed Weeks Since the Interview	Total Number of Responses (N)	χ^2	$p <$
1 & 2	133	45.1	.001
3	86	4.2	.7
4	48	8.9	.2
5	79	8.1	.3
6	71	7.0	.5
7	98	2.6	.9
8	64	4.3	.7
9 & 10	64	4.7	.7

Note. $df = 6$. From "Memory for day of the week: A 5 + 2 day cycle," by J. Huttenlocher, L. V. Hedges, and V. Prohaska, 1992, Journal of Experimental Psychology: General, 121(3). Copyright 1992 by the American Psychological Association. Reprinted with permission.

affected people's reaction time to report the day of the week of "yesterday" or "tomorrow," suggesting the possibility of a time line rather than a multiple entry representation. We examined our data to determine whether people were more likely to misremember an interview in the morning as occurring on the preceding day and an interview in the evening as occurring on the following day. In a multiple entry representation, memory for the day would be unaffected by time of the day. The percent of errors in the two directions at each time of day were not significantly different, supporting multiple entry representation.

These findings indicate that the week is a separate scheme in memory. We next asked whether the week itself is hierarchically organized with separate entries at different levels. Displayed in Table 7.2 is the percentage of people who reported a particular day for each actual interview day. The diagonal gives the percentage correct for each actual interview day. The percentage of correct responses differed for the different days. The highest percentage correct occurred on the weekend days. This may be because the weekend days are more memorable. Of course, if the weekend forms a separate unit, error would then be lower on these than other days because if just the category were remembered, 50% of reports would be correct by chance (in contrast to 20% for the weekday period).

The direction of error shows that the weekday period is hierarchically organized. Assuming unbiased but uncertain memory for the day, most errors will fall symmetrically on days that are adjacent to the actual day unless there is a boundary. When the actual day of a weekday event is adjacent to a weekend boundary, reports tend to lie in the direction away from the boundary. There are more reports for days near the middle of the weekday period as would be expected if it forms a category. Evidence is not

TABLE 7.2
Frequency (Percent) of Reported Days of
the Week for Each Actual Day of the Week

Reported Day of the Week	Actual Day of the Week							Number of Responses
	Mon.	Tues.	Wed.	Thurs.	Fri.	Sat.	Sun.	
Mon.	**38**	10	2	8	3	0	1	168
Tues.	11	**32**	8	11	15	3	1	93
Wed.	11	16	**51**	16	10	4	4	134
Thurs.	8	5	13	**31**	14	2	4	90
Fri.	5	5	5	9	**34**	6	4	77
Sat.	3	2	0	2	6	**70**	11	136
Sun.	3	2	1	2	1	4	**73**	73
"Do not know"	21	28	20	21	17	11	2	143
n	101	116	129	124	102	162	80	814

Note. Bold and underlined numbers represent correct responses. From "Memory for day of the week: A 5 + 2 day cycle," by J. Huttenlocher, L. V. Hedges, and V. Prohaska, 1992, *Journal of Experimental Psychology: General, 121*(3). Copyright American Psychological Association, 1992. Reprinted with permission.

as clear that the weekend forms a category; errors are not more likely to fall in the weekend than the weekday period for Saturday, although they are for Sunday. It seems that each of the weekend days is highly distinctive so that people are likely to remember the exact weekend day on which an event occurred.

Further evidence of hierarchical organization of the week is evident in a study by Prohaska and Fellner (1993), presented in Table 7.3. Subjects ($N = 35$) reported the day of the week of a number of public events, including three events that occurred on weekdays: John Gotti convicted of murder and racketeering (Gotti), Mike Tyson convicted of rape (Tyson), and the Rodney King verdict (King). No subject reported a weekend day for any of these events. Reports for another event, the incident involving a celebrity basketball game at City College of the City University of New York, in which several

TABLE 7.3
Frequency Distributions (Number) of Reports

Event	Number of Reports						
	Mon.	Tues.	Wed.	Thur.	Fri.	Sat.	Sun.
Gotti	3	9	8	**8**	7	0	0
Tyson	**3**	8	7	8	8	0	0
King	6	7	**12**	8	2	0	0
Incident	1	1	3	3	14	**11**	0

Note. Bold and underlined numbers represent correct responses.

8

SPATIAL CONSTRUCTIONS

Barbara Tversky
Stanford University

MEMORY FOR SPACE

Knowing where things are and keeping track of them as we move about underlies many of our interactions in the world. In fact, our lives literally depend on knowledge of place and space, knowing where our kin and foe are, knowing where to find food and where to avoid danger. Spatial knowledge is so vital that it is accessed by all of our senses, first and foremost sight, but also sound, touch, and smell. There are even those who can taste the sea air.

As we wander about the world, we seemingly effortlessly keep track of the things around us. At a party or a meeting, we are usually aware of the locations of people and objects in the room, even when we are not looking at them. In familiar environments, such as campus or town, we normally know what buildings we have passed and what buildings we are approaching. We often form vivid images of places we have been. As anyone who has gone home again knows, places evoke myriad memories of events, scenes, and emotions. Police detectives bring victims, witnesses, and suspects to crime scenes for the purpose of reviving memories. Our memory for the spatial world is important in and of itself, and serves a basis for memory of many other things. This is an ancient observation, one put to good use by the Greeks, who, in the absence of teleprompters and cue cards, used the Method of Loci to remember their orations. Stage mnemonists still use this technique, in which one takes a mental walk throughout a well-known environment where each landmark has been associated with a portion of what needs to be remembered.

According to one view, implicit or explicit in discussions of picture memory and imagery, memory for the spatial or visual world is like a series of snapshots. Like snapshots, memories may fade with time, but because the fading is general, retrieval is unbiased. The classical theories of imagery (e.g., Finke & Shepard, 1986; Kosslyn, 1980) compare images to pictures and transforming images to transforming objects. In images, searching for large parts is faster than searching for small parts, just as would be expected in searching pictures or the world. In imagery, time to transform an image—for example, mental rotation or expansion—is proportional to the extent of transformation, just as would be expected for physical transformations. Although there are many elegant experiments supporting this view, it does not seem to account for all cases of spatial thinking, in particular, the research to be reported here.

The view presented here, supported by other research, is a constructionist view. According to this view, representations of space are constructed from elements and a frame of reference. Examples of elements are figures in a scene, objects in a picture, or landmarks in an environment. They are spatially related to each other through a frame of reference. Examples of frames of reference are the sides of a page, the axes extending from a person or an object, the walls of a room, longitude, latitude, and altitude of the world. This view can account for biases in memory retrieval time and systematic errors in memory. Evidence supporting this view comes from two research programs on spatial cognition, each reviewed briefly. The first project explores spatial mental models induced by descriptions of environments rather than by experiencing them, and the second is an exploration of errors in cognitive maps.

LANGUAGE OF SPACE

Language serves as a surrogate for experience, not just perceptual experience, but emotional experience as well. Moving descriptions of human interactions can make us laugh or cry, just as moving descriptions of space can make us feel the grandeur of a mountain range or the bustle of a city or the barrenness of a desert. Many researchers in the area of language comprehension have concluded that in understanding discourse, readers construct mental representations of the situation described by the text as well as the language of the text (e.g., Bransford, Barclay, & Franks, 1972; Johnson-Laird, 1983; van Dijk & Kintsch, 1983). These mental models or situation models are presumed to represent the spatial relations among characters and objects in a scene, and to be updated as the situation changes. Evidence that narratives lead to mental representations that reflect the spatial relations among objects has come from studies of Mani and Johnson-Laird (1982) and Perrig and Kintsch (1985), among others. For example, subjects in Mani and Johnson-Laird's study recognized verbatim and gist information equally well for descriptions that allowed construction of a complete and consistent mental model, but not for descriptions that were indeterminate. Evidence that narratives lead to mental representations that reflect distance relations has come from studies of Glenberg, Meyer, and Lindem (1987), Morrow, Greenspan, and Bower (1987), and Morrow, Bower, and Greenspan (1989), among others. In those experiments, reaction times increased with distance.

Perspective in Descriptions of Space but Not in Mental Models of Space

Inspired by this work, especially a similar project by Perrig and Kintsch (1985), Taylor and I (Taylor & Tversky, 1992b) began an investigation of the role of narrative perspective in mental models of environments. Typically, environments are described from one of two perspectives, termed route or survey. In a route perspective, the description addresses the reader as "you" and takes the reader on a mental tour of the environment, adopting a view from within the environment and describing the locations of landmarks relative to the reader's left, right, front, and back, from the reader's changing point of view. A survey perspective takes a view from above, and describes the locations of landmarks relative to one another in terms of north, south, east, and west. A route description is analogous to exploring an environment and in fact provides a set of procedures for navigating; a survey description is analogous to studying a map. Therefore, both styles of description are natural ways of learning about environments. Is perspective encoded in the mental representations induced by the descriptions, or are the mental representations perspective-free; that is, more abstract than either perspective? Supporting the expectation of different mental representations depending on description perspective is evidence from many sources that different information is available from environments learned from exploration than from environments learned from maps (e.g., Evans & Pezdek, 1980; Lloyd, 1989; Presson, DeLange, & Hazelrigg, 1989; Sholl, 1987; Streeter, Vitello, & Wonsiewicz, 1985; Thorndyke & Hayes-Roth, 1982).

To investigate whether narrative perspective is reflected in spatial mental models, we wrote route and survey descriptions of each of four familiar environments, in order of size, a convention center, a zoo, a town, and a recreational area, each containing about a dozen landmarks. The descriptions included nonspatial information, such as beach activities in the recreational area, as well as spatial information to make them more interesting and natural.

For each environment, subjects studied a description from one perspective. Subjects for this and subsequent experiments were college students, participating for credit or pay. After studying a description, subjects' memories were tested in several tasks. First, they were presented with a series of statements about the environment to which they responded true or false. Some of the statements contained information about the nonspatial parts of the descriptions. The statements of primary interest were the spatial ones, those providing true or false information about the spatial relations between two landmarks, relative to a specified point of view. Of these, some were taken verbatim from the texts of each perspective. Others were inference statements, written in either route or survey perspective, containing information inferrable from the texts but not stated directly in either of them. The remaining spatial statements were false statements from the two perspectives. Subjects responded true or false to each statement; accuracy and response times were recorded. After responding to the statements, subjects drew maps of the environments they had never seen. If subjects' mental models incorporate the perspective of the text, then they should respond faster or more accurately to the inference statements from the perspective they had read than to inference statements from the other perspective.

The results of four experiments supported the claim that subjects formed mental models of the environments from descriptions but that the mental models were perspective-free. First, the maps subjects drew were excellent; that is, complete and nearly error-free, indicating that subjects learned the spatial relations among the landmarks simply from studying descriptions of them. Some of the spatial relations were stated directly, but many had to be inferred. To draw accurate maps, subjects needed to have accurate mental maps. Performance on the statements corroborate those findings. On the whole, accuracy was high, and there were no overall effects of description perspective; that is, both route and survey perspectives led to good performance. Subjects reading each perspective were equally good on the nonspatial statements. On the spatial statements, subjects were faster and more accurate responding to verbatim statements than to inference statements. This indicates that subjects formed at least two representations from the text—a representation of the language of the text and a representation of the situation described by the text. The verbatim statements seemed to be verified against a representation of the language of the description, and the inference statements against a mental model of the situation. Finally, there was no advantage to the perspective subjects had read. Responses to inference statements from the read perspective were as fast and as accurate as responses to the statements from the other perspective. The results suggest that the spatial mental models subjects formed were perspective-free; that is, they contained information about the spatial relations among landmarks in a way that allowed both perspectives to be taken equally rapidly and accurately. This is not to say that subjects did not encode the perspective of the text, but that the situation models did not reflect it.

What is the nature of the mental models subjects formed from the descriptions? They seem to consist of a mental spatial structure or skeleton to which landmarks are attached. The mental model seems to be perspective-free, but enables someone to take different perspectives on it in order to correctly respond to the statements, which were from different perspectives. We likened a perspective-free mental model of spatial relations to an architect's model of a city. It portrays the basic elements of the city in the correct spatial configuration, yet it has no perspective in and of itself. It allows a viewer to take many different perspectives on it. As Johnson-Laird (1983) noted, an image differs from a mental model in that an image has a specific perspective, whereas a model does not; an image can be conceptualized as a view on a model. Therein lies the usefulness of a model; like the structural descriptions presumed to underlie object recognition (e.g., Pinker, 1984), mental models allow recognition of objects or scenes from different points of view.

Language does not capture all our experience—not even all our visual or spatial experience. Details of individual objects, such as faces, can be difficult to describe in such a way that another person can pick one from a group of similar others, unless, of course, the target has an unusual feature. Exact metric distances and durations can be easily described, but they are not very accurate (Guzv, Leibowitz, & Fulcher, 1993). The descriptions of Taylor and Tversky (1992a, 1992b, in press) successfully conveyed information about categorical spatial relations, but did not include detailed information about appearances of landmarks or about metric distances or directions. For describing environments categorically and giving directions, language can be very effective. In fact, describing space must have been an early use of language—to tell others where to go to find water, food, and friends, and where not to go to avoid danger. We can describe routes and terrains so that someone who has never been there can successfully explore an environment. The early use of language to describe space is also suggested by the many spatial metaphors used to describe all aspects of life. Anyone needing examples should look first at graduation speeches (ignoring, as the occasion demands, the inconsistencies): "Let us go forward to explore uncharted terrain and wide-open fields, navigating by the landmarks left by our predecessors." For more examples of spatial metaphors as well as analysis of them, see Clark (1973), Cooper and Ross (1975), and Lakoff and Johnson (1980). Space is familiar, even to children, and can serve as a medium to convey more abstract and less familiar ideas.

REPRESENTATION OF SPACE
FROM DIFFERENT PERSPECTIVES

The research with Taylor provided evidence that spatial mental models of environments too large to be seen at one viewing can be perspective-free. Responding to queries from specific points of view requires taking a specific perspective, using the general spatial model to generate a particular point of view. The next project examined retrieval of information lying in specified directions from a particular perspective. How do people scan mental space? Are some directions privileged over others?

Upright Case

Franklin and Tversky (1990) began with the simplest and most prototypic spatial situation in which people find themselves: standing alone and upright in a scene, surrounded by objects to all six sides of the body; that is, beyond the head, feet, left, right, front, and back, with the simplest form of navigation, turning in place. A schematic display appears in Fig. 8.1. In subsequent experiments, we systematically complicated the spatial situation. In the initial experiments, as before, subjects learned the environments from descriptions rather than experience, so the project continues the investigation of the power of language to instill spatial mental models. They were not instructed to image the environments, just to comprehend the narratives. Each narrative placed the reader in a different setting, such as an opera house, a space museum, or a hotel lobby, as follows. "You are in the lobby

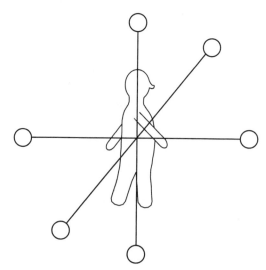

FIG. 8.1. Schematization of the internal upright spatial framework situation.

of a glamorous hotel, at the top of an escalator. While waiting for your dinner companion, you look around the lobby. To your left, you see a shimmering fountain beyond a carpeted walkway. Below you is a candlelit tavern, filled with well-dressed patrons. Straight ahead of you, you see a quaint giftshop, its window filled with the kind of porcelain statues that you collect...." Subjects studied each narrative until they learned the environment, and then turned to a computer that oriented them to face one of the objects. The computer then probed them with direction terms—head, feet, left, right, front, and back—and the subjects responded with the object lying in that direction. Subjects were reoriented until all of the objects on the horizontal plane had been faced. Then subjects learned a new narrative describing a new setting. Performance was nearly perfect, so the data of interest were the reaction times to the various directions.

Possible Models

We considered three models for times to retrieve objects in space. The first, the *Equiavailability Model*, treated all spatial directions as equally accessible, as they are in scanning the world. In scanning, eye movements are attracted to points of interest, but points of interest do not occur in specific directions (e.g., Mackworth & Morandi, 1967). According to the Equiavailability Model, people treat the scenes like pictures, where no location has precedence over any other (Levine, Jankovic, & Palij, 1982). This leads to the prediction that all directions should be equally available, that is, responded to equally quickly.

The second, the *Mental Transformation Model*, derived from the classic research on mental imagery (e.g., Kosslyn, 1980; Shepard & Cooper, 1982). The classical position treats imagery as internalized perception, where the imaginary world is analogous to the perceptual world, and is scanned or manipulated in an analog fashion. For the present situation, according to the Mental Transformation Model, subjects should imagine themselves in the three-dimensional scene, surrounded by objects and facing one of them. In order to ascertain what object is in the specified direction, subjects should mentally search that direction. Objects that are further displaced from forward, the oriented direction, should take longer to search. Therefore, the fastest times should be for "front," followed by times to directions displaced 90 degrees, "above" (or "head"), "below" (or "feet"), "left," and "right." Slowest times should be to "back," which is displaced by 180 degrees. In fact, the patterns of reaction times obtained in the five original experiments, and in many subsequent ones, failed to support either the Equiavailability or the Mental Transformation Models. Search times were not equal to all directions as predicted by the Equiavailability Model, nor did they increase with increasing distance from the forward direction, as predicted by the Mental Transformation Model. Instead, when the observer in the narrative was upright, subjects responded fastest to objects located at head and feet, next to objects located in front and back, and slowest to objects located at left and right.

This pattern of data fit the pattern predicted by the third model, the *Spatial Framework Model*. Franklin and Tversky (1990) developed this model, inspired by analyses of Clark (1973), Fillmore (1975), Levelt (1984), Miller and Johnson-Laird (1976), and Shepard and Hurwitz (1984), but differing from each of them. According to the Spatial Framework analysis, people construct a mental scaffolding, termed a *spatial framework*, based on extensions of the three axes of the body, head/feet, front/back, and left/right, and associate objects to the appropriate places on the framework. The framework preserves the relative locations of the objects independent of the observer, so that as the observer turns in the scene, the new directions relative to the observer's body are rapidly updated. At any (upright) facing, the speed of accessing objects along the axes depends on the relative salience of the body axes and the posture of the observer in the scene. For the upright observer, the head/feet axis is most salient. It corresponds to the only asymmetric axis of the world, the axis created by gravity and bounded by earth and sky. It also corresponds to an asymmetric axis of the body; people's heads differ from their feet. Of the two horizontal axes, only the front/back axis has prominent asymmetries. The front is not only physically different from the back, but that axis separates the world that can be easily perceived and manipulated from the world that cannot be easily perceived and manipulated. Like the front/back axis, the right/left axis is not correlated with a significant axis of the world, but unlike the other axes, it has no prominent asymmetries. The spatial framework model predicts that times to identify objects at head and feet should be fastest, followed by times to front and back, followed by times to left and right. This pattern was confirmed by the data in four experiments. Some of the experiments used "above" and "below" and others used "head" and "feet," but the pattern of reaction times was the same.

In contrast to the classical view of imagery, that embodied in the Mental Transformation Model, the Spatial Framework Model incorporates people's conceptions of the perceptual world, not just their perceptions of it. People's conceptions of the perceptual world reflect their long-term interactions with the world, not just their instantaneous view of it. People's typical interactions with space are not random; they are structured by their own bodies and by the world. As noted previously, people's bodies have three axes, two of which having salient perceptual and functional asymmetries, and one having no salient asymmetries. The perceptual world has three dimensions, one objectively defined by gravity and asymmetric, and two horizontal axes with no definite anchors or salient asymmetries. These facts about human bodies and the world they inhabit constrain the interactions people typically have. For example, people typically interact with the world in an upright position, moving forward rather than backward or sideways, navigating on a horizontal or sloping plane rather than on a vertical plane. In general, people move through a stationary world rather than standing still as the world moves. People's interactions occur in many situations, varying in spatial layout, in posture, in perspective, and more. Depending on the nature of the situation, the Spatial Framework theory makes different predictions about searching space. Research subsequent to that described here has systematically varied critical aspects of the spatial setting to generalize the Spatial Framework analysis.

Reclining Case

The first variant we (Franklin & Tversky, 1990) examined was the case of the reclining observer. The reclining case differs from the upright case in two significant ways. Although people may recline in bed or elsewhere, most of people's alert interactions with the world take place upright. This should lead to faster overall times to upright than to reclining. Next, when people recline, turning from front to sides to back, no axis of the body is correlated with gravity, the only salient axis of the world. For reclining, then, accessibility of axes depends solely on the relative asymmetries of the body axes. We argued that the asymmetries of the front/back axis are more important than those of the head/feet axis, as the front/back axis separates the world that can be easily perceived and manipulated from the world that cannot be easily perceived and manipulated. Therefore, for the reclining case, times should be fastest to front/back, then to head/feet, in contrast to the upright case, and slowest to left/right, as in the upright case. This pattern appeared in two experiments, one in which subjects read narratives with both upright and reclining postures, and one in which they read narratives with only the reclining posture. In both cases, reaction times were also considerably longer in the reclining than the upright case, supporting both predictions of the Spatial Framework theory.

Third-Person Observer and Probing for Directions

The next two variants were to the narratives rather than the described setting. The original narratives described the observer as "you" in order to draw the subject/reader into the narrative. According to some notions of narrative interpretation, third-person narratives are construed differently from second-person narratives. Hence, it is interesting to know if readers would take the point of view of an observer described in the third person as readily as they did for observers described as "you." In fact, the pattern of reaction times was identical for third-person narratives as for second-person narratives (Bryant, Tversky, & Franklin, 1992). Subjects had no difficulty taking the point of view of a third-person observer. In another experiment, there was a central object, such as a saddle, rather than a central observer. The object was surrounded by other objects, and turned to face each one by an external force. Even for inanimate objects, subjects appeared to adopt the point of view of the object. There was one difficulty with objects; they have tops and bottoms, whereas people have heads and feet. Those terms are ambiguous; they can refer to a specific part of an object, such as the lid of a jar, or, for objects without intrinsic sides, they can refer to the part currently facing upward or downward. When an object is upright, these two senses coincide, but when an object reclines, they conflict. This led to relatively long response times to top and bottom when the object reclined.

The original task presented subjects with direction terms, and the subjects responded with name of the object located in that direction. In a simple test of generality, we reversed the probes and responses; subjects were presented with names of objects, and asked to respond with the current direction of the object from the observer (Bryant & Tversky, 1992). This should not make a difference in the pattern of response times, and in fact, it did not.

External Spatial Array

In the initial research, the narratives described environments in which the observer was at the center of an array of objects, turning toward each in turn. However, in many spatial situations, observers are outside of a three-dimensional spatial array looking onto it. We called this the *external* situation, to contrast with the situation where the observer is *internal* to the array. Bryant et al. (1992) investigated two kinds of external scenes. In one, narratives described an observer looking at a cubic array of objects; for example, a Halloween party, with various decorations and refreshments. For the other type of external array, narratives described an observer looking at a character surrounded by an array of objects. The scenes, therefore, were similar to those in the original, internal situation, but the subject was required to respond from the observer's external point of view rather than the character's internal point of view. Schematic displays of the two settings appear in Fig. 8.2.

The Spatial Framework analysis for the external setting differs slightly from that for the internal setting. For the external setting, the mental framework that subjects construct surrounds the array of objects, as before, but does not surround the observer, as the observer is external to the array of objects. Instead, the mental framework is projected in front of the observer, and the objects are mentally associated to it in the appropriate places. The order of salience of the axes is the same as for the internal spatial framework, but for slightly different reasons. Because the observer is not included in the mental framework, characteristics of the perceptual world determine accessibility rather than characteristics of the observer's body and orientation. Above/below should dominate because of the asymmetric effect of gravity on the world. Front/behind (instead of "back") should be next, because of the asymmetries of the visual field of the observer. In the external setting, all the objects are in front of the observer, but those in "front" are closer, appear larger, and are more likely to occlude objects that are "behind." Left/right should be slowest, as there are no salient asymmetries along the left/right plane in the observer's field of view. There was one difference predicted between the internal and external cases. In the internal case, objects to the back are not in the field of view, but in the external case, they are. For the internal case, therefore, reaction times to front should be faster than those to back, but not for the external case. These patterns of data were obtained for both external situations (Bryant et al., 1992).

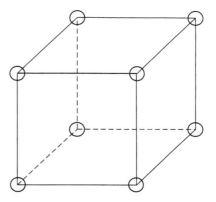

FIG. 8.2. Schematization of external spatial framework situations: Cubic array.

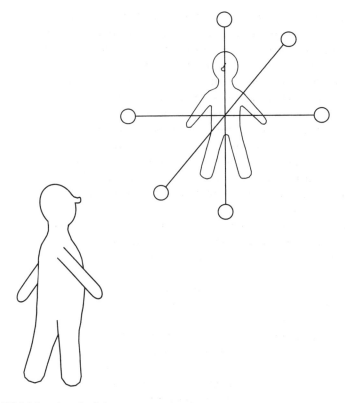

FIG. 8.2 *(continued)*. Schematization of external spatial framework situations: Array surrounding another character.

Turning Observer Versus Turning Environment

In normal human interactions in the world, it is people who move, not environments. Of course, some objects may move and change positions, but they do so individually; the environment as a whole does not move. According to the reasoning behind the Spatial Framework model, it should be easier for people to conceptualize changing spatial arrays when observers move than when environments move. To test this, we returned to the internal situation, where narratives described an observer surrounded by an array of objects (Kim, 1992). In this case, the narratives described the observer standing in various rooms of a gravity-free space house, built to study the effects of weightlessness, where the rooms could rotate as easily as the observer. In the turning-observer condition, the observer turned to face different objects, as before. In the turning-room condition, the observer stood in place, and the room rotated. Formally, the turning-observer and turning-environment conditions are identical; in terms of the locations of objects relative to the observer, having the observer turn to the right, for example, is equivalent to having the room rotate to the left. Psychologically, however, the situations are very different.

The first experiment compared the turning-room condition to the turning-observer condition, where movement was on both a horizontal and a vertical plane. Subjects reading narratives where the observer turned had no trouble with the task, and their results replicated the upright and reclining internal array findings described earlier. Subjects reading narratives where the room turned simply could not perform the task. After a few changes of orientation, they got completely disoriented, and could not figure out where things were around the observer. This occurred despite the fact that all of them realized that the turning room situation could be translated into a turning-observer situation.

In the next experiment, turning was restricted to the horizontal plane. The horizontal axis of rotation, turning leftwards or rightwards should be easier than the vertical, as this is the normal plane of navigation. With only horizontal rotation, subjects in both the turning-person and the turning-room conditions successfully performed the task. However, subjects in the turning-room condition took twice as long to reorient to a new facing as subjects in the turning-person condition, supporting the claim that conceptualizing a moving environment is more difficult than conceptualizing a moving observer. Once subjects had reoriented, their responses were as fast as subjects in the turning-person situation, and the spatial framework pattern emerged for both conditions. Obviously, this is just a first step, and more needs to be done. Nevertheless, in accordance with the Spatial Framework reasoning that normal or typical ways of interacting in space should be easier to conceptualize than atypical forms of interaction, people easily updated the spatial array when narratives described observers as turning, but not when narratives described the room as turning.

Two Viewpoints

In the previous studies, only one point of view was queried, but in many real life situations, people need to take more than one point of view in the same scene, for example, in describing a route to someone facing a different direction. Franklin, Tversky, and Coon (1992) studied perspective taking in narratives describing scenes with more than one point of view where subjects were required to answer from both. Three different situations were investigated: two characters in the same scene, either surrounded by the same set of objects or different sets of objects; two characters in different scenes, surrounded by different objects; and the same character facing a different way in the same scene at two different times. In all cases, subjects were queried from the point of view of one of the characters (or times) for a block of trials, then queried from the point of view of the other character (or time) for a block of trials, then back to the first character (or time), and so on.

There seemed to be two ways that subjects could respond alternately from two viewpoints. One way would be to take the perspective of each viewpoint in turn. If subjects adopt that strategy, then the spatial framework pattern of data should emerge for each viewpoint; that is, subjects should respond fastest to head/feet, then front/back, and slowest to left/right. Another way would be to take an inclusive viewpoint, not the viewpoint of any observer in the scene, but a viewpoint incorporating all the objects and characters in the scene. This would be a neutral viewpoint, as it is not the viewpoint of any of the participants. For example, subjects could adopt an overhead or oblique perspective that would allow imagining all the characters and objects in the scene, but would not correspond to the viewpoint of any of the characters. In this case, the subjects' body axes would not be oriented like the body axes of any character, so the conditions of the spatial framework would not hold. Subjects could compute front, back, head, and feet directly, with no clear advantage of one of those axes over another. They might have to take a perspective to calculate left and right (cf. Parsons, 1987; Shepard & Cooper, 1982), which might render times to left and right longer. Therefore, the data should correspond to the Equiavailability model, where times to all directions are equal, or to what we called *weak equiavailability*, where front/back and head/feet do not differ, but left/right is slower.

The cognitive demands for the two strategies appear to trade off the number of tokens that need to be kept in mind with the need to switch perspective. Taking one viewpoint at a time requires keeping in mind only one character and the surrounding objects at a time, but demands switching perspectives. Taking a neutral perspective of the entire scene requires keeping in mind both characters and associated objects but does not demand switching perspectives. The data from six experiments indicated that subjects could adopt either strategy, indicating that cognitive demands are not critical in this case. In some situations, the data corresponded to the spatial framework pattern, and in others, there were no differences among the axes, or a small disadvantage to left/right.

The spatial scene described in the narratives determined which strategy subjects adopted rather than processing demands. When the narratives described two viewpoints in the same scene, subjects appeared to form mental models of the entire situation and take oblique viewpoints. This pattern occurred for the two viewpoints of two different characters as well as for the two viewpoints of the same character at different times. It occurred when the two characters were surrounded by the same objects, so the memory load was small, as well as when the two characters were surrounded by different objects, so the memory load was large. In those cases, reaction times were equal to all directions (equiavailability) or slightly slower to left and right (weak equiavailability). When the narratives described two viewpoints in different scenes, the pattern of data corresponded to the spatial framework pattern, with head/feet fastest, then front/back, and then left/right, suggesting that subjects adopted each perspective in turn, using separate models for each perspective. It seems that readers take a single perspective for a single scene. When the scene had only one viewpoint—that of a single observer—subjects appeared to adopt that viewpoint. When the scene had more than one viewpoint—that of two observers (or the same observer at different times)—subjects adopted a neutral viewpoint rather than the viewpoint of either or both observers.

Comparing Perception and Language

In all of the research conducted to date, subjects learned about the scenes from reading descriptions of them. Will subjects construct the similar mental models if they learn the scenes from witnessing them rather than reading about them? Do the mental models established from descriptions resemble those that would be established from actual experience in a scene?

A related question of interest is whether responding from perception is like responding from memory. This raises issues concerning the nature of spatial mental models. Are they simply like images, or are they more abstract and based on different principles? The traditional view of imagery treats images as internalized perceptions (e.g., Kosslyn, 1980; Shepard & Cooper, 1982). As reviewed earlier, according to the classical view of imagery, properties of images are like properties of objects, so that scanning an image for a larger property should and does take less time than scanning an image for a smaller property (Kosslyn, 1980). Transforming images is like perceiving transformations on objects, so comparing the parity of two objects should and does take longer the greater the angle of displacement between the objects, as though one were being mentally rotated into correspondence with the other. Put differently, according to the classical theory of imagery, retrieval time and transformation time should follow the same patterns in both imagery and perception. If spatial mental models are like images, then responding from actual perception of a scene should follow the same pattern as responding from memory for a scene.

Bryant, Tversky, and Lanca (1994) addressed these issues in a series of experiments. To investigate performance from memory where learning was either from observation or from studying a narrative, we used the original internal spatial framework situation, of an observer surrounded by a set of objects as well as the external situation. For the internal situation, subjects entered a small room and stood on a bench. For each block of trials, the experimenter hung large pictures of objects to all six sides of the subject. For the external situation, subjects observed a foot-high doll on a table in front of them, with objects to all six sides of the doll. Subjects learned the scenes from observation, but responded from memory. For both spatial situations, the pattern of reaction times conformed to the spatial framework pattern of times. Therefore, for this task requiring accessing of spatial relations of objects to an observer turning in a scene, learning from observation was just like learning from narrative when responding was from memory.

An entirely different pattern of responding emerged when subjects responded from perception rather than from memory for the internal situation. In this case, the objects surrounding the subject were changed frequently so that subjects could not respond from memory. The reaction times corresponded to what can be termed the *Physical Transformation Model*. Subjects were fastest to respond to objects to the front and next fastest to respond to objects offset by 90 degrees, those to the left, right, head, and feet, with no differences among them. They were slowest to respond to the objects displaced by 180 degrees, those to the back. Interestingly, in a previous study where the objects were not changed frequently, subjects stopped looking; that is, they preferred to rely on their memories to access objects in specified directions to actually looking in those directions. This underscores the intimate relationship between perception and memory, and warns us that even when a scene is available to observation, people may not observe, preferring to use their memory.

CONCEPTIONS OF SPACE, NOT PERCEPTIONS OF SPACE, UNDERLIE SPATIAL MENTAL MODELS

The sharp differences between responding from observation and responding from memory add to the evidence that spatial mental models are not like images, not like internalized perceptions. Instead of being derived from people's immediate perceptions of the world, spatial mental models are derived from people's conceptions of the world. People's conceptions of the world are based on typical interactions in a three-dimensional world with a vertical axis defined by gravity and two horizontal axes orthogonal to it and each other, where people navigate, ordinarily in an upright position, and the surrounding environment usually stays still.

To say that spatial mental models are not like images or internalized perceptions is not to say that they are propositional in any simple way. A typical propositional account would need to be enriched with conceptions of space in order to explain the intricate patterns of reaction times to access objects in the six directions from the body depending on posture and perspective. The so-called "imagery–propositional" debate far oversimplifies the issues. Mental structures do not necessarily fall neatly into categories, analog or propositional, continuous or discrete.

MENTAL REPRESENTATIONS OF MAPS
AND ENVIRONMENTS

Common misconceptions of geography, such as the popular belief that Reno is east of San Diego (Stevens & Coupe, 1978), are more than a conversational curiosity or a source of trivia questions. Like visual illusions and slips of the tongue, they can provide insight into normal processing. The systematic errors that reveal underlying processing do not appear in many studies of cognitive maps. In those studies, errors appear to be random, and have often led to the conclusion that cognitive maps are like real maps, just a little noisy (see, e.g., some of the papers collected in Zube & Moore, 1989, especially a review by Golledge & Garling). To find *systematic* errors, studies must be carefully designed to produce them. A careful design is usually inspired by intuitions about causes of error, intuitions that develop into theory. I turn now to review a project investigating errors in cognitive maps, especially of two types, termed *rotation* and *alignment* (Tversky, 1981, 1991). Before recounting details of the evidence, I describe the theory that led to the research, a theory of organization of spatial memory based on scene perception and comprehension.

One early process in scene perception is distinguishing figures from ground (e.g., Hochberg, 1978). Like people, objects, and buildings in pictures or scenes, land masses, cities, roads, and the like can be regarded as figures on the backgrounds of oceans, countries, or cities. Once figures are discerned, they are identified. An integral part of identifying a figure is assigning it an orientation (Rock, 1973). Orientation can be assigned only relative to a reference frame. In the case of pictures, maps, and scenes, the natural reference frame is the canonical axes of the picture plane, the horizontal and vertical axes. In the case of maps, the vertical and horizontal axes coincide with the canonical directions, north–south and east–west. Vertical and horizontal lines have a privileged status; they are better detected and remembered than lines at other orientations, and serve as anchors for other lines (cf. Howard, 1982). Well-known figures, such as trees, houses, and faces, may have known orientations, but abstract ones may not. Nevertheless, they may have "natural" orientations. Viewers of abstract figures frequently agree on how the figures should be oriented (Braine, 1978). People prefer elongation to be aligned with one of the canonical axes, especially the vertical one, and prefer focal features at the top. Viewers encode the orientation and location of figures with respect to the canonical axes, the basis for rotation errors, and they also encode the orientation and location of figures with respect to other figures, the basis for alignment errors. Both of these encoding processes can lead to distortion. Both processes are similar to anchoring; they have the effect of drawing figures toward the anchors. When the natural orientation of a figure and its actual orientation conflict, they are brought closer into correspondence. When two figures that are grouped together are slightly misaligned, they are brought closer into correspondence.

The experimental evidence supporting rotation and alignment is too large to be reviewed in full (e.g., Byrne, 1979; Glicksohn, 1994; Lloyd, 1989; Lloyd & Heivly, 1987; Moar & Bower, 1983; Tversky, 1981). Studies have been done in a number of different countries, typically using large numbers of college students in each study. Support for alignment and rotation has been found in studies of memory for environments learned by exploration as well as environments learned by studying maps, and in memory for environments that are well-known and natural as well as for environments that are new and artificial. A few examples that illustrate the phenomena follow.

Rotation

The initial experiments tested people's knowledge of geography of areas that are well-known to them, either from years of studying classroom maps or from living in the region. In rotation, subjects are expected to misremember the orientation of a figure that has a natural orientation as closer to the orientation of the frame of reference, when they are not perfectly oriented. South America is a good candidate for rotation errors. In its correct orientation relative to the canonical axes, it appears tilted. A large group of students were asked to place a cutout of South America correctly into a rectangular frame where the sides of the frame corresponded to the north–south east–west axes. In fact, most of the subjects turned South America counterclockwise relative to its true orientation, uprighting it (Tversky, 1981). Similar errors were evident when Stanford students were asked to indicate the directions between pairs of cities in the San Francisco Bay Area. The San Francisco Bay Area actually runs as much east–west as it does north–south, clearly evident from maps of the area, including the weather and earthquake maps appearing daily in the papers. Mentally, residents appear to rotate the Bay Area to north–south. For example, students indicated that Berkeley was east of Stanford, when in fact it is west of Stanford, and they indicated that Santa Cruz was west of Stanford, when in fact it is east of Stanford. South America and the Bay Area are both elongated land masses oriented so that the axis of elongation is oblique to the canonical north–south east–west axes of the world. In both cases, what subjects seem to be doing in their minds is turning the land mass so that its major axis is in closer correspondence with one of the canonical axes, a phenomenon termed *rotation*. Rotation errors have been found not just for orientations of land masses and directions between cities in the world, but also for orientations of land masses and directions between cities in artificial maps, for orientation of streets that are directly experienced rather than acquired from maps, and for orientations of blobs not perceived as maps.

Alignment

In alignment, people group figures together, and then remember them as more closely grouped than they actually were. The land masses of the Americas, Europe, and Africa are likely candidates for alignment. It is natural to group Europe with North America and Africa with South America. In fact, however, Europe is on the whole north of North America, or at least of the United States, and Africa is north of South America. If alignment affects people's memory for relative locations in those continents, then systematic errors of memory should arise. Alignment was tested by asking a large group of students to indicate the direction between many pairs of cities in Europe, Africa, and the Americas. Consistent with alignment, people incorrectly indicated that Rome is south of Philadelphia and Algiers is south of Los Angeles. This is not just due to weather, as subjects made similar errors in indicating the directions between pairs of cities in North and South America. In fact, most of South America is east of most of North America, or at least the United States, but North and South America are large land masses likely to be grouped together. Consistent with alignment, subjects indicated that Rio is west of Boston and Lima is west of Miami, both of which are incorrect. When asked to choose between a correct map of the world and one in which the Western Hemisphere had been moved northward so that the United States and Europe and South America and Africa were more closely aligned, a majority of subjects selected the incorrect map. More subjects preferred the incorrect map when asked to choose between the correct map of the Americas, and a map in which South America had been moved westward relative to North America, so that they were better aligned. In all these cases, what subjects seem to be doing is coding the location of one land mass relative to that of another. The two land masses are then remembered as more *aligned* than they actually were. Like rotation, alignment is found for artificial maps as well as real world ones, for environments learned by experience rather than environments learned from maps, and for visual blobs not viewed as maps.

Both alignment and rotation errors occur in perception as well as in memory, but the errors are greater in memory than in perception (Tversky, 1981). One study compared perception and memory of artificial maplike stimuli. In the perception task, subjects were asked to reproduce the orientations and locations of blobs in frames of reference by attaching them correctly to a frame of reference. In the memory task, subjects studied the original stimuli and then attached the blobs to the frames of reference from memory. Alignment and rotation errors occurred in the perception task, but were considerably greater in the memory task. Encoding errors presumably occur for the same reason that memory errors occur. Subjects use other figures and the frame of reference in order to locate and orient the critical figure. In the perception task, subjects can correct their errors by looking at the original figure, something they cannot do in memory. Nevertheless, some error in the direction of rotation and alignment occurred even when subjects could check their accuracy.

Related Systematic Errors

Alignment and rotation are but two of many types of systematic error in memory for maps and environments. Some errors, like alignment and rotation, seem to have their origin more in perceptual processing, others more in judgment (for a review, see Tversky, 1992). Milgram and Jodelet (1976) found that Parisians straighten the Seine, something North Americans seem to do for the U.S.–Canadian border. These appear to occur primarily at encoding. Holyoak and Mah (1982) found evidence for the so-called New Yorker's view of the world, popularized in cartoons. They asked students (in Ann Arbor, MI) to imagine themselves either on the East Coast or on the West Coast of the United States. Then they asked subjects to make judgments of the distances between pairs of cities more or less equidistant along an east–west line across the United States. Students with a West Coast perspective overestimated the distance between San Francisco and Salt Lake City and underestimated the distance between New York City and Pittsburgh relative to students taking an East Coast perspective. Because the nature of the distortion depends on the perspective adopted, it appears to occur primarily at judgment. This and other judgments have parallels in actual perception and in social judgment. In perception, closer distances seem larger than more distant ones. In social judgment, we tend to judge the people near us, in our own group, to be highly differentiated, yet see the people in other groups, other universities, other political parties, or other countries, to be more alike (Quattrone, 1986).

Constructive Processes Again

Memory for location and orientation is relative and qualitative. It is relative to a frame of reference and to other figures. It is a consequence of the processing entailed by comprehension of a scene, by mental construction or reconstruction of it. Some degree of distortion is evident even in perception, when subjects copy the stimuli, but greater degrees are evident in memory. People's spatial knowledge is not only biased, it is also fragmented. There is no guarantee that these bits of distorted knowledge, when put together, will form a coherent picture, a knowledge structure consistent with a map. Although random errors can be accommodated by the traditional view of a "cognitive map" as maplike or imagelike or picturelike, systematic errors cannot be.

MEMORY FOR SPACE AND MISMEMORY FOR SPACE

Putting together the two projects, memory for space and mismemory for space seem to depend on similar mental spatial constructions. Critical to both is a mental reference frame to which objects in space are linked. Selection of a reference frame depends on the situation; it is content-specific. For keeping track of the objects around us, extensions of the three body axes form a natural mental reference frame. For remembering locations and orientations of land masses, cities, and landmarks, the canonical north–south east–west axes form a natural reference frame. For visual blobs, the sides of the page form a natural reference frame. Without a mental reference frame, figures would float unlocated in a space. When other objects are present, then figures are located with respect to them as well.

Selection of a reference frame depends not just on perceptual factors, but also on conceptions about the figures and their contexts. For objects around our own selves, we select the three axes of our bodies. It is through our bodies that we experience the world. For geographic entities, the north–south east–west axes have been adopted independently by many cultures. The east–west axis corresponds to the average path of the sun; the north–south axis is perpendicular to it, and globally associated with weather and seasons. For figures on a piece of paper, the sides of the paper serve as a reference frame. It is no accident that for maps, the canonical directions are normally lined up with the sides of the page. For graphs—that is, simple linear increasing functions in an x–y plot—the implicit diagonal serves as a reference frame rather than the axes of the graph (Schiano & Tversky, 1992; Tversky & Schiano, 1989). For this type of graph, the implicit diagonal, representing the identity line, provides a meaningful referent.

Analogous Errors and Processes

As noted earlier, similar distortions have been found in memory and judgment in other domains, notably time (see, e.g., Huttenlocher, chapter 7, this volume). Space and time are closely linked in language and in thought (e.g., Clark & Clark, 1977). "Before" and "after," for example, are spatial terms that have been applied to describe time. Although time is viewed as one-dimensional, humans use many different reference frames for organizing time, some of them cyclical, such as the hours of a day and the days of a week, and some of them linear, such as labeling of years (e.g., Friedman, 1993; Huttenlocher, Hedges, & Prohaska, 1988, 1992; Koriat & Fischoff, 1974). Salient events, public or private, can serve as temporal anchors, much as landmarks serve as spatial anchors (e.g., Loftus & Marburger, 1983). As for spatial reference frames, temporal reference frames can be invoked in reconstructive processes at time of retrieval as well as in constructive processes at time of experience.

IS THERE A SYSTEMATIC WAY TO THINK
ABOUT SYSTEMATIC ERRORS IN MEMORY?

The chapters in this volume discuss a variety of ways that memory can be veridical or erroneous. Here, I focus on the paradigms that produce error to enable comparisons to the research described on systematic errors in cognitive maps. A central example is the misinformation paradigm developed by Loftus, Miller, and Burns (1978) and used widely since by a number of the authors in this volume as well as many others. In that paradigm, subjects witness or experience an event. At some later time, the experimental subjects read or hear or witness information that is misleading; that is, inconsistent in some way with the original event. The control subjects do not. Still later, memory for the original event is tested. Typically, memory in the experimental group is biased toward the misleading information in comparison to the control group. In many cases, eyewitness reports have been significantly altered by misleading postevent information of the kind that can come from question sessions. Misinformation presupposed in questions can become incorporated into eyewitness reports, often with a great deal of confidence (e.g., Belli, 1989; Ceci & Bruck, 1993, chapter 16, this volume; Goodman & Quas, chapter 11, this volume; Loftus, 1979; Loftus & Hoffman, 1989; Loftus et al., 1978; Ornstein et al., chapter 4, this volume; Peters, chapter 15, this volume; Tversky & Tuchin, 1989; Zaragoza et al., chapter 17, this volume). As some of this research has shown, however, when original learning is stronger, then misinformation effects are weaker.

Loftus and her collaborators have asserted that the misleading information overwrites and replaces the original information (Loftus, Hoffman, & Wagenaar, 1992). As they are aware, this is a difficult assertion to substantiate. Any evidence for overwriting; namely, forgetting, is also evidence for retrieval failure. Because there are many substantiated cases of retrieval failure with subsequent retrieval success (e.g., Crowder, 1976), that possibility always remains. Retrieval failure is a common consequence of interference, not a surprising outcome given that the eyewitness paradigm is essentially a retroactive interference paradigm. In the retroactive interference paradigm, subjects first learn A. Then the experimental subjects learn B, which is similar to A, but the control subjects do not. At some later time, both groups are tested for A. The typical finding is poorer performance for the experimental group. The case for retrieval failure rather than overwriting is strengthened by studies that show some memory for the original information in addition to memory for the misleading information (Tversky & Tuchin, 1989; see similar accounts in Bekerian & Bowers, 1983; Christiaansen & Ochalek, 1983; Morton, Hammersley, & Bekerian, 1985; Schooler & Engstler-Schooler, 1991). According to interference theory, the original witnessed information is confused with the similar misleading information, much as a friend's previous phone number is confused with the friend's newly acquired number. At recall, the similar intervening, and presumably incorrect information or some blend of the correct and the intervening information, or both the original and the intervening information may be given instead of the original, requested information alone.

Errors in memory can also come from confusing what actually happened with what we imagined happened or confusing what we actually did with what we intended to do. These have been termed *source-monitoring errors*, where an event is remembered, but its source is forgotten or confused (see Johnson, Hashtroudi, & Lindsay, 1993, for a comprehensive review). Other source-monitoring errors include not remembering or confusing where you read a news item or who told you a bit of gossip, or whether you or your collaborator came up with a particular idea. The paradigm for source-monitoring experiments is also similar to that of retroactive interference. Subjects experience a number of events and imagine experiencing others; at some later time, they are asked to distinguish those they experienced from those they imagined, and sometimes err. The quality of source monitoring depends in part on how the events were encoded. When memories are accompanied by rich perceptual and contextual associations, people are more likely to believe that they were real rather than imagined, or that they, rather than someone else, performed the action. Of course, rich perceptual and contextual associations may be a consequence of actual stimulation or of vivid imagination. Source monitoring also depends on decision processes such as assessments of plausibility—judgments that come after events have or have not occurred, at memory retrieval.

Plausibility considerations are prominent in recollections of our own previous attitudes and assessments of changes in our own behavior (Ross, 1989), especially in cases where our recollections are weak to begin with. According to Ross, we make these judgments in large part by applying implicit theories about attitude and behavior change to our current attitudes and behaviors. People whose attitudes have been changed by experimental manipulation nevertheless often remember their previous position as similar to their current one. Presumably, their implicit theories about attitudes is the belief that attitudes do not change radically over short time periods. In other cases, people exaggerate the differences between their present and previous attributes, rather than assimilating them. For example, people who have undergone self-improvement programs often report their improvement to be greater than it actually was presumably because they believe that the program was effective. Personal histories are constructed with the help of implicit theories. Memories of the past will be consistent or inconsistent with assessments of the present, depending on the implicit theory about the trait or attitude or behavioral change.

Almost every framework for memory distinguishes three stages: encoding, storage, and retrieval. Can we assign these systematic errors to one or another of those stages? Probably not. Errors of eyewitness testimony, source monitoring, and personal histories seem to be a consequence of deficient encoding as well as intervening interfering information and judgment processes at retrieval. To the extent that the original memory is weaker, the possibility of error due to interference or judgment is greater. Systematic errors of spatial memory seem to occur as a consequence of processes at encoding as well as reconstruction processes at retrieval. They may be invoked at encoding in comprehension of a scene. They may also be invoked during retrieval, where, quite frequently, disparate items of information must be combined to provide the needed information. Because the same processes are presumed to be used at both encoding and retrieval, error may be introduced at either or both times. An analogous situation exists in memory for word lists and narratives, where categories, scripts, or story schemas may be used at encoding to organize the information and at retrieval to access it. What is remembered is patched together from different scraps of information, with schemas as patterns and plausibility as thread.

Errors can be introduced during encoding, storage, or retrieval. The best defense against error and forgetting is effective encoding (e.g., Bower, 1970), although often by the time we realize that, it is too late. In a lecture given at the Musée des Beaux Arts d'Anvers in 1938, Magritte talked about his well-known painting *The Human Condition*. This is the often-reproduced painting of an easel holding a painting of a landscape including a tree. The easel is inside, in front of a window, with the "real" landscape outside. The painting and the outside are perfectly aligned so that in some places, it appears that the landscape is on the canvas and in other places, it appears that the landscape is outside the window. Of this painting, Magritte (1940) said:

> The viewer sees the tree in the interior of the room and at the same time he sees the other tree, outside the room in the real landscape, through his mind. This is how we see the world: We see it outside ourselves, and yet we have another representation of it inside ourselves.

In Magritte's painting, the "real" landscape and the painted landscape are identical—but this is, after all, a painting. In mental representations, the real and the represented are not always the same.

ACKNOWLEDGMENTS

I am grateful to Peter Ornstein and Nancy Stein for valuable comments on a previous draft of this chapter, and to my collaborators in the research, Nancy Franklin, Diane Schiano, Holly Taylor, and David Bryant, for years of stimulating discussion. Research reviewed here was supported by the Air Force Office of Scientific Research, Air Force Systems Command, USAF, under grant or cooperative agreement number AFOSR 89–0076, NSF–IST Grant 8403273, and NSF Grant BSN 8002012 to Stanford University. Preparation of the manuscript was facilitated by a grant from Interval Research Corporation.

REFERENCES

Bekerian, D. A., & Bowers, J. M. (1983). Eyewitness testimony: Were we misled. *Journal of Experimental Psychology: Learning, Memory, and Cognition, 9*, 139–145.

Belli, R. F. (1989). Influences of misleading postevent information: Misinformation interference and acceptance. *Journal of Experimental Psychology: General, 118*, 72–85.

Bower, G. H. (1970). The analysis of a mnemonic device. *American Scientist, 58*, 496–510.

Braine, L. G. (1978). A new slant on orientation perception. *American Psychologist, 33*, 10–22.

Bransford, J. D., Barclay, J. R., & Franks, J. J. (1972). Sentence memory: A constructive versus interpretive approach. *Cognitive Psychology, 3*, 193–209.

Bryant, D. J., & Tversky, B. (1992). Assessing spatial frameworks with object and direction probes. *Bulletin of the Psychonomic Society, 30*, 29–32.

Bryant, D. J., Tversky, B., & Franklin, N. (1992). Internal and external spatial frameworks for representing described scenes. *Journal of Language and Memory, 31*, 74–98.

Bryant, D. J., Tversky, B., & Lanca, M. (1994). *Spatial mental models from observed and remembered scenes.* Manuscript submitted for publication.

Byrne, R. W. (1979). Memory for urban geography. *Quarterly Journal of Experimental Psychology, 31*, 147–154.

Ceci, S. J., & Bruck, M. (1993). Suggestibility of the child witness: A historical review and synthesis. *Psychological Bulletin, 113*, 403–439.

Christiaansen, R. E., & Ochalek, K. (1983). Editing misleading information from memory: Evidence for the coexistence of original and postevent information. *Memory and Cognition, 11*, 73–86.

Clark, H. H. (1973). Space, time, semantics and the child. In T. E. Moore (Ed.), *Cognitive development and the acquisition of language* (pp. 27–63). New York: Academic Press.

Clark, H. H., & Clark, E. V. (1977). *Psychology and language.* New York: Harcourt Brace Jovanovich.

Cooper, W. E., & Ross, J. R. (1975). World order (word order). In R. E. Grossman, L. J. San, & T. J. Vances (Eds.), *Papers from the parasession on functionalism* (pp. 63–111). Chicago: Chicago Linguistic Society.

Crowder, R. G. (1976). *Principles of learning and memory.* Hillsdale, NJ: Lawrence Erlbaum Associates.

Evans, G. E., & Pezdek, K. (1980). Cognitive mapping: Knowledge of real-world distance and location information. *Journal of Experimental Psychology: Human Learning and Memory, 6*, 13–24.

Fillmore, C. J. (1975). *Santa Cruz lectures on deixis.* Bloomington: Indiana University Linguistics Club.

Finke, R. A., & Shepard, R. N. (1986). Visual functions of mental imagery. In K. R. Boff, L. Kaufman, & J. P. Thomas (Eds.), *Handbook of perception and human performance* (Vol. 2, pp. 1–55). New York: Wiley-Interscience.

Franklin, N., & Tversky, B. (1990). Searching imagined environments. *Journal of Experimental Psychology: General, 119*, 63–76.

Franklin, N., Tversky, B., & Coon, V. (1992). Switching points of view in spatial mental models acquired from text. *Memory and Cognition, 20*, 507–518.

Friedman, W. J. (1993). Memory for the time of past events. *Psychological Bulletin, 113*, 44–66.

Glenberg, A. M., Meyer, M., & Lindem, K. (1987). Mental models contribute to foregrounding during text comprehension. *Journal of Memory and Language, 26*, 69–83.

Glicksohn, J. (1994). Rotation, orientation, and cognitive mapping. *American Journal of Psychology, 107*, 39–51.

Golledge, R. G., & Garling, T. (1989). Environmental perception and cognition. In E. H. Zube & G. T. Moore (Eds.), *Advances in environment, behavior and design* (Vol. 2, pp. 203–236). New York: Plenum.

Guzv, L. T., Leibowitz, H. W., & Fulcher, J. A. (1993). *Accuracy of quantitative estimates as a function of retrieval technique*. Unpublished manuscript, State University of New York at Oneonta.

Hochberg, J. (1978). *Perception*. Englewood Cliffs, NJ: Prentice-Hall.

Holyoak, K. J., & Mah, W. A. (1982). Cognitive reference points in judgments of symbolic magnitude. *Cognitive Psychology, 14*, 328–352.

Howard, I. P. (1982). *Human visual orientation*. New York: Wiley.

Huttenlocher, J., Hedges, L. V., & Prohaska, V. (1988). Hierarchical organization in ordered domains: Estimating the dates of events. *Psychological Review, 95*, 471–484.

Huttenlocher, J., Hedges, L. V., & Prohaska, V. (1992). Memory for day of the week: A 5 + 2 day cycle. *Journal of Experimental Psychology: General, 121*, 313–325.

Johnson, M. K., Hashtroudi, S., & Lindsay, D. S. (1993). Source monitoring. *Psychological Bulletin, 114*, 3–28.

Johnson-Laird, P. N. (1983). *Mental models*. Cambridge, MA: Harvard University Press.

Kim, J. (1992). *Changing environments in spatial mental models*. Unpublished senior honors thesis in Psychology, Stanford University, Stanford, CA.

Kosslyn, S. M. (1980). *Image and mind*. Cambridge, MA: Harvard University Press.

Koriat, A., & Fischoff, B. (1974). What day is today? An inquiry into the process of time orientation. *Memory and Cognition, 2*, 201–205.

Lakoff, G., & Johnson, M. (1980). *Metaphors we live by*. Chicago: University of Chicago Press.

Levelt, W. J. M. (1984). Some perceptual limitations on talking about space. In A. J. van Doorn, W. A. de Grind, & J. J. Koenderink (Eds.), *Limits in perception* (pp. 323–358). Utrecht, The Netherlands: VNU Science Press.

Levine, M., Jankovic, I., & Palij, M. (1982). Principles of spatial problem solving. *Journal of Experimental Psychology: General, 111*, 157–175.

Lloyd, R. (1989). Cognitive maps: Encoding and decoding information. *Annals of the Association of American Geographers, 79*, 101–124.

Lloyd, R., & Heivly, C. (1987). Systematic distortions in urban cognitive maps. *Annals of the Association of American Geographers, 77*, 191–207.

Loftus, E. F. (1979). *Eyewitness testimony*. Cambridge, MA: Harvard University Press.

Loftus, E. F., & Hoffman, H. G. (1989). Misinformation and memory: The creation of memory. *Journal of Experimental Psychology: General, 118*, 100–104.

Loftus, E. F., Hoffman, H. G., & Wagenaar, W. A. (1992). The misinformation effect: Transformations in memory induced by postevent information. In M. L. Howe, C. J. Brainerd, & V. F. Reyna (Eds.), *Development of long-term retention* (pp. 159–183). New York: Springer-Verlag.

Loftus, E. F., & Marburger, W. (1983). Since the eruption of Mt. St. Helens, has anyone beaten you up? Improving the accuracy of retrospective reports with landmark events. *Memory and Cognition, 11*, 114–120.

Loftus, E. F., Miller, D. G., & Burns, H. J. (1978). Semantic integration of verbal information into a visual memory. *Journal of Experimental Psychology: Human Learning and Memory, 4*, 19–31.

Mackworth, N. H., & Morandi, A. J. (1967). The gaze selects informative details within pictures. *Perception and Psychophysics, 2*, 547–551.

Magritte, R. (1940, April). Summary, Lecture at Musee des Beaux Arts d'Anvers, November 20, 1938. *L'Invention* (N. Shapiro, Trans.). (Taken from a wall at the Magritte exhibit at the Art Institute of Chicago, May, 1993)

Mani, K., & Johnson-Laird, P. N. (1982). The mental representation of spatial descriptions. *Memory and Cognition, 10*, 181–187.

Marr, D., & Nishihara, H. K. (1978). Representation and recognition of the spatial organization of three-dimensional shapes. *Proceedings of the Royal Society B, 200*, 269–291.

Milgram, S., & Jodelet, D. (1976). Psychological maps of Paris. In H. Proshansky, W. Ittelson, & L. Rivlin (Eds.), *Environmental psychology* (2nd ed., pp. 104–124). New York: Holt, Rinehart & Winston.

Miller, G. A., & Johnson-Laird, P. N. (1976). *Language and perception*. Cambridge, MA: Harvard University Press.

Moar, I., & Bower, G. H. (1983). Inconsistency in spatial knowledge. *Memory and Cognition, 11*, 107–113.

Morrow, D. G., Bower, G. H., & Greenspan, S. (1989). Updating situation models during narrative comprehension. *Journal of Memory and Language, 28*, 292–312.

Morrow, D. G., Greenspan, S., & Bower, G. H. (1987). Accessibility and situation models in narrative comprehension. *Journal of Memory and Language, 26*, 165–187.

Morton, J., Hammersley, R. H., & Bekerian, D. A. (1985). Headed records: A model for memory and its failures. *Cognition, 20*, 1–23.

Parsons, L. M. (1987). Imagined spatial transformations of one's hands and feet. *Cognitive Psychology, 19*, 178–241.

Perrett, D., Harries, M., Mistlin, A. J., & Chitty, A. J. (1990). Three stages in the classification of body movements by visual neurons. In H. Barlow, C. Blakemore, & M. Weston-Smith (Eds.), *Images and understanding* (pp. 94–107). Cambridge, England: Cambridge University Press.

Perrig, W., & Kintsch, W. (1985). Propositional and situational representations of text. *Journal of Memory and Language, 24*, 503–518.

Pinker, S. (1984). Visual cognition: An introduction. *Cognition, 18*, 161–193.

Presson, C. C., DeLange, N., & Hazelrigg, M. D. (1989). Orientation specificity in spatial memory: What makes a path different from a map of the path? *Journal of Experimental Psychology: Learning, Memory, and Cognition, 15*, 887–897.

Quattrone, G. A. (1986). On the perception of a group's variability. In S. Worchel & W. Austin (Eds.), *The psychology of intergroup relations* (pp. 25–48). New York: Nelson-Hall.

Rock, I. (1973). *Orientation and form*. New York: Academic Press.

Ross, M. (1989). Relation of implicit theories to the construction of personal histories. *Psychological Review, 96*, 341–357.

Schiano, D., & Tversky, B. (1992). Structure and strategy in viewing simple graphs. *Memory and Cognition, 20*, 12–20.

Schooler, J. W., & Engstler-Schooler, T. Y. (1991). Verbal overshadowing of visual memories: Some things are better left unsaid. *Cognitive Psychology, 22*, 36–71.

Shepard, R. N., & Cooper, L. A. (1982). *Mental images and their transformations*. Cambridge, MA: MIT Press.

Shepard, R. N., & Hurwitz, S. (1984). Upward direction, mental rotation, and discrimination of left and right turns in maps. *Cognition, 18*, 161–194.

Sholl, M. J. (1989). Cognitive maps as orienting schema. *Journal of Experimental Psychology: Learning, Memory, and Cognition, 13*, 615–628.

Stevens, A., & Coupe, P. (1978). Distortions in judged spatial relations. *Cognitive Psychology, 13*, 422–437.

Streeter, L. A., Vitello, D., & Wonsiewicz, S. Q. (1985). How to tell people where to go: Comparing navigational aids. *International Journal of Man–Machine Studies, 22*, 549–562.

Taylor, H. A., & Tversky, B. (1992a). Descriptions and depictions of environments. *Memory and Cognition, 20*, 483–496.

Taylor, H. A., & Tversky, B. (1992b). Spatial mental models derived from survey and route descriptions. *Journal of Memory and Language, 31*, 261–282.

Taylor, H. A., & Tversky, B. (in press). Perspective in spatial descriptions. *Journal of Memory and Language*.

Thorndyke, P., & Hayes-Roth, B. (1982). Differences in spatial knowledge acquired from maps and navigation. *Cognitive Psychology, 14*, 560–589.

Tversky, B. (1981). Distortions in memory for maps. *Cognitive Psychology, 13*, 407–433.

Tversky, B. (1992). Distortions in cognitive maps. *Geoforum, 23*, 131–138.

Tversky, B., & Schiano, D. (1989). Perceptual and conceptual factors in distortions in memory for maps and graphs. *Journal of Experimental Psychology: General, 118*, 387–398.

Tversky, B., & Tuchin, M. (1989). A reconciliation of the evidence on eyewitness testimony: Comments of McCloskey and Zaragoza. *Journal of Experimental Psychology: General, 118*, 86–91.

van Dijk, T. A., & Kintsch, W. (1983). *Strategies of discourse comprehension.* New York: Academic Press.

Zube, E. H., & Moore, G. T. (Eds.). (1989). *Advances in environment, behavior and design.* New York: Plenum.

9

CHILDREN'S FORGETTING WITH IMPLICATIONS FOR MEMORY SUGGESTIBILITY

C. J. Brainerd
University of Arizona

In June 1989, I attended a conference entitled "The Suggestibility of Children's Recollections" at Cornell University. The aim of the conference was to explore the question of whether children's memories of earlier events are acutely sensitive to impairment by later events. More specifically, Are children's memories of earlier events, in comparison to adults', inclined to be distorted by later events that conflict with the earlier events? This question had become prominent not through research on memory development, but because of the frequency with which children were being called on to testify in court cases involving allegations of child abuse. Most of the conferees approached things from that perspective, and they were particularly interested in whether false memories that conflict with prior events and produce inaccurate testimony can be retroactively implanted by attorneys, law enforcement personnel, parents, psychotherapists, and social workers.

My assigned role was to supply relevant input from basic research. The operative word was "relevant." The memory-development literature is vast and only certain segments of it are probative with respect to the suggestibility of children's memories. It seemed obvious, for two reasons, that research on the development of forgetting would be especially on-point. First, the question of childhood memory suggestibility is self-evidently a question about forgetting. The event–testimony lags associated with court cases are so protracted (months or years) that memories of original events, a key basis for accurate testimony, will undergo substantial forgetting as a matter of course. Second, the mainstream adult literature reveals a close connection between the distorting influence of later events and how much has been forgotten about earlier events. As writers from Bartlett (1932) to Piaget (1968) to Bransford and Franks (1971) have commented, it is not difficult to demonstrate false memories in adults. Indeed, there are certain experimental paradigms that were devised for just this purpose (intrusion in categorized recall, false recognition, subliminal priming, etc.). A well-known fact about those paradigms is that it becomes easier to introduce false memories as original memories fade. In recognition memory for words and sentences, for instance, subjects' tendency to accept distractors that preserve some of the features of targets (e.g., aspects of their meaning, orthography, or phonology) can increase dramatically across forgetting intervals of only a few days (Brainerd, Reyna, & Kneer, 1995; Kintsch, Welsch, Schmalhofer, & Zimny, 1990; Reyna & Kiernan, 1994).

Of course, it could be argued, and it often has been argued, that basic research cannot be generalized to questions about the suggestibility of children's memories because such questions typically involve memories of stressful and emotionally charged events. Assuming that this argument is put forward as a hypothesis, it deserves careful consideration. It has received such consideration, with the result being that available evidence does not support it. Howe, Courage, and Peterson (1994), for example, have conducted a detailed analysis of this hypothesis using a corpus of case studies of children's long-term retention of memories for traumatic events (e.g., broken bones, severe cuts that required sutures). They found that such memories obeyed the usual principles that have been identified in basic research on the development of forgetting. They also reviewed other studies in which no correlation was found between the rated stressfulness of events and children's long-term retention of memories for those events. For these and other reasons, they concluded that children's autobiographical "memories for traumatic events are subject to the same laws that govern the retention of memories in general" (p. 327).

Returning to the literature on the development of forgetting, I discovered something perplexing as I surveyed it. There was not much of it. I was puzzled by this because, in addition to children's testimony, the question of whether their memories, once formed, are highly labile is fundamental to elementary education, child psychotherapy, and other areas of importance to child welfare. Therefore, although it might seem unremarkable that basic research had overlooked other topics of applied concern, it was very surprising in this case.

I drew these facts to the attention of the conferees, and stated my belief that then-current debates about the suggestibility of children's memories turned on at least three questions that basic research had not yet answered (cf. also Brainerd, 1990; Brainerd & Ornstein, 1991). First, does the rate at which information is forgotten across long-term retention intervals vary with age, particularly between early childhood and young adulthood? Second, does reminiscence, the ability to recover forgotten information purely as a consequence of repeated interrogations, develop and is it present in children as well as adults? Third, do memory tests inoculate children's memories against forgetting the way they inoculate adults' memories?

In the interval since the Cornell conference, the situation has changed for the better. We now have some answers to each of these questions—rather detailed answers in some cases. The main things that we have learned are sketched in the present chapter, with a view to their ramifications for suggestibility. In the first section, findings from developmental studies of normal forgetting from long-term memory are summarized. Because many of these studies measured forgetting on multiple occasions, they also provide data on age changes in the ability to recover memories on later tests that could not be recovered on earlier tests. That question is considered in the second section. In the third section, the question of how memory tests influence the persistence of children's memories is examined. Here, I rely on a recent review of relevant studies by Poole and White (1995). At the end of the chapter, I outline some theoretical developments that may allow us to gather both forgetting and suggestibility under one explanatory umbrella.

DOES FORGETTING DEVELOP?

Basic research on this question has a somewhat checkered history. Therefore, it is well to begin with a few historical remarks. A procedure devised by Ebbinghaus, the retention paradigm, is the standard means of emulating everyday forgetting in the laboratory. It consists of three steps. During Step 1, the *acquisition session*, subjects are exposed to some target information (word lists, picture lists, sentences, connected discourse, a film, etc.). Memory for this information is tested at the end of the acquisition session. Step 2 is a *retention interval*. As a rule, it is just a dead space (minutes, hours, days, weeks) in which subjects resume their normal lives. During Step 3, the *retention phase*, another series of memory tests is administered. The slope of the line connecting performance at the end of Step 1 with performance during Step 3 is then the measure of forgetting; the steeper the decline, the larger the amount of forgetting. In the retroactive-interference variant of this paradigm, such as the procedure that is used to study memory suggestibility (cf. Ceci & Bruck, 1993; Loftus, 1979; Loftus & Hoffman, 1989; Tversky & Tuchin, 1989), information that conflicts with what subjects learned during Step 1 (usually in the form of leading questions) is interpolated at some point during Step 2.

When one inspects the published archive of memory development research over the past quarter of a century, one finds a handful of articles in which the retention paradigm was used (Berch & Evans, 1973; Dempster,

1984; Fajnsztejn-Pollack, 1973; Hasher & Thomas, 1973; Hudson & Nelson, 1986; Lehman, Mikesell, & Doherty, 1985; Merriman, Azmita, & Perlmutter, 1988; Morrison, Haith, & Kagan, 1980; Wagner, 1978; Wang, 1991; Wickelgren, 1975). This literature presents two striking features. First, note that it is a collection of one-shot studies; there are no two articles by the same investigators. Second, age comparisons of forgetting rates consistently failed to produce evidence of developmental variability. Lehman et al. (1985) aptly summarized the situation when they stated that "information is not lost more rapidly by children than by adults. Forgetting rates . . . were invariant from childhood to young adulthood" (p. 27), and Merriman et al. (1988) did likewise when they concluded that "acquisition and/or retrieval differences are more likely sources of memory development in early childhood than are differences in rate of forgetting" (p. 473). Obviously, this explains the noncumulative nature of the literature; forgetting does not develop.

This conclusion seemed so untenable that I thought that rather than accept it at face value, the possibility should at least be considered that it was some sort of procedural artifact. Could a design factor be identified that would have militated against detecting age differences? I found three candidates that were common across most studies: (a) recognition insensitivity; (b) ceiling effects in retention; and (c) stages-of-learning confounds.

Concerning recognition insensitivity, recognition tests were the memory measures in most studies. A familiar property of recognition tests and one that has been commented on in many articles (e.g., Brown & Scott, 1971; Ornstein & Corsale, 1979; Stein & Mandler, 1975) is that they display minimal age variability. Other things being equal, then, administering recognition tests of *any* memory ability stacks the deck against observing age trends. Concerning ceiling effects, by definition age differences in forgetting cannot be detected unless a study first produces substantial performance declines between Step 1 and Step 2. For a confluence of reasons (e.g., retention intervals of 2 days or less), however, declines were modest in most studies. In some (e.g., Morrison et al., 1980), declines were not significant in most conditions. Concerning stages-of-learning confounds, the acquisition sessions of these studies always consisted of a fixed number of learning trials, with a single trial being the norm. Because the rate at which information is learned increases as development proceeds, this factor necessarily confounds age with level of learning at the end of Step 1. This is problematical because, of course, level of learning might be related to subsequent forgetting. In particular, if the initial "primary" things that children learn about the target information are more resistant to forgetting than the subsequent "secondary" things that they learn, age differences in forgetting rates will be masked: Even if older children forget at a slower rate than younger children, a larger proportion of what they learn consists of more forgettable "secondary" information (Brainerd, Kingma, & Howe, 1985). Empirically, this is supported by the fact that forgetting curves are negatively accelerated; performance drops more rapidly at first than it does later on.

Eliminating these problems has been one objective of a series experiments that Reyna, Howe, and I have reported (Brainerd & Reyna, 1990a, 1991, in press; Brainerd, Reyna, Howe, & Kingma, 1990; Howe, 1991; Howe & Brainerd, 1989; Howe, Courage, & Bryant-Brown, 1993; Reyna, 1992; Reyna & Kiernan, 1994). The recognition insensitivity problem has been dealt with by administering some form of recall (associative, cued, free, serial) as the memory measure. The ceiling effects problem has been dealt with by lengthening the retention interval to at least 1 week, although intervals in the 2- to 6-week range have also been used. The level of learning problem has been dealt with by switching to criterion learning; whenever forgetting was compared across age levels, subjects from all age levels first learned the material to a perfect-recall criterion.[1]

Experiments incorporating these modifications have all shown the same thing: Forgetting develops. What is more, ontogenesis follows the intuitive pattern: Forgetting rates decrease between early childhood and young adulthood, rapidly at first and then more slowly, remain stable throughout much of the adult years, and then begin to increase again during late adulthood. Some illustrative data are shown in Fig. 9.1. In Panel A, forgetting rates from the five treatment combinations in Experiments 1 and 2 of Brainerd et al. (1990) are plotted. The memory task in all data sets was free recall, the retention interval was 2 weeks, and because the target material had been learned to criterion, forgetting rate was simply the error probability during the retention session. Note that this probability was twice as high in 7-year-olds as in 11-year-olds. In Panel B, life-span forgetting rates—for elementary schoolers, young adults, and aged adults—are plotted for the eight treatment combinations in Experiments 3 and 4 of Brainerd et al. (1990). Here, the memory task was associative recall, and the retention interval was 1 week. As can be seen, forgetting rates decreased by roughly half from elementary school (mean age = 9 years, 4 months) to young adulthood (mean age = 19 years, 6 months) and then increased by roughly the same amount between

---

[1]Two points should be mentioned in connection with the criterion-learning modification. First, although the other two modifications can easily be incorporated in more naturalistic studies of memory for everyday events, this one obviously cannot be. Even in naturalistic studies, however, some statistical control of the confounding effects of levels of learning can be achieved using analysis of covariance. As Reyna and Kiernan (1994) pointed out, as long as there is an initial memory test and a delayed test, performance on the initial test can be treated as a level-of-learning index and entered as a covariate when analyzing for age differences in forgetting rates. Second, it might perhaps be argued (e.g., following proposals in McGeogh, 1942, and Underwood, 1954) that once age differences in levels of learning are controlled, age differences in forgetting rates would disappear. This has proven not to be the case. Indeed, recent criterion-learning studies have revealed a surprising lack of relationship between age differences in learning rates and age differences in forgetting rates (Brainerd & Reyna, 1990a).

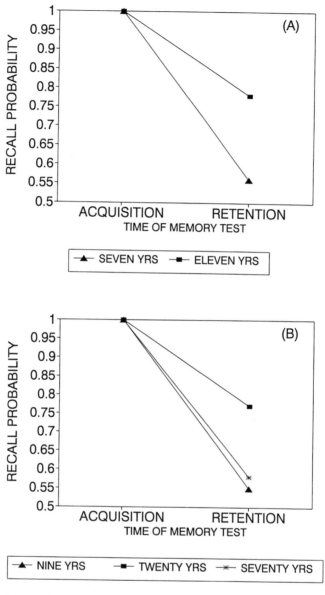

FIG. 9.1. Developmental trends in forgetting rates. Panel A contains 7- and 11-year-old data from Experiments 1 and 2 of Brainerd et al. (1990). Panel B contains life-span data from Experiments 3 and 4 of Brainerd et al. (1990).

young adulthood and late adulthood (mean age = 71 years, 8 months). Therefore, although we may not yet understand the process in theoretical terms, at least it is possible to demonstrate developmental changes in forgetting under certain conditions.

A potential problem with those conditions is that the modification that was adopted to avoid confounding age with level of learning, criterion learning, creates two interpretative difficulties. Those difficulties have been examined in some recent experiments, and, as yet, neither has proved to be problematical.

The first concerns the potential confounding influence of age differences in *learning rate* on age differences in forgetting rate. A familiar conjecture about forgetting is that individual differences in learning rate predict individual differences in forgetting rate; subjects who learn more slowly forget more rapidly (e.g., McGeoch, 1942; Underwood, 1954). Because, as a group, younger children will learn almost anything more slowly that older children, learning rate is confounded with age in a criterion design, which may explain the observed age differences in forgetting rates. For standard measures of age (e.g., months since birth), forgetting rate (e.g., mean errors on retention tests), and learning rate (e.g., mean trial of last error at acquisition), any one of the models in Panel A of Fig. 9.2 might account for the data. Model 1 is the most worrisome because it assumes that there is no relationship between age forgetting. Instead, age causes learning rate to increase, which then causes forgetting rate to decease. On the other hand, Models 2 and 3 assume that there are separate age $\rightarrow$ forgetting rate and age $\rightarrow$ learning rate relationships, with Model 3 adding a learning rate $\rightarrow$ forgetting rate relationship. Reyna and I conducted comparative evaluations of these three models (Brainerd & Reyna, 1990a) using path analysis. With the data of two experiments involving 7- and 11-year-olds, we found that Model 2 gave the best overall fit and that Model 1 gave consistently unacceptable fits. We concluded that "path analyses uniformly favored models . . . that postulated independent causal paths from development to forgetting rates" (p. 201).

The second difficulty is that this conclusion might itself be an artifact of failure to control individual differences in *opportunities to learn*. Learning rate and learning opportunities (e.g., number of learning trials at acquisition) are necessarily correlated in a criterion design; the slower learning is, the more learning opportunities will be provided prior to reaching criterion. Further, there is an intuitive relationship between learning opportunities and forgetting rate; more learning opportunities ought to translate into slower forgetting. If we add the other intuitive relationship mentioned earlier, that a faster learning rate means a slower forgetting rate, it is evident that the inverse relationship between learning rate and learning opportunities could have masked a learning rate $\rightarrow$ forgetting rate relationship in

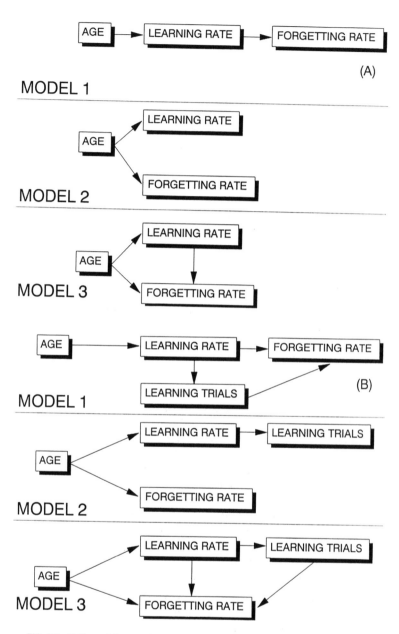

FIG. 9.2. Path models specifying potential causal relationships between age, forgetting rate, and other variables. Panel A presents three path models for age, forgetting rate, and learning rate (Brainerd & Reyna, 1990a). Panel B presents three path models for age, forgetting rate, learning rate, and opportunities to learn (Brainerd & Reyna, in press).

Brainerd and Reyna's (1990a) experiments. Specifically, slower learning rates might indeed mean faster forgetting rates, but the additional learning opportunities that were provided to slow learners might have compensated for their tendency to forget more rapidly. Therefore, any one of the three models in Panel B of Fig. 9.2, each of which is generated from the corresponding model in Panel A by adding a learning rate → learning opportunities relationship, might explain Brainerd and Reyna's results. Model 1 is again the most worrisome because it assumes that age differences in forgetting rates are artifacts of correlated age differences in learning rates and learning opportunities. Reyna and I evaluated these models in two further experiments in which age, forgetting rate, learning rate, and learning opportunities were all entered as variables in path analyses (Brainerd & Reyna, 1995). The results were consistent with our earlier findings in that the best-fitting model was Model 2. Therefore, there were independent age → learning rate and age → forgetting rate causal paths, but there was no relationship between individual differences in forgetting rate and individual differences in either learning rate or learning opportunities.

Summing up, although early developmental studies failed to detect age variability in forgetting rates, their designs included factors that would tend to obscure such variability. When those factors are eliminated, forgetting rates are found to decline markedly between early childhood and young adulthood and then to increase in late adulthood. The counterargument that this finding is a by-product of correlated developmental differences in learning rate or learning opportunities or both has not received support in follow-up studies.

The ramifications for childhood memory suggestibility seem to be straightforward. Age differences in forgetting should set the stage for age differences in memory suggestibility. Because memories for original events will normally become more suggestible as they fade, the basal developmental pattern should be that suggestibility effects decrease during birth-to-young-adult development and increase during young-adult-to-aged-adult development. Further, given what we now think we know about the ontogenesis of forgetting, perhaps the most defensible conclusion about developmental suggestibility studies that fail to produce this pattern is that, like early developmental studies of forgetting, their procedures are somehow insensitive to age change. Conveniently, basic research has identified some design variables that minimize age differences. However, this should not be taken to imply that such variables, and others that have been identified in suggestibility studies (e.g., see Stein, chapter 2, this volume), are just methodological niceties. On the contrary, these variables are theoretically and pragmatically significant because they establish boundary conditions for the development of suggestibility.

DOES REMINISCENCE DEVELOP?

Imagine that you are attending a high school reunion and your former world history teacher asks if you remember who said, "In the course of my life I have often had to eat my words, and I must confess that I have always found it a wholesome diet." At first, you cannot recollect the name, although the remark sounds familiar. A little later, your teacher asks if you have remembered yet, and you exclaim, "Churchill!" This is the phenomenon of reminiscence.

In retention studies with adults, reminiscence and what used to be called *the reminiscence effect* (e.g., Postman, 1978), but has recently been called *hypermnesia* (e.g., Erdelyi & Stein, 1981), are ubiquitous phenomena. *Reminiscence* refers to the fact that when multiple memory tests are administered during a retention session, a few items that could not be recalled on the first test are recovered on one or more of the subsequent tests. Of course, the opposite phenomenon, which I shall call *deminiscence*, occurs too; items recalled on the first test sometimes cannot be recalled on one or more of the subsequent tests.[2] Finally, *hypermnesia* is simply a positive difference between the rates of reminiscence (recalling items later that could not be recalled earlier) and deminiscence (failing to recall items later that were recalled earlier). If reminiscence is greater than deminiscence, performance will necessarily improve—thus, hypermnesia.

There are two questions about such phenomena that bear on childhood memory suggestibility. First, can reminiscence be demonstrated in children, especially young children, and do reminiscence rates vary with age? If reminiscence is present even in young children, specific memories that have been impaired by suggestion can perhaps be reconstituted and lead to accurate testimony through repeated questioning. Second, can hypermnesia be demonstrated in children, especially young children, and do hypermnesia rates vary with age? If hypermnesia is present even in young children, the general effects of both forgetting and suggestion on testimonial competence can potentially be ameliorated via repeated questioning. This is not to suggest, however, that this will be easy in most situations, or that repeated questioning might not also distort children's memories (Brainerd & Orstein, 1991).

Reminiscence

There has been some controversy over the answer to this question. To begin with, all recent studies that have (a) administered multiple memory tests during the retention session and (b) demonstrated age differences in for-

---

[2]Logically, there is a third possibility—*false reminiscence*. That is, information could be recovered on later tests that was not recalled on the first test but that is incorrect (i.e., intrusions). I do not consider this possibility because false reminiscence appears to be rare, particularly in children (Howe et al., 1994).

getting have also demonstrated some reminiscence in children, including young children. In the experiments that Reyna, Howe, and I have reported, the youngest children studied have ranged from Grade 2 down to preschool. With a variety of materials (words, pictures, sentences, stories) and a variety of retention tests (associative recall, cued recall, free recall), children within this age range have been found to recover information on subsequent retention tests that they did not recover on initial tests.

However, there is controversy concerning developmental trends in reminiscence rates. On the one hand, some investigators (e.g., Brainerd, 1991; Brainerd et al., 1990; Poole & White, 1991) claimed to have found that reminiscence rates are age invariant. On the other hand, certain other investigators (e.g., Cassel & Bjorklund, 1995; Poole & White, 1993) claimed to have found that reminiscence rates increase between early childhood and young adulthood. When one examines the data on which these claims are based, however, the inconsistency vanishes because different aspects of retention performance are being used. The age-invariance conclusion is based on the growth of recall accuracy across a series of retention tests— hypermnesia, in other words—but the age-variability conclusion is based on the conditional probability of recalling an item on Test i given that it was not recalled on Test i-1—reminiscence, in other words. I now summarize what is known about reminiscence, postponing discussion of hypermnesia until the next section.

There is consistent support for the claim that reminiscence increases between early childhood and young adulthood. As illustrations, I exhibit the mean probabilities of recalling an item on later retention tests that was not recalled on earlier tests for three experiments; two reported by Howe, Kelland, Bryant-Brown, and Clark (1992) and a third reported by Cassel and Bjorklund (1995), in Fig. 9.3. Both of Howe et al.'s experiments involved associative recall. In Experiment 1 (Panel A), the probability of recalling an item on a 16-day retention test that was not recalled on a 2-day test was computed for two age levels, as was the probability of recalling an item on a 30-day test that had not been recalled on a 16-day test. It can be seen that both probabilities were higher for older children (10 years) than for younger children (7 years). Experiment 2 (Panel B) was similar, but the two age groups were older. Again, it can be seen that reminiscence probabilities were higher for older subjects (20 years) than for younger subjects (13 years). Finally, data from Cassel and Bjorklund's experiment appear in Panel C. Their design involved administering cued and free-recall tests to subjects from three age levels at the end of acquisition, 1 week later, and 6 weeks later. Reminiscence probabilities were then computed for the immediate versus 1-week test and the 1-week versus 6-week test. As can be seen, the former probability increased between age 6 and 8 and between age 8 and 20, and the latter probability increased between age 8 and 20 but not between age 6 and 8.

CROSS-SESSION REMINISCENCE RATES FOR HOWE ET AL.'S EXPERIMENT 1

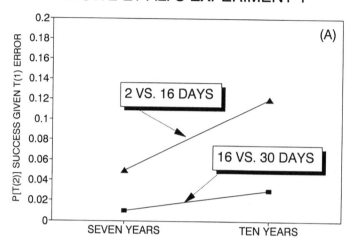

CROSS-SESSION REMINISCENCE RATES FOR HOWE ET AL.'S EXPERIMENT 2

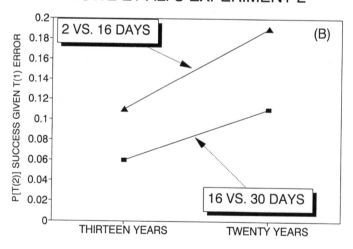

FIG. 9.3. *(Continued)*

CROSS-SESSION REMINISCENCE RATES FOR CASSEL AND BJORKLUND'S SUBJECTS

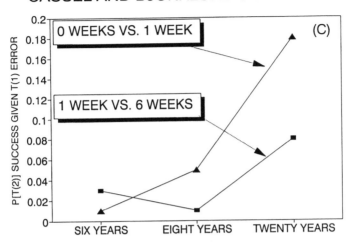

FIG. 9.3. Developmental trends in reminiscence rates. Panel A contains data from Experiment 1 of Howe et al. (1992). Panel B contains data from Experiment 2 of Howe et al. (1992). Panel C contains data from Cassel and Bjorklund (1995).

To investigate the development of reminiscence in greater detail, Howe and I reanalyzed our corpus of retention studies. The various experiments cover most of the life span, from age 4 to 70. Although a variety of materials were learned during the acquisition session and different types of recall tests were administered during the retention session, all of the experiments shared an important property: At least four independent memory tests for the target material were administered during the retention session. We thought that it would be instructive to compute the overall reminiscence rate (mean probability of correct recall of an item on Test i given incorrect recall on Test i-1) and the overall deminiscence rate (mean probability of incorrect recall of an item on Test i given correct recall on Test i-1) for our data sets. An interesting developmental pattern emerged, which is shown in Fig. 9.4. There, mean reminiscence and deminiscence probabilities have been plotted for six age levels (4, 6, 8, 12, 20, and 70) using all the data sets for those age levels. The observed pattern for reminiscence was that it remained constant until age 8, then it increased substantially between age 8 and age 20, and then it decreased by roughly the same amount between age 20 and age 70. The observed pattern for deminiscence was that it decreased dramatically between the ages of 4 and 8, reached near-floor levels by age 8, and remained there until age 70. The fact that these patterns are so different suggests the interesting possibility that reminiscence and deminiscence are not opposite sides of the same coin, but are dissociated processes that are controlled by different developmental factors.

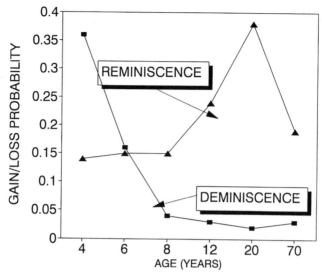

FIG. 9.4. Life-span patterns of reminiscence and deminiscence across sequences of long-term retention tests.

Hypermnesia

Available data also provide a clear answer to the second question, although
it seems counterintuitive at first. In the first place, hypermnesia has been
demonstrated in children as well as adults. In fact, hypermnesia appears to
be the norm in younger and older children, as well as adults, because all
studies that have detected age differences in forgetting have detected hypermnesia at all age levels (for a review, see Howe et al., 1992). Some
illustrative life-span trends based on three of the experiments reported by
Brainerd et al. (1990) are displayed in Fig. 9.5. In two of the experiments
(five data sets in all), 7- and 11-year-olds were administered a series of four
free-recall tests 2 weeks after they had learned lists of words to a perfect-
recall criterion. The mean proportions of correctly recalled items, pooled
across data sets, are plotted by age level and retention test in Panel A. At
both age levels, accuracy recovers steadily between the first and last test.
In the other experiment (eight data sets in all), 20- and 70-year-olds were
administered a series of four associative-recall tests 1 week after having
learned lists of word or picture pairs to a perfect-recall criterion. Again, at
both age levels, accuracy recovers steadily between the first and last test.
Therefore, although data on children younger than age 7 are as yet scarce,
it appears that hypermnesia is present fairly early in development and that
it is the norm throughout most of the life span.

The answer to the question of whether or not hypermnesia develops
seems apparent in Fig. 9.5: The recovery curves for different age levels are
parallel—that is, the amount recovered between the first and last test is the

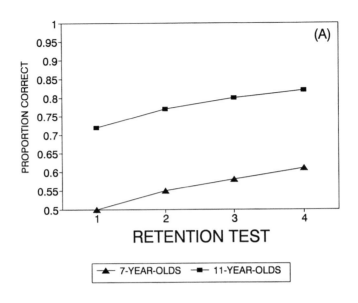

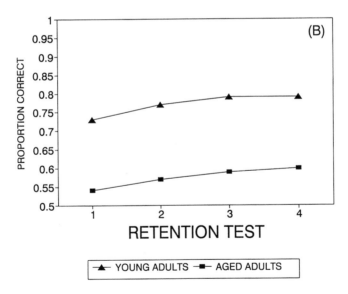

FIG. 9.5. Developmental trends in hypermnesia rates. Panel A contains 7- and 11-year-old data from Experiments 1 and 2 of Brainerd et al. (1990). Panel B contains 20- and 70-year-old data from Experiment 4 of Brainerd et al. (1990).

same for younger and older subjects. This pattern is quite typical of recent developmental studies of long-term retention (for reviews, see Brainerd et al., 1990; Howe et al., 1992; Reyna, 1992). Age invariance in hypermnesia seems incredible in light of the findings for reminiscence and deminiscence (Fig. 9.4). We know from those findings that the probability a forgotten item will be recovered on a later retention test increases with age during childhood and that the probability a remembered item will be lost on a later retention test decreases during this same age. Therefore, should it not be the case that the magnitude of recovery across retention tests increases with age during childhood?

The answer is not necessarily because the size of the hypermnesia effect is jointly dependent on the reminiscence/deminiscence rates and the forgetting rate. By definition, an item cannot be reminiscenced (and contribute to the hypermnesia effect) unless it is first forgotten. So, although older children's reminiscence rates are higher and their deminiscence rates are lower than younger children's, which favors age increases in hypermnesia, their forgetting rates are lower, which favors age decreases in hypermnesia (because the amount of forgotten information that is available to be reminisced is smaller). Therefore, the fact that amount of recovery across retention tests has tended to be equivalent for different age levels is not as deeply perplexing as it first seems. There are two sets of factors that contribute to hypermnesia rates and they vary in opposite directions with age.

Perhaps the best way to summarize the development is to make two statements. First, if hypermnesia is defined as the number of forgotten items that are recovered across retention tests, then hypermnesia has generally been found to be age invariant by this measure. However, this definition confounds age variability in reminiscence/deminiscence rates with age variability in forgetting rates. Second, if hypermnesia is defined as the proportion of forgotten items that are recovered across retention tests, then hypermnesia has been found to vary with age by this measure, increasing between early childhood and young adulthood and decreasing thereafter. This can be seen by merely replotting the data in Fig. 9.5 using relative, rather than absolute, increase in proportion recalled as the dependent variable. These replots are displayed in Fig. 9.6.

DOES MEMORY-TEST INOCULATION DEVELOP?

The issue of what sorts of factors inoculate memories against forgetting has, of course, figured prominently adult retention experiments. A well-known outcome of such experiments is that mere memory testing is a surprisingly effective inoculator. Forgetting is reduced if subjects' memory for the target material is tested sometime between exposure and the administration of

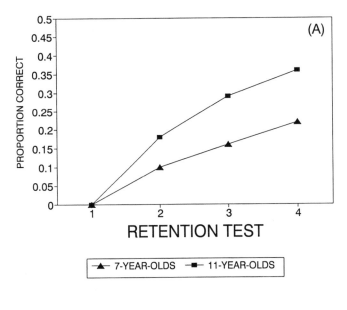

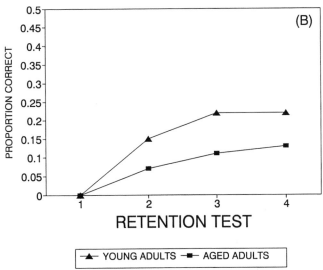

FIG. 9.6. Developmental trends in hypermnesia rates replotted as proportionate increases in recall. Panel A contains replotted data from Panel A of Fig. 9.5. Panel B contains replotted data from Panel B of Fig. 9.5.

retention measures (e.g., Runquist, 1983). The magnitude of this effect can be quite large when memory tests are administered immediately after exposure, and certain types of tests produce more inoculation than others. As Poole and White (1991) and Brainerd and Ornstein (1991) pointed out, these facts are of potential significance to child testimony. Although we have no control over the information to which child witnesses have been exposed, we are able to exercise considerable control over the timing, frequency, and content of forensic memory tests. Therefore, forensic interviewing methods could be materially improved if we knew whether memory-test inoculation effects are present in children as well as adults.

Poole and White (1995) presented a review of eyewitness memory studies that bear on this issue. Here I simply summarize their conclusions and direct readers to their article for supporting evidence. Poole and White concluded that although some studies have failed to detect memory-test inoculation effects with children, there is:

> strong corroborating evidence that multiple testing sessions preserve memories over time. Although children may benefit less than adults when early interviews do not encourage them to report details, there is no evidence that frequent retelling is more likely to introduce inaccuracies than other techniques for supporting delayed testimony such as the use of dolls to minimize verbal demands . . . predictions derived from basic research about the impact of multiple interviews on forgetting have been confirmed in studies of eyewitness memory. (p. 34)

In addition to the studies reviewed by Poole and White, two more recent articles, one by Brainerd et al. (1995) and the other by Warren and Hagood (1995), provide evidence of memory-test inoculation effects in children.

Brainerd et al. (1995) reported some experiments in which children's (5-year-olds' and 8-year-olds') recognition memory for words (concrete nouns) was tested immediately after presentation and 1 week later. One factor in their designs was whether words (both targets *and distractors*) that appeared on the 1-week recognition test had also appeared on the immediate test; some had, others had not. Relevant results are shown in Fig. 9.7. The retention data for targets (i.e., words that were actually presented) are plotted separately by age level for two types of targets, low learning (one presentation) and high learning (three presentations). Three findings are apparent. First, a prior-memory test reduced forgetting at both age levels; children recognized previously tested targets at higher rates than previously untested targets. Second, in addition to being present in the youngest children, the magnitude of the inoculation effect was about the same at the two age levels. Third, the inoculation effect interacted with level of learning. Items that had been presented once derived less benefit from a memory test than items that had been presented three times.

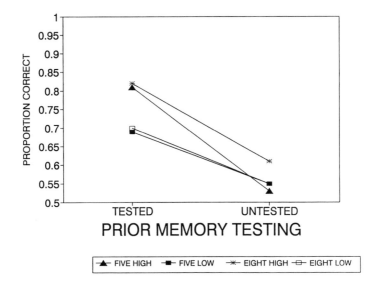

FIG. 9.7. Memory-test inoculation effects for 5- and 8-year-olds averaged across the experiments reported by Brainerd et al. (1995).

These data look promising, but their forensic interpretation requires consideration of children's performance on distractor items. Although memory testing increases the rate at which children correctly recognize targets on retention tests, it might also increase the rate at which children *falsely* recognize distractors. If so, forensically speaking, memory testing would be a two-edged sword; it would preserve true memories but at the expense of encouraging false memories. Some recent experiments by Brainerd and Reyna (in press) showed that this is, indeed, a concern with certain types of memory tests. In our experiments, 5- and 8-year-old children studied some materials, took an initial recognition test, and then took another recognition test 1 week later. On the second test, false recognition rates were higher for distractors that had appeared on the first test than for distractors that had not; a mere recognition test seemed to create false memories. This was particularly true when these distractors were conceptually related to studied targets, as they normally are in a forensic interview. Other research (Brainerd, Reyna, & Brandse, in press) has shown that the persistence over time of these test-induced false memories can equal or exceed that of true memories.

Of course, the effects of memory testing could be different for the types of materials that are used in memory suggestibility studies of children. Warren and Hagood's (1995) study partly addresses this concern because it used a standard memory suggestibility design in which degree of prior memory testing was manipulated. Children (9-year-olds) and young adults (22-year-olds) first viewed a short video of domestic events involving a mother and two children. In two of the conditions, the procedure either terminated immediately after the video (no-test), or the subjects received free-recall tests for the events in the video (test). One week later, both groups were questioned about the events. Recall accuracy for previously tested and untested children were 78% and 70%, respectively, and 79% and 66% for previously tested and untested adults. However, this experiment does not provide direct evidence on the tendency of memory testing to induce false memories. Intrusions are rare on initial free-recall tests, especially in recall of naturalistic events by children (Cassel & Bjorklund, 1995). Therefore, free recall does do not supply the sort of controlled, baseline index of false-memory responses that is provided by distractors in recognition tests.

Summing up, there is consistent support for the conclusion that memory testing reduces forgetting of target events, in children and well as adults and in suggestibility designs as well as in standard retention designs. The evidence with respect to whether testing may also introduce false memories that are then preserved on retention tests is less consistent. Poole and White (1995) stated that the bulk of the literature does not support this proposal. Some recent studies (Brainerd & Reyna, in press; Brainerd et al., in press) are supportive, however. The prudent conclusion is that this remains an open question.

FUZZY-TRACE THEORY, FORGETTING, AND SUGGESTIBILITY

The focus up to this point has been squarely on empirical matters. I conclude by considering some issues of a more theoretical nature that grow out of fuzzy-trace theory's (FTT) account of childhood forgetting and suggestibility. Although FTT is chiefly a theory of the relationship between memory development and the development of higher reasoning abilities, certain of its core assumptions have been used to analyze the development of forgetting. Those same assumptions have been used to explain memory suggestibility in children (e.g., Cassel & Bjorklund, 1995; Ceci & Bruck, 1993; Poole & White, 1993). A comprehensive account of suggestibility from the perspective of FTT appears in a recent article by Reyna (1995). The remarks that follow derive mainly from that source.

Four assumptions have been used in connection with the development of forgetting (for fuller treatments, see Brainerd & Reyna, 1990b, 1993; Reyna & Brainerd, 1991, 1992). First, during the acquisition session of a retention experiment, subjects deposit different representations of individual inputs. Of particular interest, they store dissociated records of the surface forms of inputs (*verbatim traces*) and of various senses, patterns, and meanings that those inputs instantiate (*gist traces*). Our definition of *input* is purposely broad, and has been applied to most of the types of information that subjects process in everyday life (words, pictures, connected discourse, etc.). Following Mandler (1980), verbatim traces may be formed by integrating surface information about an input (e.g., its visual appearance, its auditory properties) with relevant contextual cues to achieve a unified, reality-grounded representation of that experience. Gist traces, on the other hand, are formed by using inputs as retrieval cues to access concepts in long-term memory and then to assign episodic interpretations to those concepts. For instance, the statement "Farmer Brown, owns seven cows, five horses, and three sheep," cues the retrieval of the concept "most," which is assigned the episodic interpretation "cows." (It cues the retrieval of other concepts too, naturally, many of which are not numerical.)

Second, other things being equal, gist memories are harder to store than verbatim memories. Perhaps the most obvious reason is that verbatim memories represent information has actually been encoded, whereas as gist memories represent information that must be retrieved on the basis of what is encoded and then interpreted (Brainerd & Gordon, 1994). Third, other things being equal, although verbatim traces are easier to store, they are harder to retain than gist memories. Here, an important reason seems to be that verbatim traces are more sensitive to sources of retroactive interference (Reyna, 1992, 1995). Fourth, developmentally, there is age variability in the spread between verbatim versus gist storage rates and in the spread between verbatim versus gist retention rates. Both spreads tend to narrow between early childhood and young adulthood. The storage differential narrows because, with age, more concepts obviously can be accessed in long-term memory, and children become better practiced at retrieving and interpreting them (Brainerd & Gordon, 1994). The retention differential narrows because, with age, children become less sensitive to sources of retroactive interference (Brainerd & Reyna, 1993).

How do these ideas bear on the development of forgetting, reminiscence, and memory-test inoculation? Taking forgetting first, the designs of retention experiments imply that forgetting should be more a matter of verbatim failure than of gist failure. Tasks that ensure the storage of relevant gist at acquisition will necessarily eliminate age variability in this factor. This is what happened in the retention experiments described earlier. To begin with, as is the case in most child memory research, the learned information always consisted of familiar materials (concrete nouns, pictures, sentences describing everyday events) for which even the youngest children can access many relevant concepts in their long-term memories. (Given a list of concrete nouns in which the words blue, cow, and chair appear, for instance, even preschoolers are well aware that blue is a color, cow is an animal, and chair is a type of furniture—Bjorklund, 1995.) Further, learning was always to a perfect-recall criterion. Therefore, even if the younger children in these studies had difficulty accessing and interpreting relevant concepts on any given trial, they were given many opportunities to do so. In short, by virtue of familiar materials and criterion learning, the acquisition sessions of these studies tended to eliminate gist storage as a factor. Consequently, forgetting should be more a matter of verbatim failure than of gist failure at all age levels because, once stored, gist traces are easier to retain than verbatim traces.

That is what was found in some model-based decompositions of those trends. Howe and I developed some stochastic models that measure the probability that recall errors at the start of a retention session are due to verbatim failure versus gist failure (Brainerd, 1986; Howe & Brainerd, 1989). These models are three-state Markov processes—consisting of an initial state V (verbatim-memory failure) in which errors occur with probability 1, an intermediate state G (gist-memory failure) in which errors occur with some probability $0 < p < 1$, and a terminal state R (no memory failure) in which errors occur with probability 0. These models allow one to estimate the respective rates of verbatim and gist forgetting by simply calculating the proportions of items that occupy states V and G at the start of a retention session. Estimation of these rates for the data of developmental retention studies has produced two results. First, at all age levels, errors on retention tests were more apt to be due to verbatim failure than to gist failure. Second, the differential between the two processes remained constant during child-to-young-adult development because both types of forgetting declined at the same rate, but the differential increased during young-adult-to-aged-adult development because verbatim failure increased, whereas gist failure remained constant. Both results are illustrated in Fig. 9.8, where verbatim and gist failure rates are plotted by age for some life-span data sets in Brainerd et al. (1990, Experiments 3 and 4).

Turning to the development of reminiscence and memory-test inoculation, model-based analyses also bear on such questions. Concerning reminiscence, if verbatim memories become inaccessible more rapidly than gist, it is natural to predict (a) that reminiscence is more likely to be due to reconstruction from still-accessible gist than to restorage of inaccessible verbatim memories and (b) that developmental trends are therefore primarily due to age changes in gist-based reconstruction abilities. We were able to examine these predictions as well, because our models contain parameters that measure both the probability of reconstituting failed verbatim traces across a series of retention tests and the probability of reconstructing items from still-accessible gist. The results of the analyses have supported both predictions. Concerning memory-test inoculation, if forgetting has been mainly due to verbatim failure in developmental studies of retention, it is natural to predict (a) that memory tests primarily inoculate verbatim memory and (b) that developmental trends are therefore primarily due to age changes in the tendency of verbatim memory to benefit from inoculation.

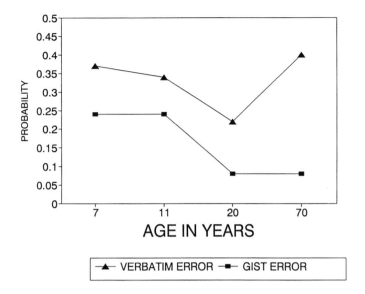

FIG. 9.8. Developmental trends in verbatim and gist forgetting rates. These data are from Experiments 3 and 4 of Brainerd et al. (1990).

Ideas of this sort were proposed by Poole and White (1995) in their literature review. Some qualitative findings that they described (e.g., that inoculation effects in eyewitness designs seem to be larger for peripheral details of events than for central themes) support such proposals. However, model-based analyses, in which the effects of prior memory tests on verbatim failure rates versus gist failure rates are independently measured, have not yet been reported in this literature.

All of this brings us to the more specific implications of this analysis of forgetting for the suggestibility of children's eyewitness memories. Reyna (1995) pointed out that childhood memory suggestibility experiments are quintessential verbatim-interference designs. Consider three facts about the designs of such experiments. First, the material to which children are exposed during acquisition sessions consists of familiar events (live or filmed; see other chapters in this volume) that follow some script that is well known to children (going to a restaurant, getting ready for school in the morning, going to the doctor, etc.) and that contains some incidental details (e.g., french fries were eaten, a red hat was worn, the eyes were examined) that are to be foci of subsequent misinformation. Like developmental retention studies, the use of familiar scripted events means that age differences in gist storage will be minimized, leaving verbatim failure as the chief source of memory suggestibility. Second, during the misinformation session, information is presented that is designed to interfere with memories of target details (e.g., it is stated that hash browns were eaten, that a green hat was worn, that the ears were examined) but not with the gist of the events. Third, during the retention session, children are administered tests that tap memory for the original incidental details.

Therefore, it is not hard to see that memory suggestibility designs have a verbatim slant and that the age trends that have been observed in such studies may be best explained in terms of what we know about developmental changes in the sensitivity of verbatim memories to retroactive interference. Reyna (1995) went on to point out that this notion helps straighten out some of the empirical disputes in this literature (e.g., over the effects of different memory tests, over the effects of different materials). Perhaps the most contentious one is what Howe (1991) called the now-you-see-it-now-you-don't quality of childhood misinformation effects. Some studies (e.g., Zaragoza, Dahlgren, & Muench, 1992) have failed to produce suggestibility effects (and therefore age trends) in children, whereas other studies (e.g., Ceci & Bruck, 1993) have produced robust effects and have found that they become less pronounced between early childhood and young adulthood. If suggestibility designs have a verbatim slant, an obvious conjecture would be that the former studies incorporated factors that would tend to protect verbatim memories against retroactive inference. Reyna noted that the interval between event presentation and misinformation would be an especially critical factor because the susceptibility of verbatim memories to retroactive interference increases as those memories are forgotten. Consistent with this observation, she found that studies that had failed to produce suggestibility effects shared a key property: Misinformation was presented during the acquisition session, a few minutes after the to-be-remembered events had been encoded and before there had been sufficient time for verbatim memories to undergo forgetting. In contrast, she found that studies that had produced suggestibility effects had delayed misinformation until a day or more after the acquisition session.

I conclude with a note of caution. On the one hand, it appears that the foregoing analysis can be productive in helping us achieve some preliminary theoretical understanding of the data of childhood suggestibility experiments. However, it must be stressed that, as yet, applications of procedures (e.g., mathematical models) that allow one to precisely measure the relative contributions of different memory processes to suggestibility have been scarce. To date, only two such applications have been reported, the first by Howe (1991) and the second by Marche (1993). In line with the foregoing analysis, misinformation effects were concentrated in parameters that measure verbatim-memory failure (falling back to State V) rather than gist-memory failure (falling back to State G). In both studies, however, misinformation effects were small, and they were not reliable in most conditions. Firm conclusions must therefore await the application of such measurement techniques to more satisfactory data sets.

REFERENCES

Bartlett, F. C. (1932). *Remembering: A study in experimental and social psychology.* Cambridge, England: Cambridge University Press.

Berch, D. B., & Evans, R. (1973). Decision processes in children's recognition memory. *Journal of Experimental Child Psychology, 16,* 148–164.

Bjorklund, D. F. (1995). *Children's thinking.* Pacific Grove, CA: Brooks/Cole.

Brainerd, C. J. (1986, November). *Development of forgetting from long-term memory.* Paper presented at Psychonomic Society, Boston, MA.

Brainerd, C. J. (1990). Issues and questions in the development of forgetting. In C. J. Brainerd, V. F. Reyna, M. L. Howe, & J. Kingma (Eds.), The development of forgetting and reminiscence (pp. 100–109). *Monographs of the Society for Research in Child Development, 55*(3–4, Whole No. 222).

Brainerd, C. J. (1991, November). *Fuzzy-trace theory and the developmental stability of reminiscence.* Paper presented at Psychonomic Society, San Francisco, CA.

Brainerd, C. J., & Gordon, L. L. (1994). Development of verbatim and gist memory for numbers. *Developmental Psychology, 30,* 163–177.

Brainerd, C. J., Kingma, J., & Howe, M. L. (1985). On the development of forgetting. *Child Development, 56,* 1103–1119.

Brainerd, C. J., & Ornstein, P. A. (1991). Children's memory for witnessed events: The developmental backdrop. In J. Doris (Ed.), *The suggestibility of children's recollections* (pp. 10–20). Washington, DC: American Psychological Association.

Brainerd, C. J., & Reyna, V. F. (1990a). Can age x learnability interactions explain the development of forgetting? *Developmental Psychology, 26,* 194–204.

Brainerd, C. J., & Reyna, V. F. (1990b). Gist is the grist: Fuzzy-trace theory and the new intuitionism. *Developmental Review, 10,* 3–47.

Brainerd, C. J., & Reyna, V. F. (1991). Acquisition and forgetting processes in normal and learning-disabled children: A disintegration/redintegration theory. In J. E. Obrzut & G. W. Hynd (Eds.), *Advances in the neuropsychology of learning disabilities* (pp. 147–178). San Diego, CA: Academic Press.

Brainerd, C. J., & Reyna, V. F. (1993). Memory independence and memory interference in cognitive development. *Psychological Review, 100,* 42–67.

Brainerd, C. J., & Reyna, V. F. (1995). Learning rate, learning opportunities, and the development of forgetting. *Developmental Psychology, 31,* 251–263.

Brainerd, C. J., & Reyna, V. F. (in press). Mere memory testing creates false memories in children. *Developmental Psychology.*

Brainerd, C. J., Reyna, V. F., & Brandse, E. (in press). Are children's false memories more persistent than their true memories? *Psychological Science.*

Brainerd, C. J., Reyna, V. F., Howe, M. L., & Kingma, J. (1990). The development of forgetting and reminiscence. *Monographs of the Society for Research in Child Development, 55*(3–4, Whole No. 222).

Brainerd, C. J., Reyna, V. F., & Kneer, R. (1995). False-recognition reversal: When similarity is distinctive. *Journal of Memory and Language, 34,* 157–185.

Bransford, J. D., & Franks, J. J. (1971). The abstraction of linguistic ideas. *Cognitive Psychology, 2,* 331–350.

Brown, A. L., & Scott, M. S. (1971). Recognition memory for pictures in preschool children. *Journal of Experimental Child Psychology, 11,* 401–411.

Cassel, W. S., & Bjorklund, D. F. (1995). Developmental patterns of eyewitness memory and suggestibility: An ecologically based short-term longitudinal study. *Law and Human Behavior, 19,* 507–532.

Ceci, S. J., & Bruck, M. (1993). The suggestibility of the child witness: A historical review. *Psychological Bulletin, 113,* 403–439.

Dempster, F. N. (1984). Conditions affecting retention test performance: A developmental study. *Journal of Experimental Child Psychology, 37*, 65–77.

Erdelyi, M., & Stein, J. (1981). Recognition hypermnesia: The growth of recognition memory (d') over time with repeated testing. *Cognition, 5*, 283–286.

Fajnsztejn-Pollack, G. (1973). A developmental study of decay rate in long-term memory. *Journal of Experimental Child Psychology, 16*, 225–235.

Hasher, L., & Thomas, H. (1973). A developmental study of retention. *Developmental Psychology, 9*, 281.

Howe, M. L. (1991). Misleading children's story recall: Forgetting and reminiscence of the facts. *Developmental Psychology, 27*, 746–762.

Howe, M. L., & Brainerd, C. J. (1989). Development of long-term retention. *Developmental Review, 9*, 301–340.

Howe, M. L., Courage, M. L., & Bryant-Brown, L. (1993). Reinstating preschoolers' memories. *Developmental Psychology, 29*, 854–869.

Howe, M. L., Courage, M. L., & Peterson, C. (1994). How can I remember when "I" wasn't there: Long-term retention of traumatic experiences and emergence of the cognitive self. *Cognition and Consciousness, 3*, 327–355.

Howe, M. L., Kelland, A., Bryant-Brown, L., & Clark, S. L. (1992). Measuring the development of children's amnesia and hypermnesia. In M. L. Howe, C. J. Brainerd, & V. F. Reyna (Eds.), *Development of long-term retention* (pp. 56–102). New York: Springer-Verlag.

Hudson, J., & Nelson, K. (1986). Repeated encounters of a similar kind: Effects of familiarity on children's autobiographic memory. *Cognitive Development, 1*, 253–271.

Kintsch, W., Welsch, D., Schmalhofer, F., & Zimny, S. (1990). Sentence memory: A theoretical analysis. *Journal of Memory and Language, 29*, 133–159.

Marche, T. A. (1993). *On the resistance of preschoolers' memories to postevent misinformation*. Unpublished doctoral dissertation, Memorial University of Newfoundland, St. John's, Newfoundland, Canada.

Lehman, E. B., Mikesell, J. W., & Doherty, S. C. (1985). Long-term retention of information about presentation modality by children and adults. *Memory & Cognition, 13*, 21–28.

Loftus, E. F. (1979). *Eyewitness testimony*. Cambridge, MA: Harvard University Press.

Loftus, E. F., & Hoffman, H. G. (1989). Misinformation in memory: The creation of new memories. *Journal of Experimental Psychology: General, 118*, 100–104.

Mandler, G. (1980). Recognizing: The judgment of previous occurrence. *Psychological Review, 87*, 252–271.

Merriman, W. E., Azmita, M., & Perlmutter, M. (1988). Rate of forgetting in early childhood. *International Journal of Behavioral Development, 11*, 467–474.

McGeoch, J. A. (1942). *The psychology of human learning*. New York: Longmans, Green.

Morrison, F. J., Haith, M. M., & Kagan, J. (1980). Age trends in recognition memory for pictures: The effects of delay and testing procedure. *Bulletin of the Psychonomic Society, 16*, 480–483.

Ornstein, P. A., & Corsale, K. (1979). Organizational factors in children's memory. In C. R. Puff (Ed.), *Organization, structure, and memory*. New York: Academic Press.

Piaget, J. (1968). *On the development of memory and identity*. Worcester, MA: Clark University Press.

Poole, D. A., & White, L. T. (1991). Effects of question repetition on the eyewitness testimony of children and adults. *Developmental Psychology, 27*, 975–986

Poole, D. A., & White, L. T. (1993). Two years later: Effects of question repetition and retention interval on the eyewitness testimony of children and adults. *Developmental Psychology, 29*, 844–853.

Poole, D. A., & White, L. T. (1995). Tell me again and again: Stability and change in the repeated testimonies of children and adults. In M. Zaragoza, J. R. Graham, G. N. N. Hall, R. Hirschman, & Y. S. Ben-Porath, (Eds.), *Memory, suggestibility, and eyewitness testimony in children and adults* (pp. 24–43). Newbury Park, CA: Sage.

Postman, L. (1978). Picture–word differences in the acquisition and retention of paired associates. *Journal of Experimental Psychology: Human Learning and Memory, 4*, 146–157.

Reyna, V. F. (1992). Reasoning, remembering, and their relationship: Social, cognitive, and developmental issues. In M. L. Howe, C. J. Brainerd, & V. F. Reyna (Eds.), *Development of long-term retention* (pp. 103–132). New York: Springer-Verlag.

Reyna, V. F. (1995). Interference effects in memory and reasoning: A fuzzy-trace theory analysis. In F. N. Dempster & C. J. Brainerd (Eds.), *Interference and inhibition in cognition* (pp. 29–59). San Diego, CA: Academic Press.

Reyna, V. F., & Brainerd, C. J. (1991). Fuzzy-trace theory and children's acquisition of mathematical and scientific concepts. *Learning and Individual Differences, 3*, 27–60.

Reyna, V. F., & Brainerd, C. J. (1992). A fuzzy-trace theory of reasoning and remembering: Paradoxes, patterns, and parallelism. In A. F. Healy, S. Kosslyn, & R. M. Shiffrin (Eds.), *From learning processes to cognitive processes: Essays in honor of William K. Estes* (pp. 235–260). Hillsdale, NJ: Lawrence Erlbaum Associates.

Reyna, V. F., & Kiernan, B. (1994). The development of gist versus verbatim memory in sentence recognition: Effects of lexical familiarity, semantic content, encoding instructions, and retention interval. *Developmental Psychology, 30*, 178–191.

Runquist, W. N. (1983). Some effects of remembering on forgetting. *Memory & Cognition, 11*, 641–650.

Stein, N. L., & Mandler, J. M. (1975). Development of detection and recognition of orientation of geometric and real figures. *Child Development, 46*, 379–388.

Tversky, B., & Tuchin, M. (1989). A reconciliation of the evidence on eyewitness testimony: Comments on McClosky and Zaragoza. *Journal of Experimental Psychology: General, 118*, 86–91.

Underwood, B. J. (1954). Speed of learning and amount retained: A consideration of methodology. *Psychological Bulletin, 51*, 276–282.

Wagner, D. A. (1978). Memories of Morocco: The influence of age, schooling, and environment on memory. *Cognitive Psychology, 10*, 1–28.

Wang, A. Y. (1991). Assessing developmental differences in retention. *Journal of Experimental Child Psychology, 51*, 348–363.

Warren, A. R., & Hagood, P. L. (1995). Effects of timing and type of questioning on eyewitness accuracy and suggestibility. In M. Zaragoza (Ed.), *Memory, suggestibility, and eyewitness testimony in children and adults.* New York: HarperCollins.

Wickelgren, W. A. (1975). Age and storage dynamics in continuous recognition memory. *Developmental Psychology, 11*, 165–169.

Zaragoza, M. S., Dahlgren, D., & Muench, J. (1992). The role of memory impairment in children's suggestibility. In M. L. Howe, C. J. Brainerd, & V. F. Reyna (Eds.), *Development of long-term retention* (pp. 184–216). New York: Springer-Verlag.

STUDIES OF EMOTIONAL AND PAINFUL MEMORIES

10

MAKING EVERYDAY EVENTS EMOTIONAL: THE CONSTRUAL OF EMOTION IN PARENT–CHILD CONVERSATIONS ABOUT THE PAST

Robyn Fivush
Janet Kuebli
Emory University

Emotions are an integral part of our daily experiences. Although it is clearly the case that some events are substantially more emotionally arousing than others, even everyday events are emotionally toned. Moreover, the emotional tone and texture of experienced events is modulated by social and cultural "rules" or understandings of emotional experience. Although the physiological experience of emotion is certainly based on our biological heritage, the interpretation, evaluation, expression and display of emotion is constructed in social interaction. Obviously, some interpretation and evaluation of emotion occurs in the moment, as the event is being experienced and processed. However, much of emotion interpretation and evaluation is done retrospectively. As we talk about our experiences with others, these event memories come to take on particular emotional meanings. Developmentally, children are learning a great deal about culturally appropriate emotional and evaluative frameworks for interpreting their experiences through participating in conversations about the past.

In this chapter, we discuss several studies that have explored the ways in which parents discuss past emotional experiences with their preschool children, and how children are learning to understand and interpret their emotional experiences through participating in these conversations. Before presenting the data, we explicate our theoretical framework and discuss the assumptions underlying our research. At the end of the chapter, we return to the issue of the emotionality of everyday events, and discuss developmental relationships between understanding events, emotions, and self.

THEORETICAL ACCOUNTS OF EMOTIONAL EXPRESSION

Many theoretical approaches to emotions have been proposed, from more biologically based accounts derived from Darwin focusing on facial expressions (e.g., Eckman & Friesen, 1971; Izard, 1977) to various perspectives emphasizing the cognitive mechanisms underlying emotion appraisal (e.g., Arnold, 1960; Lazarus, Kanner, & Folkman, 1980). In the study of emotional development, some models claim that a set of discrete emotions is present at birth (e.g., Campos, Caplovitz, Lamb, Goldsmith, & Stenberg, 1983), whereas others trace specific emotions back to one or a few early undifferentiated states (e.g., Bridges, 1932; Sroufe, 1979). Confusion arises when various theories define emotion in different ways or focus on different aspects of emotional life. For this reason, any single theory of emotion is hard put to provide a satisfactory account for the whole of emotional life. However, one useful model for thinking about the multiple dimensions of emotion was outlined by Lewis and Michaelson (1983; Lewis, 1992a). In their scheme, five central components of emotion were discussed: emotional elicitors, receptors, states, expressions, and experiences. Emotional experience, the dimension that most centrally concerns us here, refers to how individuals phenomenologically interpret and evaluate the emotions they feel or display. Therefore, emotional experience includes insights and understandings of our own and others' emotions. In this sense, it is clear why emotional experience can be viewed as the most cognitive of emotion components. Lewis and Michaelson further hypothesized that developments in emotional experience are tied to the self-concept. That is, children need a sense of an "I" who owns and knows its own emotion states and expressions in order to experience them. Essentially, emotional experience relies on certain important cognitive capacities of introspection and self-reflection.

Social factors are equally important influences on emotional experience. According to Lewis and Michaelson, socialization plays a powerful role in shaping the content of emotional experience. Indeed, despite a compelling universality in the way facial expressions for basic emotions are labeled (Eckman & Friesen, 1971), studies also show striking differences in how cultures define, express, and evaluate emotions (e.g., Lutz, 1985; Markus & Kitayama, 1991; Matsumoto & Assar, 1992; Matsumoto, Kudoh, Scherer, & Wallbott, 1988). For example, American and Chinese people identify different types of causes for pride (Stipek, Weiner, & Li, 1989), and Americans classify sadness as an emotion, whereas in Tahiti it is regarded as a physical illness (Levy, 1984). From this perspective, emotions (or, more precisely, emotional experience) can be conceptualized as largely sociocultural constructs that function to regulate social interactions. This view has become prevalent in various disciplines, including anthropology (e.g., Lutz & White, 1986), sociology (Hochschild, 1983; Mead, 1956; Thoits, 1989) and psychology (Barrett, 1993; Halberstadt, 1991; Saarni, 1985).

Emotional experience, therefore, is embedded in a social cultural context. At the most general level, the culture provides links between specific kinds of events and specific kinds of emotion states or their expressions. Cultures also develop social conventions, in the form of display rules, for expressing one's feelings in different situations. Cultures do not entirely determine emotional experience; rather, cultures provide emotional "scripts" that highlight the kinds of events that the culture deems appropriate causes of specific emotional reactions, and how those reactions should be displayed and expressed. For example, what kinds of events induce anger versus sadness? What are the culturally appropriate ways to express these emotions? However, cultural knowledge regarding emotions is displayed in more local social interactions as well. The ways in which emotional experiences are talked about in day-to-day interactions are critical in the socialization of emotions. Indeed, a basic assumption underlying our research is that language is a primary medium for the social construal of emotional experience.

THE ROLE OF LANGUAGE IN THE SOCIALIZATION OF EMOTION

Different cultures may conceptualize aspects of emotional experience in different ways. However, culture is embodied in everyday interactions; the ways in which people behave and communicate display their cultural beliefs. It is through participating in social interactions that young children learn to be competent members of their cultural group (Cole, 1985; Rogoff, 1990). Adult–child interactions carry numerous explicit and implicit messages about culturally appropriate behavior, and much of this information is communicated through language (Schiefflin & Ochs, 1986). This is not to argue that children are always explicitly taught rules about the expression and interpretation of emotion, although as we will see later when we examine some parent–child conversations about emotion, this certainly does occur. Rather, the majority of emotional socialization occurs at a much more subtle level. The ways in which adults talk with young children about their own and others' emotional experiences gives children a great deal of information about culturally appropriate ways of expressing and interpreting emotion.

It must be emphasized that the model of emotional socialization that we are outlining does not assume that cultural rules are imposed on children. Children are clearly active agents in their own socialization (Bell & Harper, 1977; Russell & Russell, 1992). Parent–child conversations about past emotional experiences are co-constructed by the parent and child and what the child brings to these conversations plays a pivotal role. Children's memories of their own emotional experiences and how they have interpreted these experiences may or may not conform to parents' understanding (see especially Stein, Trabasso, & Liwag, 1994, for discussion of this point). However, regardless of whether or not parents and children agree on their emotional interpretations, the ways in which these conversations are structured and how parents use these conversations to inform their children, both implicitly and explicitly, about emotion, provides invaluable information for children in acquiring cultural models of emotion. In turn, these cultural understandings will come to have an important influence on how children come to construct and understand their own emotional experience. Given this model of emotional socialization, what aspects of parental talk about past emotion might be important to consider?

At the simplest level, the sheer amount of talk about emotion may be critical. Children who are exposed to a great deal of talk about emotion may come to learn that emotion is an important and salient part of experience, and that it is appropriate to share emotional experiences with others. In contrast, children who are not exposed to much talk about emotion may come to believe that emotional aspects of experience are either unimportant, or at least should not be shared with others. It may also matter how particular emotions are talked about. Are certain emotions discussed more than others? Are causes and consequences of emotions emphasized over the feeling state itself? Does the conversation focus on the child's emotions, or are others' emotions included as well? One can easily envision how adult-guided conversations about emotional experiences can inform children about which emotions are appropriate to experience and express in particular situations and why (see Lutz, 1983, and Gordon, 1989, for related arguments).

Denham, Zoller, and Couchoud (1993) have proposed three specific ways in which parents may socialize their children's understanding of emotion. *Coaching* is the most explicit avenue of socialization, and involves the parent's direct encouragement of children's emotion knowledge. This strategy involves labeling emotions and drawing attention to causes and consequences of specific emotions. In *modeling*, parents display their own emotional experiences, and, in so doing, implicitly teach their children about emotion. Finally, specific parental reactions to children's emotional displays provides *contingency* information for children. The way in which parents react to emotional displays may either encourage, discourage, or modify children's emotional displays in the future (see also Harris & Olthof, 1982; Saarni, 1985). These three strategies of emotional socialization are not mutually exclusive; in fact, most parents probably use all three strategies depending on the situation and the reasons for the emotion talk. Rather, by outlining these strategies, Denham et al. highlighted the myriad ways in which parents and children may talk about emotion, and how this talk may teach children about the experience and expression of emotion.

Mother–Child Conversations About Emotion

Recent research examining mother–child talk about emotions demonstrates that maternal talk is, indeed, related to children's developing discussion of emotional experience. Interestingly, evidence from maternal reports, diary studies, and naturalistic observations indicate that mothers and children begin talking about emotion extremely early in development, perhaps as early as 13 months of age (Beeghley, Bretherton, & Mervis, 1986; Ridgeway, Waters, & Kuczaj, 1985), suggesting that emotional experience is seen as an important topic of conversation from very early on. Not surprisingly, amount of emotion talk increases over the first few years of children's lives (Beeghley et al., 1986). Most important for our arguments, observations of spontaneous family interactions at home and during mother–child free play sessions in the laboratory indicate that those children whose mothers talk about emotions frequently discuss emotions more frequently than do children whose mothers do not talk about emotions often (Beeghley et al., 1986; Dunn, Bretherton, & Munn, 1987). In addition, frequency of maternal talk about emotion during the early preschool years predicts children's later ability to identify emotions and discuss the causes and consequences of emotional experience (Denham et al., 1993; Dunn, Brown, & Beardsall, 1991). Such findings point to individual differences in how mothers discuss past emotions with their young children, and, equally important, demonstrate that these differences have consequences for children's developing understanding of emotional experience.

Some intriguing gender differences have also been found in maternal talk about emotions. Mothers may talk about emotions more overall with daughters than with sons (Dunn et al., 1987), especially for negative emotions (Zahn-Waxler, Cole, & Barrett, 1991). Although there are no differences in emotional language used by boys and girls at 18 months of age, by 24 months of age, girls use significantly more emotion words than do boys (Dunn et al., 1987). These early gender differences mirror some gender differences found in the adult literature on emotion (see Brody, in press, for a review). In particular, women report talking about emotions more frequently than do men (Allen & Hamsher, 1974), and rate emotions as more important to them than do men (Allen & Haccoun, 1976; Balswick & Avertt, 1977).

Although these findings are provocative, we must be extremely cautious in drawing any conclusions about developmental relations between these lines of research. First of all, gender differences in early mother–child emotion talk have only been reported in a few studies (Dunn et al., 1987; Zahn-Waxler et al., 1991), and it is not always clear why other studies do not find such gender differences. One possible explanation is limited power. Because this kind of research is so time and labor-intensive, any one study often includes few subjects, which would make it difficult to find existing gender differences. A second explanation concerns the kinds of emotions examined. In many of the studies of early mother–child talk about emotion, different emotions were not examined separately; at most, emotions were categorized as positive or negative. In the adult literature, gender differences emerge most strongly when separate emotions are examined. In particular, women report experiencing and expressing more sadness than anger, whereas men report the reverse (Brody, in press). Therefore, it is critical that studies of early parent–child talk about emotion look at the ways in which different emotions are talked about in more detail (see Stein, Trabasso, & Liwag, in press, for relevant data). Finally, the developmental studies have examined only mothers; given the robust gender differences in emotional communication documented with adults, it would be instructive to examine the ways in which fathers talk to their young children as well. These are all issues that we have tried to address in our research. Nevertheless, regardless of the interpretation of the gender differences, the research on mother–child talk about emotion clearly supports the contention that emotion talk is an important avenue for emotional socialization.

Emotions About Past Events

Importantly, previous research has not always made a distinction between talk about emotions as they are occurring and talk about emotions in retrospect. Conversations about the past may be a particularly critical avenue for emotional socialization for several reasons. First, as Dunn et al. (1991) and Stern (1985) argued, talking about past emotions may allow the child some distance from the "hot" emotional experience, and thus better allow the child to reflect on and interpret emotions. Further, it is through language that events are reexperienced and reevaluated. Talking about the past allows us to make sense out of our experiences, and much of this sense making involves placing the experience in an emotional and evaluative context that defines the event's significance. Moreover, in reminiscing, parents can select particular kinds of emotional experiences to highlight with their children. Regardless of how frequently the child may actually experience and display a particular emotion, by talking about those events in which particular emotions were displayed (or by not talking about such events), parents are implicitly informing their children about the appropriateness and importance of these particular emotions in their children's lives. Therefore, the ways in which parents talk with their young children about past events, and especially about the emotional aspects of these events, is critical in children's developing representations of their own experiences.

PARENT-CHILD TALK ABOUT PAST EMOTIONS

Parents and children begin engaging in conversations about past experiences virtually as soon as children begin talking (Engel, 1986; Hudson, 1990). And as Labov (1982) and others (Miller & Sperry, 1988; Peterson & McCabe, 1983) have argued, emotion and evaluations are a critical component of these personal narratives. It is the emotional evaluation of an event that gives the experience its personal meaning (Bruner, 1990). We have begun to examine the ways in which parents structure conversations about past emotions with their preschool children in a series of studies. We are critically interested in three issues: (a) How often and what kinds of emotions do parents and children discuss when reminiscing together about the past? (b) What kind of a framework do parents provide for understanding emotional experience? (c) What are the developmental relations between parents' emotion talk and children's emotion talk over time? In the next section, we briefly describe the results of several studies addressing these questions. We then present a more in-depth descriptive analysis of conversations between two mothers and their preschool children that illustrate the ways in which parents and children construe emotional experience when talking about the past.

All of our studies are conducted in the home with white, middle-class families; all of the parents have at least some college education and the majority hold college degrees. More than half of the participating mothers work full time outside the home, and the vast majority work at least part time outside the home. Within each gender group, approximately half of the participating children are first-borns and half are later-borns. Although these demographics may limit the generalizability of our findings, it is important to study a homogeneous population so as not to confound ethnic and economic factors with individual style differences in maternal emotion talk.

Parents are told we are interested in their children's memory. We ostensibly ask parents to conduct the interviews because the child is more familiar and comfortable with the parent than a stranger. In this way, we hope to keep the parent's conversational style as natural as possible. We then ask the parent to sit with the child in a quiet place, with a tape recorder between them, and to talk together about specific past experiences. Different studies used somewhat different instructions, as described later, and these differences change the conversations to some extent, but there is still remarkable consistency in findings across these studies. Most intriguing, in all our studies we have found consistent gender differences; parents talk in different ways about emotional aspects of the past with daughters than with sons.

Given the earlier discussion about interpreting gender differences, it is important to point out that the studies reported here only examined mother-child talk about the past. However, in related studies we have found few differences between mothers and fathers in the way they talk about past emotions with their young children, but both mothers and fathers show similar patterns of gender-related talk with daughters and with sons (Adams, Kuebli, Boyle, & Fivush, in press; Kuebli & Fivush, 1992).

Spontaneous Talk About Past Emotions

In the first two studies, we simply asked mothers to discuss novel past experiences with their children; no mention was made of our interest in emotion (Fivush, 1989; Kuebli & Fivush, 1992). In both studies, families were visited in their homes for one session[1] and the mother was asked to sit quietly with her child and reminisce. In the first study, mothers were free to select whatever events they wanted with no restrictions on number or type of events discussed. In the second study, we wanted events discussed to be somewhat more comparable across families, and so we asked mothers to discuss three past events that they shared with the child, that were novel experiences and that spanned no more than a day.[2] Even with the differences in instructions, conversations averaged about 30 to 40 minutes in duration for both studies. Also, events discussed in both studies tended to be child-centered, positive experiences such as a trip to SeaWorld, the circus, or visits to or from special people, although there were several exceptions such as conversations about illness, and even death, as is described later in more detail. Only those events for which the child recalled some information were included in analyses.

Table 10.1 shows the mean number of emotion words mothers use with daughters and with sons, and the number of different, unique words mothers use. That is, some mothers may use the same emotion word, such as scared, frequently, whereas other mothers may use a greater variety of words to express this emotion, such as scared, fearful, afraid, and so on. Additionally, some mothers may discuss a wider variety of emotional experiences overall than other mothers. Frequency of emotions words used is the appropriate measure, rather than proportionalizing emotion words to some other metric such as conversational length, because the emotion socialization model we propose explicitly states that the sheer amount of emotion talk is a critical factor in children' emotional socialization. Because in our methodology length

---

[1]In Study 2, the mother–child conversation about past events was one of four sessions conducted in the home during a 2-week period. The other sessions included a father–child conversation about past events, an experimenter interviewing the child about past events, a mother–child book-reading session and a mother–child free-play session.

[2]Note that using this methodology, all the events discussed were selected by the mother, not by the child. We decided to use these instructions because our major interest was in examining how mothers structured talk about past emotions. It would be interesting to compare these conversations to conversations about events that the child selects for recall.

TABLE 10.1
Number of Emotion Words and Number of Unique
Emotion Words Used by Mothers in Study 1 and Study 2

	Number of Emotion Words	Number of Unique Words
Study 1 (age = 32–35 mos.)		
with girls ($n = 8$)	4.94	3.63
with boys ($n = 8$)	6.57	4.75
Study 2 (age = 40 mos.)		
with girls ($n = 12$)	8.33	5.50
with boys ($n = 12$)	7.18	3.73

of conversation is determined by the dyad, and not by the experimenter, length of conversation and frequency of emotion language within the conversation can be considered integral aspects of the mother's style, and should be analyzed accordingly. Even assuming that some children are exposed to more emotion talk "only" because their parents talk more in general, we still must account for the fact that these children are being exposed to this kind of talk more frequently and that frequency of exposure will have a cumulative effect on children's developing understanding of emotion.

Children in the first study were between 30 and 35 months of age, and as can be seen in Table 10.1, mothers use approximately equal numbers of emotions words with daughters and with sons. Children in the second study were a bit older; they were 40 months of age. Although the differences in conversations with sons and daughters are again quite small, there is a tendency here for mothers to use more emotion words and more unique emotion words with daughters than with sons. The reason why these small differences approach significance in these data but not in the first study is because variability within the gender groups was much less in the second study than in the first. However, these are very small differences. Notice also that, comparing across studies, mothers seem to be using more emotion words and more unique emotion words with their children as they get older. Moreover, although the absolute number of emotion words used seems somewhat low, given the relatively brief duration of these conversations, emotions were mentioned about once every 5 minutes. Furthermore, only 2 mothers in the first study and none of the mothers in the second study used no emotion language at all, indicating that emotions are an integral part of mother–child talk about the past. This is even more impressive in light of the fact that mothers were given no indication of our interest in emotion talk.

Although the quantitative differences in mother–son and mother–daughter conversations are minimal, the kinds of emotions that mothers discuss with sons and daughters are quite distinct, and this is especially apparent when

TABLE 10.2
Mothers' Frequency of Mention of Specific Emotions in Study 1 and Study 2

	Type of Emotion		
	Sad	Angry	Scared
Study 1 (age = 32–35 mos.)			
with girls (n = 8)	14	0	11
with boys (n = 8)	8	12	28
Study 2 (age = 40 mos.)			
with girls (n = 12)	14	4	9
with boys (n = 12)	2	2	12

discussing negative emotions. Table 10.2 shows the frequency of mention of words referring to the emotions of sadness, anger, and fear. These three emotion categories account for at least 75% of all negative emotion words discussed across studies. In both studies, mothers talk about sadness a great deal more with daughters than with sons. In the first study, mothers talk about anger more with sons; in fact they did not talk about anger at all with daughters in this data set. For some reason, in the second study, mothers rarely talked about anger with either sons or daughters. There is also some suggestion that mothers talk about fear more with sons than with daughters.

Therefore, these two studies indicate, first, that emotions are an integral part of talk about the past. As early as 30 months of age, mothers and children include information about emotional aspects of events when they reminisce together. Second, mothers seem to increase the amount of talk about past emotion as children get older, presumably because children become more competent in participating in these conversations. Finally, although there are few overall quantitative differences in mother–daughter and mother–son conversations, mothers seem to be emphasizing different emotions in conversations with daughters than with sons; in particular, mothers seem to emphasize sadness more with daughters than with sons, and perhaps emphasize anger more with their sons than with their daughters.

Elicited Talk About Past Emotions

Although the findings are provocative, the first two studies raised many additional questions. First, possibly due to our instructions, mother–child conversations about emotions were for the most part limited to a brief mention of an emotional state or reaction; there were few instances of extended discussions about emotional experiences in these transcripts. What might more extended conversations about emotions look like? Moreover, although mothers may spontaneously mention certain emotions more or less frequently with sons and daughters, it is possible that when these emotions are discussed, they are discussed in similar ways with daughters and with sons. Alternatively, even when the "same" emotion is being discussed, mothers may talk about different aspects of the emotional experience with daughters and with sons.

In order to explore mother–child conversations about past emotions in more detail, we conducted a third study in which mothers were asked explicitly to discuss four emotional events with their 30–35-month-old child (Fivush, 1991). During a single home visit, mothers were asked to talk with their child about events in which the child felt sad, angry, scared, and happy. These emotions were chosen because they are the ones most frequently discussed in the spontaneous conversations. Notice that, as in the first two studies, it is the mother who is selecting the events to discuss. Therefore we are examining discussions about events the mother selects as illustrative of her child's emotional experience. It is entirely possible that the child would not select the same events as the mother, but that is a different question. However, it is important to point out that, even though the events were selected by the mother, there were extremely few cases where the child explicitly disagreed with the mother's interpretation of the child's emotional reaction. This contrasts to some recent findings by Stein and her colleagues (Stein et al., 1994, also this volume), who have been examining narratives in which the mother and child disagree about the child's emotional state at the time of experience. One reason why we may have seen so few disagreements in our transcripts is because mothers almost never selected an event in which they were in conflict with their child, and it seems that this is a situation in which we would be most likely to see a disagreement about each individual's emotional state. Although the discrepant findings suggest some interesting avenues for future research, here we were primarily interested in examining how mothers structured extended conversations about emotional experiences.

All conversational utterances referring to these emotions were identified, and Table 10.3 shows the number of conversational turns about each emotion with daughters and with sons. In this coding scheme, an emotion did not have to be explicitly mentioned for that conversational turn to be coded as emotion-related; rather, any conversational turn that referenced the emotional experience (e.g., by discussing the cause or consequence of the emo-

TABLE 10.3
Mean Number of Conversational Turns About Each Emotion in Study 3

	Type of Emotion			
	Sad	Angry	Scared	Happy
With girls ($n = 15$)	15.00	6.87	14.33	5.73
With boys ($n = 15$)	9.20	11.00	15.46	5.87

tion, or by elaborating on the emotion) was counted as an emotionally relevant utterance. Even using a different measure of emotion talk than in the first two studies, we again found that mothers are talking more about sadness with their daughters and more about anger with their sons, as indicated by differences in the mean length of conversation about these emotions with girls and with boys. There are no gender differences in conversations about fear or happiness.

Because in this study we specifically asked mothers to talk about an event during which the child experienced happiness, anger, sadness, or fear, we were able to examine the kind of events mothers selected to illustrate these different emotions. Events fell into two major categories: social–relational and autonomous. Social–relational themes focused on other people's roles in the emotional experience, such as happiness being due to playing with a favorite friend. Autonomous themes focused on the internal, individual state of the child, such as happiness being due to completing a difficult task. Figure 10.1 shows the number of conversations about each of the four emotions across dyads falling into each of these two categories. As can be seen, mothers are placing emotions in a social–relational framework to a much greater extent with daughters than with sons. This is especially true for sadness, for which mothers often select an event about another's misfortune, illness, or death as a time when their daughters were sad. With sons, in contrast, emotions are more frequently discussed in an autonomous framework. For example, sadness is caused by lost possessions or one's own physical ailments.

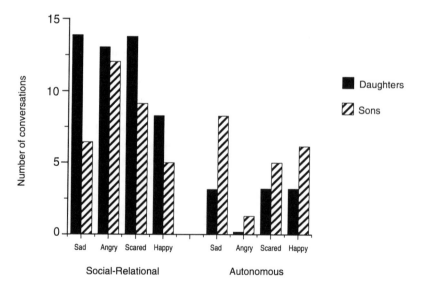

FIG. 10.1. Number of social–relational and autonomous conversations about emotions in Study 3 by gender.

The pattern of results across these studies suggests that mothers are discussing emotional aspects of past events in different ways with daughters and with sons. In particular mothers seem to emphasize sadness with daughters and anger with sons. Moreover, mothers seem to place emotions in a more social–interactional framework with daughters than with sons. Note, because the children in these first studies were so young, they engaged in very little emotion talk at all. Importantly, these studies do not allow us to investigate possible long-term effects of how mothers talk about past emotions on children's developing understanding of their past emotional experiences.

Longitudinal Relations Between Maternal and Child Talk About Past Emotions

We have begun to investigate relations between maternal and child talk about past emotions over time in a longitudinal study (Kuebli, Butler, & Fivush, 1995). The mothers and children originally seen in the second study discussed previously, were seen at two additional time points during the preschool years, for a total of three assessment points.[3] Mothers and children were seen first when the child was 40 months of age, again 18 months later when the child was not quite 5 (58 months old), and finally a year later when the child was not quite 6 (70 months old). At each of these time points, families were visited in their home and during a single session mothers were asked to sit quietly with their child and discuss three shared past experiences.[4] As in the previous studies, the conversations were about 30 to 40 minutes in duration.

Table 10.4 shows the mean total number of emotion words used at each time point for both mothers and children, as well as the mean total number of unique words used by mothers and children at each time point. Interestingly, although the means indicate an increase in both number and diversity of emotion words used by mothers over time, none of these effects reach significance. However, mothers talk more about emotions overall with daughters than with sons, and mothers talk about a greater variety of emotions with daughters than with sons, across all three time points. Moreover, mothers increase the number of unique emotion words used over time in conversations with daughters but not with sons.

---

[3]For various reasons, not all of the families that participated in the first assessment point were available for the remaining assessments; overall, six of the original families were not included in the longitudinal data. Therefore, the means presented for the first time point of this study do not exactly match the means presented earlier for Study 2.

[4]As in the first phase of this study, at all subsequent phases families participated in several other sessions conducted in the home over a 2-week period, including mother–child book reading, thematic play, and self-concept measures.

TABLE 10.4
Mean Number and Variety of Emotion Words Used by
Mothers and Children Over Time in the Longitudinal Study

	Mothers		Children	
Time	With Girls	With Boys	Girls	Boys
	Number of Emotion Words			
Time 1 (40 mos.)	8.00	6.00	1.44	1.67
Time 2 (58 mos.)	10.56	7.56	3.44	1.11
Time 3 (70 mos.)	15.89	6.89	6.44	1.33
Mean	11.48	6.82	3.77	1.37
	Number of Unique Emotion Words			
Time 1 (40 mos.)	6.33	4.11	1.33	1.56
Time 2 (58 mos.)	5.56	4.44	2.22	1.00
Time 3 (70 mos.)	10.00	3.89	4.22	1.22
Mean	7.29	4.15	2.59	1.26

When we look at the children's use of emotional language, an extremely interesting pattern emerges. Here we do see a significant increase in both number and variety of emotion words used over time; however, this increase is only apparent for girls, not for boys. Therefore, mothers are incorporating more emotion talk into conversations with daughters, and, over time, girls are coming to incorporate more emotion talk into these conversations as well. Given this pattern, it was of interest to determine who initiated discussion of emotion in these conversations. In general, mothers bring up emotions overwhelmingly more than do children; 82% of all emotion conversations are initiated by mothers across time. However, it was also the case that daughters initiated more emotion conversations than did sons; whereas 89% of mother–son emotion conversations were initiated by the mother, only 75% of mother–daughter conversations were initiated by the mother. In terms of whose emotions are being discussed, at the first time point 69% of emotions discussed were the child's emotions, but this decreased significantly over time and, at the third time point, only 42% of the emotions discussed were the child's emotions. Therefore, with both daughters and sons, mothers are increasingly talking about other people's emotions as children grow older.

Finally, when we look at the kinds of emotions discussed, as displayed in Table 10.5, we see some of the same patterns across time that we saw in the previous studies. In particular, mothers emphasize sadness more with daughters than with sons as found in all three previous studies. They also emphasize fear more with daughters than with sons in this study, in contrast to the previous research in which mothers seemed to emphasize fear more

TABLE 10.5
Mothers' and Children's Frequency of Mention of
Specific Emotions Across Time in the Longitudinal Study

	Type of Emotion Word		
	Sad	*Angry*	*Scared*
	Mothers		
With girls	27	4	26
With boys	19	2	19
	Children		
Girls	13	4	12
Boys	9	1	7

with sons than with daughters. It is possible that mothers emphasize fear with sons early in development but then begin to focus more on fear with daughters as their children grow older, but we do not yet have enough data to draw any conclusions. In addition, there is very little focus on anger in this study. In general, therefore, mothers seem to downplay anger with both sons and daughters, but when they do discuss anger, they discuss anger more with sons than with daughters, as found in two of the previous studies.

When we look at the emotion words that the children are using, we see a similar pattern, although we must be very cautious, because children are using relatively few emotion words overall. Nevertheless, the pattern suggests that girls are beginning to talk about sadness and fear more than are boys during the preschool years.

The longitudinal results support and extend the previous findings. First, although there is some suggestion from the previous studies that mothers increase their emotional language as children grow older, these data suggest that maternal emotion talk may stabilize toward the end of the preschool years. However, mothers clearly use more emotion words and a greater variety of emotion words with daughters than with sons. As in the previous studies, mothers seem to emphasize sadness more with girls than with boys. Perhaps most intriguing, although there are no gender differences in boys' and girls' use of emotion language early in development, as demonstrated in the first two studies, by the time children are about 3 or 4 years old, girls are using substantially more emotion words and a substantially larger emotion vocabulary than are boys, and this difference increases across the preschool years. Girls may also emphasize sadness more than do boys in these conversations.

These results suggest that maternal emotion language early in development may facilitate children's developing use of emotion language when reminiscing about past events. More direct evidence for this possibility comes from examining the patterns of correlations between maternal emotion language and children's emotion language over time. Pearson product correlations were computed between the frequency of maternal use of emotion terms and children's use of emotion terms at each time point and across time points. All significant correlations are displayed in Fig. 10.2. As can be seen, at the first two time points, there are no concurrent relations between maternal use of emotion language and children's use of emotion language, but at the last time point, when children are not quite 6 years old, those mothers who are talking more about emotion have children who are talking more about emotion during that same conversation. These are important findings because they indicate that mothers who use a lot of emotion language are not doing so simply because their children are using a great deal of emotion language at that same point in time. Rather, it seems that mothers who use a great deal of emotion language have children who begin to use a great deal of emotion language 18 months later, suggesting that maternal focus on emotional aspects of the past facilitates children's developing discussion of past emotions. The fact that there are no longitudinal relations between children's use of emotion language and their mother's subsequent use of emotion language further suggests that it is mothers who are primarily responsible for the relations between maternal and child emotion language at the last time point.

Summary

The longitudinal pattern, along with the previous findings of differences in the ways in which emotions are talked about with daughters and with sons, suggests that girls and boys may come to have very different emotional understandings of their past experiences. Across the studies, several themes

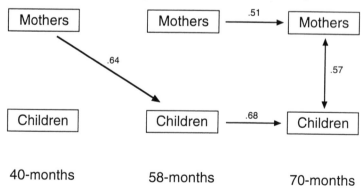

FIG. 10.2. Correlations between maternal and child emotion talk across time in the longitudinal study.

emerge. First, mothers talk about emotions more overall with daughters than with sons, and they talk about a greater variety of emotions with daughters than with sons. Moreover, whereas girls may be socialized to think about sadness as an important evaluative framework for understanding their past experiences, boys may be socialized to focus on anger. Finally, girls may be socialized to understand emotions as interpersonal constructs, whereas boys may come to understand emotions more as individual, internal constructs.

Of course, we need to be careful about inferring causal relations from mother to child from data such as these. Although the correlations over time certainly suggest that maternal use of emotion language influences children's developing use of such language, there are other possible interpretations. For example, we did not measure nonverbal expression of emotion; it is possible that mothers talk more about emotions with daughters because girls display more emotion nonverbally in these conversations. It would be extremely interesting to analyze videotaped conversations about past emotions to explore this idea. As we argued at the beginning of the chapter, children are active agents in their own socialization. In reminiscing about the past, both participants play an active role in maintaining and developing the conversation. Although our analyses have focused on what mothers are doing in these conversations, it is essential to examine what children are doing in these conversations as well in order to provide a full explanation for the gender effects we have documented.

Moreover, in all of our studies, the mother selects the events to discuss. It might be that mothers do not select events that are very salient or emotionally laden for their children, and this may be especially true with sons for some reason. If children were asked to select events themselves, the gender difference in emotion language used by children might be attenuated. Nevertheless, our task is ecologically valid, in that mothers frequently initiate conversations with their preschool children about the past; in fact, research on spontaneous conversations about the past indicates that mothers initiate a much higher number of such conversations than do children (Engel, 1986; Miller, 1994; Ratner, 1984). Our results demonstrate that when mothers initiate such conversations, they are also the ones to initiate talk about emotions associated with the past event. Most importantly, in this situation, mothers initiate more talk about emotion with daughters than with sons.

Because girls are exposed to and develop a larger vocabulary for describing past emotional experience than boys, girls may come to think about emotional aspects of their past experiences more than do boys, and girls may come to understand their emotional experiences as more interpersonally situated than do boys. In these ways, girls may come to understand both their own past experiences and the past experience of others as emotionally richer and more varied than do boys. As adults, females report more emotionally laden memories than do males (Davis, 1991), supporting this possibility. Girls may also come to focus on sadness when thinking about their past more so than boys. Again, research with adults indicates that women report feelings of sadness more frequently than do males (Brody, in press), and, indeed, may even ruminate on sad experiences so much that they become depressed (Nolen-Hoeksema, 1987; Stapley & Haviland, 1989). As noted earlier, we must be extremely cautious in relating the developmental findings to the findings with adults, but the patterns of convergence are provocative. Certainly, as the longitudinal data demonstrate, the ways in which mothers talk about emotional aspects of past experiences with their young children may influence children's developing discussion of their emotional experiences, and mothers seem to structure these conversations in different ways depending on whether they are reminiscing with a daughter or a son.

However, it must also be stressed that gender is only one variable among many that are important to consider when thinking about the socialization of emotion. Although there are differences in the ways in which mothers talk about emotions with daughters and with sons, it is also true that there is a great deal of variability within gender groups. In addition, there are similarities as well as differences in the ways in which mothers talk about emotions with sons and daughters. Moreover, we studied only white, middle-class families. Gender-related patterns of emotion talk may be very different in other subcultures, where gender is constructed in different ways. Nevertheless, the pattern of results across these studies clearly demonstrates that, at least in this population, gender is a critical factor in mother–child talk about past emotions.

QUALITATIVE ANALYSIS OF CONVERSATIONAL EXCERPTS

The quantitative data provide important information about how mothers and children are incorporating emotion into their conversations about the past. Numbers alone, however, do not always illustrate the richness and complexity of these conversations. Therefore, in this section we provide in-depth discussion of four conversational excerpts. These excerpts come from the longitudinal study just discussed. Recall that in this study, mothers were asked to select novel events to discuss with their children at three points in time. Although most of the events selected were fun family outings, some mothers selected more negatively toned events as well. Two of our mothers discussed a death at the second time point when the children were 58 months old, and these mothers were asked to discuss the same event again a year later at the last time point, when the children were 70 months old; these are the excerpts that are presented.

The first excerpt is from a mother and daughter, in which they discuss going to the wake of the child's preschool teacher after the teacher dies of cancer. At the time of this interview, the child was not quite 5 years old. They had attended the wake about a month before the interview, and according to the mother, they had discussed the event about four to five times since it had occurred:

M: Well I think what we're going to talk about neeext is going to Karen Butler's (wake).

C: Unh. Well I remember when they were crying and Molly, Molly started crying.

(6 conversational turns about who Karen Butler is)

M: Mmm hmm and it was very sad to see her so sick.

C: Yes.

M: And theeen what happened?

C: Well she they they did everything but it didn't work and she died.

M: Yeah. And it was sad wasn't it?

C: Yeah (softly).

M: And you begged Mommy and Daddy to go to her wake.

C: Yeah (softly).

M: And what was the wake like?

C: Well it had sadly music and it was really sad to talk about. So I didn't want to talk about it.

(10 conversational turns about what happened at the wake)

M: Didn't we go talk to her daughter?

C: (softly) Yes.

M: And we gave her big hugs.

(4 conversational turns about who was there)

C: Yeah. . . . But I don't want to talk about this cause you're almost gonna make me cry.

M: Okay. I won't, we won't talk about it anymore.

Several things should be noted about what is happening in this conversation. First, it is the child who brings up the emotional tone of the event, in the second conversational turn. This is relatively unusual, as mothers initiated 75% of all conversations about emotions with daughters. Moreover, the emotional tone is set by someone else's emotional reaction, not the child's own reaction. Again, as discussed earlier, by this time point about half of all emotions talked about were other people's emotional reactions, so this was not unusual. After talking about the teacher's illness, the mother summarizes by saying how sad it was. Notice that the mother is not attributing the emotion to a particular person, but rather to the situation. In this way, the mother is placing the emotion as a shared interpersonal understanding and evaluation of an event, rather than an intrapersonal evaluation. They continue to discuss how sad this event was, until the child says that it is essentially too sad to talk about. Here, the child seems to understand both that emotions are enduring, that one can continue to feel an emotion even after the event is over, and also that one can manage one's emotions; one can choose not to talk about or think about events that make one feel distressed. However, even though the daughter states she does not want to talk about the event, the mother continues the conversation, quite possibly because they were participating in our study and the mother may have felt obligated to continue discussing the event. After discussing what happened at the wake, the mother turns the conversation to the other people present. In particular, she mentions talking with and hugging the teacher's daughter, Molly. Here again we see a focus on sharing emotions with others, as well as a life lesson in appropriate comforting behaviors for those in distress. At this point, the child again states that she does not want to talk about this event, but in much stronger terms. Here it seems that the child is really disturbed by this event and is still feeling very sad about it all, and now the mother accepts this and ends the conversation. The tone throughout the conversation is very much one of sharing a sad experience together; this mother is engaged in eliciting and interpreting this sad experience with her child.

A year later, this mother–daughter pair again talked about this event. Now the child is not quite 6 years old. According to the mother, they have only discussed this event once or twice in the previous year:

M: Well we're gonna talk about going to Karen Butler's wake.
C: I don't want to talk about sad parts.
M: Well don't talk about the sad parts, talk about the happy parts. Were there any happy parts to that? Was it good s–, to see Molly?
(14 conversational turns about who was at the wake)
C: I don't want to talk about this anymore.
M: You don't want to remember Karen's wake? That is a sad time. But you know what, Meagan, I mean, Patty?
C: I even got to see her body when she was dead.
M: Yeah, she was definitely dead. It's hard to, to go to wakes, but you know what? Sometimes it helps us face the reality that the person is really dead.
C: I can't understand, when she came back she was gonna die, I don't understand how she c–, how she took it.
M: Yeah, I'm sure we'll never know how she took it. I'm sure she took it real sad. Anyway–
C: I'm sure she went back to sleep when it hurted.
M: Okay.

Again, the child is the first to emotionally label the event. Notice that again, the emotional tone of the event is the very first thing recalled. Clearly, it is the emotional tone that gives this event its meaning. Here, the child begins right away stating that she does not want to talk about the sad parts, so even more than a year after the wake, we see that this child is still experiencing sadness when discussing this event. The mother makes a very interesting move; she asks about the happy parts of this event, thus indicating that even very sad events are not all-or-none emotional experiences. Emotional aspects of events are complex and may even involve mixed emotions. What was happy about this event? The happiness was in being able to share it with other people, so again we see the emphasis on sharing emotional experiences with others as positive. After talking about the people they saw at the wake, the child states, as she did in the previous conversation a year earlier, that she does not want to talk about it anymore. The mother confirms that it is sad to think about these kinds of events, but then goes on to explain that cultural rituals surrounding some kinds of sad events help us to deal with our strong and disturbing emotions, again emphasizing the value of sharing our emotional experiences with others. The child then takes the perspective of her teacher who died; not only was this sad for the child, but the child begins to realize how sad it was for the person who died. Here, the mother and child agree that some emotions may be difficult for us to share fully. Again, the overall tone of the event is very much one of sharing and trying to come to terms with very strong, sad feelings for both the mother and the child.

The second set of excerpts come from a mother–son pair who are discussing the death of the family pet cat, Winston, which occurred about 5 months earlier. The mother reported that they had talked about this event about 5 to 10 times since it occurred, but had not discussed it at all during the previous month. Now clearly, the death of a pet is not the same as the death of a person, but as you will see in these conversations, there are very strong emotions expressed:

M: Can we talk about something that's kind of sad for Mommy for a minute?

(13 conversational turns about what happened to Winston)

M: ...and we had to put him to sleep. And how did Mommy feel?

C: Very very sad (quietly)

M: ...And what did Mommy do?

C: Cried.

M: I cried a lot, didn't I?

C: Why?

M: Honey, because when somebody dies, that somebody has been your friend for a long time you miss them. And Mommy, and Winston was Mommy's friend for a long time and I miss him.

C: Are you crying?

M: I might, a little bit, because I miss him. Who else died this year that we miss an awful lot?

C: Granddaddy.

M: Granddaddy, Granddaddy died last year.

C: Grandmother.

M: No, Mommy didn't, my mother didn't die this year, but somebody else did that we really miss. Who, who died this year?

C: Grandpa's mother.

M: No, she died a long time ago. But who, remember somebody else died (unin) that made Mommy really really sad.

C: Granddaddy.

M: No, Aunt . . .

C: Aunt—

M: Aunt—Aunt who died?

C: Aunt Amy.

M: Aunt Amy died too and what did Mommy do?

C: Cried.

M: I cried soo much. 'Cause it was really sad, we miss Aunt Amy, don't we?

This mother is quite different from the first mother. She begins the conversation by emotionally labeling the event, but notice that she labels her own emotion, not the child's or the family's feelings in general. In contrast to the first mother, this mother makes no implicit assumption that other's might feel the same way about the event. The emotion seems to be an individual, intrapersonal occurrence rather than an interpersonal shared evaluation of the event. After discussing the events surrounding going to the vet and putting Winston to sleep, the mother asks the child to recall how she, the mother, felt about the event, again focusing on her own emotion rather than the child's or the family's reactions. When the child asks for more information, the mother provides a very explicit explanation of how a certain class of events should be emotionally evaluated. At the end of the excerpt, the mother brings up a related event, the death of a relative, and again focuses on her own emotional reaction. Notice that as in the first mother–child pair, emotions are enduring states; they are not limited to the event as experienced, but continue to be part of the event as re-experienced through thought and language. However, whereas it was the child's emotional state that endured in the first examples, it is the mother's state that endures in this example.

A year later, when the child is not quite 6 years old, they discuss this event again. According to the mother the event had been talked about rarely during the previous year and not at all during the previous month:

M: Do you remember last year? Who died?

C: I don't know.

M: (overlaps with C) That it was really sad and Mommy missed him so much.

(48 conversational turns about who died and the burial procedures)

M: ... what did Mommy do?

C: Cry?

M: I cried a lot huh?

C: (sounds like laughing noises).

M: 'Cause I was really sad. You know you shouldn't laugh when somebody's sad, honey.

C: Ha, ha. Well, I was just, well, I was just faking real sad.

M: Oh, okay.

(15 conversational turns about burying)

C: ... I didn't do anything when (unin few words) Winston.

M: You know what, except you were good to me, I think you took good care of me when we were burying Winston, didn't you?

C: Yeah.

M: I mean you just were supportive and you gave me hugs and made me feel really good.

C: But ... I shoulda given him a little kiss and a little hug (unin).

M: (overlaps with C) You know what, I think you might have before we took him outside, I think you might have. 'Cause remember we sat in here and petted him and I cut off some of his fur so I'd have it.

C: Mm.

M: I think we all kissed him good-bye.

C: Gave him a hug.

Again, the mother begins by labeling the event emotionally by focusing on her own emotions and again, these emotions are linked to a particular emotional display—in this case crying. It is not exactly clear what happens next, but it appears that the child is trying to make crying sounds but instead seems to make laughing sounds, to which the mother provides an explicit rule about appropriate and inappropriate emotional expressions in relation to other people's feelings. Notice also that this child seems to understand that emotional expression may not always match the underlying emotional state. The mother then goes on to discuss how supportive the child was when the mother was so sad. Here, therefore, we do see a concern with others, but in a very different way than in the first mother–child pair. For the first mother–child pair, comforting was a way of sharing an emotional experience; for this pair, comforting seems more a matter of the appropriate behavioral response to another's feelings. The child then expresses some concern that he, himself, did not do much for Winston when he died; perhaps we are seeing some regret over not feeling or doing what is culturally appropriate in this situation. The mother reassures the child that, in fact, he probably did do something to mark the sad occasion, and the conversation ends. Again, the overall tone focuses on the mother's emotional experience; emotions are discussed as internal, individual events rather than as shared experiences. In contrast to the first mother, who elicits and interprets emotional experience with her child, this mother interprets emotional experience for her child.

In these excerpts, we see different ways in which mothers may discuss emotional experiences with their children and how these conversations guide children to an understanding and interpretation of that emotional experience. Moreover, as these examples make clear, the child is playing an active role in these conversations. These two children seem to be experiencing and discussing their emotional experiences in very different ways. The longitudinal data presented earlier indicate that maternal language about emotional experience influences children's developing use of emotional language in describing their past, but most likely, this process is bidirectional. Just as maternal emotional language influences children, children's understanding and ability to express their own emotions will influence maternal language. These examples provide powerful evidence that interpreting and evaluating emotional experiences is very much a social process.

CONCLUSIONS

Clearly, emotions are an important part of conversations about the past. Whether mothers and their preschool children are discussing somewhat mundane events, such as a trip to the zoo, or more deeply emotional events, such as the death of a friend, they include emotional aspects of the experience in their conversations. Moreover, the ways in which mothers talk about emotions seem to play an important role in the ways in which children come to talk about their own emotional experiences, and maternal differences in emotion language seem to be related to the child's gender. Mothers talk more about emotions, and about a greater variety of emotions, with girls than with boys, and by the end of the preschool years, girls are talking about more emotions and a greater variety of emotions than are boys. There is also some suggestion that mothers may talk about different emotions with girls and with boys; in particular, mothers seem to emphasize sadness more with daughters than with sons (see Fivush, 1993, for a full discussion of this issue).

As we argued earlier, language is a primary tool for emotional socialization. The ways in which adults talk to young children about emotions provide a great deal of information about culturally appropriate emotional expression.

We believe that children are not simply learning how to talk about emotion in these early conversations; they are also learning how to think about their emotional experiences. Mothers who talk more about emotional aspects of the past are implicitly informing their children that emotions are an important part of experience. Children of mothers who talk more about emotion may come to think about their past experiences in more emotional terms. Therefore, given the data presented in this chapter, girls may come to have an emotionally richer understanding of their past than will boys.

Most provocative, emotional experience is an important part of self-understanding (e.g., Fivush, 1993; Lewis, 1992b). The way we interpret and evaluate our past experiences is a critical part of how we understand ourselves. Because mothers and daughters talk a great deal about emotions, girls may come to value emotions more than do boys, and because girls think about their past experiences in more emotionally rich ways, they may come to conceptualize themselves as more emotional than do boys. Certainly, the early patterns of socialization of emotion are related in intriguing ways to adult gender differences in emotional expression and understanding.

Regardless of how we interpret the gender differences, it is abundantly clear that emotions are an important aspect of our daily experience and, beginning very early in development, adults and children discuss and interpret this experience retrospectively. Talking about past emotions is a critical avenue for emotional socialization. Most importantly, even when talking about the somewhat mundane events of our daily lives, we talk about emotion. Emotional events are not a special class of experience; rather, all of our experiences are inherently emotional, and sharing these emotional experiences with others is an integral part of everyday social interaction.

ACKNOWLEDGMENTS

Much of the research in this chapter was supported by a grant from the Spencer Foundation to the first author. Many people were instrumental in data collection, transcription, coding and analyses of the studies reported here. Thanks to Winifred Diggs, Naomi Singer, Stephen Soufer, Catherine Haden, Elaine Reese, Liza Dondonan, Laura Underwood, Marcella Eppen, and Elyse Kreiger. We are especially grateful to Susan Butler for her involvement in the longitudinal study and, of course, we are very grateful to all of the families who gave so generously of their time.

REFERENCES

Adams, S., Kuebli, J., Boyle, P., & Fivush, R. (in press). Gender differences in parent–child conversations about past emotions: A longitudinal investigation. *Sex Roles.*

Allen, J. G., & Haccoun, D. M. (1976). Sex differences in emotionality: A multidimensional approach. *Human Relations, 29,* 711–722.

Allen, J. G., & Hamsher, J. H. (1974). The development and validation of a test of emotional styles. *Journal of Counseling and Clinical Psychology, 42,* 663–668.

Arnold, M. B. (1960). *Emotion and personality.* New York: Plenum.

Barrett, K. C. (1993). The development of nonverbal communication of emotion: A functionalist perspective. *Journal of Nonverbal Behavior, 17,* 145–169.

Beeghley, M., Bretherton, I., & Mervis, C. (1986). Mothers' internal state language to toddlers. *British Journal of Developmental Psychology, 4,* 247–261.

Bell, R. Q., & Harper, L. V. (1977). *Child effects on adults.* Hillsdale, NJ: Lawrence Erlbaum Associates.

Bridges, K. M. B. (1932). Emotional development in early infancy. *Child Development, 3,* 324–334.

Brody, L. (in press). On understanding gender differences in the expression of emotion: Gender roles, socialization, and language. In S. Ablon, D. Brown, J. Mack, & E. Khantrian (Eds.), *Human feelings: Explorations in affect development and meaning.* Hillsdale, NJ: Analytic Press.

Bruner, J. (1990). *Acts of meaning.* Cambridge, MA: Harvard University Press.

Campos, J. J., Caplovitz, K. B., Lamb, M. E., Goldsmith, H. H., & Stenberg, C. (1983). Socioemotional development. In M. M. Haith & J. J. Campos (Eds.), *Handbook of child psychology: Vol 2. Infancy and developmental psychobiology* (4th ed., pp. 783–915). New York: Wiley.

Cole, M. (1985). The zone of proximal development: Where culture and cognition create each other. In J. V. Wertsch (Ed.), *Culture, communication and cognition: Vygotskian perspectives* (pp. 146–161). New York: Cambridge University Press.

Davis, P. (1991, July). *Gender differences in autobiographical memory.* Paper presented at the NATO Advanced Research Conference: Theoretical perspectives on autobiographical memory, LaGrange, England.

Denham, S. A., Zoller, D., & Couchoud, E. A. (1993). *When Mommy's angry, I feel sad: Socialization of preschoolers' understanding of emotion.* Unpublished manuscript.

Dunn, J., Bretherton, I., & Munn, P. (1987). Conversations about feeling states between mothers and their young children. *Developmental Psychology, 23,* 132–139.

Dunn, J., Brown, J., & Beardsall, L. (1991). Family talk about feeling states and children's later understanding of others' emotions. *Developmental Psychology, 27,* 448–455.

Eckman, P., & Friesen, W. V. (1971). Constants across cultures in the face and emotion. *Journal of Personality and Social Psychology, 17,* 124–129.

Engel, S. (1986, April). The role of mother–child interaction in autobiographical recall. In J. A. Hudson (Chair), *Learning to talk about the past.* Symposium conducted at the Southeastern Conference on Human Development, Nashville, TN.

Fivush, R. (1989). Exploring sex differences in the emotional content of mother–child conversations about the past. *Sex Roles, 20,* 675–691.

Fivush, R. (1991). Gender and emotion in mother–child conversations about the past. *Journal of Narrative and Life History, 1,* 325–341.

Fivush, R. (1993). Emotional content of parent–child conversations about the past. In C. A. Nelson (Ed.), *The Minnesota Symposia on child psychology: Vol. 26. Memory and affect in development* (pp. 39–78). Hillsdale, NJ: Lawrence Erlbaum Associates.

Gordon, S. L. (1989). The socialization of children's emotions: Emotional competence, culture, and exposure. In C. Saarni & P. L. Harris (Eds.), *Children's understanding of emotion* (pp. 319–349). New York: Cambridge University Press.

Halberstadt, A. G. (1991). Toward an ecology of expressiveness: Family socialization in particular and a model in general. In R. S. Feldman & B. Rimé (Eds.), *Fundamentals of nonverbal behavior* (pp. 106–160). New York: Cambridge University Press.

Harris, P., & Olthof, T. (1982). The child's concept of emotions. In G. Butterworth & P. Light (Eds.), *Social cognition: Studies of the development of understanding* (pp. 188–209). Chicago: The University of Chicago Press.

Hochschild, A. R. (1983). *The managed heart: Commercialization of human feeling.* Berkeley: University of California Press.

Hudson, J. (1990). The emergence of autobiographic memory in mother–child conversation. In R. Fivush & J. A. Hudson (Eds.), *Knowing and remembering in young children*. New York: Cambridge University Press.

Izard, C. E. (1977). *Human emotions*. New York: Plenum.

Kuebli, J., & Fivush, R. (1992). Gender differences in parent–child conversations about past emotions. *Sex Roles, 27*, 683–698.

Kuebli, J., & Boyle, P. (1993, March). *Past emotions in parent–child conversations over time*. Poster presented at the Conference on Human Development, Pittsburgh, PA.

Kuebli, J., Butler, S., & Fivush, R. (1995). Mother–child talk about past emotions: Effects of child gender over time. *Cognition and Emotion, 9*, 265–283.

Labov, W. (1982). Speech actions and reactions in personal narrative. In D. Tannen (Ed.), *Analyzing discourse: Text and talk* (pp. 219–247). Washington, DC: Georgetown University Press.

Lazarus, R. S., Kanner, A. D., & Folkman, S. (1980). Emotions: A cognitive–phenomenological analysis. In R. Plutchik & H. Kellerman (Eds.), *Emotion: Theory, research, and experience* (pp. 189–217). New York: Academic Press.

Levy, R. I. (1984). Emotion, knowing, and culture. In R. A. Shweder & R. A. Levine (Eds.), *Culture theory: Essays on mind, self, and emotion* (pp. 214–237). Cambridge, England: Cambridge University Press.

Lewis, M. (1992a). *Shame: The exposed self*. New York: The Free Press.

Lewis, M. (1992b). The role of the self in social behavior. In F. S. Kessel, P. M. Cole, & D. L. Johnson (Eds.), *Self and consciousness: Multiple perspectives* (pp. 19–44). Hillsdale, NJ: Lawrence Erlbaum Associates.

Lewis, M., & Michaelson, L. (1983). *Children's emotions and moods*. New York: Plenum.

Lutz, C. (1983). Parental goals, ethnopsychology, and the development of emotional meaning. *Ethos, 11*, 246–262.

Lutz, C. (1985). Cultural patterns and individual differences in the child's emotional meaning system. In M. Lewis & C. Saarni (Eds.), *The socialization of emotion* (pp. 37–53). New York: Plenum.

Lutz, C., & White, G. M. (1986). The anthropology of emotions. *Annual Review of Anthropology, 15*, 405–436.

Markus, H. R., & Kitayama, S. (1991). Culture and the self: Implications for cognition, emotion, and motivation. *Psychological Review, 98*, 224–253.

Matsumoto, D., & Assar, M. (1992). The effects of language on judgments of universal facial expressions of emotion. *Journal of Nonverbal Behavior, 16*, 85–99.

Matsumoto, D., Kudoh, T., Scherer, K., & Wallbott, H. (1988). Antecedents of and reactions to emotions in the United States and Japan. *Journal of Cross-Cultural Psychology, 19*, 267–286.

Mead, G. H. (1956). *On social psychology: Selected papers*. Chicago: University of Chicago Press.

Miller, P. (1994). Narrative practices: Their role in socialization and self-construction. In U. Neisser & R. Fivush (Eds.), *The remembering self: Construction and accuracy in the life narrative* (pp. 158–179). New York: Cambridge University Press.

Miller, P. J., & Sperry, L. L. (1988). Early talk about the past: The origins of conversational stories of personal experience. *Journal of Child Language, 15*, 293–315.

Nolen-Hoeksema, S. (1987). Sex differences in unipolar depression: Evidence and theory. *Psychological Bulletin, 101*, 259–282.

Peterson, C., & McCabe, A. (1983). *Developmental psycholinguistics: Three ways of looking at a child's narrative*. New York: Plenum.

Ratner, H. H. (1984). Memory demands and the development of young children's memory. *Child Development, 55*, 2173–2191.

Ridgeway, D., Waters, E., & Kuczaj, S. A. (1985). Acquisition of emotion-descriptive language: Receptive and productive vocabulary norms for ages 18 months to 6 years. *Developmental Psychology, 21*, 901–908.

Rogoff, B. (1990). *Apprenticeship in thinking*. New York: Oxford University Press.

Russell, A., & Russell, G. (1992). Child effects on socialization research: Some conceptual and data analysis issues. *Social Development, 1*(2), 163–184.

Saarni, C. (1985). Indirect processes in affect socialization. In M. Lewis & C. Saarni (Eds.), *The socialization of emotions* (pp. 187–209). New York: Plenum.

Schiefflin, B. B., & Ochs, E. (1986). *Language socialization across cultures*. New York: Cambridge University Press.

Sroufe, L. A. (1979). Socioemotional development. In J. D. Osofsky (Ed.), *Handbook of infant development* (pp. 462–516). New York: Wiley.

Stapley, J. C., & Haviland, J. M. (1989). Beyond depression: Gender differences in normal adolescents' emotional experiences. *Sex Roles, 20*, 295–308.

Stein, N. L., Trabasso, T., & Liwag, M. (1994). The Rashomon phenomenon: Personal frames and future-oriented appraisals in memory for emotional events. In M. Haith, J. B. Benson, R. J. Roberts, & B. F. Pennington (Eds.), *Future-oriented processes* (pp. 409–435). Chicago: University of Chicago Press.

Stein, N. L., Trabasso, T., & Liwag, M. (in press). The representation and organization of emotional experience: Unfolding the emotion episode. In M. Lewis & J. Haviland (Eds.), *Handbook of emotions*. New York: Guilford Press.

Stern, D. (1985). *The interpersonal world of the infant*. New York: Basic Books.

Stipek, D., Weiner, B., & Li, K. (1989). Testing some attribution–emotion relations in the People's Republic of China. *Journal of Personality and Social Psychology, 56*, 109–116.

Thoits, P. A. (1989). The sociology of emotions. *American Review of Sociology, 15*, 317–342.

Zahn-Waxler, C., Cole, P., & Barrett, K. (1991). Guilt and empathy: Sex differences and implications for the development of depression. In J. Garber & K. Dodge (Eds.), *The development of emotion regulation and disregulation. Cambridge studies in social and emotional development* (pp. 141–164). New York: Cambridge University Press.

11

TRAUMA AND MEMORY: INDIVIDUAL DIFFERENCES IN CHILDREN'S RECOUNTING OF A STRESSFUL EXPERIENCE

Gail S. Goodman
Jodi A. Quas
University of California, Davis

Not all children react to stressful events in the same way. Some children cope surprisingly well, but others suffer adverse reverberations for years. Similarly, not all children remember stressful events in the same way; over time, some children remember traumatic events with clarity, other children recall stressful events inaccurately, and some children seem to forget that the traumatic incident occurred at all. Consider the following examples: In 1993, pictures of a 4-year-old child being molested by two adults were found in an abandoned car, but when the identity of the child was discovered and the child was interviewed, she had no recollection of ever being assaulted ("Innocent Plea," 1993). A 4-year-old child who witnessed his sister being severely injured in an accident had a vivid and accurate memory of it 3 years later (Terr, 1990). Alternatively, a 4-year-old who experienced a stressful medical procedure remembered the core features of the event accurately but confabulated part of the rest (Goodman, Bottoms, Schwartz-Kenney, & Rudy, 1991). Why do some children form enduring, accurate memories of such experiences and others not? Developmental level and extent of trauma are undoubtedly influential; however, there might also be important individual differences in children's ability to remember stressful experiences.

CHILDREN'S MEMORY FOR STRESSFUL EVENTS

Many researchers agree that understanding children's memory for traumatic experiences rests on a foundation of knowledge concerning children's long-term memory for personally significant events (Goodman, 1984; Ornstein,

Larus, & Clubb, 1991). Until relatively recently, however, most theory and research on memory development has focused on emotionally neutral events, whereas most theory and research on childhood traumas has been based on clinical case studies. Necessary ethical prohibitions against imposing stressful events on children stymied researchers from conducting more controlled, scientific investigations of memory for traumatic events.

Fortunately, a breakthrough was made with the insight that scientific research could be conducted on children's memory for stressful medical procedures. Although stressful medical procedures, unlike many other traumas, are socially sanctioned and the aim is to heal rather than harm, these procedures often entail what children perceive as unpleasant, frightening violations of their bodies, and this can result in the child crying, struggling to get free, and being forcibly restrained (Steward, 1993). Pain caused by the procedure may be amplified by a feeling of betrayal (e.g., when children are lied to about whether a procedure will hurt, when a parent participates in subjecting the child to pain by holding the child down, when a parent leaves the room and seems to abandon the child; e.g., Bush, Melamed, & Cockrell, 1989). Because children's reactions to medical procedures can be intense, such procedures afford researchers an opportunity to examine children's memory for stressful real-life experiences.

The first studies of this type concerned children's memory for venipuncture and inoculations (Goodman, Hepps, & Reed, 1986; Goodman, Hirschman, Hepps, & Rudy, 1991), procedures that are quite stressful for some children and for which an objective record can be obtained. Following those studies, researchers examined children's memory for other medical procedures such as dental examinations (Peters, 1991; Vandermaas, Hess, & Baker-Ward, 1993), full-body medical checkups (Baker-Ward, Gordon, Ornstein, Larus, & Clubb, 1993; Saywitz, Goodman, Nicholas, & Moan, 1991; Steward, 1993), cancer treatment (Bearison & Pacifici, 1989), and emergency room procedures (Howe, Courage, & Peterson, 1994).

Although relatively few studies have been conducted to date, mixed results have already emerged that are similar to the mixed results from studies of adults' memory for stressful events—results that caused psychologists to debate whether stress has adverse or beneficial effects on adults' memory. If detailed "flashbulb memories" are formed for traumatic events, as some researchers have claimed (e.g., Bohannon & Symons, 1992; Brown & Kulik, 1977; see also Winograd & Neisser, 1992), one would expect particularly robust memories of medical "traumas." The existence of such memories is consistent with the notion that people often wish they could forget highly negative experiences but, no matter how hard they try, cannot. In contrast, if trauma causes memory impairment or retrograde amnesia, as others have asserted (e.g., Loftus, 1979), one would expect particularly poor memory for traumatic events. The Yerkes–Dodson Law is often relied on to explain the latter possibility (Yerkes & Dodson, 1908). According to this descriptive "law," when stress increases beyond an optimal level, performance suffers. When applied to memory, this law has been used to predict that memory for highly stressful, as opposed to moderately stressful, events will be impaired.

Recently, Christianson (1992) made strides toward resolving debates about the relation between stress and memory, arguing that when memory for information integral to a stressor is tested, enhanced memory is found, but when memory for nonintegral information is considered, stress is associated with weaker memory. One typical kind of study indicating this pattern contrasts memory for central versus peripheral information in stressful and nonstressful versions of the same basic stimuli (e.g., a picture of a woman bicyclist hit by a car versus a picture of the woman bicycling across the street; Christianson & Loftus, 1987). Christianson's formulation provides a possible conceptual fit not only for data from studies of adults' memory, but also for findings concerning children's memories for stressful experiences. Several studies of stress and children's memory have focused on less integral, more peripheral information that is not directly related to the stressor. These studies have uncovered possible inhibitory effects of stress on memory (e.g., Peters, 1991; see also Ceci & Bruck, 1993). Other studies have focused on central, integral acts, finding that stress is associated with strengthening of children's memory (e.g., Goodman, Hirschman, Hepps, & Rudy, 1991). Both kinds of findings would be expected given Christianson's ideas (see also Baddeley, 1976; Easterbrook, 1959). Although it may be difficult to determine a priori what aspects of a stressful situation will be central to a particular child, one would suspect that information directly related to the cause of the stress (e.g., the syringe if one is afraid of shots) would be central.

However, the central–peripheral distinction is not the only explanation that can potentially resolve these discrepant findings. Brainerd and Reyna's (1991) fuzzy-trace theory (FTT) provides a potentially useful conceptual framework for understanding developmental differences in memory for stressful events. A central notion of FTT is that developmental changes occur in memory for "gist" (relational) and "verbatim" (perceptual) information. Specifically, young children tend to retain information more in verbatim than in gist form. With age, gist memory becomes more prominent. Poole (personal communication, January 1994) has related FTT to children's memory for stressful events. She proposed that stress enhances memory for gist and impairs memory for verbatim information. Although the type of gist (relations) a child can abstract from a situation changes with cognitive development, the basic tendency for stress to help consolidate gist memory and impair verbatim memory would be expected to continue into adulthood.

Other researchers have proposed distinctions that remain untested in the child memory literature—for example, that focus of attention is internally versus externally directed during a victimization experience (Pynoos, 1992; Yuille & Tollestrup, 1992). Pynoos contended that once penetration occurs, a victim's attention becomes directed at internal sensations. Unfortunately, there is little supporting evidence for this interesting possibility.

However, consideration of type of information (e.g., central vs. peripheral, gist vs. verbatim) is unlikely to reveal the entire story. There may be important developmental and individual differences in how people handle stressful situations, how stressed they become, how they deal with a traumatic memory, and how easily and under what conditions they can talk about it (Bretherton, 1993; Goodman, Bottoms, Schwartz-Kenney, & Rudy, 1991; Liwag & Stein, 1993; Stein, 1991; Vandermaas et al., 1993). Indeed, recent empirical findings from our laboratory reveal important individual differences in reactions to and memory for stressful experiences (Goodman, Batterman-Faunce, Quas, Riddlesberger, & Kuhn, 1993).

INDIVIDUAL DIFFERENCES
IN CHILDREN'S MEMORY

Few studies exist in which individual-difference predictors of children's memory have been identified. However, researchers have anecdotally noted striking individual differences in the accuracy of children's memory (e.g., Rudy & Goodman, 1991), even when considering age groups particularly vulnerable to memory errors (e.g., preschoolers). Identification of personality differences that moderate basic memory processes may help resolve discrepancies concerning effects of stress on memory; it would also contribute to the integration of research on memory and personality development. Later, we consider several studies that raise questions about individual differences in children's memory for personally experienced, real-life events. We then review some of the few studies in which individual-difference predictors of memory for such events have been identified. Because our own research focuses on children's memory for stressful genital touch and children's suggestibility, we concentrate on related research here.

Saywitz et al. (1991) investigated 5- and 7-year-olds' reports of a medical checkup that involved nonpainful genital contact. Half of the children in that study experienced complete physical examinations including vaginal and anal touch, whereas for the other half the vaginal and anal examinations were omitted. For the children whose examinations included genital contact, direct questioning about vaginal and anal touch was required for the majority of children to reveal this part of the examination. Interestingly, younger children were more likely than older children to disclose such touch, probably because the older children were more self-conscious or embarrassed (Goldman & Goldman, 1988). A small percentage of children (8%) who did not experience vaginal or anal touch falsely agreed to a leading question regarding genital contact. Given that the questioning of all children was identical, it is important to figure out why 8% of the children gave false reports. What differentiates these children from the 92% who were able to resist these false suggestions? Moreover, 22% of the children who experienced the genital examination reported it in free recall. What differentiates these children from the others? Similarly, Steward and Steward (1989) found a 10% false report rate when 3- to 6-year-old boys and girls were questioned about doctor visits, some of which involved genital touch. However, the rate of recantation of genital contact (denying that genital touch occurred when in fact it did) was even higher (19.7%). Again, why did some children provide false reports and others falsely recant?

Research on children's memory for neutral events indicates that 3-year-olds are particularly suggestible (at least under a number of interview conditions), and this extends to suggestibility when being questioned about genital contact (Goodman & Aman, 1991; Goodman, Bottoms, et al., 1991). Borrowing in part the design developed by Saywitz et al., Bruck, Ceci, Francouer, and Renick (1995) found that about 40% of 2- to 3-year-olds falsely reported genital touch when interviewed in a leading manner with anatomically detailed dolls immediately after a medical checkup that did not include a genital examination. Although mean age trends indicate greater suggestibility in 3-year-olds, not all 3-year-olds cave in to false suggestion. Why not?

Only a few studies have identified significant individual differences in children's suggestibility and lack of disclosure. Clarke-Stewart, Thompson, and Lepore (1989) are among the few researchers to report significant individual-difference predictors of children's memory and suggestibility. In their study, one hundred 5- and 6-year-old children observed a janitor either clean or play with a set of toys. Some of the children were asked by the janitor to keep his activities secret. Later, the children were interviewed about the janitor's actions. Some of the children who watched the janitor clean were later questioned in a way which suggested that the janitor had actually played. Clarke-Stewart et al. found that children were more likely to change their interpretation of the janitor's activities (from cleaning to playing) if they were more suggestible about other events, less knowledgeable about lying, and had parents who were less likely to value self-direction. Of the children who were asked by the janitor to keep his activities secret, those especially likely to maintain the secret were boys, the less mature and confident, and those who were more anxious and negative about themselves. However, this study did not involve a stressful event.

Particularly relevant to research reported in the current chapter, Ornstein, Shapiro, Clubb, Follmer, and Baker-Ward (chapter 4, this volume) uncovered significant correlations between individual-difference measures of "approach/withdrawal" and "adaptability" on the one hand, and children's memory of a stressful medical procedure on the other. They propose that temperament may affect encoding (e.g., attentional focus during a stressful medical procedure) and retrieval of information during a memory interview.

In summary, these studies provide evidence that important individual differences can be identified (see also Gudjonsson & Clark, 1986). Such findings motivate further exploration of individual differences in children's reports of personally experienced events.

ATTACHMENT THEORY AND MEMORY FOR STRESSFUL MEDICAL PROCEDURES

Although we know little about individual differences in children's memory for stressful events, attachment theory, developed by Bowlby (1969, 1973) and Ainsworth (1989; Ainsworth, Blehar, Waters, & Wall, 1978), and extended to adult interpersonal styles by Main, Kaplan, and Cassidy (1985) and Hazan and Shaver (1987; Shaver & Hazan, 1993; Shaver, Hazan, & Bradshaw, 1988), provides a theoretical framework for predicting individual differences in children's reactions to and memories of stressful medical tests. According to this framework, children develop "internal working models" of self and others based on their primary caregiver's sensitivity to emotional and physical needs. The caregiver's sensitivity and responsiveness create expectations in the child regarding whether the caregiver, as well as other people, will protect and comfort the child. These expectations form an important part of children's internal working models.

Like other cognitive structures, such as "scripts" and "schemas," internal working models are hypothetical constructs assumed to be stored in long-term memory. They are automatically activated when attachment-related issues arise. According to attachment researchers, internal working models are composed of autobiographical memories, beliefs, goals, and individual plans (Collins & Read, 1994). Unlike traditional cognitive approaches to mental structures, the attachment approach to working models emphasizes motivational and behavioral tendencies (Shaver, Collins, & Clark, 1995). Therefore, internal working models are knowledge structures that concern self and others, but that include both cognitive and affective components.

To elaborate, children with loving, consistently responsive caregivers will develop models of other people as loving and trustworthy. In contrast, if caregivers consistently reject children's attempts to gain comfort, children develop models of others as untrustworthy. Inconsistencies in caregivers' responsiveness lead to internal working models—that is, expectations—that others will be unreliable and unpredictable. According to Bowlby (1969, 1988) and other researchers (Bretherton, 1993; Main et al., 1985) internal working models of relationships are the underlying structures that shape children's interpersonal expectations and behavior, and that lead to their particular style of attachment.

Ainsworth et al. (1978) identified three types of infant–caregiver attachment in a laboratory procedure called the *Strange Situation*. In this situation, a parent and an infant (typically 12–18 months of age) are observed in the laboratory while they engage in a series of activities. The infant's reactions are noted during play, presence of a stranger, and separation from and subsequent reunion with the parent with and without a stranger present. The three patterns of attachment identified by Ainsworth are termed *secure* (Type B), *anxious–ambivalent* (Type C), and *avoidant* (Type A). As assessed in the Strange Situation, core features of a secure relationship include that the child plays happily and independently in the presence of the parent, and is moderately distressed when the parent leaves, but is quickly comforted by the parent on reunion. In an anxious–ambivalent relationship, the child is vigilant about the parent's whereabouts, is particularly upset when left by the parent, and approaches the parent on reunion. However, the child in an anxious–ambivalent relationship also angrily protests or resists the parent's attempts to provide comfort, as if the parent's attempts are less than satisfactory (perhaps "too little, too late"). In an avoidant relationship, the child shows relatively little reaction to separation and reunion, and may actively avoid the parent's attempts to establish contact on reunion.

In longitudinal studies, these attachment orientations in infancy have been predicted accurately by home observations of parenting style and have subsequently predicted preschoolers' and elementary school children's play behavior, self-concept, and social relations with teachers and peers (see Rothbard & Shaver, 1994, for a review). Continuity in attachment patterns has been observed for as long as 10 years (from 12 months to 11 years of age; see Elicker, Egelund, & Sroufe, 1992; Grossman & Grossman, 1991). For example, in a follow-up study of children whose attachment status was measured in infancy, Elicker et al. (1992) studied children's self-esteem and social interactions at a summer camp when the children were 11 years old. When camp counselors ranked children in terms of self-esteem, self-confidence, and social interaction skills, the children with secure attachment histories scored significantly higher than children with insecure attachment histories. Secure children were also significantly more likely to interact in groups of other children than children with insecure attachment histories (38% vs. 27%, respectively), who tended to be more isolated.

Since Ainsworth et al.'s initial studies, a fourth type of attachment has been identified, termed *A/C* by Crittenden (1988) and *D* by Main (Main & Hesse, 1990). Children classified into this fourth category exhibit odd behavior during reunion, such as freezing, staring off into space, and rocking. (Main and her associates refer to this behavior as "disorganized, disoriented.") It is believed that such behavior is associated with having a parent who is troubled or suffering from unresolved grief concerning attachment-related losses or abuse.

A number of studies have uncovered intergenerational transmission of attachment style from parents to children. For example, there is empirical support for the notion that mothers' attachment status (sometimes measured by interview even before their infants are born) predicts infants' attachment classification in the Strange Situation at 12 months of age (e.g., Fonagy, Steele, & Steele, 1991; Main et al., 1985). Fonagy et al. administered the Adult Attachment Interview (AAI) to 100 mothers expecting their first child. The AAI is a structured interview consisting of 18 questions about attachment, primarily concerning the individual's relationship to his or her own mother or father during childhood. In the interview, the individual is asked about global attachment issues (e.g., to provide several adjectives describing mother). The goal of this initial questioning is to obtain a measure of the individual's semantic representations of important attachment figures. The individual is then asked to provide specific episodic memories of childhood experiences with those attachment figures. Scoring of the AAI concerns such matters as coherence of discourse, fluency of speech, and the consistency of an individual's global attachment representations as compared to the individual's specific memories.

Using the AAI, Fonagy et al. (1991) questioned expectant mothers about their own attachment histories. One year after the expectant mothers' children were born, the children were tested in Ainsworth's Strange Situation. High intergenerational concordance was found, with 75% of the secure mothers having children who were securely attached and 73% of the insecurely attached mothers having insecurely attached children. When all three attachment classifications were considered, the intergenerational concordance rate was 66% (with 44% expected by chance, $p < .001$). Main et al. (1985) also found that security of children's attachment to their mothers was highly correlated with the mothers' security of attachment as measured by a continuously scaled version of the AAI ($r = .62$). Genetically based temperament may also be a factor in intergenerational transmission, but the weight of the evidence (e.g., different patterns of child behavior with mother and father when the parents have different styles) points more to nongenetic factors (Rothbard & Shaver, 1994).

One interpretation of these findings is that mothers' "internal working models" of attachment or "state of mind with respect to attachment" (concepts proposed by Bowlby and Main, respectively) affect parenting behavior, which in turn affects children's affect-regulation strategies as measured in the Strange Situation. Because attachment orientations show considerable intergenerational continuity, there is a basis for using measures of adult attachment classifications as indirect predictors of children's attachment classifications. Until attachment measures for children are validated for use across a broad age range, adult attachment measures may prove, for certain purposes, to be the best available estimates of children's attachment styles.

Attachment, Stress, and Memory

Attachment theory is compatible with cognitive theories that focus on schema memory (Bartlett, 1932; Brewer & Nakamura, 1984; Schank & Abelson, 1977) and schema development (Mandler, 1984; Nelson, 1986). Schemas are organized sets of expectations concerning a specific domain. The domain of interest to attachment theorists is interpersonal relationships, and in attachment theory the schemas concerning such relationships are called internal working models (see earlier discussion). Although internal working models are conceptualized as involving affect-regulation strategies as well as expectations, and in that sense go beyond "cold" cognitive structures, like other cognitive schemas, internal working models would be expected to influence attention, interpretation, and memory. When a stressful event relates to attachment issues, internal working models should automatically come into play.

One implication of attachment theory for children's memory of stressful events is that internal working models will influence children's interpretations of potentially stressful experiences and thus children's level of stress. Differences in attachment may also influence children's memory reports by influencing the way children store and retrieve information from memory (Bretherton, 1993; Collins & Read, 1994; Crittenden & Claussen, 1993). Differences in attachment style are believed to reflect underlying differences in internal working models. As would be true for other mental schemas (e.g., see Schank & Abelson, 1977), internal working models would thus be expected to guide perception, storage, and retrieval.

According to Bowlby (1969), children who lack coherent, security-related internal working models interpret events related to attachment issues differently than children who have internal working models associated with security. Insecure children may overreact in ambiguous or stressful situations because they are unsure of the receptivity of adult caregivers to their needs. Compared to parents of secure children, parents of insecure children may not provide them with enough feedback in ambiguous situations to permit them to determine whether or not certain situations pose a threat, and parents of insecure children are more likely to reprimand or punish children in stressful situations (Bowlby, 1988; Bretherton, 1993). Insecure versus secure children may thus become more stressed in ambiguous or stressful situations.

A study by Main et al. (1985) provides support for the contention that attachment style may influence children's reactions to and interpretation of stimuli that raise attachment issues. In a longitudinal study of children's internal working models and attachment classifications, Main et al. found differences in 6-year-old children's emotional reactions to a photograph of a child whose parents were leaving him or her alone to go on vacation. These differences in emotional reaction when the children were 6 related to their earlier attachment classifications in the Strange Situation when they were 1. Insecure–avoidant and insecure–anxious children were much more overtly upset when questioned about the photograph than were securely attached children. Insecure–avoidant children tended to avoid answering questions about the photograph altogether. Main et al. concluded that security-related internal working models provide children with rules for directing and organizing their attention and emotion regulation when attachment issues are being directly or indirectly addressed.

Therefore, to the extent that attachment issues are raised in the course of experiencing a stressful event, attachment styles may influence children's memory by affecting children's encoding and interpretation of events and thus, through affect regulation, influence children's level of stress. Children with anxious–ambivalent attachment styles should have gaining approval and avoiding rejection as important interpersonal goals. They may be particularly vigilant to signs of abandonment and attend more exclusively than secure or avoidant children to information relevant to these interpersonal needs, especially in stressful situations, and have few resources left to process other aspects of the environment. Anxious–ambivalent children would thus be expected to make more memory errors when queried about the types of information often tested in memory research (e.g., features of the environment). Regarding memory for stressful situations that raise attachment issues, avoidant children might also be expected to make more errors than secure children, but for somewhat different reasons. Avoidant children attempt to avoid attachment issues and would thus direct their attention away from features of the environment that make attachment issues salient. Furthermore, to the degree that both anxious–ambivalent and avoidant children have difficulty forming and communicating coherent representations of attachment-related experiences, they also would be expected to make errors or produce inconsistencies in recounting a stressful event that raised attachment issues. In contrast, secure children would be expected to make fewer errors in recounting a stressful event than insecure children. Because of their increased ability to integrate positive and negative feelings about experiences and to form coherent representations of their experiences (Main, 1991), secure children would be expected to make fewer errors.

Attachment style may also be related to children's suggestibility. To the extent that memory and suggestibility are linked (Loftus, 1979), insecurely attached children may be more suggestible than securely attached children, for the reasons mentioned earlier. In addition, through a history of responsive caregiving and support for autonomy by a caregiver, secure children should develop a sense of self-worth, self-reliance, and efficacy that insecure children lack (Elicker et al., 1992). A sense of self-worth and efficacy may be related to decreased suggestibility (Eagly & Carli, 1981; Gudjonsson & Clark, 1986). In contrast, insecurely attached children, especially those with anxious–ambivalent attachment styles, may be particularly dependent on or needy of adult approval (Sroufe, Carlson, & Shulman, 1993). They may therefore conform more readily to adults' suggestions, regardless of the suggestion's truth value.

Attachment theory also suggests that an important aspect of parental behavior is communication about emotions aroused by stressful situations (Bretherton, 1990), and studies confirm that parent–child communication is related to attachment status (Main et al., 1985). Children whose parents do not spend time in balanced interactions with them may not have learned how to communicate information effectively to others. They may lack coherence in their memory reports or lack a desire to discuss past stressful events. This leads to the hypothesis that parental attachment style will be predictive of the parent's communication with his or her child following a stressful medical procedure. Style of communication may in turn affect children's memory for stressful experiences (Bretherton, 1993; Goodman et al., 1993).

From a strictly cognitive perspective, parent–child discussion of a stressful event provides the child a chance to learn more about and review what happened. Increased knowledge and rehearsal of either emotional or nonemotional events is often associated with more complete and resilient memory (e.g., Bohannon & Symons, 1992; Brainerd & Ornstein, 1991; Kail, 1990). Through careful discussion, the parent can correct misconceptions (Bretherton, 1993), which might otherwise lead to inaccuracies in children's memory reports. From a more clinical perspective, parent–child discussion about a stressful event can be seen to facilitate the release of pent-up or frightening feelings, which may eventually permit the child to recall and think about the event in a calmer, more controlled way, with less interference from negative emotions and associated defenses (e.g., by facilitating coherence of mind and discourse in children of secure parents and emotional disruption or blocking in children of insecure parents; see Bretherton, 1990).

In summary, based on attachment theory, one would predict individual differences in children's memory for stressful events, especially if the event activates attachment issues (e.g., children's expectations about parental or adult protection). One may speculate that securely attached children will display less stress than children who are insecure–ambivalent or insecure–avoidant when children encounter a potentially stressful situation that evokes attachment issues. Additionally, insecure–ambivalent children will evidence more stress than insecure–avoidant and securely attached children, especially when faced with parental abandonment.

Based on studies of stress and children's memory, there are at least two possibilities concerning the relations among attachment style, stress, and memory for a traumatic event that evokes attachment issues. One possibility is that the degree of stress experienced may influence the accuracy of a child's memory directly (e.g., Goodman et al., 1986; Peters, 1991). For example, if stress is associated with less accurate memory, one would predict that insecure children would have less accurate memories because they were more stressed than secure children during the event. A second possibility is that attachment is related to memory for a stressful event independently of the level of stress experienced. According to this possibility, when attachment issues are a salient part of a stressful event, insecure children have more difficulty fully and accurately encoding and retaining information about the event. They would also be expected to have a more difficult time coherently communicating their experiences and would obtain less parental support for accurate memory. Furthermore, they might be particularly susceptible to false suggestion. Therefore, insecure children would be predicted to make more errors than securely attached children.

Stressful medical procedures may activate internal working models relevant to attachment issues. Stressful medical procedures may involve parents comforting or scolding the child, holding children down, or abandoning the child by leaving the room (as often required by doctors), all of which may raise attachment issues. Moreover, to the extent that internal working models generalize and affect expectations that other people (in this case, medical staff) will be responsive and caring, attachment issues might be raised regarding the actions of doctors, nurses, and technicians. These features of medical procedures may thus facilitate the study of individual differences in children's memory for stressful events. This possibility is supported by our research, as explained in the next section.

DEVELOPMENTAL DIFFERENCES

Attachment style is not expected to be the sole influence on children's memory for a stressful event; there is ample reason to expect developmental differences as well. Studies of children's memory for inoculations and venipuncture, for example, indicate that older children are better able to recall the event and answer questions about it accurately than are younger children (Goodman, Bottoms, et al., 1991; Goodman, Hirschman, et al., 1991). Older children's more complete and accurate memories may reflect greater knowledge about the events (Chi, 1978), as well as increased memory capacity and skill level afforded by cognitive development (Case, 1985; Fischer, 1980). Older children may also form more forgetting-resistant gist memories than do younger children (Brainerd & Reyna, 1991) and evidence more strategic control of the memory process (Kail, 1990; Ornstein & Naus, 1985).

Developmental differences in the intensity of children's reactions to medical settings must also be considered. Previous research indicates that children below the age of about 8 years are particularly upset during medical procedures such as inoculations (Melamed, 1976). Part of young children's greater fear seems to stem from their lack of understanding of the event and poorer abilities to utilize strategies of distraction and self-soothing (e.g., Pinto & Hollandsworth, 1989).

In summary, developmental differences in the intensity of children's reactions to stressful medical procedures and in children's knowledge base, cognitive development, and memory abilities may all be relevant to their ability to tell later what happened.

REPEATED VERSUS ONE-TIME STRESSFUL EVENTS

Another influence of potential importance in understanding memory for stressful events is the number of times the event is experienced. To date, there is very little published scientific research on children's reports of repeated stressful events, and yet this is an extremely important issue both theoretically and practically. Do children form "scripts" (Fivush, 1993; Nelson, 1986) for repeated traumatic events and thus evidence typical schema memory effects? Do children form "flashbulb memories" (i.e., particularly detailed, vivid memories) for each incident? Related to the earlier discussion, repetition of a stressful event should establish a more elaborate knowledge base for the event, which might strengthen memory; but how does knowledge base affect memory for a stressful as opposed to a nonstressful event? Given that many similar stressful events can be experienced, it is important to determine whether children are more accurate or more error-prone and suggestible about a single (as opposed to a repeatedly experienced) event.

In an attempt to understand the effects of repeated stressful events on children's memory, Terr (1988, 1990) conducted a clinical case study of children who had experienced or witnessed either one-time or repeated traumatic events (e.g., intrafamilial sexual abuse, kidnapping, accidents resulting in disfigurement). She concluded:

> the type of traumatic event bore a significant influence upon whether and how completely a child would be able, verbally, to remember what had happened. Short, single events were by far the best remembered.... The accuracy of those children exposed to very long or to repeated events at or after age twenty-eight months was considerably poorer than was the accuracy of those youngsters exposed to one short event at these very same ages. (Terr, 1990, pp. 182–183)

Terr attributed this finding to the role of defense mechanisms:

> Why does the nature of the traumatic event exert so much influence over whether what happened will be remembered in words? It appears that sudden, fast events completely overcome any defenses that a small child can muster.

Long standing events, on the other hand, stimulate defensive operations—denial, splitting, self-anesthesia, and dissociation. These defenses are completely overrun by one sudden, unanticipated terror, and brilliant, overly clear verbal memories are the result. On the other hand, when the defenses are set up in advance in order to deal with terrors the child knows to be coming, blurry, partial, or absent verbal memories are retained. The child may even develop blanket amnesia for certain years in the past. (p. 183)

Terr (1991) linked these ideas to the notion of repressed memories; specifically, she has hypothesized that one-time traumatic events are less likely than repeated events, such as incest, to lead to repressed memories.

Although Terr attributed the phenomenon she documented to defense mechanisms, her observations are in some ways consistent with what is known about children's memories for repeated events generally. One-time novel events of a more neutral nature are retained well by children (Nelson, 1986). However, memories of repeated events often combine to form a script or schema (i.e., an organized set of expectations; Bartlett, 1932; Schank & Abelson, 1977). When a script is formed, details of specific instances can become lost. Depending on the complexity of the event and the number of repetitions, the loss of detail and merging of instances is especially likely among young children (Farrar & Goodman, 1992, but see Hudson, 1990). However, the gist of the events and certain distinctive features are still typically retained in accurate detail (Nelson, 1986).

There are virtually no scientific studies comparing children's memory for a one-time stressful event with memory for a repeated stressful event. Terr's work consists of clinical case studies in which the nature of the events varied widely and there was little control over such important variables as age, gender, and SES. Basic research on the development of script memory tightly controls such factors but has not focused on memory for repeated traumatic events (but see Bearison & Pacifici, 1989; Reynolds, Johnson, & Silverstein, 1990). Thus there is a need to determine whether the aforementioned principles hold true when children are questioned about one-time versus repeated stressful events and when the events are standardized and an objective record exists.

THE PRESENT RESEARCH

At Children's Hospital of Buffalo, we conducted a study to examine children's memory for a stressful medical test (Goodman et al., 1993). The study was initially motivated mainly by a desire to examine age differences in children's memory for a traumatic experience involving genital contact. However, we were also interested in individual-difference predictors of children's memory and suggestibility about a traumatic event. The findings reveal important individual differences, as well as age differences, in memory for stressful medical experiences. Specifically, the results indicate that parents' orientation to intimate relationships (adult attachment style, as assessed with a measure devised by Hazan & Shaver, 1987, 1990) is significantly related to children's affect-regulation strategies in stressful medical situations, as well as to their memory. The strength of these relations was surprisingly strong.

The study concerned children's memory for a medical test called voiding cystourethrogram fluoroscopy (VCUG). It took advantage of the fact that VCUG is often ordered by doctors when a child has urinary tract infections, is incontinent, or wets the bed. Although indications for VCUG include a variety of urinary tract problems (Kirks, 1991; Noe, Wyatt, Peeden, & Rivas, 1992), by the age of 3 years, most children undergo VCUG because of urinary tract infections, problems with micturition, or enuresis. With parents' and children's consent, we were permitted to observe and videotape children who were receiving the VCUG test, in order to obtain an objective record of the procedure and the child's level of distress, about which we could later interview the children.

Receiving a VCUG test is stressful for many, if not most, children. In fact, it can be a painful, frightening, and embarrassing procedure even for an adult. The procedure starts with simple X-rays of the child. However, it progresses to catheterization of the child through the urethra (involving insertion of a 12″ to 15″ plastic tube), infusion through the catheter of a liquid contrast medium which fills the child's bladder, and the taking of X-rays while the child voids publicly onto the examination table. Parents play a role in the event by holding the child down as the child is catheterized, by trying to distract the child, and by various degrees of emotional comforting or demands for cooperation. At the hospital where our data were collected, parents were also required to leave the room midway through the procedure.

For our study, 46 children (18 boys and 28 girls), ranging in age from 3 to 10 years ($M = 5$ years 6 months), were observed during their VCUG test and interviewed later. Most of the children were experiencing VCUG for the first time, although 17 had experienced VCUG at least once before, some as many as six times. Individuals were excluded from the study if they were mentally retarded, paralyzed, hyperactive, or chronically ill (e.g., cancer patients).

Our typical procedure was for the child and parent to come to our university-based laboratory for an initial pre-VCUG session (Session 1), at which time the child was administered various individual-differences tests (e.g., the Peabody Picture Vocabulary Test), and the parent completed the Hazan and Shaver (1987, 1990) Close Relationship Questionnaire concerning the parents' own feelings and behaviors in close relationships (see Table 11.1).[1] The Hazan and Shaver measure is based on Ainsworth's parent–child

---

[1]Due to scheduling constraints, an initial session was not always possible. In that case, parental consent was obtained at Session 2 and the Session 1 measures were administered at Session 3, as possible.

TABLE 11.1
Close Relationships Questionnaire

This questionnaire is concerned with your experiences in *romantic love relationships*. Take a moment to think about these experiences and answer the following questions with them in mind.

1. Read each of the three self-descriptions below (A, B, and C) and then place a checkmark next to the single alternative that best describes how you feel in romantic relationships or is the nearest to the way you are. (Note: The terms "close" and "intimate" refer to psychological or emotional closeness, not necessarily to sexual intimacy.)

_____ A. I am somewhat uncomfortable being close to others; I find it difficult to trust them completely, difficult to allow myself to depend on them. I am nervous when anyone gets too close, and often, love partners want me to be more intimate than I feel comfortable being.

_____ B. I find that others are reluctant to get as close as I would like. I often worry that my partner doesn't really love me or won't want to stay with me. I want to get very close to my partner, and this sometimes scares people away.

_____ C. I find it relatively easy to get close to others and am comfortable depending on them. I don't often worry about being abandoned or about someone getting too close to me.

2. Now please rate each of the relationship styles above according to the extent to which you think each description corresponds to your general relationship style.

Not at All Like Me			Somewhat Like Me			Very Much Like Me	
Style A	1	2	3	4	5	6	7
Style B	1	2	3	4	5	6	7
Style C	1	2	3	4	5	6	7

From "Love and Work: An Attachment–Theoretical Perspective," by C. Hazan and P. R. Shaver, 1990, *Journal of Personality and Social Psychology, 59*.

attachment typology, and includes three attachment categories (secure, avoidant, and anxious–ambivalent) which characterize adults' intimacy styles in close relationships. The Hazan and Shaver measure consists of a brief description of the three attachment styles followed by 7-point scales on which the respondent indicates how much each of the three descriptions applies to her or him. Of most interest to the current study were the parents' responses on the 7-point scales, as opposed to their category classification as secure, anxious–ambivalent, or avoidant. Unfortunately, a direct measure of the children's attachment patterns was not possible given the relatively broad age range of interest (3 to 10 years). This is because there is no single, generally accepted measure of attachment that covers this broad age range. Although a direct measure of the children's attachment status would have been preferable, the Hazan and Shaver parent measure proved quite useful.

When the family arrived at the hospital for the VCUG test (Session 2), the parent completed a brief questionnaire concerning the child's expectations about the medical test and knowledge of the procedure. A researcher then accompanied the parent and child into the X-ray room. On 6-point scales, the researcher rated the child's level of distress (1 = *extremely happy* and 6 = *extremely unhappy*) and degree of crying (1 = *not crying at all* and 6 = *hysterical crying*) at several key points during the VCUG test (e.g., when the child was first placed on the examination table; during the catheterization; and when the parent left the room, which occurred right after catheterization). In addition, the entire VCUG procedure was videotaped.

From 1 to 4 weeks later, the child returned to the laboratory for a memory interview (Session 3). The memory interview consisted of a free-recall question (i.e., "Tell me everything you can remember about what happened") followed by a set of open-ended questions (e.g., "What did the doctor look like?"), specific questions (e.g., "Did the nurse touch you down there?"), and misleading questions (e.g., "Your mother stayed with you the whole time, didn't she?"). Free-recall and open-ended questions were scored for units of correct or incorrect information, and all other questions were scored for proportion of correct responses, commission errors, and omission errors (see Goodman, Quas, Batterman-Faunce, Riddlesberger, & Kuhn, 1994).

As expected, there were age differences in the level of stress children displayed and in their memory performance. During the catheterization, children's mean stress rating per age group was: 3- to 4-year-olds, $M = 4.82$; 5- to 6-year-olds, $M = 3.56$; 7- to 10-year-olds, $M = 3.83$, $F(2, 42) = 3.51$, $p < .05$. Planned comparisons revealed that the 3- to 4-year-olds were significantly more stressed than the 5- to 6-year-olds, $p < .05$, and somewhat more stressed than the 7- to 10-year-olds, $p < .10$. Age was also associated with how much the children cried when their parent left the room: 3- to 4-year-olds, $M = 2.82$; 5- to 6-year-olds, $M = 1.50$; 7- to 10-year-olds, $M = 1.33$, $F(2, 42) = 5.66$, $p < .01$. Planned comparisons revealed that the youngest children cried more when the parent left the room than did the older children, $p < .05$. These findings are consistent with those of other researchers who find that younger children display more upset and crying during stressful medical procedures than do older children (Melamed, 1976).

Age differences in memory were also consistent with predictions (see Table 11.2). Significant age differences appeared across virtually all dependent measures, most typically with the 3- to 4-year-olds providing fewer correct answers and more incorrect answers than older children. However, age differences were not significant for incorrect information provided in response to free-recall or open-ended questions.

Interestingly, repetition of the VCUG experience did not seem to affect children's memory, at least as far as we could detect statistically. When memory performance was compared for children who experienced the medical test once versus those who experienced it several times, there were no significant differences in memory performance, even when age was statistically controlled (Goodman et al., 1994). The number of VCUGs the child experienced was also not significantly associated with the child's age or display of stress during the VCUG that we observed.

TABLE 11.2
Memory Performance for Each Age Group

	3 to 4 Years	5 to 6 Years	7 to 10 Years	F	p
Free recall (mean number of units)					
Correct	8.88[a]	17.00[ab]	26.23[b]	6.02	.01
Incorrect	2.59	1.38	1.00	n.s.	
Specific questions (mean proportions)					
Correct	0.47[a]	0.63[b]	0.82[c]	21.81	.001
Commission	0.15[a]	0.08[b]	0.06[b]	7.87	.001
Omission	0.16[a]	0.10[b]	0.04[c]	14.97	.001
Misleading questions (mean proportions)					
Correct	0.48[a]	0.67[b]	0.82[c]	13.71	.001
Commission	0.26[a]	0.11[b]	0.06[b]	14.18	.001
Omission	0.15[a]	0.08[b]	0.06[b]	7.01	.01
Open-ended questions (mean number of units)					
Correct	7.76[a]	19.44[b]	43.00[c]	24.22	.001
Incorrect	6.12	7.75	5.23	n.s.	

Note. Proportions may total less than 1.00 due to "do not know," no response, changing the topic, or ambiguous and unscorable responses. Across rows, a different superscript letter indicates a significant planned mean comparison: all Fs(1, 43) ≥ 5.04, p < .05.

Knowledge base should be an important determinant of memory (Chi, 1978), including memory for stressful events (Liwag & Stein, 1993; Ornstein et al., chapter 4, this volume). Experiencing VCUG several times would be expected to contribute to more complete knowledge of the test. Therefore, it was surprising that there were no significant relations between memory and repeated VCUG experience. However, we obtained another indicator of knowledge base; specifically, what the child expected to happen during the medical test at the hospital. Based on parent report provided on the day of the VCUG, we created a variable concerning what the child expected/knew about the VCUG exam (0 = nothing, 1 = child knew she or he would have a medical test to see what was wrong, 2 = child knew she or he would have an X-ray, 3 = child knew she or he would be catheterized, 4 = child knew full details of the VCUG test). There were several significant correlations between this variable and memory accuracy, particularly in regard to free-recall and misleading questions, rs = .35 and .43, respectively, ps ≤ .05 (with age and parental attachment partialled). The knowledge variable was not, however, significantly related to inaccuracy. Therefore, at least one indicator of knowledge base was predictive of children's correct responses, as would be expected based on memory development research.

The findings of major interest, however, concerned the relation between the children's level of stress, their memory, and their parents' attachment style. Concerning the children's level of stress, Hazan and Shaver's adult attachment measure (completed by *parents*) significantly predicted how stressed the *children* were by the VCUG test. If parents rated their attachment style as high on the anxious–ambivalent or avoidant scales (both of which indicate insecure attachment in Ainsworth's scheme), the child tended to show the highest levels of stress during key parts of the VCUG test, with correlations in the .21 to .61 range. (For these correlations and those reported here later, child age was statistically controlled through partial correlations.) Security of parental attachment style was associated with children being less stressed during the VCUG procedure; *r*s ranged up to −.61. This was quite remarkable because, as mentioned earlier, the Hazan and Shaver measure consists only of a brief description of three adult attachment styles (one of which, for example, focuses on the respondent's difficulty getting emotionally close to relationship partners) followed by a 7-point scale on which to indicate how much the description characterizes the respondent, not the child (see Table 11.1). The raters of the children's stress were completely blind to the parents' attachment style; they were simply rating the child's visible level of stress. However, the correlations were quite robust. They indicate that children of insecure parents are more likely to be upset during the VCUG test, whereas children of secure parents are more likely to be calm.

An important question for our study concerned the relation between stress and memory. Interestingly, there were no significant correlations between any of the stress ratings and *correct* responses on the various memory-test indices. However, the pattern of correlations indicated that stress was associated with more memory errors. Simply attending to correlations would have thus led us to conclude that stress was associated with children being more incorrect (*r*s ≤ .38, with age partialled). This was especially evident for children's errors of omission to both specific and misleading questions.

However, the full story was more complicated and more interesting than that. Path analyses revealed that stress was not related to memory errors. Instead, parents' attachment style was significantly related to children's error rates, and parental attachment style accounted for the relation between stress and memory errors. To further articulate what we found, details of the path analyses are presented next.

To conduct the path analyses, several initial steps were taken. The first step concerned the adult attachment measure. Because parents' attachment-style ratings (i.e., parents' ratings of their similarity to secure and avoidant romantic attachment styles) were fairly strongly correlated, the ratings were subjected to factor analysis, using varimax rotation, to reduce redundancy. A two-factor solution emerged, which is consistent with past research employing adult attachment scales (e.g., Brennan, Shaver, & Tobey, 1991). Low scores on the first factor correspond to greater similarity to the secure attachment style and high scores correspond to greater similarity to the avoidant attachment style. High scores on the second factor correspond to high similarity to the anxious/ambivalent attachment style.

Then, to reduce the number of variables involved, the children's memory scores were factor analyzed using varimax rotation. Two factors emerged, one indicating correctness and the other incorrectness. Note that a child may have scored highly on both factors if he or she provided a substantial amount of correct and incorrect information.

Finally, to conduct the path analyses, we selected amount of crying when the parent left the room as our measure of stress. This measure was selected because of its importance from an attachment-theory perspective and because a parent leaving his or her child alone with strangers is a central component of Ainsworth's Strange Situation. Furthermore, the level of stress children displayed during the catheterization showed considerably less variability because many children were quite stressed during that time. Of importance to our argument, our basic path-model findings still hold regarding stress and memory even when other stress measures are selected (e.g., initial stress level).

The results of the path analyses can be seen in Fig. 11.1. (Two separate path analyses were conducted, one for correct information and one for incorrect information. The results are combined in Fig. 11.1.) Children's age and parents' anxious–ambivalent attachment ratings were significantly related to how much the children cried when their parents left the room.

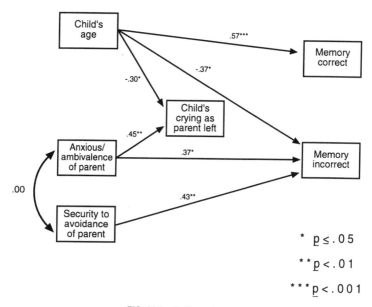

FIG. 11.1. Path analyses.

Specifically, the children's level of crying decreased with age. Additionally, the more similar parents were to the anxious–ambivalent romantic attachment style, the more their children cried when the parents left the room, as would be predicted by attachment theory.

Age was the only variable in the path analyses that influenced how correct children were on the memory test, with older children providing more correct information.[2] Age also predicted how much incorrect information children provided. As expected, younger children were more inaccurate.

In the path analyses, there was no indication that stress was related to children's memory errors; the relation between stress and memory was not significant. However, children whose parents indicated an avoidant attachment style made more errors, as did children whose parents indicated an anxious–ambivalent attachment style. Therefore, parent attachment style was a better predictor of children's memory errors than was the children's level of crying during the VCUG exam.

Attachment theory would also lead to the prediction that, after the VCUG exam, parents would talk to their children in different ways, depending on their attachment style. During Session 3 of our study, the child's parent (usually the mother) completed a questionnaire concerning her post-VCUG discussions with and comforting of the child. Consistent with this prediction, a higher score on the secure-attachment scale was positively related to indicating "yes" to questions about whether or not the mother discussed the VCUG exam with the child, explained the VCUG exam to the child, physically comforted the child, and asked the child questions about the VCUG exam, $rs \geq .33$, $p < .05$. In contrast, a higher score on the insecure-attachment scales was inversely associated with discussing the VCUG exam with the child, explaining the exam to the child, and physically comforting the child, $rs \leq -.28$, $ps < .05$.

In summary, the results of our path analyses suggest that the relation between stress and memory is in part explained by individual differences. Such individual differences may be based in what attachment theorists call internal working models, reflecting individual differences in children's concerns and interpretations of events. Although further research will be needed to determine the exact mechanisms involved, we can speculate based on attachment theory that children of anxious–ambivalent parents may become preoccupied with attachment issues during a stressful event that raises such concerns. These children may display particularly high levels of distress (e.g., cry more) once attachment issues are activated, which may influence their encoding of the stressful event in the first place and the amount of inaccurate information they report on a later memory test. We can further

---

[2]Our measure of children's knowledge of the VCUG exam was not included in the path analysis because it reduced the number of subjects in relation to the number of variables to a low level.

speculate that, as predicted by attachment theory, children with avoidant parents may try to repress or deny their feelings in recounting a stressful event, which may contribute to memory errors. In contrast, children of secure parents may have increased ability to form coherent representations of their experiences (e.g., to accurately integrate and differentiate semantic and episodic representations of events, to integrate and differentiate positive and negative feelings about experiences). Children of secure parents may also evidence greater understanding of the stressful event in part because of greater coherence of mind, but also due to parental discussion (see Goodman et al., 1994), more appropriate emotional regulation before, during, or after, or at all three stages of a stressful experience. Further research is clearly needed to test these possibilities. In any case, our results imply that in order to understand the effects of fear on children's memory, we may need to take into consideration individual differences in children's personality and concerns (fear of parental abandonment, fear of lack of protection) and in family factors (parental communication and emotional support), in addition to developmental differences in children's encoding and retention of traumatic experiences.

OTHER INTERPRETATIONS AND CONSIDERATIONS

Although attachment theory provides a framework for understanding children's memory for stressful events that raise attachment issues, alternative explanations should be considered. Temperament (e.g., neuroticism) poses one alternative explanation. Perhaps parents who are more neurotic by nature have children who are also more neurotic. Such children may be particularly upset during the VCUG test because of genetically based temperament factors, and may also make more errors in memory because of temperamental differences as well. It can be difficult to untangle effects of attachment from effects of temperament, and vice versa, but note that in our path analysis, the two attachment factors were created through varimax rotation and are thus orthogonal, making it less likely that a single dimension such as neuroticism accounts for our findings. Furthermore, the path analysis indicates that children with parents who score high on the anxious–ambivalent attachment scale differ from children with parents who score high on the avoidant scale in important and predictable ways (e.g., children of anxious–ambivalent parents cry more). Therefore, these findings make it less likely that a simple neuroticism explanation can account for our results.

It is also possible that the children who remembered the VCUG test most accurately were more intelligent or more verbal. Although we did not include a measure of intelligence in our study, we did include a test of receptive vocabulary skills, the Peabody Picture Vocabulary Test (PPVT). Unfortunately, we were not able to obtain this measure for all of the children. For the subset that did take the test, there were a few significant correlations between memory and PPVT scores. However, PPVT scores were also significantly correlated with parental attachment (secure, $r = .31$; avoidant, $r = -.47$, and anxious–ambivalent, $r = -.37$, all $ps < .05$). If secure parents talk to their children more, one would expect the children to have better vocabularies. Alternatively, one could argue that more intelligent parents produce children who have better receptive vocabularies and who are better able to recount their VCUG experiences.

As alluded to earlier, parents' extent of talking to the children after the VCUG test may have influenced the children's memory. Such discussion may stabilize or reinstate children's memory, correct misconceptions, elaborate on the experience, and serve a rehearsal function. Indeed, we found that securely attached parents talked to their children more than did insecurely attached parents, just as attachment theory would predict. However, if discussion accounted for our findings, one might expect that the parents' discussion with their children would have led to more complete reporting of the event. Instead, parental discussion after the VCUG test was associated only with fewer errors. (For further findings from the present study regarding parental discussion and children's memory, see Goodman et al., 1994.) Therefore, although parental discussion may be influential, it does not fully account for our findings. Again, further research is needed to explore various alternative explanations.

Even if attachment theory, in the end, provides the best explanation of our findings, it will still be necessary to determine the exact mechanisms involved. For example, do children who experience parenting by securely attached parents have better memory skills generally, perhaps because of greater practice in narrative communication and experience sharing? Do children with securely attached versus insecurely attached parents encode different features of the situation initially? We also do not know how attachment concerns might affect performance on a memory interview, during which children are typically separated from their parents. By varying parent absence and presence during the memory test, we may be able to learn if parent–child separation differentially affects children's performance as a function of attachment status.

Perhaps the most serious problem with our preliminary study is, as mentioned earlier, that a measure of children's own attachment classification was not available, because of the age range tested. Therefore, we had a less-than-perfect measure of children's own attachment category. Future research should include direct measures of children's attachment as such measures become available. Even when one is available, it is still reasonable to question how well all children and adults fall into the three or four

attachment categories usually studied. However, regardless of these problems and even with an imperfect measure, our findings fit surprisingly well
with predications based on attachment theory.

CONCLUSION

Despite the importance—for both theory and application—of understanding
children's memory for stressful and traumatic experiences, scientists are
only beginning to study the complex mechanisms involved. It is unlikely
that simple relations, such as the Yerkes–Dodson Law, can capture the
complex mental phenomena of interest. It is more likely that some combination of factors will influence children's memory for stressful experiences:
for example, the child's developmental level and interpretation of the experience; the child's focus of attention, goals, and knowledge base; delay
between the stressful event and memory testing; social influences, such as
parental support and discussion; and level and type of trauma. Our findings
suggest that, in addition to developmental level, individual differences in
the meaning of traumatic events, based in part on internal working models,
and in how such experiences are handled within the context of a child's
family may be especially critical. Such individual difference factors may help
determine when a child's memory for a traumatic event is accurate, inaccurate, or a blending of truth and falsehood.

ACKNOWLEDGMENTS

The contributions of Jennifer M. Batterman-Faunce, Debra Dorfman-Botens,
and Ann E. Tobey in helping to conduct the research described in this
chapter are gratefully acknowledged, as is the substantial assistance provided by Bridgette Doherty, Teresa Drost, Colleen Flanagan, Felicia Katz,
Michelle Larro, Holly Orcutt, Michelle Schweitzer, Cheryl Shapiro, and April
Smith. Special thanks also go to James Blascovich for bringing the VCUG
procedure to our attention and to Phillip R. Shaver for commenting on a
previous version of this manuscript. Staff of the Department of Radiology
at Children's Hospital of Buffalo aided the project. We are particularly in-
debted to Connie Ryan, M. Riddlesberger, Jerold Kuhn, and Diane Deck. The
research was supported in part by grants to Gail S. Goodman from the Baldy
Center on Law and Social Policy at the State University of New York at
Buffalo; the University of California, Davis Discretionary Research Fund; and
the National Center on Child Abuse and Neglect. Finally, thanks are owed
to the children and families who participated.

REFERENCES

Ainsworth, M. D. S. (1989). Attachment beyond infancy. *American Psychologist, 44,* 709–716.

Ainsworth, M. D. S., Blehar, M. C., Waters, E., & Wall, S. (1978). *Patterns of attachment: A psychological study of the strange situation.* Hillsdale, NJ: Lawrence Erlbaum Associates.

Baddeley, A. (1976). *The psychology of memory.* New York: Basic Books.

Baker-Ward, L., Gordon, B., Ornstein, P., Larus, D., & Clubb, P. (1993). Young children's long-term retention of a pediatric examination. *Child Development, 64,* 1519–1533.

Bartlett, F. (1932). *Remembering.* Cambridge, England: Cambridge University Press.

Bearison, D. J., & Pacifici, C. (1989). Children's event knowledge for cancer treatment. *Journal of Applied and Developmental Psychology, 10,* 469–486.

Bohannon, N., & Symons, V. (1992). Flashbulb memories: Confidence, consistency, and quantity. In E. Winograd & U. Neisser (Eds.), *Affect and accuracy in recall* (pp. 65–94). New York: Cambridge University Press.

Bowlby, J. (1969). *Attachment and loss: Vol. 1. Attachment.* New York: Basic Books.

Bowlby, J. (1973). *Attachment and loss: Vol. 2. Separation.* New York: Basic Books.

Bowlby, J. (1988). *A secure base.* New York: Basic Books.

Brainerd, C., & Ornstein, P. (1991). Children's memory for witnessed events. In J. Doris (Ed.), *The suggestibility of children's recollections* (pp. 10–20). Washington, DC: American Psychological Association.

Brainerd, C., & Reyna, V. (1991). Gist is the grist: Fuzzy-trace theory and the new intuitionism. *Developmental Review, 10,* 3–47.

Brennan, K. A., Shaver, P. R., & Tobey, A. E. (1991). Attachment styles, gender, and parental problem drinking. *Journal of Social and Personal Relationships, 8,* 451–466.

Bretherton, I. (1990). Open communication and internal working models: Their role in the development of attachment relationships. In R. A. Thompson (Ed.), *Socioemotional development: Nebraska Symposium on Motivation* (Vol. 36, pp. 57–113). Lincoln: University of Nebraska Press.

Bretherton, I. (1993). From dialogue to internal working models: The co-construction of self relationships. In C. Nelson (Ed.), *Memory and affect in development: Minnesota Symposium on Child Psychology* (Vol. 26, pp. 237–263). Hillsdale, NJ: Lawrence Erlbaum Associates.

Brewer, W., & Nakamura, G. V. (1984). The nature and functions of schemas. In R. S. Wyer & T. R. Srull (Eds.), *Handbook of social cognition* (Vol. 1, pp. 119–160). Hillsdale, NJ: Lawrence Erlbaum Associates.

Brown, R., & Kulik, J. (1977). Flashbulb memories. *Cognition, 5,* 73–99.

Bruck, M., Ceci, S. J., Francouer, E., & Renick, A. (1995). Anatomically detailed dolls do not facilitate preschoolers' reports of a pediatric examination involving genital touch. *Journal of Experimental Psychology: Applied, 1,* 95–109.

Bush, J. P., Melamed, B. G., & Cockrell, C. S. (1989). Parenting children in a stressful medical situation. In T. W. Miller (Ed.), *Stressful life events* (pp. 643–657). Madison, CT: International Universities Press.

Case, R. (1985). *Intellectual development.* New York: Academic Press.

Ceci, S. J., & Bruck, M. (1993). The suggestibility of child witnesses: A historical review and synthesis. *Psychological Bulletin, 113,* 403–439.

Chi, M. T. H. (1978). Knowledge structures and memory development. In R. Siegler (Ed.), *Children's thinking: What develops?* (pp. 73–96). Hillsdale, NJ: Lawrence Erlbaum Associates.

Christianson, S.-A. (1992). Emotional stress and eyewitness memory: A critical review. *Psychological Bulletin, 12,* 284–309.

Christianson, S.-A., & Loftus, E. F. (1987). Memory for traumatic events. *Applied Cognitive Psychology, 1,* 225–239.

Clarke-Steward, A., Thompson, J., & Lepore, S. (1989, April). Manipulating children's interpretations through interrogation. In G. Goodman (Chair), *Can children provide accurate eyewitness reports?* Symposium presented at Society for Research on Child Development Meetings, Kansas City, MO.

Collins, N. L., & Read, S. J. (1994). Cognitive representations of attachment: The structure and function of working models. *Advances in Personal Relationships, 5,* 53–90.

Crittenden, P. (1988). Relationships at risk. In J. Belsky & T. Nezworksi (Eds.), *Clinical implications of attachment* (pp. 136–174). Hillsdale, NJ: Lawrence Erlbaum Associates.

Crittenden, P., & Claussen, A. H. (1993, March). *Validation of a theory-based system for assessing quality of attachment in the preschool years.* Paper presented at the Society for Research in Child Development Meetings, New Orleans, LA.

Eagly, A., & Carli, L. L. (1981). Sex of researchers and sex-typed communications as determinants of sex differences in influenceability: A meta-analysis of social influence studies. *Psychological Bulletin, 90,* 1–20.

Easterbrook, J. A. (1959). The effect of emotion on cue utilization and the organization of behavior. *Psychological Review, 66,* 183–201.

Elicker, J., Egelund, M., & Sroufe, L. A. (1992). Predicting peer competence and peer relationships in childhood from early parent–child relationships. In R. Parke & G. Ladd (Eds.), *Family–peer relations: Modes of linkage* (pp. 77–106). Hillsdale, NJ: Lawrence Erlbaum Associates.

Farrar, M. J., & Goodman, G. S. (1992). Developmental differences in event memory. *Child Development, 63,* 173–187.

Fischer, K. (1980). A theory of cognitive development: The control of hierarchies of skill. *Psychological Review, 87,* 477–531.

Fivush, R. (1993). Developmental perspectives on autobiographical recall. In G. Goodman & B. Bottoms (Eds.), *Child victims, child witnesses* (pp. 1–24). New York: Guilford.

Fonagy, P., Steele, H., & Steele, M. (1991). Maternal representations of attachment during pregnancy predict the organization of infant–mother attachment at one year of age. *Child Development, 62,* 891–905.

Goldman, R., & Goldman, J. (1988). *Show me yours.* New York: Penguin.

Goodman, G. S. (Ed.). (1984). The child witness. *Journal of Social Issues, 40*(2), 1–176.

Goodman, G. S. (1993, August). *Child victims, child witnesses.* Invited address, American Psychological Association, Toronto, Canada.

Goodman, G. S., & Aman, C. J. (1991). Children's use of anatomically detailed dolls to recount an event. *Child Development, 61,* 1859–1871.

Goodman, G. S., Batterman-Faunce, J., Quas, J., Riddlesberger, M., & Kuhn, G. (1993, March). Children's memory for stressful events: Theoretical and developmental considerations. In N. Stein (Chair), *Emotional events and memory.* Symposium presented at the Society for Research in Child Development, New Orleans, LA.

Goodman, G. S., Bottoms, B. L., Schwartz-Kenney, B., & Rudy, L. (1991). Children's memory for a stressful event: Improving children's reports. *Journal of Narrative and Life History, 1,* 69–99.

Goodman, G. S., Hepps, D., & Reed, R. S. (1986). The child victim's testimony. In A. Haralambie (Ed.), *New issues for child advocates* (pp. 167–176). Phoenix: Arizona Council of Attorneys for Children.

Goodman, G. S., Hirschman, J., Hepps, D., & Rudy, L. (1991). Children's memory for stressful events. *Merrill-Palmer Quarterly, 37,* 109–158.

Goodman, G. S., Quas, J., Batterman-Faunce, J. M., Riddlesberger, M., & Kuhn, M. (1994). Predictors of accurate and inaccurate memories of traumatic events experienced in childhood. *Consciousness and Cognition, 3,* 269–294.

Grossman, K. E., & Grossman, K. (1991). Attachment quality as an organizer of emotional and behavioral responses in a longitudinal perspective. In C. M. Parks, J. Stevenson-Hinde, & P. Marris (Eds.), *Attachment across the life cycle* (pp. 93–114). London: Tavistock/Routledge.

Hazan, C., & Shaver, P. R. (1987). Romantic love conceptualized as an attachment process. *Journal of Personality and Social Psychology, 52*, 511–524.

Hazan, C., & Shaver, P. R. (1990). Love and work: An attachment-theoretical perspective. *Journal of Personality and Social Psychology, 59*, 270–280.

Howe, M., Courage, M. L., & Peterson, C. (1994). How can I remember when "I" wasn't there: Long-term retention of traumatic experiences and the emergence of the cognitive self. *Consciousness and Cognition, 3*, 327–355.

Hudson, J. (1990). Constructive processes in children's event memories. *Developmental Psychology, 26*, 180–187.

Innocent plea in snapshot molest case. (1993, October 16). *The Napa Valley Register*, Part A, p. 3.

Kail, R. (1990). *The development of memory in children*. San Francisco: Freeman.

Kirks, D. (1991). *Practical pediatric imaging: Diagnostic radiology of infants and children*. Boston: Little, Brown.

Liwag, M. D., & Stein, N. L. (1993, March). *The effects of retrieval instructions on children's memory for emotion episodes*. Paper presented at the Society for Research in Child Development, New Orleans, LA.

Loftus, E. F. (1979). *Eyewitness testimony*. Cambridge, MA: Harvard University Press.

Main, M. (1991). Metacognitive knowledge, metacognitive monitoring, and singular (coherent) vs. multiple (incoherent) models of attachment. In C. M. Parkes, J. Stevenson-Hinde, & P. Marris (Eds.), *Attachment across the life cycle* (pp. 127–159). New York: Routledge.

Main, M., & Hesse, E. (1990). The insecure disorganized/disoriented attachment pattern in infancy: Precursors and sequelae. In M. Greenberg, D. Cicchetti, & E. M. Cummings (Eds.), *Attachment during the preschool years: Theory, research, and interventions* (pp. 121–160). Chicago: University of Chicago Press.

Main, M., Kaplan, N., & Cassidy, J. (1985). Security in infancy, childhood, and adulthood: A move to the level of representation. *Monographs of the Society for Research in Child Development, 50*(1–2), 66–104.

Mandler, J. (1984). *Stories, scripts, and scenes: Aspects of schema theory*. Hillsdale, NJ: Lawrence Erlbaum Associates.

Melamed, B. G. (1976). Psychological preparations for hospitalizations. In S. Rachman (Ed.), *Contributions to medical psychology* (pp. 43–74). Oxford, England: Pergamon.

Nelson, K. (1986). *Event memory*. Hillsdale, NJ: Lawrence Erlbaum Associates.

Noe, H., Wyatt, R., Peeden, J., & Rivas, M. (1992). The transmission of vesicoureteral reflux from parent to child. *Journal of Urology, 148*, 1869–1871.

Ornstein, P., Larus, D., & Clubb, P. A. (1991). Understanding children's testimony: Implications of research on the development of memory. In R. Vasta (Ed.), *Annals of child development* (Vol. 8, pp. 145–176). London: Jessica Kingsley.

Ornstein, P. A., & Naus, M. J. (1985). Effects of knowledge base on children's memory strategies. In H. W. Reese (Ed.), *Advances in child development and behavior* (Vol. 19, pp. 113–148). New York: Academic Press.

Peters, D. (1991). The influence of stress and arousal on the child witness. In J. Doris (Ed.), *The suggestibility of children's recollections* (pp. 60–76). Washington, DC: American Psychological Association.

Pinto, R. P., & Hollandsworth, J. G. (1989). Using videotaped modeling to prepare children psychologically for surgery: Influence of parents and cost versus benefits of providing preparation services. *Health Psychology, 8*, 79–95.

Pynoos, R. (1992, June). *A model of post-traumatic stress disorder and memory in children*. Paper presented at the Developmental Psychobiology Research Group Conference, Estes Park, CO.

Reynolds, L., Johnson, S. B., & Silverstein, J. (1990). Assessing daily diabetics management by 24-hour recall interview. *Journal of Pediatric Psychology, 15*, 493–509.

Rothbard, J., & Shaver, P. R. (1994). Continuity of attachment across the life span: An attachment-theoretical perspective on personality. In M. Sperling & W. Berman (Eds.), *Attachments in adults: Clinical and developmental perspectives* (pp. 31–71). New York: Guilford.

Rudy, L., & Goodman, G. S. (1991). Effects of participation on children's reports: Implications for children's testimony. *Developmental Psychology, 27,* 1–26.

Saywitz, K., Goodman, G. S., Nicholas, E., & Moan, S. (1991). Children's memories of physical examinations involving genital touch: Implications for reports of child sexual abuse. *Journal of Consulting and Clinical Psychology, 59,* 682–691.

Schank, R., & Abelson, R. (1977). *Scripts, plans, goals and action.* Hillsdale, NJ: Lawrence Erlbaum Associates.

Shaver, P. R., Collins, N., & Clark, C. L. (1995). Attachment styles and internal working models of self and relationship partners. In G. J. O. Fletcher & J. Fitness (Eds.), *Knowledge structures in close relationships: A social psychological approach* (pp. 25–61). Mahwah, NJ: Lawrence Erlbaum Associates.

Shaver, P. R., & Hazan, C. (1993). Adults' romantic attachment: Theory and evidence. In D. Perlman & W. Jones (Eds.), *Advances in personal relationships* (Vol. 4, pp. 29–70). London: Jessica Kingsley.

Shaver, P. R., Hazan, C., & Bradshaw, D. (1988). Love as attachment: The integration of three behavioral systems. In R. Sternberg & M. Barnes (Eds.), *The psychology of love* (pp. 68–99). New Haven, CT: Yale University Press.

Sroufe, L. A., Carlson, E., & Shulman, S. (1993). Individuals in relationships: Development from infancy through adolescence. In D. C. Funder, R. D. Parke, C. Tomlinson-Keasey, & K. Widman (Eds.), *Studying lives through time* (pp. 315–342). Washington, DC: American Psychological Association.

Stein, N. (1991, March). *Children's and parents' memory for emotional events.* Paper presented at the Society for Research in Child Development Meetings, Seattle, WA.

Steward, M. (1993). Understanding children's memories of medical procedures. In C. Nelson (Ed.), *Minnesota Symposium on Child Psychology* (pp. 227–236). Hillsdale, NJ: Lawrence Erlbaum Associates.

Steward, M., & Steward, D. (1989). *The development of a model interview for young child victims of sexual abuse.* Final report to the National Center on Child Abuse and Neglect, Washington, DC.

Terr, L. C. (1988). What happens to early memory of trauma? A study of twenty children under age five at the time of documented traumatic experiences. *Journal of the American Academy of Child and Adolescent Psychiatry, 27,* 96–104.

Terr, L. (1990). *Too scared to cry.* New York: Harper & Row.

Terr, L. (1991). Childhood trauma: An outline and overview. *American Journal of Psychiatry, 148,* 10–20.

Vandermaas, M. O., Hess, T. M., & Baker-Ward, L. (1993). Does anxiety affect children's reports of memory for a stressful event? *Journal of Applied Psychology, 7,* 109–128.

Winograd, E., & Neisser, U. (1992). *Affect and accuracy in recall.* New York: Cambridge University Press.

Yerkes, R. M., & Dodson, J. D. (1908). The relation of strength of stimulation to rapidity of habit formation. *Journal of Comparative Neurology of Psychology, 18,* 459–482.

Yuille, J., & Tollestrup, P. (1992). A model of diverse effects of emotion on eyewitness memory. In S. Christianson (Ed.), *Handbook of emotion and memory* (pp. 202–216). Hillsdale, NJ: Lawrence Erlbaum Associates.

12

MEMORY FOR THE EXPERIENCE
OF PHYSICAL PAIN

Peter Salovey
Yale University

Albert F. Smith
The Cleveland State University

Imagine the following scenario. You are pacing nervously on the front porch of your home while speaking to a friend on a cordless telephone. As the phone call progresses, you become increasingly agitated. Not paying attention to much other than the voice on the other end of the telephone, you absentmindedly walk off the end of the porch and fall about three feet, landing with all of your weight on your left foot, which is turned sideways. You roll on the ground in blinding pain; the foot is swollen and turning unusual colors. A few hours later in the X-ray department of the local hospital, where you find out that you have torn a tendon in your ankle, an overtired resident asks, "On a scale of 1 to 10, with 10 being the most excruciating pain imaginable, how would you rate the pain that you experienced immediately after falling? Would you say that your pain was 'throbbing?' 'cramping?' 'achy'? 'pounding?' "

One of the authors of this chapter had this unfortunate experience recently. To make these judgments about the intensity and quality of past pain, he had to rely on a memorial representation of the painful experience. And, although untold numbers of medical decisions are based on these retrospective accounts, very little is known about their accuracy, or even the manner in which an individual transforms a representation of pain into a verbal judgment. We know even less about the representation of pain itself. In exploring the conditions under which memory for painful experiences is more and less accurate, distinctions need to be drawn regarding the contribution of different memorial processes to reliable pain recall. In so far as retrospective reports of pain are inaccurate, these problems can be attributed to variability in the actual pain representation itself or in the laying down of retrieval operations that will access them on tests. Moreover, there can be subsequent inaccuracies in the reconstructive or reminiscence processes that precede judgments about past pain. Difficulties in the recall of acute versus chronic pain may map on to these different processes as acute pain often has a clear, episodic, triggering event but chronic pain is ongoing and may be generic in its memorial representation. The research summarized here, both ours and that of others, does not provide opportunities to makes these distinctions about memory subprocesses or types of pain easily. We suspect that future work, however, will begin to address these issues.

The contributors to this volume primarily have addressed memory for autobiographical *events*, with a particular focus on the veracity of traumatic events of childhood reported by the children themselves or provided retrospectively as adults. The growing literature in this area points to the many ways in which these events may be misconstrued, suggested unwittingly by interviewers, or invented whole-cloth by well-meaning therapists and social workers (see Ceci & Bruck, 1993). These are events that, in principle, could have been observed by individuals other than the one from whom the report is obtained. In contrast, the focus of this chapter is on memory for an aspect of subjective experience not directly observable by other people. In particular, we address memory for physical pain. Our concern is not with the event that caused the pain, but rather with the quality and intensity of the pain itself. Although retrieval of memories for pain-causing events may play an important role in generating retrospective reports about pain, our interest is in reports about pain, not about the events that caused the pain.

We argue that although it is very difficult to report on such nonobservable events—indeed it was Jones (1957) who first remarked on the difficulties involved in summoning a graphic image of the sensory experiences of pain—retrospective descriptions of pain are surprisingly accurate. In making this argument, we divide this chapter into three sections. First, we review the literature on memory for physical pain, a literature suggesting that memory for pain is *not* accurate, but that also suggests that biases in recall are not necessarily systematic (for a more thorough literature review see Erskine, Morley, & Pearce, 1990). Second, we describe some of our studies of memory for physical pain (for a complete presentation of these studies, see Salovey et al., 1992). Finally, we provide a critique of this research domain and provide some thoughts about future research directions.

RELEVANT LITERATURE

Numerous investigators have suggested that memory for pain is not particularly accurate. In these studies, correlations between rated pain at the time of some injury or medical procedure and retrospective ratings some time later are reported as rather modest (e.g., Roche & Gijsbers, 1986). However, this research design does not permit the identification of systematic biases in pain recall such as over- or underestimation. Others, however, have been more concerned with the direction of bias (i.e., with nonrandom error as opposed to mere unreliability). Some of these investigators have produced evidence for overestimation, although others provide contradictory findings. An issue that transcends all of these investigations is precisely what constitutes evidence for accurate versus inaccurate recall of pain? In general, two approaches are common: reporting correlations between pain reports at one point in time with those at a later point in time or reporting mean differences between pain reports at the two points in time. There are advantages to each approach, depending on the context in which pain is recalled. For instance, if one is not especially concerned with scale values but considers pain to have been accurately recalled when the ordinal relations among subjects' pain reports are preserved, then correlations are appropriate. However, if error in the use of a particular scale or assessment device is of primary concern or one is investigating experimentally systematic sources of bias in pain ratings, then differences between mean ratings should be reported. In the literature review that follows, as well as in our own work, both measures of accuracy are used (see Jonides & Naveh-Benjamin, 1987, for a detailed discussion of these issues in the context of memory for frequency).

Recalled Pain Is Overestimated

The most familiar finding in the pain and memory literature is that when individuals are asked to recall a past painful experience, they recall its intensity as more severe than the original experience itself. For example, Kent (1985) asked dental patients to rate pain expected prior to the dental procedure, actual pain experienced as a result of the procedure, and then to recall the amount of pain they had experienced 3 months after the dental appointment. Only modest correlations between recalled and actual pain were obtained ($r = .42$), indicating that factors other than the initial pain experience accounted for most of the variance in pain recall after 3 months. Interestingly, among individuals who were not anxious about dental work, the recalled–experienced correlation was much higher ($r = .79$), but there was virtually no correlation between the two among highly anxious individuals ($r = -.11$). In general, recall drifted in the direction of anxiety; that is, highly anxious individuals remembered the pain experience as much more severe than it actually was, so much so that the correlation between actual and recalled pain dropped nearly to zero.

Linton and Melin (1982) studied 12 back and joint pain patients undergoing a 3- to 11-week treatment and found that ratings of pain at the initiation of treatment were higher when estimated at termination as compared with ratings actually made prior to the beginning of the program. Of course, patients may have been motivated to inflate their estimates of pretreatment pain in order to confirm that the effort expended in the treatment program was justified, as Ross' (1989) work suggests they would. In a follow-up study, Linton and Götestam (1983) asked similar patients to rate their pain on both a verbal scale (0 to 5 with each point labeled) or on a visual analogue scale (100-mm line). After 4 to 9 weeks, 12 of the 15 patients recalled their pain at baseline as more intense than they had actually reported it to be, and the biggest discrepancies were noted on the visual analogue scale. This latter effect is probably due to the retrieval cue provided by the verbal content of the 5-point scale.

The aforementioned studies are typical of the literature claiming that memory for pain is not especially accurate and usually overestimated. These studies, although among the first reported in the pain literature, are characterized by their use of notoriously small samples of nonrandomly selected individuals. Further, the measures of pain are not necessarily the ones on which self-report accuracy would be maximized. Other reports of recall overestimation have appeared in the literature since, but these studies are plagued by similar methodological limitations and often compare remembered pain with a recalled rather than actual baseline (e.g., Pakula & Milvidaite, 1983; Roche & Gijsbers, 1986).

Recalled Pain Is Underestimated

There are occasions when retrospective accounts of pain may be underestimates of actual pain. This situation seems to result when the consequences of pain are associated with positive affect. For example, a football player charging down the field in an important game despite having sustained an injury earlier might later report, while celebrating the victory, that he had not experienced much pain at all.

Perhaps the prototype of this sort of pain is labor, obviously quite painful, yet many mothers are unlikely to dwell on the intensity of such pain after the child is born (Guerra, 1986). Norvell, Gaston-Johansson, and Fridh (1987) found that pain ratings on visual analogue scales made during three phases of labor revealed considerably more intense pain than retrospective ratings made two days postpartum. Similarly, Lowe and Roberts (1988) found that recall of pain during the first phase of labor was remembered as significantly lower than pain indicated by ratings made at the time (although pain during the third phase of labor may be remembered as even worse than first reported). It may be that when pain intensity is low—for example, several days after the birth of a child—memory for the original experience of pain in underestimated, but that when existing pain intensity is high, memory for the original pain experience is augmented (Eich, Reeves, Jaeger, & Graff-Radford, 1985). Alternatively, the affective state of the mother during labor (fearful, anxious) and her affective state after the birth of the child (joy, relief) are so incongruent that there may be considerable interference with recall of material in the latter state that was encoding during the former (Bower, 1981).

Accuracy in Memory for Painful Experiences

Although such findings are atypical, some investigators have reported relatively accurate memory for painful experiences. For example, in perhaps the best study of pain associated with childbirth, Rofe and Algom (1985) asked more than 200 women to rate their pain immediately postpartum and then to recall its intensity 1 or 2 days later. Mean pain ratings at these two time points did not differ; as many subjects inflated as deflated their ratings. Nearly half the sample provided the exact same rating (on a 5-point scale) both times. Similarly, Jamison, Sbrocco, and Parris (1989) asked a heterogeneous sample of nearly 100 chronic pain patients to keep an hourly pain diary for 1 week and, at the end of the period, to recall their average pain intensity during the diary-keeping phase of the study. Although 60% of the subjects overestimated their previous pain, these discrepancies were extremely small on average, and the correlation between recalled and diary reported pain was .85. Reconsider Kent's (1985) study of dental pain. He reported very low correlations between recalled and experienced pain among individuals who were quite anxious about dental procedures. However, his low-anxiety group was quite accurate; correlations between actual and recalled pain after 3 months were close to .80. At least for pain that is acute and relatively novel, recall accuracy might be expected (see the discussion in Erskine et al., 1990).

FINDINGS FROM OUR LABORATORY

The extent of biases in pain reporting and even their direction may vary considerably. In the next section of this chapter, we discuss findings from three of our experiments investigating the accuracy of memory for pain (see Salovey et al., 1992, for more thorough descriptions of these studies and several others). In the first experiment, we describe how pain and pain behaviors collected over the course of a month are later recalled quite accurately. The second experiment demonstrates that pain reports may be robust against the influence of transient moods. The third experiment confirms that pain at the time of recall does, indeed, influence pain recall systematically. We argue that with the exception of the biasing influence of present pain on the reporting of past pain, the accuracy of recalled pain is surprisingly high.

Recall of Pain and Pain Behaviors

Many investigators have suggested that one way to avoid the inaccuracies thought to be inherent in the self-report of pain is to ask patients to recall changes in pain-related behaviors and changes in daily activities as a result of pain rather than the qualities of the painful experience itself (Richards, Nepomuceno, Riles, & Suer, 1982). We assigned 107 chronic pain patients recruited from a pain clinic to four experimental conditions, three of which required the completion of daily diaries for 30 consecutive days. All subjects had to have experienced pain on a daily basis for more than 6 months but could not be receiving treatment for their pain while participating in the study. The experimental conditions involved recording either (a) usual daily pain intensity, (b) daily pain-related and other behaviors, (c) both pain intensity and behaviors, or (d) a control group who kept no records at all. The pain-rating diary asked subjects to estimate their usual level of pain for that day on a 10-point scale. Subjects in the behavior diary and combination diary conditions indicated on a checklist those behaviors engaged in each day from a list of 10 pain-related behaviors and 6 other (non-pain-related) behaviors. Patients returned their diary records daily on postcards. At the conclusion of diary keeping, they recalled the number of days during which they engaged in each of the behaviors, and the number of days they experienced various levels of pain. They also estimated on a 10-point scale their usual amount of pain during the diary period.

Table 12.1 lists the actual (based on the diaries) and recalled (based on the follow-up interview) frequencies for the behaviors in each diary condition, and the actual and estimated level of pain intensity during the diary keeping month. Even using a series of one-way analyses of variance (ANOVAs) that undoubtedly maximizes capitalization on chance differences, subjects assigned to the four diary conditions did not differ significantly in their recall of pain or pain behaviors. More importantly, we compared recalled versus actual pain estimates and frequencies for the 16 behaviors. Two-way ANOVAs with diary condition as a between subjects variable and actual versus recall as a within subjects variable indicated that there were no significant mean differences in reports due to either diary condition or actual behavior/recall of behavior. We obtained only one significant interaction: Subjects in the behavior-diary condition recalled complaining more often than they actually reported in their diaries. This was, however, the only difference between a recalled and an actual mean in all of Table 12.1. Among subjects for whom we could compare actual versus recalled frequencies of pain and control behaviors, recall was quite accurate on all but one item.

TABLE 12.1
Actual and Recalled Pain Intensity and Behaviors

	Condition							
	Behavior Diary (n = 26)		Pain Diary (n = 23)		Both Diaries (n = 23)		No Diary (n = 35)	
	Act[a]	Rec[b]	Act	Rec	Act	Rec	Act	Rec
Pain intensity								
Average pain	—	6.00	6.18	6.09	6.07	5.91	—	6.71
Pain behaviors								
Take aspirin	7.16	8.92	—	5.78	8.52	7.09	—	6.20
Take other med	6.45	5.85	—	7.70	6.83	9.43	—	4.54
Take prescr	14.79	13.73	—	14.39	19.29	19.43	—	16.37
Use heat pad	9.96	10.00	—	7.00	6.64	7.30	—	8.71
Use ht wtr btl	1.12	1.00	—	1.17	0.84	0.74	—	2.11
Take nap	11.14	10.54	—	12.43	12.21	10.39	—	11.43
Use crutch	2.65	1.85	—	6.13	9.22	9.30	—	5.20
Ask for help	8.22	9.88	—	10.78	9.72	11.74	—	14.89
Complain	11.05	14.69	—	18.00	10.89	11.87	—	17.94
Avoid phys act	11.27	13.08	—	9.52	11.19	11.87	—	14.00
Other behaviors								
Pay bill	6.47	5.35	—	4.91	5.40	5.30	—	4.33
Read news	20.71	21.31	—	20.70	19.74	19.61	—	20.69
Eat chicken	6.79	7.00	—	5.43	5.40	7.70	—	5.00
Talk phone	24.64	24.77	—	27.78	21.89	22.87	—	25.77
Use stamp	9.23	7.00	—	7.35	6.64	7.83	—	7.03
Write letter	3.99	2.96	—	0.96	2.45	2.87	—	1.23

Note. From Salovey, Smith, Turk, Jobe, & Willis, *American Pain Society Journal, 2*, 184. © 1993, Churchill Livingstone. Reprinted with permission.
[a]Act = Actual ratings and frequencies based on diaries. [b]Rec = Recalled ratings and frequencies.

Consider Table 12.2; it represents another way of thinking about these data. In Table 12.2, each entry is the mean difference score between patients' actual and recalled pain intensity and behavior frequencies. These difference scores can be considered the net error for each item. We were interested in two aspects of these means: Do they differ according to diary condition and, more importantly, do they differ from zero? The only entry significantly different from zero (by *t* test) was complaining about pain by subjects in the behavior only diary condition. When we combined all diary-keeping participants, there was also a significant tendency to recall asking for help more frequently than reported in the diary. However, once again, the more profound findings are that these discrepancy scores are not significant for most of the behaviors, nor for the recall of pain intensity (where they are especially small), and that diary condition likewise had no significant effect on the magnitude of these discrepancy scores.

TABLE 12.2
Mean Deviation Scores (Actual–Recalled) by Diary Condition

	Condition			
	Behavior Diary (n = 26)	Pain Diary (n = 23)	Both Diaries (n = 23)	All Diary Conditions
Pain intensity				
Average pain	—	0.09	0.16	0.12
Pain behaviors				
Take aspirin	−1.77	—	1.44	−0.26
Take other	0.60	—	−2.60	−0.90
Take prescr	1.06	—	−0.15	0.49
Use heat pad	−0.04	—	−0.66	−0.33
Use ht wtr btl	0.12	—	0.11	0.11
Take nap	0.60	—	1.82	1.17
Use crutch	0.81	—	−0.09	0.39
Ask for help	−1.66	—	−2.02	−1.83*
Complain	−3.64*	—	−0.98	−2.39*
Avoid phy act	−1.36	—	−0.68	−1.02
All pain behav	−5.51	—	−3.81	−4.70
Other behaviors				
Pay bill	1.12	—	0.10	0.64
Read news	−0.60	—	0.13	−0.26
Eat chicken	−0.21	—	−2.30	−1.19
Talk phone	−0.13	—	−0.98	−0.53
Use stamp	2.23	—	−1.18	0.63
Write letter	1.03	—	−0.42	0.35
All oth behav	3.45	—	−4.66	−0.36

Note. From Salovey, Smith, Turk, Jobe, & Willis, *American Pain Society Journal, 2,* 184. © 1993, Churchill Livingstone. Reprinted with permission.

*Deviation score is significantly different from zero, $p < .05$.

This experiment represents one of the more systematic attempts to explore bias in the recall of pain and pain behaviors. Further, although it is risky to base arguments on failures to disconfirm the null hypothesis, it seems that both pain intensity and pain-related behaviors are recalled rather accurately. Power analyses did indicate that our sample size was sufficient to detect even small but reliable differences had they been present. Moreover, what error there was in the recall of pain intensity and behavior was generally not systematic. Depending on the item, it was either inflation or deflation. Moreover, the keeping of diaries does not seem to influence subsequent recollection, a finding that should come as some relief to investigators and clinicians relying on systematic self-monitoring in the assessment of pain. When recall inaccuracy on a pain behavior was revealed, it was located primarily on "complaining," which is rather vague compared with other pain behaviors (e.g., taking aspirin, using a heating pad). Asking about concrete pain-related behaviors seems more or less free from systematic biases of the kind documented by other investigators and reviewed earlier.

Mood Influences on Pain Reporting

A frequently cited cause of inaccuracy in the retrieval of pain episodes is related to emotional experience (e.g., Edwards, Pearce, Collett, & Pugh, 1992; Pearce et al., 1990). Recall how respondents who experienced *fear* of going to the dentist remembered dental pain as more severe than it actually was (Kent, 1985). Mothers experiencing the *joy* of a new baby tended to under-report the intense pains of labor after the birth of their children (Lowe & Roberts, 1988). In previous work involving the induction of moods in the laboratory, 66 college students with the flu recalled their symptoms as being more uncomfortable if they were assigned to a condition in which a sad mood was induced as compared with a happy or neutral mood condition (Salovey & Birnbaum, 1989). Such results are consistent with laboratory research on mood and memory suggesting that individuals are more likely to recall material that is congruent with their current moods (Singer & Salovey, 1988).

To investigate the influence of induced mood on pain reporting, we recruited 89 individuals from the surrounding community (nearly equally divided by sex) and assigned them randomly to a happy, sad, or neutral mood-induction condition. Moods were induced by asking these individuals to sit in a darkened room with their eyes closed and to imagine scenes from their childhood in which they felt happy, sad, or neither happy nor sad, depending on assigned condition. Mood measures taken shortly after this procedure revealed that moods had, indeed, been appropriately induced. Participants were then asked to recall their most recent painful experience and to rate the average and maximum levels of pain experienced at the time. They were also asked to indicate on a checklist the number of painful conditions (e.g., headaches, stomachaches) that they had experienced during the previous year.

We were surprised to find that none of these tasks proved to be mood sensitive, at least in this experiment. Subjects assigned to the three mood groups did not differ in the types of painful experiences recalled for the prior year, the number of days of pain reported, or in the usual and maximum pain they reported as associated with various physical conditions experienced during the prior year. Interestingly, a growing literature has demonstrated that induced and naturally occurring moods have powerful and robust influences on social judgments of all kinds (Forgas, 1995; Mayer, Gaschke, Braverman, & Evans, 1992), from the likelihood of future catastrophic events (Johnson & Tversky, 1983) to impressions of other people

(Forgas & Bower, 1987). However, at least for the kinds of judgments about recalled pain measured here, these systematic influences of mood were not revealed.

Recalling Pain When Ongoing Pain Fluctuates

Eich et al. (1985) noted that because affect is an integral component of pain behavior and experience, pain may produce assimilative effects on memory that parallel those thought to be engendered by emotions (although not demonstrated by us). This line of theorizing suggests that prior pain is remembered as being more severe than it actually was when the intensity of present pain is high, but less severe when the present pain is low. Eich and his colleagues asked 57 headache patients to maintain pain diaries during a treatment program by asking them to record hourly ratings of pain on a 10-point scale. In addition, during weekly scheduled appointments, they were asked to rate their present pain intensity on the usual visual analogue scale. They were then asked to recall the "maximum," "usual," and "minimum" levels of pain experienced since their last visit. Patients' ratings of present level of pain were strongly associated with their recall of maximum, usual, and minimum pain levels since the last visit. When present pain was high, patients' recalled pain levels were higher than their pain diaries indicated. When present pain was low, their recalled pain ratings were less severe than indicated by the diaries. Eich and his colleagues' results suggest that studies of pain recall in which currently pain-free subjects are asked to recall past pain episodes should result in underestimations of past pain, but that when subjects who are still experiencing pain are asked to recall past pain, they should overestimate it. Therefore, respondents may use easily available information about their present pain as a basis for judging past pain episodes, and present pain may make memories for previous painful situations more available. A cautionary note should be sounded, however, as some studies have not observed a relationship between pain at recall and recall accuracy (Jamison et al., 1989).

We asked 80 patients undergoing pain assessment at a pain clinic (who had experienced pain for at least 6 months duration but were not yet undergoing active treatment at the time of the study) to provide a rating of their pain on an hourly basis for 2 weeks. Subjects were asked to circle a number between 0 (*no pain at all*) and 9 (*pain as bad as it could be*) hourly on a postcard for each day during the 14-day diary-keeping period. At the end of each day, subjects were asked to mail the postcard to us. At the conclusion of the diary period, patients were contacted by phone and asked to (a) rate their present pain intensity on a 10-point scale and (b) complete the Pain Rating Index of the McGill Pain Questionnaire, and also to (c) rate on 10-point scales their estimates of the usual amount of pain they experienced during the 2-week diary period, (d) rate the maximum and minimum amount of pain experienced during the diary period, and (e) estimate the number of days during the diary period that their pain exceeded various predetermined criteria.

A daily mean of the hourly pain ratings was computed, and then for each subject a mean of these daily means across the 14-day diary period was calculated. As a measure of variability in a subject's hourly pain ratings, we computed the standard deviation in hourly ratings each day and then calculated the mean of these standard deviations across the 14-day period. The mean daily pain rating was 5.53 on the 0 to 9 scale with a mean daily standard deviation of 0.92. Means collected at recall were compared with those calculated from the diary reports. Subjects remembered their "usual" level of pain as 5.61, which is quite close to the actual diary average of 5.53. However, on frequency-oriented questions, subjects showed some tendency to recall pain as more severe than indicated by the diaries. Subjects remembered 3.62 days with an average pain rating above 8, but in reality there were only 1.95. Similarly, they recalled 9.00 days on which their pain averaged more than a 5, when in fact there were only 7.86 such days. Discrepancy scores created by subtracting recalled ratings from diary ratings for these two measures were significantly different from zero. This drift in the direction of overestimating previous pain is consistent with much of the literature reviewed earlier. Perhaps the pervasiveness of this bias can be attributed to the fact that the psychophysical function for numerical magnitude is negatively accelerated, so that any fixed numerical difference is seen as larger between smaller numbers (e.g., 2 and 3) than between larger numbers (e.g., 4 and 5; Moyer & Landauer, 1967). Subjects evaluating past pain may thus tend to err in a positive rather than in a negative direction. Investigators and clinicians might consider counterbalancing scale direction when measuring pain.

In Table 12.3, Pearson correlations are provided between ratings from the diary scales and the recall measures. Associations between pain level at the time of recall and the other recall measures are listed as well. Obviously, people experiencing more intense pain at the time of recall were more likely to be those individuals who experienced more intense pain during diary keeping. Therefore, it is not surprising that there were many positive correlations between pain intensity on the diaries and pain intensity at recall. Once again, recalled average pain seemed fairly accurate; there was a .83 correlation between average pain ratings on the diaries and estimates of "usual" pain at recall. Similarly, recall of days with greater pain ratings than 8 was correlated with the actual number of such days at .75, and for days greater than 5, the correlation was .71.

Multiple regression analysis was used to test the magnitude and direction of influence that pain at time of recall has on remembered pain intensity. The dependent variable for this analysis, which is presented in Table 12.4,

TABLE 12.3
Pearson Correlations Between Diary Scales and Recall Measures

	Diary Scales			
Recall Measures	Mean Pain	Mean SD	Days > 5	Days > 8
Current pain	.74	−.16	.66	.46
Usual pain	.83	.01	.71	.59
Worst pain	.68	.19	.58	.33
Least pain	.87	−.28	.78	.66
Days > 5	.70	−.13	.71	.30
Days > 8	.62	−.07	.47	.75

Correlations between current level of pain (at recall) and recall measures

Recall Measures	Current Level of Pain
Usual pain	.73
Worst pain	.58
Least pain	.61
Days > 5	.55
Days > 8	.44

Note. $N = 80$. $|r| > .22$, $p < .05$. $|r| > .29$, $p < .01$. $|r| > .36$, $p < .001$. From Salovey, Smith, Turk, Jobe, & Willis, *American Pain Society Journal, 2*, 184. © 1993, Churchill Livingstone. Reprinted with permission.

was recalled "usual" amount of pain. We entered into the analysis as predictors (a) actual mean daily pain from the diaries, (b) the mean standard deviation of daily pain from the diaries (to control for amount of pain fluctuation—we were concerned that if pain rarely fluctuated, its intensity is easier to recall), and (c) pain at the time of recall. Not surprisingly, the best predictor of recalled pain was actual mean pain during the diary period. However, after entering this variable and controlling for fluctuation (mean standard deviation), pain at the time of recall contributed significant variance to recalled "usual" level of pain in a positive direction. Subjects who reported the greatest pain at the time of recall were most likely to inflate

TABLE 12.4
Predicting Recalled Usual Levels of Pain From Actual Mean During
Diary Phase, Variability During Diary Phase, and Current Level of Pain

Predictor	Beta	T	p
Mean pain/day (diary)	0.54	5.27	.0001
Mean SD/day (diary)	0.12	1.80	.08
Current pain (at recall)	0.38	3.62	.0006

Note. $R^2 = .73$, $F(3, 76) = 55.43$, $p < .0001$. From Salovey, Smith, Turk, Jobe, & Willis, *American Pain Society Journal, 2*, 184. © 1993, Churchill Livingstone. Reprinted with permission.

their recall of pain intensity. Level of pain at the time of report does appear to influence the reporting of past pain intensity, even controlling for fluctuation in pain. Moreover, although average intensity ratings tended to be recalled reasonably accurately in this experiment (as they were in the first experiment), ratings regarding the number of days on which pain of different levels is experienced tended to be overestimated.

Conclusions

Compared with much of the literature reviewed, which generally reports considerable inaccuracy in recall of pain among small samples of patients undergoing treatment in pain clinics, recall among our subjects across the studies reported here (and several others) was characterized by its accuracy. It is difficult to deduce generalizations that account for our findings of relative recall accuracy vis-à-vis the literature reviewed earlier questioning the validity of memory for pain. Some of the published findings in this area are based on relatively limited samples of fairly idiosyncratic subjects on whom pain reports are collected using nonstandard methods in the context of clinical examinations. It is possible that these features maximize unreliability and that what looks like recall bias may in fact be error variance, although it is very hard to determine whether such error is indeed random or not. Of course, the goal in this domain of research is not to determine merely if pain is accurately or inaccurately recalled. Rather, investigators need to turn their attention to the conditions under which pain is accurately recalled and those under which it is more susceptible to distortion.

In our studies, diary keeping had minimal impact on memory for pain, and it was not systematically affected by transient mood. Pain intensity and pain-related behaviors were recalled with about equal (and fairly high) accuracy. The one systematic influence on pain reporting, a finding anticipated by the work of Eich and his colleagues, is severity of pain at the time of recall. Although we encourage investigators and pain clinic professionals to be mindful of this source of bias in pain recall, we also believe that our data suggest that self-reports of pain can generally be trusted; they appear to be recalled with reasonable accuracy, and pain-related behaviors are recalled with equal but not greater accuracy. Although much maligned, retrospective self-reports of pain collected systematically with measures of proven reliability seem relatively trustworthy.

CRITIQUE

In this section, we examine more critically studies of memory for pain, and we do not spare ourselves from our critical assessment. Despite our efforts to study memory for pain, documented in the last section, we have some profound concerns about the extent to which such efforts can be successful. This does not mean that we see the issue memory for pain as unimportant. Rather, we see it as very important: The experience of pain will continue to be one about which individuals will report, and many of these reports will be memory-based. However, we recognize that for the study of memory for pain to be fruitful, questions must be more focused than they have been to this point and need to be asked within the context of a coherently specified theoretical framework.

The most fundamental open questions are these: What is meant by "memory for pain"? To what extent does memory for pain involve recollection of specific experiences? How do memory-based reports about an acute pain experience differ from memory-based reports about chronic pain? In what aspects of a pain experience are we interested? What constitutes evidence of memory for pain?

The area of memory for pain is plagued by both conceptual and methodological problems. Among the most significant conceptual problem is that investigators have not distinguished adequately among the various subproblems that they study. This may lead to confusion about the significance of empirical results for memory for pain. For example, in some situations, pain appears to serve as a cue that enhances memory performance (e.g., a situation in which one must recall pain-related words), whereas in others, it appears to serve as a context rather than as a cue (e.g., a situation in which one must recall stimuli originally encoded during a painful episode). Each of these situations differs from those in which an individual is asked to introspect about pain that he or she has experienced and to provide a verbal report. Although each of these situations involves, in some sense, memory for pain, they are not equivalent. It does not seem to be the case, for example, that if pain leads to improved performance in some learning task that the pain has been remembered. It is important to distinguish between the arousal properties of pain and any cuing properties that it may have. Most salient among the methodological problems is that researchers are unable to apply to experimental subjects stimulation that results in experiences like those afflicted by pains of interest, and even if this were technologically possible, there would be ethical obstacles.

Representation

As we have noted elsewhere (Smith, Salovey, Turk, Jobe, & Willis, 1993), questions about memory for pain are essentially questions about the existence and nature of a memorial representation of the sensations of pain. Investigators in this area—and we include ourselves—have not specified well the nature of the representation that is contemplated. Indeed, a crucial need in this area is better hypotheses about the memory representation of pain, so that more incisive tests can be carried out.

In several studies, we were unable to reject the hypothesis that there is a representation of pain experience that subserves reports about previously experienced pain. The results of these studies led us to argue that some reports about previously experienced pain are credible—specifically, reports of average pain and reports about the frequency, during a reference period, that pain of specified intensities was experienced. Unfortunately, we did not conduct these particular studies in a way that confirms either the existence of a memory representation or that permits statements about it. It is perfectly conceivable that the very same results might have been obtained even if people have no enduring memory representation of experienced pain; instead of recollecting specific representations, people may report retrospectively about pain based on other autobiographical knowledge. When one speaks of memory for pain, one assumes a representation that permits recollection, and it is not clear that data of the sort that we (and others) have described permit incisive tests of hypotheses.

For significant progress to be made in the study of memory for pain, specific hypotheses about the nature of the memory representation and their implications for performance are required. For example, some investigators (e.g., Clark & Bennett-Clark, 1993) have argued that any representation of pain experience must be semantic and that there is no evidence that sensations and emotions can be stored in long-term memory in other than a semantic form. Although we disagree with this view, it can be seen as a statement that might be developed into specific testable hypotheses. In contrast, Wyer and Srull (1989) hypothesized that memory representations of emotion concepts include clusters of physiological reactions. If memorial representations of emotion concepts include clusters of physiological reactions, then surely it is reasonable to contemplate the possibility that pain experiences are represented as clusters of physiological reactions. We are sympathetic to the Wyer and Srull view—we find the notion of pain imagery quite plausible, as do Jerome (1993) and Melzack (1993). If pain images are not retrieved from memory, they may be constructed from information stored in memory. The form in which such information is stored is perhaps less important than the form in which it is used. During the last decade, experimental psychologists have investigated successfully visual and auditory imagery using behavioral methods (see Farah & Smith, 1983; Kosslyn, 1980; Reisberg, 1991). We have suggested that for guidance in developing and evaluating hypotheses about whether there are images of pain that are analogues of actual pain percepts, the appropriate domain in which to look is the investigation of visual and auditory imagery (Smith, Salovey, et al., 1993), although we recognize (as we discuss further later) that investigators of pain are more limited in the methods available to them than are investigators of imagery for other sensory modalities.

Methodological Obstacles

Experimental psychologists have devised procedures that have permitted convincing tests of hypotheses about memories for, and images of, various sorts of experience. Most of these are not available to the investigator of memory for pain. Whereas many kinds of experience can be administered experimentally, institutional review boards restrict the administration of nociceptive stimuli. However, this sort of procedure would seem to be required for research that follows the model of investigations of other sorts of sensory stimuli. Investigators of memory for pain are therefore limited primarily to the study of naturally occurring pains. In general, the attributes of these pains are not publicly verifiable, and do not correspond to specifiable external stimulation, so that recall validity is not measurable in any satisfying way. Recognition is not generally available as an empirical strategy. We do not see any clear ways to circumvent these methodological problems. Two possible ways to improve somewhat the state of affairs are better conceptualizations of what we want to know about ecological pains and the consideration of work on memory for emotional feelings as a model of memory for pain.

Improved Conceptualizations. In our discussion of representational issues, we argued that better hypotheses about memorial representations of pain are required. Clearly, a better specification of the contemplated memory representation would permit better tests of the nature of the representation. We require better statements about what it is we want to know about what is remembered. Although the studies that we described illustrate certain aspects of pain reports, they tell us less than we would like about memory for pain. Much research on this problem, including our own, likely makes unwarranted assumptions that threaten the interpretability of the data. There is no general statement about what evidence is acceptable evidence for accurate memory for pain. Consider several examples of weaknesses in method and alternative strategies that would constitute improvements.

One method that we used to collect reports of pain involved asking subjects to record numeric ratings of pain intensity. Later, these subjects were asked to report their usual pain during the reference period. We found that reports of usual pain correlated highly with average recorded pain levels. Although we took the high correlation as evidence of accurate memory for pain, it is not clear that a low correlation would have been sufficient to exclude the notion that people can remember pain experience. Pain experiences must be transformed into a verbal response, and the mapping of experience to a verbal response may be variable within individuals and inconsistent over individuals. One can imagine circumstances under which people would remember pain accurately, in the sense of being able to retrieve from memory a high-fidelity representation of pain, but in which the correlation of diary averages with final reports of usual pain, over subjects, would be low. Finding a high correlation requires both that subjects have stable memories and use the rating scale consistently over time. When we write about the need for tests of specific hypotheses, motivated by a theoretical view of the memorial representation of pain, we mean that we require data sets that lead to unambiguous conclusions. This means being able to identify variables according to which the memory representation of pain, if it exists, should change systematically.

Consider a second example: We asked subjects to record their pain hourly for approximately 2 weeks and then to report their average pain. It is clear that this is a very weak way of discriminating among subjects; subjects in all four conditions reported the same average pain. Suppose, however, the hypothesis that individuals afflicted with chronic pain maintain in memory a temporal record of the pain. Then a better test of memory might have involved determining whether subjects could recognize their own pain records. If asked to choose between a graphic representation of his or her own record over time and that of another subject, or between his or her record and its reflection or its complement, would the subject have selected the correct record? Would choice accuracy deteriorate with time after the end of the reference period? If the reference period were divided into temporal slices, would choice probability for a late slice be better than that for an early slice?

In any case, we feel that it is important that whenever one is faced with a situation in which one is inclined to draw conclusions from the absence of differences (as we did in several of our studies), the design include control variables that are sensitive to some experimental manipulation (for an example, see Smith, Jobe, & Mingay, 1993).

Memory for Emotional Feelings as a Model for Memory for Pain? Intuitively, there seem to be similarities between memory for emotional feelings and memory for pain experiences. Both come in chronic and acute forms, and both involve physiological reactions. Emotional feelings are abundant ecologically, and such feelings may be induced in the laboratory more easily and ethically than pain sensations. Investigation of emotional feelings may be more tractable than that of pain, and the substantial amount of theoretical work on emotion suggests that such investigations may be carried out within a coherently specified framework.

For instance, Thomas and Diener (1990) studied whether individuals could estimate accurately the intensity and frequency of pleasant and unpleasant feelings as originally established through an experience sampling method. These subjects tended to overestimate the intensities of both positive and negative emotions retrospectively. There was also some tendency, surprisingly enough, for subjects to underestimate the frequency of positive emotions. Accuracy was improved, however, when subjects were asked to rate their feelings in comparison to others. Our point here, however, is that the emotions area provides a wealth of technologies for the induction and measurement of mood that have been refined through decades of laboratory research. Investigators of memory for pain may find these procedures useful, at least as models for building a better technology for the study of memory for pain.

FINAL REMARKS

Unlike some of the everyday and emotional events described in this volume, memory for pain may be quite accurate under certain circumstances. With the exception of the assimilative influence of pain at the time of recall, we have been unable to demonstrate consistent biases in the recall of physically painful events, experiences, and behaviors. Of course, this does not mean they do not exist; as procedures for measuring pain are refined and recall tasks, perhaps, become more implicit, systematic biases may be discovered. Meanwhile, perhaps we have identified a domain of human experience that is relatively robust against the usual frailties of the cognitive system.

ACKNOWLEDGMENTS

The experiments described in this chapter (supported by contract number 200–88–7001 from the National Center for Health Statistics, Department of Health and Human Services to Peter Salovey) were part of a larger project entitled "National Laboratory for Collaborative Research on Cognition and Survey Measurement" conducted by the NCHS under grant SES–8612320 from the National Science Foundation.

A full report of the findings from this program of research was published by Salovey, P., Sieber, W. J., Smith, A. F., Turk, D. C., Jobe, J. B., and Willis, G. B. (1992) as "Reporting chronic pain episodes on health surveys" in *Vital and Health Statistics, 6*(6), 1–71. Some of the findings described in this chapter were also discussed in Salovey, P., Smith, A. F., Turk, D. C., Jobe, J. B., and Willis, G. B. (1993). The accuracy of memory for pain: Not so bad most of the time. *American Pain Society Journal, 2,* 184–191.

We thank Charles Brainerd and Peter Ornstein for their comments on an earlier version of this chapter.

REFERENCES

Bower, G. H. (1981). Mood and memory. *American Psychologist, 36*, 129–148.

Ceci, S. J., & Bruck, M. (1993). Suggestibility of the child witness: A historical review and synthesis. *Psychological Bulletin, 113*, 403–439.

Clark, W. C., & Bennett-Clark, S. (1993). Remembrance of pains past? *APS Journal, 2*, 195–200.

Edwards, L., Pearce, S., Collett, B. J., & Pugh, R. (1992). Selective memory for sensory and affective information in chronic pain and depression. *British Journal of Clinical Psychology, 31*, 239–248.

Eich, E., Reeves, J. L., Jaeger, B., & Graff-Radford, S. B. (1985). Memory for pain: Relation between past and present pain intensity. *Pain, 23*, 375–380.

Erskine, A., Morley, S., & Pearce, S. (1990). Memory for pain: A review. *Pain, 41*, 255–265.

Farah, M. J., & Smith, A. F. (1983). Perceptual interference and facilitation with auditory imagery. *Perception and Psychophysics, 33*, 475–478.

Forgas, J. P. (1995). Mood and judgment: The affect infusion model (AIM). *Psychological Bulletin, 117*, 39–66.

Forgas, J. P., & Bower, G. H. (1987). Mood effects on person–perception judgments. *Journal of Personality and Social Psychology, 53*, 53–60.

Guerra, F. (1986). Awareness and recall. *International Anesthesiology Clinics, 24*, 75–99.

Jamison, R. N., Sbrocco, T., & Parris, W. C. V. (1989). The influence of physical and psychosocial factors on accuracy of memory for pain in chronic pain patients. *Pain, 37*, 289–294.

Jerome, J. (1993). Transmission or transformation? Information processing theory of chronic human pain. *APS Journal, 2*, 160–171.

Johnson, E. J., & Tversky, A. (1983). Affect, generalization, and the perception of risk. *Journal of Personality and Social Psychology, 45*, 20–33.

Jones, E. (1957). Pain. *International Journal of Psychoanalysis, 38*, 255–257.

Jonides, J., & Naveh-Benjamin, M. (1987). Estimating frequency of occurrence. *Journal of Experimental Psychology: Learning, Memory, and Cognition, 13*, 230–240.

Kent, G. (1985). Memory for dental pain. *Pain, 21*, 187–194.

Kosslyn, S. M. (1980). *Image and mind*. Cambridge, MA: Harvard University Press.

Linton, S. J., & Götestam, K. G. (1983). A clinical comparison of two pain scales: Correlation, remembering chronic pain, and a measure of compliance. *Pain, 17*, 57–65.

Linton, S. J., & Melin, L. (1982). The accuracy of remembering chronic pain. *Pain, 13*, 281–285.

Lowe, N. K., & Roberts, J. E. (1988). The convergence between in-labor reports on postpartum recall of parturition pain. *Research Nursing and Health, 11*, 11–21.

Mayer, J. D., Gaschke, Y. N., Braverman, D. L., & Evans, T. W. (1992). Mood-congruent judgment is a general effect. *Journal of Personality and Social Psychology, 63*, 119–132.

Melzack, R. (1993). Pain and the brain. *APS Journal, 2*, 172–174.

Moyer, R. S., & Landauer, T. K. (1967). Time required on judgments of numerical inequality. *Nature, 215*, 1519–1520.

Norvell, K. T., Gaston-Johansson, F., & Fridh, G. (1987). Remembrance of labor pain: How valid are retrospective pain measurements? *Pain, 31*, 77–86.

Pakula, A., & Milvidaite, I. (1983). Memory for acute coronary pain: Decay with time versus reliability of measures. In J. J. Bonica, U. Lindblom, & A. Iggo (Eds.), *Advances in pain research and therapy* (Vol. 5, pp. 877–888). New York: Raven.

Pearce, S. A., Isherwood, S., Hrouda, D., Richardson, P. H., Erskine, A., & Skinner, J. (1990). Memory and pain: Tests of mood congruity and state dependent learning in experimentally induced and clinical pain. *Pain, 43*, 187–193.

Reisberg, D. T. (Ed.). (1991). *Auditory imagery*. Hillsdale, NJ: Lawrence Erlbaum Associates.

Richards, J. S., Nepomuceno, C., Riles, M., & Suer, Z. (1982). Assessing pain behavior: The UAB pain behavior scale. *Pain, 14*, 393–398.

Roche, P. A., & Gijsbers, K. (1986). A comparison of memory for induced ischemic pain and chronic rheumatoid pain. *Pain, 25,* 337–343.

Rofe, Y., & Algom, D. (1985). Accuracy of remembering postdelivery pain. *Perceptual and Motor Skills, 60,* 99–105.

Ross, M. (1989). Relation of implicit theories to the construction of personal histories. *Psychological Review, 96,* 341–357.

Salovey, P., & Birnbaum, D. (1989). The influence of mood on health-relevant cognitions. *Journal of Personality and Social Psychology, 57,* 539–551.

Salovey, P., Sieber, W. J., Smith, A. F., Turk, D. C., Jobe, J. B., & Willis, G. B. (1992). Reporting chronic pain episodes on health surveys. *Vital and Health Statistics,* Series 6, No. 6, 1–71 (DHHS Publication No. 92–1081). Washington, DC: U.S. Government Printing Office.

Salovey, P., Smith, A. F., Turk, D. C., Jobe, J. B., & Willis, G. B. (1993). The accuracy of memory for pain: Not so bad most of the time. *American Pain Society Journal, 2,* 184–191.

Singer, J. A., & Salovey, P. (1988). Mood and memory: Evaluating the network theory of affect. *Clinical Psychology Review, 8,* 211–251.

Smith, A. F., Jobe, J. J., & Mingay, D. J. (1993). *Concerning the suitability of diarykeeping to validate report of health-related information.* Manuscript under review.

Smith, A. F., Salovey, P., Turk, D. C., Jobe, J. B., & Willis, G. B. (1993). Theoretical and methodological issues in assessing memory for pain: A reply. *APS Journal, 2,* 203–206.

Thomas, D. L., & Diener, E. (1990). Memory accuracy in the recall of emotions. *Journal of Personality and Social Psychology, 59,* 291–297.

Wyer, R. S., & Srull, T. K. (1989). *Memory and cognition in its social context.* Hillsdale, NJ: Lawrence Erlbaum Associates.

PSYCHOLOGICAL ISSUES IN EYEWITNESS TESTIMONY

13

ADULT PERCEPTIONS OF CHILDREN'S MEMORY FOR THE TRAUMATIC EVENT OF SEXUAL ABUSE: A CLINICAL AND LEGAL DILEMMA

Mary Ann Mason
University of California at Berkeley

The childhood traumatic event that has most occupied the adult world's attention in recent years is the event of sexual abuse. As thousands of cases are brought to the attention of children's protective services or the police, two very different populations of adults are forced to deal with the allegations: the therapeutic community and the criminal justice establishment. These populations have very different goals: The aim of the therapeutic community, usually social workers and clinical psychologists, is to deal with effect of the trauma on the child; the aim of the criminal justice establishment, from police through prosecuting attorneys, defense attorneys, and judges, is to seek justice for the accused abuser (Mason, 1991b). However, to help overcome their evidentiary problems in dealing with child witnesses, prosecutors rely increasingly on expert witnesses from the therapeutic community to inform the court about the behavioral chracteristics of sexually abused children. Many of these experts describe patterns or syndromes of characteristics that include information on how a child remembers and relates the incident of abuse.

Although patterns, profiles, or syndromes of characteristics regarding sexually abused children are now widely used in therapy and in the courts, there is a great deal of controversy about the reliability of any of these models and about the appropriateness of their use in court. This chapter first explores the controversy among courts in dealing with this type of expert testimony. Judicial concern is based in part on the reliability of expert testimony regarding behavioral characteristics of sexually abused children, but also on procedural constraints which limit the admissibility of evidence. The chapter then examines the controversy within the mental health community regarding the reliability of a profile of a sexually abused child, particularly relating to the communication issues of straightforwardness, delay, inconsistency, and recantation in recalling the event of sexual abuse. Although many of the chapters in this book are devoted to the child's remembrance of a traumatic event, the conceptions that adults hold about how a child remembers and relates the event is its own story, with serious implications for criminal justice.

CONTROVERSY IN THE COURTS

Prosecutors are faced with a frustrating problem. Often they must prove a case with no corroborative evidence, no witnesses, and a victim who is reluctant or unable to testify against the defendant. Sometimes that victim is less than 5 years old. Even when the victim does testify, the nature of the testimony may be halting, inconsistent, and may completely contradict pretrial testimony. In addition, the child may recant, or deny that he or she ever made the allegations.

To compensate for lack of evidence, prosecutors rely increasingly on expert witnesses. In addition to medical witnesses who testify as to the physical symptoms of abuse if there are any, mental health professionals: Clinical psychologists, social workers, and sometimes psychiatrists are regularly called on. The core of their testimony is usually to explain to the court how a child reacts to sexual abuse. In doing so they will recite a profile of the characteristics of a sexually abused child, sometimes referring to it as a child sex-abuse syndrome. A major part of this syndrome, as well shall see, is how the child remembers and relates the story of abuse.

Mental health experts, almost always clinicians, usually offer two kinds of testimony: First, they may testify, based on their experience and training, that they consider a particular child to fit the profile of a sexually abused child. To prepare for this testimony the expert interviews the child extensively, often with the help of an anatomically correct doll, notes symptoms and behavior patterns, and formulates a diagnosis. This evaluation is sometimes derived over the course of several sessions of therapy. The parents and others who have observed the child may be questioned as well. The expert may claim, based on his clinical training and experience, that the child fits the particular characteristics of a specific syndrome associated with sexually abused children or that the child fits a looser description of characteristics often found in sexually abused children. Usually the expert will not reach this conclusion directly, but will recite the characteristics of an abused child and then describe most of the same characteristics that he or she has observed with this particular child witness.

The second kind of expert testimony addresses only the general characteristics of a sexually abused child, but not the behavior of a particular child. With this kind of testimony, the expert may or may not have evaluated the child and addresses general clinical patterns observed in sexually abused children by the expert and others. Here also the testimony may be presented as a specific syndrome, or more loosely described as general behavioral characteristics of a sexually abused child.

Behavioral syndrome testimony in child sex-abuse cases has provoked serious controversy in the courts, with contradictory appellate court decisions as to its admissibility within the same jurisdiction. There is also a serious split regarding the conditions under which such testimony is allowed, with some courts allowing this kind of expert testimony not as direct testimony, but only to rehabilitate the reputation of a child witness who has been accused of being untruthful.

Although testimony regarding the characteristics of sexually abused children is relatively recent (within the last 13 years), a fairly large body of appellate court decisions has ruled on its admissability. In all of these cases the expert testimony was allowed at the trial court level and the appellate court is asked to reverse the decisions against the defendant on the grounds that the expert testimony was wrongfully admitted. From these opinions it is possible to discern definite patterns of expert testimony and of appellate courts' responses. Although this does not tell the whole story, because we are only seeing those cases that are on appeal, it does provide a representative sample of appellate court judges' responses and reasoning, and probably fairly represents the nature of the expert testimony and the identity of the experts with whom they must deal on appeal.

The Experts and Their Testimony

My study of the appellate court decisions between 1980 and 1990 (122 cases identifiable) reveals several facts regarding the identity of the expert witnesses and the nature of their testimony (Mason, 1991a). Nearly all the experts have a clinical orientation, with social workers (all are licensed clinical social workers, either LCSWs or ACSWs), the largest group (34%), closely followed by clinical psychologists (31%), and trailed by counselor/therapists (12%), psychiatrists (8%), and physicians (8%). All other groups are sparsely represented (see Table 13.1).

Almost all the experts in these cases are hands-on clinicians, rather than behavioral scientists. The great majority are therapists, with a significant number serving as the therapist for that particular child witness. Eighty-seven percent interviewed the child, and a large group among those (45.9%) treated the child as well. Twenty-three experts specified that they employed anatomical dolls in their interview (Mason, 1991a).

TABLE 13.1
Expert Witness by Profession

Profession	n	%
Social worker	54	(34%)
Clinical psychologist	49	(31%)
Counselor/therapist	19	(12%)
Psychiatrist	12	(8%)
Physician	12	(8%)
Other (includes professor, police investigator, school principal, etc.)	14	(9%)
Total	160	

Note. There is more than one expert in many cases.

In qualification discussions, many mentioned attending workshops but conducted no independent research (with the exception of Roland Summit, who is identified in three cases). Nonetheless, none of the courts excluded their testimony on the basis of lack of qualifications. The criteria for acceptance most often used by the courts was experience in working with sexually abused children (Mason, 1991a).

Characteristics of Sexually Abused Children

Seventy-three of these appellate decisions specify indicators of sexual abuse offered by the experts in their trial court testimony. The experts claim this knowledge is based on their clinical experience and training, not on specific research. The three largest groupings of indicators deal with truthfulness, sexual behavior, and emotional upset (see Table 13.2). The largest cluster, cited by experts 54 times, focuses on how a child recalled and communicated the traumatic event. This group claimed that delayed reporting, retraction/recantation conflicting, and inconsistent accounts are all frequently presented by the experts as characteristics of sexually abused children. As we shall see, this emphasis was in part a function of the rules under which the testimony was admitted. The anomaly of this central core of descriptors is that by their very denials children strengthen the expert's belief in their abuse and the jury is given the same message. Furthermore, 15 experts testified to the complete opposite. This group claimed that sexually abused children do *not* lie about their abuse and 6 stated that consistency in accounting are characteristics of sexually abused children. According to which experts are testifying, therefore, straightforward truth telling is a characteristic of a sexually abused child, but so also is delay, denial, and recantation. This contradictory testimony reflects the same opposite extremes in describing the way that children remember and report the event of sexual abuse as noted earlier in the aforementioned survey of 212 therapists.

There are other contradictions as well. The second largest category of descriptors deals with the child's sexual behavior. Although 14 experts cite

TABLE 13.2
Description of Sexually Abused Children Offered in Testimony

Truthfulness		Sexual Behavior		Emotional Behavior	
Delay, denial, inconsistency	n	*Overly sexual*	n		n
Delayed reporting	21	Knowledge of sex in-		Nightmares, sleep	
Retraction, recantation	19	appropriate for age	8	disorders	13
Conflicting & uncon-		Sexual preoccupation	6	Helplessness	10
vincing disclosure/				Fear	10
inconsistent accounts	14	*Aversion to sex*	n	Depression	8
Fabrication	1	Negative attitude		Bedwetting	7
		toward sex	3	Anxiety	7
Truthful, consistent	n	Naive in sexual matters	1	Withdrawal	6
Children do not lie/false		Fear of men	2	Regression	6
accounts rare	15			Guilt	5
Consistency in account				Anger	5
(children unable to				Eating disorders/lack	
maintain consistent lie				of appetite	4
over time)	6			Embarrassment	2
Child can tell reality from				Confusion	2
fantasy	3			Suicidal	1
				Sense of loss	1
				Emotional behavior	1
				Dissociative behavior	1
				Trauma	1

inappropriate knowledge of sex and sexual preoccupation as characteristics of an abused child, 6 believe naivety and aversion to sexual matters are marks of abuse. In two of the cases, fear of men was recited as a trait of an abused child, whereas two experts testified that a desire to protect or to continue to see the abuser was consistent with abuse. In yet another contradiction, pseudomaturity was cited by two experts as evidence of sexual abuse, whereas one expert cited emotional immaturity (Mason, 1991a).

In the third cluster many experts described emotional or acting out behavior consistent with sexual abuse that may be considered typical of many children at some point. These general characteristic include: depression and anxiety (15); anger (5); regressive or withdrawn behavior (12); sleep or eating disorders, including nightmares and bedwetting (24); and behavioral problems such as running away, problems at school, and other forms of acting out behavior (17) (Mason, 1991a).

This examination of characteristics offered by expert witnesses in this sample indicates, at the least, an imprecise behavioral profile with a number of critical contradictions. Part of the reason that these characteristics are so contradictory and diverse may be that the expert is tailoring the list to suit a particular child. For example, in *State v. Myers* (1984), the court allowed testimony that the child was abused because she showed symptoms such as fear, confusion, poor mother–daughter relationship, fear of men, nightmares with assaultive conduct, and sexual knowledge beyond her years. On the other hand, the expert in *Ward v. State* (1988) testified that a child could show signs of abuse by sexual behavior, passiveness or aggressiveness, changes in eating habits, underachievement, sleep disturbances, or depression.

Labels Given to Syndrome Testimony

What experts called these indicators generically varied widely. Many of the earlier cases label the characteristics they present as the child sex-abuse accommodation syndrome (CSAAS), or some variation of that term (see Table 13.3) and often mention Roland Summit (1983), the psychiatrist who is generally credited with formulating this syndrome to describe intrafamilial sex abuse. The five characteristics that Summit noted and are frequently mentioned, even when not identified as CSAAS, are secrecy, helplessness, accommodation, fear of disclosure, and retraction. In later cases the term CSAAS or some variation is less frequently noted, and most experts describe their testimony generally as characteristics of sexually abused children without mentioning the word syndrome. This may well be a response to the refusal of some courts to admit the CSAAS on the grounds that it lacked scientific reliability as evidenced by its exclusion from the *DSM–III–R*. A few of the more recent cases move away entirely from sexual abuse classifications and instead refer to the posttraumatic stress disorder (PTSD), which is included in the *DSM–III–R* (Matter of E.M., 1987; *State v. Catsam*, 1987; *State v. Reser*, 1989; *Townsend v. State*, 1987). This testimony emphasizes the reluctance of children to report the event immediately or at all.

Judicial Rulings on Expert Testimony

There are two legal rules regarding the admissibility of expert testimony that judges must consider. The first is the well-established general rule that the issue of credibility is the sole province of the jury. As one court said,

TABLE 13.3
How Experts Label Descriptions

Syndrome	n
CSAAS (Child Sex Abuse Accommodation Syndrome)	10
PTSD (Posttraumatic Stress Disorder)	4
Child Sexual Abuse Syndrome	3
Intrafamilial Child Sex-Abuse Syndrome	3
Child Abuse Accommodation Syndrome	2
Post-Child-Molest Traumatic Stress Disorder	1
Child Molest Syndrome	1
No syndrome named	49

"It is hornbook law that the credibility of a witness and the weight to be given his testimony rests exclusively with the jury or trier of fact" (*United States v. Rosenberg*, 1952). This would be the case, for instance, with the introduction of the results of the polygraph or of an expert who actually claimed that he could tell if a witness was lying.

The second rule is that the judge must consider whether the expert testimony is reliable. In making this judgment, appellate courts are guided by the Federal Rules of Evidence or their state's version of them. According to Rule 702, "If scientific technical or other specialized knowledge will assist the trier of fact to understand the evidence or to determine a fact in issue, a witness qualified as an expert by knowledge, skill, experience, training, or education, may testify thereto in the form of an opinion or otherwise." This rule is balanced by Rules 401 and 403, which insist respectively that the evidence must be relevant, and that it must not create a substantial likelihood of undue prejudice by confusing the issues or misleading the jury (Fed. R. Evid., 1991).

In addition to these broad rules, some jurisdictions, including the federal courts, have adopted the more stringent Frye Test (*Frye v. United States*, 1923) which permits expert testimony only where the trial court has found that the scientific principle or discovery underlying the testimony is "sufficiently established to have gained general acceptance in the particular field in which it belongs."

In the appellate cases that were decided between 1980 and 1990, fairly clear patterns of acceptance and rejection can be identified (Mason, 1991a). In the 122 cases examined, there is an overall trend in favor of the trial court's admission of expert testimony: 67 appellate courts approved admission, 44 disallowed testimony, 11 approved admission in part and disallowed in part. The majority of appellate courts which allow the expert's testimony generally state that it is within the trial court's discretion, or that the testimony is helpful. They allow it even when it is applied to a particular child, rather than presented as a general phenomenon. The Supreme Court of Hawaii, the first court to allow this testimony, explained that the expert's opinion regarding the complainant's credibility logically followed from his testimony about the behavior of sexually abused children. Therefore, the testimony respecting the credibility of the complainant "cannot be considered to be substantially more prejudicial than the testimony which led to the conclusion" (*State v. Kim*, 1982).

By far the most important reason given for disallowing the trial court's use of expert testimony is that it is an inappropriate support of child's credibility (see Table 13.4). In a similar vein, experts who say directly that children do not lie about sexual abuse are disallowed in nine cases. The rejection of testimony that children do not lie about sexual abuse has an important bearing on expert testimony. Overall, as is described later, re-

TABLE 13.4
Reasons for Exclusion of Expert Testimony

Reasons	n
1. Inappropriate support of child's credibility	27
2. Inappropriately defines characteristics of defendant	13
3. Not helpful/irrelevant	10
4. Claim that "children do not lie"—usurps jury function	9
5. Anatomical dolls not scientifically accepted	7
6. Syndrome not accepted in scientific community	3
7. Syndrome testimony not allowed to prove abuse occurred	3
8. Too prejudicial	1

Note. Some courts offer more than one reason for exclusion.

search indicates that therapists who deal with sexually abused children believe that they are straightforward and consistent (Conte, Sorenson, Fogarty, & Rosa, 1991). This kind of testimony, however, is likely to be rejected as bearing directly on the credibility of the child.

Only about 13 of these appellate courts reject the admission of expert testimony on the grounds that their testimony is not established in the scientific community. These rejections focus on syndrome testimony and on the use of anatomically correct dolls. These appellate courts are less likely to accept testimony about the behavior of sexually abused children; namely, CSAAS (or some other, similar label), than a more flexible list of descriptors with no title. Some courts challenge the scientific reliability of the syndrome on the basis that it is not recognized as a diagnostic category by the American Psychiatric Association or the American Psychological Association. As the California court observed in *In Re Sara M* (1987):

> The Third District concluded the evidence adduced at the jurisdictional hearing failed to meet the Kelly–Frye Standard. The psychologists testified the syndrome is neither included in the *Diagnostic and Statistical Manual of Mental Disorders (DSM–III–R)* of the American Psychiatric Association nor recognized by the American Psychological Association or other professional organizations. The psychologists described the syndrome as being the beginning stages of development and acceptance.

Although the Psychiatric Association's diagnostic system does not recognize the CSAAS or any other diagnostic profile of the sexually abused child, the *DSM–III–R* does recognize PTSD, and at least one court made this distinction in allowing testimony labeled PTSD about a child's reluctance to admit that sexual abuse had occurred (American Psychiatric Association, 1987).

Nevertheless, some courts do not seem troubled by this lack of acceptance in the relevant scientific community and readily accept syndrome testimony (*People v. Gray*, 1986; *People v. Luna*, 1988).

When directly challenged on this issue of testimony based on observations with anatomical dolls, most of these appellate courts refuse to accept testimony that a child's play with anatomical dolls, although widely used by therapists to aid in assessment, reveals evidence of sexual abuse. This technique is sometimes challenged under the Frye rule as a new scientific principle not "sufficiently established to have gained general acceptance in the particular field in which it belongs" (*Frye v. United States*, 1923; see also Levy, 1989). The court in *In Re Amber B* (1987) reversed a dependency adjudication based on dolls-assisted testimony, arguing that, "The purpose [of the California version] of the Frye rule is to prevent factfinders from being misled by the 'aura of infallibility' that may surround unproven scientific methods" (see also Levy, 1989).

The Rebuttal Phenomenon

A close look at the patterns of acceptance or rejection of the admissibility of expert testimony reveals an extremely significant pattern. The overall pattern of acceptance of expert witness testimony is greatly skewed toward rebuttal rather than direct. Although on direct testimony appellate courts are more likely to disapprove rather than approve expert witness testimony, they are enthusiastic about admitting expert testimony to rehabilitate the credibility of the witness who has been attacked by the defense. The usual cause of attack is that the child delayed, denied, recanted, or was inconsistent in pretrial testimony. Twenty-seven courts admitted expert testimony on rebuttal, whereas only 7 rejected it. Courts that reject affirmative testimony sometimes express in dicta that they would have allowed it for the purpose of rehabilitating the child witness. There has been a movement in this direction among legal scholars as well (see, e.g., Myers et al., 1989).

Although there is an element of fair play in allowing expert testimony when the child's credibility has been attacked, there two significant problems with how most appellate courts handle the rebuttal exception. First, courts allow expert witness testimony on recantation, which associates a child's behavior with a syndrome used to diagnose sexual abuse, and second, opportunity for rebuttal becomes an open window through which all kinds of testimony not allowed on direct testimony is thrown.

TABLE 13.5
Pattern of Admission of Rebuttal Testimony

	Admit n	Exclude n
Direct testimony	57	73
Rebuttal testimony	27	7

Note. $\chi^2(1, N = 164) = 13.64, p < .001$.

The typical rebuttal situation occurs when the defense points out that the child delayed, sometimes for months or even years, in telling about the alleged incident of abuse, or that the child recanted regarding the original accusation of abuse. For example, in *State v. Middleton* (1983), a 14-year-old girl reported that her father had raped her. Within 1 week, she made consistent reports to her mother's friend, a children's services worker, a doctor, the police, and the grand jury. Six weeks later she recanted, in front of her mother, the father's attorney, and another witness. When evidence of the child's change of story were brought forth at trial, the expert was then allowed to explain this supposedly incomprehensible behavior by testifying that a characteristic of a sexually abused child is frequent denial following an allegation of sexual abuse, presumably out of fear of the abuser. The Middleton court stated on appeal:

> If a complaining witness in a burglary trial, after making the initial report, denied several times before testifying at trial that the crime had happened, the jury would have good reason to doubt seriously her credibility at any time. However, in this instance we are concerned with a child who states she has been the victim of sexual abuse by a member of her family. The experts testified that in this situation the young victim often feels guilty about testifying against someone she loves and wonders if she is doing the right thing. . . . Explaining this bizarre behavior by identifying its emotional antecedents could help the jury better assess the witness' credibility.

Although it may seem fair to allow the expert to counter charges by the defense that recantation indicates lying, the anomaly is that recantation is presented as a characteristic of a sexually abused child, thereby not just persuading the jury that this kind of delay for a child is explainable (as it might be by other theories of children's testimony), but that it is a characteristic of a sexually abused child. This provides a form of "linkage," which, it could be argued, is highly prejudicial.

Perhaps even more problematic is that the expert's testimony is often not limited to the fact of recantation. In *Allison v. State* (1987), the child witness was not accused of recantation, but rather of fact complicity with her mother in creating the story. The court then allowed the experts to bring in a very wide range of syndrome testimony, with no regard to its reliability, that had little to do with complicity, and nothing to do with recantation.

In *People v. Gray* (1986), the 9-year-old child witness was initially reluctant to disclose the alleged acts of lewd behavior perpetrated by her stepfather and was inconsistent initially in her account; naming a stranger, not her stepfather. The expert witness was permitted to testify that:

> There are certain behavioral traits seen in molestation victims; i.e., delayed reporting, inconsistent disclosure, accommodation in the sense of outward

affection toward an adult a child also fears, and increased likelihood of immediately reporting a stranger than a family member.

In this case the allegation was brought by the girl's father in the course of a child-support battle, whereas the girl's mother reported that the girl had a very good relationship with the stepfather and had shown no signs of emotional distress.

Overall, the rebuttal exception skews the nature of the expert testimony in the courts toward recantation, inconsistency, and delay, as indicated in the previous discussion of the indicators mentioned in the experts' testimony. These indicators become the password by which a wide range of expert testimony is permitted into the courtroom.

THE CONTROVERSY REGARDING A PROFILE OF SEXUALLY ABUSED CHILDREN WITHIN THE MENTAL-HEALTH COMMUNITY

From the other side of the bench, the mental-health community, which provides the experts, is also divided about testimony regarding behavioral characteristics of sexually abused children. There are severe disagreements within the relevant community of mental-health professionals and scientists regarding the reliability of any sort of syndrome that attempts to describe the characteristics of sexually abused children. The major division may be described as being between the research scientists and the clinicians. Generally speaking, clinicians are most likely to treat sexually abused children and most likely to serve as expert witnesses, and these clinicians are generally more confident about the reliability of behavioral indicators of abuse, based largely on their own clinical observations (MacFarlane, 1992; Summit, 1992). On the other side, research scientists are more likely to test the reliability of syndrome testimony in controlled scientific studies and they are generally more critical of testimony regarding behavioral indicators of sexual abuse (Berliner & Conte, 1993; Kendall-Tackett, Williams, & Finkelhor, 1993). The scientists have now had many years to test the validity of this syndrome testimony, and the clinicians have had the same number of years to work with sexually abused children. Their disagreement has, for the most part, grown stronger, focusing now on the appropriate role for syndrome testimony, if any, and the ethics of testifying in court on such matters.

There is a second issue, usually raised outside the clinical community, about the self-regulating standards that the profession sets or does not set with regard to this type of expert testimony. Of particular concern is the relationship of the expert to the child witness (Garbarino et al., 1989).

There has now been over a decade of research and publication focusing on the symptomology of sexually abused children. In general, it is fair to say that the research community has grown wary regarding the existence of distinct behavioral characteristics. The original profile, CSAAS, is credited to Summit (1983), who identified this syndrome based on his clinical experience with children who had experienced intrafamilial sex abuse. As noted earlier, the five characteristics that Summit noted and are still frequently mentioned, even when not identified as CSAAS, are secrecy, helplessness, accommodation, fear of disclosure, and retraction. Because of the powerless position of children in this circumstance, Summit claimed that there were unlikely to be forthcoming about the event, and when they did reveal it, they often denied it later.

Summit's model has elicited a good deal of research over the past nearly 10 years, which focuses on the characteristics of sexually abused children. Two recent studies by two groups of researchers (Berliner & Conte, 1993; Kendall-Tackett et al., 1993) evaluate a large number of the studies that have investigated the existence of behavioral characteristics. Both are critical of the presence of clear indicators of sexual abuse. Berliner and Conte, in part, discussed the difficulty in making a determination between abused and nonabused children. The authors focus specifically on the issue of whether or not sexually abused children withhold information about the event of abuse:

> Fundamentally, all the indicator-based assessment strategies suffer the same essential problems. For most criteria there is little or no evidence that the variables actually discriminate between abused and nonabused children. For many of the criteria offered as evidence that abuse did or did not take place, it is just as plausible that alternative hypothesis is true. For example, several commentators argue that a relevant criterion for a true case of sexual abuse is if the child is very hesitant to talk about the abuse. This is because of an assumption that a sexually abused child will feel ashamed and will have been threatened or bribed not to tell. However, it is just as possible that a child who has told several other adults about the abuse and been supported in that telling or a child who is too young to know what the sexual abuse represents, or a child with high self-esteem or a high level of assertiveness may show no hesitancy in describing the abuse. (Berliner & Conte, 1993, pp. 114–115)

Kendall-Tackett et al. (1993) reviewed 45 studies. Their finding is that, although sexually abused children demonstrated more symptoms than non-sexually abused children, these symptoms covered a wide range and fell into no clear pattern. In addition, about one-third showed no symptoms at all. In assessing their findings, the authors stated:

> The range of symptoms, the lack of a single predominant symptom pattern, and the absence of symptoms in so many victims clearly suggest that diagnosis

is complex. Because the effects of abuse can manifest themselves in too many ways, symptoms cannot be easily used, without other evidence, to confirm the presence of of sexually abuse. Yet the absence of symptoms certainly cannot be used to rule out sexual abuse. There are too many sexually abused children who are apparently asymptomatic. This finding is especially important for those conducting forensic evaluations. (p. 175)

Many clinicians would not agree with the general criticism of the lack of a definable pattern, or the difficulty in interpreting symptoms, such as fear of disclosure and delay or recantation of allegations. They feel that they have been dealt with unfairly by criticism from within their community and from the courts. Kee MacFarlane (1992), a clinician and Director of the Children's Institute International commented:

In sexual abuse cases, the defense will always try to avoid the unpopular appearance of attacking the character of a child. The target becomes whatever else is in the arsenal of the prosecution: the witnesses, the experts, the materials, the research, the literature. It has been particularly difficult for many clinicians to watch the language and tools of the therapeutic process become ammunition for prosecutors and a bull's eye for the defense. (p. 166)

Summit (1992), the originator of the concept of CSAAS, recently lamented the fate of this syndrome in the courts:

The polarization which inflames every issue of sexual abuse has been kindled further here by the exploitation of a clinical concept as ammunition for battles in court. The excess heat has been generated by false claims advanced by prosecutors as well as a primary effort by defense interests to strip the paper of any worth or relevance. (p. 153)

Although Summit believed his concept had been wrongly applied as a sex-abuse test, he claimed that it still has validity to explain delayed disclosure or inconsistent testimony. "The CSAAS is used appropriately in court testimony not to prove a child was molested but to rebut the myths which prejudice endorsement of delayed or inconsistent disclosure" (p. 154).

Although Summit insisted that delayed or inconsistent disclosure is still a reliable characteristic of a sexually abused child, the clinical community is by no means unanimous in their endorsement of this indicator; in fact, for many clinicians who work with allegedly sexually abused children, just the opposite is true. They believe that sexually abused children always tell the truth about the abuse and are consistent in their account of the event. For instance, in a recent survey of 212 professionals asked to rank 41 criteria often employed in indicator assessment models, 96% claimed that the "child's report of abuse is consistent over time," whereas 60% claimed that "child's disclosure contains retractions or is conflicted" (Conte, Sorenson, Fogarty, & Rosa, 1991, p. 120). According to this survey, one might infer that both telling a consistent tale and telling an inconsistent tale are positive indicators of sexual abuse for a majority of therapists and that some professionals also hold both beliefs.

Another issue of concern to some mental-health professionals, particularly with regard to interviewing a child for indications of sexual abuse that may be reported on at trial, is the relationship between the child and the expert. Garbarino et al. (1989) criticized the use of therapists to investigate a child's credibility, claiming that a therapeutic approach is conducive to eliciting a response, and to dealing with the subjective reality of the child, but not to determining credibility. At least one court has held this position as well. In *People v. Leon* (1989), the court rejected the testimony of an expert witness regarding the CSAAS, arguing:

> On the one hand is the need to care and treat an abused child and the need as a treatment device to accept as true his report, whether truthful or not; and on the other hand the preservation of the constitutional right to presumption of innocence in a criminal case. (p. 939)

The neutrality of the expert is a concern for the professional community as well. The American Psychological Association Ethical Principles warn psychologists to "avoid relationships that limit their objectivity or create a conflict of interest" ("Ethical Principles," 1981, p. 631).

CONCLUSION

How therapists perceive children's response to sexual abuse has had an important impact in both therapy and the criminal justice system. Children may be misdiagnosed in treatment, or, more seriously, criminal defendants may be convicted based on a therapist's incorrect conviction about the typical response of children. However, as this chapter has demonstrated, there is no consensus on what this response is, and, in fact, it appears therapists may endorse completely contradictory behavioral indicators as evidence of abuse.

One of the central contradictions relates to how children remember and relate the facts of sexual abuse. One group believes that abused children most often delay in relating the event, and when they do relate the event their testimony is often inconsistent. They are also likely to recant and claim they were not telling the truth. Another group believes that most children who are abused never lie about the event and tell a consistent story.

Because of the nature of the trial procedure, therapists are more likely to focus on the inconsistent, recanting behavior in court. A judge is most likely to allow expert testimony regarding a syndrome or behavioral indicators on rebuttal when the child's credibility has already been attacked. This happens when the defense points out that the child's story is inconsistent, or that the child retracted the story and said it was a lie. The judge is far less likely to admit expert testimony which claims that children never lie about sexual abuse. This is considered inappropriately bolstering the credibility of a child witness. Outside court, according to the survey noted earlier, therapists are more likely to focus on consistency and straightforwardness in relating the event as an indicator of sexual abuse.

Judges are not aware of these inconsistencies, because they are only judging one case at a time and are not likely to question the scientific basis of experts' testimony. Whereas appellate courts are reluctant to look beyond the form to critically examine the content, the scientific community is very critical of the scientific validity of the content, particularly outside the context of therapy (Berliner & Conte, 1993; Kendall-Tackett et al., 1993). The many studies that have been performed on the indicators of sexual abuse fail to reveal any consistent pattern of behavior that can be identified in the majority of sexually abused children. Moreover, many of the symptoms that do occur in some children can be found in children who are not sexually abused. The clinical community is likely to divide with the scientific community on this issue and claim that there are clear behavioral indicators, although the clinical community maintains no consensus on what these might be, even on the issue of delay or recantation.

Given the confusion and contradictory opinions regarding children's recall and relation of facts pertaining to the event (or multiple events) of sexual abuse (as well as some other indicators of sexual abuse), it would be appropriate, first, for the therapeutic community to carefully reconsider its diagnostic scheme, and second, for the courts to take a more critical view of the reliability of expert testimony in this arena. This happened recently in the much publicized Kelly Michaels trial where a young preschool teacher was convicted on 155 counts of sexual offense involving 20 children who were students in the Wee Care Nursery School. The New Jersey Superior Court Appellate Division reversed this conviction on the basis of the improper introduction of expert testimony regarding child sex-abuse syndromes (*State of New Jersey v. Michaels*, 1993). The court claimed that evidence presented regarding the scientific reliability of such testimony was insufficient. The court stated, "Unquestionably, this erroneously admitted evidence was capable of producing an unjust result and thus requires the reversal of defendant's convictions."

For the behavioral science community, the first step is to look carefully at how abused children actually remember and relate the fact of abuse, as well as to examine the other identified characteristics of sexual abuse. Many of the contributors of this book are already conducting this type of research. A second challenge is to study carefully the preconceptions that adults who work with children have about children's memory and their relation of events of sexual abuse. It is the adult therapists and criminal justice personnel who are currently carrying on the interrogations, the therapy and the criminal prosecutions. Their attitudes and beliefs have a significant impact on the outcome of criminal trials.

REFERENCES

Allison v. State, 346 S.E.2d 380 (Ga. 1986) revsd. 353 S.E.2d 805 (Ga. 1987).

American Psychiatric Association. (1987). *Diagnostic and statistical manual of mental disorders* (3rd ed., rev.). Washington, DC: Author.

Berliner, L., & Conte, J. (1993). Sexual abuse evaluations: Conceptual and empirical obstacles. *Child Abuse & Neglect, 17,* 111–125.

Conte, J. R. (1991). Evaluating children's reports of sexual abuse: A survey of professionals. *American Journal of Orthopsychiatry, 61,* 428–437.

Ethical principles of psychologists. (1981). *American Psychologist, 36,* 631.

Fed. R. Evidence (West 1991), Secs. 702, 401, 403.

Frye v. United States, 293 F. 1013, (D.C. Cir. 1923).

Garbarino, J., Stott, F., & Faculty of the Erikson Institute. (1989). *What children can tell us.* San Francisco: Jossey-Bass.

In Re Amber B, 191 Cal. App.3d 682 (1987).

In Re Sara M, 194 Cal. App.3d 585 (1987).

Kendall-Tackett, K., Williams, L., & Finkelhor, D. (1993). Impact of sexual abuse on children: A review and synthesis of recent empirical studies. *Psychological Bulletin, 13*(1), 164–180.

Levy, (1989). Using "scientific" testimony to prove child sexual abuse. *Family Law Quarterly, 383*(23), 401.

MacFarlane, K. (1992). Summit's "Abuse of the CSAAS." *Child Abuse 1*(4), 164–175.

Mason, M. A. (1991a, Fall/Winter). A judicial dilemma: Expert witness testimony in child sex abuse cases. *Journal of Psychiatry and Law,* 185–219.

Mason, M. A. (1991b). The McMartin case Revisited: The conflict between social work and criminal justice. *Social Work, 36*(5), 391–395.

Matter of E.M., 520 N.Y.S. 2d 327 (Fam. Ct. 1987).

Myers, J., Bays, D., Becker, M., Berliner, L., Corwin, D., & Saywitz, K. (1989). Expert testimony in child sexual abuse litigation. *Nebraska Law Review, 68,* 100.

People v. Gray, 187 Cal. App.3d 213 (Cal. 1986).

People v. Leon, 214 Cal. App.3d 925 (1989).

People v. Luna, 204 Cal. App.3d (1988).

State of New Jersey v. Michaels, March 26, 1993, slip op. A–199–88T1.

State v. Catsam, 534 A.2d 184 (Vt. 1987).

State v. Kim, 645 P.2d 1330 (Haw. 1982).

State v. Middleton, 657 P.2d 1215 (Or. 1983).

State v. Myers, 359 N.W.2d 604 (Minn. 1984).

State v. Reser, 767 P.2d 1277 (Kan. 1989).

Summit, R. (1983). The child sexual abuse accommodation syndrome. *Child Abuse & Neglect, 177,* 183.

Summit, R. (1992). Abuse of the child sexual abuse accommodation syndrome. *Child Abuse 1*(4), 153–165.

Townsend v. State, 734 P.2d 705 (Nev. 1987).

U.S. v. Rosenberg, 108 F.Supp. 798 (S.D.N.Y. 1952) *aff'd.* 200 F.2d 666 (2d Cir. 1952).

Ward v. State, 519 S.W.2d 1082 (Fla. App. 1988).

14

Lying and Deception

Paul Ekman
University of California, San Francisco

Questions about truthfulness occur in many contexts—when parents ask their children if they are using recreational drugs, when an employer ask applicants about the reasons they left their last job, when international leaders consider each others' threats or promises, when voters evaluate candidates' promises, when physicians consider a patient's complaint, when at the start of a romantic encounter claims about the number of prior sexual partners are evaluated, and when juries evaluate witness testimony. In all of these instances many sources of information are used to evaluate whether someone is being truthful. My focus here has solely been on those judgments that are based on a person's demeanor.

Before I turn to this, I first explain my definition of lying and how I distinguish lies from secrets, self-deception, and other kinds of deceit. I then discuss some of the difficulties in using that definition, when people believe what is false to be true. Next I consider the different motives that underlie the decision to tell a lie. I then discuss two principal reasons why lies fail and close by reviewing some of our most recent research on how difficult it is to judge whether someone is lying or telling the truth.[1]

---

[1]Much of what I cover has been published in the second edition of *Telling Lies* (Ekman, 1992) or in articles listed in the reference section of this chapter. An exception is new distinctions between concealment lies and secrets I introduce in the first section of this chapter.

LYING AND SELF-DECEPTION

The intent of the liar is one of the two criteria for distinguishing lies from other kinds of deception. The liar *deliberately* chooses to mislead the target. Liars may actually tell the truth, but that is not their intent. Truthful people may provide false information—bad advice may come from stock brokers—but that is not their intent. The liar has choice; the liar could choose not to lie. Presumably, a pathological liar is compelled to lie and, by my definition, therefore is not a liar.

The second criterion for distinguishing lies from other deceptions is that the target is not notified about the liar's intention to mislead. A magician is not a liar by this criterion, but Uri Geller is a liar, because Geller claimed his tricks were not magic. An actor is not a liar but an impostor is. Sometimes notification of an intention to mislead is implicit in the *framing*, to use Goffman's (1974) term, of the situation. Let the buyer beware is one example of an explicit warning that products or services may not be what they are purported. (Of course, that warning does not appear in advertisements, nearly all of which are designed to convey the opposite message.) In real estate transactions, the potential buyer is implicitly notified that the seller's asking price is not the actual price the seller would accept. Various forms of politeness are other instances in which the nature of the situation notifies the target that the truth may not be spoken. The host would not properly scrutinize the dinner guest to determine if the guest's claim to have enjoyed the evening is true anymore than the aunt should worry whether the nephew is lying when he says that he appreciated being given a tie for Christmas. Deception is expected; even if the target might suspect that the truth is not being told it is improper to question it. Poker is still another situation in which the rules of the game sanction and notify the players that deception will occur, and therefore one can not consider bluffing to be a lie. In some situations only certain types of deception are allowable. The poker player cannot use marked cards, nor can the home seller conceal a known defect.

Courtship is probably an ambiguous situation regarding expectations of truthfulness. The saying "all's fair in love and war" would seem to warn lovers not to believe all they are told. Recent public opinion polls suggest that lies that diminish the number of previous sexual partners are common among college-aged adults. However, I expect that lovers want to believe in the truthfulness of their partners and popular songs testify to the betrayal felt when lies are discovered. Poets have brilliantly explained how romance may be considered a form of collusion to develop and maintain myths about each other.

I differ from Bok (1982), who only considered false statements to be lies. I (Ekman, 1985) argued that concealment is just as much a lie as falsification, as long as there is an expectation that concealment will not occur. My daughter knows that if she gets into trouble at school and the head teacher gives her a "slip"—a formal warning that she may be suspended if the offense is repeated—she must tell me about it. If she does not inform me, she is lying. I do not need to ask her each evening, "Did you get into trouble at school?" She is obligated to reveal that information, and to conceal it is to deliberately mislead me without giving notification.

Marriages differ regarding the obligation to report without being asked if an extramarital affair has begun. If there is an explicit agreement to that effect, then I consider the failure to volunteer such a report a lie. If there is no such agreement, then such a concealment would not qualify to be designated a lie. Commonly partners differ about their expectations, or at least about their memory of what their mutual obligations were regarding the reports of such liaisons.

Suppose a president had a minor stroke during the middle of his term of office, and the doctors concealed it. They would have committed a concealment lie, because the American public expects to be told about a change in a president's health that affects his ability to do his job. Concealment and falsification are two different techniques for accomplishing the same objective. There are many reasons why liars will always prefer concealment to falsification if the situation allows it: The liar does not need to remember the false story; if caught, she can always claim she was just about to reveal the truth, or that she did not because she was certain the target knew what was going on.

Concealment and falsification are not the only techniques of lying, although they are the most common. I (Ekman, 1985) distinguished three other techniques. *Telling the truth falsely* is when the liar speaks the truth in such a way as to seem to mean the opposite of what is said. Consider the situation in which a wife asks her husband whether he met any attractive women on his business trip and he replies, "I sure did, I slept with a different one every night, and sometimes another one during the lunch break." If that was indeed the case, then the philandering husband would be telling the truth, but in a manner which implies that he was faithful. Another technique is to tell a *half truth* as if it was a whole truth. The wife who is asked by her husband if she is attracted to the next door neighbor is telling a half truth if she replies "he's nice" if she indeed is having an affair with him. What she has said is true, but she is deliberately leaving out crucial information to mislead her husband. The *incorrect inference dodge* was identified by a newspaper columnist who recommended it as the solution to the problem of not wanting to be truthful to a friend who puts you on the spot. Suppose your friend has, for example, an exhibition of her paintings, and you think her work is terrible. The incorrect inference dodge would be to reply to her question about whether you like the paintings by saying, "Incredible, I can't believe it, how did you do that!"

Bok (1982) defined intentional concealment as *secrecy*. I think that confuses matters, for notification is the issue in distinguishing secrecy from concealment lies. I reserve the term secrecy for a situation in which notification *is* given about the intention not to reveal information. By calling something a secret we state our right not to reveal, to maintain privacy. Secrets may remain within one individual, or two or more people may maintain information they consider secret from others. To return to earlier examples, if my daughter has not told me about the trouble in school, it is not a secret, but a concealment lie. When I ask her if she has a boyfriend, she may properly tell me, "That is a secret." If she does indeed have a boyfriend, then she has concealed that from me, but because it is acknowledged it is termed a secret. Suppose I have not asked her about this, but she knows of my interest from past conversations. If she does have a boyfriend but does not tell me, she is engaging in concealment but it is not a secret, because she has not acknowledged her right to conceal the truth, and it is not a lie because she has not agreed that there is an obligation to inform.

Self-deception presumably occurs when the deceiver does not realize he is misleading himself, and does not know his own motive for deceiving himself. My discussion of the actions that led up to the Challenger space shuttle disaster in Ekman (1992) illustrates the subtle issues involved in distinguishing self-deception from rationalization, an attempt to excuse bad judgment, or repression:

> The space shuttle launch on January 28, 1986 was seen by millions on television. This launch had been highly publicized because the crew included a schoolteacher, Christa McAuliffe. The television audience included many schoolchildren including Ms. McAuliffe's own class. She was to have given a lesson from outer space. But just seventy-three seconds after launch, the shuttle exploded killing all seven on board.
>
> The night before the launch a group of engineers at Morton Thiokol, the firm that had built the booster rockets, officially recommends that the launch be delayed because the cold weather forecast for overnight might severely reduce the elasticity of the rubber O-ring seals. If that were to happen, leaking fuel might cause the booster rockets to explode. The engineers at Thiokol called the National Aeronautic and Space Administration (NASA), unanimously urging postponement of the launch scheduled for the following morning.
>
> There had already been three postponements in the launch date, violating NASA's promise that the space shuttle would have routine, predictable launch schedules. Lawrence Mulloy, NASA's rocket project manager, argued with the Thiokol engineers, saying there was not enough evidence that cold weather would harm the O-rings. Mulloy talked that night to Thiokol manager Bob Lund, who later testified before the Presidential commission appointed to investigate the Challenger disaster. Lund testified that Mulloy told him that night to put on his "management hat" instead of his "engineering hat." Apparently doing so Lund changed his opposition to the launch overruling his own engineers. Mulloy also contacted Joe Kilminister, one of the vice presidents at Thiokol, asking him to sign a launch go ahead. He did so at 11:45 p.m., faxing a launch recommendation to NASA. Allan McDonald, who was

director of Thiokol's rocket project refuses to sign the official approval for the launch. Two months later McDonald was to quit his job at Thiokol.

Later the Presidential commission discovered that four of NASA's key senior executives responsible for authorizing each launch never were told of the disagreement between Thiokol engineers and the NASA rocket management team on the night the decision to launch was made. Robert Sieck, shuttle manager at the Kennedy Space Center; Gene Thomas, the launch director for *Challenger* at Kennedy; Arnold Aldrich, manager of space transportation systems at the Johnson Space Center in Houston; and Shuttle director Moore all were to later testify that they were not informed that the Thiokol engineers opposed a decision to launch.

How could Mulloy have sent the shuttle up knowing that it might explode? One explanation is that under pressure he became the victim of self-deceit, actually becoming convinced that the engineers were exaggerating what was really a negligible risk. If Mulloy was truly the victim of self-deceit can we fairly hold him responsible for his wrong decision? Suppose someone else had lied to Mulloy and told him there was no risk. We certainly would not blame him for then making a wrong decision. Is it any different if he has deceived himself? I think probably not, if Mulloy truly has deceived himself. The issue is was it self-deception or bad judgment, well rationalized?

To find out let me contrast what we know about Mulloy with one of the clear cut examples of self deceit discussed by experts who study self-deception (Lockard & Paulhus, 1988). A terminal cancer patient who believes he is going to recover even though there are many signs of a rapidly progressing, incurable malignant tumor, maintains a false belief. Mulloy also maintained a false belief, believing the shuttle could be safely launched. (The alternative that Mulloy knew for certain that it would blow up I think should be ruled out). The cancer patient believes he will be cured, despite the contrary strong evidence. The cancer patient knows he is getting weaker, the pain is increasing, but he insists these are only temporary setbacks. Mulloy also maintained his false belief despite the contrary evidence. He knew the engineers thought the cold weather would damage the O-ring seals, and if fuel leaked the rockets might explode, but he dismissed their claims as exaggerations.

What I have described so far does not tell us whether either the cancer patient or Mulloy is a deliberate liar or the victim of self-deceit. The crucial requirement for self-deceit is that the victim is unaware of his motive for maintaining his false belief. [It might seem that self-deceit is just another term for Freud's concept of repression. There are at least two differences. In repression the information concealed from the self arises from a deep-seated need within the structure of the personality, which is not typically the case in self-deception. And some maintain that confronting the self-deceiver with the truth can break the deceit, while in repression such a confrontation will not cause the truth to be acknowledged. See discussion of these issues in Lockard and Paulhus, 1988.] The cancer patient does not consciously know his deceit is motivated by his inability to confront his fear of his own imminent death. This element—not being conscious of the motivation for the self deceit—is missing for Mulloy. When Mulloy told Lund to put on his management hat, he showed that he was aware of what he needed to do to maintain the belief that the launch should proceed.

Richard Feynman, the Nobel laureate physicist who was appointed to the Presidential commission which investigated the *Challenger* disaster, wrote as follows about the management mentality that influenced Mulloy. "[W]hen the moon project was over, NASA . . . [had] to convince Congress that there exists a project that only NASA can do. In order to do so, it is necessary—at least it was *apparently* necessary in this case—to exaggerate: to exaggerate how economical the shuttle would be, to exaggerate how often it could fly, to exaggerate how safe it would be, to exaggerate the big scientific facts that would be discovered" (Feynman, 1988). *Newsweek* magazine said, "In a sense the agency seemed a victim of its own flackery, behaving as if space-flight were really as routine as a bus trip."

Mulloy was just one of many in NASA who maintained those exaggerations. He must have feared Congressional reaction if the shuttle had to be delayed a fourth time. Bad publicity which contradicted NASA's exaggerated claims about the shuttle might affect future appropriations. The damaging publicity from another postponed launch date might have seemed a certainty. The risk due to the weather was only a possibility, not a certainty. Even the engineers who opposed the launch were not absolutely certain there would be an explosion. Some of them reported afterwards thinking only seconds before the explosion that it might not happen.

We should condemn Mulloy for his bad judgment, his decision to give management's concerns more weight than the engineers' worries. Hank Shuey, a rocket-safety expert who reviewed the evidence at NASA's request said, "It's not a design defect. There was an error in judgment." We should not explain or excuse wrong judgments by the cover of self deception. We should also condemn Mulloy for not informing his superiors, who had the ultimate authority for the launch decision, about what he was doing and why he was doing it. Feynman offers a convincing explanation of why Mulloy took the responsibility on himself. "[T]he guys who are trying to get Congress to okay their projects don't want to hear such talk [about problems, risks, etc.]. It's better if they don't hear, so they can be more 'honest'—they don't want to be in the position of lying to Congress! So pretty soon the attitudes begin to change: information from the bottom which is disagreeable—'We're having a problem with the seals; we should fix it before we fly again'—is suppressed by big cheeses and middle managers who say, 'If you tell me about the seals problems, we'll have to ground the shuttle and fix it.' Or, 'No, no, keep on flying, because otherwise, it'll look bad', or 'Don't tell me; I don't want to hear about it. Maybe they don't say explicitly 'Don't tell me', but they discourage communication which amounts to the same thing" (Feynman, 1988).

Mulloy's decision not to inform his superiors about the sharp disagreement about the shuttle launch could be considered a lie of omission, [a concealment lie]. . . .

If Feynman is correct, if the NASA higher-ups had discouraged communi-cation, essentially saying "don't tell me," then this might constitute notification. Mulloy and presumably others at NASA knew that bad news or difficult decisions were not to be passed to the top. If that was so then Mulloy should not be considered a liar for not informing his superiors, for they had authorized the deceit, and knew they would not be told. In my judgment the superiors who were not told share some of the responsibility for the disaster with Mulloy who did not tell them. The superiors have the ultimate responsibility not only for a launch decision but for creating the atmosphere in which Mulloy operated. They contributed to the circumstances which led to his bad judgment, and for his decision not to bring them in on the decision.

Feynman notes the similarities between the situation at NASA and how mid level officials in the Iran-Contra affair, such as Poindexter, felt about telling President Reagan what they were doing. Creating an atmosphere in which subordinates believe that those with ultimate authority should not be told of matters for which they would be blamed, providing plausible deniability to a President, destroys governance. Former President Harry Truman rightly said "the buck stops here." The President or Chief Executive Officer must monitor, evaluate, decide and be responsible for decisions. To suggest otherwise may be advantageous in the short run, but it endangers any hierarchal organization, encouraging loose cannons and an environment of sanctioned deceit. (pp. 308–315)

A *broken promise* is not a lie. A week before President Clinton took office, a reporter charged that he had broken his campaign promise about Haitian immigration because he was now adopting the position of former President Bush—a policy he had criticized during the election campaign. With a trace of anger Clinton defended himself, saying that the American people would think he was foolish if he did not change his policies when circumstances change. From my framework Clinton was lying only if he had known at the time he criticized Bush that he intended to follow the same policy himself. Consider the charge that when President Bush raised taxes near the end of his term of office he should be considered a liar. Certainly he had earlier in his campaign promised not to raises taxes, but he could only be branded a liar if it could be proven he knew when he made that promise that the intended to break it.

The *failure to remember* is not a lie, although liars will often try to excuse their lies, once discovered, by claiming a memory failure. It is not uncommon to forget actions that one regrets, but if the forgetting truly has occurred, we should not consider that a lie, for there was no choice involved. Often it will not be possible to determine whether a memory failure has occurred or whether its invocation is itself a lie.

BELIEVING WHAT IS FALSE TO BE TRUE

If someone provides a false account of what truly occurred, it does not necessarily mean the person intended to mislead, and, as I explained earlier, if there is not a deliberate intent to mislead, a false statement should not be considered a lie. Why should it matter what we call a false statement? It is not simply a matter of semantics or definition. If the person is not lying, if the person does not believe he is engaged in deception at the moment he is doing it, then I expect his demeanor will be that of a truthful person. There should be no behavioral clues that the account is untrue if the person giving the account does not believe he is lying at the moment he gives the account. Although I have no direct evidence for this prediction, it is consistent with my (Ekman, 1985) general theory of when demeanor will betray a lie, and other evidence (Ekman, Friesen, & O'Sullivan, 1988; Ekman, O'Sullivan, Friesen, & Scherer, 1991) does support that account. There are a number of ways in which people may provide false information that they believe to be true.

People do misinterpret events, especially the meaning of other people's actions and the motives that lead people to act in one way or another. The fact that someone interprets matters in a way that reflects well on her, a way that allows her to engage in actions she finds desirable, does not mean that she is necessarily lying rather than misinterpreting. I would not necessarily consider such an occurrence an instance of self-deception. Not every misunderstanding or misinterpretation is self-deception.

Consider an alleged rapist who claims that his victim wanted to have sex with him. Even though rapists who do know they had totally unwilling victims could often make this claim, lying to avoid punishment, the claim itself does not tell us that it is false. Even if it is improbable, it conceivably might be true. Suppose it was a date rape, and the victim was shy or very fearful, protested only once, and not very strongly, and then did not resist. A rapist could misinterpret the initial protest and construe the subsequent lack of protest and passivity as consent. Would that rapist be a victim of self-deceit? Not, I believe, unless it was certain that he had no awareness that his misinterpretation of his victim's behavior was motivated by a wish to gratify his own needs. Did a rape occur? I believe the answer must be yes, although the rapist may not think it did, and may be telling his truth when he claims his victim implicitly consented. And one of the reasons why someone who makes such a claim might appear believable in their demeanor is that they believe their claim, and do not believe they are lying. (See Cross & Saxe, 1992, for a discussion of this problem in the context of their critique of the use of polygraph testing in child sexual abuse cases.)

Of course, that is not the only reason why someone may appear totally believable. I initially (Ekman, 1985) used the term *natural liar* to designate those people whose lies are seamless, whose demeanor is totally believable when they know they are lying. I have since (Ekman, 1992) changed the term to *natural performer*, because my studies suggest that they are not psychopaths, nor necessarily antisocial. Natural performers have the capacity to become the role they are playing, to near instantly believe for at time whatever they are saying, and because they believe they are saying the truth, their demeanor is totally credible.

Misinterpreting is not the only route by which someone may believe their false account is true. A person may initially know he is lying, but over time he may come to believe in his lie. If that happens, once he has come to believe his lie is a faithful account of what transpired, he may appear truthful. Consider a child molester who, when first accused, claimed that he was only cuddling the child, doing nothing that was really wrong, nothing the child did not want and enjoy. Even though he initially knew he was lying in his account, over time, with many repetitions of his lie, a molester could, I believe, come to believe his false story is true. It is conceivable that he could maintain in consciousness both the memory of the true event, that he forcibly abused the child, and the constructed belief that he only cuddled a willing child. In addition, the true memory might over time become much less accessible that the constructed belief, or perhaps not accessible at all.

Consider a child who deliberately lies, alleging that a teacher molested her, knowing that never occurred. Suppose the lying child was motivated by a wish to punish the teacher for having humiliated the child in class for not having done well on a test. If the child felt entitled to her revenge, she might reason that this was the kind of teacher who might have molested her, probably wanted to molest her, probably had molested other children, and so on. I believe we cannot rule out the possibility that, over time, with many repetitions and elaborations, the child could come to believe she had been molested.

These examples are troublesome because we do not know often they may occur; nor do we know if children are more vulnerable than adults to believing what is false is true, or whether there are specific personality characteristics associated with this phenomena. We have no certain way as yet to determine whether a memory is true, partially, or totally constructed. We do have ways, which I describe later to distinguish a false account, but only when the person giving that account knows he or she is giving a false account.

MOTIVES FOR LYING

My interviews with children (Ekman, 1989) and my data on adults from questionnaires suggests nine different motives for lying:

1. To avoid being punished. This is the most frequently mentioned motive by either children or adults. The punishment may be for a misdeed or for an accidental mistake.
2. To obtain a reward not otherwise readily obtainable. This is the second most commonly mentioned motive, by both children and adults.

3. To protect another person from being punished.

4. To protect oneself from the threat of physical harm. This is different from being punished, for the threat of harm is not for a misdeed. An example would be a child who is home alone telling a stranger at the door that his father is asleep now, to come back later.

5. To win the admiration of others.

6. To get out of an awkward social situation. Examples are claiming to have a babysitter problem to get out of dull party, or ending a telephone conversation by saying there is someone at the door.

7. To avoid embarrassment. The child who claims the wet seat resulted from water spilling, not wetting her pants, is an example if the child did not fear punishment, but only embarrassment.

8. To maintain privacy, without giving notification of the intention to maintain some information as private.

9. To exercise power over others, by controlling the information the target has.

I am not certain that every lie would necessarily fit under one of these nine motives, but these are the motives that emerged from the interview data I collected. There are a variety of trivial deceits, the lies of politeness and tact that are not easily subsumed by these nine motives. By my definition these are not lies, because the rules of politeness imply notification. A more difficult case is a lie required to maintain a surprise birthday party. Perhaps it should fit under the privacy motive.

WHY LIES FAIL

Many lies succeed. It is incumbent on those interested in detecting lies to account for when lies will fail and when they will succeed. Such an account will not only tell us when behavioral clues may betray a lie, and what we should therefore attend to, but will also provide guidelines for deciding which types of experimental deceptive scenarios can provide information relevant to which real-life settings.

Certainly, it is not the arena that determines the success or failure of a lie. It is not that all spousal lies succeed and all political lies fail. Within every arena of life (and when one begins to consider the matter, there are few arenas in which deception does not occur), some lies fail and others succeed.

Lies fail for a variety of reasons that will not concern us here. For example, liars are often betrayed by someone in whom the liar had confided. Liars may also be betrayed by many other kinds of evidence that expose the liar's claims as false. My focus is not on these types of betrayal, but on instances in which the liar's own behavior betrays the lie. I omit from such considerations instances in which the liar confesses (although much of my discussion is relevant to predicting when a liar will confess) or instances in which the liar might be judged to have acted in a way so that he or she would be caught. Instead, I am interested in those cases in which some aspect of the liar's behavior, despite his or her best intentions, betrays the liar's false pretense.

To put it briefly, before expanding on this, there are two reasons why lies fail; one has to do with thinking and the other with feeling. Lies fail either because the liar failed to adequately prepare, or because of the interference of emotions.

I would predict that in general (disregarding the type of lie, who is the liar, and who the target, and recognizing that disregarding these issues to make a general assertion is a very risky stance to take), most lies fail because the liar has not adequately prepared the false line he or she intends to maintain. One obvious, if not very interesting, example is when the liar forgets what he has said on one occasion and thoroughly contradicts himself on another occasion. Here, the source of clues to deceit is in the verbal content. One must be cautious about this, however, because truthful people will contradict themselves. However, I believe it would be possible, although I have not tried to do so, to specify the type of contradictions that are reliable signs of lying.

Another consequence of the failure to adequately prepare is being caught off guard when asked questions the liar had not anticipated and for which the liar has no ready reply. In such a jam the liar must think of a credible answer on the spot. When doing so most people will evidence various behaviors that signify they are thinking about what they are saying as they are talking. Pauses, gaze aversion, speech disfluencies, and speech mannerisms may all increase over what is usual for that person. In addition, the use of the hands to illustrate speech (what Ekman & Friesen, 1969a, termed *illustrators*) may decrease and voice intonation may flatten. Bear in mind that these are not signs of lying per se. There is no behavioral sign of lying itself, I maintain. However, when these signs of thinking about a reply occur in contexts in which answers should be known without thought, they can betray the liar.

Lies are also betrayed by signs of emotions. The simplest case is one in which the liar attempts to convincingly fabricate an emotion that is not felt. Few people are very good at this, although most of the time people get away with it, because rarely does the target of such a lie care whether the emotion displayed is feigned or real. There are what I call "reliable" behavioral signs of emotion; reliable in the sense that few people can display them at all or correctly. Narrowing the red margins of the lips in anger is an example of such a reliable sign of anger, typically absent when anger is feigned, because most people can not voluntarily make that movement. There are ways around this for the inventive liar, such as utilizing a Stanislavski-like technique to create the actual emotion, so that its involuntary signs will then appear unbidden.

More typically, lies about emotions do not simply involve fabricating an emotion, but concealing an emotion that is actually being experienced. Often, concealment goes hand in hand with fabrication, in which the liar uses a feigned emotion to mask signs of the emotion to be concealed. Such concealment attempts may be betrayed in either of two ways. Some sign of the concealed emotion may escape efforts to inhibit or mask the felt emotion, providing what Ekman and Friesen (1969b) termed *leakage*. What they called a *deception cue*, which does not leak the concealed emotion but betrays the likelihood that a lie is being perpetrated, occurs when only a fragment leaks that is not decipherable. A deception clue also occurs when the very effort of having to conceal produces alterations in behavior that do not fit the liars' line.

Even when the lie is not about emotions, the liar's feelings about lying can betray the lie. Chief among these feelings about lying are the fear of being caught, guilt about lying, and what I have called *duping delight*—the pleasure and excitement of putting one over. Not all lies will call forth these emotions. Whether they do will depend on characteristics of the liar, the target of the lie, and the content of the lie. Elsewhere (Ekman, 1985) I have described in some detail a lying checklist that facilitates making a prediction about the likelihood that any of these emotions about lying will occur.

To give just a few examples, the fear of being caught is highest when the stakes for being caught, the reward that is lost, and especially the punishment for being caught lying is very high. The fear of being caught will also be greater if the liar has not practiced the lie and has not had the experience of having succeeded before in this very lie with this target. If the target is known to be both suspicious and of extraordinary acumen, the fear of being caught will be greater. Guilt about lying will be highest when the liar shares values with and respects the target, when the target is not collusively aiding the lie and does not benefit from the lie, and when the lie is in no way authorized by any social group or institution. Duping delight is enhanced when others who are allies of the liar observe the liar's actions.

Although the arousal of any strong emotion—fear, guilt, or delight—produces changes in behavior that may be detectable, and thereby betray the lie if they do not fit the liar's line, each of these emotions produces some unique behavioral signs. Elsewhere I have explained in detail how these emotions, and the very process of managing emotions, are manifest in face, body, voice, and paralinguistic behavior (Ekman, 1985). Perhaps here it would be useful to mention that there is no one channel that is the best or most sensitive source for clues to deceit. Every aspect of behavior can provide such clues. There are hints of individual differences as well, in terms of what behavioral source may be most profitable to scrutinize.

An astute lie catcher will assess the likelihood of any of these emotions, so as to better know what behaviors to be especially alert to. Also, such an exercise will alert the lie catcher as to when the truthful person may appear to be lying. One must not make *Othello's error* of presuming that a sign of fear is a sign of lying. The truthful person may, under some circumstances, be afraid of being disbelieved, or guilty, or manifesting delight. The crucial issue is to examine the circumstances, and evaluate whether or not a truthful or lying person would be experiencing these emotions.

Why Is It So Hard to Discern Truthfulness From Demeanor?

Our behavioral measurements of facial expressions and voice can distinguish when someone is lying, in a high stakes lie about emotion felt at the moment, for 85% of the subjects (Ekman et al., 1991). Most observers, however, who are shown the videotapes and asked to judge who is lying do little better than chance, and that is so even for members of the criminal justice community, such as FBI, local police, or judges, as well as for members of the mental health community (Ekman & O'Sullivan, 1991).

I believe there are two reasons why most people are such poor judges of lying. The first reason I have no data to support, but nevertheless I believe that few people obtain corrective feedback about the accuracy of their judgments about who is lying and who is truthful. In workshops in which I try to improve the ability to detect deceit I provide numerous examples of lying, providing such feedback. The second reason why most people do so poorly in judging deceit is that they rely too much on what people say and ignore the discrepancies between the expressive behaviors and what is said. I have three kinds of evidence that are consistent with this explanation.

We have consistently (Ekman & O'Sullivan, 1991; Frank, Ekman, & Friesen, 1993) found that those observers who are accurate in identifying facial expressions when they are shown in a fraction of a second are more accurate in judging lying. The second type of evidence is that patients with left-hemisphere damage, rendering them more impervious to the content of speech, are more accurate than normal subjects in detecting lying (Etcoff, Ekman, Frank, Torreano, & Magee, 1992). The third type of evidence comes from a set of studies in which separate groups of observers were shown the face only, the body only, the voice (speech frequencies filtered out), and typescripts of what was said during the lying and truthful interviews. We then correlated our behavioral measurements with the judgments made by the observers who had seen either the full audio–video or the separated channels. The overall finding was that when the subjects were lying, the observers judgments correlated only with the text measures. Duchenne's smile, leakage smiles, illustrators and pitch—all of which differentiated the deception from the honest interview—were not correlated with the judgments of the deception interview made by the observers who were exposed to the full audio–video record.

It is not that the other nonverbal and vocal behaviors are not detectable, for when we examined the judgments made by observers who only saw the face, we found that Duchenne's smiles were correlated with judgments. Similarly, when we examined the judgments made by observers who saw only the body, illustrators correlated with judgments of those who saw only the body and changes in pitch were correlated with the judgments made by observers who heard only the speech.

In contrast to the nonverbal measures that were not correlated with the judgments of the audio–video presentation of the deception interview, nearly every measure of the verbal text and many of the vocal measures were correlated with observers' judgments of the audiovisual version of the deception interview. The only text measure not correlated with observers' judgments—the number of "I"'s—and the only vocal measure not correlated with observers' judgments—pitch—were the only text and vocal measures that differentiated the honest from deception interviews.

To sum up these findings, the face, body, voice, and text clues that are most relevant to spotting deceit were ignored. Those behaviors that were least useful for differentiating when someone was lying were most relied on when the observers responded to the audio–visual presentation of the deception interview. (These findings are reported in detail in Ekman et al., 1991.) This apparent failure of the observers to make use of the behaviors most relevant to detecting deceit fits with my (Ekman, 1985) notion that, in social life, people unwittingly collude in maintaining rather than uncovering deception.

ACKNOWLEDGMENT

The preparation of this chapter was supported by a Research Scientist Award from the National Institute of Mental Health (MH06092).

REFERENCES

Bok, S. (1982). *Secrets*. New York: Pantheon.

Cross, T. P., & Saxe, L. (1992). A critique of the validity of polygraph testing in child sexual abuse cases. *Journal of Child Sexual Abuse, 1*, 19–33.

Ekman, P. (1985). *Telling lies: Clues to deceit in the marketplace, marriage, and politics*. New York: Norton.

Ekman, P. (1989). *Why kids lie*. New York: Scribner's.

Ekman, P. (1992). *Telling lies: Clues to deceit in the marketplace, marriage, and politics* (2nd ed.). New York: Norton.

Ekman, P., & Friesen, W. V. (1969a). The repertoire of nonverbal behavior: Categories, origins, usage, and coding. *Semiotica, 1*, 49–98.

Ekman, P., & Friesen, W. V. (1969b). Nonverbal leakage and clues to deception. *Psychiatry, 32*, 88–105.

Ekman, P., Friesen, W. V., & O'Sullivan, M. (1988). Smiles when lying. *Journal of Personality and Social Psychology, 54*, 414–420.

Ekman, P., & O'Sullivan, M. (1991). Who can catch a liar. *American Psychologist, 46*, 913–920.

Ekman, P., O'Sullivan, M., Friesen, W. V., & Scherer, K. R. (1991). Face, voice and body in detecting deception. *Journal of Nonverbal Behavior, 15*, 125–135.

Etcoff, N. L., Ekman, P., Frank, M., Torreano, L., & Magee, J. (1992, August). *Detecting deception: Do aphasics have an advantage?* Paper presented at meeting of International Society for Research on Emotion, Pittsburgh, PA.

Feynman, R. (1988). *What do you care what other people think? Further adventures of a curious character*. New York: Norton.

Frank, M. G., Ekman, P., & Friesen, W. V. (1993). Behavioral markers and recognizability of the smile of enjoyment. *Journal of Personality and Social Psychology, 64*, 83–93.

Goffman, E. (1974). *Frame analysis*. New York: Harper & Row.

Lockard, J. S., & Paulhus, D. L. (Eds.). (1988). *Self-deception: An adaptive mechanism?* Englewood Cliffs, NJ: Prentice-Hall.

DEVELOPMENTAL PERSPECTIVES ON EYEWITNESS TESTIMONY

15

STRESS, AROUSAL, AND CHILDREN'S EYEWITNESS MEMORY

Douglas P. Peters
University of North Dakota

The topic of stress and children's eyewitness memory is the central focus of the research on which I report in this chapter. After providing a brief introduction to the area, including a review of my early studies done in the mid 1980s, I present in some detail my two most recent experiments on the effects of stress (or fear) on children's eyewitness memory. The discussion that follows evaluates differing theories and perspectives on the stress–children's memory relationship, as well as examine the need for improved methodology and new directions in this area of study.

Studies of the effect of arousal on witness identification accuracy of adult subjects have been reviewed by Deffenbacher (1983, 1991). Deffenbacher concluded that for those studies in which the "violence level or intensity of personal threat has been successfully manipulated" (Deffenbacher, 1991, p. 388), higher levels of stress are associated with reduced eyewitness accuracy for the majority of subjects across 15 studies. This finding runs counter to the assumption among most criminal court judges that the veridical perception of eyewitnesses is aided by high arousal (Deffenbacher, 1983), and is contrary to a similar view expressed by a large number of prosecuting attorneys. In contrast, the sentiments of law enforcement personnel and criminal defense attorneys in several surveys are consistent with the finding that high arousal or stress will negatively impact eyewitness identification (Brigham, 1981; Brigham & Wolfskeil, 1983). Studies of laypeople's opinions, including those in mock jury studies, have produced equivocal findings. Some report a strong belief in stress as a facilitator of eyewitness accuracy (e.g., Hastie, 1980), whereas others find little support for this position (e.g., Deffenbacher & Loftus, 1982).

If elevations in arousal or stress at the time of witnessing can impair eyewitness accuracy in adults, would similar results be seen with children? To answer this question, a series of studies were run using naturalistic settings where high levels of anxiety or fear might be present or live-event methodology where staged events could be introduced and later examined for retention (see Peters, 1991). Particular attention was given to selecting settings that were personally meaningful and involving for the subjects. Eyewitness research (mostly laboratory-based studies at this time) had been criticized on grounds of poor ecological validity or limited generalizability (Clifford, 1978). Therefore, children's eyewitness memory was studied in the context of visiting a dentist, having a strange man visit a day-care center, receiving a shot at an immunization clinic, and experiencing a realistic theft of money. Across these studies, a number of stress or arousal measures were employed. They included the use of subjective rating scales and behavioral indices of arousal (e.g., the Preschool Observational Scale of Anxiety, Glennon & Weisz, 1978). Memory tests evaluated the children's ability to recognize voices, previously seen faces, and physical surroundings, and to recall details associated with the events they witnessed. Although comparisons between the high-stress and low-stress subjects (or comparisons across high- and low-stress conditions in cases of within-subject stress manipulations) did not always yield significant effects on eyewitness memory, the impact, when reliable, was *always* negative. It appeared that event stress could, at times, degrade recognition and recall accuracy relative to controls.

In each of my early stress studies, at least one significant negative effect of stress on children's eyewitness memory was found. However, I was not satisfied in several cases with measuring stress or arousal solely on the basis of subjective ratings made by parents or other adults, nor was I willing to conclude with certainty that high levels of arousal could not facilitate eyewitness performance in children. I had never found this in my work and the adult literature, as reviewed by Deffenbacher (1983, 1991) suggested otherwise, but I was aware of two studies that made such claims (Goodman, Aman, & Hirschman, 1987; Goodman, Rudy, Bottoms, & Aman, 1990). For these reasons I decided to conduct additional stress studies with children, but in order to provide a more objective and reliable assessment of arousal, I discarded all subjective rating procedures and used blood pressure and pulse rates instead. If my stress manipulations were successful, then these measures of autonomic responding should provide independent validation. I was also concerned that the failure to observe a stress effect across comparison groups or conditions in parts of my earlier work might have been due to the lower than anticipated level of high arousal associated with the "high"-stress group or condition. A fair test of any stress effects on memory requires significant differential stress experiences for experimenter-defined high- and low-stress conditions. What I needed was a powerful stressor that could be easily manipulated—one capable of inducing strong arousal or fear, but was within ethical boundaries. My answer, based on some piloting work with several types of stimuli, was a fire-alarm procedure that is described in detail in Study 1. The last addition to my stress work was the inclusion of a postevent misleading information variable. The topic of children's suggestibility had become increasingly important among psycholegal and developmental scholars (cf. Ceci & Bruck, 1993). The impact of eyewitness stress on children's suggestibility was unclear and needed to be examined experimentally.

STUDY I

Method

Subjects.　A total of 64 children (6–9 years old, $M = 7.3$ years) of parents taking psychology classes at the University of North Dakota or living in the local community were recruited.

Procedure.　The subjects were told that they were participating in a study of children's physical characteristics and skills. Although their parents knew about the true nature of the study, including the possibility of a false fire-alarm and suggestive questioning, the children did not. The overall design was a 2×2 factorial design with two levels of stress (fire alarm vs. no fire alarm) and two levels of question bias (misleading vs. neutral). The subjects were randomly assigned to one of the factorial combinations. Analysis of mean age differences across groups was not significant.

On arriving at the testing room, the parents discovered what experimental treatment their children were to receive. First, all children were measured for body weight, blood pressure, and pulse rates. This was followed by a card-sorting task in which all subjects received a monetary reward (25¢) for their good performance (i.e., all were told they were in the top half of the children in their age group). Then they were asked a few personal questions, such as what was their favorite TV show, holiday, food to eat, and school activity, before the stress manipulation was introduced. For half of the subjects, a fire alarm (a high-pitch smoke detector) was set off, while the other half, the no-fire-alarm subjects, had a loud radio turned on for the same duration of time, approximately 60 seconds. During this period a second set of blood pressure and pulse recordings were taken, thus providing physiological measures of the children's arousal. Ten seconds after the alarm was triggered, a confederate (20-year-old female) entered the testing room appearing anxious and very concerned about the alarm, for the fire-alarm condition. She expressed concern about the possibility of a fire and wanted to see if anyone in the room had smelled smoke. She looked out a window to see if others were leaving the building, made several comments, dropped a set of keys on the floor, and then departed, indicating that she was going to check with others in the building about the fire. In the no-fire-alarm condition, the confederate entered the testing room and asked to look out the window to see if a delivery truck had arrived with equipment to move into the building. She said a few things to the adults, dropped a set of keys, and departed, saying she was going to look out another side of the building for the delivery truck. Ten seconds after the confederate left, the fire alarm and radio were turned off. The fire-alarm subjects were told that the alarm must have been false, and that there had been several such false alarms in the past week. Following this, a second card-sorting task was given. All subjects received a 25¢ reward.

Finally, a series of memory tests was administered. The children were first asked to provide a free narrative of what had transpired when the confederate had entered the room, including a description of the confederate's appearance. The narratives were recorded on audiotape and later analyzed for the number of correct and incorrect items of information, Next, 10 objective questions (answered "yes" or "no") concerning the confederate were asked (e.g., "Did the girl wear glasses on her face?" "Was the girl carrying a cup in her hands?"). Five of these were tagged as *critical* questions. Half of the fire-alarm and no-fire-alarm subjects received misleading information with such critical questions as "Did the girl wearing a yellow sweater (she had worn a white sweater) have brown hair?" (vs. the neutral question, "Did the girl have brown hair?"), "Was the girl angry when she dropped her purse (she had dropped a set of keys) on the floor?" (vs. the neutral question, "Was the girl angry when she dropped something on the floor?"). The other half of subjects received the neutrally worded critical questions. The children were then asked to draw a picture of their home (a filler task). At the end of 5 minutes they were asked to explain their drawings while being praised by the researcher. Following this, the children were asked a series of questions to evaluate the influence of the misleading questions given earlier. This suggestibility test of the five critical questions included two alternative answers for such questions as "Did the girl wear a white or yellow sweater?", "Did the girl drop her purse or keys on the floor?" The final test that was administered consisted of an assessment of the children's recognition memory for the confederate's appearance. Subjects were given a six-person photo lineup (full-face, color photographs) and instructed to determine if the confederate was in the lineup, and, if so, which person was it. They were told that she may or may not be in the lineup. Half of the children received target-present lineups and half received target-absent lineups. The children also were asked to give confidence ratings of their lineup decision using a 7-point scale.

Results and Discussion

Stress Scores. There was ample evidence that the fire-alarm manipulation was effective in producing substantial arousal. Although both groups showed nonsignificant differences in blood pressure and pulse measures when initially tested, the fire-alarm group displayed systolic and diastolic increases of 11.2 and 7.0 points, respectively, when examined during the fire alarm, as compared to a slight 1.8 and 3.0 rise in systolic and diastolic pressure for the no-fire-alarm subjects ($ps < .05$). The pulse differences across the two testing periods were even more marked. The fire-alarm group showed an average 23-point elevation in pulse rate versus a –0.7 change for the no-fire-alarm subjects ($p < .001$).

As a further check on the stress manipulation, subjects' performance on the second card-sorting task (i.e., time to completion) was examined. Deffenbacher (1983) described several studies where task performance was adversely affected by heightened arousal, such as enlisted soldiers in the high-stress condition falsely believed that incoming artillery rounds were mistargeted for their position and had to repair field radio equipment in order to communicate this error. If this effect is robust, then one would predict that the fire-alarm subjects might perform more poorly on a task immediately following the stressing event than the no-fire-alarm subjects. (This assumes that the fire-alarm subjects were still in an aroused condition.) The card-sorting test was administered for a second time immediately after the confederate had exited the experimental room. Both groups performed comparably in time to complete the first card-sorting task (a nonsignificant mean difference), but did reliably differ on the second card sort; fire-alarm group $M = 43.1$ sec. (a 10.7 increase from the first test) versus no-fire-alarm group $M = 32.6$ sec. (a 2.9 sec. decrease from the first test, $p < .025$). The card-sorting data thus provide additional support for the success of the stress manipulation, and indicate that the emotional aftereffects of the fire alarm persisted for at least the duration of the second card-sorting task.

In order to determine if the two treatment groups differed in how much time each spent visually focused on the confederate (a possible source of bias that could confound the results), analyses were made of the videotapes showing the children's behavior throughout the episode with the confederate. Results did not show a reliable time difference in looking at the confederate between the fire-alarm and no-fire-alarm groups ($Ms = 40.2$ sec. vs. 43.3 sec., respectively).

Free Recall. Although the no-fire-alarm subjects averaged more correct items of information and made fewer commission errors than subjects in the fire-alarm condition for the free recall narratives, these differences were not statistically significant ($p > .05$).

Objective Questions. In answering the 10 objective questions about the events associated with the confederate entering the testing room, the no-fire-alarm group performed better than the fire-alarm group, $Ms = 82.5\%$ vs. 72.5% correct ($p < .05$).

Suggestive Questions. The effect of misleading information was assessed by way of a 2 (Arousal Condition) × 2 (Question Bias) analysis of variance performed on the suggestibility data (proportion correct for the five critical items of information). Results indicate a significant interaction ($p < .01$) between question bias (misleading vs. neutral) and arousal condition (fire-alarm vs. no-fire-alarm). As seen in Table 15.1, subjects in the no-fire-alarm condition were more correct if given neutrally worded versus misleading questions ($Ms = 77.5\%$ vs. 56.6% correct recall), but an even larger effect ($Ms = 68.8\%$ vs. 36.6% correct recall) was observed when the subjects were in the fire-alarm condition. Both main effects, question bias and arousal condition, were significant with recognition scores being superior for the no-fire-alarm subjects ($Ms = 67.1\%$ vs. 52.7% correct, $p < .05$) and the neutrally worded questions ($Ms = 73.2\%$ vs. 46.6% correct, $p < .01$). In looking at the data in Table 15.1, it appears that the combination of conditions most adversely affecting eyewitness performance was that of high arousal (fire-alarm) coupled with misleading questions.

Facial Recognition. A 2 (Lineup Condition) × 2 (Arousal Condition) ANOVA was performed on the recognition accuracy data. As seen in Table 15.2, subjects were more accurate (correctly identifying the confederate when in the lineup or correctly indicating the absence of the confederate when not in the lineup) when given a lineup that included the target versus one that did not ($Ms = 61.5\%$ vs. 48.0% correct identification, a significant main effect of lineup condition, $p < .05$). It is not uncommon for young children to have more difficulty with target-absent lineups (e.g., see Peters, 1991). A main effect of arousal condition was also significant. Subjects in the no-fire-alarm condition were better in recognition accuracy across both target-present and target-absent lineups versus the fire-alarm group (65% vs. 44% correct identification, $p < .01$). The lineup condition × arousal condition interaction was not significant

TABLE 15.1
Mean Proportion Correct Recall as a Function
of Question Bias and Arousal Level

Question Bias	Arousal Condition	
	Fire Alarm	No Fire Alarm
Misleading	0.366	0.566
Neutral	0.688	0.775

TABLE 15.2
Facial Recognition Accuracy (Mean Proportion Correct)
as a Function of Arousal Level and Lineup Condition

	Arousal Condition	
Lineup Condition	Fire Alarm	No Fire Alarm
Target present	0.52	0.71
Target absent	0.36	0.60

($p > .05$). In looking at the confidence the children had about their recognition accuracy in identifying the confederate from lineups, a small but significant confidence–accuracy correlation was obtained ($r = .23$, $p < .05$).

STUDY 2

The results of Study 1 showed that the unexpected experience of hearing a loud fire alarm was a powerful stressor for children, one producing significant elevations in blood pressure and pulse. Further, this strong emotional reaction impaired the ability of child witnesses to remember event information accurately, a finding consistent with the majority of adult eyewitness stress studies (see Deffenbacher, 1983, 1991). The high-stress, fire-alarm condition also affected the degree to which misleading information could alter eyewitness memory. Subjects most susceptible to the biasing effects of postevent misleading information were those who had experienced the fire-alarm treatment.

Study 2 was designed to provide a replication of the findings of Study 1, and to examine a variable that had received little experimental attention in the context of stress and children's eyewitness memory. Would memory deficits observed in high stressed subjects shortly following the emotionally eliciting event dissipate over time? Would the influence of stress on children's vulnerability to suggestive questioning, seen in Study 1, be moderated by delay in testing? Would recall or recognition performance improve for children in high arousal conditions with delayed testing? If the locus of stress effects on memory is at time of encoding, then most likely the answer should be no. However, if a child's emotional state can interfere or disrupt memory at time of recall, then one would suspect that waiting for the arousal to subside could lead to an improvement in how much accurate information can be retrieved. This view has received some empirical support in a few adult memory experiments using the emotionality of words as the arousing stimuli (Kleinsmith & Kaplan, 1963, 1964). In one experiment, subjects learned to associate words with numbers. Some of the words were categorized as emotional (e.g., "vomit" and "rape"), and when memory was tested 2 minutes following learning, subjects recalled less well the emotional words versus the neutral ones. However, a week later the recall scores reversed with the emotional words being remembered better than the neutral words (Klein-smith & Kaplan, 1963).

Beyond theoretical considerations, the interaction of delay, stress, and memory has practical implications in cases where young children are unable to supply much in the way of detail after witnessing or experiencing a highly fearful event. Should these child witnesses be questioned repeatedly over time, and, if so, how much trust can be placed on their subsequent recall, assuming that they are no longer fearful or stressed when interviewed? We also know that children often witness criminal events a considerable time before they are questioned or have to recount what they observed in court (Goodman et al., 1988). Study 2 was designed to determine what effect delaying memory tests would have on recall, recognition, and suggestibility for children who had experienced a highly stressful event—an unexpected fire alarm—relative to less stressed control subjects.

Method

Subjects. A total of 96 children, ages 6 to 10 ($M = 7.6$ years), participated. They were recruited in a fashion identical to that of the first study. Although the children were naive as to the exact purpose of the study, their parents were fully informed and consented prior to the beginning of testing.

Procedure. Subjects were randomly assigned to one of the eight conditions in a 2 (Time of Testing: Immediate vs. Delayed) × 2 (Arousal: Unexpected vs. Expected Fire Alarm) × 2 (Question Bias: Misleading vs. Neutral) factorial design. The general procedures were similar to Study 1, with the addition of a time-of-testing variable and an "expected" fire alarm replacing the loud radio music for the low-stress subjects. The sound and duration of the fire alarm were identical for subjects in both the unexpected and expected fire-alarm conditions, but for the expected fire-alarm group, they were told at the beginning of testing to ignore any fire alarms heard during testing. These children were told that there had been numerous false alarms all week in the building, as a new system was being installed on each floor, and they should not worry about any alarms. Half of the subjects had their memories of the event with the confederate tested within 15 minutes of the event's conclusion (immediate testing), whereas the other half were contacted 6 months later for their memory tests (delayed testing). Those subjects in the delay condition were not aware that they would be returning for testing.

Results and Discussion

Stress Scores. The arousal manipulation once again proved successful. Mean differences in blood pressure and pulse rates between the expected and unexpected fire-alarm groups were not significant during the initial recordings, but were for the second testing, when the confederate acted out her script. The unexpected fire-alarm subjects increased their systolic and diastolic levels by 13.6 and 8.9 points, respectively, whereas the expected fire-alarm subjects averaged smaller increases of 4.1 and 3.5, respectively. The systolic difference between these two groups proved significant ($p < .05$). The unexpected fire-alarm subjects displayed an average rise in pulse rates across the two testing sessions of 19.4 points ($p < .01$). The expected fire-alarm subjects showed a nonsignificant rise of 4.7 points. Despite the fact that all subjects were exposed to the identical fire-alarm stimulus, the physiological measures indicate that only the unexpected fire-alarm subjects were undergoing high levels of emotional distress or arousal.

The amount of time the subjects in both stress conditions spent visually focused on the confederate did not reveal a significant time difference between the fire-alarm and no-fire-alarm groups ($Ms = 38.2$ sec. vs. 34.5 sec., respectively).

As was done in Experiment 1, subjects' time-to-completion scores for the card-sorting tasks were analyzed to see if the stress variable had produced differences between groups. The results were similar to Experiment 1. The subjects in the unexpected fire-alarm condition took longer to complete the second card-sorting task than those receiving the expected fire alarm, $Ms = 38.5$ sec. (an 8.9 sec. increase over the first card-sort) vs. 28.7 sec. (a 3.7 decrease over the first card-sort), $p < .05$. Once again, the card-sorting findings provide converging evidence with the physiological measures for the successful induction of a powerful stress variable.

Free Recall. A 2 (Arousal Condition) × 2 (Time-of-Test) ANOVA was run on the number of correct and incorrect items of information recalled by each subject during the free narrative phase. A main effect of time of test on the average number of correct items recalled was the only significant finding. The amount of correct information given was significantly less for the subjects tested 6 months after witnessing the event versus those questioned immediately ($Ms = 7.3$ vs. 2.1, respectively, $p < .01$). The arousal × time-of-test interaction was not significant ($p > .05$). The delay effect was consistent across arousal conditions; that is, the unexpected fire-alarm subjects showed the same pattern of reduced free recall at the 6-month delay as did the subjects given the expected fire-alarm. A separate correlational analysis of age with number of correct and number of incorrect items of information revealed a significant relationship ($r = .57, p < .05$) between age and correct recall, but not with age and incorrect information. As the children got older, the number of correct details increased, whereas the amount of incorrect information remained unchanged.

Objective Questions. The proportion of the 10 objective questions related to the presence of the confederate in the experimental room answered correctly by each subject was entered into a 2 (Arousal Condition) × 2

TABLE 15.3
Mean Proportion of Correct Answers to Objective Questions
as a Function of Arousal Condition and Time of Test

	Time of Test	
Arousal Condition	Immediate	6-Month Delay
Unexpected fire alarm	0.77	0.63
Expected fire alarm	0.88	0.75

(Time-of-Test) ANOVA. The main effect of arousal condition was significant with subjects who had received the unexpected fire alarm performing more poorly overall than those in the expected fire-alarm condition (Ms = 82.5% vs. 69% correct, p < .05). The main effect of time of test was also significant. As seen in Table 15.3, subjects were better overall at recalling event details when questioned immediately versus a 6-month delay (Ms = 82.5% vs. 69%, p < .05). Arousal condition did not interact significantly with time of test (p > .05).

Suggestive Questions. The effect of misleading information was examined with a 2 (Arousal Condition) × 2 (Question Bias) × 2 (Time-of-Test) ANOVA performed on the suggestibility data (proportion correct for the five critical items of information). Group scores can be seen in Table 15.4, with lower scores indicating more influence of misleading information (i.e., subjects were selecting the misleading information choice over the correct answer). There was a main effect of question bias with those subjects in the misleading information condition performing most poorly overall (Ms = 60% vs. 73.2% correct, p < .025). The main effect of time of test was also significant. Children were more suggestible following a 6-month delay than in immediate testing (Ms = 61.7% vs. 71.5% correct, p < .05). The only other analysis that yielded significance was a main effect of arousal condition. Overall, those subjects in the expected fire-alarm treatment were superior to those in the unexpected fire-alarm condition (Ms = 73% vs. 60.2% correct, p < .05). None of the interactions reached significance (ps > .05).

TABLE 15.4
Mean Proportion Correct Answers for Critical Items as a
Function of Question Bias, Arousal Condition, and Time of Test

	Time of Test			
	Immediate		6-Month Delay	
Question Bias	Unexpected Fire Alarm	Expected Fire Alarm	Unexpected Fire Alarm	Expected Fire Alarm
Misleading	0.56	0.74	0.49	0.61
Neutral	0.72	0.84	0.64	0.73

Similar to the results for the objective questions, there is no evidence here to suggest that the poorer memory performance seen in the high-arousal subjects (unexpected fire alarm) relative to the less stressed subjects (expected fire alarm) would be improved when testing is delayed for at least 6 months.

Facial Recognition. A 2 (Lineup Condition) × 2 (Arousal Condition) × 2 (Time-of-Test) ANOVA was performed on the recognition accuracy data. Group scores (proportion correct) are presented in Table 15.5. The only significant main effect was time of test. Recognition accuracy (correctly identifying the confederate when in the lineup or correctly indicating the absence of the confederate when not in the lineup) was much poorer following a delay of 6 months compared to immediate testing ($Ms = 32.5\%$ vs. 61.75%, $p < .01$). Although there was no significant overall effect of arousal condition, there was a significant interaction of time of test × arousal condition ($p < .05$). The recognition scores collapsed across lineup condition revealed that at immediate testing, subjects in the unexpected fire-alarm condition were inferior to those who had received the expected fire alarm ($Ms = 54.5\%$ vs. 69% recognition accuracy), but this 14.5% difference disappeared when memory tests were delayed 6 months. At this time both groups showed a drastic reduction in recognition accuracy and differed little from each other, perhaps indicating a floor effect (unexpected fire alarm $M = 31.5\%$ vs. expected fire alarm $M = 33.5\%$). The time-of-test × lineup condition interaction was also significant ($p < .05$). At immediate testing, subjects were 13.5% more accurate with target-present lineups versus target-absent lineups. However, at the 6-month delay, the lineup effect reversed with target-absent lineups now producing a 14% superiority in recognition accuracy compared to the target-present lineups.

The outcome of this study basically replicated the findings of Study 1. The observed stress effects, when they occurred, *negatively* affected eyewitness memory for event details and facial recognition. The biasing effect of misleading information was again most pronounced for those children in

TABLE 15.5
Mean Proportion Correct Response as a Function of
Time of Test, Arousal Condition, and Lineup Condition

	Time of Test			
	Immediate		6-Month Delay	
Lineup Condition	Unexpected Fire Alarm	Expected Fire Alarm	Unexpected Fire Alarm	Expected Fire Alarm
Target present	0.61	0.76	0.25	0.26
Target absent	0.48	0.62	0.38	0.41

the high-stress (unexpected fire-alarm) condition. The 6-month delay in testing degraded memory performance for both the high- and low-stress subjects, and children were more suggestible over time, a finding also reported in a recent eyewitness study where children, 4 to 7 years of age, were retested after a 1-year delay (Goodman, Hirschman, Hepps, & Rudy, 1991, Study 4). If it is argued that memories for highly arousing, emotional events improve over time, the evidence from the present study along with those of Goodman et al. (1991) would not seem to support such a position.

GENERAL DISCUSSION

When I first began to investigate the relationship between stress/arousal and children's memory, my results suggested that the impact of high arousal or stress was negative, but there were an equal number of studies reporting the opposite effect (see Goodman et al., 1991). Fortunately, the empirical picture has cleared considerably since those early studies by Goodman and her colleagues and myself. As of this writing there are 18 reported studies that have examined the influence of stress or arousal on children's ability to remember events they have witnessed or experienced. The results of these investigations are presented in Table 15.6. Of the 18 studies, only two find a

TABLE 15.6
Summary of Stress Studies: Memory and Suggestibility Effects

Study	Memory Effect	Suggestibility
1. Goodman et al., 1991 (Exp. 2)	+	o
2. Goodman et al., 1991 (Exp. 3)	+	o
3. Peters, 1991 (Exp. 1)	–	
4. Peters, 1991 (Exp. 2)	–	
5. Peters, 1991 (Exp. 3)	–	
6. Peters, 1991 (Exp. 4)	–	
7. Peters, 1991 (Exp. 5)	–	+
8. Vandermass, 1991	–	
9. Bugental et al., 1992	–	
10. Ornstein et al., 1992	–	
11. Goodman et al., 1993	–	
12. Ornstein et al., 1993	–	
13. Peters, 1993	–	+
14. Merritt et al., in press	–	
15. Steward, 1989	o	
16. Goodman et al., 1991 (Exp. 1)	o	o
17. Goodman et al., 1991 (Exp. 4)	o	o
18. Oats & Shrimpton, 1991	o	o
19. Warren & Swartwood, 1993		o

Note. "+" = significant positive associations, "–" = significant negative associations, and "0" = no significant associations between stress and either memory or suggestibility.

positive association between stress and measures of memory. (In another paper, Peters, 1991, I have commented on the methodological limitations of some of this work, including small treatment groups, low statistical power of tests, and the questionable validity of classifying subjects according to subjective ratings scales.) The majority of reports, 12 (66.7%), have found evidence of a *negative* relationship, and 4 (22.2%) have reported no significant associations.

A total of eight studies (Goodman et al., 1991, Exp. 1, Exp. 2, Exp. 3, Exp. 4; Oats & Shrimpton, 1991; Peters, 1991, Exp. 5; Peters, 1993; Warren & Swartwood, 1993) have also looked at the association between stress and suggestibility with children. Six of the studies reported no significant relationship, whereas two have found a positive one. It seems apparent that, if anything, heightened stress will *not* inoculate children against the biasing effects of misleading information. At the present time it is not clear why heightened stress can make subjects more vulnerable to leading questions in some studies, like those I have reported, and not in others. Obviously, additional work needs to be done in this area to explain these inconsistencies.

Theoretical Issues

Deffenbacher (1983, 1991) invoked the Yerkes–Dodson law (Yerkes & Dodson, 1908) to account for the range of effects of arousal on eyewitness identification. For tasks of moderate difficulty or complexity, which presumably incorporate all of the stress–eyewitness memory studies, the relationship between arousal and performance is an inverted U, with maximal performance occurring at intermediate levels of stress. Deffenbacher argued that the inferior eyewitness performance of subjects in the studies where personal threat or violence levels were high is due to the fact that the descending portion of the curve is operational; that is, it occurs in 13 of 15 studies he reviewed. The present results of Experiments 1 and 2 are consistent with this type of analysis. The high-stress subjects were past their optimal level of arousal, whereas the control subjects were nearer this point and, as a consequence, memory performance either suffered or benefited. However, this explanation is circular. What is required is an a priori determination of the placement of stress manipulations on the hypothetical Yerkes–Dodson curve that is independent of their effects on performance.

A second theoretical perspective that can be applied to the stress and eyewitness performance findings is the Easterbrook hypothesis (Easterbrook, 1959), which states that heightened arousal causes a narrowing of the range of attention. At low arousal a great breadth of information is taken in or encoded, including information relevant to the task at hand. With more arousal, less information is encoded, but performance can improve if nonessential information is differentially excluded at this point. At high levels of arousal, attentional focus has become so constricted that performance may suffer, because some of the task-relevant information is now being left out; that is, was not encoded. Attempting to predict the eyewitness perform-ance of any single subject using this framework would require knowledge about what aspects or features of an emotional event, like fear, command the highest attentional priority. These core features, according to the Eas-terbrook hypothesis, will likely be encoded and later remembered, although the overall verbatim memory is quite impoverished and could result in very poor eyewitness.

Yuille and Tollestrup (1992) have recently proposed a model of emotion and eyewitness memory that is also relevant to the discussion of eyewitness memory and stress. According to this analysis the memorial outcome of witnessing an event is dependent on the "impact" features of an event. High-impact events are highly stressful and emotionally arousing, and cause witnesses to constrict his or her focus of attention. Witnesses may direct attentional focus either internally or externally. If the focus is internal, the encoding of core detail is likely to be impoverished. Further, internal focus can be of two types. One, the witness might be preoccupied or overwhelmed with his or her own emotional response to the event; for example, becoming frightened. Such a witness will have little memory for much of the event. Instead, when questioned, he or she will claim to have been too scared during the event, and that is all that can be clearly remembered; that is, the emotion of being afraid. It is also possible as a second type of internal focus that the witness would focus on some coping or psychological response to threat, such as imagining oneself elsewhere. Whatever the form, an inter-nally focused individual would be expected to store very limited information about the event they witnessed and have more prominent memories of their internal response to the event. Alternatively, witnesses may focus externally on the high-impact event itself. In such cases a witness will likely store core details; that is, those that represent the witness's "central thematic ele-ments," at the expense of peripheral details. For low-impact events, those involving little or no stress, there is little narrowing of attentional focus, and, consequently, both core and peripheral detail should be encoded and stored in memory. This perspective and the preceding Easterbrook hypothe-sis have received some empirical support by eyewitness researchers study-ing the so-called "weapon focus" effect. Subjects exposed to confederates pointing weapon-like objects at them or others in live-event simulations showed adverse effects on their eyewitness memory for peripheral detail, particularly face recognition of the confederate (e.g., Cutler, Penrod, & Mar-tins, 1987; Loftus, Loftus, & Messo, 1987; Tooley, Brigham, Maass, & Bothwell, 1987).

Cutshall and Yuille (1989) did mention the possibility of an event being so traumatic and painful to recall that the witness shows psychogenic amnesia for a period of time after the event. This appears similar to the concept of "repressed" memories, and today there is a growing controversy over the validity of such a belief (see Loftus, 1993). The position I have taken regarding the effects of event stress is one that places the locus of action on the encoding process, which I believe is severely impaired when subjects are experiencing high levels of stress or fear. Those who argue for a strong repressed memories position assert that retrieval failure underlies the memory deficits, and that the inferior performance of highly stressed subjects might be expected to improve at a later point in time. However, in my second study, the high-stress subjects did not show any memory improvement when testing was delayed 6 months; in fact, they did worse when compared to high stress subjects examined immediately after the stressing event, the unexpected fire alarm. I do realize that experiencing an unexpected fire alarm is unlikely to be equivalent to the trauma of witnessing a parent being murdered. However, as Loftus (1993) pointed out, there is little scientific support for the concept of repressed memories, and until those long-delayed memories are scientifically observed and validated, the scientific value of this particular view of stress and memory remains questionable.

Reyna (in press) argued that most suggestibility studies of children's eyewitness memory are verbatim- (as opposed to gist-) interference designs. Her review of the literature led to an interesting observation. Studies that failed to find suggestibility effects typically separated the to-be-remembered information from the misinformation by only a few minutes, and this procedure, she reasoned, will protect verbatim memories against retroactive interference because there has been little time for verbatim memories to undergo forgetting. Conversely, studies reporting significant suggestibility effects have delayed misinformation by at least a day following the significant event and, consequently, verbatim recollections are more likely to undergo forgetting. However, in the present experiments, reliable suggestibility effects were obtained under conditions where misleading information was presented within 15 minutes of the critical event, the confederate entering the testing room. This finding perhaps underscores the need to consider children's memory from a multidimensional perspective that includes the child's emotional state. Unlike the suggestibility studies Reyna reviewed, the present ones have experimentally manipulated stress at time of encoding. The addition of this stress or fear variable complicates the misleading information–eyewitness memory equation. If environmental conditions produce high levels of subjectively experienced stress, and this heightened arousal disrupts effective encoding of information flow, then subsequent misleading information may indeed fill memory "gaps" (or predominate over a weak original memory trace; see Brainerd & Reyna, 1990, 1993; Reyna & Brainerd, 1992 for a discussion of fuzzy-trace theory) that control (non-stressed) subjects are much less likely to have. Furthermore, this vulnerability to suggestion would be most probable when children are exposed to novel and unscripted events, as was the case for the subjects in these fire-alarm studies, but *atypical*, as Reyna (in press) pointed out in her review of the suggestibility literature. Generally, children have been exposed to material from familiar events that follow some well-known script.

Does the source of arousal in the stress studies have anything to do with the phenomenon being remembered? Yuille and Tollestrup (1992) argued that it does. They suggest that differences in stress effects might be due to the wide variety of stressors employed, including violent films, inoculations, venipuncture, white noise, electric shock (adults), fire alarms, witnessing a simulated fight or frightened faces on video, receiving a physical exam by a pediatrician, or undergoing a voiding cystourethrogram procedure (see Merritt, Ornstein, & Spicker, in press, for a description of this stressful event). What is the equivalence (or nonequivalence) of these sources of arousal? The answer is unknown at this time. Christianson, Nilsson, Mjorndal, Perris, and Tjellden (1986) have results suggesting that the outcome of strong emotional arousal will be memory impairment only when the source of arousal is *related* to the to-be-remembered material. Although Study 1 and 2 were not designed to directly test this view, we do know from videotape analyses that the children in the high-stress conditions did visually direct their attention to the confederate when she was in the room. From their perspective, the confederate was, in part, a source for the arousal. She was indicating concern about a possible fire, wanted to know if anyone had smelled smoke, etc., and thus the subsequent poor showing on memory tests with these children would be with consistent with the view expressed by Christianson et al. regarding adult subjects experiencing emotional arousal.

Unresolved Problems and Future Directions

The present discussion has been limited to evaluating *event stress* (emotional arousal at time of witnessing) and the possible mechanisms to account for observed stress effects on children's eyewitness memory. Stress or arousal at the time of recall can be another important potential determinant of a subject's memory. It has been documented, for example, that emotion can produce state-dependent effects. Happy subjects can better remember happy past events; sad subjects are better able to remember sad past events (e.g., Blaney, 1986; Eich & Metcalfe, 1989; Gilligan & Bower, 1984). Therefore, emotional states at both encoding and recall or emotional matching (or mood congruence) must be factored into any comprehensive account of emotion and memory. Little in this area has been done with child witnesses, although a few studies (e.g., Clarke-Stewart, Thompson, & Lepore, 1989; Goodman et al., 1990; Saywitz, Geiselman, & Bornstein, 1992) have begun looking at the effects of emotional states and interviewing styles (e.g., accusatory, supportive, neutral) on children's testimony.

In studying arousal and stress effects with children, a major problem is selecting the most appropriate measure of arousal. Some studies rely on self-reports, bystander reports made by parents or adult observers, behavioral rating scales, physiological recordings (GSR, heart rate, blood pressure, pulse, respiration rates), and biochemical assays (salivary cortisol). An added difficulty is the fact that the correlations between objective rating scales and various self-reports and the correlation between different subjective reports of stress (a parent's, child's, and other adult's) are often weak. Related to problems of measuring stress or arousal is the issue of how valid are the stress classifications given to some of the subjects. For example, on a 6-point stress scale that has *extremely happy or relaxed* and *extremely frightened or upset* as endpoints (Goodman et al., 1987) is it appropriate to label subjects as showing "high" stress if they are rated 3.7, only 0.2 points above 3.5, the neutral midpoint? It should be noted that these problems are not restricted to child witness research. Of the 12 published adult eyewitness articles reviewed by Deffenbacher (1983), 2 contained no measure of arousal, 2 contained nonvalidated, single-item self-report measures of arousal, and the remaining 8 studies utilized measures of state or trait anxiety.

It would also seem important to know if the stress manipulations are confounded with existing knowledge differences among children. For example, children visiting a doctor's office (classified as a high-stress occurrence in some studies) may have an advantage on subsequent memory tests compared to control subjects who meet a friendly stranger in the school library, due to the highly scripted nature of a visit to a doctor's office. Children knowledgeable about a particular domain will process information about that domain rapidly and display enhanced levels of memory performance. If scripts exist for the events and settings eyewitness researchers have studied with children, how do they interact with strong emotional states like fear or anxiety?

What is the utility of viewing children's stress and arousal reactions in terms of Stein and Jewett's (1986) higher order emotional construct *fear*, which they define as "a state of anticipation of possible state change" (p. 240). In their language of want-attainment states, fear is associated with *not want* (do not want something bad or painful to happen) and *not attain* (it has not happened yet). The emotional experience of fear is the conjoint occurrence of autonomic nervous system (ANS) arousal and cognitive evaluation. For example, a 6-year-old is sitting quietly in an unfamiliar room in a strange building, and suddenly a loud, piercing fire alarm goes off. The child encodes enough information about the event to recognize a warning signal (maybe associated with a possible fire), infers that this outcome is undesirable (a fire or something harmful taking place), recognizes that a safety goal is in jeopardy, experiences elevated ANS arousal, which in turn leads to experiencing the emotion of fear. I think this fear orientation and framework could be useful in future work on stress and children's eyewitness memory.

In viewing scripted memory for children along with the want-attainment states perspective of Stein and Jewett (1986) and Stein, Trabasso, and Liwag (in press), it may be possible to explain some of the individual differences in the literature on stress and children's memory (e.g., some of Goodman's subjects show better memory under high-stress conditions, whereas most others report the opposite finding; there are also wide ranges of test scores within individual stress groups). Consider the child that has received numerous blood draws or allergy shots in a doctor's office. It is likely that the child will have formed scripted memory of the event that not only includes the pain of the needle (anticipation of a possible undesirable state change), but also the expectation of receiving a sucker, sticker, or balloon at the end of the doctor visit. Initial processing of the event may induce stress and arousal (fear) in anticipation of the painful needle, thus narrowing attentional focus, but further cognitive appraisal is activated by an expectation of a reward (desirable goal), which in turn may attenuate the initial encoding deficit brought on by the fear response to the needle. As a consequence of this, the child's memory of the experienced event will prove superior to the child who lacks such a developed script and simply reacts to the fear of the needle.

Unfortunately, the children's stress and eyewitness memory literature does not contain adequately designed studies that would permit this detailed level of analysis, and thus we are at a loss regarding questions of children's underlying knowledge structure and what is the nature of these representations. Recently, Trabasso, Stein, Rodkin, Munger, and Baughn (in press) began online, moment-to-moment tracking of children's knowledge of goals and plans during a storytelling episode. At the 1994 University of Chicago conference on Memory for Everyday and Emotional Events, Stein and Trabasso indicated that they have expanded their online moment-to-moment tracking to include emotional responses, like fear, with young children. This tracking includes physiological measurements along with ongoing narratives. Future investigators studying children's stress and memory would be well advised to consider this type of analysis. I suspect that important gains in the understanding of individual differences in memory performance, as affected by emotional states like fear or stress, will develop within this methodological and conceptual framework.

REFERENCES

Blaney, P. (1986). Affect and memory: A review. *Psychological Bulletin, 99,* 229–246.

Brainerd, C. J., & Reyna, V. F. (1990). Gist is the grist: Fuzzy-trace theory and the new intuitionism. *Developmental Review, 10,* 3–47.

Brainerd, C. J., & Reyna, V. F. (1993). Memory independence and memory interference in cognitive development. *Psychological Review, 100,* 42–67.

Brigham, J. C. (1981, November). The accuracy of eyewitness evidence: How do attorneys see it? *The Florida Bar Journal, 55*, 714–721.

Brigham, J. C., & Wolfskeil, M. P. (1983). Opinions of attorneys and law enforcement personnel on the accuracy of eyewitness identifications. *Law and Human Behavior, 7*, 337–349.

Bugental, D., Blue, J., Cortez, V., Fleck, K., & Rodriguez, A. (1992). Influences of witness affect on information processing in children. *Child Development, 63*, 774–786.

Ceci, S. J., & Bruck, M. (1993). Suggestibility of the child witness: A historical review and synthesis. *Psychological Bulletin, 113*(3), 403–439.

Christianson, S., Nilsson, L., Mjorndal, T., Perris, C., & Tjellden, G. (1986). Psychological versus physiological determinants of emotional arousal and its relationship to laboratory induced amnesia. *Scandinavian Journal of Psychology, 27*, 300–310.

Clarke-Stewart, A., Thompson, W., & Lepore, S. (1989, May). *Manipulating children's interpretations through interrogation.* Paper presented at the Biennial Meeting of the Society for Research on Child Development, Kansas City, MO.

Clifford, B. R. (1978). A critique of eyewitness research. In M. M. Gruneberg, P. E. Morris, & R. N. Sykes (Eds.), *Practical aspects of memory* (pp. 199–209). London: Academic Press.

Cutler, B. L., Penrod, S. D., & Martens, T. K. (1987). The reliability of eyewitness identification: The role of system and estimator variables. *Law and Human Behavior, 11*, 233–258.

Cutshall, J. L., & Yuille, J. C. (1989). Field studies of eyewitness memory of actual crimes. In D. C. Raskin (Ed.), *Psychological methods in criminal investigation and evidence* (pp. 97–124). New York: Springer.

Deffenbacher, K. (1983). The influence of arousal on reliability of testimony. In B. R. Cliford & S. Lloyd-Bostock (Eds.), *Evaluating witness evidence* (pp. 235–251). Chichester, England: Wiley.

Deffenbacher, K. (1991). A maturing of research on the behaviour of eyewitnesses. *Applied Cognitive Psychology, 5*, 377–409.

Deffenbacher, K., & Loftus, E. F. (1982). Do jurors share a common understanding concerning eyewitness behavior? *Law and Human Behavior, 6*, 15–30.

Easterbrook, J. A. (1959). The effect of emotion on the utilization and organization of behavior. *Psychological Review, 66*, 183–201.

Eich, E., & Metcalfe, J. (1989). Mood dependent memory for internal versus external events. *Journal of Experimental Psychology: Learning, Memory, and Cognition, 15*, 443–455.

Gilligan, S. G., & Bower, G. H. (1984). Cognitive consequences of emotional arousal. In C. Izard, J. Kagan, & R. Zajonc (Eds.), *Emotions, cognition and behavior.* New York: Cambridge University Press.

Glennon, B., & Weisz, J. R. (1978). An observational approach to the assessment of anxiety in young children. *Journal of Counseling and Clinical Psychology, 46*, 1246–1257.

Goodman, G. S. (1993). Understanding and improving children's testimony. *Children Today, 22*, 13–15.

Goodman, G. S., Aman, C., & Hirschman, F. (1987). Child sexual and physical abuse: Children's testimony. In S. J. Ceci, M. P. Toglia, & D. Ross (Eds.), *Children's eyewitness memory* (pp. 1–23). New York: Springer-Verlag.

Goodman, G. S., Hirschman, J. E., Hepps, D., & Rudy, L. (1991). Children's memory for stressful events. *Merrill–Palmer Quarterly, 37*, 109–158.

Goodman, G. S., Jones, D. P. H., Phyle, E., Prado, L. P., England, T., Mason, R., & Rudy, L. (1988). The child in court: A preliminary report on the effects of criminal court testimony on child sexual assault victims. In G. Davies & J. Drinkwater (Eds.), *The child witness: Do courts abuse children?: Issues in criminological and legal psychology* (pp. 46–54). Leicester: British Psychological Association.

Goodman, G. S., Rudy, L., Bottoms, B., & Aman, C. (1990). Children's concerns and memory: Issues of ecological validity in the study of children's eyewitness testimony. In R. Fivush & J. Hudson (Eds.), *Knowing and remembering in young children* (pp. 249–284). New York: Cambridge University Press.

Hastie, R. (1980). *From eyewitness testimony to beyond reasonable doubt.* Unpublished manuscript, Harvard University.

Kleinsmith, L. T., & Kaplan, S. (1963). Paired associate learning as a function of arousal and interpolated interval. *Journal of Experimental Psychology, 65,* 190–193.

Kleinsmith, L., & Kaplan, S. (1964). The interaction of arousal and recall interval in nonsense syllable paired-associate learning. *Journal of Experimental Psychology, 67,* 124–126.

Loftus, E. F. (1993). The reality of repressed memories. *American Psychologist, 48,* 518–537.

Loftus, E. F., Loftus, G. R., & Messo, J. (1987). Some facts about "weapon focus." *Law and Human Behavior, 11,* 55–62.

Merritt, K. A., Ornstein, P. A., & Spicker, B. (in press). Children's memory for a salient medical procedure: Implications for testimony. *Pediatrics.*

Oates, K., & Shrimpton, S. (1991). Children's memories for stressful and non-stressful events. *Medicine, Science, and the Law, 31,* 4–10.

Ornstein, P. A., Gordon, B. N., & Larus, D. (1992). Children's memory for a personally experienced event: Implications for testimony. *Applied Cognitive Psychology, 6,* 49–60.

Peters, D. P. (1991). The influence of stress and arousal on the child witness. In J. L. Doris (Ed.), *The suggestibility of children's recollections* (pp. 60–76). Washington, DC: American Psychological Association.

Peters, D. P. (1993, June). *Stress, arousal, and eyewitness memory in children.* Paper presented at Memory for Everyday and Emotional Events Conference, University of Chicago, Chicago, IL.

Reyna, V. F. (in press). Interference effects in memory and reasoning: A fuzzy-trace theory analysis. In F. N. Dempster & C. J. Brainerd (Eds.), *New perspectives on interference and inhibition in cognition.* San Diego, CA: Academic Press.

Reyna, V. F., & Brainerd, C. J. (1992). A fuzzy-trace theory of reasoning and remembering: Paradoxes, patterns, and parallelism. In A. F. Healy, S. Kosslyn, & R. M. Shiffrin (Eds.), *From learning processes to cognitive processes: Essays in honor of William K. Estes* (pp. 235–260). Hillsdale, NJ: Lawrence Erlbaum Associates.

Saywitz, K., Geiselman, R., & Bornstein, G. (1992). Effects of cognitive interviewing, practice, and interview style on children's recall performance. *Journal of Applied Psychology, 77,* 744–756.

Stein, N. L., & Jewett, J. (1986). A conceptual analysis of the meaning of negative emotions: Implications for a theory of development. In C. Izard & P. Reid (Eds.), *Measuring emotions in infants and children* (Vol. 2, pp. 238–267). Cambridge, England: Cambridge University Press.

Stein, N. L., Trabasso, T., & Liwag, M. (in press). The representation and organization of emotional experience: Unfolding the emotion episode. In M. Lewis & J. Haviland (Eds.), *Handbook of emotions.* New York: Guilford.

Steward, M. (1989). *The development of a model interview for young child victims of sexual abuse* (Tech. Rep. No. 90CA1332). Washington, DC: U.S. Department of Health and Human Services.

Tooley, V., Brigham, J. C., Maass, A., & Bothwell, R. K. (1987). Facial recognition: Weapon effect and attentional focus. *Journal of Applied Social Psychology, 17,* 845–849.

Trabasso, T., Stein, N. L., Rodkin, P. C., Munger, M. P., & Baughn, C. R. (in press). Knowledge of goals and plans in the on-line narration of events. *Cognitive Development.*

Vandermas, M. (1991, April). *Assessment of young children's anxiety during dental procedures.* Paper presented at the biennial meeting of the Society for Research in Child Development, Seattle, WA.

Warren, A. R., & Swartwood, J. N. (1993). Developmental issues in flashbulb research: Children recall the Challenger event. In E. Winograd & U. Neisser (Eds.), *Affect and accuracy in recall: The problem of flashbulb memories* (pp. 142–151). New York: Cambridge University Press.

Yerkes, R. M., & Dodson, J. D. (1908). The relation of strength of stimulus to rapidity of habit formation. *Journal of Comparative Neurology and Psychology, 18,* 459–482.

Yuille, J. C., & Tollestrup, P. A. (1992). A model of the diverse effects of emotion on eyewitness memory. In S. Christianson (Ed.), *The handbook of emotion and memory: Research and theory* (pp. 210–215). Hillsdale, NJ: Lawrence Erlbaum Associates.

16

THE DESCRIPTION OF CHILDREN'S SUGGESTIBILITY

Maggie Bruck
McGill University

Stephen J. Ceci
Cornell University

Since the turn of the century, social scientists have examined the topic of children's suggestibility (see Ceci & Bruck, 1993, 1995, for a historical review). Although there were a few studies carried out in the United States from 1900 until the middle of the 1980s, it is only in the last few years that this topic has attained an important status within the fields of developmental and cognitive psychology. Over the past 5 or so years, social scientists from a number of different disciplines have mounted studies in this field. This flurry of important work has been mainly spurred by an applied issue—children's ability to give reliable legal testimony. As we show in this chapter, the methodologies as well as the primary issues of many studies address applied concerns rather than theoretical ones; and yet the results of these studies have expanded, and at times challenged, some important theoretical concepts.

To illustrate these advances and to present an overview of our present state of knowledge about children's suggestibility, we present an abbreviated version of an amicus brief that we prepared for the Supreme Court of New Jersey in the case of *New Jersey v. Michaels* (Bruck & Ceci, 1995). We show how general issues involved in this case of alleged child sexual abuse can be addressed by the existing literature and how cases such as this one have provided researchers with paradigms as well as hypotheses for study. First, however, we provide the reader with a background of this case.

Margaret Kelly Michaels, a 26-year-old nursery-school teacher, was accused of sexually abusing children at the Wee Care Nursery School. Based on the children's reports, she was said to have licked peanut butter off of children's genitals, played the piano while nude, made children drink her urine and eat her feces, and raped and assaulted them with knives, forks, spoons, and Lego blocks. She was accused by the children of performing these acts during school hours over a period of 7 months. None of the alleged acts were noticed by staff or reported by children to their parents. No parent noticed signs of strange behavior or genital soreness in their children, or smelled urine, peanut butter, or feces on them.

The first suspicion that Kelly Michaels abused her charges occurred 4 days after she had left the Wee Care Nursery School. A 4-year-old former student of Kelly's was having his temperature taken rectally at his pediatrician's office, and said to the nurse, "That's what my teacher does to me at school." When asked to explain, he replied, "Her takes my temperature" (Manshel, 1990, p. 8). On the advice of the pediatrician, the child's mother notified the State's child protection agency. Two days later, when interviewed by the assistant prosecutor, the child inserted his finger into the rectum of an anatomical doll, and reported that two other boys also had their temperature taken. When later questioned, these two boys denied the claim, but one indicated that Kelly Michaels had touched his penis. The first child's mother then told a parent, who was a board member of the Wee Care Nursery School, of her son's disclosures. This board member interrogated his son about Kelly Michaels touching him inappropriately, remarking that "he was his best friend and that he could tell him anything." His son then told him that Kelly had touched his penis with a spoon. The Wee Care Nursery School sent out a letter to parents, informing them of an investigation of a former employee "regarding serious allegations." In a subsequent meeting, a social worker explained to the parents that sexual abuse of children is very common, with one out of three children being victims of an "inappropriate sexual experience" by the age of 18 years. She encouraged parents to examine their children for genital soreness, nightmares, bed wetting, masturbation, or any noticeable changes in behavior, and to have them examined by pediatricians for injury. Soon, there were many more allegations against Kelly Michaels. Two and a half years later, she was convicted of 115 counts of sexual abuse against twenty 3- to 5-year-old children. After spending 5 years in jail, her case was successfully appealed.[1]

---

[1]At the request of Ms. Michaels' defense lawyers, we wrote an amicus brief to the Supreme Court of New Jersey that argued that the testimony of the child witnesses was potentially tainted by poor interviewing techniques so that one may never come to know the true facts of the case. This brief, parts of which are presented in this chapter, was signed by 45 prominent social science researchers.

RESEARCH ON CHILDREN'S SUGGESTIBILITY:
HISTORICAL OVERVIEW

At the time of Kelly Michaels' initial trial in 1987, the relevant research in the area of children's suggestibility was quite limited, and this may have influenced her conviction. That is, although children's suggestibility has been a focus of research since the turn of the 20th century, most of the studies up until the middle of the 1980s examined the influences of a single misleading question on children's reports of neutral, nonscripted, and often uninteresting events that occurred in a laboratory setting. For example, children would be shown a movie or read a story and later asked questions about what happened. Some of these questions would be misleading (e.g., "What color was the boy's hat?" when in fact the boy was not wearing a hat). A common finding in most of these studies was that there was a correlation between the age of the subject and accurate responses to suggestive or misleading questions; younger children were more prone than older children or than adults to accept the suggestions in misleading questions. Therefore, in the earlier example, younger children would be more likely to reply that the hat was "yellow" or "red," whereas older children or adults would be more likely to reply that the boy was not wearing a hat.

Although the results of these studies were often important for theory development (e.g., the degree to which a suggestion impairs an original memory trace or coexists with it; or, the degree to which suggestibility reflects memory impairment or social compliance), they were of limited practical and legal relevance in cases such as Kelly Michaels', which tend to share the following characteristics: The allegations in these cases involve the child in the role of an active participant rather than in the role of a passive bystander; they involve the child's recall of salient, central events rather than peripheral, unimportant events; these cases often involve *repeated* interviews that are highly suggestive rather than a single misleading question as is true of the bulk of laboratory studies; and they frequently involve emotionally charged and traumatic events such as sexual molestation as opposed to the kinds of nontraumatic events we have typically studied in our laboratories. These differences between the modal laboratory study and actual child witness situations has led some commentators to assert that the former research provides few clues about the latter.

For example, in 1989, 2 years after the conviction of Kelly Michaels, an international conference was held at Cornell University that brought together basic and applied researchers in the area of memory development and children's testimony. Based on their review of the literature at that time, one group of researchers wrote:

> Most research on children as eyewitnesses has relied upon situations that are
> very different from the personal involvement and potential trauma of sexual

abuse. Researchers have used brief stories, films, videotapes or slides to simu-
late a witnessed event. A few have used actual staged events but these events
are also qualitatively different from incidents of child abuse. (Goodman &
Clarke-Stewart, 1991, pp. 92–93)

As we show in this chapter, such dismissive claims are less true today
than they were in 1989. Since the Cornell conference, many researchers have
developed paradigms to examine children's reports of salient and personally
experienced events that involve their own bodies, sometimes in painful or
embarrassing contexts. In addition, researchers have turned their attention
from studying the effects of an isolated misleading question on children's
recall to studying the effects of larger sections of social interaction; in some
of these studies the interview itself is the unit of analysis. Taking a cue from
actual forensic contexts, this new research often entails questioning children about events that occurred weeks, months, or even years previously;
the children are sometimes asked multiple leading questions by interviewers who possess erroneous hypotheses.

Changes in the paradigms to study children's suggestibility reflect researchers' attempts to challenge previously held views about the nature of
children's suggestibility; these views have changed dramatically over the
past 100 years. For the first 70 years of the century, the common view was
that child witnesses were hopelessly susceptible to adult influences (Ceci
& Bruck, 1993). This view began to change in the 1980s when researchers
began to examine children's reports of more salient events (e.g., an inoculation, a physical examination). Based on the results of these studies, a
common view was that when children are inaccurate in their reporting about
salient, personally experienced events involving their own bodies, it is because they make "errors of omission" (i.e., they fail to report actual events)
rather than "errors of commission" (i.e., they report false events). The result
is that it is now common to hear the view expressed that if children are
prone to suggestion, it is for unimportant details, not salient ones:

There is now no real question that the law and many developmentalists were
wrong in their assumption that children are highly vulnerable to suggestion,
at least in regard to salient details. Although some developmentalists may be
challenged to find developmental differences in suggestibility in increasingly
arcane circumstances, as a practical matter who really cares whether 3-year-
old children are less suggestible about peripheral details in events that they
witnessed than are 4-year-old children? Perhaps the question has some significance for developmental theory, but surely it has little or no meaning for
policy and practice in child protection and law. (Melton, 1992, p. 154)

As we discuss in this chapter, such views of the young child witness are
now being challenged. Our best evidence is that suggestibility is not con-

fined to "arcane circumstances" and that the existing research does seem to hold important meaning for policy and practice.[2]

In order to investigate the dimensions of children's suggestibility, it has been necessary to expand our definition of suggestibility. As defined traditionally, suggestibility is "the extent to which individuals come to accept and subsequently incorporate post-event information into their memory recollections" (Gudjonsson, 1986, p. 195; see also Powers, Andriks, & Loftus, 1979). The traditional definition implies that: (a) suggestibility can only be unconscious (i.e., misleading information is unwittingly incorporated into memory), (b) suggestibility results from the provision of information following an event as opposed to preceding it, and (c) suggestibility is a memory-based, rather than a social, phenomenon. Recently, however, we argued (Ceci & Bruck, 1993) that suggestibility concerns the degree to which children's encoding, storage, retrieval, and reporting of events can be influenced by a range of internal and external factors. A core implication of this latter definition is a sensitivity to context, such that the insinuations of leading questions and the tone of an interviewer's voice may affect the degree to which information is incorporated into a person's account. Our expanded definition implies that (a) it is possible to accept information and yet be fully aware of its incompatibility with originally perceived information, as in the case of acquiescence to social demands, or lying—hence, these forms of suggestibility do not involve the alteration of memory; (b) suggestibility can result from the provision of information either preceding or following an event; and (c) suggestibility can result from social as well as cognitive factors. This broadened view of suggestibility is consistent with both the legal and lay usage of the term, referring to how easily one is influenced by subtle suggestions, expectations, stereotypes, and leading questions that can unconsciously alter reports, as well as by explicit bribes, threats, and other forms of inducement that can consciously influence reports.

Armed with this expanded definition, we now summarize some of the major findings of this area of research. We utilize the Wee Care interviews to provide examples of different suggestive interview techniques.[3]

---

[2]Some researchers in the field have remarked that Melton got it exactly backwards; that is, although it may be true that children are better at remembering the gist than the precise verbatim components of an eyewitness episode, that adjudication of guilt almost invariably turns on memory for the latter rather than for the former. Although all eyewitnesses, including young children, agree that when they went to the convenience store last Saturday evening, there was a robbery, the guilt of the accused may turn on whether the robber was wearing a grey or a tan coat. This scenario calls for the study of children's recall and suggestibility for peripheral details. We thank Chuck Brainerd for making this interesting point.

[3]In this chapter we provide excerpts from some of the initial interviews that were carried out with the preschool witnesses in this case. All these interviews were conducted by two or three investigators within a 6-week period.

CURRENT RESEARCH ON CHILDREN'S
SUGGESTIBILITY: EXAMINING THE INTERVIEW

When researchers have the opportunity to examine actual interviews of child witnesses conducted by therapists, forensic investigators, or even parents, it quickly becomes apparent that there are often several glaring disjunctions between these real-world interviews and the highly structured question-and-answer dialogues that take place in experimental studies. We have come to the conclusion that experimental studies, although immensely important in revealing the underlying mechanisms of suggestibility, underestimate the potency of suggestive techniques in the real world. This is because the latter often entail more extreme forms of suggestion, combinations of suggestive techniques, or both.

First, it is rarely the case that actual child witnesses are interviewed only one time, by one interviewer, under relaxed conditions. The modal child witness has been officially interviewed between 3.5 and 11 times before appearing in court (Gray, 1993; McGough, 1994), and some children have been interviewed weekly for years about the same event prior to testifying in court. Some researchers, ourselves included, have suggested that the incessant use of leading questions and suggestions in these repeated interviews may result in a qualitatively different type of report distortion to that which arises in experimental studies from a single misleading question in a single postevent interview. Second, in many actual cases there are other elements besides suggestive questions that create a suggestive interview: Both implicit and explicit suggestions are sometimes woven into the fabric of interviews through the use of bribes, threats, repetitions of certain questions. and the inductions of stereotypes and expectancies. Third, in actual forensic cases children are questioned by parents, therapists, and legal officials—adults who carry greater status and power in their eyes than may be the case in experimental studies. In such situations, children may be more likely to comply with the suggestions of the interviewers than in analogous experimental situations, where interviewers are generally less important to them, less imposing, or both. It is also true that when children come to court, they are frequently questioned weeks, months, or even years after the occurrence of an event (as opposed to the very brief delays that are common in most experimental studies). Although the effect of delay on children's reports has been examined in some previous studies, these effects may be increased when paired with some of the suggestive interview techniques just described.

When suggestive elements appear in an interview with some frequency, they may reflect a more general phenomenon that we term *interviewer bias*. Interviewer bias characterizes those interviews where interviewers have a priori beliefs about the occurrence of certain events and, as a result, mold the interview to elicit statements from the interviewee that are consistent with these prior beliefs. Later, we elaborate on the concept and effects of interviewer bias. We then examine the effects of certain suggestive strategies that are used by biased interviewers (e.g., the use of leading questions, stereotype inducement).

Interviewer Bias

A review of interviews of children suspected of sexual abuse reveals that some interviewers blindly pursue a single hypothesis that sexual abuse has occurred. In such situations the interviewer typically fails to rule out rival hypotheses that might explain the behavior of the child. As a result, the interviewer may erroneously conclude that the child was sexually abused. Therefore, while gathering evidence to support his hypothesis, the interviewer also fails to gather any evidence that could potentially disconfirm his hypothesis. The interviewer does not challenge the child who provides abuse-consistent evidence by saying things like, "You're kidding me, aren't you?" The interviewer does not ask questions that might provide alternate explanations to the allegations (e.g., "Did your mommy and daddy tell you that this happened, or did you see it happen?"). And the interviewer does not ask the child about events that are inconsistent with his hypothesis (e.g., "Who else beside your teacher touched your private parts? Did your mommy touch them, too?"). When children provide inconsistent or bizarre evidence, it is either ignored or interpreted within the framework of the interviewer's initial hypothesis.

Some investigative and therapeutic interviewers claim that the relentless pursuit of the young child's memory is necessary, because child victims are so scared or embarrassed that they will never willingly or spontaneously tell an interviewer, including their own parents, of their abuse. Therefore, they claim, it is necessary, to use all available strategies to get the child to reveal abuse. These strategies include the use of repeated leading questions, repeated interviews, bribes or threats, and the induction of stereotypes and expectancies. Such strategies may prove extremely successful when the child has truly been abused; that is, the interviewer will be successful in drawing out an accurate report of abuse from the child. As we document later, however, when interviewers have strong preconceived impressions of what happened, such biases can also result in the generation of false reports from children who were not abused.

Clarke-Stewart, Thompson, and Lepore (1989) conducted a study in which 5- and 6-year-olds viewed a staged event that could be construed as either abusive or innocent. Some children interacted with a confederate named "Chester" as he cleaned some dolls and other toys in a playroom. Other children interacted with Chester as he handled the dolls roughly in a mildly abusive manner. Chester's dialogue reinforced the idea that he was either cleaning (e.g., "This doll is dirty, I had better clean it."), or playing with the doll in a rough suggestive manner (e.g., "I like to play with dolls. I like to spray them in the face with water.").

The children were questioned about this event several times on the same day, by different interviewers who differed in their interpretations of the event. The interviewer was either (a) accusatory in tone (suggesting that the janitor had been inappropriately playing with the toys instead of working), (b) exculpatory in tone (suggesting that the janitor was just cleaning the toys and not playing), or (c) neutral and nonsuggestive in tone. In the first two types of interviews, the questions changed from mildly to strongly suggestive as the interview progressed.

Following the first interview, all children were asked to tell in their own words what they had witnessed. They were then asked some factual questions (e.g., "Did the janitor wipe the doll's face?"), and some interpretive questions regarding the janitor's activities (e.g., "Was the janitor doing his job or was he just being bad?"). Then, each child was interrogated by a second interviewer who either reinforced or contradicted the first interviewer's tone. Finally, children were asked by their parents to recount what the janitor had done.

When questioned by a neutral interviewer, or by an interviewer whose interpretation was consistent with the activity viewed by the child, children's accounts were both factually correct, and consistent with the janitor's script. However, when the interviewer contradicted the activity viewed by the child, those children's stories quickly conformed to the suggestions or beliefs of the interviewer. By the end of the first interview, 75% of children's remarks were consistent with the examiner's point of view, and 90% answered the interpretive questions in agreement with the interviewer's point of view, as opposed to what actually happened.

Children changed their stories from the first to second interviews only if the two interviewers differed in their interpretation of the events. Therefore, when the second interviewer contradicted the first interviewer, the majority of children then fit their stories to the suggestions of the second interviewer. If the interviewer's interpretation was consistent across two interviews, the suggestions planted in the first session were quickly taken up and mentioned by the children in the second session. Moreover, when questioned by their parents, the children's answers were consistent with the interviewers' biases. Finally, although the effects of the interviewers' interpretations were most observable in terms of the children's responses to the interpretive questions about what the janitor had done, 20% of the children also made errors on the factual questions in the direction suggested by the biased interpretation, even though no suggestions had been given regarding these particular details.

In the second study, preschoolers played a game similar to "Simon Says" (Ceci, Leichtman, & White, in press). One month later they were interviewed by a trained social worker. Before the interview, the interviewer was given a written report containing two types of information about the play episode: accurate and erroneous. For example, if the event involved one child touching her own stomach and then touching another child's nose, the interviewer would be told that the child touched her own stomach and then touched the other child's toe. The interviewer was not told that some the information in the report was inaccurate. She was merely told these actions *might* have occurred during the play episode. She was asked to conduct an interview to determine what each child could recall about the original play episode. The only instruction given to the social worker was that she should begin by asking the child for a free narrative of what had transpired and that she should try to avoid all forms of suggestions and leading questions. Otherwise, she was allowed to use any strategies that she felt necessary to elicit the most factually accurate recall from the child.

The information provided on the one-page sheet influenced the social worker's hypothesis (or beliefs) about what had transpired, and powerfully influenced the dynamics of the interview, with the social worker eventually shaping some of the children's reports to be consistent with her hypothesis, even when it was inaccurate. When the social worker was accurately informed, the children correctly recalled 93% of all events. However, when she was misinformed, 34% of the 3- to 4-year-olds and 18% of the 5- to 6-year-olds corroborated one or more events that the interviewer falsely believed had occurred, even though they had not. Interestingly, it was our impression that the children seemed to become more credible as their interviews unfolded. Many children initially stated details inconsistently or reluctantly, but as the interviewer persisted in asking leading questions about nonevents that were consistent with her hypothesis, a significant number of these children abandoned all contradictions and hesitancy, and endorsed the interviewer's erroneous hypothesis (see Poole & White, 1991, for similar evidence on how statements become more confident with repeated interviews).

These two studies provide evidence that interviewers' hypotheses can influence the accuracy of children's testimony. These results illustrate the risks of having only a single hypothesis about the event in question—especially when it is incorrect.

Examples of interviewers' biases, blind pursuit of a single hypothesis, and failure to test alternate, equally believable, explanations of the children's behavior are rife in the interviews conducted with the Wee Care children. These biases are apparent when interviewers persistently maintained one line of inquiry (through the use of repeated leading questions, bribes, and threats) even when children consistently denied that the hypothesized events occurred. Interviewer biases are also revealed by a failure to follow up on some of the children's inconsistent or bizarre statements when doing so might undermine the interviewer's primary hypothesis. The following dialogue in which the interviewer (Q) engages one child (A) during an early interview is indicative of the failure to consider any evidence that was contrary to the interviewer's hunch:

Q: Do you think that Kelly was not good when she was hurting you all?

A: Wasn't hurting me. I like her.

Q: I can't hear you, you got to look at me when you talk to me. Now when Kelly was bothering kids in the music room . . .

A: I got socks off.

Q: Did she make anybody else take their clothes off in the music room?

A: No.

Q: Yes.

A: No.

In this next section, the interviewers had developed the belief that Kelly had abused the children with various utensils and also that part of the abuse involved smearing peanut butter on their bodies. Here is an example of how the investigator pursued this hypothesis with a child who was given an anatomically correct doll and some utensils:

Q: Okay, I really need your help on this. Did you have to do anything to her with this stuff?

A: Okay. Where's the big knife at. Show me where's the big knife at.

Q: Pretend this is the big knife because we don't have a big knife.

A: This is a big one.

Q: Okay, what did you have to do with that? What did you have to . . .

A: No . . . take the peanut—put the peanut butter.

Q: You put what's that, what did you put there?

A: I put jelly right here.

Q: Jelly.

A: And I put jelly on her mouth and on the eyes.

Q: You put jelly on her eyes and her vagina and her mouth.

(Note: The child never mentions "vagina.")

A: On her back, on her socks.

Q: And did you have to put anything else down there?

A: Right there, right here and right here and here.

Q: You put peanut butter all over? And where else did you put the peanut butter?

A: And jelly.

Q: And jelly?

A: And we squeezed orange on her.

Q: And you had to squeeze an orange on her?

A: Put orange juice on her.

Q: And did anybody—how did everybody take it off? How did she make you take it off?

A: No. Lick her all up, eat her all up and lick her all up.

Q: You had to lick her all up?

A: And eat her all up.

Q: Yeah? What did it taste like?

A: Yucky.

Q: So she made you eat the peanut butter and jelly and the orange juice off of the vagina too?

A: Yeah.

Q: Was that scary or funny?

A: Funny, funny and scary.

As is clear from this last excerpt, when children's responses contained inconsistent, incomprehensible, or no information, the interviewers either regarded these responses as evidence that abuse had taken place or else they chose to ignore these statements. The techniques used by the Wee Care interviewers directly reflected their preconceived belief that the children were abused.[4]

As is clear from some of these examples, when interviewers have a bias, they use certain types of strategies in their interviews to elicit reports from their child witnesses. Some of these components of biased interviews have been the focus of experimental studies that document their suggestive influences. Later, we provide some examples of this research (see Ceci & Bruck, 1995, for an extensive analysis of the components of suggestive interviews).

---

[4]For example, a child therapist, who presided over two heavily attended parent meetings when allegations were first made and who eventually assessed or treated 13 of the 20 child witnesses, stated that her goal was to induce the children to discuss sexual abuse. In the first group therapy session, she told the children that they were assembled together because of some of the things that had happened at Wee Care and with Kelly.

Lou Fonolleras, an investigator from the Division of Youth and Family Services, who conducted most of the initial investigatory interviews during a 6-week period, described his interviewing techniques as follows: "The interview process is in essence the beginning of the healing process." To rationalize his use of persistent questions with the children, he stated, "because it is my professional and ethical responsibility to alleviate whatever anxiety has arisen as a result of what happened to them."

The Effects of Repeated Questions

When interviewing children, adults frequently repeat a question because the child's first response may not provide enough information. In forensic interviews, questions may be repeated in order to check the consistency of a child's reports. Sometimes, interviewers' repetition of questions signals their specific biases: They keep asking a child the same question until they receive the answer they are looking for.

A number of studies from different domains demonstrate that when young children are asked the same question more than once in an interview they change their answer. A number of studies have shown that asking children the same yes/no question repeatedly within or across interviews (e.g., Poole & White, 1991) often results in the child changing his or her original answer. Preschoolers are especially susceptible to such influences. Some researchers have argued that children often do this because they seem to reason, "The first answer I gave must be wrong, that is why they are asking me the question again. Therefore, I should change my answer." Sometimes children may change their answer to please the interviewer, they reason that the "adult must not have liked the first answer I gave so I will give another answer." For example, Siegal, Waters, and Dinwiddy (1988) showed young children a videotape of a puppet being given a Piagetian conservation test. Sometimes the puppet was asked the same question twice; in these cases, the puppet changed its answer. After the puppet made a response, the children were asked if it had responded to please the adult or because that was what the puppet really thought was true. The children were more likely to say that the puppet pleased the experimenter when he gave an incorrect response in a two-question interview. In contrast, they were more likely to say that the puppet really thought the answer was true in the one-question procedure.

Sometimes children's answers may change because the interviewer's suggestions become incorporated into their memories (e.g., see Cassel & Bjorklund, 1995). However, we think that this is more likely to occur when questions are repeated across rather than within interviews.

The Wee Care interviews contain many instances of questions repeated after a child denied abuse or after the child's answer was inconsistent with the interviewer's hunch. Although there are instances when children tenaciously rejected the interviewer's persistent suggestive questions, upon repetition of a question, children sometimes changed their answers to become consistent with the interviewer's suspicion of sexual abuse:

> Q: When Kelly kissed you, did she ever put her tongue in your mouth?
> A: No.
> Q: Did she ever make you put her tongue in her mouth?

A: No.

Q: Did you ever have to kiss her vagina?

A: No.

Q: Which of the kids had to kiss her vagina?

A: What's this?

Q: No that's my toy, my radio box. Which kids had to kiss her vagina?

A: Me.

This second example of a child changing her answer in response to repeated questioning within one interview is taken from the Grand Jury hearing:

Prosecutor: Did she touch you with a spoon?

A: No.

Prosecutor: "No?" OK. Did you like it when she touched you with the spoon?

A: No.

Prosecutor: "No?" Why not?

A: I don't know.

Prosecutor: You don't know?

A: No.

Prosecutor: What did you say to Kelly when she touched you?

A: I don't like that.

The Effects of Repeating Misinformation Across Interviews

Numerous studies illustrate the deleterious effects of repeatedly giving children misleading information over a series of interviews (for a review, see Poole & White, 1995). We have conducted one study that highlights the deleterious effects of repeating misinformation across interviews on young children's reports (Bruck, Ceci, Francouer, & Barr, 1995); these effects are particularly pernicious because not only can the repeated misinformation become directly incorporated into the children's subsequent reports (they use the interviewers' words in their inaccurate statements) but it can also lead to fabrications or inaccuracies that, although not directly mirroring the content of the misleading information or questions, are inferences based on the misinformation.

The children in our study visited their pediatrician when they were 5 years old. During that visit, a male pediatrician gave each child a physical examination, an oral polio vaccine, and an inoculation. During that same visit, a female research assistant talked to the child about a poster on the wall, read the child a story, and gave the child some treats.

Approximately 1 year later, the children were reinterviewed four times over a period of 1 month. During the first three interviews, some children were falsely reminded that the male pediatrician showed them the poster, gave them treats, and read them a story, and that the female research assistant gave them the inoculation and the oral vaccine. Other children were given no misinformation about the actors of these events. During the final interview, when asked to recall what happened during the original medical visit, children who were not given any misleading information were highly accurate in their final reports. They correctly recalled which events were performed by the male pediatrician and by the female research assistant. In contrast, the misled children were very inaccurate; not only did they incorporate the misleading suggestions into their reports, with more than half the children falling sway to these suggestions (e.g., claiming that the female assistant inoculated them rather than the male pediatrician), but 45% of these children also included nonsuggested but inaccurate events in their reports by falsely reporting that the female research assistant had checked their ears and nose—inferences that are consistent with the erroneous suggestion that she had administered the shot, therefore she must have been the doctor, and did things that doctors usually do. None of the control children made such inaccurate reports. Therefore, young children use suggestions in highly productive ways to reconstruct and at times distort reality (see the aforementioned Chester Study by Clarke-Stewart et al., 1989, and the Sam Stone Study by Leichtman & Ceci, 1995, which is discussed later, for similar results).

Unfortunately, this is one area where we cannot provide any direct examples from the Wee Care Case, and we can only speculate about the effects of repeated interviews on the accuracy of children's reports. The reason for the absence of examples is that we do not have any of the initial interviews with the children. Therefore, we cannot ascertain the degree to which the allegations that emerge in later taped investigatory interviews are consistent with the first reports made by these children versus the degree to which they reflect earlier implantation of suggestions. We also do not have records of the conversations that the children had with their parents; it is possible that some of the allegations that occurred in these later investigatory interviews reflect suggestions incorporated from earlier conversations with parents who were urged by other parents and professionals to look for signs of abuse in their children. Nonetheless, the fact that parents of the child witnesses reported that their children had never disclosed abuse until after the investigatory interviews and the fact that allegations continued to emerge for several years after the investigatory interviews raises the hypothesis that these allegations were the result of multiple suggestive interviews.

Accusatory Nature of the Interview

Children are apt to be affected by the emotional tone of an interview. Implicit and explicit threats, bribes, and rewards can be conveyed by the emotional tone of an interview. For example, in some studies when an accusatory tone is set by the examiner (e.g., "We know something bad happened" or "It isn't good to let people kiss you in the bathtub" or "You'll feel better once you tell" or "Don't be afraid to tell"), then children in these studies are likely to fabricate reports of past events. The study of Chester the janitor described earlier provides an example of how an interviewer's accusatory tone (which reflects their bias of what had transpired) affected the children's reports. Other studies document how accusatory tone can also affect children's reports of sexual events (see Ceci & Bruck, 1993; Ceci, DeSimone, Putnick, & Nightingale, 1993).

For example, in one study 3- and 6-year-old children played with an unfamiliar male for 5 minutes while seated across the table from him. Four years later, Goodman, Wilson, Hazan, and Reed (1989; also described in Goodman & Clarke-Stewart, 1991) reinterviewed the children. At this time, the researchers created "an atmosphere of accusation" by telling the children that they were to be questioned about an important event, and by saying such things as, "Are you afraid to tell? You'll feel better once you've told." Although few of the children remembered the original event from 4 years earlier, their performance on suggestive-abuse questions was, according to the researchers, "mixed." Five out of the 15 children incorrectly agreed with the interviewer's suggestive question that they had been hugged or kissed by the confederate, 2 of the 15 agreed that they had their picture taken in the bathroom, and one child agreed that she had been given a bath. The important conclusion of this study is that children may begin to give incorrect information to misleading questions about events for which they have no memory, when the interviewer creates an atmosphere of accusation.

The Wee Care interviewers often tried to enlist the children's cooperation by creating an atmosphere of conspiracy. For example:

Investigator: Your mommy tells me that you guys are interested in busting this case wide open with us, is that right?

and:

Investigator: That's why I need your help, especially you older kids . . . because you can talk better than the younger kids . . . and you will be helping to keep her in jail longer so

that she doesn't hurt anybody. Not to mention that you'll
also feel a lot better once you start.

The Effects of Being Interviewed
by Adults With High Status

Young children are sensitive to the status and power of their interviewers.
If their account is questioned, for example, children may defer to the chal-
lenges of the more senior interviewer. To some extent, the child's recognition
of this power differential may be one of the most important causes of their
increased suggestibility. Children are more likely to believe adults than other
children, and they are more willing to go along with the wishes of adults
and to incorporate adults' beliefs into their reports (e.g., Ackerman, 1983;
Sonnenschein & Whitehurst, 1980. This fact has long been recognized by
researchers since the turn of the century and has been demonstrated in
many studies (see Ceci & Bruck, 1993, for a review). For example, children
are less open to suggestive influences when the suggestions are planted by
their peers than when they are planted by adults (Ceci, Ross, & Toglia, 1987).

However, children may also be sensitive to status and power differentials
among adults. This is a particularly important issue for the testimony of
child witnesses who are interviewed by police officers, judges, and medical
personnel. The Wee Care children were interviewed by law enforcement
agents or by social workers who made reference to their connection to law
enforcement agents. The children were explicitly made aware of the status
of their interviewers by such comments as: "I'm a policeman. If you were a
bad girl, I would punish you, wouldn't I? Police can punish bad people" and
"I'm going to introduce you to one of the men who arrested Kelly and put
her in jail."

A recent study by Tobey and Goodman (1992) suggests that interviews
by high-status adults who make such statements may have negative effects
on the accuracy of children's reports. In their study, 4-year-olds played a
game with a research assistant who was called a "baby-sitter." Eleven days
later, the children returned to the laboratory. Half of the children met a
police officer, who said:

> I am very concerned that something bad might have happened the last time
> that you were here. I think that the baby-sitter you saw here last time might
> have done some bad things and I am trying to find out what happened the
> last time you were here when you played with the baby-sitter. We need your
> help. My partner is going to come in now and ask you some questions about
> what happened.

A research assistant dressed up as a police officer then questioned these
children. Other children never met the police officer; they were only ques-

tioned by a neutral interviewer (who was also dressed up as a police officer) about what had happened with the baby-sitter. When the children were asked to tell everything they could remember, the children in the police condition gave fewer accurate statements and more inaccurate statements than children in the neutral condition. The results of this study not only reflect some potentially negative effects of interviews between law enforcement agents and child witnesses but more generally how a child's reports may be negatively influenced by interviewers who refer to their power or status.

The Influence of Stereotypes on Children's Report Accuracy

Some suggestive interviews involve the creation of stereotypes. If a child is repeatedly told that a person "does bad things," then the child's report might come to reflect this belief. Recently, Leichtman and Ceci (1995) demonstrated the deleterious influence of stereotypes when paired with repeated suggestive questioning. Although their procedure entailed assignment to one of four experimental conditions, we confine our description to only two conditions here; namely, a control condition that did not contain any stereotype induction or suggestive questioning, and an experimental condition that contained *both* a stereotype induction plus a series of suggestive questioning.[5]

In the control condition, a stranger named Sam Stone visited a day-care center. Following his visit, 3- to 6-year-olds who were present during his visit were interviewed four times over a 10-week period. During these interviews, the questioner refrained from using suggestive questions. Finally, the children were interviewed a fifth time, by a new interviewer who asked about two "nonevents" entailing Sam Stone doing something to a teddy bear and a book. In reality, Sam Stone never touched either one. When asked: "Did Sam Stone do anything to a book or a teddy bear?", only 10% of the 3- to 4-year-olds' answers contained claims that Sam Stone did anything to a book or teddy bear. When asked if they actually saw him do anything to the book or teddy bear, as opposed to "thinking they saw him do something," or "hearing he did something," now only 5% of their answers contained claims that anything occurred. Finally, when these 5% were gently challenged ("You didn't really see him do anything to the book/the teddy bear, did you?"),

---

[5]There was also a condition that contained only a stereotype induction but no suggestive questioning and a condition that contained only suggestive questioning condition but no stereotype induction; these two conditions resulted in performances midway between that of the control condition, on the one hand, and the stereotype plus suggestive condition, on the other.

only 2.5% still insisted on the reality of the fictional event. None of the 5- to 6-year-olds claimed to have actually seen Sam Stone do either of the fictional events.

Preschoolers assigned to the experimental condition were presented with a stereotype of Sam Stone before he visited their day-care center. Each week, beginning a month prior to Sam Stone's visit, these children were told a new Sam Stone story, in which he was depicted as very clumsy. For example:

> You'll never guess who visited me last night. [pause] That's right. Sam Stone! And guess what he did this time? He asked to borrow my Barbie and when he was carrying her down the stairs, he tripped and fell and broke her arm. That Sam Stone is always getting into accidents and breaking things!

Following Sam Stone's visit, these children were given four suggestive interviews over a 10-week period. Each suggestive interview contained two erroneous suggestions, one having to do with ripping a book and the other with soiling a teddy bear (e.g., "Remember that time Sam Stone visited your classroom and spilled chocolate on that white teddy bear? Did he do it on purpose or was it an accident?" and "When Sam Stone ripped that book, was he being silly or was he angry?").

Ten weeks later, when a new interviewer probed about these events ("Did anything happen to a book?" "Did anything happen to a teddy bear?"), 72% of the 3- to 4-year-olds claimed that Sam Stone did one or both misdeeds—a figure that dropped to 44% when asked if they actually saw him do these things. Importantly, 21% continued to insist that they saw him do these things, even when gently challenged. Eleven percent of the 5- to 6-year-olds claimed they saw him do one or both of these misdeeds.

The Sam Stone study demonstrates the powerful effects of suggestive questioning that is paired with stereotype induction. In this study the induction occurred prior to the children's first and only meeting with Sam Stone. Similar patterns of results have been obtained when a stereotype is induced after an encounter or an experience. For example, the study of Chester the janitor provides an example of how induction of a stereotype after an event influenced children's reports.

The Wee Care interviews are riddled with examples of stereotype induction. The interviewers explicitly repeated in various interviews that Kelly was bad. The investigators also promoted fear by asking leading questions about whether Kelly had threatened them or their families if they were to tell on her. Sometimes the investigators suggested that she had claimed to have supernatural powers ("Kelly said a lot of things to some kids and I think that she might have said them to you too, like she had some special powers like she can come through a wall and she could lift your bed and stuff like that . . .").

It is interesting that despite these statements, in the early interviews at least, the children did not completely incorporate the suggested stereotypes of Kelly. Sixteen of the 34 children never said they were afraid of her (but it is also the case that in the experimental studies, not all children are influenced by the stereotype inductions). Some children claimed that Kelly was bad, but they never completely justified their claims. In one of the examples we have of two transcribed interviews for the same child, we see that in the first of the transcribed interviews the child is repeatedly asked about bad things that Kelly did. She denies that Kelly did anything bad to her. In the next (transcribed) interview, the following exchange takes place:

> *Q:* Was Kelly a good girl or a bad girl?
> *A:* She was a bad girl.
> *Q:* She was a bad girl. Were there any other teachers who were bad?
> *A:* No.
> *Q:* Kelly was the only bad girl? What did Kelly do that made her a bad girl?
> *A:* She readed.
> *Q:* She what?
> *A:* She readed and she came to me and I said no, no, no.
> *Q:* Did she hurt you?
> *A:* I hurted her.
> *Q:* How did you hurt her?
> *A:* Because I didn't want to write and she write and I said no, no, no, no and I hit her.

Source Amnesia

As can be seen, the preceding factors that we have been discussing are quite salient; their presence can be easily isolated in transcribed interviews. Less salient and less easily detectable suggestions, however, can also exert a significant influence on children's report accuracy. In this section we focus on source monitoring errors.

Source monitoring is a task that we perform continuously and often unconsciously. It involves identifying the origins of our memories in order to elucidate them or to validate them. For example, it involves remembering when or where an event occurred, identifying the speaker of a remembered utterance, keeping track of who did what, and monitoring the origins of our experiences. Whereas a more specific term, *reality monitoring*, is used to refer to the determination of whether an event was imagined or real, source monitoring generally refers to the monitoring of sources that did occur. These are sometimes indistinguishable in cases where the task involves trying to remember whether something actually happened to us or whether someone said that something happened to us.

Source monitoring was initially studied in the context of adult memories, because adults occasionally misidentify the sources of their recollections. They may, for example, remember someone telling them about an event when in actuality they had read about the event in a newspaper. Recently, however, a number of developmental psychologists have begun to examine source monitoring in children (see Zaragoza et al., chapter 17, this volume, for full details). In these studies children experience an event, then later are told a number of details about the event, some of which did not occur. Later, when asked to recall the details of the original event, subjects often cannot monitor the source of the information; that is, they report that some of the nonoccurring details that were provided after the event actually happened during the event. This effect happens at all ages, but it seems that younger children make disproportionately more of these errors. Some recent work also suggests that these errors are true reflections of confusions; when subjects are warned before their final recall not to believe anything that was said to them after the event because it was not true, they continue to make source errors. This pattern is most prominent for preschoolers (Lindsay, Gonzales, & Eso, 1995).

Ceci, Crotteau, Smith, and Loftus (1994) designed a study to examine whether preschoolers exhibit source misattributions when they are repeatedly encouraged to think about events that never occurred. These children completed a minimum of 7 interviews about past events in their lives. Each week, an interviewer asked preschoolers to think about both actual events that they had experienced in their distant past (e.g., an accident that eventuated in having stitches) and fictitious events that they had never experienced (e.g., getting their hand caught in a mousetrap and having to go to the hospital to get it removed). The parents supplied the real events and confirmed that the false events had never occurred. Each of these events and nonevents was written on a separate card. The child selected a card, the interviewer would read it aloud, and then ask if the event ever happened. For example, when the child selected the card that read: "Got finger caught in a mousetrap and had to go to the hospital to get the trap off," the interviewer would ask: "Think real hard, and tell me if this ever happened to you. Can you remember going to the hospital with the mousetrap on your finger?" (This study will be henceforth referred to as "The Mousetrap Study.")

After 7 to 10 weeks of thinking about both real and fictitious events, these preschool children were interviewed by a second interviewer. Initially, the interviewer asked: "Tell me if this ever happened to you: Did you ever get your finger caught in a mousetrap and have to go to the hospital to get the trap off?" Following the child's reply, the interviewer asked for additional details (e.g., "Can you tell me more?").

When exposed to these very mild manipulations, 58% of the preschool children produced false narratives to one or more of these fictitious events;

25% produced false narratives to the majority of them. Furthermore, the children's reports did not solely contain one-word responses; their narratives contained elaborated and embellished descriptions of events that never occurred. Some accounts were internally coherent, containing not only details and sequences of events that never occurred but also containing descriptions of the child's affect during these nonevents. These data indicate that children can come to make false reports about nonoccurring events, even ostensibly painful bodily events, when suggestions are mildly made in the course of a conversation or a story-telling activity.[6]

If children are repeatedly asked by investigators, therapists, and parents to try to remember "how someone touched you" or "if someone touched your vagina," will children eventually come to make statements that they had been sexually abused, when abuse had never taken place? Furthermore, when parents or therapists read books with abuse themes to children, do children come to believe what happened in the book actually happened to them? For example, Dr. Susan Esquilin, one of the therapists for the Wee Care children, read *Where the Wild Things Are* to some of her clients. One of the pictures contains a child with a fork running after a monster. After reading this book, some children began reporting abuse with utensils. The possible link between these two events was raised by the defense lawyer at the trial. There are no data on these important issues. However, the results of the studies that we have just reviewed provide a theoretical and empirical framework for suspecting that such activities could lead to significant source misattributions.

To recap, we have presented a number of features of biased interviews that may significantly undermine the accuracy of children's reports, including the use of repeated questions, the repetition of misleading information, and the creation of an accusatory atmosphere. In addition, children's reports may be biased by an intimidating interviewer, such as a police officer, or by stereotype induction. Some recent evidence suggests that simply asking children to repeatedly think about whether an event occurred may have a negative effect on their future report accuracy. Finally, when the designs of studies allowed for developmental comparisons, the effects of suggestive interviews were predominantly larger for younger compared to older children.

CHILDREN'S CREDIBILITY

Although children's reports may be highly influenced by a number of suggestive influences, this does not necessarily mean that the children will appear credible when they parrot interviewers' erroneous suggestions. Of

---

[6]It should be noted that similar patterns of results have been recently reported for adult subjects (Hyman, Billings, Husband, Husband, & Smith, 1993; Loftus, 1993).

particular concern is whether a juror, a child development researcher, or a child therapist can differentiate between children's accurate and false reports. The existing evidence suggests that one cannot tell the difference between these two kinds of children.

For example, Leichtman and Ceci (1995) examined the believability of the children's reports in the Sam Stone Study, by showing the videotapes of their final interviews to 119 researchers and clinicians who work on children's testimonial issues. These researchers and clinicians were told that all the children observed Sam Stone's visit to their day-care centers. They were asked to decide which of the events reported by the children actually transpired and then to rate the overall credibility of each child.

The majority of the professionals were highly inaccurate. Experts who conduct research on the credibility of children's reports, who provide therapy to children suspected of having been abused, and who carry out law enforcement interviews with children generally failed to detect which of the children's claims were accurate and which were not, despite being confident in their judgments. The highly credible yet inaccurate reports obtained from the children may have resulted from a combination of repeated interviews with persistent and intense suggestions that built on a set of prior stereotypes. Similarly, it may become difficult to separate credibility from accuracy when these children, after repeated interviews, give a formal videotaped interview or testify in court.

Similar results were obtained when psychologists who specialize in interviewing children were shown videotapes of the children in the Mousetrap study (Ceci et al., 1994). Recall that these children had been simply asked to repeatedly think about whether a fictitious or real event had actually happened. Again, professionals could not reliably detect which of the events in the children's narratives were real and which were not. One reason for their difficulty may be that they cannot imagine such plausible, internally coherent narratives being fabricated. In addition, the children exhibited none of the telltale signs of duping, teasing, or tricking. They seemed sincere, their facial expressions and affect were appropriate, and their narratives were filled with the kind of low-frequency details that make accounts seem plausible, as shown in the following account:

> My brother Colin was trying to get Blowtorch (an action figure) from me, and I wouldn't let him take it from me, so he pushed me into the wood pile where the mousetrap was. And then my finger got caught in it. And then we went to the hospital, and my mommy, daddy, and Colin drove me there, to the hospital in our van, because it was far away. And the doctor put a bandage on this finger (indicating).

One might argue that the content of the children's narrations in these studies is quite different from that of children who report sexual abuse.

Perhaps well-trained professionals can reliably differentiate between true and false reports of sexual abuse. Unfortunately, the existing literature suggests that there is little consistency among these professionals' judgments. There are two programs of research to illustrate this point.

Realmuto, Jensen, and Wescoe (1990) asked a highly trained child psychiatrist to interview children and then to determine which of the children had been sexually abused. Next, videotapes of these assessments were shown to 14 professionals (pediatricians, psychiatrists, social workers, psychologists, attorneys) each with more than 10 years of experience in the field of child sexual abuse. The professionals were asked to classify the children as abused or nonabused. Although there was high concordance between the interviewer and the raters in terms of which children they classified as abused and nonabused, the overall rates of accurate classification were low. The interviewing psychiatrist correctly identified 33% of the abused children and 67% of the nonabused children. The group of professionals correctly classified 23% of the abused children and 85% of the nonabused children.

Homer, Guyer, and Kalter (1993a, 1993b) presented an actual case of alleged sexual abuse of a 3-year-old to mental health specialists. These clinicians heard a detailed presentation of the court-appointed clinician's findings, which included parent interviews and videotaped child–parent interaction sequences. The case presentation lasted approximately 2 hours, during which time the participants questioned the clinician who evaluated the child and her family. After the presentation, the clinicians estimated the likelihood of sexual molestation. The range of estimated probabilities of abuse was extreme—many clinicians were confident that abuse did not take place, and others were just as confident that abuse had occurred. The same patterns were obtained when the analyses were restricted to a smaller group of experts who were uniquely qualified to assess child sexual abuse.

Although surprising to some, these results are depressing to all. They suggest that when allegations of child sexual abuse are made in many cases, there is no "Pinocchio" test that can be used even by the most qualified to definitively ascertain whether or not abuse occurred.

THE ARGUMENT THAT CHILDREN ARE NOT SUGGESTIBLE

It could be argued that this chapter contains a one-sided presentation of the literature in view of numerous studies demonstrating that young children are no more suggestible than older children or adults. In this chapter we have focused on studies that emphasize the weaknesses of children's memories because the conditions in these studies are the most relevant to the forensic interviewing conditions exhibited in cases such as Wee Care, which we have used to illustrate the growing applicability of the developmental research.

Studies that emphasize the accuracy of young children's reports (e.g., see Goodman, Batterman-Faunce, & Kenney, 1992, for a review) do not contain the same types of suggestive interviewing procedures found in many of the best-known cases. Instead, many of these studies are characterized by the neutral tone of the interviewer, the limited use of misleading questions (usually a single occasion), and the absence of strong stereotypes or motives to make a false report. When children are interviewed in these neutral settings, it is a common (although not a universal) finding[7] that children are less susceptible to suggestive influences, particularly about sexual details, than when interviewed under the suggestive conditions that have been discussed in this chapter. Hence, studies of children's strengths were not the focus of this chapter because the interviewing conditions used in these studies do not typify those under which the Wee Care children and many other child witnesses have been interviewed; therefore, such studies have limited relevance to the issues in such cases. However, there are two important implications of the studies that focus on the strength of children's reports.

A first implication of studies that emphasize the strength of children's memories is that they illustrate the conditions under which children should be interviewed if one wishes to obtain the most reliable reports. Again, when children are interviewed by unbiased, neutral interviewers, and when leading questions are kept to a minimum, and there is the absence of threats, bribes and stereotype induction, then children's reports are most accurate.

The second point is that although children are mainly accurate in studies in which they are interviewed by a neutral experimenter, asked minimal leading questions, and not given any motivation to produce distorted re-

---

[7]For example Ornstein and his colleagues (Baker-Ward, Gordon, Ornstein, Larus, & Clubb, 1993; Gordon, Ornstein, Clubb, & Nida, 1991) found that when children were later questioned on one occasion about their memories of the visit to the pediatrician, 3-year-olds were more prone than 6-year-olds to make false claims in response to suggestive questions about silly events involving body contact (e.g., "Did the nurse lick your knee?"). Other examples are provided by the research of Goodman and her colleagues. Goodman & Aman (1990) found that 3- and 5-year-old children frequently gave false answers to abuse-related questions such as, "Did he touch your private parts?" (32% of 3-year-olds and 24% of 5-year-olds gave inaccurate answers to these types of questions) and to misleading abuse related questions such as, "How many times did he spank you?" (24% of 3-year-olds and 3% of 5-year-olds gave inaccurate answers to these types of questions). Nor were these effects limited to this one study. When 3–4-year-olds were interviewed by a neutral interviewer about events surrounding an inoculation, there was an error rate of 23% on questions such as, "How many times did she kiss you?" and "She touched your bottom, didn't she?" (Goodman, Rudy, Bottoms, & Aman, 1990). That is, many of these children replied "yes" even though these events did not occur.

ports, there are nevertheless a few children in such studies who do give bizarre or sexualized answers to some leading questions. For example, in one study of children's reports of their medical examinations (Saywitz, Goodman, Nicholas, & Moan, 1991), one child, who never had a genital exam, falsely reported that the pediatrician had touched her buttocks and on further questioning claimed that it tickled and that the doctor used a long stick. In a study of children's recalls of their visit to a laboratory (Rudy & Goodman, 1991) one young child claimed that he had seen bones and blood in the research trailer (see Goodman et al., 1992, for additional examples). Therefore, when interviewed under ideal circumstances, small numbers of children do make spontaneous, strange, and unfounded allegations. However, as Goodman and her colleagues pointed out, many of these allegations can be understood by sensibly questioning the child and parents further. Often these allegations reflect the child's source confusions or anxieties.

CONCLUSIONS

We have illustrated that the investigation of child sexual abuse allegations is a complex matter fraught with problems. Scientists have begun to contribute important insights to these problems, although clearly more research is needed. Regardless of the complexities of the research, the present state of scientific knowledge permits us to make the following general statements about the reliability of the testimony of the child witnesses:

1. There are reliable age effects in children's suggestibility, with preschoolers being more vulnerable than older children to a host of factors that contribute to unreliable reports.

2. Although young children are often accurate reporters, some do make mistakes—particularly when they undergo suggestive interviews; these errors can involve not only peripheral details, but also central, predictable (i.e., scripted) events that involve their own bodies. It is also the case that suggestive questioning not only distorts children's factual recall, but also has a strong influence on their interpretation of events.

3. Measures can be taken to lessen the risk of suggestibility effects. To date, the factors that we know most about concern the nature of the interview itself—its frequency, degree of suggestiveness, and demand characteristics.

- A child's report is less likely to be distorted, for example, after one interview than after several interviews (the term "interviews" here includes informal conversations between parents and child about the target events).

- Interviewers who ask nonleading questions, who do not have a confirmatory bias (i.e., an attachment to a single hypothesis), and who do not repeat close-ended yes/no questions within or across interviews, are more likely to obtain accurate reports from children.
- Interviewers who are patient, nonjudgmental, and who do not attempt to create demand characteristics (e.g., by providing subtle rewards for certain responses) are likely to elicit the best quality reports from young children.

Therefore, at one extreme we can have more confidence in a child's spontaneous statements made prior to any attempt by an adult to elicit what they suspect may be the truth. At the other extreme, we are more likely to be concerned when a child has made a statement after prolonged, repeated, suggestive interviews.

5. It is also important to appreciate the complexity of the interrelationships of the factors affecting children's suggestibility. As in most areas of social science, effects are rarely as straightforward as one might wish. Even though suggestibility effects may be robust, the effects are not universal. Results vary between studies and children's behavior varies within studies. Therefore, even in studies with pronounced suggestibility effects, there are always some children who are highly resistant to suggestion. We have seen this in our own studies as well as in the transcripts of the Wee Care interviews: In some cases, no matter how much an interviewer may try to suggest that an event occurred, some children will consistently resist and not incorporate the interviewer's suggestion or point of view. On the other side, although suggestibility effects tend to be most dramatic after prolonged and repeated interviewing, some children incorporate suggestions quickly, even after one short interview (e.g., Clarke-Stewart, et al., 1989).

6. Although the focus of chapter is on children's suggestibility, there is a substantial literature on how adults' reports and memories can be influenced, changed, distorted, or created by a variety of factors, many of which are suggestive in nature (the interested reader should consult Lindsay & Read, 1994; Ross, chapter 3, this volume).

Having pointed out the great advancements that have been made in this field, there are still many important issues remaining to be tackled. Most of the work that we described in this chapter focuses on descriptions of the phenomenon of children's suggestibility; the hard work, however, remains. It is now time to link these behaviors to psychological mechanisms and to theoretical processes.

The following issues represent gaps in our knowledge; their exploration is crucial to our understanding of the phenomenon of suggestibility in general and of children's suggestibility, in particular. Some of this work is already in progress and is described in various chapters in this volume.

First, we have an incomplete understanding of the mechanisms underlying suggestibility. Ongoing and future work on this topic will provide a basis for accounting for age differences in suggestibility and for individual differences in suggestibility (i.e., why are some individuals so resistant to suggestions whereas other fall sway so easily?). A number of different mechanisms have been proposed. Some researchers posit that age differences in suggestibility can be directly linked to age differences in memory. Namely, children's greater susceptibility to suggestion is a direct outgrowth of their relatively weaker ability to accurately encode, store, and retrieve different types of information. At present, the evidence is inconsistent. Some researchers report a link between suggestibility and memory in children (Pezdek & Roe, 1995; Warren, Hulse-Trotter, & Tubbs, 1991); but there are other researchers who have argued that there is no relationship between a memory's strength and children's susceptibility to suggestion (Howe, 1991; Zaragoza, 1991).

Some researchers are investigating the link between knowledge and suggestibility effects. This topic is addressed in chapter 4 of this volume by Ornstein and his colleagues. Other explanatory candidates include language comprehension and production factors (e.g., Snyder, Nathanson, & Saywitz, 1993), source monitoring difficulties (see Zaragoza et al., chapter 17, this volume), and social factors. In experimental situations, some have argued that suggestibility effects arise out of social pressures: The subject accepts the misleading information in order to please the experimenter or because the experimenter is trusted. At other times the pressures may be more subtle, suggestibility may reflect gap-filling strategies (e.g., McCloskey & Zaragoza, 1985): Subjects accept the misleading information because they have no memory for the original event. Instead of telling the experimenter that they cannot remember or do not know, they revise or fill in memory gaps in order to please the experimenter. Social factors may play a very prominent role in children's suggestibility.

Some researchers have attempted to determine the relative importance of social versus cognitive factors in accounting for suggestibility effects. The results of these studies are inconsistent; thus, the issue remains unresolved. As we have argued in previous work (Ceci & Bruck, 1993, 1995), it seems that for now we can conclude that although social factors are quite important, they clearly do not fully account for all suggestibility effects. A variety of cognitive factors—specifically, memory impairment and source monitoring errors—appear to play an important role in explaining suggestibility effects in children. Of course, these conclusions are based on laboratory studies, where children are usually interviewed about an event only one time. Therefore, they tell us little about the time course of suggestibility effects or how reports become increasingly distorted over repeated interviews.

Furthermore, it seems that a focus on whether cognitive or social factors are more important obscures the possibility that both factors interact in producing suggestion. For instance, when memory traces are weak (or when there is no memory for the original event), children may be more compliant and willing to accept suggestions because there is no competing memory trace to challenge the suggestion. On the other hand, when the traces are strong, the child (or adult) is less likely to incorporate misleading suggestions into memory. It is also possible for social factors to underpin the effectiveness of cognitive mechanisms in producing suggestibility; for example, a child may attend more to suggestions from authority figures (a social factor), thus insuring greater encoding (a cognitive factor). However, these are hypotheses in need of data.

Finally, it is possible that a child's report may initially be the result of some social factor, but over time the report may become a part of the child's actual memory. In the legal arena, in response to strongly suggestive—even pressurized—interviews, children may initially realize that they are providing the interviewer with an erroneous account in order to please him, but after repeated retellings to different interviewers, the erroneous account may become so deeply embedded as to be indistinguishable from an actual memory.

Although cognitive as well as social factors may play a role in suggestibility effects, the important question, for which we have no empirical data, is whether there are age-related differences in the interaction of these factors. Specifically, do younger children differ from older children and from adults in terms of how quickly false reports, which may have been initially motivated by social factors, come to be believed?

REFERENCES

Ackerman, B. (1983). Speaker bias in children's evaluation of the external consistency of statements. *Journal of Experimental Child Psychology, 35,* 111–127.

Baker-Ward, L., Gordon, B., Ornstein, P. A., Larus, D., & Clubb, P. (1993). Young children's long-term retention of a pediatric examination. *Child Development, 64,* 1519–1533.

Bruck, M., Ceci, S. J., Francoeur, E., & Barr, R. (1995). "I hardly cried when I got my shot": Young children's reports of their visit to a pediatrician. *Child Development, 66,* 193–208.

Bruck, M., & Ceci, S. J. (1995). Amicus Brief to the Supreme Court of New Jersey in *New Jersey v. Michaels. Psychology, Policy and the Law, 1,* 272–322.

Cassel, W. S., & Bjorklund, D. F. (1995). Developmental patterns of eyewitness memory, forgetting, and suggestibility. An ecologically based short-term longitudinal study. *Law and Human Behavior, 19,* 507–532.

Ceci, S. J., & Bruck, M. (1993). The suggestibility of the child witness: A historical review and synthesis. *Psychological Bulletin, 113,* 403–439.

Ceci, S. J., & Bruck, M. (1995). *Jeopardy in the courtroom. A scientific analysis of children's testimony.* Washington, DC: American Psychological Association.

Ceci, S. J., Crotteau, M., Smith, E., & Loftus, E. W. (1994). Repeatedly thinking about non-events. *Consciousness & Cognition, 3*, 388–407.

Ceci, S. J., DeSimone, M., Putnick, M., & Nightingale, N. (1993). Age differences in suggestibility. In D. Cicchetti & S. Toth (Eds.), *Child witnesses, child abuse, and public policy* (pp. 117–137). Norwood, NJ: Ablex.

Ceci, S. J., Leichtman, M., & White, T. (in press). Interviewing preschoolers: Remembrance of things planted. In D. P. Peters (Ed.), *The child witness in context: Cognitive, social, and legal perspectives.* Holland: Kluwer.

Ceci, S. J., Ross, D., & Toglia, M. (1987). Age differences in suggestibility: Psycholegal implications. *Journal of Experimental Psychology: General, 117*, 38–49.

Clarke-Stewart, A., Thompson, W., & Lepore, S. (1989, May). *Manipulating children's interpretations through interrogation.* Paper presented at Biennial Meeting of the Society for Research on Child Development, Kansas City, MO.

Goodman, G., & Aman, C. (1990). Children's use of anatomically detailed dolls to recount an event. *Child Development, 61*, 1859–1871.

Goodman, G. S., Batterman-Faunce, J. M., & Kenney, R. (1992). Optimizing children's testimony: Research and social policy issues concerning allegations of child sexual abuse. In D. Cicchetti & S. Toth (Eds.), *Child abuse, child development, and social policy* (pp. 139–166). Norwood, NJ: Ablex.

Goodman, G. S., & Clarke-Stewart, A. (1991). Suggestibility in children's testimony: Implications for child sexual abuse investigations. In J. L. Doris (Eds.), *The suggestibility of children's recollections* (pp. 92–105). Washington, DC: American Psychological Association.

Goodman, G. S., Rudy, L., Bottoms, B., & Aman, C. (1990). Children's concerns and memory: Issues of ecological validity in the study of children's eyewitness testimony. In R. Fivush & J. Hudson (Eds.), *Knowing and remembering in young children* (pp. 249–284). New York: Cambridge University Press.

Goodman, G. S., Wilson, M. E., Hazan, C., & Reed, R. S. (1989, April). *Children's testimony nearly four years after an event.* Paper presented at the Annual Meeting of the Eastern Psychological Association, Boston, MA.

Gordon, B., Ornstein, P. A., Clubb, P., & Nida, R. E. (1991, November). *Visiting the pediatrician: Long-term retention and forgetting.* Paper presented at the annual meeting of The Psychonomic Society, San Francisco, CA.

Gray, E. (1993). *Unequal justice: The prosecution of child sexual abuse.* New York: Macmillan.

Gudjonsson, G. (1986). The relationship between interrogative suggestibility and acquiescence: Empirical findings and theoretical implications. *Personality and Individual Differences, 7*, 195–199.

Horner, T. M., Guyer, M. J., & Kalter, N. M. (1993a). Clinical expertise and the assessment of child sexual abuse. *Journal of the American Academy of Child and Adolescent Psychiatry, 32*, 925–931.

Homer, T. M., Guyer, M., J., & Kalter, N. M. (1993b). The biases of child sexual abuse experts: Believing is seeing. *Bulletin of the American Academy of Psychiatry and Law, 21*, 281–292.

Howe, M. L. (1991). Misleading children's story recall: Reminiscence of the facts. *Developmental Psychology, 27*, 746–762.

Hyman, I., Billings, F., Husband, S., Husband, T., & Smith, D. (1993, November). *Memories and false memories of childhood experiences.* Paper presented at the Annual Meeting of The Psychonomic Society, Washington, DC.

Leichtman, M. D., & Ceci, S. J. (1995). The effects of stereotypes and suggestions on preschoolers' reports. *Developmental Psychology, 31*, 568–578.

Lindsay, D. S., Gonzales, V., & Eso, K. (1995). Aware and unaware uses of memories of postevent suggestions. In M. S. Zaragoza, J. R. Graham, C. N. Gordon, R. Hirschman, & Y. Ben-Porath (Eds.), *Memory and testimony in the child witness* (pp. 86–108). Newbury Park, CA: Sage.

Lindsay, D. S., & Read, J. D. (1994). Psychotherapy and memories of childhood sexual abuse: A cognitive perspective. *Applied Cognitive Psychology, 8,* 281–338.

Loftus, E. F. (1993). The reality of repressed memories. *American Psychologist, 48,* 518–537.

Manshel, L. (1990). *Nap time.* New York: Kensington.

McCloskey, M., & Zaragoza, M. (1985). Misleading postevent information and memory for events: Arguments and evidence against the memory impairment hypothesis. *Journal of Experimental Psychology: General, 114,* 1–16.

McGough, L. (1994). *Fragile voices: The child witness in American courts.* New Haven, CT: Yale University Press.

Melton, G. (1992). Children as partners for justice: Next steps for developmentalists. *Monographs of the Society for Research in Child Development, 57*(Serial No. 229).

Pezdek, C., & Roe, C. (1995). The effect of memory trace strength on suggestibility. *Journal of Experimental Child Psychology, 60,* 116–128.

Poole, D., & White, L. (1991). Effects of question repetition on the eyewitness testimony of children and adults. *Developmental Psychology, 27,* 975–986.

Poole, D., & White, L. (1995). Tell me again and again: Stability and change in the repeated testimonies of children and adults. In M. S. Zaragoza, J. R. Graham, C. N. Gordon, R. Hirschman, & Y. Ben-Porath (Eds.), *Memory and testimony in the child witness* (pp. 22–43). Newbury Park, CA: Sage.

Powers, P., Andriks, J. L., & Loftus, E. F. (1979). Eyewitness accounts of females and males. *Journal of Applied Psychology, 64,* 339–347.

Realmuto, G., Jensen, J., & Wescoe, S. (1990). Specificity and sensitivity of sexually anatomically correct dolls in substantiating abuse: A pilot study. *Journal of the American Academy of Child and Adolescent Psychiatry, 29,* 743–746.

Rudy, L., & Goodman, G. S. (1991). Effects of participation on children's reports: Implications for children's testimony. *Developmental Psychology, 27,* 527–538.

Saywitz, K., Goodman, G., Nicholas, G., & Moan, S. (1991). Children's memory of a physical examination involving genital touch: Implications for reports of child sexual abuse. *Journal of Consulting and Clinical Psychology, 5,* 682–691.

Siegal, M., Waters, L., & Dinwiddy, L. (1988). Misleading children: Causal attributions for inconsistency under repeated questioning. *Journal of Experimental Child Psychology, 45,* 438–456.

Snyder, L. S., Nathanson, R., & Saywitz, K. (1993). Children in court: The role of discourse processing and production. *Topics in Language Disorders, 13,* 39–58.

Sonnenschein, S., & Whitehurst, G. (1980). The development of communication: When a bad model makes a good teacher. *Journal of Experimental Child Psychology, 3,* 371–390.

Tobey, A., & Goodman, G. S. (1992). Children's eyewitness memory: Effects of participation and forensic context. *Child Abuse & Neglect, 16,* 779–796.

Warren, A. R., Hulse-Trotter, K., & Tubbs, E. (1991). Inducing resistance to suggestibility in children. *Law and Human Behavior, 15,* 273–285.

Zaragoza, M. (1991). Preschool children's susceptibility to memory impairment. In J. L. Doris (Eds.), *The suggestibility of children's recollections* (pp. 27–39). Washington, DC: American Psychological Association.

17

CONFUSING REAL AND SUGGESTED MEMORIES: SOURCE MONITORING AND EYEWITNESS SUGGESTIBILITY

Maria S. Zaragoza
Sean M. Lane
Jennifer K. Ackil
Karen L. Chambers
Kent State University

It is now well documented that the accuracy of eyewitness testimony can be severely compromised by exposure to misleading postevent suggestions. Many studies have shown that the eyewitness reports of subjects who have witnessed an important event such as an auto accident or an office theft are easily contaminated by misleading information that occurs after the event in question (Bekerian & Bowers, 1983; Belli, 1989; Ceci, Ross, & Toglia, 1987a, 1987b; Christiaansen & Ochalek, 1983; Gibling & Davies, 1988; Gudjonsson, 1986; Hammersley & Read, 1986; Kohnken & Brockmann, 1987; Lindsay & Johnson, 1987, 1989; Loftus, 1975, 1977, 1979a, 1979b; Loftus & Hoffman, 1989; McCloskey & Zaragoza, 1985a; Metcalfe, 1990; Pirolli & Mitterer, 1984; Smith & Ellsworth, 1987; Tversky & Tuchin, 1989; Wagenaar & Boer, 1987; Zaragoza, McCloskey, & Jamis, 1987).

Although eyewitness suggestibility has been the focus of extensive research, several key aspects of suggestibility phenomena remain unexplained and even unexplored. In this chapter, we focus on one such fundamental question with regard to eyewitness suggestibility: To what extent do witnesses come to believe they actually remember witnessing the suggested information they report? We first show that the extant suggestibility literature does not address this question in a direct fashion and then describe the results of a research program that we have developed for the explicit purpose of answering this question.

A second goal of this chapter is to advance the notion that eyewitness suggestibility effects reflect a failure to accurately monitor the *source* of information in memory (see also Lindsay, 1990, 1994; Lindsay & Johnson, 1987, for similar proposals), and to advocate a source-monitoring approach to the study of suggestibility phenomena. A clear advantage of a source-memory approach is that the theoretical bases of source-monitoring processes are well established and fairly well understood (see Johnson, Hashtroudi, & Lindsay, 1993, for a recent review), and as such provide a rich source of hypotheses about the factors that are likely to influence the occurrence of these errors. In this chapter we show that the source-monitoring framework makes novel predictions about the magnitude and incidence of suggestibility effects that are confirmed by empirical research.

Laboratory studies of eyewitness suggestibility have focused primarily on a phenomenon known as the *misinformation effect*. This is the well-documented and highly reliable finding that subjects exposed to misleading postevent information about a witnessed event are quite likely to later report the suggested information rather than the events they actually saw (e.g., Loftus, Miller, & Burns, 1978). In studies of the misinformation effect, subjects are first shown a film clip or slide show depicting a forensically relevant event, such as a theft or a traffic accident. A subset of these subjects are then exposed to verbal misinformation that contradicts selected aspects of the event they saw. For example, in Loftus et al., some subjects who had viewed a traffic accident involving a stop sign were later asked a series of questions, one of which incorrectly referred to the stop sign as a yield sign. Finally, all subjects are tested on their memory for the event they saw. Subjects were given a forced choice between the slide depicting the stop sign they had actually seen and a nearly identical slide depicting a yield sign. The finding was that 75% of the control subjects (who had not been misled) correctly chose the slide with the stop sign, whereas only 41% of the misled subjects did so. Many other studies have replicated this effect.

To date, most of the theorizing about misinformation effects has focused on the controversial claim that misleading postevent information impairs subjects' ability to remember what they originally saw, a hypothesis we refer to as the *memory-impairment* hypothesis. One version of the memory impairment claim posits that misinformation transforms the original memory representation by erasing and ultimately replacing the originally stored information that it contradicts (e.g., Loftus, 1979b; Loftus & Loftus, 1980; Loftus et al., 1978). According to this view, the misinformation is integrated with the original memory representation, resulting in a single, altered-memory representation of the witnessed event. Another version of the memory-impairment claim holds that misinformation does not alter the original memory representation, but merely renders it difficult to retrieve (e.g., Bekerian & Bowers, 1983).

We (McCloskey & Zaragoza, 1985a, 1985b; Zaragoza & McCloskey, 1989; Zaragoza et al., 1987) have argued that misinformation does not impair original memories but merely influences the reports of subjects who either never encoded or otherwise failed to remember the original details they were misled about. We proposed that these subjects, who do not remember the original detail they saw, respond on the basis of the misinformation because they have no reason to believe it is not true. These conclusions were based on the results of studies where we used memory tests that did not permit the misinformation as an option. For example, subjects who had seen a thief holding a hammer and were later misinformed that the thief had been holding a screwdriver were given a test that asked them to choose between the original item, "hammer," and a novel item, such as "wrench." What we have found in numerous experiments with this modified test procedure is that the performance of misled subjects is just as accurate as that of control subjects (Bowman & Zaragoza, 1989; McCloskey & Zaragoza, 1985a; Zaragoza & McCloskey, 1989). We have also obtained the same result in several studies with preschool children (Zaragoza, 1987; Zaragoza, Dahlgren, & Muench, 1992).

Our findings and conclusions about the memory-impairment hypothesis have not gone unchallenged, however. There have recently been reports of small but reliable memory-impairment effects obtained with the modified test procedure we developed (Ceci, Ross, & Toglia, 1987b; Chandler, 1989; Belli, Windschitl, McCarthy, & Winfrey, 1992). Hence, the status of the memory-impairment hypothesis is still somewhat uncertain, and a number of researchers continue to seek evidence of memory impairment (e.g., Belli, Lindsay, Gales, & McCarthy, 1994).

In summary, the claim that exposure to verbal misleading postevent information can permanently transform memory representations of originally witnessed events (e.g., Loftus, 1979b; Loftus & Loftus, 1980) has dominated research and theorizing about suggestibility phenomena. At this time, the evidence in favor of this claim is very mixed. Moreover, the memory-impairment effects that have been obtained have been very small and inconsistent (e.g., Belli et al., 1992) and thus cannot fully account for the highly robust misinformation effects that Loftus and others have reported.

Our claim that misinformation does not impair preexisting memories of originally seen details (e.g., McCloskey & Zaragoza, 1985a) is not really in conflict with the general view that misinformation can lead to erroneous memories, although it has often been interpreted that way. In other words, there has been a general tendency to equate evidence against the memory impairment hypothesis with evidence for accurate memory of originally witnessed events, and similarly, to equate the no-impairment position with the claim that misinformation effects are due entirely to "social" or nonmnemonic factors (e.g., demand, conforming to authority). This tendency to equate no impairment with accurate memory is apparently due to the implicit assumption that trace integration is the only mechanism that can lead to erroneous memories. According to the integration claim, the mechanism that leads to impaired memory for original details (i.e., the merging of traces) also leads to the false memory that the suggested information was part of the originally witnessed event. Therefore, if one adopts the integration view, evidence of no impairment is evidence that no integration occurred, and thus implies that misinformation had no deleterious effect on memory at all. However, impaired memory for original details and false memory of having seen suggested items need not go hand in hand. For example, if it is assumed that memory representations of the original event and postevent episodes are stored separately rather than integrated, inaccuracies in memory can occur even if the original memory representation is unaffected. For example, it would be possible for subjects to confuse memories of suggested items for their real memories of the witnessed event, even though memory records of the originally witnessed events are preserved unharmed in memory. It is important to note, however, that one need not abandon the integration assumption to show that false memories of having witnessed suggested items can exist in the absence of memory impairment. Memory impairment (of the erase and update variety) can occur only in situations where the misinformation directly contradicts some piece of information in memory. Many eyewitness suggestibility situations, however, do not satisfy this requirement. For example, in many situations subjects are exposed to suggestions that fill a gap in memory (e.g., McCloskey & Zaragoza, 1985a) or that otherwise serve to supplement subjects' memory for what they saw (e.g., Loftus & Palmer, 1974). Although these sorts of suggestions cannot cause memory impairment (because there is no contradictory original memory to replace), they may nevertheless lead to inaccurate memories if subjects ultimately come to believe they remember seeing these suggested items at the original event.

In summary, whether or not exposure to misinformation impairs the original memory, it is possible that subjects come to confuse misleading postevent suggestions for their "real memories" of witnessed events. However, much of the suggestibility literature cannot be brought to bear on this issue because the procedures traditionally employed in these studies do not allow one to pinpoint the reasons why subjects incorporate misinformation into their reports. It is possible that subjects report the suggestions because they are going along with the experimenter or simply because they believe the misinformation is true. In the typical eyewitness suggestibility study the misinformation is presented to subjects as an accurate description of the events they witnessed by an experimenter whom they are likely to view as knowledgeable and credible. Our own experience with suggestibility experiments provides informal support for these claims: On more than one occasion we have had subjects tell us during debriefing that they went along with the suggestions because they never thought we would lie to them! If subjects believe that the postevent information is simply a description of the events they actually witnessed, they may be likely to report everything they know about the event, without regard to whether they specifically recollect witnessing it at the original event or whether they learned it from a postevent source.

One way to more directly assess the extent to which subjects confuse memories of suggested items for memories of events they actually witnessed is to ask subjects specific questions about the *source* of the suggested items (e.g., "Do you remember seeing this item at the original event? Do you remember hearing about this item from the experimenter?"). Determining whether subjects misremember witnessing suggested items is in essence a question about subjects' ability to monitor the *source* of their memories. The belief that one remembers witnessing a suggested item is an example of a situation where a memory derived from one source (e.g., misleading suggestions provided by an experimenter) is misattributed to another source (e.g., the witnessed event), an error we refer to as a *source-misattribution* error.

At this writing, very few studies in the suggestibility literature have employed a test procedure wherein subjects were asked to make overt judgments about their memory for the source of suggested items (Lindsay & Johnson, 1989; Zaragoza & Koshmider, 1989; Zaragoza & Lane, 1994). More-over, two of these studies (Lindsay & Johnson, 1989; Zaragoza & Koshmider, 1989) failed to find evidence that subjects misremembered the suggested items as being from the originally seen event, even though both studies showed that they could replicate the misinformation effect when the traditional test procedures were used. In contrast, the results of recent studies we have conducted have established that misled subjects do experience genuine source confusions (Zaragoza & Lane, 1994; see also Lindsay, 1990, for converging evidence using a different test procedure[1]). In this chapter we review the evidence for source misattributions that result from exposure to suggestion,

---

[1]Lindsay (1990) found that misled subjects reported suggested items on a cued-recall test of the witnessed event even though they had been explicitly warned that all of the information they had read in the postevent narrative was wrong (i.e., definitely not in the event they saw). Therefore, although subjects in this study were not asked overt questions about their memory for the source of suggested items, it is clear that these subjects could not remember the true source of the suggested items or they would have refrained from reporting them on the test. It should be noted, however, that Lindsay found evidence of source misattribution errors only in a condition that was designed to make the original and misleading episodes difficult to discriminate (e.g., the original slides were accompanied by a tape-recorded narrative that was in the same female voice as the postevent narrative, subjects were explicitly instructed to form visual images of the events described in the postevent narrative, and the final test occurred after a 48-hr. interval)—under less extreme conditions no source misattribution errors were observed. In contrast, the results we report here provide evidence of source misattributions under conditions in which the two sources are much more discriminable (e.g., they occur in different modalities, subjects are tested immediately), conditions that more closely approximate those of the typical suggestibility study. It is probably the case that Lindsay's procedure underestimated the incidence of source misattributions because it does not detect the proportion of subjects who believe that they both saw and read about the misleading suggestion.

and discuss some of the factors that influence the incidence and magnitude of this source-misattribution effect. Of particular interest is the finding that young children may be especially susceptible to confusing misleading suggestions for their actual memories of witnessed events.

A THEORETICAL FRAMEWORK

Our investigations of source misattributions in the misinformation paradigm follow directly from the source monitoring framework of Johnson and colleagues (see Johnson et al., 1993, for a recent review). This framework, which is an elaboration and extension of the reality-monitoring model of Johnson and Raye (1981), has received an impressive amount of empirical support (see Johnson & Raye, 1981; Johnson et al., 1993, for reviews). According to this framework, information about the source of a memory is typically not directly coded as some sort of "tag" or proposition. Rather, source memory is assumed to be the product of a decision process that involves evaluating the characteristics of memories. For example, some of the characteristics that allow us to distinguish between real and imagined memories are the vividness of the memory and the amount of sensory details; memories based on perception tend to have more of these characteristics than do memories that are self-generated through imagination. Nevertheless, because these are "average" differences, attribution errors are sometimes made.

Consistent with the source monitoring framework, we assume that memory representations of the original and misleading episodes consist of characteristics or *attributes* (cf. Bower, 1967) that reflect the conditions under which each memory was acquired (e.g., where and when each piece of information was acquired, their mode and medium of presentation, emotional reactions to the information, and records of reflective processes) as well as their semantic content. Second, we assume that source monitoring results from a decision process that involves evaluating the characteristics of these memories. In general, the likelihood of source misattribution errors is expected to vary as a function of the similarity and differences between the characteristics of the two kinds of memories. For example, the greater the overlap in the memory characteristics of the original and misleading episodes, the greater the chances that source misattributions will occur.

Johnson et al. (1993) argued that many (if not most) source judgments are made rapidly and automatically on the basis of the qualitative characteristics of the memory representation, with little awareness of any decision-making process. However, source-monitoring judgments are sometimes made more deliberately and strategically, and may be influenced by reasoning based on additional information from memory. Therefore, for example, even if a memory has characteristics that are typical of perceived events (e.g., visual detail), one might decide that the memory is not "real" on the basis of other knowledge one has (e.g., "I couldn't have seen the color of the thief's eyes because it was very dark outside and I saw him from a distance"). In addition, because source memory is the product of a judgment process, it can involve a variety of criteria and can be influenced by biases, metamemory assumptions, and current goals and agendas. So, for example, one might expect people to be more careful about the source of their memory when questioned by a police officer than when engaging in a casual conversation with a friend.

Finally, an important aspect of the source monitoring account is that people can mistake the origin of some item in memory even if memory for the item itself is very good. For example, one might be quite sure someone said there was an assassination attempt on the president, but be unsure which of two people said it. Consistent with this idea, several of the studies described in this chapter show that people can have highly accurate memories of the content of misleading suggestions yet misattribute their source.

EMPIRICAL EVIDENCE FOR SOURCE MISATTRIBUTIONS FOLLOWING MISINFORMATION

In order to illustrate the type of evidence we have garnered in support of the claim that subjects misattribute suggested items to the original event, we first describe a representative experiment from Zaragoza and Lane (1994, Expt. 3). We discuss the experiment in some detail because all of the studies to be reviewed here employed the same general experimental paradigm.

A Method for Assessing Source Misattributions

In this study subjects first viewed a series of slides depicting an office theft. Immediately following the slide sequence, subjects were exposed to misleading postevent information presented in the form of either (a) a narrative description of the event that subjects read (Narrative Group) or (b) questions about the event that subjects answered (Questions Group). For each subject, the postevent narrative/questions suggested 6 items that were not in the original slide sequence. Across the experiment a total of 12 items (objects) were used as misleading suggestions, but each subject was exposed to only 6 of these. For example, for some subjects the postevent information mentioned a *coat rack* when there was no coat rack in the original office scene. Note that this is a departure from many previous studies of suggestibility in that the misleading suggestions employed in this and all of the other studies we report *supplemented*, rather than contradicted, the events that subjects had actually seen. For subjects in the Questions condition who were misled about a coat rack, the misinformation was presented in the context of the following question that subjects were required to answer: ". . . As she gathered her purse and blue umbrella from a nearby *coat rack*, what was she preparing to do?" For the corresponding subjects in the Narrative condition, this misleading item was presented in the following statement embedded in the context of a paragraph that subjects read: ". . . As she gathered her purse and blue umbrella from a nearby *coat rack*, she was preparing to leave the office. Those subjects who were not exposed to misinformation about a coat rack (and hence for whom *coat rack* served as a control item) received the same question (or statement) with the exception that the word *coat rack* was deleted.

Source-Memory Groups. After a 10-minute filler task subjects received a source memory test. The test consisted of a list of 24 items presented via audiotape at a rate of one item every 8 sec. The test list consisted of the 12 critical items (6 suggested or read items and 6 control or new items) interspersed with 12 filler items (6 of which had appeared in the slides only, and 6 of which appeared in both the slides and the postevent narrative). The subjects' task was to indicate their memory for the source of each test item by selecting either "saw," "read," "both," or "new" as a response. Subjects were accurately informed that the test list contained items from each of the four categories. In other words, subjects were explicitly told that the postevent questions/narrative had mentioned items that were not in the slides they had seen, and that some of these items were in the test list.

The question of primary interest in this study was whether subjects would be more likely to incorrectly claim they remembered witnessing the critical items when they had been suggested to them than when they were new (i.e., when they served as control items). This source-misattribution error was measured as the proportion of times subjects claimed to remember seeing items they had not in fact seen by selecting either the "saw" or "both" response.

Standard Test Groups. In addition to the Question and Narrative source-memory groups described earlier we tested an additional two groups of subjects (half in the questions condition and half in the narrative condition) using the experimental procedure typically employed in studies of eyewitness suggestibility. We did so in order to assess how the goals and motivations of the rememberer might affect the accuracy of source monitoring. Recall that with the exception of the test phase, these subjects were treated identically to the source memory test subjects just described. At the time of test subjects were given the same list of 24 test items and simply told to indicate whether or not they remembered seeing the test items in the original event by responding "yes" or "no." Therefore, what distinguishes the standard procedure from the source-memory procedure is that in the former subjects are led to believe that the postevent information is an accurate description of the events they saw, and are never informed that the postevent questions/narrative contained information that was not in the original event. Hence, in the standard procedure subjects are not given any reason to distinguish between original and postevent information in memory, because they are led to assume that the postevent information corresponds to the events they witnessed. Moreover, the fact that subjects are not asked to make overt source judgments (i.e., choose among multiple possible sources) further discourages retrieval of source relevant information. For these reasons, we hypothesized that subjects would be more likely to claim they remembered seeing the suggested items in the standard test groups than in the source test groups.

Considering first the results of the Source test groups, we tested a total of 144 subjects, with half the subjects in the Questions condition and half the subjects in the Narrative condition. The leftmost panel of Fig. 17.1 shows the proportion of times subjects incorrectly claimed to remember seeing the suggested and control items (by selecting either the "saw" or "both" response). Of primary interest for present purposes was the finding that subjects were more likely to claim they remembered seeing the suggested items than the control items, although the magnitude of this *source-misattribution effect* (i.e., the difference in errors to suggested and control items) was greater in the Questions condition than in the Narrative condition. Post hoc analyses revealed that although the source misattribution effect obtained in the Questions condition was highly reliable, the effect observed in the Narrative condition did not reach statistical significance (see Zaragoza & Lane, 1994, for a more detailed discussion of these results). Therefore, the results demonstrate that subjects exposed to misleading suggestions in the context of questions they answered came to believe they actually remembered witnessing these items—a finding we have replicated in several other experiments (see, e.g., Zaragoza & Lane, 1994, Experiments 1 and 4). In contrast, exposure to misleading suggestions in the context of a narrative subjects read did not lead to a reliable source-misattribution effect, although in other experiments we have obtained evidence of small but reliable source-misattribution effects in narrative conditions (see, e.g., Zaragoza & Lane, 1994, Expt. 1). Putting aside for the moment the possible reasons for the differences between these two conditions, the results of this experiment show that source misattributions are a real, although not inevitable, consequence of exposure to suggestion.

In the standard test groups we tested a total of 120 subjects with equal numbers of subjects in the questions and narrative conditions. As illustrated in the rightmost panel of Fig. 17.1, there were striking differences between

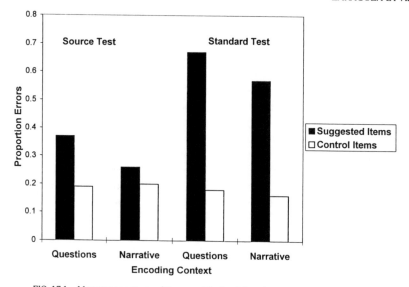

FIG. 17.1. Mean percentage of times subjects claimed to remember witnessing suggested and control items as a function of test condition (source or standard) and whether the suggestions had been encountered in the context of misleading questions or misleading narratives. From Zaragoza and Lane (1994, Experiment 3). © 1994 by the American Psychological Association, Inc. Adapted with permission.

performance in the source memory and standard test groups, with errors to suggested items in the standard test groups far exceeding those observed in the source-memory test groups. It is especially noteworthy that we found a robust misinformation effect in the narrative/standard test condition even though we failed to find evidence of a source-misattribution effect with the very same materials when subjects were tested in the context of the source test.

The contrast between performance in these two test conditions has several important implications. First, these results demonstrate that subjects' source-monitoring performance depends heavily on the specific demands of the retrieval environment. Clearly, the standard paradigm typically used in suggestibility studies greatly underestimates subjects' ability to discriminate between original and postevent sources of information. When subjects are motivated to make use of source information in memory (as in the source test conditions), they show significant improvements in source-monitoring ability. Finally, it should be noted that although the source-misattribution effect is highly reliable (see Zaragoza & Lane, 1994, Experiments 1–5) the magnitude of the effect is considerably smaller than the misinformation effects typically obtained with standard test procedures, a finding that is clearly illustrated in Fig. 17.1. Although these data do not permit clear inferences about the basis for the high incidence of errors in the standard condition, they are consistent with the notion that subjects tested under the standard procedure may report misinformation they know they do not remember witnessing at the original event.

The astute reader may have surmised that a possible reason for the differences between performance in the standard and source test conditions is the fact that the source test employed a four-alternative forced-choice format, whereas the standard test used a yes–no test format. We propose to the contrary that it is the differences in the demands of the retrieval environment, and not test format per se, that is responsible for the large differences in performance between the two sets of groups. In several different studies (Ackil & Zaragoza, 1995; Chambers & Zaragoza, 1993; Zaragoza & Lane, 1994, Experiment 5) we have used a source test with a yes–no format (i.e., subjects were asked two yes–no questions: "Did you see it in the video?" and "Did you read about it in the questions?") and we have nevertheless obtained source misattribution effects that are virtually identical to those obtained with the four-alternative forced-choice source test procedure. Therefore, our results suggest that source monitoring will improve under conditions that alert subjects to the need for retrieving source-relevant information, regardless of the format of the test (i.e., yes–no or forced-choice).

Confidence in Source Misattribution Errors

Although we have argued that the results of the foregoing experiment strongly support the claim that subjects come to believe they remember witnessing suggested items, there is a potential alternative explanation. In the source memory test we have described, subjects were forced to choose between one of four test alternatives: "saw," "read," "both," or "new." The potential problem with this test is that subjects who were unsure of the suggested item's source may have been likely to select the "both" response because this response category may have been perceived as a compromise option. Given that a "both" response is considered a source-misattribution error, the selection of this response category by subjects who were unsure of the suggested item's source may have artificially inflated the incidence of such errors.

To test this alternative explanation, Zaragoza and Lane (1994, Experiment 5) employed a test procedure where subjects were asked to rate their confidence in their source judgments, thereby giving subjects the opportunity to indicate when they were unsure about an item's source. Specifically, subjects were asked to answer two questions for each of the test items: (a) saw in slides? and (b) read in questions? Subjects indicated their responses to each question on a 7-point scale that had the following values: 1 = *definitely yes*, 2 = *probably yes*, 3 = *maybe yes*, 4 = *unsure*, 5 = *maybe no*, 6 = *probably no*, and 7 = *definitely no*. Therefore, another advantage of this test procedure is that it eliminated "both" as a response option. With the exception of the test format, subjects were treated identically to subjects tested in the other source test experiments described earlier.

The results provided strong evidence that subjects came to believe they remembered seeing suggested items. Specifically, even though a substantial proportion of subjects selected the "unsure" response, a robust source-misattribution effect comparable in size to that observed in other experiments was obtained. Collapsing across the 1, 2, and 3, responses to get an overall measure of "yes" responses to the "saw in slides" question, the results revealed that subjects were significantly more likely to claim they remembered seeing suggested items ($M = .42$) than control items ($M = .17$). Moreover, a substantial proportion of source misattributions to suggested items were accompanied by the highest confidence rating—the proportion of times subjects claimed they definitely remembered seeing the suggested items ($M = .24$) far exceeded the proportion of times subjects claimed to definitely remembered seeing the control items ($M = .06$). In sum, by demonstrating that a source-misattribution effect of comparable magnitude was obtained when a different test procedure was used, the results of this experiment provide clear-cut evidence for the validity and reliability of the source-misattribution effect (see Zaragoza & Lane, 1994, Experiment 5, for a more detailed discussion of this experiment).

In summary, the results of the experiments discussed thus far provide strong evidence that subjects sometimes come to believe they remember witnessing suggested items. In the next section, we discuss some of the encoding and retrieval factors that influence the incidence and magnitude of these effects. All of the experiments employed the same general experimental procedure we have already described.

The Role of Visual Imagery

According to the source monitoring model (e.g., Johnson et al., 1993), source-misattribution errors will be a function of the overlap between the memory characteristics of the original and suggested information. For example, reality monitoring studies have shown that subjects are more likely to confuse imagined items with perceived ones when the imagined items are similar to perceived items in sensory and perceptual detail (e.g., Johnson, Foley, & Leach, 1988). On this basis we predicted that memories of suggested items would be confused with perceived details to the extent that they include visual information (albeit imagined) about what the suggested details look like. The results of a study by Carris, Zaragoza, and Lane (1992) are consistent with this prediction (see Fig. 17.2). Specifically, subjects who were instructed to form a visual image of the events described in the misleading narrative were more prone to claiming they remembered seeing the suggested items

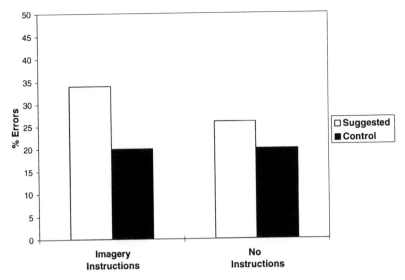

FIG. 17.2. Mean percentage of times subjects claimed to remember witnessing suggested and control items as a function of whether or not they were instructed to form a visual image of the events described in the postevent narrative.

than subjects who simply read the narrative (i.e., did not receive explicit instructions to imagine the events), even though there was a significant source misattribution effect in both groups.

Limiting Resources at Test

There is considerable evidence that retrieval of source relevant information is an effortful and attention demanding process (Begg, Anas, & Farinacci, 1992; Jacoby, Woloshyn, & Kelley, 1989; Johnson, Kounios, & Reeder, 1992). On this basis we (Zaragoza & Lane, 1991) assumed that severely restricting the amount of time subjects have to make a source judgment would render them less able to access the information they need to identify the test items' source, and would force them to base their source judgments on more accessible aspects of the target memory such as the item's familiarity. To the extent that subjects have a bias which leads them to assume that familiar items are items they have seen, we predicted that severely restricting the amount of time in which subjects have to make a source judgment would increase the incidence of source misattribution errors.

We tested these ideas in an experiment where one group of subjects was given 8 sec to make each source judgment (ample time) and another group was given only 3 sec to make each source judgment (minimal time). The results (see Fig. 17.3) revealed that although there was a significant source-

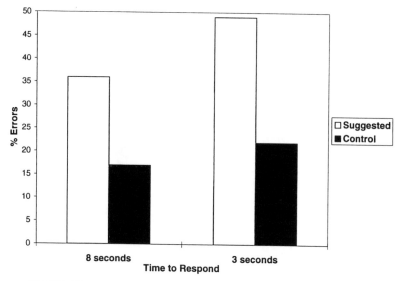

FIG. 17.3. Mean percentage of times subjects claimed to remember witnessing suggested and control items as a function of whether they were given 8 seconds or 3 seconds to make each source judgment.

misattribution effect in both groups, the magnitude of the source-misattribution effect was greater in the 3 sec group than in the 8 sec group, as evidenced by a significant interaction ($p < .05$). That is, severely restricting the amount of time subjects have to make source judgments led to a disproportionate increase in the errors committed to suggested items.

The results also revealed that although the 3 sec group committed more source misattributions, their old/new recognition of the suggested items (.84) was identical to that of the 8 sec group (by old/new recognition, we mean subjects' ability to recognize that the suggested item occurred in the experiment as evidenced by the subjects' ability to identify the item as one they either saw and/or read about). In sum, severely restricting time to respond at test selectively impaired retrieval of source relevant information, leaving recognition of the target item intact. This, in turn, led to an increase in the magnitude of the source misattribution effect under conditions of limited resources. These results parallel the finding by Jacoby, Woloshyn, and Kelley (1989) from a somewhat different domain that subjects' ability to make correct attributions about people's fame breaks down under conditions of limited attention.

The results reported underscore the important role that retrieval conditions play in the incidence and magnitude of source misattribution effects. These results demonstrate that the tendency to commit source misattribution can and does vary substantially simply as a function of the circumstances at recall. It is clear that a complete theory of source misattributions must ultimately explain the interaction between retrieval conditions and the memory characteristics of the underlying memory representations that support source monitoring judgments. In the next study we show how retrieval conditions can reduce source-misattribution errors.

Discrediting the Source of Suggested Information

In a recent experiment (Chambers & Zaragoza, 1993), we showed that source-monitoring performance improves when subjects are exposed to a cue that discredits the source of the suggestions in a highly salient manner. In this study subjects viewed a videotape of a police training film that depicted a house robbery and an ensuing car chase involving the police. The critical manipulation came after the subjects were misled. Half the subjects (discounting cue group) observed a male confederate, who was posing as a subject in the experiment, raise his hand and angrily state, "There were things in these questions that really weren't in the video, weren't there? You were trying to trick us, weren't you?" The experimenter responded by acting rather flustered and admitted that the questions did in fact contain phony information that was not in the video. The experimenter then informed the subjects that they were to proceed with the experiment anyway and gave subjects the source test. Subjects in the no discounting cue group were simply given the source test after completing the postevent questions.

We were somewhat surprised to find that discrediting the source of the suggested information did reduce the magnitude of the source misattribution effect (the groups differed in errors committed to suggested, but not control, items, $p < .05$; see the left side of Fig. 17.4). Although previous studies had shown that discrediting the source of the misleading suggestions prior to being misled reduces suggestibility (e.g., Dodd & Bradshaw, 1980; Greene, Flynn, & Loftus, 1982), this was the first study to demonstrate that discrediting information encountered *after* exposure to suggestion could induce resistance to suggestibility. It is worth noting, however, that although the discounting cue improved performance, it did not eliminate the source-misattribution effect altogether.

We (Chambers & Zaragoza, 1993) then conducted a second experiment that took its inspiration from the "sleeper effect" well known in the social persuasion literature. Studies of the sleeper effect have typically used a procedure where subjects read a message from either a highly credible source or a noncredible source. The usual finding is that subjects are persuaded by the argument when it is provided by a highly credible source, but are dissuaded by the argument when it is provided by a noncredible source. Of particular interest is the finding that after a delay, subjects in the low-credibility condition come to be equally persuaded as subjects in the high-credibility condition. One interpretation of the sleeper effect is that the source of the

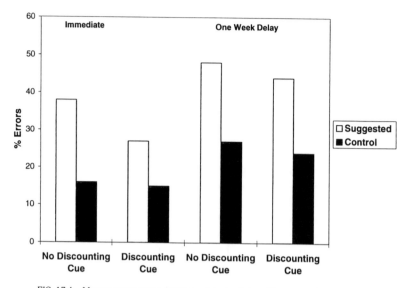

FIG. 17.4. Mean percentage of times subjects claimed to remember witnessing suggested and control items as a function of discounting cue condition (discounting cue or no discounting cue) and retention interval (immediate or 1-week delay).

message decays faster than the facts conveyed by the messenger (however, see Pratkanis, Greenwald, Leippe, & Baumgardner, 1988, for a critical analysis of this hypothesis). These findings suggested to us the possibility that although witnesses may be able to discount misinformation from a discredited source initially, the discredited misinformation may be a potent source of errors after a delay.

We tested this hypothesis in an experiment that was identical to the one just described except that subjects were tested on their memory for source after a 1-week retention interval (only the source test was administered after the retention interval; everything else, including the discounting cue, occurred in the first session). As revealed in the right side of Fig. 17.4, a very different pattern of results emerged when subjects were tested after 1 week. Although subjects in both groups made more errors to suggested items than control items, the magnitude of this effect did not differ as a function of group. Therefore, after a 1-week retention interval, the discounting cue had no effect.

The results also provided evidence consistent with the hypothesis that memory for the source of the suggested items decayed faster than memory for their content. Specifically, although subjects in the immediate test groups had good memory for having read about the suggestions, with the majority of subjects identifying the suggestion as coming from the postevent source (by claiming they read it or both read and saw it), there was a 50% decline in memory for having read the suggestions after the 1-week retention interval. Given that the discounting cue should be effective only to the extent that subjects can identify which items were from the postevent source, it is perhaps not surprising that the discounting cue was ineffective after the 1-week delay.

Developmental Differences in Source Monitoring and Suggestibility

Although laboratory studies of eyewitness suggestibility have established that children's testimony can be heavily influenced by misleading suggestions, these studies have failed to uncover a simple relationship between suggestibility and age (see Ceci & Bruck, 1993, for a review). What has emerged from this research is the understanding that suggestibility arises from a variety of cognitive and social factors, many of which interact with age. To date, research on the cognitive factors that underlie children's suggestibility has paralleled work with adults in that it has focused on the memory-impairment issue (Ceci et al., 1987a, 1987b; Toglia, Ross, Ceci, & Hembrooke, 1992; Zaragoza, 1987; Zaragoza et al., 1992). Unfortunately, attempts to investigate potential age differences in susceptibility to memory impairment have yielded inconsistent results, with contradictory findings across studies using extremely similar material and procedures (see Zaragoza et al., 1992, for a review).

Are young children especially likely to confuse suggested information for their "real" memories of a witnessed event? To our knowledge no studies have examined any age-related changes in the prevalence of this sort of memory error. Nevertheless, an answer to this question is central to the study of developmental differences in suggestibility and, ultimately, for assessing children's competence to testify.

Even though there is no research on children's ability to monitor the source of suggested information in an eyewitness sort of situation, we do know a fair amount about children's ability to make other sorts of source monitoring decisions (Johnson & Foley, 1984). In fact, research has shown that in many instances children are as accurate as older subjects at discriminating between the sources of their memories (e.g., Foley, Aman, & Gutch, 1987; Foley & Johnson, 1985; Foley, Johnson, & Raye, 1983; Johnson, Raye, Hasher, & Chromiak, 1979). For example, 6- and 7-year-olds are just as good as adults at distinguishing what they said from what they heard someone else say, at remembering which of two people said what, and at distinguishing words they actually heard from those they only imagined hearing. Nevertheless, 6-year-olds are more likely than 9-year-olds and adults to confuse what they said and what they imagined saying (Foley et al., 1983), and 6- and 9-year-olds are more likely than adults to confuse what they did and what they imagined doing (Foley & Johnson, 1985). By and large, age differences in source monitoring have been observed when children are asked to make discriminations between memories derived from similar sources. For example, when 4- to 6-year-olds are asked to remember which of two people said what, they have more difficulty than adults if the two people speaking share similar physical characteristics such as voice, gender, and appearance (Lindsay, Johnson, & Kwon, 1991). Similarly, 7- and 10-year-olds make more source confusions than adults when asked to remember what another person did and what they merely imagined that same person doing.

The typical eyewitness suggestibility situation also requires that subjects discriminate between memories derived from similar sources in that the suggested information and the actual eyewitness situation both refer to the same set of events. Therefore, it seems reasonable to hypothesize that there may be age-related changes in subjects' tendency to confuse their memories of suggested information for their memories of the actually witnessed event.

In a recent study (Ackil & Zaragoza, 1995) we reported the results of two experiments designed to assess whether young children are more likely than older children and adults to come to believe they remember witnessing suggested details. Because the two experiments were identical with the exception that one employed an immediate test and the other employed a 1-week retention interval before testing, they will be discussed together here.

The two experiments involved a total of 474 subjects from four age groups (with roughly equal numbers of subjects in each age × experiment condition): first grade, third grade, fifth grade, and college age. The eyewitness event was an 8-min video segment from a Walt Disney movie titled *Looking for Miracles*. The movie depicts the story of a young boy's experience at a summer camp where his older brother is a camp counselor. Immediately following the video, an experimenter verbally summarized the main events of the movie segment. Embedded within the summary were five suggested items or events. As before, the suggestions were designed to be plausible within the context of the video without contradicting or duplicating any details that were actually in the video. Following a short filler task, subjects in the first experiment were given the source-memory test by an experimenter who was different from the one who had provided the misleading summary (subjects in the second experiment returned 1 week later to take the source test). Before beginning the test we told subjects that the person who had summarized the video had made some mistakes, and that some of the things she talked about were *not* in the video they had seen. We then told subjects that we needed them to help us decide which things were in the video and which things were not. In this way, we hoped to motivate subjects to attend to source-relevant information in memory, and to eliminate any perceived demand to go along with the suggestions provided by the experimenter who summarized the video.

Figure 17.5 depicts the proportion of times subjects claimed to remember seeing the suggested and control items as a function of age and retention interval. We outline the major findings here. Overall, subjects were more likely to claim they remembered seeing critical items when they had been suggested to them than when they were new, as evidenced by highly significant source misattribution effects in both experiments (both $ps < .0001$). However, in both experiments, the magnitude of the source misattribution effect varied as a function of age, as evidenced by highly significant age × item type interactions at both retention intervals (both $ps < .01$). Planned comparisons confirmed that, in both experiments, there was a significant source-misattribution effect in every age group. Therefore, although there were age differences in suggestibility, no age group was immune to these errors.

Subsequent analyses confirmed that in both experiments first graders were more likely to claim they remembered seeing suggested items than all of the other age groups ($ps < .05$), even though they did not differ from the other elementary-school-aged groups in their tendency to claim they remembered seeing the control items ($ps > .05$). Hence, there was no evidence that the increased suggestibility of the first graders was related to a general tendency to claim they remembered seeing items they had not in fact seen.

The second source of age differences in suggestibility was the finding, in both experiments, that college-age subjects were less likely to claim they remembered seeing suggested items than all of the other age groups. There was some evidence that college-age subjects were also less likely to claim they remembered seeing the control items, although this effect reached statistical significance in experiment two only. It is nevertheless the case

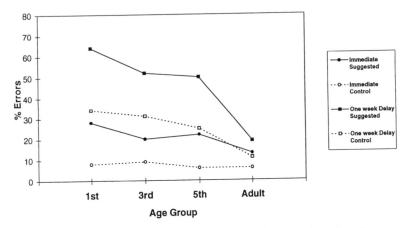

FIG. 17.5. Mean percentage of times subjects claimed to remember witnessing suggested and control items as a function of age group (1st, 3rd, or 5th grade, and adults) and retention interval (immediate or 1-week delay). From Ackil and Zaragoza (1995). © 1995 by Academic Press, Inc. Adapted with permission.

that in both experiments the magnitude of the source-misattribution effect was smaller for the college-age subjects than for the other age groups.

In order to determine whether the aforementioned developmental differences in suggestibility simply reflect a more general age-related memory deficit, we also assessed potential age-related differences in old/new recognition of suggested items. Old/new recognition of suggested items refers to subjects' ability to both (a) recognize that the suggested items were presented in the context of the experiment (by claiming they saw and/or heard it) and (b) recognize that the control items were never presented. From these data a d' score was computed for each subject as an overall index of recognition.

Although we found evidence of age differences in d' in both experiments, the pattern of recognition scores did not correspond with the pattern of age differences in suggestibility. An analysis of d' scores for subjects in Experiment 1 revealed that first graders had significantly poorer recognition than all of the other age groups, but that none of the latter groups differed from each other. In Experiment 2 the pattern of age differences in d' scores was somewhat different, with the college-age subjects performing better than all of the other age groups, but with none of the elementary-school-age groups differing from each other.

In sum, both experiments provided evidence of situations where source misattribution errors varied as a function of age and old/new recognition did not. Specifically, in Experiment 2 first graders made more source-misattribution errors to suggested items than the third- and fifth-grade subjects, even though their recognition of suggested items was as good as that of older children. Similarly, in Experiment 1, college-age subjects made fewer source misattributions than fifth-grade subjects, even though their recognition of suggested items was not better than that of the fifth-grade subjects. Taken together, the results show that source-misattribution errors are not simply another measure of memory for occurrence.

In summary, this study (Ackil & Zaragoza, 1995) is the first to provide evidence that young children are more susceptible to a serious memory error; namely, the tendency to believe they remember seeing details that were merely suggested to them. We want to emphasize, however, that no age group was immune to suggestibility errors, and as such the age difference is a relative one. Although the results of this study should be replicated and extended before firm conclusions about children's suggestibility can be drawn, the findings are consistent with the claim that young children's memories are more suggestible.

Our plans are to extend this work to situations involving live events that have greater personal relevance to the child and where misleading suggestions are provided in a context that better resembles an actual interview situation. We know from the literature on source monitoring in other domains that developmental differences in source monitoring appear and disappear as a function of the difficulty of the discrimination subjects have to make. To the extent that more naturalistic sorts of situations are likely to result in memories of original and postevent episodes that have more distinctive cues to source (both because there should be less overlap between the episodes when they are not two phases of a single experimental session, and because the more naturalistic context is likely to result in a richer array of contextual cues due to its higher interactional content), developmental differences may very well be minimized under such situations, at least in the short run. In addition, it will be important to investigate how the pattern of developmental differences interacts with variables such as repeated questioning over time (cf., Bruck & Ceci, chapter 16, this volume).

SUMMARY AND CONCLUSIONS

The research we have reviewed here provides strong evidence that misled subjects commit genuine source misattributions, and provides new information about the nature and incidence of these errors. Although there is still much to be learned about the mechanisms that give rise to source-misattribution effects, continued research along these lines promises to lay the groundwork for a general model of eyewitness suggestibility. Much of the theorizing about misinformation phenomena to date has centered on their implications for theories of forgetting (e.g., is originally stored information permanently lost as a consequence of misinformation, or is it merely rendered inaccessible?). Although it is certainly important to understand forgetting that results from exposure to suggestion, it is equally important to understand the inaccuracies in memory that exposure to suggestion may cause. The study of source misattributions provides one means of satisfying the need for theory development along these lines.

In addition to documenting a new phenomenon, the research reviewed here illustrates the application of a novel theoretical framework to the study of suggestibility phenomena, one that has proven very fruitful in understanding source monitoring in other domains (see Johnson et al., 1993; Johnson & Raye, 1981, for reviews). Traditionally, memory theorists have viewed "remembering" as a direct manifestation of a particular kind of memory representation. This is especially true in the study of misinformation phenomena, where the finding that subjects incorporate misleading suggestions into their testimony has been taken as evidence that the memory traces of the original and misleading episodes are integrated in memory, such that what remains is a single memory for the originally seen event (e.g., Loftus & Palmer, 1974). In other words, it has been assumed that distortions in testimony reflect distortions in an underlying trace. However, as we demonstrate in the studies presented here, the problem with this perspective is that it fails to take into account that the magnitude and incidence of these effects is heavily influenced by the retrieval context (e.g., the instructions at the time of test, the attentional resources available, the motivations and goals of the rememberer). In short, our results show that source-misattribution errors are as much a function of the circumstances at recall as they are a function of the underlying memory trace (see also Jacoby, Kelley, & Dywan, 1989). Therefore, one advantage of the "remembering-as-attribution" approach is that it accurately captures the dynamic nature of suggestibility.

Finally, we have shown that the source-monitoring approach has many advantages as a framework for studying children's suggestibility. A problem that has often plagued attempts to assess developmental differences in the suggestibility of memory is the fact that young children are more likely to conform to suggestions simply because of the perceived pressure to go along with an adult authority figure. Consequently, age differences in the tendency to report suggested information become very difficult to interpret. A clear advantage of the source test procedure is that it eliminates any demand to conform with the suggestion—if anything, it creates demand in the opposite direction. As we have shown, the source test procedure provides a relatively clean, unambiguous assessment of the extent to which children confuse misleading suggestions for events that they have actually witnessed. Moreover, this same approach has been successful in advancing our understanding of the development of other source monitoring skills, such as reality monitoring. For this reason we believe that the source-monitoring approach is an especially fruitful one that promises to provide a much clearer understanding of possible age-related changes in the suggestibility of memory.

ACKNOWLEDGMENTS

The research reported in this chapter was supported by NIMH grant MH47858 to Maria Zaragoza. We thank Karen Mitchell for helpful comments on an earlier version of this chapter.

REFERENCES

Ackil, J. K., & Zaragoza, M. S. (1995). Developmental differences in eyewitness suggestibility and memory for source. *Journal of Experimental Child Psychology, 60*, 57–83.

Begg, I. M., Anas, A., & Farinacci, S. (1992). Dissociation of processes in belief: Source recollection, statement familiarity, and the illusion of truth. *Journal of Experimental Psychology: General, 121*, 446–458.

Bekerian, D. A., & Bowers, J. N. (1983). Eyewitness testimony: Were we misled? *Journal of Experimental Psychology: Learning, Memory, and Cognition, 1*, 139–145.

Belli, R. F. (1989). Influences of misleading postevent information: Misinformation interference and acceptance. *Journal of Experimental Psychology: General, 118*, 72–85.

Belli, R. F., Lindsay, D. S., Gales, M. S., & McCarthy, T. T. (1994). Memory impairment and source misattribution in postevent misinformation experiments with short retention intervals. *Memory and Cognition, 22*, 40–54.

Belli, R. F., Windschitl, P. D., McCarthy, T. T., & Winfrey, S. E. (1992). Detecting memory impairment with a modified test procedure: Manipulating retention interval with centrally presented event items. *Journal of Experimental Psychology: Learning, Memory and Cognition, 18*, 356–367.

Bower, G. (1967). A multi-component theory of the memory trace. In K. W. Spence & J. T. Spence (Eds.), *The psychology of learning and motivation: Advances in research in theory* (Vol. 1, pp. 229–325). New York: Academic Press.

Bowman, L. L., & Zaragoza, M. S. (1989). Similarity of encoding context does not influence resistance to memory impairment following misinformation. *American Journal of Psychology, 102*, 249–264.

Carris, M., Zaragoza, M., & Lane, S. (1992, May). *The role of visual imagery in source misattribution errors.* Poster presented at the annual meeting of the Midwestern Psychological Association, Chicago, IL.

Ceci, S. J., & Bruck, M. (1993). The suggestibility of the child witness: A historical review and synthesis. *Psychological Bulletin, 113*, 403–439.

Ceci, S. J., Ross, D. F., & Toglia, M. P. (1987a). Age differences in suggestibility: Narrowing the uncertainties. In S. J. Ceci, M. P. Toglia, & D. F. Ross (Eds.), *Children's eyewitness memory* (pp. 79–91). New York: Springer-Verlag.

Ceci, S. J., Ross, D. F., & Toglia, M. P. (1987b). Suggestibility of children's memory: Psycholegal implications. *Journal of Experimental Psychology: General, 116*, 38–49.

Chambers, K. L., & Zaragoza, M. S. (1993, November). *The effect of source credibility and delay on eyewitness suggestibility.* Poster presented at the annual meeting of the Psychonomic Society, Washington, DC.

Chandler, C. C. (1989). Specific retroactive interference in modified recognition tests: Evidence for an unknown cause of interference. *Journal of Experimental Psychology: Learning, Memory, and Cognition, 15*, 256–265.

Christiaansen, R. E., & Ochalek, K. (1983). Editing misleading information from memory: Evidence for the co-existence of original and post-event information. *Memory & Cognition, 11*, 467–475.

Dodd, D. H., & Bradshaw, J. M. (1980). Leading questions and memory: Pragmatic constraints. *Journal of Verbal Learning and Verbal Behavior, 21*, 207–219.

Foley, M. A., Aman, C., & Gutch, D. (1987). Discriminating between action memories: Children's use of kinesthetic cues and visible consequences. *Journal of Experimental Child Psychology, 44*, 335–347.

Foley, M. A., & Johnson, M. K. (1985). Confusions between memories for performed and imagined actions: A developmental comparison. *Child Development, 56*, 1145–1155.

Foley, M. A., Johnson, M. K., & Raye, C. L. (1983). Age-related changes in confusion between memories for thoughts and memories for speech. *Child Development, 54*, 51–60.

Gibling, F., & Davies, G. (1988). Reinstatement of context following exposure to post-event information. *British Journal of Psychology, 79*, 129–141.

Greene, E., Flynn, M. S., & Loftus, E. F. (1982). Inducing resistance to misleading information. *Journal of Verbal Learning and Verbal Behavior, 21*, 207–219.

Gudjonsson, G. H. (1986). The relationship between interrogative suggestibility and acquiescence: Empirical findings and theoretical implications. *Personality and Individual Differences, 7*, 195–199.

Hammersley, R., & Reed, J. D. (1986). What is integration? Remembering a story and remembering false implications about the story. *British Journal of Psychology, 77*, 329–341.

Jacoby, L. L., Kelley, C. M., & Dywan, J. (1989). Memory attributions. In H. L. Roediger & F. I. M. Craik (Eds.), *Varieties of memory and consciousness: Essays in honor of Endel Tulving* (pp. 391–422). Hillsdale, NJ: Lawrence Erlbaum Associates.

Jacoby, L. L., Woloshyn, V., & Kelley, C. M. (1989). Becoming famous without being recognized: Unconscious influences of memory produced by dividing attention. *Journal of Experimental Psychology: General, 118*, 115–125.

Johnson, M. K., & Foley, M. A. (1984). Differentiating fact from fantasy: The reliability of children's memory. *Journal of Social Issues, 40*, 33–50.

Johnson, M. K., Foley, M. A., & Leach, K. (1988). The consequences for memory of imagining another person's voice. *Memory & Cognition, 16*, 337–342.

Johnson, M. K., Hashtroudi, S., & Lindsay, D. S. (1993). Source monitoring. *Psychological Bulletin, 114*, 3–28.

Johnson, M. K., Kounios, J., & Reeder, J. A. (1992, November). *Time course studies of reality monitoring and recognition.* Paper presented at the annual meeting of the Psychonomic Society, St. Louis, MO.

Johnson, M. K., & Raye, C. L. (1981). Reality monitoring. *Psychological Review, 88*, 67–85.

Johnson, M. K., Raye, C. L., Hasher, L., & Chromiak, W. (1979). Are there developmental differences in reality-monitoring? *Journal of Experimental Child Psychology, 27*, 120–128.

Kohnken, G., & Brockmann, C. (1987). Unspecific postevent information, attribution of responsibility, and eyewitness performance. *Applied Cognitive Psychology, 1*, 197–207.

Lindsay, D. S. (1990). Misleading suggestions can impair eyewitness's ability to remember event details. *Journal of Experimental Psychology: Learning, Memory, and Cognition, 16*, 1077–1083.

Lindsay, D. S. (1994). Memory source monitoring and eyewitness testimony. In D. F. Ross, J. D. Read, & M. P. Toglia (Eds.), *Adult eyewitness testimony: Current trends and developments* (pp. 27–55). New York: Springer-Verlag.

Lindsay, D. S., & Johnson, M. K. (1987). Reality monitoring and suggestibility: Children's ability to discriminate among memories from different sources. In S. J. Ceci, M. P. Toglia, & D. F. Ross (Eds.), *Children's eyewitness memory* (pp. 92–121). New York: Springer-Verlag.

Lindsay, D. S., & Johnson, M. K. (1989). The eyewitness suggestibility effect and memory for source. *Memory & Cognition, 17*, 349–358.

Lindsay, D. S., Johnson, M. K., & Kwon, P. (1991). Developmental changes in memory source monitoring. *Journal of Experimental Child Psychology, 52*, 297–318.

Loftus, E. F. (1975). Leading questions and the eyewitness report. *Cognitive Psychology, 7*, 560–572.

Loftus, E. F. (1977). Shifting human color memory. *Memory and Cognition, 5*, 696–699.

Loftus, E. F. (1979a). *Eyewitness testimony.* Cambridge, MA: Harvard University Press.

Loftus, E. F. (1979b). The malleability of human memory. *American Scientist, 67*, 312–320.

Loftus, E. F., & Hoffman, H. G. (1989). Misinformation and memory: The creation of new memories. *Journal of Experimental Psychology: General, 118*, 100–104.

Loftus, E. F., & Loftus, G. R. (1980). On the permanence of stored information in the brain. *American Psychologist, 35*, 409–420.

Loftus, E. F., Miller, D. G., & Burns, H. J. (1978). Semantic integration of verbal information into a visual memory. *Journal of Experimental Psychology: Human Learning and Memory, 4*, 19–31.

Loftus, E. F., & Palmer, J. E. (1974). Reconstruction of automobile destruction: An example of the interaction between language and memory. *Journal of Verbal Learning and Verbal Behavior, 13*, 585–589.

McCloskey, M., & Zaragoza, M. (1985a). Misleading postevent information and memory for events: Arguments and evidence against memory impairment hypotheses. *Journal of Experimental Psychology: General, 114*, 3–18.

McCloskey, M., & Zaragoza, M. (1985b). Postevent information and memory: Reply to Loftus, Schooler, and Wagenaar. *Journal of Experimental Psychology: General, 114*, 381–387.

Metcalfe, J. (1990). Composite holographic associative recall model (CHARM) and blended memories in eyewitness testimony. *Journal of Experimental Psychology: General, 119,* 145–160.

Pirolli, P. L., & Mitterer, J. O. (1984). The effect of leading questions on prior memory: Evidence for the coexistence of inconsistent memory traces. *Canadian Journal of Psychology, 38,* 135–141.

Pratkanis, A. R., Greenwald, A. G., Leippe, M. R., & Baumgardner, M. H. (1988). In search of reliable persuasion effects: III. The sleeper effect is dead. Long live the sleeper effect. *Journal of Personality and Social Psychology, 54,* 203–218.

Smith, V. L., & Ellsworth, P. C. (1987). The social psychology of eyewitness accuracy: Misleading questions and communicator expertise. *Journal of Applied Psychology, 72,* 294–300.

Toglia, M. P., Ross, D. F., Ceci, S. J., & Hembrooke, H. (1992). The suggestibility of children's memory: A social–psychological and cognitive interpretation. In M. L. Howe, C. J. Brainerd, & V. F. Reyna (Eds.), *Development of long-term retention* (pp. 217–241). New York: Springer-Verlag.

Tversky, B., & Tuchin, M. (1989). A reconciliation of the evidence on eyewitness testimony: Comments on McCloskey and Zaragoza. *Journal of Experimental Psychology: General, 118,* 86–91.

Wagenaar, W. A., & Boer, H. P. A. (1987). Misleading postevent information: Testing parameterized models of integration in memory. *Acta Psychologica, 66,* 291–306.

Zaragoza, M. S. (1987). Memory, suggestibility, and eyewitness testimony in children and adults. In S. J. Ceci, M. P. Toglia, & D. F. Ross (Eds.), *Children's eyewitness memory* (pp. 53–78). New York: Springer-Verlag.

Zaragoza, M. S., Dahlgren, D., & Muench, J. (1992). The role of memory impairment in children's suggestibility. In M. L. Howe, C. J. Brainerd, & V. F. Reyna (Eds.), *The development of long-term retention* (pp. 184–216). New York: Springer-Verlag.

Zaragoza, M. S., & Koshmider, J. W. (1989). Misled subjects may know more than their performance implies. *Journal of Experimental Psychology: Learning, Memory, & Cognition, 15,* 246–255.

Zaragoza, M. S., & Lane, S. (1991, November). *The role of attentional resources in suggestibility and source monitoring.* Paper presented at the annual meeting of the Psychonomic Society, San Francisco, CA.

Zaragoza, M. S., & Lane, S. (1994). Source misattributions and the suggestibility of eyewitness testimony. *Journal of Experimental Psychology: Learning, Memory, & Cognition, 20,* 934–945.

Zaragoza, M. S., & McCloskey, M. (1989). Misleading postevent information and the memory impairment hypothesis: Comment on Belli and reply to Tversky and Tuchin. *Journal of Experimental Psychology: General, 118,* 92–99.

Zaragoza, M. S., McCloskey, M., & Jamis, M. (1987). Misleading postevent information and recall of the original event: Further evidence against the memory impairment hypothesis. *Journal of Experimental Psychology: Learning, Memory, & Cognition, 13,* 36–44.

COMMENTARIES

18

WHOSE MEMORY IS IT?
THE SOCIAL CONTEXT
OF REMEMBERING

Tom Trabasso
The University of Chicago

Suppose that a child is being questioned by an adult about an experience. The adult asks questions in an effort to learn what the child "remembers." The child attempts to answer the questions. The child's answers constitute a *verbal account* of what may or may not have occurred. This *conversational situation* is common to a number of investigations of memory in this volume but may go unrecognized as such. For this reason alone, I have chosen conversational interaction as a context for discussion of issues and problems that pertain to the study of memory for everyday and emotional events. Although I pay particular attention to the co-constructive aspects of an adult interacting conversationally with a child in an effort to find out what the child "remembers," I touch on ideas, issues, questions, and problems raised in all chapters.

In experimental studies of this volume that focus on children as "subjects" of investigation (Brainerd; Goodman & Quas; Ornstein et al.; Peters; Zaragoza et al.; chapters 9, 11, 4, 15, and 17, this volume), the child is asked to "remember" an actual experience. The experiences are drawn, in several instances, from real-life occurrences: a routine visit to a doctor's office for an examination, a painful laboratory test, or a physically stressful event. In others, they are novel learning tasks that ask children to "remember" the content of what they experienced such as triplets of words or camping activities. The primary focus in these studies is on "accuracy." The central question is whether what the child "remembers" is "accurate" or is influenced by "misleading questions" or "confusion of sources." Accuracy, however, as Ross (chapter 3, this volume) indicated, is here operationally defined as how well what the child reports matches or approximates what and how the experimenter interprets the event. It is not possible to know what "veridical" means when the child underwent, say, an examination of her heartbeat. The child reporting "Then, the doctor listened to my heart" is a summary phrase of a complex set of activities and experiences on the part of the doctor and the child. It does not report in any detail what occurred. It is "accurate" because it matches the adult summary or "gist" of the event. "Veridicality" probably does not obtain either for more trivial tasks such as recalling three words on a card such as "orange," "fish," and "house." What the child is "remembering" is an answer to the experimenter's question of what were the words on the card, and not the details of what the child was asked to do, what the experimenter did, what the child did, who was there, what was the lighting of the room, and so on. What we are treating as "memories" are highly selected aspects of experience expressed as verbal reports in answers to questions about a past experience.

The fact that an adult is involved in experimental studies is treated as incidental. The "influence" of the experimenter is taken to be minimal. However, the context in which the "memory" of the child is assessed is a social and communicative situation. It involves someone asking the child questions. The child, in turn, responds to the questions. This question–answer exchange is one of the key units of a conversational interaction. Even though the experimental questions try to minimize influence by being "open-ended" (e.g., "Tell us what happened" or "Tell us what the doctor did"), they guide the child's search and select or constrain what the child reports. Asking a child to report on what happened constrains the child to use narrative forms to talk about the past and to focus on summary or referential states, events, and actions. When more highly constrained recognition probes of particular events are given as affirmation or negation questions (e.g., "Where did the doctor touch you?"), they provide detailed information that may assist the child in retrieval of some prior experience but they also communicate presuppositions (e.g., that the doctor touched the child), and, as such, impose demands of affirmation and compliance. Questions to remember are not neutral probes into the life of the child. They are, at best, attempts to obtain information that the child may have about a past experience. They do influence what and how much is reported. Their influence operates at retrieval and during the construction of a verbal report. In short, one major influence on the child's "memory" is what is asked and what the child "remembers" is not solely the child's creation.

In chapters that analyze conversations, per se (Ceci & Bruck; Fivush & Kuebli; chapters 16 and 10, this volume), transcripts of interactions are presented where an adult interviews and questions a child about a past event. These studies had the strongest influence on the theme of this chap-

ter and more will be said below about their context for the study of the
child's "memory." For the moment, these chapters represent an extreme
opposite of the experimental investigations in that they report on what
occurs during real life interviews or interactions where an adult collaborates
with a child on "remembering."

Other chapters in the volume fall somewhere in between the experimental question asking of children and the complex social interactions where
an adult seeks to find out what a child knows. In these investigations,
children and adult caregivers provide verbal accounts of what they experienced as an emotional or stressful event (Stein et al.; Folkman & Stein;
chapters 2 and 5, this volume). Here, too, the questioning begins with
"open-ended" procedures (e.g., "Tell us what happened") in an effort to
minimize the interviewer's influence. However, the questioning also moves
to more specific probes as in the experimental studies, asking questions
about the person's feelings, appraisals, and general coping (e.g., "How did
you feel?" or "What did you do? What did you want to do?") These kinds of
questions could produce verbal reports that involve appraisals or interpretations and renderings that occur at the time of reporting as well as at the
time of the original experience.

Few studies use "reconstruction" or "reenactment" as a procedure. The
only exceptions are those of Stein et al. (this volume) who varied the degree
to which children are allowed to act out their "memory" for emotional
events and Mandler and McDonough (chapter 6, this volume) who had
infants enact motor sequences as "imitation" after they observed the sequence performed by an adult. Because the enactment situation differs
substantially from what the child experienced or witnesses, the transformation from the originally experience to that which is reported is something
also accomplished at retrieval and is not, by definition, a veridical memory.
What the child reports can be influenced by attempts on the part of the
child to influence the interviewers and is clearly from the perspective of the
child. What the infant does is constrained by what objects are provided for
the infant, whether the infant understands that she is supposed to reproduce what was done in the order in which it was done, and what motor and
representational skills the infant has. In both cases, what is "remembered"
is reported or shown to adult observers. Anatomically correct dolls, cited
as a problem by Mason (chapter 13, this volume) and Goodman and Quas
(this volume), may be viewed as an attempt to use reenactment as a measure of memory, but this procedure with children 2 years of age and older
would be heavily laden with verbal communication and provides considerable opportunity for improvisation by the child (see later discussion).

As indicated at the outset, the conversational situation of remembering
by a child in collaboration with an adult serves as a referential source for
several issues and problems raised by authors throughout this volume. The

child may have had an experience that was shared with the adult, as was the case in the studies of real emotional experience of children reported by Fivush and Kuebli and by Stein et al. (both, this volume). It may be an experience observed or known by the experimenter as in the case of studies by Brainerd, Goodman, Ornstein et al., Peters, and Zaragoza et al. (all this volume). On the other hand, in the studies of Ceci and Bruck and Folkman and Stein (both this volume), the experience being reported was not known to the investigators or to anyone else other than the participant or participants until it was reported. Not knowing what occurred originally is the more likely state of the interviewer in cases where real life experiences are being reported. Where the experience is not known, the "remembering" may be based on an interpreted or imagined experience on the part of either of the participants, not just the one making the "memory" report. Issues of interpretation or encoding of the original experience (Ornstein et al.; Stein et al., this volume), false memories (Mason, this volume), suggestibility (Ceci & Bruck; Goodman & Quas; Ornstein et al.; Peters; Zaragosa et al.; all, this volume), lying (Ekman, chapter 14, this volume), fabrication and compliance (Ceci & Bruck, this volume), and veridicality (Ross, this volume) may all come into play.

In the study of memory, the focus is primarily on the individual person who is assumed to have or "possess" the memory. The question is: What does the person possess? The issues and concerns, not surprisingly, are with an individual's accuracy, suggestibility, lying, false memory, or veridicality. However, as the chapters by Ceci and Bruck and by Fivush and Kuebli (both, this volume) remind us, two or more people are involved in a communicative transaction. It is important to keep in mind that what is communicated is a product of mutual influences and constraints of the participants on one another, not only the questions asked but the participants' roles, knowledge, beliefs, convictions, values, social and personal relationships, linguistic competencies, and respective motivations. If each participant shared in the original experience, their perspectives and personal representations are likely to be different and would affect what is discussed during the "memory" conversation. Motivation always comes into play, be it to know, to assist, to withhold, to express, or to comply. Differences in knowledge about the events prior to the experience can affect both the initial interpretation of them and the subsequent remembering, as Ornstein et al.'s (this volume) studies demonstrate so well. The "memory product" is not one of merely encoding, storage, and retrieval of a particular, past event on the part of one person. The memory or, at least, its report, occurs in a social context that deeply influences what is co-constructed at retrieval (cf. Rogoff, Baker-Sennett, & Matusov, 1994). What is "remembered" may differ substantially from what was initially understood, encoded, represented, and stored about the experience by the child or the adult participant.

It is also important to keep in mind that it is the adult who is seeking *information* primarily, but not exclusively, by asking the child questions. This seeking of information involves various tactics and strategies of social influence by the adult. It also involves various tactics and strategies of children in dealing with another person in a conversation where questions are being asked. What the adult thinks is being asked does not necessarily correspond to what the child thinks is being asked (Siegal, 1991a, 1991b). If so, answers to questions are not what the adult believes them to be. For example, Siegal showed that if an question is repeated, the child thinks that something has changed in the situation and that the prior answer was not accepted by the adult. Siegal showed that if one asks the conservation question of volume ("Do the jars contain the same amount of water?") after rather than before and after pouring one jar into another, children answer the question appropriately. When the question is posed twice, once before the transformation and one after the transformation, they shift from "Yes" to "No" and seemingly "fail" the conservation test. This kind of implicit conversational demand leads to a biased view that children do not understand a concept when in fact they do.

The adult, who is seeking information, may "assist" the child in "remembering" by introducing information that is intended to serve as "retrieval cues" for the child. Although this information may well be used by the child as a retrieval cue to something that was stored and represented as a memory, the child may also use the new information to elaborate on the stored representation during the conversation in ways that depart from the child's original memory representation or at least from consensus on what occurred. The child may construct an imagined experience as the result of the new information introduced by the adult. If the adult asks "Did you put peanut butter on Kelly?" the child may interpret this question in line with a real experience, such as asking "Did you get peanut butter from Kelly?" or "Did Kelly put peanut butter on your bread?" If so, a "Yes" answer is a correct one for the child but a false one to the adult's interpretation of the question. Alternatively, in using the doll, the child might imagine putting peanut butter on Kelly (the doll) as a result of the question. This mental representation then becomes part of the conversational situation model for the child. If the adult then elaborates by asking where child put the peanut butter on her (referring to the doll who is supposed to represent Kelly), then the child might reply, "On eyes and mouth." The adult then asks if peanut butter was put somewhere else on the doll's body. The child might respond, "On her back and socks." And so the "game" continues. If the adult accepts the Gricean principle (Grice, 1975) that the speaker is telling the truth, then the adult might ask, "You put the peanut butter on her eyes, mouth, vagina, socks, and back?", accepting what the child has said as true but adding information not previously communicated by the child. Because

the affirmation–negation question contains many body parts already introduced by the child, one new body part introduced by the interviewer may
be accepted as part of the game of "Where Do We Put the Peanut Butter on
The Kelly Doll?". It becomes a simple matter within this frame for the child
to say "Yes." Although this might be a pretend game for the child, it is
serious business for an adult bent on seeking information that might convict
someone of a felony. In this kind of conversational pretend game, it is not
likely that the child understands the consequences of the answers to the
question for Kelly the doll or Kelly the real person. If several children share
these conversations with their parents, with themselves, or with a therapist,
a shared fantasy becomes a shared and dangerous reality to the person
being accused (cf. Mason, chapter 13, this volume).

Conversational interviews for a young child with an engaging and interested adult might well be a situation for pretend play of the type investigated
between children by Garvey (Garvey, 1974, 1979, 1982, 1984; Garvey & Berndt,
1977; Garvey & Kramer, 1989) and between adults and children by Leslie
(1987). The child may assume that when the adult refers to unusual events
such as adults "peeing" on one another or putting peanut butter on genitalia
or wiping "Doo-Doo" on faces that the adult is using indirect strategies for
an entry into a pretend frame in which a shared fantasy is to be elaborated
on by the child. Pretense is a major form of thinking and social interaction
and learning by children from 2 to 6 (Harris & Kavanaugh, 1993).

The power of pretense in conversational interaction with and between
children is not to be underestimated. The high frequency of false alarms in
the use of "anatomically correct" dolls (Ceci & Bruck; Goodman; both, this
volume) indicates that children may view these enactment situations as a
form of pretense rather than as a reference to some prior situation, especially if the prior situation did not occur. It certainly is not veridical, because
use of a toy or any object is an opportunity for pretense and for construction
of a meaning episode at the time of enactment and, at best, "stands for" a
past experience. Sympathetic and accepting adults, be they parent, therapist, or police investigator, may unwittingly enter into a pretend play frame
with the child. Once entered, they may unknowingly assist in the co-construction of an elaborate story about the imagined actions by the child or
by an innocent parent or nursery school teacher. The subtlety of entering
into and out of pretense in an conversational situation (cf. the volume edited
by Corsaro & Miller, 1992) with a child is likely to be lost on an adult intent
on gathering veridical information. The literature on social play in young
children and the role of conversational exchanges in this play is central to
understanding how children can fabricate an experience with the assistance
of an adult (see Sawyer, 1994, for an extensive review of this literature).

It is a mistake to assume that the ways children construe an event have the
same meanings as it does for adults. The use of "anatomically correct" dolls

can serve to illustrate differences in assumptions on the part of the adult and child. Adults are likely to assume implicitly that the child thinks of the doll as representative of themselves or another person in the original context. The child may not make this assumption of reference but may treat the doll as a pretend play object where anything might be tried or said within the limits of what the doll and other objects afford. If the child puts a pencil into the anus of the doll, this does not necessarily mean that the child is enacting a prior experience. Rather, the child might be exploring the parts of doll, especially those not normally shown, and does this by probing any orifice with a pencil. On the other hand, the child might be pretending to be a doctor who is examining the doll with a pencil but this pretense has little to do with what occurred between the doctor and the child in the examination room. If the adult unknowingly enters into the pretense frame and asks the child what else the doctor did, it would not be surprising within the pretend play frame for the child to insert the pencil in the mouth or nose or ear or anus or vagina of the doll. It is the gullible and biased adult who is "misled" into thinking that sexual activity of this nature occurred. The child is not lying in the sense that Ekman (chapter 14, this volume) defined it, because the child is not deliberately misleading the adult. The child is playing; the adult is misleading himself or herself by the adult preconceptions that are used to interpret the meaning of what the child does.

Through pretend play, the child may use the new information to begin a shared, conversational fantasy or fabrication with an unknowing but willing adult that results in the adult constructing a "story" that has no basis in fact. The child might begin to believe or be forced to justify a false memory of this sort as having happened, especially if the parent or interrogator persist, act as if they believe it, put demands on the child to be consistent, justify what occurred, or use collaborative statements from peers. If what the child reports is influenced *in any way* by the adult, then one has to ask "Whose 'memory' is it?" What is "remembered"? Better yet, what is constructed as a "memory" is not likely to be that of the child but that of a child in conversational collaboration with an adult. Fivush's (chapter 10, this volume; see also Fivush, 1989, 1991, 1993; Hudson, 1990) conversations have exactly this feel—the mother is so actively involved that one is uncertain whose memory is being constructed, the child's or the adult's or both the child and adult in a transaction. A substantial part of what is remembered, then, is likely to be what the child and the adult *co-construct* at the time of the interview rather than what was stored or not as an experience by the child.

Suppose that the adult and the child witness the same series of events as in the case of the child's visit to the doctor in Ornstein's experiments or in the emotional events reported on by Folkman and Stein (chapter 5, this volume) or in the studies of Fivush and Kuebli (chapter 10, this volume).

The latter two investigations show that differences in "memory" exist, despite common participation—the so-called Rashomon effect (Stein, Trabasso, & Liwag, 1994). The child's initial representation of what occurred may, in all cases, be very different from that of the adult. Ornstein, Shapiro, Clubb, Follmer, and Baker-Ward (chapter 4, this volume) differences in knowledge about medical examinations predict differences in "memory" as measured by the number of events recalled. In the Stein et al. studies, adults who differ from their children in memory for what is reported by the child express surprise and try to influence directly the child's memory by persistent questioning or attempts through retrieval cues. In the Fivush and Kuebli's (chapter 10, this volume) protocols, the mothers actively socialize the child about feelings and how to deal with them. In the Ceci and Bruck (chapter 16, this volume) protocols, the adults do not accept what the child says when it goes against what the investigator wishes to prove and the investigator introduces new concepts that implicate the accused (see further discussion on this kind of influence later). The differences in memory representations in general may lead adults to try, in subtle and in not so subtle ways, to persuade or influence the child on how one should interpret what occurred. In the case where the adult believes that something happened which may or may not have happened, the adult may be motivated to persuade the child that something occurred, not only by suggestion but by persistence in framing questions about the event contrary to the child's representation and by ignoring protests on the part of the child. If the adult wants the child to act or believe something to be the case, as occurs in socialization, then the adult will also be motivated to have the child adopt beliefs and values that were not present in the original context.

Another condition by which a child might be influenced by the adult's conversational input arises because the child does not remember much about a given experience. Given the extensive data in this volume on "forgetting" or failure to report information by children, fabrications and false reports may result from the child's failure to remember what occurred (this point was made by Brainerd and, in a different kind of context on adult bias in memory by Huttenlocher & Prohaska, chapters 9 and 7, this volume). When this occurs, the child may wish to appear as if he remembers and complies with the presuppositions of what the adult asks. A child who did not experience or did not "remember" experiencing sadness at a funeral may say that sadness was experienced it because the child thinks that what she or he should have experienced or that is what the adult wanted her or him to say. The high false-alarm rates in the studies of Ornstein et al. (chapter 4, this volume), Goodman (chapter 11, this volume), and Zaragoza, Lane, Ackil, and Chambers (chapter 17, this volume) may be a result of young children who willingly comply when they do not know or have forgotten or cannot retrieve that something happened.

Another source of misrepresentation of the child's memory can come from adult investigators and expert witnesses, who, in testifying about an interview with a suspect or witness, do not rely on video and cassette tape recordings of the conversation. Rather, they rely on notes of what occurred. They, in effect, construct a story about what occurred based on the adult's memory of the conversation with the child and the notes that they wrote down during the conversation. Because note taking is guided by what one knows or wishes to know, they can be a major source of selection as to who said what to whom. In this regard, imagine in the Wee Care Nursery School case, the investigator reporting that the child told him the following (please compare this to the transcript in Ceci and Bruck's chapter 16, this volume, pp. 380–381):

> The child told me that she (the child) *had to* use a big knife to put peanut butter and jelly *all over her body*, on *Kelly's* eyes, mouth, *vagina*, back, and socks. The children *had to* squeeze orange juice on her. Then, *everybody took it off* by licking her up and it *tasted* yucky. Kelly *made the children eat the peanut butter, jelly, and orange juice off the vagina*. It was *scary* for the children.

In this fabricated report, I have italicized those terms introduced into the conversation by the police interrogator and *not* by the child. Note that the police interrogator is the first one who asked what Kelly made the children do, whether the peanut butter was placed all over the body, and, in particular, on the vagina, how the children had to take it off, how it tasted, whether it was licked off the vagina, and whether it was scary. None of these ideas were introduced by the child, although, when introduced in the context of the child enacting with the doll, they are assented to by the child. Without the original testimony, however, how could one know what the child actually said, who initiated the concepts, and to what the child agreed to? Even with the transcripts, the reference may not be to Kelly the school teacher but Kelly the doll. This hypothetical account would have a very damaging effect on a defendant. However, I was easily able to concoct it from the "data" in the transcript. This kind of practice of selectively in recording and in reporting by police or therapists is highly probable. Because prosecutors treat such statements as "facts" about what was said to have occurred, it is a serious source of bias in trials.

RECOMMENDATIONS FOR FUTURE PRACTICES AND RESEARCH

Audio–Video Recordings of Interviews

All interviews with subjects in experiments or with potential witnesses should be recorded on audio and videotape, showing both the interviewer and the person being interviewed throughout the conversational interaction.

If all attempts at remembering were videotaped, we would have observational information on a memory as it is being co-constructed. As a result, a permanent, public record would be created of who said what to whom and how and when it was said.

These tapes would constitute a database for analyses of conversational interactions, assessment of the contribution of each participant to the "remembering," and other possible mutual influences by the participants on one another. In the event that the interview is of a potential witness, be it child or adult, tapes, transcripts, or both of the spoken dialogue could be made available to the prosecution and the defense in legal proceedings.

The value of a complete record is that testimony by witnesses could be corroborated. Accuracy, consistency, and attribution as to initiation of content could be determined. The possible influence of the interrogator on a child and the crucial information by the child witness might then be assessed with more confidence.

I am aware of client–therapist confidentiality, but in the event that a therapist is called in to obtain "facts" in an investigation, this privilege should be waived in the interests of fairness and accuracy of reporting. In cases where the therapist serves as an interviewer or interrogator, audio and video recording should be required by law.

Analysis of Conversational and Nonverbal Interactions

Systematic analyses of questions and information sources during testing and interviews should be carried out to reveal possible effects of co-constructive processes. For example, it would be a worthwhile exercise to score transcripts as to (a) who initiates key information in a question or in an answer, (b) what is the child's initial answer, (c) how often the answer is accepted or ignored, (d) whether the question is repeated, and (e) whether the child changes his answer. From these analyses, one could construct a "memory" representation that originates from the adult or from the child as well as agreements or disagreements of the child with the adult. Furthermore, it might be possible to trace the verbal reports of the same witness over more than one interview. Later interviews could show an influence of earlier ones. In this way, over a transcript or set of transcripts, one could show patterns of influence on what the child "remembers."

Individual Recall Prior to and After Co-Construction

To deal with the Rashomon effect and its possible influence in conversational interaction between adults and children in remembering, it is recommended that each party give an open-ended, "what happened," narrative account prior to the interaction. In legal contexts, this would ask that potential witnesses simply narrate what happened in a particular time and place before the interrogator intervenes with further questions. In conversational situations with parent and children, it means that each participant tell what happened in a particular time and place without prompting before the mother is asked to talk with the child about the experience.

If one had separate verbal reports by the mother and by the child, one could assess the mother's and the child's separate contributions based on their respective perspectives. One could also examine what the new information contributions of each party were as well as what emerges as a result of the interaction. Stein, Trabasso, and Liwag (1994) analyzed separate narratives of parents and children in terms of overlapping and different elements in this way.

If one asked the child and the interviewer to report what occurred in the conversational interaction, one could assess the resistance or assimilation by the child of the adult's suggestions. One could also assess possible bias on the part of the adult.

Children's Encoding of Events

One of the most serious problems facing our understanding of memory for everyday and emotional events, especially when adults impose their meanings and standards on what the child says in answer to memory questions, is information on how the child understood and encoded the event as it occurred—so called online comprehension. In our laboratory, we have used three procedures to find out how children interpret, represent, and encode events that they witness or read about. In one procedure, the child narrates a picture sequence, one picture at a time (Trabasso & Nickels, 1992; Trabasso & Rodkin, 1994; Trabasso & Stein, 1994; Trabasso, Stein, Rodkin, Munger, & Baughn, 1992). This online procedure allows the child to interpret what events are occurring as they are witnessed. The verbal protocols of the children reveal how they identify, describe, and explain what they see. These abilities develop substantially over the 3- to 5-year-old age range.

In a second procedure, the person reads one sentence at a time in a story that tells a sequence of events. The person is instructed to try to understand what it is that she is reading and to tell us what she understands (Suh & Trabasso, 1993; Trabasso & Magliano, 1996; Trabasso & Suh, 1993; Trabasso, Suh, & Payton, 1995; Trabasso, Suh, Payton, & Jain, 1994). This think-aloud procedure reveals inferences that are made about the events as they are comprehended. In the study by Trabasso et al. (1994), data show that 9-year-old children explain, associate, and predict information relevant to the events and show memory operations of maintaining or carrying over information from sentences or prior thoughts, retrieval of prior sentences and thoughts to explain (or associate and predict), and activation of relevant world knowledge for use in making inferences.

In a third procedure, an adult and a young child (5 years in age) interact in different ways over a trade book that contains brief, three-sentence texts supported by pictures on successive pairs of pages. In her PhD thesis, Lo (1995) used three such texts and carried out three different conditions on the same group of five-year-old children. In all three conditions, she read the text to the children. In a control, the child had a second reading and then "remembered" the text. In a question-answering condition, Lo asked questions after reading each brief text; in a co-construction condition, she engaged the child in a conversational interaction over the text and pictures. In the conversational exchanges, she asked questions, accepted answers, and elaborated text, pictures, or both. The child answered questions, initiated identification and elaborated the text, pictures, or both. Because all the children recalled all texts, it was possible to assess, within subjects, the effects of each condition on "remembering" the text. She found that question answering facilitated memory but that co-construction tended to lead to less of the text being recalled spontaneously. Children in the co-construction condition needed considerably more prompting during remembering. Current analyses of what was done during the interaction and what is "remembered" are being carried out at this time.

The Lo (1995) study has an advantage over that of the Fivush and Kuebli (this volume) and other mother–child "memory" studies (Fivush, 1989, 1991, 1993; Hudson, 1990) in that it varies the child over the same adult conversational participant. In the mother–child studies, there is only one dyad so that mother style and gender differences are confounded. If the children differ in what they know and understand, their effect on the adult conversational partner can be assessed. Lo, in fact, found that individual differences in memory were independent of what she did during co-construction.

Question Understanding

Research on how children understand questions is needed. Siegal (1991a, 1991b) has demonstrated powerful effects of the communicative context on inferences and conclusions that are drawn on the cognitive competence of children. In his investigations, considerable variance is accounted for by the kind and repetition of questions. In addition to the pragmatic considerations of the conversations that are addressed by Siegal, research is need on how questions reveal what a child understands, what the effect is of multiple questioning, how repeated questions alter what the child says, how new information is accepted or not by the child, and whether children are sensitive to changes, subtle or otherwise, in repeated questions. Ceci and Bruck's (chapter 16, this volume) work on therapist bias is a step in this direction and should help inform us on how therapists as expert witnesses may influence the "remembering" of the children they interview.

In addition to studying how children understand questions, it might be of value to understand how adults understand the same questions that are posed on the children. Differences in understanding would help us to guard against interpretation of what a child says from an adult perspective.

CONCLUDING COMMENTS

I am aware that I did not deal with the substantial findings of many of the chapters in this volume. My comments were strongly affected by those chapters that dealt with conversational interactions (Ceci & Bruck; Fivush & Kuebli; Folkman & Stein; Mason; Stein, Wade, & Liwag, all this volume). My intent was not to slight the clever experimental simulations of stressful everyday events and problems with children as witnesses. I felt that the conversational interactions were closer in spirit to what occurs when adults try to find out about another person's "memory" for everyday and emotional events. The Clarke-Stewart, Thompson, and Lepore (1989) study, cited by Ceci and Bruck (chapter 16, this volume) is one that should be repeated and emulated. Children's experiences with a real person in their world contexts provide experiences that would permit one to study both how children report "remembrances" and investigate possible influences of adult interviewers in contexts more closely approximating real life.

ACKNOWLEDGMENT

The writing of this chapter was supported by a grant to the author from the Spencer Foundation.

REFERENCES

Clarke-Stewart, A., Thompson, W., & Lepore, S. (1989, May). *Manipulating children's interpretations through interrogation.* Paper presented at Biennial Meeting of the Society for Research on Child Development, Kansas City, MO.

Corsaro, W. A., & Miller, P. J. (Eds.). (1992). *Interpretive approaches to children's socialization.* San Francisco: Jossey-Bass.

Fivush, R. (1989). Exploring sex differences in the emotional content of mother–child conversations about the past. *Sex Roles, 20*, 675–691.

Fivush, R. (1991). Gender and emotion in mother–child conversations about the past. *Journal of Narrative and Life History, 1*, 325–341.

Fivush, R. (1993). Emotional content of parent–child conversations about the past. In C. A. Nelson (Ed.), *The Minnesota Symposia on Child Psychology: Vol. 26. Memory and affect in development* (pp. 39–78). Hillsdale, NJ: Lawrence Erlbaum Associates.

Garvey, C. (1974). Some properties of social play. *Merrill-Palmer Quarterly, 20*, 163–180.

Garvey, C. (1979). Contingent queries and their relations in discourse. In E. Ochs & B. B. Schief-felin (Eds.), *Developmental pragmatics* (pp. 363–372). New York: Academic Press.

Garvey, C. (1982). Communication and the development of social role play. In D. Forbes & M. T. Greenberg (Eds.), *Children's planning strategies* (pp. 81–101). San Francisco: Jossey-Bass.

Garvey, C. (1984). *Children's talk.* Cambridge, MA: Harvard University Press.

Garvey, C., & Berndt, R. (1977). *The organization of pretend play.* Corte Madera, CA: Select Press.

Garvey, C., & Kramer, T. L. (1989). The language of social pretend play. *Developmental Review, 9,* 364–382.

Grice, H. P. (1975). Logic and conversation. In P. Cole & J. L. Morgan (Eds.), *Syntax and semantics, Vol. 3: Speech acts* (pp. 41–58). New York: Academic Press.

Harris, P. L., & Kavanaugh, R. D. (1993). Young children's understanding of pretense. *Monographs of the Society for Research in Child Development, 58*(1, Serial No. 231).

Hudson, J. (1990). The emergence of autobiographic memory in mother–child conversation. In R. Fivush & J. A. Hudson (Eds.), *Knowing and remembering in young children* (pp. 166–196). New York: Cambridge University Press.

Leslie, A. M. (1987). Pretense and representation: The origins of "theory of mind." *Psychological Review, 94,* 412–483.

Lo, D. (1995). *Social construction of meaning in story book readings with young children.* Unpublished doctoral dissertation, The University of Chicago.

Rogoff, B., Baker-Sennett, J., & Matusov, E. (1994). Considering the concept of planning. In M. Haith, J. Benson, B. Pennington, & R. Roberts (Eds.), *Future-oriented processes* (pp. 353–374). Chicago: University of Chicago Press.

Sawyer, R. K. (1994). *The performance of pretend play: Enacting peer culture in conversation.* Unpublished doctoral dissertation, The University of Chicago.

Siegal, M. (1991a). *Knowing children: Experiments in conversation and cognition.* Hove, England: Lawrence Erlbaum Associates.

Siegal, M. (1991b). A clash of conversational worlds: Interpreting cognitive development through communication. In L. B. Resnick, J. M. Levine, & S. Teasley (Eds.), *Perspectives on socially shared cognition* (pp. 23–40). Washington, DC: American Psychological Association.

Stein, N. L., Trabasso, T., & Liwag, M. (1994). The Rashomon phenomenon: Personal frames and future-oriented appraisals in memory for emotional events. In M. M. Haith, J. Benson, B. Pennington, & R. Roberts (Eds.), *The development of future-oriented processes* (pp. 409–435). Chicago: University of Chicago Press.

Suh, S., & Trabasso, T. (1993). Inferences during on-line processing: Converging evidence from discourse analysis, talk-aloud protocols, and recognition priming. *Journal of Memory and Language, 32,* 279–301.

Trabasso, T., & Magliano, J. (1996). How do children understand what they read and what can we do to help them? In M. Graves, P. van den Broek, & B. Taylor (Eds.), *The First R: A right of all children* (pp. 158–181). New York: Teachers College, Columbia University Press.

Trabasso, T., & Nickels, M. (1992). The development of goal plans of action in the narration of picture stories. *Discourse Processes, 15,* 249–275.

Trabasso, T., & Rodkin, P. C. (1994). Knowledge of goal/plans: A conceptual basis for narrating *Frog, Where are You?.* In R. A. Berman & D. I. Slobin (Eds.), *Relating events in narrative: A crosslinguistic developmental study* (pp. 85–106). Hillsdale, NJ: Lawrence Erlbaum Associates.

Trabasso, T., & Stein, N. L. (1994). Using goal/plan knowledge to merge the past with the present and the future in narrating events on-line. In M. M. Haith, J. Benson, B. Pennington, & R. Roberts (Eds.), *The development of future-oriented processes* (pp. 323–349). Chicago: University of Chicago Press.

Trabasso, T., Stein, N. L., Rodkin, P. C., Munger, G. P., & Baughn, C. (1992). Knowledge of goals and plans in the on-line narration of events. *Cognitive Development, 7,* 133–170.

Trabasso, T., & Suh, S. (1993). Understanding text: achieving explanatory coherence through on-line inferences and mental operations in working memory. *Discourse Processes, 16,* 3–34.

Trabasso, T., Suh, S., & Payton, P. (1995). Explanatory coherence in communication about narrative understanding of events. In M. A. Gernsbacher & T. Givon (Eds.), *Text coherence as a mental entity* (pp. 189–214). Amsterdam: John Benjamins.

Trabasso, T., Suh, S., Payton, P., & Jain, R. (1994). Explanatory inferences and other strategies during comprehension and their effect on recall. In R. Lorch & E. O'Brien (Eds.), *Sources of coherence in text comprehension* (pp. 219–239). Hillsdale, NJ: Lawrence Erlbaum Associates.

19

MEMORY AS KNOWLEDGE-BASED INFERENCE: TWO OBSERVATIONS

Gerd Gigerenzer

Max Planck Institute for Psychological Research, Munich

Nancy Stein opened her talk at the conference from which this volume stems with two bold statements. I could not find these as bluntly stated in her chapter (with Wade and Liwag, chapter 2, this volume), although they can be read between the lines. Therefore, I take the liberty to reconstruct these two statements from my notes and memory: "Before we will make any progress in the studies of memory and emotion, (a) we need to investigate the content of the information to be remembered, and (b) we need to understand memory as inductive inference." These two assertions are linked to each other. If memory is inductive inference, then such an inference about what happened in the past needs to be based on what one *knows* in the present. If memory is inferred from present knowledge, then the content of a memory task is crucial for performance indicators such as accuracy, because knowledge is content-specific. In this chapter, I elaborate on these two assertions.

THE DOCTRINE OF INFORMATION EQUIPOTENTIALITY

There are two opposing strategies for asking questions about the nature of memory, depending on how one handles content. These two ways are by no means peculiar to memory research; they are symptomatic of a more general, important conflict in cognitive psychology, behaviorism, and beyond.

The first strategy is to ask questions about memory processes or outcomes *independent of the content of the information* to be remembered. I will

445

label the underlying assumption *information equipotentiality*, in analogy to B. F. Skinner's doctrine of *stimulus equipotentiality*, which assumes that all stimuli can be treated as interchangeable for the purpose of designing the laws of conditioning. For instance, several contributors to this volume who are concerned with the accuracy of memory ask questions that implicitly assume information equipotentiality: Is children's recall under stress less accurate than that of adults? Are children more suggestible, and to what degree? Is less information encoded when arousal is high? These questions are about the amount of information remembered and about accuracy measured in terms of misses or false alarms, and they have in common that they treat the content of the information as interchangeable. The questions ask "how much" rather than "what" information.

The second strategy mistrusts information equipotentiality. Its goal is to design theories about how memory is inferred from what one knows about the kind of information in question. This view needs to address the question of how the mind categorizes the *particular* information to be recalled into a *kind* of information, which I will call a *domain*. We do not yet seem to understand well what these domains are, but we do have examples and hypotheses. A particular information to be remembered (e.g., "Did the doctor check your temperature?") may be inferred by the child by mapping the particular event into a larger domain, such as "visiting the doctor." What the child knows about the domain at the time of recall can be used to infer what actually happened. In this view, measures of accuracy will depend on the domain of content and on what a person knows about that domain. This view has two consequences. First, "how much" questions about accuracy, such as those mentioned earlier, seem to have little promise for making progress. Second, once knowledge about particular domains is included, motivation and emotion associated with the domain can no longer be excluded. If a child is asked to remember what her rival sibling has done to her before she hit him over his head, the emotions and motives that are part of sibling interactions are integral parts of a behavioral domain. Therefore, abandoning the doctrine of information equipotentiality invites the researcher to cross the fenced territories in which psychology has become divided up—reasoning, motivation, and memory, as well as others.

The contributors to this volume are divided between, and sometimes seem torn inbetween, these two ways of posing questions to nature.

Most of the hundreds of studies on children's eyewitness testimonies in the 1980s and 1990s have had relatively little concern over the content of the memory; that is, *what* is remembered. Typically, the accuracy of memory for things (as opposed to actions), of details (as opposed to a story line or a narrative structure), and of peripheral events (as opposed to central events) has been measured (see Ceci & Bruck, 1993). Consider, as an example, the question "Does stress have an effect on the encoding of information?" In the fire-alarm study (Peters, chapter 15, this volume), 10 seconds after the alarm was triggered, a female confederate entered the testing room, appearing anxious and very concerned about the alarm. After the alarm was turned off, the children's memory, including the effect of misleading information, was tested; however, memory of what information? Some questions asked were whether the girl wore glasses on her face, carried a cup in her hand, or what color her sweater and her hair was. These details seem arbitrary, exchangeable, and peripheral to the situation from the children's point of view. They are not of functional importance; that is, not relevant for an appropriate action in a potentially dangerous situation. A fire alarm might focus children's attention to verbal and nonverbal signals from their parents (who were present)—rather than to the color of a girl's sweater—in order to find out whether to worry or cry, and what to do.

Now, there is a good reason why peripheral details of things are studied. The testimony about circumstantial evidence may play an important role in legal trials—the color of a T-shirt, the shape of spectacles. However, if the accuracy of memory depends on *what* information is encoded or retrieved, because memory is knowledge-based inference, then posing research questions that treat information as of one kind will most likely lead to inconsistent results.

What is the evidence on information equipotentiality in children's recall? Ornstein et al. (chapter 4, this volume) have analyzed *what* children recall from a physical examination, and found that accuracy depends highly on the content of the examination. Recall values at the initial interview varied between 93% for blood test and 0% for the pediatrician's check of the wrist. In addition, there seemed to be an interaction over time: After 6 weeks, it was the prize that was most frequently remembered. That is, depending on what information one looks, one can claim anything from impressive accuracy of children's memory to total inaccuracy (here: misses). Other studies seem to confirm the dependency of memory processes and accuracy of the kind of information (see Ross, chapter 3, this volume; Stein, Trabasso, & Liwag, in press).

The Larger Context of the Information Equipotentiality Doctrine

A historical perspective may help to place this pressing issue in memory research in a larger context. In this century, logic and mathematics are prime examples of content-independent theories. This was not always so. *Mixed mathematics*, a term derived from Aristotle's explanation of how harmonics and optics mixed the forms of mathematics with the matter of sound and light, had no existence independent of its subject matter (Gigerenzer et al., 1989). For instance, Euclidean geometry once described the space we live in and probability theory once described the intuitions reasonable humans have. In the late 19th and early 20th centuries, however, these systems had been divorced from their original subject matter and exist now as theories that may apply to any content, or even for none.

Piaget assumed that this development in the history of science—from mixed mathematics to pure mathematics—is recapitulated in ontogeny. Children's cognitive operations are first attached to concrete contents, and by the stage of formal operations, the child finally is assumed to be able to use operations in a content-independent way. Piaget's doctrine that cognitive processes finally become independent of any content is shared or implicitly assumed by many. Examples abound in research on deductive and probabilistic reasoning (note that even these research categories are logical categories and as such, content-independent). Like in logic, where it does not matter whether a syllogism is about white and black swans, or something else, in many contemporary cognitive theories content does not matter much either. For instance, it makes no difference for Johnson-Laird's (1983) mental models whether they deal with beekeepers and artists or something else, and only a little for Tversky and Kahneman's (1980) heuristics and biases whether Bayes' theorem is about blue and green taxicabs or something else.

Mainstream behaviorism used to be built on a similar doctrine. Skinner's laws of operant conditioning were designed to be content-independent; that is, to hold true for all stimuli and responses (the notion of the "equipotentiality" of stimuli). The experiments by Garcia (Garcia & Koelling, 1966) and his colleagues showed the limitations of this approach. For instance, when the taste of flavored water was repeatedly paired with electric shock immediately after tasting, rats had great difficulty ever learning to avoid the flavored water. However, in just one trial the rat can learn to avoid the water when the aversive stimulus is experimentally induced nausea (even with 2 hours delay) rather than electric shock. Stimulus equipotentiality, the law of contiguity, and other content-independent principles have turned out to be empirically inadequate in behaviorism. It is ironic that the doctrine survived the cognitive revolution and now flourishes in cognitive science. Domain-specificity, as in mixed mathematics, however, has reemerged in cognitive science, such as in expert systems, cognitive development, and evolutionary views of cognition (Cosmides & Tooby, 1992; Gigerenzer & Hug, 1992; Hirschfeld & Gelman, 1994).

KNOWLEDGE-BASED INDUCTIVE INFERENCE

The theoretical challenge posed by the many interesting facts reported in this volume is to design models that specify how memory "jumps" from the present knowledge about a domain to the particular past event. Nancy Stein's and my personal bias is to assume that the mechanism of this "jump" is some form of inductive inference.

For instance, Ornstein et al. (chapter 4, this volume) reported that those events in individual checkups which correspond to the child's knowledge about what generally happens in a pediatrician's examination are remembered better and more consistently by the child. Children's recall seems to be here, to some substantial degree, inductive inference based on knowledge about what usually happens. The research by Ornstein et al. and others demonstrates that knowledge matters for memory. However, what exactly does the mechanism of the inductive inference involve? How is knowledge about what generally happens in a pediatrician' s examination transformed into a recall of the particular event? Here we seem to be far from having an answer, much less an algorithm.

Reiteration and Belief. I comment here on one particular cue on which inductive inferences about the truth of observations and assertions can be based: reiteration. David Hume and David Hartley had postulated that the repeated correlation of sensations produced associations of ideas; the more frequent and constant the observed correlations, the stronger the mental associations and beliefs. This link between frequency and belief applies to the repetition of assertions as well (e.g., Hasher & Zacks, 1979) and has been labeled the reiteration effect (Hertwig, Gigerenzer, & Hoffrage, in press). The reiteration effect describes how mere repetition of an assertion, independent of its actual truth or falsity, can increase one's confidence that the assertion is actually true. Thus far, however, the effect concerns only confidence, not recall. Hertwig et al. (in press) have proposed a theoretical model of how the reiteration effect merges with the hindsight bias to produce systematic changes in recall. This model applies to the situation in which subjects recall their initial reports rather than an external reality (Ross, chapter 3, this volume), and may be useful for understanding the conditions under which witnesses change their memory without noticing it.

Thus, there are two ways in which reiteration seems to be used more or less automatically as a cue in inductive inference. First, mere repetition of an assertion (e.g., by an interviewer) tends to increases the listener's (e.g., witnesses) confidence in the truth of the assertion; second, repetition and feedback about the truth of an assertion tends to change the memory of the listener as to what she had believed earlier. The change in memory is larger if the feedback confirms rather than disconfirms the original belief (Hertwig et al., in press).

There is a third way in which reiteration can function as a cue for inferring the past. This third way concerns the repetition of *questions* rather than *assertions*. The repetition of a question, in particular by a person with higher social status, can be a powerful cue for indicating to the listener that his answer was either wrong or inappropriate. Again, this is not a new insight; it was well known by the mathematicians in the 17th and 18th century for whom the trustworthiness of eyewitness testimony was a big topic (Daston, 1988). They weighed the testimony of witnesses according to their legal status. For instance, at times, two full witnesses were needed to convict a defendant. Women and children did not count as full witnesses, but only as fractions. The mathematicians took into account that the reports of minors often resulted from a combination of intimidation and inference.

Ceci and Bruck (1993, chapter 16, this volume) pointed out the intimidation combined with the repetition of questions by some interviewers in the Wee Care investigation, the case of 26-year-old nursery school teacher Kelly Michaels, who was accused and convicted of sexually abusing children at the Wee Care Nursery School. The Wee Care interviews contain many instances of the same or similar questions repeated when a child denied abuse or after a child disagreed with the interviewer's hunch:

Q: Did you ever have to kiss her vagina?
A: No.
Q: Which of the kids had to kiss her vagina?
A: What's this?
Q: No that's my toy, my radio box. Which kids had to kiss her vagina?
A: Me.

In general, the repetition of questions as well as of interviews tends to change a child's report. Grice's conversational axioms could provide a basis for modeling the functional significance of reiteration in a conversation between speakers with different status and power.

Postscript: Methodological Observations

Statistical Rituals. Some chapters in this volume perform what Luce (1988) called *mindless hypothesis testing.* Mindless hypothesis testing is mechanical null-hypothesis testing: Testing only a null hypothesis (e.g., no difference between two groups), and basing conclusions on whether a result comes out significant on the 5% level or not. Adherents of this method typically do not construct substantive theories of some depth, do not specify precise alternative hypotheses, do not predict or measure effect sizes, do not calculate the power of their tests to guard them against Type-II errors, and above all, replace good statistical reasoning with mechanical behavior. This ritual is—contrary to what statistical texts written by psychologists often suggest—alien to the sciences and amusing to the contemporary statistician. Rituals can hurt the respectability of otherwise good research. If you are still in the ritual, read Bakan (1966), Gigerenzer et al. (1989) or Gigerenzer (1993).

A Tendency Toward Inductivism. Francis Bacon might have enjoyed some of the chapters in this volume for the very reason that they collect mere observations without merging these with some "idol" or pet theory. Karl Popper, in contrast, who taught us to construct rich theories that have surprising ("bold") predictions, used to demonstrate to his students that mere induction based on neutral observation is a fiction. In his lectures, he asked his students to take paper and pencil and to write down everything they observed. They could not do it. "What should we look for?" his students asked.

Observations that are not connected with a causal structure, such as a story or theory, tend to be forgotten, unless they are baffling like visual illusions (Stein et al., chapter 2, this volume). Similarly, data in memory research that are not connected with a causal theory are likely to be rapidly forgotten. Data without theory have a low life expectancy, like a baby without a parent.

Let me summarize. Further studies are needed, true. More important, however, more theoretical courage is needed.

REFERENCES

Bakan, D. (1966). The test of significance in psychological research. *Psychological Bulletin, 66*, 423–437.

Ceci, S. J., & Bruck, M. (1993). Suggestibility of the child witness: A historical review and synthesis. *Psychological Bulletin, 113*, 403–439.

Cosmides, L., & Tooby, J. (1992). Cognitive adaptions for social exchange. In J. H. Barkow, L. Cosmides, & J. Tooby (Eds.), *The adapted mind: Evolutionary psychology and the generation of culture* (pp. 163–228). New York: Oxford University Press.

Daston, L. J. (1988). *Classical probability in the Enlightenment.* Princeton, NJ: Princeton University Press.

Garcia, J., & Koelling, R. A. (1966). The relation of cue to consequence in avoidance learning. *Psychonomic Science, 4*, 123–124.

Gigerenzer, G. (1993). The superego, the ego, and the id in statistical reasoning. In G. Keren & G. Lewis (Eds.), *A handbook for data analysis in the behavioral sciences: Methodological issues* (pp. 311–339). Hillsdale, NJ: Lawrence Erlbaum Associates.

Gigerenzer, G., & Hug, K. (1992). Domain-specific reasoning: Social contracts, cheating, and perspective change. *Cognition, 43*, 127–171.

Gigerenzer, G., Swijtink, Z., Porter, T., Daston, L., Beatty, J., & Krüger, L. (1989). *The empire of chance: How probability changed science and everyday life.* Cambridge, England: Cambridge University Press.

Hasher, L., & Zacks, R. T. (1979). Automatic and effortful processes in memory. *Journal of Experimental Psychology: General, 108*, 356–388.

Hertwig, R., Gigerenzer, G., & Hoffrage, U. (in press). The reiteration effect in hindsight bias. *Psychological Review.*

Hirschfeld, L. A., & Gelman, S. A. (1994). *Mapping the mind. Domain specificity in cognition and culture.* Cambridge, England: Cambridge University Press.

Johnson-Laird, P. N. (1983). *Mental models.* Cambridge, England: Cambridge University Press.

Luce, R. D. (1988). The tools-to-theory hypothesis. Review of G. Gigerenzer and D. J. Murray, "Cognition as intuitive statistics." *Contemporary Psychology, 32*, 151–178.

Stein, N. L., Trabasso, T., & Liwag, M. (in press). The Rashomon phenomenon: Personal frames and future-oriented appraisals in memory for emotional events. In M. Haith (Ed.), *Future-oriented processes*. Chicago, IL: University of Chicago Press.

Tversky, A., & Kahneman, D. (1980). Causal schemas in judgments under uncertainty. In M. Fishbein (Ed.), *Progress in social psychology* (pp. 49–72). Hillsdale, NJ: Lawrence Erlbaum Associates.

CHILDREN'S EYEWITNESS MEMORY RESEARCH: IMPLICATIONS FROM SCHEMA MEMORY AND AUTOBIOGRAPHICAL MEMORY RESEARCH

William F. Brewer
University of Illinois at Urbana–Champaign

BASIC VERSUS APPLIED RESEARCH

One of the fundamental themes that runs though the literature on children's eyewitness memory research is a conflict between basic research and applied research (cf. Ceci & Bruck, chapter 16, this volume). Researchers coming out of a basic research tradition (such as myself) have a tendency to believe that the solution to applied problems is to work out the basic laws in the laboratory and then apply those laws to the practical problem at hand. However, it seems to me that the actual history of the relations of science and technology show that the relationships are much more varied and complex than the view just outlined.

Temporal Order

In the history of science and technology, applied solutions were sometimes developed before the relevant basic science was understood. For example, animal breeding was developed before genetics, and bridge building before physics. However, on other occasions the science came first and the technology second. For example, nuclear physics preceded the development of nuclear energy, and solid-state physics preceded the development of the transistor.

Knowledge Transfer

The relationships between basic science and technology in terms of knowl-edge transfer show the same diversity. Some areas of science have little impact on applied issues (e.g., modern cosmology). Other areas of science show a direct one-way transfer (e.g., the impact of Newtonian mechanics on space probe navigation), whereas other areas of science show two-way interactions between science and technology (e.g., research on superconduc-tivity). One finds the same patterns when one looks at technology. Some aspects of technology have little impact on basic science (e.g., current refinements on the internal combustion engine). Occasionally, there is a one-way transfer from technology to science (e.g., the discovery of the cosmic background radiation while trying to eliminate noise from radio antennas).

Implications for Eyewitness Research

What are the implications of these historical examples for the area of chil-dren's eyewitness memory research? First, given the diversity of the histori-cal relationships it seems clear that we should be suspicious of any writer who *proscribes* a particular relationship for this area.

It seems to me that currently there has been relatively limited interaction between the basic research on memory and the applied studies of children's eyewitness memory. I see few indications that the eyewitness researchers have been applying the basic research. For the most part, these researchers have been working very hard to develop experimental paradigms that mimic important aspects of real-world situations involving children's memory and testimony in legal settings. Similarly, I see few examples of information from the applied work influencing basic memory research.

However, research on the applied problems of children's eyewitness memory reports is a relatively immature area, and the relationships between basic and applied work may change. In fact, this chapter is an attempt to bring some basic research to bear on the issues of children's eyewitness memory research.

ECOLOGICAL VALIDITY

Another theme that runs though discussions of the child eyewitness litera-ture is the problem of ecological validity. I take "ecologically valid" research to be research that uses tasks that are similar to some real-world situation along dimensions that the researcher thinks are theoretically important. The goal of designing ecologically valid research is to reduce the size of the inductive leap in going from the results of the study to the target phenomena in the real world.

An issue that becomes tangled up with ecological validity is the issue of laboratory versus nonlaboratory research. I personally do not see a problem here. In science our goal is to develop explanatory theories and gather data to test these theories. One of the great insights of the scientific revolution was that theories could be tested with laboratory experiments that controlled unwanted variables. I cannot believe that any modern researcher wants to give up this insight.

However, note that some phenomena do not lend themselves easily to laboratory research. For example, astronomy developed into a very successful science without the benefit of laboratory control of its objects of investigation. Astronomers to this day are troubled by the problems of working in a nonlaboratory environment (e.g., cloudy nights). The same thing is true in psychology. Some tasks simply do not lend themselves to the laboratory. For example, one cannot ethically study flashbulb memory in the laboratory, so researchers have been forced to use more ecological techniques of gathering data (cf. Winograd & Neisser, 1992), with the accompanying problems of lack of experimental control. Certain types of child eyewitness phenomena also cannot be studied in the laboratory, and much of the research in this area in the last 5 to 10 years has involved finding naturally occurring events (e.g., dentist visits, inoculations) that could be used to investigate children's memory in more ecologically valid situations.

Another aspect of this problem is that one cannot know, a priori, how well a given theory tested in the laboratory will apply to a particular real-world problem. For example, it turns out that the laws Galileo developed with the nonecological task of rolling balls down an inclined plane apply very well to objects dropped on the surface of the moon and apply fairly well to lead spheres dropped on the earth, but do not apply as well to balls of wadded up paper dropped on the earth. The validity of laws developed in the laboratory simply have to be worked out for each real-world phenomenon.

Researchers in the area of human memory have good reason to be cautious on this issue. For many years laboratory studies of human memory used nonsense materials in order to gain better experimental control over the phenomena. However, in the last 25 years we have come to realize that the research paradigms used in those studies excluded phenomena such as the role of knowledge and linguistic structure in human memory. Therefore, the findings derived from these laboratory studies did not apply well to most real-world memory tasks, where knowledge and linguistic factors play an enormous role.

The issue of making the leap from empirical studies to the relevant real-world phenomena is crucial for research on child eyewitness memory. Most of the work in this area is directed at the applied problem of determining the validity of child witness testimony in courts of law. This is a very important problem in current society and one in which it is important to be very certain of the validity of the inferential leap from the research studies to the applications in the real world.

I had not read the recent research on child eyewitness testimony before being invited to this conference on everyday and emotional events. I was actually quite impressed with the literature on the issue of ecological validity. It appears that Goodman (1984; Goodman, Aman, & Hirschman, 1987) initially raised consciousness on this issue by criticizing the earlier laboratory-based work as not ecologically valid with respect to the real-world phenomena of child witness testimony. Then Goodman (Goodman et al., 1987; Goodman, Hirschman, Hepps, & Rudy, 1991; Goodman & Reed, 1986; Rudy & Goodman, 1991; Saywitz, Goodman, Nicholas, & Moan, 1991), Peters (1987, 1991b, chapter 15, this volume), and Ornstein (Baker-Ward, Gordon, Ornstein, Larus, & Clubb, 1993; Ornstein, Gordon, & Larus, 1992; Ornstein et al., chapter 4, this volume) all began playing "ecological poker"—"I'll match your ecological design and raise you one more point of ecological validity with my new design." This poker game has reduced the inferential leap needed to generalize this memory research to the real world through the use of more realistic stimuli, more realistic experimental manipulations, and more realistic time intervals. It appears that Ceci (Bruck, Ceci, Francoeur, & Barr, 1995; Ceci & Bruck, chapter 16, this volume; Ceci, Leichtman, & White, in press) has raised the ante one more time by including multiple leading questions during memory retrieval. In general, I think these researchers ought to be pleased with the progress that they have made toward the study of more ecological tasks. It seems to me that the inductive leap is much reduced from the situation of only 10 years ago. However, later in this chapter I argue that some important aspects of the real world situations are still not being captured by the current experimental designs.

REPEATED EVENTS AND TYPES OF AUTOBIOGRAPHICAL MEMORY

There is a distinction among types of memory that has been made in the autobiographical memory literature that I think may have important implications for the study of child eyewitness memory. In my 1986 paper on the nature of autobiographical memory, I argued that one must distinguish between personal memory and generic personal memory (I now use the terms *recollective memory* and *generic recollective memory*).

Recollective Memory

Recollective memory is memory for a particular episode from an individual's life (cf. Brewer, 1986, 1996). It typically appears to be a "reliving" of the individual's phenomenal experience during that earlier episode and almost always includes reports of visual imagery. It is experienced as occurring at a unique time and place, often accompanied by a belief that the recollective memory is a veridical record of the originally experienced event. Thus I have a recollective memory of parking my car the first day of the Everyday and Emotional Event Conference and then walking into the lobby of the conference hotel.

Generic Recollective Memory

A generic recollective memory is a generic memory produced by having experienced a number of similar individual episodes. It frequently includes generic visual imagery and is not experienced as representing a unique event from the individual's life. For example, I have a generic recollective memory of sitting in a dark, wood-paneled room at the University of Chicago at a U-shaped table with the other members of the conference listening to someone talk. I am not recollecting a specific moment at the conference (such as the moment Nancy Stein got up to give the welcoming speech), but am having a generic recollection of my repeated experiences over several days.

Repetition and Memory

What are the implications of these distinctions for research on children's eyewitness memory? A number of researchers in the area of children's eyewitness memory have stated that repetition leads to improved memory (e.g., Brainerd & Ornstein, 1991, p. 16; Davies, 1991, p. 183; Goodman & Helgeson, 1988, p. 112). The assertion that repetition improves memory is probably a reasonable conclusion from the laboratory situation in which the exact same stimuli can be presented to the subject over and over again.

However, this is one of those instances where there is a disanalogy between the laboratory paradigms and the real-world phenomena of interest. In the real world, events are rarely repeated exactly. For example, think of the repeated instances of having a physical exam. Over the course of a number of physical exams the medical personnel are likely to vary, the examining room is likely to vary, the particular tests and the order of the tests is likely to vary. In the real world, repetition typically means repetition with variation. This difference between exact repetition in the laboratory and repetition with variation in the real world has important implications for human memory.

Dual-Process Theory

Both Linton (1982, p. 79) and I (Brewer, 1986, p. 45, 1988, p. 76) have argued that in autobiographical memory, repetition improves generic memory for events, but impairs memory for the instances. In my 1986 paper I stated this dual-process theory of repetition as "repetition of events leads to the development of generic personal memories at the expense of the individual personal memories that were repeated" (p. 45).

The data from my study of randomly selected events from the lives of undergraduates (Brewer, 1988) provides considerable empirical support for the dual-process theory. This study showed that by far the best predictor of event memory was event and location frequency. Rare events and rare locations showed much better memory than did instances of repeated events and locations. This finding is strong evidence that event repetition leads to impairment of memory for individual autobiographical events.

Real-World Situation

One of the frequent types of cases that involve child testimony are cases of repeated sexual abuse. If the dual-process theory of repetition is correct, then the child may have a strong and accurate generic recollective memory of the events, but a relatively poorer ability to recollect any one incident. This leads to an important conflict between the way human memory works and the current requirement of the legal system that the child testify about a particular incident.

Child Eyewitness Memory Research

This discussion of types of autobiographical memory also suggests one aspect of current child eyewitness studies that is not ecologically valid. Most child eyewitness studies involve a single event that is to be recalled later and thus the data may not be valid for an important subset of real-world cases (i.e., those involving frequently repeated events). See Goodman et al. (1987, p. 19) for a similar suggestion.

SCHEMA RELATIONS AND HUMAN MEMORY

Tenpenny and I have carried out a series of experiments (Brewer & Tenpenny, 1991, in preparation) that attempt to work out the consequences for memory of the various ways in which information can be related to some form of generic knowledge structure (schema). This work is an extension of an earlier schema memory framework outlined in Brewer and Nakamura (1984). I think that the data and the theory in these papers can be used to explain some of the apparently inconsistent data in the child eyewitness literature.

Three Types of Schema Relations

We argue that a new piece of information can have three basic relations with a schema.

Schema Consistent. A schema-consistent item is an item that would be expected given knowledge of a particular schema. For example, in the context of a doctor's physical exam, the information that "The doctor listened to the child's heart with a stethoscope" is schema consistent.

Schema Irrelevant. A schema-irrelevant item is an item that is not expected but not inconsistent with a particular schema. For example, in the context of a doctor's physical exam, the information that "The doctor tied his shoe" is schema irrelevant.

Schema Inconsistent. A schema-inconsistent item is an item that is incompatible with a particular schema. For example, in the context of a doctor's physical exam, the information that "The doctor rolled a bowling ball" is schema inconsistent. We argue that schema inconsistency is not a problem for schema theory as has been suggested by some (e.g., Alba & Hasher, 1983). Instead, we point out that inconsistency must be a part of schema theory, given that most cases of inconsistency in the real world are schema-based. Note that in the physical exam example, there is nothing intrinsically odd about rolling a bowling ball; in fact, carrying out this action would be expected at a bowling alley. It is the occurrence of this action in the context of a physical exam schema that makes it inconsistent.

Schema Relations and Memory Performance

The data that Tenpenny and I have gathered suggest that the various schema relations give rise to different levels of memory performance for recall and recognition testing. A general account of these findings is given in Table 20.1.

TABLE 20.1
Memory Performance for Presented and
Nonpresented Items for Different Schema Relations

Information Originally Presented (Test Items)		
Schema Relations	*Recall*	*Recognition*
Consistent	(apparently) good	poor
Irrelevant	poor	fairly good
Inconsistent	good	very good

Information Not Originally Presented (Foil Items)		
Schema Relations	*Recall*	*Recognition*
Consistent	many intrusions	poor
Irrelevant	rare	fairly good
Inconsistent	rare/never	very good

SCHEMA MEMORY AND CHILD EYEWITNESS DATA

Testing Present Information

Schema Consistent. A number of the studies in the child eyewitness area involve memory for visits to a doctor—an activity for which young children probably already have a reasonably developed script (cf. Clubb, Nida, Merritt, & Ornstein, 1993). These studies have tended to show that children have fairly good memory for the visit (Baker-Ward et al., 1993; Ornstein et al., 1992; Saywitz et al., 1991).

Studies of memory for scripts (i.e., schema for a repeated event) are complex and hard to interpret. Graesser (Graesser & Nakamura, 1982; Graesser, Woll, Kowalski, & Smith, 1980) has argued that the apparently good memory in script memory experiments is an illusion. He pointed out that in recalling scripted material subjects often make script intrusions. In a recognition task they often select nonpresent script foils. Therefore, much of the apparent superiority shown in script memory experiments may not be true episodic recall, but may simply be due to information already present in the subject's long-term memory.

We (Brewer & Tenpenny, 1991, in preparation) have pointed out that to clarify these issues one must distinguish between an abstract script item (e.g., "The nurse gave the child a treat") and an instantiated script item (e.g., "The nurse gave the child a sticker of a unicorn"). The data in Brewer and Tenpenny show that memory for abstract script information is relatively poor, whereas memory for instantiated script information is relatively good. Thus, if a child eyewitness researcher carries out a study of a scripted activity such as a doctor visit and then receives a positive answer to the question "Did the doctor look in your ears?", it is not clear if this response shows memory for the specific visit being tested or simply reflects the child's long-term knowledge about what goes on during doctor visits. Note that Ornstein and his coworkers (Baker-Ward et al., 1993; Ornstein et al., chapter 4, this volume) have been sensitive to this problem and have developed several lines of evidence to suggest that the children in their studies are showing true episodic memory for the event being tested.

Schema Inconsistent. Ornstein (Ornstein et al., 1992) found good recall of the schema inconsistent event of a doctor taking a Polaroid picture during a physical exam. This is in agreement with our finding that recall of schema inconsistent information is good. We argue that the good recall is produced by attention processes being directed at the inconstant information that results in attaching the information to the underlying schema structure.

Testing Absent Information

Schema Consistent. As discussed earlier, the work of Graesser and others (Graesser & Nakamura, 1982; Graesser et al., 1980) shows that if subjects in a script memory task are presented with an abstract script item that was not present in the original stimuli they will show a high degree of false alarms (i.e., poor memory performance).

Schema Inconsistent. Brewer and Tenpenny (1991, in preparation) have shown that in a script memory task if subjects are presented with a script-inconsistent item that was not present in the original stimuli they show a strong ability to reject the foil (i.e., good memory performance). We argue that subjects' performance is due to their ability to use a metamemory process ("If that item had occurred I would have noticed it and recalled it—I do not recall it, so it must not have occurred"). My ecological study of memory for rooms provides additional evidence for this metamemory strategy (Brewer & Treyens, 1981, pp. 220–221). In that study, subjects showed a strong ability to reject foils that were highly salient or highly schema inconsistent, thus strongly suggesting that they were using the metamemory strategy.

Eyewitness Studies. The schema-theory analysis just outlined may help resolve some of the controversies in this area over the quality of children's memory in naturalistic settings (e.g., Goodman, 1991; Peters, 1991a).

Goodman and Reed (1986, p. 326) have noted that children (over age 5) rarely give schema-inconsistent information in free recall. This is in keeping with the schema framework, which predicts few recalls of nonpresent schema inconsistent information. One presumes that many other studies in this area have data relevant to this issue, but have chosen not to mention it because it would amount to saying that something you would not expect did not occur. However, this experimental condition has extremely important analogs in real-world cases of child testimony and so ought to be included in discussions of child eyewitness free-recall data.

In studies of children's eyewitness memory three very different types of probe/recognition memory tasks have been used to examine children's memory: (a) questions with incorrect presuppositions, (b) questions about nonpresent, schema-consistent information, and (c) questions about non-present, schema-inconsistent information. Unfortunately, at various times all three types of probes have been referred to as "misleading questions."

The effects of the use of postevent questions containing presuppositions have been well studied. This type of biased question typically leads to impaired memory performance for children (e.g., Ceci, Ross, & Toglia, 1987; Cole & Loftus, 1987).

There have been fewer child eyewitness studies that have asked children about nonpresent, schema-consistent information. However, this condition has been studied under several labels (Baker-Ward et al., 1993, *absent feature*; Ornstein et al., 1992, *intrusions*; Ornstein et al., chapter 4, this volume, *absent feature*). All of these studies show a moderate degree of false alarms (i.e., moderate memory performance). As discussed earlier, the laboratory studies with adults using verbal materials typically show high false alarms for abstract script items and low false alarms for instantiated script items. Therefore, if the items used in the child eyewitness studies were a mixture of abstract script and instantiated script items, the data are roughly as would be expected.

A number of studies in the child eyewitness literature have asked questions about nonpresent, schema-inconsistent information (Baker-Ward et al., 1993; Goodman et al., 1987, 1991; Ornstein et al., chapter 4, this volume; Rudy & Goodman, 1991). The questions used in these studies are items such as, "Did the nurse sit on top of you?" These studies are consistent in showing few false alarms to nonpresent, schema-inconsistent items and thus are in agreement with the Brewer and Tenpenny schema framework.

Note that this analysis of the child eyewitness literature in terms of the schema memory framework gives a partial account of the disagreement between Goodman (1991) and Peters (1991a) over the general accuracy of children's memories in naturalistic experiments. Peters, who has argued that children do make a considerable number of errors in naturalistic memory tasks, has typically used questions with incorrect presuppositions (Peters, 1991b, chapter 15, this volume) and has interpreted his data as favoring his position. Goodman, who has argued that children make relatively few errors in naturalistic memory tasks, has typically used nonpresent, schema-inconsistent questions (Goodman et al., 1987, 1991; Rudy & Goodman, 1991) and has interpreted her data as supporting her position. The current analysis of these tasks suggests that each side has been obtaining the expected data on memory accuracy, but that the choice of type of "misleading" question used in their respective experiments have led to at least a part of the apparent inconsistency in their results.

Goodman has often used abuse-related, schema-inconsistent items (e.g., "Did the [nurse] hit you?") and has interpreted the low rate of false alarms as due to the fact that these items "violate [children's] concerns" about their bodies (Goodman, Rudy, Bottoms & Aman, 1990, p. 279). It should be easy to test Goodman's account versus the more cognitive account given in this chapter. The two views can be tested by carrying out a standard doctor-visit study and then asking two types of schema-inconsistent questions: (a) bodily concern items (e.g., "Did the doctor stick his finger in your eye?") and (b) nonbodily concern items (e.g., "Did the doctor stand on his head?"). The bodily concern hypothesis predicts that children will be particularly good at rejecting the first type of question, whereas the schema account predicts that the children will be quite good at rejecting both types of items.

Several authors (e.g., Peters, 1991a; Steller, 1991) have criticized Goodman for using schema-inconsistent items because these questions bias the data in the direction of showing that children have accurate memories. Although I differ with Goodman's interpretation of her data, I strongly agree with her in believing that this type of question is of crucial ecological importance and should be asked. In questioning a child about a single (nonrecurring) instance of physical or sexual abuse, it is vital to know what the base rate is for answers to this type of question, so that one can know how to interpret the answers of a possibly abused child who may (or may not) have experienced an event that is inconsistent with his or her past experience.

Overall, this analysis of the child eyewitness literature in terms of schema memory theories suggests that it might be quite productive for researchers in this area to systematically include the various forms of schema relations in ecological child eyewitness studies. One would like to have data on the impact of these schema relations on children's memory in a variety of ecologically valid situations.

The second point brought up by this analysis is that it is crucial to assess the child's knowledge about the ecological task being studied. One cannot carry out an analysis of the schema relations unless one knows the current state of the subject's knowledge. In laboratory studies using undergraduate subjects it is usually clear what schemata the subjects are bringing to the experiment, but with young children this may not be so obvious (see Clubb et al., 1993, for an example of the type of work needed).

OVERALL IMPLICATIONS FOR CHILD TESTIMONY

The application of the dual-process theory of repetition to children's memory suggests that children may have a strong generic memory for a repeated event, but more limited memory for the individual events that led to the generic memory. It would thus appear useful if the legal system would allow reports of generic memory into court testimony.

Our examination of child eyewitness memory suggests that children's memory does not show any qualitative differences from adult memory. It therefore seems unreasonable for the courts to arbitrarily exclude the testimony of children below a certain fixed age. It would appear that the decision to exclude the testimony ought to be made on an individual basis, taking into account what is known about child memory in naturalistic settings.

The finding that children rarely make schema-inconsistent recalls and give relatively few false recognition responses to nonpresent, schema-inconsistent information needs further investigation and elaboration. Once there is a firm baseline on this issue then the data can be used in legal settings to evaluate the veracity of children's reports of schema-inconsistent information.

This analysis suggests that individuals dealing with children's testimony should have information about the background rate of children's knowledge of relevant schemata and should try and ascertain what information about relevant schemata is known by the particular child who is testifying. For example, note the impact of explicit television reporting and drama and recent attempts to make children more aware of potential sexual abuse. In earlier periods, when this type of information was withheld from children, one would have been more confident in assuming that a child reporting some aspect of adult sexual behavior was recalling valid, schema-inconsistent information. However, now the case would not be so clear.

A final suggestion relates to the problems of the impact of previous interviews on the child's current memory reports. When the chemists are concerned that something they have found might be due to impurities or other problems in their techniques, they run a chemically pure blank through the chemical process. If one of their reagents is impure it will contaminate the blank, and they will know that the original finding was in error. It seems to me that we can use a similar procedure to examine the problems that may arise when children are exposed to multiple (biased?) interviews before a crucial recall. One can select some nonoccurring event that is similar to the actual event in which one is interested and then treat it just as the experimental event is treated. The overall rate of erroneous recall or recognition of the control event should give a fair index of the degree to which the previous questioning is distorting the child's memory.

In the usual circumstances of child testimony many of the adults interviewing the child have to assume that some unlawful event may have occurred and feel that it is their job to get a possibly reluctant child to tell them about the event. Under these conditions it seems quite likely that the interviewer is going to ask leading questions. However, if it became standard procedure to ask about some nonoccurring event (e.g., "Daddy let you drive his car to the store, didn't he?") with the same frequency and intensity as those about the suspected event, there could be two important consequences. First, one would have information for each individual child on the degree to which the child's memory for the nonoccurring event was distorted, and that could be compared with the information obtained on the suspected event. Second, the professionals who interview children would obtain feedback on the degree to which their interview techniques were producing distortions and they could modify their procedures accordingly.

CONCLUSIONS

In this chapter I have attempted to use certain findings from basic research on human memory to derive some consequences for the practical problem of assessing the memory of children giving court testimony. To the degree that I have been successful, this chapter can be considered a demonstration of how basic research can inform work in this area.

REFERENCES

Alba, J. W., & Hasher, L. (1983). Is memory schematic? *Psychological Bulletin, 93*, 203–231.

Baker-Ward, L., Gordon, B. N., Ornstein, P. A., Larus, D. M., & Clubb, P. A. (1993). Young children's long-term retention of a pediatric examination. *Child Development, 64*, 1519–1533.

Brainerd, C., & Ornstein, P. A. (1991). Children's memory for witnessed events. In J. Doris (Ed.), *The suggestibility of children's recollections* (pp. 10–20). Washington, DC: American Psychological Association.

Brewer, W. F. (1986). What is autobiographical memory? In D. C. Rubin (Ed.), *Autobiographical memory* (pp. 25–49). Cambridge, England: Cambridge University Press.

Brewer, W. F. (1988). Memory for randomly sampled autobiographical events. In U. Neisser & E. Winograd (Eds.), *Remembering reconsidered: Ecological and traditional approaches to the study of memory* (pp. 21–90). Cambridge, England: Cambridge University Press.

Brewer, W. F. (1996). What is recollective memory? In D. C. Rubin (Ed.), *Remembering our past: Studies in autobiographical memory* (pp. 19–66). Cambridge, England: Cambridge University Press.

Brewer, W. F., & Nakamura, G. V. (1984). The nature and functions of schemas. In R. S. Wyer, Jr., & T. K. Srull (Eds.), *Handbook of social cognition* (Vol. 1, pp. 119–160). Hillsdale, NJ: Lawrence Erlbaum Associates.

Brewer, W. F., & Tenpenny, P. (1991, July). *The role of schemas in the recall and recognition of episodic information.* Paper presented at the International Conference on Memory, Lancaster University, Lancaster, England.

Brewer, W. F., & Tenpenny, P. L. (in preparation). *The role of schemata in the recall and recognition of episodic information.*

Brewer, W. F., & Treyens, J. C. (1981). Role of schemata in memory for places. *Cognitive Psychology, 13*, 207–230.

Bruck, M., Ceci, S. J., Francoeur, E., & Barr, R. (1995). "I hardly cried when I got my shot!": Influencing children's reports about a visit to their pediatrician. *Child Development, 66*, 193–208.

Ceci, S. J., Leichtman, M. D., & White, T. (in press). Interviewing preschoolers: The remembrance of things planted. In D. P. Peters (Ed.), *The child witness in context: Cognitive, social, and legal perspectives.* Dordrecht, The Netherlands: Kluwer.

Ceci, S. J., Ross, D. F., & Toglia, M. P. (1987). Suggestibility of children's memory: Psycholegal implications. *Journal of Experimental Psychology: General, 116*, 38–49.

Clubb, P. A., Nida, R. E., Merritt, K., & Ornstein, P. A. (1993). Visiting the doctor: Children's knowledge and memory. *Cognitive Development, 8*, 361–372.

Cole, C. B., & Loftus, E. F. (1987). The memory of children. In S. J. Ceci, M. P. Toglia, & D. F. Ross (Eds.), *Children's eyewitness memory* (pp. 178–208). New York: Springer-Verlag.

Davies, G. (1991). Concluding comments. In J. Doris (Ed.), *The suggestibility of children's recollections* (pp. 177–187). Washington, DC: American Psychological Association.

Goodman, G. S. (1984). The child witness: Conclusions and future directions for research and legal practice. *Journal of Social Issues, 40*(2), 157–175.

Goodman, G. S. (1991). Commentary: On stress and accuracy in research on children's testimony. In J. Doris (Ed.), *The suggestibility of children's recollections* (pp. 77–82). Washington, DC: American Psychological Association.

Goodman, G. S., Aman, C., & Hirschman, J. (1987). Child sexual and physical abuse: Children's testimony. In S. J. Ceci, M. P. Toglia, & D. F. Ross (Eds.), *Children's eyewitness memory* (pp. 1–23). New York: Springer-Verlag.

Goodman, G. S., & Helgeson, V. S. (1988). Children as witnesses: What do they remember? In L. E. A. Walker (Ed.), *Handbook on sexual abuse of children* (pp. 109–136). New York: Springer.

Goodman, G. S., Hirschman, J. E., Hepps, D., & Rudy, L. (1991). Children's memory for stressful events. *Merrill–Palmer Quarterly, 37*, 109–157.

Goodman, G. S., & Reed, R. S. (1986). Age differences in eyewitness testimony. *Law and Human Behavior, 10*, 317–332.

Goodman, G. S., Rudy, L., Bottoms, B. L., & Aman, C. (1990). Children's concerns and memory: Issues of ecological validity in the study of children's eyewitness testimony. In R. Fivush & J. A. Hudson (Eds.), *Knowing and remembering in young children* (pp. 249–284). Cambridge, England: Cambridge University Press.

Graesser, A. C., & Nakamura, G. V. (1982). The impact of a schema on comprehension and memory. In G. H. Bower (Ed.), *The psychology of learning and motivation* (Vol. 16, pp. 59–109). New York: Academic Press.

Graesser, A. C., Woll, S. B., Kowalski, D. J., & Smith, D. A. (1980). Memory for typical and atypical actions in scripted activities. *Journal of Experimental Psychology: Human Learning and Memory, 6*, 503–515.

Linton, M. (1982). Transformations of memory in everyday life. In U. Neisser (Ed.), *Memory observed: Remembering in natural contexts* (pp. 77–91). San Francisco: Freeman.

Ornstein, P. A., Gordon, B. N., & Larus, D. M. (1992). Children's memory for a personally experienced event: Implications for testimony. *Applied Cognitive Psychology, 6*, 49–60.

Peters, D. P. (1987). The impact of naturally occurring stress on children's memory. In S. J. Ceci, M. P. Toglia, & D. F. Ross (Eds.), *Children's eyewitness memory* (pp. 122–141). New York: Springer-Verlag.

Peters, D. P. (1991a). Commentary: Response to Goodman. In J. Doris (Ed.), *The suggestibility of children's recollections* (pp. 86–91). Washington, DC: American Psychological Association.

Peters, D. P. (1991b). The influence of stress and arousal on the child witness. In J. Doris (Ed.), *The suggestibility of children's recollections* (pp. 60–76). Washington, DC: American Psychological Association.

Rudy, L., & Goodman, G. S. (1991). Effects of participation on children's reports: Implications for children's testimony. *Developmental Psychology, 27*, 527–538.

Saywitz, K. J., Goodman, G. S., Nicholas, E., & Moan, S. F. (1991). Children's memories of a physical examination involving genital touch: Implications for reports of child sexual abuse. *Journal of Consulting and Clinical Psychology, 59*, 682–691.

Steller, M. (1991). Commentary: Rehabilitation of the child witness. In J. Doris (Ed.), *The suggestibility of children's recollections* (pp. 106–109). Washington, DC: American Psychological Association.

Winograd, E., & Neisser, U. (Eds.). (1992). *Affect and accuracy in recall: Studies of "flashbulb" memories.* New York: Cambridge University Press.

AUTHOR INDEX

N

O

P

Subject Index